MACROECONOMICS

ROGER N. WAUD
UNIVERSITY OF NORTH CAROLINA
CHAPEL HILL

**WITH "ECONOMIC THINKERS" ESSAYS BY
HUGH S. NORTON, UNIVERSITY OF SOUTH CAROLINA**

1817

HARPER & ROW, PUBLISHERS, New York
Cambridge, Hagerstown, Philadelphia, San Francisco,
London, Mexico City, São Paulo, Sydney

Photo credits: Smith, p. 13, *Culver;* von Hayek, p. 51, *UPI;* Galbraith, p. 53, *UPI;* Marshall, p. 79, *Historical Pictures Service;* Kuznets, p. 95, *UPI;* Mitchell, p. 123, *Columbia University in the City of New York;* Say, p. 143, *Dictionnaire de l'economie politique;* Keynes, p. 179, *Brown Brothers;* Samuelson, p. 205, *Wide World;* Tobin, p. 269, *Pictorial Parade;* Friedman, p. 285, *The University of Chicago;* Malthus, p. 391, *Brown Brothers;* Ricardo, p. 413, *Brown Brothers.*

The news items in this text are based on articles that originally appeared in *The Wall Street Journal, Time* magazine, *The New York Times,* and the *First Chicago World Report.*

Sponsoring Editor: John Greenman
Special Projects Editor: Claudia M. Wilson
Project Editor: Claudia Kohner
Senior Production Manager: Kewal K. Sharma
Photo Researcher: Myra Schachne
Compositor: Lehigh/ROCAPPI, Inc.
Printer and Binder: Halliday Lithograph Corporation
Art Studio: J & R Technical Services, Inc.

MACROECONOMICS

Library of Congress Cataloging in Publication Data

Waud, Roger N   1938-
    Macroeconomics.

    Includes index.
    1. Macroeconomics.   I. Norton, Hugh Stanton, 1921-   II. Title.
HB171.5.W249   339   79-23022
ISBN 0-06-046965-X

To Myra

BRIEF
CONTENTS

DETAILED CONTENTS

PREFACE

One of this book's major aims is to demonstrate how principles of economics can be used to analyze real-world events and problems. Moreover, it presents these events and problems in the way that people usually encounter them—namely, via the news media. This approach is motivated by the view that a basic education in economic principles should develop the facility to apply an economic way of thinking to a news item of economic interest.

Economics professors are not readily available to the concerned citizen to help interpret the implications of the day's news. Those who report the news are often as befuddled by its meaning as those to whom they report. Clearly, it is not enough to know that economics is relevant. And it is not enough to understand basic economic principles spoon-fed from a textbook. Ultimately, a basic education in economic principles should develop a facility, indeed a habit, for disentangling and making sense out of the economic matters presented to us in our daily lives via the news media. Every chapter of this book uses real news reports to repeatedly demonstrate how to do this.

ADVICE FOR THE STUDENT

You don't have to have had a course in economics to be aware of economic problems. Newspapers, radio, and television bombard you with them daily. You no doubt are well aware of inflation, unemployment, and gasoline shortages. Tuition bills, finding a job, and just getting a few bucks to spend on a favorite pastime already have given you experience at economic problem solving. In short, you're not a novice to the subject of economics in the same way you might be to college physics. Nonetheless, economics is a rigorous subject. It should be studied in the same way that you would study a course in one of the sciences—a little bit *every day*.

Before reading a chapter always look at the learning objectives that are set out at the beginning. This will give you a brief outline of what you are about to read and what you want to learn from the chapter. Also, always read the news item before proceeding with the chapter. Typically you will find the content of the news item puzzling. At various points in the chapter your attention will be drawn back to the news item as basic economic principles are developed that will enable you to understand the news story better. After you have read and studied the chapter, read the news item again. You should find that you have gained considerable insight into the main points it raises. You will find that the economic way of thinking, which at times may seem somewhat abstract, is a powerful tool for analyzing real-world problems. Also, after completing a chapter, you should go back and see how well you have accomplished the learning objectives set out at the beginning. This will provide a self-check on your grasp of the concepts and principles developed in the chapter.

When reading this book, read for understanding, not speed. Each chapter is broken into major sections that focus on important concepts. At the end of a major section, you will encounter a Checkpoint: a brief series of questions that will enable you to test your understanding of what you have just read. You should always stop and measure your progress with these Checkpoints.

Economics is a problem-analyzing discipline. In order to give you more practice, further questions are provided at the end of each chapter. Try your hand at these as well. Discuss them with fellow students and your instructor whenever you feel unsure about the answers. Further problems and questions designed for this book are contained in John E. Weiler's *Study Guide*. The *Study Guide* will give you considerable practice at economic problem solving and aid your understanding of important economic principles.

Beginning with Chapter 5, you will find a News Item for Your Analysis at the end of each chapter. The news item has been chosen because it illustrates many of the concepts and principles just developed in the chapter. You should read it and then try to answer the questions about it that follow. Doing so will help develop your ability to analyze economic events as you encounter them.

Finally, always bear in mind that the concepts and principles studied in each chapter are typically used again and again in subsequent chapters. Mastering the material as you go makes the chapters that follow that much easier.

TO THE INSTRUCTOR

Writing a principles text is an indulgence of ego—I felt it could be done better. I have been motivated in part by my experiences as a teacher and researcher. My exposure to the policy-making environment of the Federal Reserve Board, where I worked while on a two-year leave of absence from the university, provided added impetus.

As a teacher of principles, I have long felt that students need exposure to actual economic problems in a way that is also realistic—the way that people are in fact exposed to them every day. This led me to the strategy of presenting a news item at the beginning of every chapter, a news item that cries out for the application of the economic principles that are developed in the chapter. As the chapter unfolds, the news item then provides a convenient and obviously relevant vehicle for showing beginning students why the study of economics is useful. They don't have to be told it's useful—they can discover that fact as they go along.

In brief, not being satisfied with the presentation of economic principles and policies in currently available texts, and not wishing to be evicted from the kitchen for taking up room and only complaining, I've decided to become a chef. Let me highlight what I think are the important features in my menu.

Macroeconomics

Recent years have brought new developments to the subject of macroeconomics. The standard Keynesian models that are used to teach principles students focus almost exclusively on total demand to explain the determination of total income, output, and employment. The rapid rise in the price of imported oil and other shocks to the supply side of the economy during the 1970s made it painfully apparent to instructors that aggregate supply must somehow be worked into the analysis. Without taking explicit account of aggregate supply, we have no way of explaining either cost-push inflation or the simultaneous occurrence of inflation and rising unemployment—the problem of stagflation. These concerns are so much a part of the contemporary world that students expect, and should receive, a meaningful analysis of them in an introductory course in economics. We owe it to them.

Such an analysis is one of the major innovations of this text. After developing the standard Keynesian aggregate demand model in Chapters 7 and 8, the concept of aggregate supply is introduced. The last major section of Chapter 8 shows the relationship between total demand and supply and illustrates why it is possible to have an increase in the general price level and the unemployment rate at the same time. This framework is used in Chapter 13 to facilitate a comparison of Keynesian and monetarist views. More significantly perhaps, it provides a framework for the analysis of stagflation and the contemporary problems of fiscal and monetary policy in Chapter 14. I should emphasize that *the standard Keynesian income analysis, with which instructors are so familiar, is fully developed in this text.* There is no scrimping on that. But the supply side of economy is then integrated with this analysis in a carefully explained fashion to enable the instructor to deal with cost-push inflation, supply shocks to the economy, and the problem of stagflation and its policy implications.

Inflation is a topic that calls for and receives extensive treatment in this text. The questions of who gains and who loses from inflation, and why, are addressed early on in Chapter 6. Cost-push and demand-pull inflation are first dealt with in Chapter 8, and in the comparison of Keynesian and monetarist views in Chapter 13. The problem of inflation obviously figures prominently in the discussion of stagflation and the problems of contemporary fiscal and monetary policy in Chapter 14. Roughly two-thirds of Chapter 15 is devoted to an analysis of wage-price guidelines and controls, their effectiveness and shortcomings, and the question of indexing. There we examine recently proposed guideline policies such as wage insurance and the tax-based income policy (TIP), as well as the indexing of income and capital gains taxes, and the indexing of government bonds and other financial assets. Chapter 15 also examines methods for dealing with unemployment other than the conventional tools of fiscal and monetary policy. These include manpower programs of the 1960s and 1970s, public works projects, and the concept of employment tax credit that has received much attention in recent years.

Another major feature of the text is an explicit treatment of the implications for the economy of the way in which government budget deficits are financed. Too often, it seems to me, currently available texts do not give sufficient attention to these implications. Yet they figure prominently in the comparison of the Keynesian and monetarist views, particularly as they relate to the issue of crowding out and the effectiveness of fiscal and monetary policy discussed in Chapter 13. These implications are also quite relevant to the discussion of the contemporary problems of fiscal and monetary policy and to the stagflation dilemma discussed in Chapter 14. There I set out an analysis of the current problems of macroeconomic policy that, I find, students want ("Why are we in such a mess?") but in my opinion is not given in currently available principles texts.

Money, the money supply process, and financial institutions are given careful coverage in Chapters 10, 11, and 12. Chapter 12 brings money and the interest rate explicitly into the model. I believe that the treatment has benefited from my own experience and research activities in this area.

On Explaining Things

It may seem an odd pitch to make about a textbook, but this book places an emphasis on explanation. In recent years many economics principles texts seem to put a premium on being terse—even to the point of being "slick." But there is a trade-off between brevity and explanation. Given the need to explain, the ideal is to be as brief as possible but not briefer than necessary. As a practical matter, books typically and unavoidably end up somewhat to one side or the other of the ideal. I have decided that, if I am condemned to err, I would opt for explaining too much rather than too little. Every effort has been taken to make the book as readable as possible. Numerous examples are provided to give concreteness to difficult concepts.

MORE ABOUT THE NEWS ITEMS
AND OTHER FEATURES AND INNOVATIONS

News Items

Every chapter begins with a news item based on a bona fide newspaper article (most often, but not always, taken from the *Wall Street Journal*). Each news item has been selected because it illustrates economic problems and concepts that are directly related to the economic principles to be developed in the particular chapter. As these principles are developed during the course of the chapter, it is shown how they can be applied to clarify and provide understanding of the economic problems discussed in the news item. Hence, in addition to engaging the student's attention in a relevant way at the outset of each chapter, the news item and the subsequent references to it aid in showing how and why economic analysis is a powerful and useful tool. *Care was taken to select news items that are as enduring as the fundamental economic principles they illustrate. The names of the actors may change but, in almost every case, the central themes most likely will be as timely a generation from now as they are today.*

News Items for Your Analysis: Case Studies

In order to give the student practice in analyzing economic problems as they are presented in the news, News Items for Your Analysis are presented at the end of every chapter starting with the fifth chapter. Like those at the beginning of each chapter, each end-of-chapter news item is adapted from an actual newspaper article that directly illustrates the basic economic principles developed in the chapter. However, end-of-chapter news items are generally, though not always, somewhat longer and more elaborate. The questions which follow the article encourage the student to apply the economic principles just learned. The end-of-chapter news items and the questions about them constitute case studies typical of those that we encounter every day.

Checkpoints

Checkpoints appear throughout every chapter, generally at the end of major sections. At each Checkpoint the student is signaled to stop and answer a series of questions about concepts just presented— to stop and check on his or her progress and grasp of the material. Questions and problems placed at the end of chapters are all too often easily ignored, like so much litter at the back of a closet that one is rarely forced to face. The Checkpoints are intended to get around this problem and help the student to reconsider what has just been read. They try to check on the student's understanding of concepts as they are encountered, rather than after many curves and several compounded misunderstandings accumulated at the journey's end. Often the Checkpoints will include questions that require the student to apply a concept just learned to a particular aspect of the news item at the beginning of the chapter. Frequently, the Checkpoints provide grist for class discussion.

Learning Objectives

Learning objectives are listed and set off from the main text at the beginning of each chapter. They outline a plan of study for the chapter as well as provide an overview of what's to be done. After completing the chapter, the student can also use the list of learning objectives as a quick check to see whether the material in the chapter has been mastered or not.

Economic Thinkers

These are biographies of famous economists and others who have had a significant impact on economic events and economic thinking. They are not so much personal biographies as studies in the history of economic thought. Their major purpose is to highlight the development of economic thinking on major problems and concerns while indicating the significant role that particular individuals have played in this development.

Key Terms and Concepts

Terminology is unavoidably abundant in economics. In addition, words that have several meanings in common everyday usage often have a more precise meaning when used in economics. Such words, along with other important economic terms, appear in boldface type whenever they are first introduced and defined in the text. Key Terms and Concepts, at the end of each chapter, lists these. These terms and concepts are defined again in the Glossary at the end of the book.

Summaries

The Summaries at the end of each chapter are fairly comprehensive. They are intended to tie together the main concepts developed in the chapter as well as alert the student to areas that may require rereading.

Questions and Problems

Questions and Problems are also located at the end of each chapter. These are generally more complex and extended than the questions found in the Checkpoints. Some are almost case studies. Many may be readily used for class discussion. The News Items for Your Analysis appear after the Questions and Problems. The Checkpoints, the Questions and Problems, and the News Items for Your Analysis, with its Questions, provide significantly more in-text questions, problems, and case studies with questions than are provided by most economic principles texts currently available.

Figures, Graphs, and Tables

There is liberal use of real-world data that appear in tables and figures throughout the book. Quite often tables containing hypothetical data are used to illustrate particularly difficult concepts. Graphs and figures are also used extensively—more liberally than in most principles texts. The captions describing each graph and figure generally begin with a brief summary statement followed by a reasonably complete description of what is portrayed.

ACKNOWLEDGMENTS

Many people have provided helpful comments and contributions to this book throughout the course of its development. I would like especially to thank the following:

David Able, Mankato State University
Alan B. Batchelder, Kenyon College
Allan E. Bergland, Northern Arizona University
Dudley W. Blair, Clemson University
Charles W. Brown, Stephen F. Austin State University
Stephen Buckles, University of Missouri, Columbia
Malcolm R. Burns, University of Kansas
Robert Campbell, University of Oregon
David Conn, Wayne State University
David Denslow, Jr., University of Florida
Hartmut Fischer, University of San Francisco
John M. Gemello, San Francisco State University
Warren S. Gramm, Washington State University
Nicholas D. Grunt, Tarrant County Junior College
Salim Harik, Western Michigan University
James R. Jeffers, University of Iowa
Hirschel Kasper, Oberlin College
Lester S. Levy, Northern Illinois University
John W. Lowe, Arizona State University
David C. Loy, University of Wisconsin, Oshkosh

Robert Mackay, Virginia Polytechnic Institute
Robert McNown, University of Colorado
H. Lynn Miller, Central Florida Community College
W. Douglas Morgan, University of California, Santa Barbara
Ronald Mulcahey, San Diego Mesa College
John E. Peck, Indiana University
Robert C. Puth, University of New Hampshire
James F. Ragan, Kansas State University
John Rapp, University of Dayton
David M. Rees, North Dakota State University
James M. Rock, University of Utah
Morton Schnabel, U.S. Department of Commerce
Mark B. Schupack, Brown University
Donald A. Smith, West Los Angeles College
Philip E. Sorensen, Florida State University, Tallahassee
Robert M. Stern, University of Michigan
Douglas O. Stewart, Cleveland State University
Howard Swaine, Northern Michigan University
Rick Tannery, University of Pittsburgh
Lloyd B. Thomas, Kansas State University
James R. Thornton, University of Delaware
Arthur Welsh, University of Iowa
Harvey Zabinsky, University of Kentucky
Robert Owen Zimmerman, Xavier University
Armand J. Zottola, Central Connecticut State College

ROGER N. WAUD

ONE

INTRODUCTION

1

ECONOMICS AND ECONOMIC ISSUES

ELECTRICITY USE TOPS FORECASTS

WASHINGTON, Aug. 17—Utility companies report demand may exceed the forecasts previously made in the wake of the surge in fuel costs caused by the Arab oil embargo. They fear unexpected strains on their capacity. Skeptical environmentalists argue that utility companies are crying wolf.

The evidence is deceptive. Last year a sizeable decline in use by industry, operating below capacity because of the recession, masked a substantial rise in residential and commercial use. Now with economic recovery, industrial use is on the rise.

Power companies claim to be caught in a pinch between rising electricity demand and fuel shortages. Diminishing gas supplies will put increased pressure on nuclear, coal, and oil supplies. This puts electricity users on a collision course with environmentalists. Air-quality standards in some areas practically rule out anything but low-sulphur oil, the most expensive of fuels.

Utilities claim a constricting net of environmental legislation and regulation is stifling their plant-building plans. They say plant costs have soared because of big wage settlements with construction unions and the extra expense of legally mandated safety and pollution-control gear. Utility companies have asked for huge rate increases to cover these costs. Aghast, rate-setting regulators have dug in their heels. Rate hearings have dragged on for 18 months or more. When increases are finally granted, the new rates will have already been outstripped by inflation. Investors, noting the havoc, have cooled on utility stocks, and share prices have slumped.

Environmentalists still consider utilities' demand projections too high, building plans excessive, and their encouragement of conservation unconvincing. However, other observers are wondering whether the cost of protecting the environment is outrunning the benefits. Some have also noted that the recent recession and inflation have further confused the issue.

We have all come across items like this one in the news media. As ordinary citizens, we often feel overwhelmed by the complex nature of the issues involved. To understand this particular item, we must have some knowledge of:

1. the implications of an international oil embargo;
2. the conflict between energy needs and environmental considerations;
3. the world's dwindling reserves of oil, which cannot be replaced;
4. the role of government in regulating the oil industry;
5. the possible reaction of investors in credit markets;
6. how these issues relate to each other against a background of recession, inflation, and recovery.

How can the study of economics help you to find your way through this maze? Most importantly, a knowledge of economics will help you to organize and analyze issues like these so that they may be understood. Although the laws of economics may not be as absolute as the law of gravity, they will help you deal with facts and opinions like those set forth in this news item. As a result, you will be able to come to intelligent, informed conclusions when faced with both day-to-day problems and questions of national policy. Near the end of this chapter we will briefly consider how an economist might analyze the issues raised in the news item.

It has been said that there are three kinds of people: those that make things happen; those that watch things happen; and those that wonder what happened. If you sometimes find yourself among the wonderers, the study of economics is for you.

ECONOMY AND ECONOMICS

The word **economy** typically brings to mind ideas of efficiency, thrift, and the avoidance of waste by careful planning and use of resources. We might say that some job was done with an "economy of motion," meaning that there was no unnecessary effort expended. The word comes from the Greek *oikonemia,* which means the management of a household or state. In this sense, we often speak of the U.S. or the Chinese economy; of a capitalist, socialist, free-market, or planned economy; or of industrialized and underdeveloped economies. We use the term in this last sense when we refer to a particular system of organization for the production, distribution, and consumption of all things people use to achieve a certain standard of living.

The term **economics**, on the other hand, is not so simple. It covers such a broad range of meaning that any brief definition is likely to leave out some important aspect of the subject. Most economists would agree, however, that economics is a social science concerned with the study of economies and the relationships between them. Paul Samuelson, America's first Nobel prizewinner in economics, has suggested the following definition:

> Economics is the study of how people and society end up *choosing,* with or without the use of money, to employ *scarce* productive resources that could have alternative uses, to produce various commodities and distribute them for consumption, now or in the future, among various persons and groups in society. It analyzes the costs and benefits of improving patterns of resource allocation.[1]

[1] Paul A. Samuelson, *Economics,* 10th ed. (New York: McGraw-Hill, 1976), p. 3.

In this definition, Samuelson touches upon several important ideas—scarcity, choice, resources, and so forth—with which we will be concerned both in this chapter and throughout this book.

Before reading any further you should understand that, whatever it is, economics is not primarily a vocational subject such as accounting, marketing, or management. Nor is it primarily intended to teach you how to make money, though it may help. Economics studies problems from society's point of view rather than from the individual's. Nevertheless, it is likely you will find the study of economics helpful in whatever career you choose. Moreover, it should make you a more knowledgeable and able citizen.

THE LANGUAGE OF ECONOMICS

As is the case with many subjects, the words used in economics often seem strange to the beginner. Physicists talk about neutrons, quarks, and hystoresis; football coaches about fly patterns, look-in patterns, and flex defenses. To make sense of a typical news item about economic issues, such as the one at the beginning of this chapter, you must be familiar with the language of economics. Economists frequently use common words to mean something more precise than is generally expected in everyday conver-

sation. For instance, when you say someone has a lot of money, common usage suggests that you mean a person who owns a lot of things such as cars, houses, buildings, bonds, stocks, cash, and so on. In economics, however, we generally accept that "money" means one's holdings of currency and demand deposits at a commercial bank. When we mean something else, we would always spell out exactly what other items we mean to include in our definition of money. Certain basic terms, such as money, will come up again and again throughout this book. The following definitions will help you understand and use them correctly.

Economic Goods

The news item about electricity use concerns the production of an economic good—electricity. An economic good is any item that is desired and scarce. In general, economic goods may be classified as either commodities or services. Commodities are tangible items such as food or clothing. (Tangible means, quite literally, able to be touched.) Commodities do not have to be consumed when they are produced. That is, they may be stored. Services are intangibles (that is, non-touchables) such as shoeshines or haircuts. They cannot be stored or transferred. For example, I cannot give you my haircut (a service), but I can give you my coat (a commodity). Such distinctions are not always

After reading this chapter, you will be able to:

1. Define the terms "economy" and "economics."
2. List and define the basic economic terms used most often in economic discussions.
3. Distinguish between and give examples of positive and normative statements.
4. Identify the basic elements that make up any economic theory.
5. Construct a simple graph from data given in a table.
6. Define and give examples of the three major fallacies that may be found in statements of economic theory or analysis.
7. Define the terms "macroeconomics" and "microeconomics."
8. Explain the role of economic theory and analysis in economic policy making.

clear cut. For example, the economic good electricity might be called a service by some who say it is intangible, and a commodity by those who note that it can be stored in a battery. Most often, an economic good is simply referred to as a good. You may have heard of the output of the economy referred to as "goods and services." This is done largely to remind us of the existence of services.

Whether they are commodities or services, all economic goods share the quality of being **scarce**. That is, there are not enough of them to supply everyone's needs and desires. As a result, people have to pay to obtain them. What they have to pay is called the **price** of the good. The price of electricity is referred to as a rate in the news item. As we will see in Chapter 4, price is determined to a large extent by the number of people who desire and are able to pay for a particular good.

People desire economic goods because these goods provide some form of satisfaction. A refrigerator provides satisfaction by keeping food cold. A stereo system provides satisfaction by giving us entertainment. Because an economic good gives us satisfaction, we say that it is useful to us. As a result, economists sometimes refer to the satisfaction a good yields as its utility. The creation of goods which have utility is called production. Production is carried out through the use of economic resources.

Economic Resources

Economic resources, also called the factors of production, are all the natural, man-made, and human resources that are used in the production of goods. These resources may be broken down into two broad categories, nonhuman resources (capital and land) and human resources (labor).

CAPITAL

Capital is an example of a term that is used to mean one thing in everyday conversation and another in economics. We often speak of capital when referring to money, especially when we are talking about the purchase of equipment, machinery, and other productive facilities. It is more accurate to call the money used to make

the purchase financial capital. An economist would refer to this purchase as investment. An economist uses the term capital to mean all the man-made aids used in production. Sometimes called investment goods, capital consists of machinery, tools, buildings, transportation and distribution facilities, and inventories of unfinished goods. A basic characteristic of capital goods is that they are used to produce other goods. For example, electricity is produced with capital goods consisting of boilers, turbines, fuel storage facilities, poles, and miles of wire.

LAND

To an economist, land is all natural resources which are used in production. Such resources include water, forests, oil, gas, mineral deposits, and so forth. As we were informed by the news item that began this chapter, these resources are scarce and, in many cases, rapidly becoming more scarce.

LABOR

Labor is a very broad term that covers all the different capabilities and skills possessed by human beings. The labor referred to in our news item consists of welders, carpenters, masons, hod carriers, and others involved in the actual construction of a power plant. Although not specifically mentioned, there is another type of labor involved in the functioning of utility companies. This is management. The term manager embraces a host of skills related to the planning, administration, and coordination of the production process. A manager may also be an entrepreneur (or enterpriser). This is the person who comes up with the ideas and takes the risks that are necessary to start a successful business. The founders of electric utility companies were entrepreneurs, while those currently running them are more accurately called managers.

The Firm

These economic resources of land, capital, and labor, are brought together in a production unit that is referred to as a business or a firm. The firm uses these resources to produce goods which are then sold. The money obtained from the sale of these goods is used to pay the economic resources. Payments to those providing labor services are called wages. Payments to those providing buildings, land, and equipment leased to the firm are called rent. Payments to those providing financial capital (those who own stocks and bonds) are called dividends and interest.

Gross National Product

The news item refers to a recession. A recession is usually defined in terms of an important concept known as GNP. The total dollar value of all the final goods (as distinguished from goods still in the process of production) produced by all the firms in the economy is called the gross national product (GNP). In order to make meaningful comparisons of the GNP for various years, economists often use real GNP—GNP adjusted so that it only reflects changes in quantity of output, and not changes in prices. When the real GNP goes down, we say the economy is in a state of recession. A severe recession is called a depression, although there is no general agreement as to how to decide exactly when a recession becomes a depression.

Inflation and Unemployment

The economic health of the nation, of which GNP is one measure, is directly affected by two other important factors, inflation and unemployment. Inflation is an ongoing general rise in prices. The steeper this rise, the faster is the decline of a dollar's purchasing power. The reference in the news item to electricity rates being "outstripped by inflation" simply means that the prices of many other goods are rising faster than the price of electricity. The unemployment rate measures the percentage of the total number of workers in the labor force who are actively seeking employment but are unable to find jobs. The higher the unemployment rate, the more the economy is wasting labor resources by allowing them to stand idle. However, it is generally believed that a decrease in the unemployment rate will lead to an increase in inflation, all other things remaining the same. ("All other things remaining the same" is an important phrase in economics that we will look into later in this chapter.)

Normative and Positive Statements

Intelligent discussion of economic issues requires that we distinguish between normative and positive statements. In the previous paragraph we made the statement that "a decrease in unemployment leads to an increase in inflation." This is a statement of fact which may be supported or refuted by examining data. As such, we can say it is a **positive statement**. *Positive statements tell us what is, what was, or what will be. Any disputes about a positive statement can be settled by looking at the facts.* "It rained last Thursday" and "the sun will rise in the East tomorrow" are positive statements. In the news item, for example, "now with economic recovery, industrial use is on the rise" is a positive statement.

But now let's change our statement about inflation and unemployment slightly. Let's say that "it is *better* to decrease unemployment and live with the resulting increase in inflation than to allow a large number of people to go without jobs." This is a **normative statement**—*an opinion or value judgment.* Those of you who are looking for jobs would probably tend to agree with this statement. But your grandparents who are retired and living on fixed incomes would probably disagree. Since they are not seeking employment, an increase in the number of jobs available would in no way compensate them for a rise in prices. As far as they are concerned, it would probably be better to slow the rise in prices. This, of course, would lead to an increase in unemployment, which would make all job-seekers very unhappy. The dispute between these two groups cannot be settled by facts alone.

Normative statements tell us what should be (normative means establishing a norm or standard). *Although normative statements often have their origin in positive statements, they cannot be proven true or false by referring to objective data.* For example, I may make the normative statement "you shouldn't drink and drive." This statement has its origin in the positive statement "drinking alcoholic beverages slows down one's ability to react." We could disagree forever over the first statement, but statistical studies could be brought to bear on any dispute over the second. In the news item the statement "the evidence is deceptive" is a normative statement that has its origin in positive statements about data on the economy and utility companies. But two people might argue endlessly about whether or not the data are "deceptive."

In any discussion about economic issues, as soon as voices rise you can almost be certain that the discussion has shifted from evidence and fact to value judgment and opinion. However, don't forget that value judgments and opinion often parade in the clothes of logic and fact.

■ CHECKPOINT 1-1

Go back over the news item at the beginning of this chapter and make a list of all the positive statements and a list of all the normative statements. Examine the normative statements and try to determine what kinds of positive statements they may be based on.

ECONOMIC REALITY AND ECONOMIC THEORY

Economic reality—making a living, paying the rent, shopping for food, paying taxes, and so forth—forces us to deal with a large and confusing swarm of facts, figures, and events. The activities of households, firms, and federal, state, and local governments all have a direct effect on our economic lives. In order to make some sense out of the world around us we all have formulated some economic theories, even without being aware of doing so.

How to hold down inflation is a topic about which practically everyone has a theory. One individual, having just filled out an income tax return, might say, "if we don't curb all this government spending, inflation will get worse." The owner of a small business, on the other hand, feels that "if something isn't done to break up the big unions and big corporations, we'll never bring inflation under control." Based on observations of the way certain groups, organizations, and institutions function, each individual has focused on the relationship that appears to be most relevant to an explanation of inflation. From these examples, we can say that *an economic theory is an attempt to describe reality by abstracting and generalizing its basic characteristics. Economists often refer to an economic theory as a law, principle, or model.* Each of these terms may be taken to mean the same thing.

Observations and Predictions: The Scientific Method

The inflation-control theories of the individuals above share two common features: (1) each is based on observation of facts or events; and (2) each makes a prediction about the consequences of certain events. We can now add to our definition of an economic theory by saying that *an economic theory provides an explanation of observed phenomena which may be judged by its ability to predict the consequences of certain events.*

Although economics is not a science like chemistry or physics, it does make use of the scientific method in arriving at and testing theories. The aspects of the **scientific method** that we are most concerned with here are induction and deduction. **Induction** *is the process of formulating a theory from a set of observations.* **Deduction** *is the process of predicting future events by means of a theory.* The predictions made by deduction are then tested by once again observing facts or events to see if what was predicted actually takes place. If not, the theory will have to be changed to conform with reality, and the whole process begins again. For example, suppose there is an increase in government spending, the crucial event in the first individual's theory, but we do not observe the predicted increase in inflation. Following the scientific method, we must either modify or discard the theory because of its failure to predict. The process of induction and deduction is never-ending, since all theories must be continually retested in light of new facts and events.

Constructing a Theory

Our income-tax payer and our small-business owner, needless to say, did not really use the scientific method in drawing up their theories. But now let's see how an economist would go about formulating a theory. As an example, we will analyze the law of demand, a theory which will be referred to many times throughout this book.

ELEMENTS OF ECONOMIC THEORY

Every formal statement of a theory has four basic elements:

1. a statement of variables;
2. a set of assumptions about conditions which must be present for the theory to work;
3. a hypothesis about the way the variables are related;
4. one or more predictions about future happenings.

The law of demand states that the quantity of a good demanded per unit of time will increase as the price of the good decreases, all other things remaining the same. Let's break this statement down into the four elements listed above.

Variables. The law of demand is concerned with two variables, price and quantity demanded. We call these variables because they can vary, that is, they are subject to change. As we noted in our discussion of the language of economics, price is the amount that must be paid to obtain a good. Quantity demanded is the amount of that good that people want and can pay for per unit of time.

Assumptions. The law of demand makes the assumption that, except for price, all other factors that might influence demand will remain the same. This assumption, which is a feature of all economic theories, is often referred to as *ceteris paribus*. Logically enough, that's Latin for "all other things remaining the same." This assumption is important when we come to the point of testing our theory. Real-world events may not turn out as the theory says they should. We must be sure to find out whether this is because the theory is wrong or because something other than just price has changed, thus violating the *ceteris paribus* assumption.

Hypothesis. A hypothesis is a statement of the way we think the variables in question relate to each other. Our hypothesis in the law of demand is that as price decreases, quantity demanded will increase. This is known as an **inverse relationship**, since the variables are changing in opposite ways. If the variables change in the same way (an increase in one leads to an increase in the other), we say they have a **direct relationship**.

Prediction. Here we move directly into the realm of the real world. Armed with our theory, what can we say will likely happen if the manager of our local clothing store reduces the price of Irish knit sweaters from $35 to $25? While customers might not break down the doors to get in, our theory tells us that we can safely bet that the number of sweaters they want to buy will increase. Historically, the development of the automobile is a good example of the validity of the law of demand. The original cars, which were made on an individual basis, were so expensive that only the rich could afford them. Then Henry Ford developed the assembly-line method of production, which made them less costly to produce. As a result of using this method, he was able to reduce prices. The quantity demanded soared.

How Exact Is Economic Theory?

Since economic theory tries to explain and predict human behavior, you probably wonder how it is possible to be very exact. Economic theory cannot be as exact as Newton's three laws of motion. But economic behavior is on average more predictable than the behavior of many subatomic particles currently studied in high energy physics. If economic behavior weren't predictable, stores wouldn't hold sales, banks wouldn't need vaults and security guards, and traffic tickets wouldn't carry fines. If you don't think economic behavior is predictable, drop a pail of quarters in a public swimming pool some summer afternoon. Make a practice of this and see if you notice a predictable pattern of behavior.

The law of demand is a good predictor because people's behavior on average is such that they will buy more of a good the lower is its price. True, there is the occasional person who will buy more of a good the higher its price because of "snob appeal." But this is unusual. When we look at the behavior of a large group of individuals, the on-average similarity of the behavior of the majority of them dominates the unusual behavior of the few.

■ CHECKPOINT 1-2

During the Arab oil embargo of 1973–1974, people waited in long lines to fill up their tanks with gas. What does the law of demand suggest to you about a way in which those lines could have been shortened?

Theories into Graphs

So far, we have been using words to explain how the law of demand works. But when we come to the point of relating the theory to data obtained through research, it is time to use pictures. In economics, the pictures we use take the form of graphs. Returning to the topic of our news item, let's construct a graph from data about electricity use.

BASIC ELEMENTS OF A GRAPH

An ordinary graph starts out with two lines, which are called axes. One of the lines is drawn vertically, the other horizontally. The point at

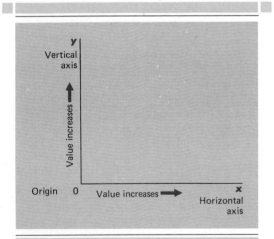

FIGURE 1-1 BASIC ELEMENTS OF A GRAPH

Every graph starts out with two lines. One is called the vertical (or *y*) axis. The other is called the horizontal (or *x*) axis. The point at which they meet is called the origin and has a value of 0. The value of the variable being measured on each axis increases as you move farther away from the origin. This means moving up along the vertical axis and to the right along the horizontal axis.

TABLE 1-1 DEMAND FOR ELECTRICITY AT DIFFERENT PRICES
(Hypothetical Data)

	Price per Kilowatt Hour	Kilowatt Hours Demanded (in Millions per Month)
(*a*)	$.06	15
(*b*)	.05	17
(*c*)	.04	20
(*d*)	.03	25
(*e*)	.02	35
(*f*)	.01	50

This table tells us how much electricity will be demanded per month at various prices. If the price is $.06 per kilowatt hour, the quantity demanded will be 15 million kilowatt hours per month (combination *a*). If the price is $.03 per kilowatt hour, the quantity demanded will be 25 million kilowatt hours (combination *d*).

which they meet is called the origin and has a value of 0 (see Figure 1-1). The value along each axis increases as we move away from the origin. This means moving up along the vertical axis and to the right along the horizontal axis.

In the case of the law of demand, we noted that we would be looking at two variables, price and quantity demanded. In economics, it is customary to use the vertical axis to measure price. Quantity demanded, therefore, is measured along the horizontal axis. What does this mean in terms of our investigation into the demand for electricity? We now have to find out what numbers to use on each axis. In other words, we must determine how much electricity is demanded at various prices. Let's suppose that our research into electricity demand in one city comes up with the data given in Table 1-1.

CONSTRUCTING A GRAPH

Returning to our graph, we can now label the vertical axis "Price per Kilowatt Hour" and the horizontal axis "Kilowatt Hours Demanded (in Millions per Month)," as shown in Figure 1-2. (These labels correspond to the column headings in Table 1-1.) We divide the vertical axis evenly into units representing $.01 increases in

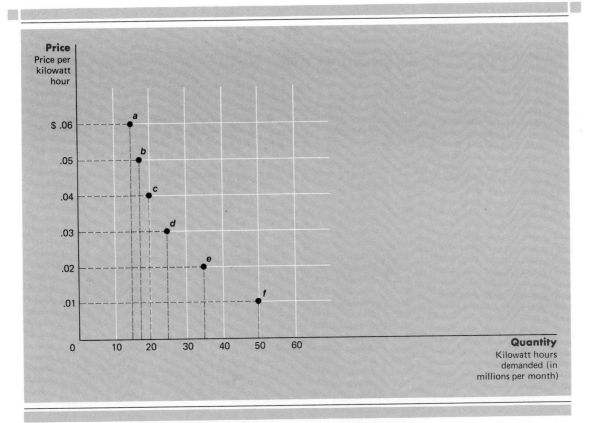

FIGURE 1-2 DEMAND FOR ELECTRICITY AT VARIOUS PRICES

Using the data obtained from Table 1–1, we are able to locate points on the graph which represent the various price-quantity demanded combinations for electricity. To locate combination b, for example, we move right along the horizontal axis until we come to 20 million kilowatt hours. We then move directly upward from this point until we are opposite the $.04 mark on the vertical axis. The same procedure is used to find the other combinations listed in Table 1–1.

price. We divide the horizontal axis evenly into units representing 10-million kilowatt-hour increases in quantity demanded. Our next task is to find the points on the graph corresponding to the quantity demanded per hour figure and the price per kilowatt-hour figure for each of the six pairs of numbers given in Table 1–1. (We have labeled these pairs of numbers a, b, c, d, e, and f in our table.)

For combination a, we first move right along the horizontal axis to a point equal to 15-million kilowatt hours. We then move directly upward from that point until we are opposite the point

on the vertical axis that represents a price of $.06. We label the point at which we have arrived a, since it corresponds to combination a on our table. We use the same procedure to locate points b, c, d, e, and f. Our graph now looks like Figure 1-2.

If we draw a line connecting points a through f, we have what is called a demand curve. Our graph now looks like Figure 1-3. In this case, we see that the demand curve slopes downward and to the right. This tells us that as price decreases (moves down along the vertical axis), quantity demanded increases (moves right

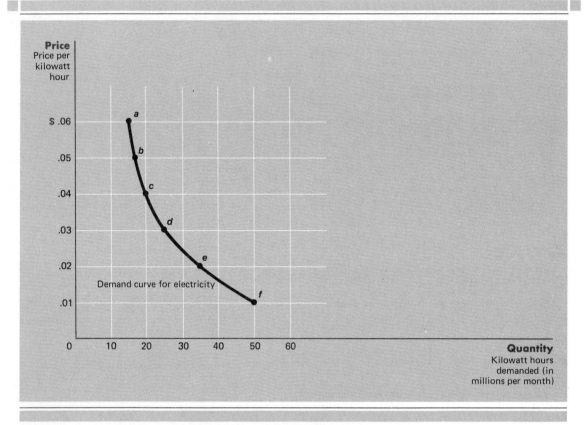

FIGURE 1-3 DEMAND CURVE FOR ELECTRICITY

After we have located all the points that correspond to the price-quantity demanded combinations in Table 1–1, we draw a line connecting them. This line is called the demand curve. In this case, because the relationship between price and quantity demanded is an inverse relationship, the curve slopes downward and to the right.

along the horizontal axis). Thinking back to our discussion of the elements of a theory (p. 9), you will remember that we called this type of relationship between two variables an inverse relationship. All inverse relationships (one variable increasing while the other is decreasing) produce this type of downward, rightward-sloping curve. It is one of the major purposes of a graph to show us, without even having to read the specific numbers involved, what the relationship between the variables is. When we compare the picture of demand provided by our graph with our theory, we see that the theory is consistent with the facts. The downward, rightward slope

of the demand curve shows us that as price decreases, quantity demanded increases.

■ CHECKPOINT 1-3

The news item at the beginning of this chapter tells us that utility companies say they are finding it difficult to produce all the electricity their customers are demanding. Keeping in mind the graph we have just constructed in Figure 1–3, let us suppose we were able to obtain information on electricity demand in another city. In this case, let us suppose that the data indicate that the demand in this other city is less sensitive to

ECONOMIC THINKERS

ADAM SMITH
1723–1790

Adam Smith is often thought of as the father of modern economics, although his great work, *An Inquiry into the Nature and Causes of the Wealth of Nations* (1776), would not look very much like a modern economics textbook to today's reader.

One of Smith's most significant contributions to economic thought was his explanation of the importance of the division of labor and its relationship to the development of the economy. In his famous description of operations in a pin factory, Smith shows how output can be greatly increased by dividing tasks into small segments, each performed by specialists who require little training.

Smith's central theme was the value of enlightened self-interest, and he preached the doctrine of laissez faire. In Smith's view, the role of government should be minimized, in contrast with the power governments had exercised over all types of commerce in the past. Beyond maintaining national security, preserving internal order, and undertaking a few tasks such as public education, government was, according to Smith, to exercise little power. An advocate of economic freedom, Smith generally accepted the idea of "natural order" taught by the Scottish philosopher Francis Hutcheson, which implied the removal of restrictions of all kinds. Such a theory well suited the rising commercial class in Western Europe, particularly in England, who found government regulations irksome. Freedom allowed the natural instincts provided by a wise providence (in other words, self-interest) to prevail and provide the drive to turn the wheels of trade and commerce.

As Smith saw it, it would be foolish to assume that people satisfy the needs of others simply as a result of feelings of altruism. On the contrary, the baker, the brewer, and the candlestick maker each undertakes to satisfy the needs of others as a means of satisfying his or her own. By seeking to fulfill personal needs, each individual is helping to increase the wealth of society:

> He generally, indeed, neither intends to promote the public interest nor knows how much he is promoting it. By preferring the support of domestic to that of foreign industry, he intends only his own security; and by directing that industry in such a manner as its produce may be of the greatest value, he intends only his own gain; and he is in this, as in many other cases, led by an invisible hand to promote an end which was no part of his intention.

FOR FURTHER READING

Clark, John J., and others. *Adam Smith, 1776–1926.* University of Chicago Press, 1928.

Smith, Adam. *An Inquiry into the Nature and Causes of the Wealth of Nations.* Modern Library Edition. New York: Random House, Inc., 1937.

changes in price than the demand in the city we've been looking at so far. What sort of shape do you think the demand curve for electricity would have compared with the one shown in Figure 1–3? In which city do you think an increase in price would most relieve the strain on the utility companies? Why?

ECONOMIC REASONING: COMMON PITFALLS

In order to analyze an economic issue or problem correctly, we must avoid certain common pitfalls of economic reasoning. One of the most common fallacies arises from the difficulty of distinguishing between cause and effect. Another is commonly known as the fallacy of composition.

Cause and Effect

As we have seen in our analysis of the law of demand, a key interest of economics is to determine how events in the real world can be explained and even predicted. In other words, we are looking for causes. We want to be able to say with reasonable certainty that if A happens, B will be the result. Having analyzed the law of demand, we are able to say that if prices are decreased, quantity demanded will increase, all other things remaining the same. Unfortunately for us, it is not always easy to tell if some event was the cause of another event or if it just preceded it in time. The situation is especially tricky when event B regularly follows event A.

In economics there are many times when it is very difficult to tell whether A caused B or B caused A. Perhaps there is no causal relationship between B and A at all, but both occur together because event C always causes both A and B to happen. A fire causes smoke and light, but smoke doesn't cause light and light doesn't cause smoke. People in high-income brackets tend to have better health and more education than people in low-income brackets. Possibly they were born with a hardier constitution and more than the average amount of energy. These factors would enable such people to attend school more regularly and have a greater capacity for work. If so, it is possible that high income and education are no more causally related than smoke and light, but that being born with a hardy constitution causes both. On the other hand, it may be that higher education causes higher income, which makes it possible to afford a better diet and better medical care.

The rather common fallacy of concluding that A caused B simply because A occurred before B is known as the **post hoc, ergo propter hoc** ("after this, therefore because of this") fallacy. I carried an umbrella and "after this, therefore because of this" it rained.

Fallacy of Composition

Common sense will tell you that if you find yourself in a burning building, you should get out as fast as you can. However, if the burning building is a crowded movie theater, and each individual in it tries to get through the door at the same time, the results are likely to be tragic. What is good advice for you as an individual is not good advice for the group as a whole. *The false assumption that what is true for a particular part of the whole is also true for the whole itself is called the* **fallacy of composition**. (The whole is made up, or composed, of two or more individual parts.)

We can see how this fallacy works on an economic level if we consider the following example. If you are unemployed and have a mortgage on your house, you might be wise to sell the house. You can use the money obtained from the sale to pay off the mortgage and buy a cheaper house. In this way you can eliminate the burden of monthly mortgage payments. But if everyone on your block decides to do the same thing, the glut of houses on the market may drive prices down so low that you may not be able to get enough money to pay off the mortgage and buy a new house. What makes good economic sense for the individual does not necessarily make good economic sense for the whole economy.

In judging what is true for the whole of society, we must not go to the opposite extreme and assume that what is true for the whole is also true for the individual parts. Such an assumption is known as the **fallacy of division**. For example, while it is true that society as a whole may benefit from a highly competitive marketplace, some individual firms with weak management skills may go bankrupt.

■CHECKPOINT 1-4

Think up some examples where confusions about cause and effect might arise. Can you think of a fallacy of composition that frequently occurs when a crowd watches a football game?

MACROECONOMICS VERSUS MICROECONOMICS

Economists often use the terms macroeconomics and microeconomics to distinguish between different levels of economic analysis.

In **macroeconomics** we are concerned with the workings of the whole economy or large sectors of it. These sectors include government, business, and households. For the purposes of analysis, the smaller groups that make up these large sectors are often lumped together and treated as one unit. For example, the consumer sector may be treated as though it were one large household. The business sector might be considered to be one large business. Macroeconomics deals with such issues as economic growth, unemployment, recession, inflation, stagflation, and monetary and fiscal policy.

Microeconomics, on the other hand, focuses on the individual units that make up the whole of the economy. Here we are interested in how households and businesses behave as individual units, not as parts of a larger whole. Microeconomics studies how a household spends its money. It also studies the way in which a business determines how much of a product to produce, how to make best use of the factors of production, what pricing strategy to use, and so on. Microeconomics also studies how individual markets and industries are organized, what patterns of competition they follow, and how these patterns affect economic efficiency and welfare.

An analysis of the problems of the utility companies, reported in our news item, would be an exercise in microeconomics. However, some of the utility companies' problems have been aggravated by inflation and recession. These are problems that affect the whole economy and are the subject of macroeconomic analysis.

ECONOMIC POLICY

From the previous discussion it seems obvious that some way has to be found for dealing with both the problems of individuals and the problems of society as a whole. Economic theories have by and large evolved as responses to problems. In other words, necessity has been the mother of invention. But theory is only a tool, a way of looking at economic reality. It does not provide ready-made solutions to problems. John Maynard Keynes, a highly regarded policy maker as well as theorist, put it this way:

The theory of economics does not furnish a body of settled conclusions immediately applicable to policy. It is a method rather than a doctrine, an apparatus of the mind, a technique of thinking, which helps its possessor to draw correct conclusions.

Economic policy *is concerned with finding solutions to economic problems.* While policy makers use economic theory to help them, they must go beyond it as well. They must consider the cultural, social, legal, and political aspects of an issue if they are to formulate a successful policy. In the end, making economic policy involves making value judgments such as those we explored when we looked at the conflict between unemployment and inflation. And an economist has no special claim over anybody else to making these judgments.

Economic Analysis and Economic Policy Making

While economic theory and analysis may not always be able to tell policy makers what they should do, it usually can tell them what they shouldn't do. An understanding of economic principles can keep us from both pursuing unwise policies and chasing conflicting goals. A few examples will illustrate how this is so.

AN UNWISE POLICY

The printing of money by a government in order to finance its expenditures has long been considered by economists to be an unwise move. Despite their warnings, however, history is a graveyard of fallen governments which have yielded to this temptation. Somehow it always seems easier to turn on the printing press than to raise taxes. After World War I, the German government printed money at such a clip that the rate of inflation reached several thousand percent. At this point the deutsche mark ceased to have any value at all as a medium of exchange. No one would accept it in payment for goods or services. Faith in the government's ability to manage was seriously shaken. The resulting political instability contributed directly to the rise of Adolf Hitler and the Nazi party.

CONFLICTING GOALS

In the conflicting goals category, an election year is often marked by talk of achieving full employment and reducing inflation—both at the same time. Full employment today is usually defined as an unemployment rate of roughly 5 to 6 percent. Most everyone would agree that a 1 percent rate of inflation is low. But almost any economist will tell you that these two goals conflict with one another. A 5 percent unemployment rate goal is probably not compatible with a 1 percent inflation rate goal. Research findings, while not final or always clearcut, might indicate that a 5 percent unemployment rate is possible only if we are willing to accept a 10 percent inflation rate. On the other hand, in order to cut inflation to 1 percent, we might have to live with an unemployment rate of 10 percent. This serves to remind us that an economy's behavior can only be modified within limits. (You can't expect a large bus to take corners like a sports car, or a sports car to carry 50 passengers.) Economic analysis can help us to form realistic policy objectives that don't conflict with one another.

The conflict between goals can be illustrated further by looking at the case of a retail clothier. Suppose the clothier stocked a large number of winter coats—the goal, to make money from their sale. But suppose the winter season is drawing to a close and the clothier still has a large number of winter coats on hand. The clothier has another goal—to make room for new spring fashions. Economic analysis, in particular the law of demand, tells the clothier to lower prices, in other words, to have a sale. But this may mean that the coats will have to be sold for less than what they cost the clothier. As a policy maker, the clothier has had to choose between making money on coats and making room for the new fashions.

Economic Policy, Special Interests, and the Role of the Economist

Making economic policy forces us to choose among alternatives that have different consequences for different groups. Each of us is a member of one or more special interest groups. As students and educators, we might find it in our interest to pay special attention to any proposed legislation that affects education and institutions of learning. Similarly, labor unions are concerned about legislation on right-to-

work laws and the powers and rights of unions to help one another enforce strikes and deal with strikebreakers. Business interests are also concerned with such labor legislation, but their stands on such matters are usually opposed to those of labor. Farmers and consumers are both concerned with agricultural policy, but once again their interests are often in conflict. Resolution of conflicts like these typically involves choices such as those we have discussed in connection with the inflation-unemployment trade-off or the clash between environmentalists and the utility companies. That is, we must make choices that are matters of value judgment. As we have noted, economists have no special calling to make subjective judgments as to what particular group should gain at another's expense. Economists probably do their greatest service to policy making when they take the goals of all parties concerned as given and confine themselves to exploring and explaining which goals are compatible and which conflict, and what economic consequences will result from different policy actions.

AN ECONOMIST LOOKS AT THE NEWS ITEM

Let's take a brief look at the way an economist would probably analyze the news item at the beginning of this chapter. The conflict between producing electricity and maintaining certain environmental standards has led utility companies to ask rate regulators for permission to increase the rates charged electricity users. Economic analysis of the situation would probably suggest to rate regulators, the policy makers in this case, that this request is reasonable. For now, in addition to the usual costs of producing electricity, utility companies are going to have to buy antipollution devices. If they are not allowed to charge a higher price for electricity to help cover these costs, the rate of return on financial capital invested in utility companies will fall. This will make it more difficult to induce lenders to loan funds to utility companies, and hence hamper their ability to expand capacity to supply the growing demand for electricity. Economic analysis indicates that if the goal is to produce electricity in a cleaner manner, then it is not a realistic goal to hold the price of electricity down and also expect to realize the goal of having adequate capacity to meet demand in the future.

MAJOR ECONOMIC POLICY GOALS
IN THE UNITED STATES

A list of economic policy goals which most economists, policy makers, and citizens feel are important in the United States would probably look like this:

1. *Price stability:* in recent years this has meant checking inflation.
2. *Full-employment:* in recent years most economists would take this to mean keeping the unemployment rate down around 5.2 to 5.8 percent.
3. *Economic growth:* continued growth in the standard of living for the average citizen.
4. *Environmental standards:* more control over the pollution and wastes that our production processes produce and impose on the environment.
5. *Economic security:* provision of an adequate standard of living for those who are unable to work either because of age, illness, and other handicaps beyond their control, or because there are simply not enough jobs for all who want them.
6. *An equitable tax burden:* people, especially the middle-income groups, have shown increasing concern that our tax system favors those, typically in higher income brackets, who are in a position to take advantage of various loopholes in our tax laws to avoid or greatly reduce their "fair share" of the tax burden.
7. *Economic freedom:* the idea that businesses, consumers, and workers should be given much freedom in their economic activities.

We have already pointed out how economic experience has suggested that goals 1 and 2 may not be compatible, and that there seems to be a trade-off between the achievement of one at the expense of the other. The same may be true of goals 3 and 4, and goals 4 and 7. Goals 2, 3, and 5 all seem compatible in the sense that if we achieve 2 and 3, we will very likely enhance economic security, goal 5. With respect to goal 6,

some would argue that certain of the so-called loopholes are important as a spur to risky business ventures and that without the tax breaks for these activities there would be less of the sort of enterprising activity essential to economic growth and full employment, goals 2 and 3. They would contend that goal 6, therefore, may not be compatible with goals 2 and 3.

ECONOMIC ANALYSIS
AND THE ECONOMIST

The examples we have considered illustrate why economic analysis is useful in formulating economic policy. In sum, economic analysis: (1) helps to predict what the consequences of any policy action are likely to be, (2) indicates from among several ways to achieve a given goal which ones are most efficient in that their side effects are least detrimental, or possibly even helpful, to the achievement of other goals, (3) suggests which goals are compatible with one another and which are not, (4) indicates what the likely trade-offs are between goals which are not mutually compatible.

If economic analysis does nothing else but keep policy makers from pursuing foolhardy policies, this alone is justification for its use as a policy tool. When economists go beyond the exercise of economic analysis summarized by points 1 to 4 they join the ranks of the various parties to any policy dispute. Their opinions and programs are then properly treated as those of a special interest group. Because, just like everyone else, economists usually do have opinions on matters of value judgment, they often use their economic expertise in support of a cause. In the end, therefore, the burden of separating objective economic analysis from value judgment must rest with you, the citizen. This fact alone should justify the time you devote to the study of economics.

SUMMARY

1. Economics is a social science concerned with the study of how society chooses to use its scarce resources to satisfy its unlimited wants. Economics studies the many issues and problems associated with this process from an overall point of view.

2. Goods are produced by using economic resources. Economic resources are of two basic kinds—human resources (labor) and nonhuman resources (capital and land). Economic resources are also referred to as the factors of production.
3. Discussions of economic issues make use of two kinds of statements. Positive statements are statements of fact. Normative statements, which may be based on positive statements, are statements of opinion.
4. In an effort to explain "how things work," economic analysis makes use of the scientific method. This method uses induction to formulate a theory from observation of facts and events. This theory is then used to predict future events (deduction).
5. Every economic theory has four basic elements: (1) a statement of variables, (2) a set of assumptions, (3) an hypothesis, (4) one or more predictions about future happenings. Economic theories may also be called economic laws, principles, or models. Economic theory is exact to the extent that economic behavior is predictable.
6. Economic theories, such as the law of demand, may be represented graphically.
7. In economics, it is important to determine whether one event is the cause of another event or simply preceded it in time (the *post hoc, ergo propter hoc* fallacy).
8. The assumption that what is true of the parts is true of the whole is known as the fallacy of composition. The assumption that what is true of the whole is true of the parts is known as the fallacy of division.
9. Economic analysis has been divided into two broad areas. Macroeconomics is concerned with the functioning of the whole economy or large sectors within it. Microeconomics focuses on individual units such as households and firms.
10. Economic policy makers use economic theory and analysis to help them formulate ways in which to solve the problems posed by economic reality. In most cases, the solution to these problems involves resolving a conflict between special interest groups. Such a resolution usually depends upon

value judgments, and economists are no more qualified than anyone else to make such judgments. Economic analysis is most useful in determining the possible consequences of various policies.

KEY TERMS AND CONCEPTS
ceteris paribus
deduction
direct relationship
economic policy
economics
economic theory
economy
fallacy of composition
fallacy of division
induction
inverse relationship
macroeconomics
microeconomics
normative statement
positive statement
post hoc, ergo propter hoc
price
scarce
scientific method

QUESTIONS AND PROBLEMS
1. Why is economics called a social science instead of a social study?

2. Why is it that economists, who supposedly use scientific methods when analyzing economic issues, are so often in disagreement?

3. Go back over the news item at the beginning of the chapter and find instances in which a concept or subject is mentioned or discussed which is related to one or more of the economic terms introduced in this chapter.

4. Open today's newspaper to the financial and business section. Pick a story at random and calculate the ratio of positive statements to the total number of statements in the story. Now go to the financial and business *editorial* section and do the same.

5. *Think* about the following experiment. Suppose you were to run an ad in your local paper this week stating that you own a vacant one-acre lot and that somewhere on the lot is buried a metal box containing $10. You state that any and all are welcome to come dig for it and that you will give the $10 to whoever finds it during the coming week. How many people do you think will show up to dig? Suppose, instead, you had said the box contained $30 instead of $10. How many diggers do you think would show up during the same week? Estimate how many would show up during the same week if the reward were $60, $120, or $150. Now construct a graph which measures dollars of reward on the vertical axis and number of diggers on the horizontal axis. Find the points on the graph representing each combination of dollars and diggers and draw a line connecting them.

a. Is the relationship you observe between the size of the dollar reward and the number of diggers an inverse relationship or a direct relationship?

b. What led you to hypothesize the relationship you did between the size of the dollar reward and the number of diggers?

c. If you actually ran the ads over the course of a year and tabulated the number of diggers who showed up for each reward, plotted the results, and found a relationship opposite to the one you have predicted, what would you conclude about your theory? Might the season of the year during which you ran each ad have had something to do with the difference between your theory and what actually happened? Suppose when you ran the $150 reward ad it rained for the whole week the offer was good. Suppose when you ran the $120 reward ad it was sunny the first day of the week and rained the next six. Suppose for the $90 reward ad it was sunny for the first two days and rained the next five. Suppose for the $60 reward ad it was sunny for the first three days and rained the next four. Suppose for the $30 reward ad it was sunny the first five days and rained the next two.

Finally, for the $10 reward ad suppose it was sunny the whole week. How do you think the curve obtained by plotting the combinations of dollar reward and number of diggers might look now? Looking back at the first curve you drew, how important do you think your "other things remaining the same" assumption was?

d. Suppose your original curve was based on the assumption that it was always sunny. If instead it was always raining, where would the curve be—to the left or to the right of the original curve?

e. What would you predict would happen if you raised the amount of the reward money to $1,000?

f. Can you, as my economic policy adviser, recommend how I might clear off and dig up a one-acre lot that I own in town?

g. Can you, as my economic policy adviser, tell me how to deal with the racial tensions that might arise between the people who show up to dig on my lot?

h. Do you think people respond to economic incentives?

i. Do you think human behavior is predictable?

6. The following item appeared in the *Wall Street Journal* of September 14, 1976:

> Election Returns: Who holds the presidency "has an effect on the workers' ability to organize into unions," the AFL-CIO argues in its analysis of the past 16 years. It cites figures showing that in the Kennedy-Johnson years 57 percent of workers voted for unions in NLRB [National Labor Relations Board] elections, while only 44 percent favored unions in the Nixon-Ford years.

a. What do you think of the merits of this cause-and-effect argument?

b. Are there other explanations that might be offered for these facts?

2

SCARCITY, CHOICE, AND THE ECONOMIC PROBLEM

ECOLOGY'S MISSING PRICE TAG

NEW YORK, June 5—In "The Closing Circle," Barry Commoner states as the fourth law of ecology that "there is no such thing as a free lunch." This is also the first law of economics. Mr. Commoner's use of this phrase is intended to mean that we cannot go on doing damage to the environment indefinitely without paying a price for it. What is equally true, however, is that to reduce the damage of economic activity to the environment we must also pay a price.

There have been numerous attempts to assess the cost of federal pollution-control legislation. Suppose we combine the cost estimates for water-pollution control, made by the National Commission on Water Quality (NCWQ), and the National Economic Research Associates' (NERA) cost estimates for air-pollution control for the Electric Utility industry, with the Council on Environmental Quality's (CEQ) estimates for all other pollution-control costs. We come up with a total capital investment from 1974 to 1983 of $175 billion to $263 billion and annual costs in 1983 of $55 billion to $66 billion, or $679 to $815 per household per year (in 1975 dollars). Allowing for possible underestimates in the CEQ data, annual costs in 1983 could be as high as $89.4 billion or $1,098 per household.

On the basis of these estimates, by 1983 between 3 percent and 6 percent of GNP and between 7 percent and 10 percent of total gross private domestic investment would be expended to comply with federal clean air and water legislation. To put this in perspective, in 1974 about 7 percent of GNP was allocated to all educational programs in the United States, the same percentage to health, and about 1 percent to law enforcement.

The size of these figures does not mean such expenditures are unwarranted. However, they do suggest that environmental legislation represents a significant reordering of our national priorities. And this can come about only at the expense of other important objectives.

The subject of this news item is a typical example of the kind of economic issue that confronts modern industrial economies. Moreover, it has all the ingredients of the basic economic problem that has always confronted human beings. In the first chapter we talked about economics, economic methodology, and the nature of economic issues. In this chapter we will focus on the basic economic problem and the fundamental questions it poses. Then we will look into the ways economies may be organized to answer these questions. Although, as we shall see, the answers may vary considerably, the need to answer these questions is inescapable. The answers an economy gives to these questions are related to the fundamental issues of how well people live, how hard they work, and how choices about these matters are to be made.

THE ECONOMIC PROBLEM

The basic **economic problem** *that underlies all economic issues is the combined existence of scarce resources and unlimited wants.* Ben Franklin put it this way: "The poor have little,—beggars none; the rich too much,—enough not one." As we noted in Chapter 1, the economic resources of land, labor, and capital exist only in limited amounts. As a result, there is a limit to the quantity of economic goods which can be produced with these scarce resources. But unfortunately, people's desires for goods are really unlimited for all intents and purposes of economic analysis. While in theory it may be possible to attain a level of abundance which would satisfy everybody's appetites for all things, no such state has ever existed. And at this time, the prospects of ever achieving such a state seem remote enough to be considered nonexistent. One only has to consider the standard of living

in the world's richest nation, the United States, to realize that there is hardly a person who couldn't draw up a list of wanted goods which far exceeds his or her means to obtain them. Ask yourself, or anyone else, what you would do with an additional hundred dollars. If you felt completely without want, you might say that you would give it to a charity. But why does charity exist? Because some other group or person has unsatisfied wants.

The combination of scarcity and unlimited wants continually forces us to make choices. You might decide to spend almost all your income on a fancy new car or the latest in sophisticated stereo gear or a wardrobe of the latest fashions or all three at once. However to do so, you may have to be willing to live on peanut butter sandwiches and share a one-bedroom walk-up with two winos over a sleazy bar in a low-rent district of town. It's your choice if you want to do it. Or you might choose to allocate your income so that you forgo the car, clothes, and stereo gear in favor of a college education. This is a decision that may still force you to live in the sleazy part of town with two wino roommates posing as students. In the latter case, you've probably chosen to forgo some of the "better things in life" now in order to get an education which will give you greater opportunities to obtain them later. If you have a generous parent, relative, or other benefactor who can give you a great deal of money now you might be able to have all of the things you want and move out of the sleazy apartment as well. Even then, you would still have to make choices. Your time is scarce. Should you spend it majoring in economics, fine arts, or engineering? In Calcutta, three women may share one dress. They have to choose which one wears it and when, while the other two stay indoors.

Scarcity, Production, and Efficiency

Given that resources are limited and people's wants are unlimited, the problem that faces any economy is how to use scarce resources and organize production so as to satisfy to the greatest extent possible society's unlimited wants. This means that the available resources must be used as efficiently as possible. In other words, the maximum output must be obtained from the resources at hand.

There are two major problems that can prevent a society from achieving **economic efficiency**. These are **unemployment** and **underemployment** or **resource misallocation**.

UNEMPLOYMENT

Maximum economic efficiency cannot be achieved while available resources are not fully used. This holds true for both human and non-human resources. As long as there are workers looking for work and unable to find it, or if plant capacity remains unused, maximum economic efficiency cannot be achieved. Notice that we stress that in order to have economic efficiency all *available* resources must be employed. Some parts of the population may not seek employment. By custom and law some people, such as children and the aged, may be prevented from working. Certain kinds of land are prohibited by law from use for certain types of productive activity. However, whenever there

are available resources standing idle, there are fewer inputs into the economy's productive process. As a result, there is a lower output of goods to satisfy society's wants.

UNDEREMPLOYMENT OR RESOURCE MISALLOCATION

If certain available resources are used to do jobs for which other available resources are better suited there is underemployment or misallocation of resources. For example, if cabinetmakers were employed to make dresses and seamstresses were employed to make cabinets, the total amount of cabinets and dresses produced would be less than if each group were employed in the activity for which it was trained. Similarly, if Florida's orange groves were planted with wheat while Minnesota's farms were planted with orange trees, the same total land area would provide the country with substantially less of both crops than is the case with the conventional arrangement. Resource underemployment also results whenever the best available technology is not used in a production process. A housepainter painting with a toothbrush and a farmer harvesting wheat with a pocketknife are both underemployed. A forty-ton bulldozer is underemployed when used to mow a half-acre yard once a week. *Whenever there is resource underemployment or misallocation, a reallocation of resources to productive activities for*

After reading this chapter, you will be able to:
1. Explain why the combination of scarce resources and unlimited wants makes choice necessary.
2. Define the term "economic efficiency" and distinguish between unemployment and underemployment of resources.
3. Explain the concept of the production possibilities frontier and show why when an economy is on the frontier it can have more of one good only by giving up some of another.
4. Demonstrate why the selection of an output combination on today's production possibilities frontier affects the location of tomorrow's frontier.
5. Formulate the basic questions posed by the fundamental economic problem that every economy must answer.
6. Distinguish among pure market economies, mixed economies, and planned economies.

which they are better suited will result in a larger output of some or all goods and no reduction in the output of any.

Production Possibilities Trade-off

When an economy's available resources are fully employed (that is, there is no unemployment or underemployment), we say that economy is producing its maximum possible output of goods. Given that resources are limited, the maximum possible output level is, of course, limited too. Therefore, producing more of one kind of good will of necessity mean producing less of another. The amount of reduction in the production of one good that is necessary in order to produce more of another is called **opportunity cost**, a very important economic concept.

Let us illustrate this concept by focusing on the subject of the news item at the beginning of this chapter. Suppose that the output of an economy may be divided into two categories—antipollution devices and bundles of all other goods. One bundle will contain one of each and every good produced in the economy *except* antipollution devices. A bundle may be thought of as a good—the composite good. The issue to be illustrated here is of more than academic interest. Central to the news item on electricity demand in the previous chapter is the dispute between the electrical utility companies and the environmentalists. Environmentalists would impose stricter pollution standards on utility companies. Utility companies claim that the costs of meeting these standards are reducing their ability to meet the growing demand for electricity. The fundamental issue raised by this particular dispute is relevant for the whole economy, as the news item at the beginning of this chapter suggests. If we are to have a cleaner environment, we are going to need to use antipollution devices in many production processes that cause pollution. How do we measure the cost to society of providing these devices?

PRODUCTION AND CHOICE

In answering this question we will make certain assumptions, as follows:

1. The existing state of technology will remain unchanged for the period in which we are examining this issue.

2. The total available supply of resources (land, labor, and capital) will remain the same. However, these resources may be shifted from producing antipollution devices to producing bundles of all other goods and vice versa.

3. All available resources are fully employed (there is no unemployment or underemployment in the economy).

Given the existing supply of resources and level of technology, society must make choices. Should its fully employed resources be devoted entirely to the production of bundles of all other goods? Or should it reduce its output of bundles and use the factors of production released from that activity to produce antipollution devices? If so, what combinations of bundles and antipollution devices can it produce, given that its resources are fully employed? Clearly, the more antipollution devices the economy produces, the more resources will have to be devoted to their production. Fewer resources will then be available for the production of bundles. Given that resources are fully employed, whatever combination of bundles and devices the economy might think of producing, any other combination will necessarily contain more of one and less of the other. In short, you can't get something for nothing. If the economy wants to produce more antipollution devices, it will have to give up a certain number of bundles. If it wants to produce more bundles, it will have to give up a certain number of antipollution devices.

CHOICES FOR POLLUTION CONTROL

Some of the possible combinations of bundles and antipollution devices which the economy we have been considering can produce per year when all resources are fully employed are listed in Table 2-1. If this economy was to devote all of its resources to producing bundles of all other goods, it would be able to produce 80 million bundles per year and no antipollution devices (combination *A*). Although it seems very unrealistic and highly unlikely, the economy could devote all of its fully employed resources to producing antipollution devices and go without all other goods (combination *E*). Such a choice would certainly carry environmental considerations to the extreme, in the sense that the cost would amount to giving up the production of all other goods. However, at the other extreme, combination *A* would probably not be very desirable either. With this combination, the economy would not be doing anything at all about pollution. If it were deemed desirable to do something about pollution, the economy could be moved away from point *A* toward point *E*. *To do this, resources would have to be moved away from the production of bundles and into the production of antipollution devices.* How much of a shift in this direction society chooses to make will depend upon the degree of concern about pollution. A cleaner environment will cost something. Suppose society's concern is such that it chooses to produce combination *B* instead of combination *A*. The cost of the 50,000 antipollution devices it will now have is the 20 million bundles of all other goods it must give up to achieve this combination. If society has an even greater concern about pollution, combination *C* or even combination *D* could be chosen. However, to have the greater quantities of antipollution devices associated with combination *C* or combination *D* requires that society forgo the production of more bundles of all other goods.

THE OPPORTUNITY COST OF CHOICE

In summary, because economic resources are scarce, a full-employment, two-good economy cannot have more of both goods. To have more of one good, it must give up some of the other. The cost of having more of one good is the opportunity cost, or the amount of the other good that must be given up. By choosing combination *B* in Table 2-1 *instead* of combination *A*, society must forgo the opportunity of having 20 million bundles of all other goods (the difference between 80 million and 60 million). The opportunity cost of the 50,000 antipollution devices is therefore 20 million bundles. The opportunity cost of choosing combination *C instead* of combination *B*, or the opportunity cost of having an additional 30,000 antipollution devices, is another 20 million bundles. The opportunity cost of choosing *C instead* of *A*, or the opportunity cost of having 80,000 antipollution devices, is 40 million bundles, the difference between

TABLE 2-1 POSSIBLE COMBINATIONS OF ANTIPOLLUTION DEVICES AND BUNDLES OF ALL OTHER GOODS THAT MAY BE PRODUCED IN A FULL-EMPLOYMENT ECONOMY (Hypothetical Data)

Product	Production Possibilities (Output per Year)				
	A	B	C	D	E
Antipollution devices (in thousands)	0	50	80	100	110
Bundles of all other goods (in millions)	80	60	40	20	0

the number of bundles associated with combination *A* and the number associated with combination *C*.

Whenever scarcity forces us to make a choice, we must "pay" an opportunity cost. This cost is measured in terms of forgone alternatives. All costs are opportunity costs (often simply referred to as costs). If you buy a notepad for a dollar, you forgo the opportunity of spending that dollar on something else. Since the pad cost you a dollar, you now have a dollar less to spend on all other goods, unless you have an infinite supply of money, which is impossible. There is no free lunch.

■CHECKPOINT 2-1

What is the opportunity cost of choosing combination *C* instead of combination *B*? Of choosing combination *B* instead of combination *C*? Of choosing combination *A* instead of combination *D*?

The Production Possibilities Frontier

To get a better idea of what opportunity cost is all about, let's plot the data from Table 2-1 on a graph. We begin, as always, with our two axes. On the horizontal axis we measure the number of antipollution devices. On the vertical axis we measure the number of bundles. As we did in Chapter 1, we now locate all the points

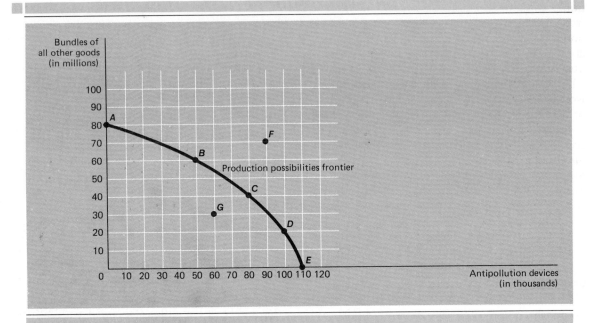

FIGURE 2-1 THE PRODUCTION POSSIBILITIES FRONTIER

Each point on the downward-sloping curve represents some maximum output combination of two goods for an economy whose available resources are fully employed. (In this case, the two goods are bundles and devices.) Because no combination to the right or above the curve is possible, it is called the production possibilities frontier.

Point *G* represents a combination of goods produced when the economy is operating inefficiently. Unemployment or underemployment of economic resources has resulted in a smaller output than is actually possible. Point *F*, on the other hand, represents a combination of goods that cannot be produced given available resources and technology. This point can only be achieved if the production possibilities curve shifts outward as a result of economic growth.

on the graph that represent the possible devices/bundles combinations listed in our table. If we draw a line connecting the points, the result looks like Figure 2-1. The curve slopes downward because when available resources are fully employed, more devices can be produced only by producing fewer bundles.

ON AND OFF THE FRONTIER

The curve we have drawn by connecting all the points on the graph is called the **production possibilities frontier**. *Each point on a production possibilities frontier represents a maximum output combination for a two-good economy whose available resources are fully employed.* The term fron-

tier is used because it is not possible for the economy to produce any combination of the two goods (in this case bundles and devices) represented by a point above or to the right of the curve. Therefore, a combination of quantities of bundles and devices represented by the point *F* in Figure 2–1 is not possible.

Now let's change one of our assumptions so that the economy's available resources are not being used efficiently (they are either unemployed or underemployed). In this case, the economy cannot produce any combination of devices and bundles represented by any point on its production possibilities frontier. Rather, it will only be able to produce output combinations represented by points located inside the frontier, such as point *G*, for example. Any point inside the production possibilities frontier is attainable given available resources. To produce any such output combination would be inefficient, however, since available resources would either be unemployed or underemployed or both.

Finally, we should note that *if any of the economy's available resources are increased, or if there is an increase in technological know-how, the production possibilities frontier will shift outward (up and to the right)*. This is **economic growth**.

THE LAW OF INCREASING COSTS

Figure 2-1 illustrates how graphs plotted from economic data can make the relationship between two economic variables immediately obvious. In Figure 2-1 we are struck at once by the change in the trade-off between bundles and antipollution devices as we move from combination *A* to *B* to *C* and so on to *E*. When we move from *A* to *B*, a sacrifice (or cost) of 20 million bundles allows us to have 50,000 antipollution devices. However, a move from *B* to *C*, which costs another 20 million bundles, allows us to have only an additional 30,000 devices. The additional quantity of antipollution devices obtained for each succeeding sacrifice of 20 million bundles continues to get smaller as we move from *C* to *D* to *E*. The reason for the deteriorating trade-off is that economic resources are more adaptable to some production processes than others. As more and more resources are shifted from the production of bundles into the production of antipollution devices, we are forced to use factors of production whose productivity at making devices is lower and lower relative to their productivity at making bundles. For example, when we move from *A* to *B*, a large number of engineers and scientists might be moved from bundle production to the highly technical production of devices. As we continue moving from *B* to *E*, it becomes harder and harder to find labor resources of this nature. When moving from *D* to *E*, only the labor least suited for producing devices will be left—poets, hod carriers, and so forth.

The decrease in the number of additional antipollution devices obtained for each additional sacrifice of 20 million bundles as we move from *A* to *E* is a common economic phenomenon. It is sometimes called the **law of increasing costs**. To illustrate this law more clearly, divide the number of bundles that must be sacrificed by the additional number of devices obtained by moving from one combination to the next. In the move from *A* to *B*, it costs 20 million bundles to obtain 50,000 devices, or 400 bundles per device. In the move from *B* to *C*, it costs 20 million bundles to obtain 30,000 devices, or 666.6 bundles per device. The move from *C* to *D* costs 1,000 bundles per device. The move from *D* to *E* costs 2,000 bundles per device. We are accustomed to measuring costs in dollars— so many dollars per unit of some good. Since dollars merely stand for the amounts of other goods they can buy, we have simply represented the cost of devices in terms of bundles of other goods. *The law of increasing costs says that when moving along the production possibilities frontier the cost per additional good obtained measured in terms of the good sacrificed rises due to the difference in productivity of resources when used in different production processes.*

Choice of Product Combination: Present Versus Future

By now you may be puzzled by the fact that antipollution devices have been discussed only in terms of the cost of producing them. Don't antipollution devices provide benefits? Yes, but only once they've been installed. Remember the first two assumptions underlying our construction of the production possibilities frontier? We assumed that the existing state of technology and the total available supply of factors of production would remain the same. These assumptions tell us something about the length of time involved in our analysis. Since antipollution devices are used to produce other goods—clean air and water—they are capital goods. As capital goods, they become factors of production once they are built. *During the time period* to which the production possibilities frontier we drew in Figure 2-1 applies, existing factors of production are given and fixed in place to be used for production during that same period. Antipollution devices to be built in that time period cannot be used then. Once they are built and put in place, the supply of available economic resources will be larger. But then we must construct a new production possibilities frontier to account for this increase in available resources.

PRESENT SACRIFICE
FOR FUTURE BENEFIT

But why would an economy want to give up any bundles to build devices in the first place? Such a sacrifice is only made because it is felt that the antipollution devices produced will yield benefits in the future. The production possibilities frontier tells us that in order to build antipollution devices now we have to pay for them by giving up the production of a certain amount of bundles of all other goods now. By giving up more bundles now, more antipollution devices can be built, which will provide more of the goods (clean air and water) we want in the future. More clean air and water and a generally cleaner environment will lead to less fouling of equipment and an increase in the general health of the population. This will in turn increase efficiency and thereby increase the economy's productive capacity. However, we must bear in mind that some of the goods in each of the bundles we are giving up now are other capital goods. If we sacrifice too many bundles now to produce antipollution devices, the future increases in productive capacity resulting from a cleaner environment may be offset by decreases in future productive capacity resulting from a lack of other capital goods. These other capital goods are needed as factors of production in the future.

SHIFTING THE FRONTIER

This concept is illustrated in Figure 2-2. Here we will use the same curve we drew in Figure 2-1 to represent the economy's 1985 production possibilities frontier. We will call this Frontier 1. An increase in the economy's productive capacity will cause the frontier to expand outward. A decrease will cause the frontier to contract inward. The degree to which the frontier will expand or contract depends upon the com-

bination of goods the economy decides to produce in 1985. If the economy chooses to produce a combination of devices and bundles such as A (all bundles, no devices), the increase in capital goods will cause the frontier to expand outward to 1986 Frontier 2. A choice such as B will result in fewer bundles but the addition to productive capacity from devices will more than offset whatever loss in productive capacity may result from producing fewer bundles. As a result, the frontier will expand even farther, to 1986 Frontier 3. If, however, the economy chooses to produce a combination such as D on its 1985 frontier, the small production of bundles (which, remember, contain all other capital goods) will result in a loss of productive capacity which cannot be offset by the gain from the large number of devices that will be produced. This is so because the production of other capital goods is reduced below the level needed simply to replace existing capital goods as they wear out. Consequently, the loss of productive capacity will cause the production possibilities frontier to contract inward to the 1986 Frontier 4. Finally, if combination E is chosen in 1985, nothing but devices will be built and the society will have no other goods at all to sustain itself. Since people can't live on antipollution devices alone, they will starve and the 1986 frontier will collapse to the origin.

In summary, we can say that an economy's present choice of a point on its production possibilities frontier influences the future location of that frontier. To this extent, present choices imply future choices as well.

ECOLOGY'S PRICE TAG

The news item on electricity demand in the previous chapter noted that some people are wondering whether the cost of protecting the environment is outrunning the benefits of doing so, a theme also stressed by this chapter's news item. The production possibilities frontier shows us the nature of the choices and the associated costs that must be considered when answering this question. The economist can objectively say that society would be making an inefficient use of resources if it decided to produce a combination of goods inside the frontier. Similarly, an economist can objectively say that a combina-

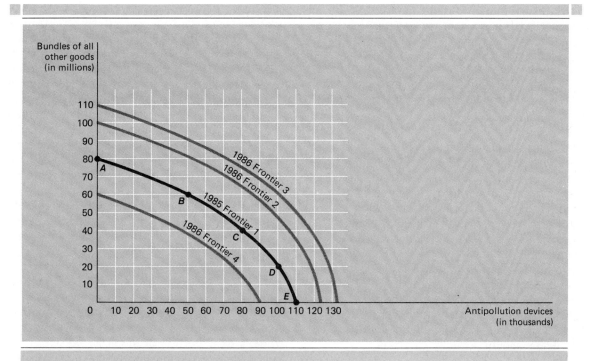

FIGURE 2-2 PRESENT CHOICES AND FUTURE PRODUCTION POSSIBILITIES FRONTIERS

An economy's choice of a point on its present production possibilities frontier influences the location of its future frontier. A choice such as *A* on 1985 Frontier 1 will produce enough capital goods to expand the frontier outward to 1986 Frontier 2. But a choice such as *B*, which includes production of some antipollution devices, will increase productive capacity even further. The frontier would then be able to expand outward to Frontier 3. However, if the economy chooses *D*, the smaller production of bundles (which, remember, contain all other capital goods) will result in a loss of productive capacity, which cannot be offset by the gain from the large number of devices that will be produced. At *D* the economy would not even be able to replace its present supply of capital goods as they wore out, and the production possibilities frontier would actually contract inward, to 1986 Frontier 4. Finally, a choice such as *E*, which would produce only antipollution devices, would cause mass starvation and privation. The production possibilities frontier would then collapse to the origin.

tion above or to the right of the frontier is not possible. But the following also needs to be said. In an economy such as that summarized in Table 2-1, it must be pointed out to those who would like to produce 80,000 antipollution devices that they cannot also produce 80 million bundles as well. Almost everyone is for God, mother, and country—and environmental protection. The question is, How much are we willing to pay for it?

■ CHECKPOINT 2-2

Suppose we always redistribute all the food in the world so that each person has an equal share. Suppose, however, that the rate of population growth continues to exceed the rate of growth of the food supply. As a policy maker, what choices do you now have? In Table 2-1 what is the opportunity cost of choosing combination *C* instead of *D*; *B* instead of *C*; *A* instead of *D*? Consider the

movement from *E* to *A* in Figure 2–1 and represent the law of increasing cost measured in terms of antipollution devices.

BASIC PROBLEMS FOR ANY ECONOMY

Given an economy's available resources and technology, we have seen how the production possibilities from which it may choose can be characterized by a production possibilities frontier. A frontier can be determined for any economy, whatever its form of government. A knowledge of what is possible is necessary in order to answer a number of important questions or problems that any economy, be it that of the Soviet Union or the United States or Pakistan, must solve. These questions confront socialist, communist, and capitalist countries, developed and underdeveloped economies alike. These questions are what and how much to produce, how should production be organized, and for whom should goods be produced.

What and How Much to Produce

We could draw up an incredibly large list of goods that could be produced in the United States. These goods would include everything from needles and thread to space vehicles and kidney dialysis machines. Some of the goods on the list, while possible to produce, might not be desired by anybody. Other goods, such as various kinds of food, might be desired by nearly everyone. If we were to draw up a list of goods that could be produced by one of the less developed countries in the world, it would probably be considerably shorter. Nevertheless, given its respective list, each country would have to decide what goods and how much of each to produce.

In the economy summarized in Table 2-1, the answer to the question "what to produce" was antipollution devices and bundles of all other goods. The question "how much" really asks what point on the production possibilities frontier would be selected. The answer to this question must be decided by society's tastes and priorities. The answer is thus a value judgment. As we noted in Chapter 1, an economist's value

judgment has no superior claim over anyone else's. It may be that a relatively underdeveloped country seeking rapid economic growth and industrialization would feel little concern about the environmental impact of these processes. It would therefore not want to divert resources to antipollution devices. However, a country such as the United States, having experienced growth and industrialization, may be more aware of their adverse environmental impact. It would therefore be willing to divert a larger share of resources to producing antipollution devices. Whether the cost of protecting the environment is outrunning the benefits will depend on who is assessing the benefits.

Who makes the decisions about what and how much to produce? The answer to this question varies greatly from one economy to another. In countries like the Soviet Union or Communist China, these decisions are made by a central planning bureau of the government. In the United States, Canada, and Western Europe, a large portion of the decisions about the allocation of resources is made by the pricing system, which is often referred to as a **free-market economy**. However, as indicated by the news item on electricity demand in the previous chapter, the political process has legislated government intervention in some decisions. In the United States, electric utility companies set rates subject to approval by government regulatory agencies. Similarly, decisions about pollution control have to a considerable degree been made through congressional action. Government intervention seems desirable in certain cases because society has decided that the resource allocations made by free markets have been unsatisfactory in some areas. Pollution control is one of these. National defense is another.

How Should Production Be Organized?

In discussing the production possibilities frontier, we emphasized that to be on the frontier it is necessary to use economic resources in the most efficient way. Once society has determined what goods to produce, the amount of each of those goods it will be able to produce will depend on how available resources are allocated to various productive activities. If we try to grow oranges in Minnesota and raise wheat in Florida, we are not going to have as much of either as we would if those land resources were used just the other way around. In addition, even when resources are allocated to their most productive activities, the most efficient known productive processes must be used. Harvesting wheat in Minnesota with pinking shears and making orange juice in Florida by squeezing them by hand is still not going to give us as much wheat or orange juice as is technologically possible. Ideally, *society should allocate available resources to productive activities and use known productive techniques in such a way that no reallocation of resources or change of technique could yield more of any good without yielding less of another. This is true of any combination of goods represented by any point on the production possibilities frontier.*

This ideal is easy enough to understand and describe. But it may have struck you by now as a little like being told that the way to make money on the stock market is to buy low and sell high. You can understand that perfectly and wouldn't disagree a bit. But only a moment's reflection will lead you to ask the inevitable question: "Yes, but how do I *know* when a stock is at its low and when it is at its high?" Similarly, an economy doesn't have a big television screen up in the sky with a picture of its production possibilities frontier and a white dot which can be moved around by turning knobs until society has got itself right at the desired spot on the frontier. Society can't "see" the economy's production possibilities frontier, nor is it a simple matter of turning a few control knobs to "move" onto it. So how should an economy go about organizing its available resources in order to use them most efficiently? What regulating mechanisms or rules of thumb can be used to do this? How will the most efficient production techniques be determined? Which are the best combinations of resources to use with these techniques? What regulating mechanisms or management techniques can be used to assure that the appropriate kinds and necessary amounts of resources will be directed to indus-

tries producing desired goods? Any economy, be it centrally planned or completely free market, wants to be on its production possibilities frontier. The question is, How does it get there?

For Whom to Produce

For whom should the output of the economy be produced? Put another way, how should the economy's total output be distributed among the individual members of the economy? Should it be distributed to individuals according to their productive contribution to the making of that output? Or should we take from each according to his or her ability and give to each according to his or her need? If people receive strictly according to their productive contribution, it's clear some people are going to be terribly poor. On the other hand, if there is no relationship between an individual's productive contribution and the reward received for it, what will be the incentive for hard work? If the able and productive members of society do not have incentives to work hard, the total output of the economy will not be as large. If the total pie is smaller, there simply will be less to go around. All societies must wrestle with this problem. They must decide how to distribute output in such a way as to encourage the productive members to work up to their ability, and at the same time try to maintain a minimum standard of living for all. In short, they must decide what degree of income inequality can be tolerated given these conflicting goals. The range of opinion on this is wide indeed and can fire the most heated debates. It is a matter of politics, cultural values, and moral issues.

In addition to solving this problem, all economies must decide how much of the total output should go to government, how much to business, and how much to households. This, of course, raises questions about how taxes should be levied and who should pay them. It raises questions about how much of the decision-making process for allocation of resources should be in the hands of the government rather than of the private sector (households and businesses). In wartime, any society is likely to give to the government whatever portion of output it needs to ensure survival. In peacetime, without the pressure of such a common goal, decisions about how to distribute total output are not usually made with such a consensus.

Full Utilization of Resources

In our discussion of economic efficiency and the problem of how to organize production, we emphasized that *an economy can fall short of its production possibilities frontier if resources are misallocated or if the best known production techniques are not used. Another kind of economic inefficiency, also noted earlier, occurs whenever available resources are allowed to stand idle. This kind of inefficiency will also keep an economy from operating on its production possibilities frontier.*

In twentieth-century capitalist economies, such as that of the United States, there have been frequent periods of recession, which means that significant amounts of labor and other available resources have been idle, or unemployed. During the depression of the 1930s, the measured unemployment rate was around 25 percent. Economists estimate that the actual rate of unemployment may have been considerably higher than this. (This is because some of the unemployed were not reported.) In capitalist economies we often refer to the recurring pattern of increasing and decreasing unemployment associated with decreasing and increasing output as **business fluctuations** or **business cycles**. Centrally planned economies such as those of the Soviet Union, Communist China, and the Eastern European nations are not free from the problem of fluctuations in their production of output. The underlying reasons why they have these difficulties are different, and for ideological reasons they describe the problem differently. An economist visiting the United States from the central planning bureau of an Eastern European country was asked if they experienced anything like our business fluctuations. He said, "Oh, no." The question was then rephrased, "Well, don't you ever experience fluctuations in production cycles?" He responded, "Oh, you mean 'technical cycles'!"

In the industrialized economies of the Western world, the problem of eliminating or reducing unemployment of labor and other available

resources is a high priority of economic policy. In the United States, Congress passed the Employment Act of 1946, declaring that it shall be the continuing policy and responsibility of the federal government "to promote maximum employment, production, and purchasing power." Responsibility for carrying out the intent of this act is given to the executive branch of the government. The president, assisted by the Council of Economic Advisors established by the act, must submit an annual economic report. This report describes the current state of the economy and recommends policy actions aimed at fulfilling the objectives of the act.

Unemployment of economic resources is similar in its effects to the underemployment of economic resources which results from their misallocation to inappropriate activities or when the best known techniques of production are not used. Both unemployment and underemployment cause the economy to produce at a point inside its production possibility frontier. However, the appropriate ways to deal with these two problems are quite different. *The underemployment problem requires an answer to the question of how to organize production.* Remedies there require establishing ways to see to it that Minnesota is planted with wheat and not oranges, and that harvesting machines instead of pinking shears are used to cut it. These kinds of problems are generally studied in microeconomics.

Remedies for the unemployment problem generally take the form of assuring that there is enough demand for goods and services to require the full utilization of all available resources to meet that demand. You might think it strange that resources could be idle at all, and that it could be due to a low demand for goods. After all, don't people work in order to earn income to buy goods? Unfortunately, in a money-using economy producing many kinds of goods, a person's offer of labor services in one place is quite removed from his or her desired purchase of goods in another. A line of unemployed jobseekers at a steel mill's gate does not mean that each wants to work in direct exchange for a ton of cold-rolled steel to be carried home at the end of the day. The mill manager's plans to produce steel and hire workers are affected quite differently by a line of job-seeking, unemployed steel workers than they are by a line of customers wanting to place orders. It is not obvious that if workers were employed in the back, customers would materialize out front to purchase their output. This is true even though the workers would most likely use their earned money to buy a multitude of items requiring steel. All firms in the economy producing all kinds of goods are in the same situation as the steel mill. Clearly when there are unemployed laborers and other resources in the whole economy, it is a result of the totality of these situations. The remedies for this sort of problem are studied in macroeconomics.

Change, Stability, and Growth

All economies are subject to change. The underlying causes of change are sometimes quite predictable. Population growth and the increase of technological know-how is a main impetus to economic growth. These kinds of change are fairly steady and ongoing. Population growth in underdeveloped countries is typically higher than in more industrialized countries. It is so high, in fact, that it poses a problem for those economies. Namely, it makes it very difficult to increase the standard of living. The growth in the number of people to be fed makes it difficult to divert resources from agricultural production to the capital formation needed for industrialization. This applies not just to the formation of physical capital, but to the investment in human capital needed to provide the level of literacy and know-how required of the labor force in an industrialized economy. In other countries, such as Australia, it is felt that the rate of population growth is too low to spur the kind of economic growth desired. Depending on the particular economy, the level of population growth can pose a problem by being either too high or too low. In India birth control measures are a primary policy concern. In Australia, population policy has been aimed at creating incentives to encourage immigration from abroad and the settlement of the vast interior of the continent.

Other kinds of change are often less predictable and pose severe problems for maintaining stable economic processes in a country. The abrupt onset of the energy shortage in the United States in 1973 and 1974 was not widely predicted or anticipated. It is felt by most economists that it was a major contributing factor to the recession which began in late 1973 and lasted through the first quarter of 1975. This was the severest recession in the United States since the depression of the 1930s.

Often, drastic institutional and political changes, even when well intended, can cause severe economic problems for an economy. After the Communists took over in China in 1949, they instituted a new agricultural and industrialization program. This program increased grain production from 108 million tons in 1949 to 182 million tons in 1956, and steel production from 360,000 tons in 1950 to 3.32 million tons by 1956. Then in 1958 the Chinese leadership attempted to institute what they called the Great Leap Forward. They constructed backyard steel furnaces throughout the country, mandated 18-hour workdays, and transferred half a billion peasants into giant communes. All this, combined with three years of bad weather, proved to be too much change for the economy to adapt to. In some places, there was near starvation for the first time since the Communist takeover. Production dropped sharply and economic progress may have been set back by as much as a decade.

A major cause of instability in industrialized Western economies in recent years has been change in the general levels of prices. This phenomenon is more commonly referred to as inflation. Since World War II, the general direction of prices in the United States has been continually upward. But in more recent years the rate of increase of prices seems to have risen. Perhaps of equal concern from the standpoint of stability has been the variation in the rate of increase. For example, during the recession lasting from November 1973 through March 1975, the consumer index rose at a compound annual rate of 10.9 percent. During the subsequent year of recovery, it rose at a compound annual rate of 6.1 percent. This kind of variation creates uncertainty among consumers and businesses. Consumers often become more cautious about making major purchases, such as for housing and automobiles. Businesses and labor unions spend more time haggling about cost-of-living clauses in union contracts. Economists are in broad agreement that price stability is a most undesirable source of change in the economy.

Every economy has to contend with various kinds of change at one time or another. Some are thought to be desirable, such as the growth in technological knowledge. In industrialized economies of the West, change in consumer tastes and an economy's ability to adapt to meet those changes is generally considered desirable. Other kinds of change, including inflation, recession, and external shocks to the economy, such as that caused by the Arab oil embargo, are on everybody's bad list. About some forms of change we have mixed feelings. A prime example in the United States in recent years is economic growth. We like it to the extent that it provides employment and an increase in goods and services. On the other hand, we don't like the accompanying increase in pollution, congestion in urban areas and on highways, and what many feel is a growing rootlessness and depersonalization of our way of life.

A major problem to be solved by an economy is how to adapt to various kinds of change so as to maximize the benefits derived from the desirable aspects of change, and minimize the losses caused by the undesirable.

■ CHECKPOINT 2-3

Do you think the questions of what to produce and for whom to produce it are of a normative or a positive nature? Why? Does the news item at the beginning of this chapter focus on the nature of the production possibilities frontier or on the issues of what and how much to produce, and for whom?

THE VARIETY OF ECONOMIC SYSTEMS

There are a wide variety of ways of organizing an economy to answer the basic questions we have discussed in this chapter. How an economy deals with the basic problem of scarcity—

the questions it poses—is also an expression of its vision of the relationship between the individual and society. The way in which a society chooses to organize its economy is therefore to a large extent a reflection of its cultural values and political **ideology**. It was in recognition of this fact that the subject of economics was originally called political economy. Most any debate over the relative merits of various types of economic systems cannot avoid dealing with the different political ideologies on which they are based. In the following section we will consider three basic types of economic systems without dwelling at any length on their political and ideological implications. Nonetheless, it should be kept in mind that these implications are usually regarded as matters of considerable importance.

Pure Market Economy, Laissez Faire Capitalism

Laissez faire is a French expression which means "let [people] do [as they choose]." Especially in matters of economics, it means allowing people to do as they please without governmental regulations and controls. *The ideological basis of such an economic system is the belief that if each economic unit is allowed to make free choices in pursuit of its own best interests, the interests of all will be best served.*

What are the main features of a pure market economy based on laissez faire **capitalism**? The means of production are privately owned by private citizens and private institutions. Private property is the rule. Government ownership is generally limited to public buildings and other facilities needed by the government in order to provide such things as national defense, a judicial system, police and fire protection, and public schools and roads. There is freedom of choice for consumers, businesses, and all resource suppliers. Consumers may purchase what they want subject to the limits of their money incomes—there is consumer sovereignty. Businesses are free to purchase and utilize resources to produce whatever products they desire and sell them in markets of their choice—there is free enterprise. Suppliers of resources such as labor, land, and financial capital are likewise free to sell them in whatever markets they please. The major constraint on businesses and resource suppliers is imposed by the marketplace where consumer sovereignty decides what goods and services can and cannot be produced and sold profitably. Freedom of choice and all market activities are subject to the broadest legal limits consistent with maintaining law and order, and the enforcement of contracts freely entered into by consenting parties.

THE MARKET MECHANISM

The mechanism which serves to coordinate the activities of consumers, businesses, and all suppliers of resources is the market. A **market** is defined as an area within which buyers and sellers of a particular good are in such close communication that the price of that good tends to be the same everywhere in the area. The answers to the question of what and how much to produce are determined by the signals communicated between buyers and sellers via the interacting network of markets and prices. The potential buyers of a good make contact with the sellers or suppliers in the market. Then a price must be determined such that suppliers will provide just the quantity of the good that buyers wish to purchase. On the buyers' (demand) side of the market, the level of the price determines who will buy the good and how much will be bought. On the suppliers' side of the market, the price level determines who will supply the good and how much will be supplied. If buyers want more than is being supplied at the prevailing price, they will signal their desires for more by bidding up the price. Suppliers will then respond by providing more of the good. If at the prevailing price sellers are providing a larger quantity of the good than buyers demand, prices will be bid down. This will be a signal to sellers to reduce the quantity of the good they supply to the market. In this way prices serve as the communicating link between buyers and sellers in a market economy.

MARKETS DETERMINE
WHAT, HOW, FOR WHOM

The markets for different goods are interrelated because the alternative to using one good is to use another. If the price of beef is felt to be too high, one alternative would be to buy poultry. And if the price of poultry is likewise thought to be too high, another alternative might be to buy ham. Hence the amounts of these goods buyers will demand will depend on the price of beef, relative to the price of poultry and ham. Similarly, suppliers will be induced to supply those goods which are selling for the highest prices, relative to the prices of other goods. Changes in the price in one market will set up a chain reaction of adjustments in quantities demanded and supplied in related markets. For example, an increase in demand for new housing will cause an increase in the price (wages) of architects, bricklayers, carpenters, furniture sales personnel, and so on. This will induce labor resources to move from other activities into those which now appear relatively more rewarding. All markets in the economy are interrelated with one another to varying extents in this way. It is the "invisible hand" of the marketplace which determines the allocation of resources, *what* goods will be produced, and *how much* of each.

Competition among suppliers of goods and labor services will ensure that the most efficient and productive will ask the lowest price for any good and thus make the sale to shopping buyers. Hence the forces of the marketplace will cause labor and other resources to flow into those occupations and uses for which they are best suited. This is the way a market economy determines *how production should be organized.*

For whom are goods produced in a market economy? Obviously, for whoever is able to pay the price for them. And who are these people? Those who are able to sell their labor services and any other resources they own which can be used in the production of other goods. The emphasis is on competition and a reward structure oriented toward the most efficient and productive. The vision of the individual's relation to society that underlies pure market, laissez faire capitalism has sometimes been characterized as an ideology of the survival of the fittest. All are free to go into any line of work or business they choose, to take any risks at making as much or losing as much money as they care to. The individual is entitled to all the rewards of good decisions and must bear the full consequences of bad ones.

RESOURCE UTILIZATION

How fully do pure market systems utilize their available resources? This is difficult to evaluate, because history provides few, if any, examples of a pure market economy without any form of government intervention. However, many of the industrialized economies of the Western world have a significant portion of their economic decisions determined by free-market forces. This was even more so in the nineteenth century and the twentieth century prior to World War II. The Great Depression, which afflicted these nations during the 1930s, together with the record of previous decades, suggests that pure market economies have difficulty keeping their available resources fully employed all the time.

CHANGE, STABILITY, AND GROWTH

As to change, stability, and growth, economies which most closely approximate pure market, laissez faire capitalism have achieved some of the highest standards of living in the world. Such systems seem particularly well suited to responding to the changing tastes of consumers. They are also able to develop new products and bring new technologies to the everyday use of the masses. From the standpoint of stability, fluctuations in economic activity as measured by GNP, employment, and the behavior of prices have always been a source of concern in such economies.

Obviously, one would be hard pressed to find a pure form of this type of economy today. In the late eighteenth century at the beginning of the Industrial Revolution, England and the United States came pretty close. Nonetheless, there are still many economies today where free markets play a dominant role. Moreover, the concept of pure market, laissez-faire capitalism may be viewed as one extreme on a spectrum of ways of organizing an economy.

The Mixed Economy

A **mixed economy** is one in which free markets are not allowed to be the only determinant of what, how, and for whom goods are to be produced. The *underlying rationale of a mixed economy is that not all of the outcomes provided by pure market, laissez faire capitalism are desirable.* Therefore, it is felt that some government intervention is necessary to improve upon the results. The amount and extent of government involvement can vary a great deal, but virtually all economies are subject to government intervention in some form or other.

GOVERNMENT INTERVENTION IN WHAT, HOW, FOR WHOM

In the United States, for example, the public became concerned around the turn of the century over the tendency of free-market forces to give rise to a few large firms dominating the supply side of the market in certain areas of the economy, such as the oil and aluminum industries. As a result, Congress passed antitrust legislation. These laws made such forms of market and production organization illegal because they were considered anticompetitive and not consistent with the best interests of the economy. In a similar vein, it was recognized that the production and distribution of electricity, clean water, and telephone service naturally tended (due to production technology) to be provided by a large single firm. Because consumers lacked any competitive alternative source of supply, such a firm could charge exorbitant prices. As a result, government regulates the prices these industries may charge the public. One of the points of contention reported in the news item in the previous chapter concerned the electrical utilities' request to raise electricity rates. The government rate regulators were reluctant to do so in that instance. In part, the request was motivated by the increase in the cost of producing electricity caused by government regulations aimed at pollution control. In recent years the opinion has been growing that free markets alone do not adequately dispose of the bads (pollution) produced by many production processes. As a result, government intervention has been deemed necessary.

In some mixed economies, government intervention extends even to the ownership of certain industries—such industries are called **nationalized industries**. In Great Britain, for example, the steel, the airplane, and the railroad industries are nationalized. The public by and large felt that these industries would operate better under complete government control, rather than under private ownership subject to varying degrees of government regulation as is the case with the railroads and airlines in the United States. Hence, a mixed economy may involve not only a mixture of private and public decision making, but a mixture of private and public ownership as well.

In a mixed economy the answers to the questions what and how much to produce, how to organize production, and for whom to produce are determined by a mixture of government intervention, regulation, and control in some areas of the economy, coupled with a certain amount of private enterprise and a reliance on free markets in other areas. Mixed economies typically provide for the unemployed and others unable to work.

RESOURCE UTILIZATION

How good are mixed economies at maintaining a *full utilization of their available resources?* The Great Depression of the 1930s which plagued the industrialized economies of the West led these countries to call for more government intervention in the future. In this way, these economies hoped to avoid another episode of such dramatic underemployment of resources. The ideas put forward at that time by the British economist John Maynard Keynes provided a rationale for how government intervention could prevent such a calamity. Income tax reductions and stepped-up government expenditures to offset the fall in expenditures by businesses and consumers are among the measures to be used. Most economists today are of the opinion that such government intervention would be appropriate and quite effective in averting another Great Depression. However, there is considerable debate among economists as to whether such intervention has been either practicable or effective in alleviating the recessions that have occurred in the United States since World War II.

CHANGE, STABILITY, AND GROWTH

As for *change, stability,* and *growth,* mixed economies justify government intervention, at least in part, as a means of promoting stability and growth, and those kinds of change which are considered desirable. How well mixed economies have succeeded is a matter of continual debate among economists. In the United States some economists think that the antitrust activities of the government on the whole have helped to prevent the growth of monopoly and thereby promoted competition in some areas of the economy. It is felt that more competition better serves changing consumer tastes and leads to more innovation in products, which is a spur to economic growth. On the other hand, the government has intervened to save large faltering corporations from bankruptcy, as in the case of Lockheed Aircraft. Many economists feel that this interferes with the beneficial working of the marketplace, which serves to weed out inefficient producers, a form of change felt to be desirable. Furthermore, they ask, why should the government prop up certain large failing corporations when many smaller businesses fail every day because they are unable to meet the rigors of the marketplace? With regard to economic growth and stability, many economists feel that in the United States greater growth and stability have been promoted by government intervention. Others say, not so, that the increasing growth of government has stifled the private sector with heavy personal income and corporate profits taxes. The reply to this is often "Well, even if there is some truth to that, at least we have not had another Great Depression." Debates over the pros and cons of mixed economies and the appropriateness or folly of government intervention in different areas of the economy are unending. We will encounter these issues again and again throughout this book.

The Command Economy

In the **command economy**, also called the planned economy, the government answers the questions of how to organize production, what and how much to produce, and for whom. These answers take the form of plans which may extend for as far as 10 to 20 years into the future. In such a planned economy, the government literally commands that these plans be carried out.

GOVERNMENT DOMINATION

Typically, the government owns the means of production, as in the Soviet Union or Communist China, but this is not always so. In Nazi Germany the government controlled and planned the economy, but ownership remained largely in private hands. *In economies where planning is the most centralized and complete, the government must be very authoritarian. Therefore, it is typically a totalitarian regime—ideologically committed to communism or to fascism.* Even in these economies the government may allow free markets to operate in certain areas of the economy if it is consistent with, or helpful to, the achievement of other planning objectives. The Soviet Union allows this to some extent in its agricultural sector, for example. In a command economy, all forms of labor, including management, are essentially government employees. The state is the company store, the only company.

PLANNING WHAT, HOW, AND FOR WHOM

The underlying rationale for a command economy is that the government knows best what is most beneficial for the entire economy and for its individual parts. In a command economy there are differences between what consumers may want and what the planners have decided to produce. If planners do not want to devote resources to television sets, consumers simply will go without. Once the plan for the entire economy has been drawn up, each producing unit in the economy is told *what* and *how much* it must produce of various goods to fulfill its part of the plan. This determines each unit's need for labor, capital equipment, and other inputs. Obviously it is not easy to centrally coordinate all of the component parts of the plan to ensure that the right kinds and amounts of labor, capital, and other inputs are available to each producing unit, so that each may satisfy its individual plan. *How to organize production* is quite a task for central planners overseeing the economy of an entire nation. Managing General Motors, AT&T, or IBM pales in comparison.

For *whom* is output produced? Centrally planned economies typically provide for all citizens regardless of their productive contribution to the output of the economy. However, planners cannot avoid the fact that human nature does respond to material incentives. As a result, government-determined wage scales vary from one occupation or profession to the next, depending on where planners feel there are shortages or surpluses of needed labor skills. This, of course, depends on how authoritarian the government wants to be in allowing people to pick and choose their occupation or profession. For example, it appears that Communist China is more authoritarian in this regard than some of the Eastern European countries.

RESOURCE UTILIZATION

Full utilization of available resources presumably does not pose a problem in a command economy. Remember that by full utilization we mean that there are no available resources standing idle. This is a different issue from whether or not resources may be underemployed due to poor planning. In the Soviet Union planners seem to have continual difficulty meeting their agricultural goals. If they think their goals are reasonable, their relatively frequent shortfalls from these goals suggest that the resources devoted to agriculture may not be as efficiently employed as possible, even allowing for setbacks caused by bad weather.

CHANGE, STABILITY, AND GROWTH

How do planned economies deal with *change* and *growth?* Obviously, in a planned economy growth and many kinds of change can be engineered by the central planning bureau to a large extent. If the government wants more economic growth, the central planning agency will draw up plans devoting a larger share of the economy's resources to the production of capital goods. On the other hand, critics argue that authoritarian control, large bureaucratic structure, and centrally dictated goals put a damper on individual initiative and innovation. Because of this it is argued that technological discovery and change are inhibited. This is considered a major factor in economic growth, a factor that critics feel is weak in planned economies. The *stability* of planned economies depends on how well the government is able to set realistic goals and structure the appropriate plans to attain them. If goals are too ambitious, and if the amount of reorganization in the economy is too great for the time allowed, the loss of economic stability can be severe. This was the case with Communist China's ill-fated Great Leap Forward discussed earlier.

SUMMING UP

The planned or command economy may be viewed as representing the other extreme on the spectrum of economic organization from that of pure market, laissez faire capitalism. The mixed economy represents all the in-betweens. No two economies in the world are exactly alike, but each may be thought of as lying somewhere on the spectrum between the two extremes we have described. Most fall under the very broad category of the mixed economy. All have to grapple with the economic problem posed by scarcity, unlimited wants, and the consequent need for choice.

■CHECKPOINT 2-4

Describe the likely process of selecting a point on the production possibilities frontier of Figure 2-1 (that is, the combination of antipollution devices and bundles) for: a free-market economy, a mixed economy, and a planned or command economy. For each of these three kinds of economies, what difference do you think it makes, in terms of the point chosen on the frontier, if they are industrially underdeveloped as compared to the likely outcome if they are industrially advanced?

SUMMARY

1. While available economic resources are limited, human wants are virtually unlimited. This creates the fundamental problem of scarcity, which makes it necessary to make choices.
2. Economic efficiency requires that there be no unemployment or underemployment of resources. Unemployment exists whenever some available resources are idle. Underemployment (or resource misallocation) exists if

certain available resources are employed to do jobs for which other available resources are better suited. It also exists whenever the best available technology is not used in a production process.
3. When there is no unemployment or underemployment of available resources, an economy is able to produce the maximum amount of goods possible. When producing this maximum, the economy is said to be on its production possibilities frontier. This frontier is a curve connecting the maximum possible output combinations of goods for a fully employed economy. In this situation, the production of more of one kind of good is possible only if the economy produces less of another. The cost of having more of one good is the amount of the other that must be given up. This cost is often called the opportunity cost of a good.
4. Economic growth occurs when an economy's available supply of resources is increased or when there is an increase in technological know-how. As a result, the production possibilities frontier expands outward. The output combination chosen on today's frontier affects the amount of capital goods that will be available tomorrow. Therefore, today's choice will affect the location of tomorrow's production possibilities frontier.
5. Any economy, whatever its political ideology, must answer certain questions that arise because of the basic economic problem of scarcity. Every economy must decide what goods to produce, how much to produce, how to organize production, and for whom output is to be produced. The answer to the question of what to produce determines the nature and location of the production possibilities frontier. The answer to the question of how much to produce determines the point chosen on the frontier. How to organize production determines whether the chosen point on the frontier will be reached. For whom to produce is largely determined by ideological orientation as to the proper mix of free markets, government regulation, and central planning.
6. Every economy must concern itself with

maintaining full employment of its resources (avoiding unemployment). This has frequently been a problem for the industrialized economies of the West. Every economy must also deal with change. The stability of an economy depends very much on how well it is able to adjust to change. An important kind of change is economic growth, and economies are often judged on how well they promote economic growth.

7. There are three basic kinds of economies, or ways of organizing the process of deciding what and how much, how, and for whom to produce. Each kind presumes a particular relationship between the individual and the state. They are basically distinguished by the amount of government intervention they permit in the decision-making process of the economy.

a. *Pure market or laissez faire capitalism.* Individual economic units are given free choice in all economic decisions, which are completely decentralized. There is no interference by government in the form of regulations or controls. Markets and prices are the sole coordinating mechanisms for allocating resources and organizing production.

b. *Mixed economy.* Government intervenes so that free markets are not allowed to provide the only answers to the questions of what and how much, how, and for whom to produce. The underlying rationale is that not all of the answers provided by pure market, laissez faire capitalism are desirable. The mixed economy is a very broad, descriptive category because the amount and extent of government intervention varies a great deal from one economy to another.

c. *Command, or planned, economy.* An authoritarian government decides what and how much, how, and for whom to produce. Government typically owns the means of production, plans economic activities, and commands that these plans be carried out. The underlying rationale is that the government knows best what is most beneficial for the entire economy and its individual parts.

KEY TERMS AND CONCEPTS

business cycles
business fluctuations
capitalism
command economy
economic efficiency
economic growth
economic problem
free-market economy
ideology
laissez faire
law of increasing costs
market
mixed economy
nationalized industry
opportunity cost
production possibilities frontier
resource misallocation
underemployment
unemployment

QUESTIONS AND PROBLEMS

1. Think about the following situation in terms of the concept of opportunity cost. If you choose not to go to college, suppose your best alternative is to drive a truck for $12,000 per year. If you choose to go to college, suppose that you must pay a tuition fee of $2,000 per year and buy books and other school supplies amounting to $400 per year. Suppose that your other living expenses are the same regardless of which choice you make. Suppose you choose to go to college. What is the opportunity cost of your college diploma?

2. The following is a production possibilities table for computers and jet airplanes:

| Product | Production Possibilities | | | | |
	A	B	C	D	E
Computers (in thousands)	0	25	40	50	55
Jet airplanes (in thousands)	40	30	20	10	0

a. Plot the production possibilities frontier for the economy characterized by this table.
b. Demonstrate the law of increasing costs using the data in this table.

c. Suppose technological progress doubles for the productivity of the process for making computers and also of that for making jet airplanes. What would the numbers in the production possibilities table look like in that case? Plot the new production possibilities frontier.

d. Suppose technological progress doubles the productivity of the process for making computers, but there is no change in the process for making jet airplanes. What would the numbers in the production possibilities table be now? Plot the new production possibilities frontier.

e. Suppose technological progress doubles the productivity of the process for making jet airplanes, but there is no change in the process for making computers. What would the numbers in the production possibilities frontier be now? Plot the new production possibilities frontier. Why is it that, despite the fact that there is no change in the productivity of producing computers, it is now possible at any given level of production of jet airplanes to have more computers?

3. Consider a production possibilities frontier for consumer goods and capital goods. How would the choice of a point on that frontier affect the position of tomorrow's frontier? Choose three different points on today's production possibilities frontier and indicate the possible location of tomorrow's frontier that is associated with each.

4. Construct your own production possibilities frontier by putting a grade-point scale on the vertical axis to measure a grade in your economics course and the number of waking hours in a typical day (say 16) on the horizontal axis. Out of those 16 hours per day, how many do you think you would have to give up to get a D? a C? a B? an A? Plot the frontier determined by these combinations.

5. Compare and contrast the ways in which each of the three economies we have discussed deals with the five basic questions or problems any economy faces.

3

THE NATURE
OF THE
MIXED ECONOMY

PROFITS: HOW MUCH IS TOO LITTLE?

LOS ANGELES, Feb. 5—A forum of European and U.S. business leaders and economists gathered recently to discuss new challenges to the role of profits in Western economies. Almost without exception, the speakers testified to the pressures and pinches afflicting the profit system. In some instances, such as Sweden, socialist governments are levying confiscatory taxes on corporate profits and insisting on huge contributions to pension funds, which in turn are being used to buy up the companies. In Britain, the Labour party's left wing continues to demand the nationalization of shipbuilding, aircraft production, and banking. This despite the fact that most of Britain's already nationalized industries are chronic money losers whose inefficiencies are a major cause of the country's dismal economic plight.

In the United States no excess-profits tax has been levied on U.S. corporations since the Korean War. In fact, the regular federal tax on corporate profits has been lowered over the past three years from 52 percent to 48 percent. Hardly anyone questions the basic right of business to make *some* profit. The question has been, How much?

Opinion polls suggest that a majority of the public believes that corporations earn much more than they actually do, and favor higher taxes on profits. In a poll conducted by the Opinion Research Corporation of Princeton, New Jersey, a majority of those questioned thought that companies averaged $.33 profit on each dollar of sales. A sampling of college students by Standard and Poor's yielded an even higher estimate: $.45. The actual figure is below $.05, and the overall trend has been downward. In 1950, 64.1 percent of corporations' domestic income was used to pay wages, salaries, and fringe benefits, while profits comprised 15.6 percent. A quarter century later, the share of wages and salaries had risen to 76 percent, while profits had fallen to only 8.3 percent.

This news item typifies the continuing controversy over the proper role of capitalism and free markets in present-day mixed economies. You also may have some fairly strong opinions and impressions about the nature and role of profits in our economy. In the previous chapter, we observed that the government's role in mixed economies in the world today varies noticeably from one mixed economy to the next. And this, of course, reflects the varying shades of opinion on these issues in different countries. Nonetheless, there are certain characteristics common to all mixed economies. They all have markets where the exchange of goods and services takes place using money as the medium of exchange. They all have had a strong tradition of capitalism stemming from their history of economic development, particularly the fact that they experienced the Industrial Revolution.[1] They all have felt the need to modify capitalism and the workings of free markets through government intervention.

In this chapter we will get a brief overview of some of the main characteristics of mixed economies like our own. Much of the analysis in the rest of this book will focus on mixed economies. In this chapter we will briefly explore the role of markets, money, profits, and government in such an economic system. Of course a good deal of what we say about each of these subjects is true whether or not we are speaking of a mixed economy. Finally we will depict the structure of the mixed economy in terms of a circular-flow diagram.

[1] Countries which most commonly come to mind are the United States, Great Britain, Canada, the Scandinavian countries, France, West Germany, Italy, Australia, New Zealand, and Japan.

MARKETS AND MONEY

Specialization gives rise to the need for trade, and trade creates markets. Money makes trade easier and therefore encourages specialization and a more extensive development of markets. Let's consider the truth of each of these statements in turn.

Specialization and Markets

Why do markets exist in the first place? Why are goods traded? What is it that leads people to go to market? The answer lies in the fact that each of us is better at doing some things than at doing others. We often refer to our best skill as "my thing," "my bag," or my "long suit." We tend to specialize in that thing we are best at. We "trade on it." Have you ever heard it said of movie stars that "they trade on their good looks"?

When each of us specializes in that particular thing he or she is best at, the whole economy is able to produce more of everything than if each of us tries to be self-sufficient. Of course when each specializes in producing one thing, each is dependent on others for the production of everything else. *With specialization most of what one produces is a surplus that must be traded for the other things that one wants. Hence the more* **specialization of labor** *there is in an economy, the greater is the need for trade.* And as trade becomes more important to the functioning of an economy, markets in all kinds of goods and services become more commonplace.

The Role of Money

A prominent characteristic of markets with which you are familiar is that goods are traded for money. *In a* **barter economy** *goods are traded* *for goods.* The more an economy is characterized by specialization of labor, the less likely is it that we will observe goods being traded directly for goods. What led people to start using money in the first place? The fundamental reason for the invention and existence of money is that it makes specialization and trade much easier. This is most obvious if we consider the difficulties of trade in a barter economy.

TRADE IN A BARTER ECONOMY

Suppose you are a member of an economy in which each individual in the economy specializes in the production of a particular good. Like everyone else, you produce more of your particular good than you need for yourself and trade the surplus for other goods. Suppose you specialize in chopping wood and today you decide to go shopping for a pair of sandals. Lugging your wood on your back, you go in search of a sandalmaker. Finding one at last, you are disappointed to find that the sandalmaker has no need for chopped wood. No trade takes place, and so with aching back and sore feet you continue on your quest. Your problem is two-fold. You must first find someone who has sandals to trade. Second, while you may encounter several such people, you must find among them one who wants to acquire chopped wood. In other words, you are looking for an individual who coincidentally has sandals to trade *and* also wants chopped wood. Should you find such an individual, your wants will coincide with that person's. If you have enough

chopped wood, you should be able to negotiate a trade. Hence, in order to have a trade, it is necessary to have a **coincidence of wants**.

At this point you might ask, is it not possible that someone who has sandals to trade, but no need for chopped wood, might accept the wood and then trade it for something he or she does want? Yes, it is possible, but very inconvenient. If that person accepts the wood, the problem of finding a coincidence of wants has really just been transferred from you to him or her.

In sum, *the difficulties involved in finding a coincidence of wants tend to discourage specialization and trade in a barter economy.* Given the effort and time that must be spent just to find a coincidence of wants, many individuals in a barter economy would find it easier to be more self-sufficient and produce more items for their own consumption. To this extent, the gains from specialization and trade cannot be fully realized.

MONEY AS A MEDIUM OF EXCHANGE

How does the use of money allow us to get around these difficulties? *Money eliminates the need for the coincidence of wants.* If the economy uses money to carry on trade, you can sell your chopped wood to whoever wants it and accept money in exchange. Whether the purchaser makes something you want is now irrelevant. As long as you can use the money received to buy what you want you are satisfied. You can use the money to buy a pair of sandals or whatever. Similarly, the sandalmaker will accept

After reading this chapter, you will be able to:
1. Explain why markets exist.
2. Explain how money makes trading much easier and therefore promotes specialization and trade.
3. Define "normal profit."
4. Define the role of profit in the creation and allocation of capital.
5. State the nature and rationale of government intervention in a mixed economy.
6. Explain the interconnecting economic relationships between households, businesses, and government as characterized in flow diagrams.

your money even though he or she may have no need for your chopped wood. We say money serves as the medium of exchange.

At different times and in different societies, the medium of exchange used as money has taken many forms—from houndsteeth, to precious stones, to gold coin, to currency, checks, and credit cards. Whatever its form, *money's common characteristic is that it must be acceptable to people because they know they can use it as buyers. Because money eliminates the need for coincidence of wants it promotes specialization and trade, and thereby makes possible the gains which stem from specialization and trade. The incentive for societies to use money in exchange derives from these gains. The introduction of money into a barter economy essentially causes that economy's production possibilities frontier to be shifted outward.*

■ CHECKPOINT 3-1

Suppose there are three people, A, B, and C, and that A specializes in growing corn, B in catching fish, and C in growing wheat. A has a surplus of corn, B a surplus of fish, and C a surplus of wheat. Suppose A would like to get some wheat from C, but C doesn't have any desire for A's corn. Suppose that C would like to get some fish from B, but B doesn't want any of C's wheat. And suppose that B would like to get some corn from A, but A doesn't want any of B's fish. Each wants something from one of the others, but has nothing to offer in exchange. What is lacking here? Further, suppose each lives alone on an island 20 miles from each of the others and that each has a boat. Describe how trade would have to be carried on under a barter system, if it were carried on at all. By comparison, describe how trade would be carried on if A, B, and C used money.

MARKETS AND PROFITS

A money-using economy with extensive markets fosters specialization among workers and in the methods of production. This specialization leads to the development of more sophisticated production processes which typically require large amounts of investment in capital goods. In a capitalistic economy where the productive units or firms are privately owned, either by those who run them or by shareholders, sizeable amounts of funds, or financial capital, must be raised by the owners in order to acquire the capital goods. Whether or not it is worthwhile to commit funds to such investments depends on that controversial thing called profit. And the amount of profit is determined by the markets where the goods produced by the capital goods are sold. Another key role played by profit in a capitalistic economy is to provide an incentive for entrepreneurial activity. The entrepreneur described in Chapter 1 is a key factor in the creation and organizing of new production techniques and the founding of firms which employ them to satisfy the demands of new and continually changing markets.

What Is a Normal Profit?

It is clear from the news item at the beginning of this chapter that profit is one of the most controversial and least understood concepts in economics. For some people the mere mention of the word conjures up images of exploitation and robber barons carving out their pound of flesh from the downtrodden. But what is a "reasonable" profit, or what economists call a **normal profit**? When we say that a firm is earning a normal profit, what must be the relationship between its total sales revenue and its total costs?

In order to answer these questions, recall that we emphasized in the previous chapter that all costs are opportunity costs due to the fact that resources are scarce and have alternative uses. Our discussion of the production possibilities frontier indicated that if resources are used to produce one good, they are not available to produce other goods. The cost of the one good is thus the alternative goods which must be forgone in order to produce it. This notion of cost is directly applicable to the individual firm. All the resources, including financial capital and entrepreneurial skills, that a firm needs in order to produce its product have alternative uses in the production of other products by other firms. Hence *the costs of production for a firm are all those payments it must make to all resource sup-*

pliers in order to bid resources away from use in the production of alternative goods. When the firm's total sales revenue is just sufficient to cover these costs, all resources employed by the firm are just earning their opportunity costs. In particular, the financial capital and the entrepreneurial skills used by the firm are being compensated just enough to keep them from leaving and going into some other line of productive activity. They are earning a normal profit.

Profit and the Allocation of Resources

Changes in the level of profits which are earned in different markets play an important role in the efficient allocation of resources in a dynamic, changing economy. Suppose a market for a new product develops or that there is a sudden increase in demand for an existing product. Firms already in the market or those first to enter will find they can earn above-normal profits. This happens because demand so exceeds the existing capacity to meet it that prices considerably in excess of cost can be charged. Above-normal profits serve as a signal to entrepreneurial skills and financial capital in other areas of the economy that they can earn more by moving into the new and expanding markets. Resources will continue to move into these areas so long as above normal profits exist. Eventually, enough resources will have moved into these markets and increased capacity sufficiently that above-normal profits will no longer exist. In this way *above-normal profits serve to allocate resources to those areas of the economy where they are most in demand. Similarly, of course, below-normal profits in one area of the economy will cause entrepreneurial skills and financial capital to move out of that line of productive activity and into those where they can earn their opportunity cost.*

Controversy About the Role of Profit

Any time you read something or hear a discussion about profit, you should ask yourself how the term is being used. The news item at the beginning of this chapter suggests that there is a good deal of misunderstanding about the nature of profit in mixed economies.

EARLY VIEWS ON PROFIT

Suspicion of profit is an ancient theme in Western culture. A sixteenth-century French thinker, Michel de Montaigne, wrote an essay entitled "The Profit of One Man Is the Damage of Another." His thesis was that "man should condemn all manner of gain." However, with the dawn of the era of capitalism two centuries ago, the profit motive found an able defender in Adam Smith—the renowned author of *The Wealth of Nations*. In this book, published in 1776, Smith argued that profits are the legitimate return for risk and effort. He put forward the notion that the "invisible hand" of market forces turns private greed into productive activity, which provides goods for the benefit of all. A century later, Karl Marx argued the opposite view. He maintained that labor, not capital, was the ingredient that added value to goods or raw materials in the production process. He asserted that profit was the "surplus value" that the capitalist unjustifiably added on to the real worth of the product.

TWENTIETH-CENTURY VIEWS ON PROFIT

In the early part of the twentieth century, the Fabian socialists argued that profits should be "taxed into oblivion" to create a new socialist order. If they meant above-normal profit, they might have a good case in certain circumstances. In the mixed economy of the United States, public policy has recognized that due to the technology of producing certain kinds of goods and due to the size and nature of certain kinds of markets, one firm can become dominant and exclude any others from the market. In that case, the monopoly position of the firm allows it to charge high prices and earn above-normal profit because consumers who want the product have no alternative but to buy the product from that firm. Electric power companies, telephone companies, and gas companies are examples. Without some type of government intervention, such firms could go on earning above-normal profits until technological innovation provides some substitute good not yet existent. Because of this, utility companies are subject to government regulation of the prices they can charge. In this way, profit in excess of normal profit, frequently called monopoly profit, is supposed to be taxed into oblivion. Most economists, policy makers, and the general public feel this is justified in such "natural" monopoly situations. In practice such regulation has not always been able to achieve this goal.

Suppose the Fabians' expressed desire to tax profits into oblivion were meant to apply to normal profits. This would effectively remove any return to financial capital and entrepreneurial skill. It would, therefore, remove the incentive for anybody to provide the financial capital necessary for the creation of physical capital goods or the innovative effort necessary to create new technology and supply new markets. When an economy ceases to build capital goods, the growth in its capacity to produce other goods stops. If the Fabians meant by profits normal profits, taxing profits out of existence would certainly be an extreme position. There would definitely be a new social order.

Controversy over the taxation of profits such as that reported in the news item will undoubtedly always be a much debated issue in mixed capitalistic economies. Unfortunately, much of the debate is often the result of misunderstanding over the meaning or meanings of the word profit.

PROFIT IN TODAY'S ECONOMY

Today the average individual directly or indirectly owns a sizeable portion of the shares (or stock) of corporations in the United States. The dividends paid on these shares derive directly from the profits of these corporations. Nearly half of all corporate shares, measured in dollar value, are owned by institutions such as pension funds, insurance companies, college endowments, and churches. Hence, for millions of Americans such things as the assurance of a retirement income, the soundness of an insurance policy, and the availability of a college scholarship are heavily dependent on the continued profitability of U.S. corporations. When profits go down, or turn into losses, the average person in the street often has as much cause for concern as the corporate board of directors. It should be said, however, that large profits de-

rived from situations where competition in the marketplace is nonexistent or inhibited are generally considered not to be in the economy's best interest.

■ CHECKPOINT 3-2

Samuel Gompers (1850–1924) was an American labor leader. He was the first president of the American Federation of Labor, a position he held from 1886 until his death (except for one year, 1895). He once said: "The worst crime against working people is a company which fails to operate at a profit." What do you suppose he meant by this? Like Gompers, Marx championed the working class. How do their views on profit seem to differ?

GOVERNMENT'S ROLE IN THE MIXED ECONOMY

As with profits, there is always a good deal of controversy over the appropriate role of government versus that of markets in determining what, how, and for whom to produce. "Be thankful you don't get all the government you pay for" say some who are skeptical of what government does and how efficiently it does it. A critic of the market system once said, "competition in the marketplace brings out the best in products and the worst in people."

Government, whether it be local, state, or federal, performs four main functions in a mixed economy: (1) it provides the legal and institutional structure in which markets operate; (2) it intervenes in the allocation of resources in areas of the economy where public policy deems it beneficial to do so; (3) it redistributes income; (4) it seeks to provide stability in prices, economic growth, and economic conditions generally. Of course, government actions in any one of these spheres almost invariably have implications for the others.

Legal and Institutional Structure for Markets

Even in pure market, laissez faire capitalism, the government must provide for legal definition and enforcement of contracts, property rights, and ownership. It must also establish the legal status of different forms of business organizations from the owner-operated small business to the large corporation. It must provide a judicial system so that disputed claims between parties arising in the course of business may be settled. Government also provides for the supply and regulation of the money supply, the maintenance of a system of measurement standards, and the maintenance of a police force to maintain order and protect property.

You will find little disagreement anywhere as to the need for government to provide this basic legal and institutional structure. Since the turn of the century, however, the legal sanctions and constraints on the functioning of markets and the economic relationships between business, labor, and consumers have become more complex. In the United States the government has taken an active role in trying to maintain competition in markets. We have already noted how government regulates pricing activities in the utilities industries where technological and market conditions do not naturally encourage competition. In an attempt to maintain competitive conditions in all markets, Congress has enacted a number of antitrust laws, which are essentially aimed at preventing market domination by one or a small number of large firms. Starting with the Sherman Act of 1890, these laws also made it illegal for firms in any particular market to collude (get together) in setting prices or conspire to restrict competition. Legislation such as the Taft-Hartley Act of 1947 was enacted to impose legal constraints on the way unions are organized and run and on collective bargaining procedures. These laws also prescribe how strikes that threaten the general well-being of the nation are to be handled. Government intervention to protect consumers has been the subject of legislation throughout the twentieth century, starting with the Pure Food and Drug Act of 1906. More recently the government has actively intervened in the area of pollution control. In 1969 Congress established the Environmental Protection Agency in order to develop quality standards for air and water with the assistance of state and local governments.

Government intervention in the marketplace through creation and change of certain aspects of the legal and institutional structure has often proved beneficial. In other instances, it has not. One of the most disastrous examples was the Volstead Act passed in Congress in 1919. It prohibited the production and sale of alcoholic beverages. The act became so unpopular that Congress repealed it in 1933. Many observers feel that it provided a tremendous economic windfall to the underworld, which did a thriving business in the illicit production and sale of the liquor which a thirsty public would not do without. This is felt to have laid the foundation for modern organized crime as a big business.

Resource Allocation

Government affects resource allocation in our economy through its spending activities, its tax policies, and its own production of certain goods and services.

GOVERNMENT SPENDING

In the United States about 70 percent of all output is produced and sold in markets. The quantity and variety of goods and services represented by this 70 percent of total output is the result of decisions made by numerous firms and consumers—the private sector of our economy. The other 30 percent of the economy's output is the result of government (public sector) expenditure decisions. Though much of this output of goods and services is produced by private businesses, it is done under government contract and reflects government decisions about what to produce and for whom—highways for motorists, schools for young people, and military hardware for national defense are just a few examples.

TAXATION

Another way in which the government affects the allocation of resources is through its power to levy taxes. For example, we have already noted how changes in profit affect the incentive to create new capital goods. From our discussion of the production possibilities frontier in the previous chapter, we know that there is a trade-off between producing capital goods and producing goods for present consumption. In order to produce more of one kind of good, it is necessary to obtain the resources to do so by cutting back on production of the other. That is, it is necessary to reallocate resources from one line of productive activity to another. By changing the rate of taxation of profit, the government changes the incentive to produce capital goods relative to the incentive to produce goods for current consumption. For instance, suppose the government increased taxes on profits. This would discourage the production of capital goods relative to consumer goods. Some resources would therefore be reallocated from capital goods production to consumer goods production. This is but one example of a way in which the government can affect the allocation of resources through tax policy.

GOVERNMENT PRODUCTION OF GOODS AND SERVICES

Another way that the government affects resource allocation is by producing goods and services itself. There are certain kinds of goods and services that would not be produced at all if the choice were left up to the market mechanism, even though it might be acknowledged by everybody that such goods provide benefits for all. Such goods are **public goods**.

An essential feature of a public good is that it cannot be provided to one person without providing it to others. If the government provides a dam to protect your property from floods, the benefits accrue to your neighbor as well. Public goods are *not* subject to the so-called **exclusion principle**. *Any good whose benefits accrue only to those who purchase it is said to be subject to the exclusion principle.* Those who do not buy the good are excluded from its benefits. The exclusion principle almost invariably applies to goods produced and sold in a market economy. When producers cannot prevent those who don't pay for the good from having it, the exclusion principle does not hold for that good. If one can have a good without paying for it, then there is no way for producers to charge and receive a price to cover the costs of producing it. Hence there will be no incentive for firms to produce it in a market economy. If I build a lighthouse, there is no way I can exclude any ship at sea from benefiting from its beacon.

Hence there is no way I can charge ships at sea for its service, so I won't build it, despite the fact that shipping companies all agree that it cuts down their economic losses due to shipwrecks. Similarly, it is difficult to privately produce and sell the services of a dam, national defense, cloud seeding, and clean air.

Another feature of a public good is that once it is provided for one citizen, there is no additional cost to providing it for others. This is really just another aspect of the fact that when a public good provides benefits to one it unavoidably provides them to others. It costs no more to protect one ship at sea than to protect several with the same lighthouse.

Of course, there are many goods which are not by nature public goods, but which the government provides anyway. Examples of goods and services that can be privately produced and sold in markets, but are provided by state, local, or federal government are education, police and fire protection, certain kinds of preventive medical treatment, sewage treatment, garbage collection, bridges, toll roads, and air shows financed by the government through the Defense Department. In most of these cases, it is usually argued that there are substantial social benefits, and that if their provision were left strictly to private producers and markets, less of these goods would be produced than is desirable.

Income Redistribution

In virtually all modern, industrialized, mixed economies there are specific government policies aimed at alleviating the hardships of poverty. If people cannot earn some minimal standard of living in the marketplace, it is generally agreed that they should be given economic assistance in some form. Whatever form it takes, this assistance makes it necessary to redistribute income from those judged to have enough to those who do not.

One obvious way to do this is for the government to simply levy heavier income taxes on people in higher income brackets and use the money collected to help those in lower brackets. The money may simply be transferred to those in lower income brackets in the form of cash payments made by various public assistance

ECONOMIC THINKERS

FRIEDRICH A. VON HAYEK
1899-

Hayek, who won the Alfred Nobel Memorial Prize in Economics Science in 1974, is probably best known for his book *The Road to Serfdom* (1944), in which he attacked big government and all forms of collectivism.

According to Hayek, government's role should basically be limited to providing those services that the free market does not provide but that are necessary for the general welfare:

> Let us consider, first, the distinction between the coercive measures of government and those pure service activities where coercion does not enter or does so only because of the need of financing them by taxation. In so far as the government merely undertakes to supply services which otherwise would not be supplied at all (usually because it is not possible to confine the benefits to those prepared to pay for them), the only question which arises is whether the benefits are worth the cost. Of course, if the government claimed for itself the exclusive right to provide particular services, they would cease to be strictly non-coercive. In general, a free society demands not only that the government have the monopoly of coercion but that it have the monopoly only of coercion and that in all other respects it operate on the same terms as everybody else.

Hayek also saw some merit in government regulations that limited entry into various trades and professions to those technically qualified. Such regulations, he felt, were not incompatible with the idea of a free society.

Extensive control over prices (and thus over allocation) was another matter, however. According to Hayek, such control was not only outside the proper bounds of government's role but also beyond its technical capability. In putting forth his theory of limited government intervention in the economy, Hayek did not go so far as to advocate a return to a pure laissez faire system, however.

In essence, Hayek would rely on the impersonal decisions of the market and would, in fact, exclude almost all nonmarket phenomena from economic calculations. Unlike many of his contemporaries, Hayek deplores the use of economic research methods based on those used in the physical sciences. He refers to the use of such methods as "scientism," and believes they are inappropriate to the study of human beings.

FOR FURTHER READING

Hayek, F. A. von. *The Constitution of Liberty*. University of Chicago Press, 1960. Pp. 251-261.

A good account of Hayek's contemporary position in the field of economics is found in "The Unknown Nobel Prize Winner," *The Wall Street Journal*, October 23, 1974.

---

programs. **Public assistance programs** *are a way of providing help to those who would otherwise have little or no income at all.* They are aimed at dependent families, the sick, the handicapped, and the aged—those who, largely for reasons beyond their control, cannot work.

Many government transfers of income and wealth between citizens do not necessarily redistribute from rich to poor. Social security payments to retired persons are financed by social security taxes paid by all those citizens presently working as well as by their employers. Any retired citizen over 62 years of age, even a multimillionaire, is eligible for these benefits.

And even the lowest paid worker is obliged to pay the social security taxes used to finance these benefits.

A good deal of the transfer of income and wealth among citizens takes the form of the government provision of goods and services at zero or below cost to the citizens who use them. The costs of providing such goods and services are covered by tax revenue, much of which is collected from citizens who may not themselves use these governmentally provided goods and services. Public education, parks and recreation areas, public libraries, and a partially subsidized postal service are but a few examples. Again, a wealthy person might choose to use these facilities while someone with a much lower income may use them little or not at all, even though he or she pays taxes used to subsidize the government provision of such goods and services.

Another way in which the government affects income distribution is by direct intervention in the marketplace. Well-known examples of this are governmentally enforced price supports in agricultural markets and minimum-wage laws in labor markets. Farm price supports reflect a desire to maintain the income levels of farmers. Minimum-wage laws supposedly reflect a desire to see to it that laborers' wage levels assure some minimum standard of living. In the case of agriculture such direct market intervention has been criticized for unjustly favoring special interests and distorting resource allocation. It has also been charged that minimum-wage laws aggravate unemployment and contribute to poverty rather than alleviate it. Some argue that minimum wage laws reflect the desire of skilled or unionized workers to diminish the competition they face from low-wage workers.

Economic Stabilization

In the previous chapter we noted the difficulties which market-oriented economies have in avoiding recessions in economic activity, fluctuations in employment and GNP, and unacceptable levels of inflation. In most capitalistic, mixed economies, we observed that a good deal of responsibility for avoiding these difficulties has been vested in the government—witness the Employment Act of 1946 in the United States. Governmental efforts to carry out the spirit of that act are an example of how the exercise of a government responsibility in one area invariably affects other areas. Fiscal policy—government expenditure and tax changes aimed at smoothing out fluctuations in economic activity—unavoidably affects resource allocation, income distribution, and even the competitive market structure of industries in which the government buys goods and lets contracts for public projects. By changing the levels of interest rates, monetary policy has similar effects on resource allocation and income distribution.

Controversy About the Role of Government

In recent years there has been a growing skepticism about the ability of government to provide services to the public, direction to the economy, and solutions for a number of social problems. This has led to a critical examination of how government functions in our economy, a search for the reasons why once optimistic expectations about the government's role have often not been fulfilled.

EFFICIENCY IN GOVERNMENT

Many critics point out that government bureaucracies by their very nature do not have the built-in incentives for efficiency that exist in the typical business firm. The reward of profit and the threat of loss are absent. Moreover, it is typically difficult to measure either output or performance. It is often impossible for a government bureaucrat to show how and where he or she has saved the taxpayers money. How can one tell how efficiently the Department of the Interior, the local library, or a city school system are being operated? If efficient performance is hard to demonstrate, it is likely to be unrecognized and unrewarded, so why try so hard? Similarly, an inefficient performance is equally hard to detect. Neither the carrot nor the stick is much in evidence under these circumstances. In short, because the relationship between taxpayer dollars and benefits produced is hard to establish, the incentives for efficiency are weak.

SPECIAL INTEREST LEGISLATION

Special interest groups often push hard for legislation that provides special benefits for

ECONOMIC THINKERS

JOHN KENNETH GALBRAITH
1908–

A Canadian by birth, Galbraith emigrated to the United States in the early 1930s and obtained a Ph.D. from the University of California at Berkeley. In 1949 he became professor of economics at Harvard, where he remained until he retired in 1974.

While most economists write for a narrow and specialized audience, Galbraith addresses a broad spectrum of intelligent laypeople and is no doubt the best-known economist in the country. Two of his books, *The Affluent Society* (1958) and *The New Industrial State* (1967), remained on best-seller lists for weeks after publication.

In *The Affluent Society* Galbraith argued that America in the mid-twentieth century had a superabundance of consumer goods compared with earlier generations or other nations. But conventional wisdom continued to analyze the marketplace as though consumers were living in dire poverty. Orthodox price theory, which was formulated at a time when economics concentrated on basic wants, was therefore no longer adequate to deal with the realities of modern American society.

According to Galbraith, the two basic propositions underlying the traditional theory of demand—the law of diminishing marginal utility and the assertion that wants are generated from the individual—are not valid in today's world. How can production be defended as want-satisfying if that production itself creates wants?

The end result of Galbraith's reasoning is the doctrine of "social imbalance," in which the supply of private goods outstrips the supply of necessary public goods. Private goods that are not urgently needed are produced in abundance, while public goods are not produced in adequate supply.

The contrast was and remains evident not alone to those who read. The family which takes its mauve and cerise, air-conditioned, power-steered, and power-braked automobile out for a tour passes through cities that are badly paved, made hideous by litter, blighted buildings, billboards, and posts for wires that should long since have been put underground. They pass on into a countryside that has been rendered largely invisible by commercial art. . . . They picnic on exquisitely packaged goods from a portable ice box by a polluted stream . . .

In *The New Industrial State,* Galbraith examined the socioeconomic scene of the 1950s and 1960s, in which, he felt, education, social arrangements, and government institutions were all influenced by the changes brought about by the modern Industrial Revolution. In this society, the major goals of the firm are survival and stability and much emphasis is put on planning and market analysis. While aggregate economic planning is of course beyond the scope of any individual firm, the upper levels of industry, in their quest for stability, come to appreciate the stimulation that resulted from government economic policies.

Many economists disagree with Galbraith, and perhaps the most admired part of his work from their viewpoint is his analysis of the modern U.S. economy in *American Capitalism* (1956), which was later embodied in *Economics and the Public Purpose* (1973). Galbraith argued that as big business and big unions have evolved over the years, they have each come to exercise great power, which is often offset by the power of the other. Galbraith called this concept "countervailing power" and maintained that government needed to be large to itself countervail against and control these forces.

FOR FURTHER READING

Galbraith, John Kenneth. *The Affluent Society.* 2nd ed. Boston: Houghton-Mifflin, 1969.

————. *The New Industrial State.* 2nd rev. ed. Boston: Houghton-Mifflin, 1971.

them and possibly little or no benefit for anyone else. Special interest groups often get their way even when it may not serve the broader public interest. Why?

Suppose some special interest group presses for a program that will cost each individual taxpayer only a dollar. The total cost of the program may be tens of millions of dollars. But as far as the individual taxpayer is concerned the extra dollar of taxes will hardly be noticed. For the individual taxpayer it is scarcely worth the effort to become informed about the program. However, those in the special interest group may stand to benefit substantially, so that they have very strong feelings about whether the program is approved or not. Consequently a politician who doesn't vote for the special interest group's program stands to lose the group's vote in the next election, and quite likely a helpful financial contribution to his or her campaign as well. On the other hand, a vote for the program will probably cost the politician few if any votes among the other largely uninformed voters. Consequently the politician votes for the special interest group's program, even though it may not be in the broader public interest.

For example, you are a congressman from a district where a large company dumps toxic wastes into a river. Downstream the river runs through heavily populated areas creating a health hazard and requiring costly water treatment plants. Suppose the citizens downstream are ill-informed about the source of their dirty water. An antipollution law is proposed in Congress that would require offending companies, like the one in your district, to clean up their toxic wastes. The company and its employees, who fear a loss of jobs, are a special interest group on this issue. You can't afford to lose their vote and so you vote against the legislation, to the detriment of the larger, but ill-informed, public downstream.

CONSUMER PREFERENCES
AND THE BUNDLE PROBLEM

When you buy goods in the marketplace, you shop for them on an item-by-item basis. You are able to be very selective. Your selection of governmentally provided goods and services is much more limited because you must select them through an intermediary, the candidate for political office. Each candidate really represents a bundle of public goods and services, the ones that the candidate will support and vote for if he or she is elected. Your choice of bundles is limited by the number of candidates running for an office. Each candidate may have certain goods and services in his or her bundle that you want and others that you don't want. You vote for that candidate whose bundle most closely matches your preferences. Even then you are forced to take some public goods and services you don't want in order to get those that you do want.

For example, you choose to vote for candidate A because A supports the construction of a dam that you want very much. But the candidate may also be in favor of price supports for wheat and corn which you don't want, but you don't feel as concerned about price supports as you do about the dam. Candidate B is against the price supports, but does not favor the dam either. You vote for A instead of B. Even though A's bundle of goods and services doesn't match your preferences perfectly, it comes closer than the alternative bundle represented by B.

BIAS TOWARD CURRENT
BENEFIT, HIDDEN COST PROJECTS

Because politicians must worry about getting reelected, there is a natural tendency for them to favor projects and programs that have immediate, highly visible benefits and less visible costs. An objective economic analysis of project A might show it to be more worthwhile than a number of other projects. But suppose project A's benefits are spread over a distant future, while tax increases will be required to cover its immediate costs. Project A is therefore likely to lack support, while other economically less worthwhile projects that have more immediate benefits and less visible costs will be pushed forward.

It should be emphasized that none of these criticisms of the way government functions to provide goods and services is a criticism of politicians and government bureaucrats. They respond to rewards and incentives just like people in other walks of life. Given that, these criticisms are directed at the ways in which the reward and incentive structure of our political and governmental institutions are not always geared to provide goods and services in the most economically efficient manner.

■CHECKPOINT 3-3

Explain how the government's power to enforce contracts contributes to the development of markets. Is the postal service a public good or not? Why or why not? Is the military draft a form of government transfer of income or wealth? Why or why not? It appears that sometimes when a government agency isn't working very efficiently its budget is increased. What happens when a private business doesn't operate very efficiently? In order to eliminate some of our present political system's shortcomings for providing governmentally produced goods and services, it has been suggested that limits should be placed on the number of terms that politicians can remain in office. Explain why you think this might or might not help.

THE CIRCULAR FLOW OF GOODS AND MONEY

In a capitalistic, mixed economy money is used by households, businesses, and government to buy and sell goods and resources in markets, to pay and collect taxes, and to borrow and lend in financial markets. The flow of goods and resources in exchange for money, the flow of money to fulfill tax obligations to government and to redistribute income from one group to another, the flow of money from lenders to borrowers in exchange for borrowers' IOUs, and the expenditure of the borrowed funds on goods can all be envisioned schematically in a flow diagram.

The Exchange Flow Between Households and Businesses

Consider first a flow diagram representing an economy in which there is no government inter-

vention in economic activities. For the moment, we will also ignore the existence of financial markets and simply assume that businesses and households are the only two groups of decision makers. The relationship between these two groups is shown in Figure 3-1. The upper channel represents the flow of economic resources (land, labor, and financial capital) owned and provided by households to businesses. The direction of this flow is indicated by the counterclockwise arrow running from households to businesses. In exchange for these services, businesses make money payments in the form of wages, rents, interest, and the distribution of profits. The direction of this flow is indicated by the clockwise arrow running from businesses to households. All of these exchanges take place at mutually agreeable money rates of exchange (or prices), determined by the functioning of markets for production inputs. *Wages* go to labor, *rents* to landowners, *interest* and *profits* to those providing the use of financial capital and entrepreneurial skills (a particular kind of labor service). All of these money payments received by households constitute income.

The lower channel represents the flow of goods and services produced by businesses using all the inputs provided by the upper flow channel. This flow of goods and services in the lower channel runs from businesses to households, as indicated by the counterclockwise arrow. The goods and services are purchased by the households with the money receipts (or income) obtained by selling the services of their resources, as indicated in the upper channel. The money payments made to businesses in exchange for goods and services are indicated in the lower channel by the arrow running clockwise from households to businesses. These exchanges also take place at mutually agreeable prices determined by the functioning of markets.

The money payments made by businesses in the upper channel are viewed as costs by them, while their receipt by households is viewed as income. The money payments received by businesses in the lower channel are viewed by them as sales revenue. For households these payments are the expenditures of the income they

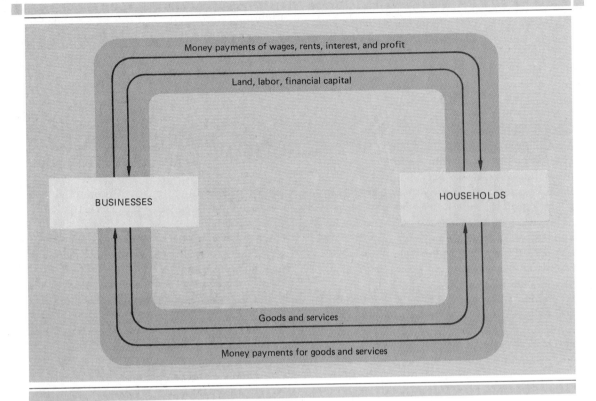

Money payments of wages, rents, interest, and profit

Land, labor, financial capital

BUSINESSES

HOUSEHOLDS

Goods and services

Money payments for goods and services

FIGURE 3-1 THE EXCHANGE FLOW
BETWEEN BUSINESSES AND HOUSEHOLDS

In a money-using economy, businesses obtain the resources (land, labor, and financial capital) necessary for production from households in exchange for money payments (wages, rents, interest, and profit) as indicated in the upper flow channel. These payments are income to the households, which spend it on goods and services produced by businesses. This is indicated by the money payments made to businesses in exchange for goods and services in the lower flow channel. Businesses use the money proceeds from sales to purchase the resources in the upper flow channel, thus completing the loop.

receive for supplying the resources that were used to produce the goods and services. Hence, in this money-using, pure market economy we have a clockwise flow of money payments made against a counterclockwise flow of resources, goods, and services. The clockwise circular flow of money expenditures may be thought of as the cause of the counterclockwise circular flow of resources, goods, and services, although both flows take place at the same time. These simultaneous flows reflect the ongoing and repetitive exchanges between buyers and sellers in the many markets of the economy.

The Exchange Flows
with Financial Markets

The exchange flows shown in Figure 3-1 are oversimplified in several respects. For one thing, businesses produce and sell goods to each other—capital equipment, for example. Similarly households buy and sell labor services from each other, such as domestic services like babysitting.

HOUSEHOLDS AND BUSINESSES SAVE

We also know that households do not typically spend all their income on goods and services, nor do businesses pay out all of their sales revenue for the current use of land, labor, and financial capital. *Households save part of their income, usually by putting it in banks and other financial institutions. Similarly, businesses save part of their sales revenue. Some of this saving takes the form of* **depreciation allowances**. *These allowances are funds which are set aside for the replacement of capital equipment when it wears out. The rest of their saving usually takes the form of* **retained earnings**. Like households, businesses put savings in banks and other financial institutions. Often they use their savings to purchase bonds and other forms of IOUs issued by parties that want to borrow money. Banks and other financial institutions perform the function of taking the savings of households and businesses and lending this money to borrowers who in turn use it to buy goods and services. When businesses, and sometimes households, use their savings to buy bonds and IOUs directly without the assistance of the intermediary role played by banks and other financial institutions, the effect is the same—savings are lent to borrowers.

THE ROLE OF FINANCIAL MARKETS

The markets which perform the function of taking the funds of savers and lending them to borrowers are called **financial markets**. The households and businesses that lend their savings to borrowers through these financial markets receive compensation in the form of interest payments. Financial markets serve the function of taking the funds from the saving flows of businesses and households and lending them to borrowers at interest rates mutually agreeable to both lenders and borrowers. Who are the borrowers? Other businesses and households. What do they do with the borrowed funds? Spend them on goods and services. *In effect, financial markets take the savings, or the flow of funds provided by those businesses and households that do not want to spend them on goods and services, and put them in the hands of those that do want to spend them on goods and services.*

FLOW DIAGRAM WITH
FINANCIAL MARKETS AND SAVINGS

The role of financial markets can be represented in diagram form by making some

changes in Figure 3-1. Figure 3-2 reproduces Figure 3-1 with the addition of savings flows and financial markets. Note now that not all of the sales revenue of businesses is immediately paid out in wages, rents, interest, and profit. Some is retained and saved, and flows from businesses into the financial markets as indicated by the counterclockwise arrow labeled "business saving." (It should be emphasized that these savings are still owned by the stockholders of the businesses who have provided financial capital.) Similarly, households do not spend all of their income on goods and services. That which is not spent is saved and flows into financial markets as indicated by the clockwise arrow labeled "household saving." The financial markets in the lower part of the diagram lend out the savings of businesses and households to other businesses and households that want to borrow funds. These borrowers do not borrow money and make interest payments on their loans just for the privilege of holding the money. They use it to buy goods and services from businesses, as indicated by the upward directed arrow labeled "expenditures on goods and services by borrowers." These goods and services are part of the flow labeled "goods and services," indicated by the counterclockwise arrow running from businesses to households. The business borrowers purchase goods and services from other businesses. The main point is this: *The flow of money diverted by saving away from further expenditure on goods and services is redirected through the financial markets into the hands of those who will spend it on goods and services.* In performing this function financial markets play a crucial role in capitalistic, market-oriented economies. Because there is no government economic intervention indicated in Figure 3-2, it may be taken to represent an economic system of pure market, laissez faire capitalism.

The Exchange Flows
Between Businesses, Households,
and Government

In order to characterize a capitalistic, mixed economy in a flow diagram, it is necessary to bring government into the picture. This has been done in Figure 3-3. (The term government

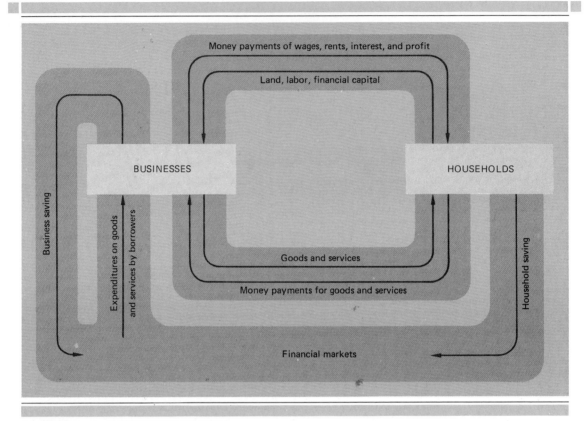

Money payments of wages, rents, interest, and profit

Land, labor, financial capital

BUSINESSES

HOUSEHOLDS

Business saving

Expenditures on goods and services by borrowers

Household saving

Goods and services

Money payments for goods and services

Financial markets

FIGURE 3-2 EXCHANGE FLOWS WITH SAVINGS AND FINANCIAL MARKETS

This diagram elaborates on Figure 3–1 by adding the savings flows from households and businesses. These feed into the financial markets where they are loaned to borrowers at some mutually acceptable rate of interest. The borrowers then spend the funds on goods and services produced by businesses. The financial markets thus serve to redirect the savings money flows, otherwise diverted from expenditure on goods and services, back into the hands of those who will spend them on goods and services. Figure 3–2 may be viewed as representing a pure market, laissez faire capitalist economy.

as used here includes federal, state, and local government.)

GOVERNMENT EXPENDITURES, TAXES, AND TRANSFERS

In order to carry out its functions, government must hire labor and other resources owned by households. This is indicated by the counterclockwise arrow running from households to government and labeled "labor and other resources." The money payments by government for these resources are indicated by the clock-

wise arrow running from government to households and labeled "transfer and factor payments." The factor payments are made to cover wage, rent, and interest payments to households in exchange for labor services, buildings and land rented to the government, and the financial capital provided through household holdings of government bonds. These factor payments are viewed as expenditures by the government and as income by the households. Transfer payments represent government payment to households of social security benefits and other bene-

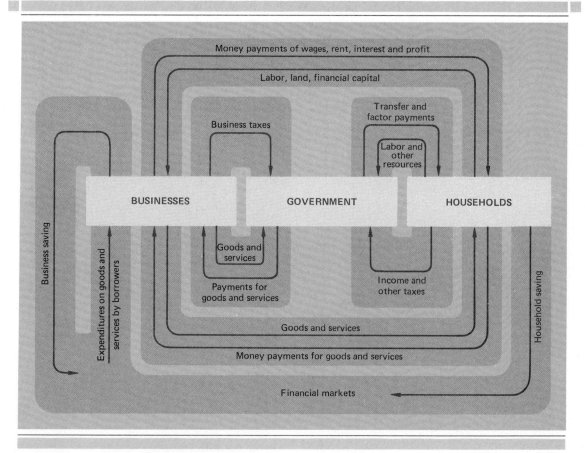

Money payments of wages, rent, interest and profit

Labor, land, financial capital

Transfer and factor payments

Business taxes

Labor and other resources

BUSINESSES   **GOVERNMENT**   **HOUSEHOLDS**

Business saving

Expenditures on goods and services by borrowers

Goods and services

Payments for goods and services

Income and other taxes

Household saving

Goods and services

Money payments for goods and services

Financial markets

FIGURE 3-3 EXCHANGE FLOWS WITH SAVINGS AND FINANCIAL MARKETS AND GOVERNMENT

This diagram elaborates on Figure 3–2 by adding government, which is financed by taxes from businesses and households. Government uses the tax proceeds to make transfer payments to households as well as to hire labor and purchase other resources from households. Government also uses the tax revenue to purchase goods and services from businesses. In this way government reallocates resources and redistributes income. Also, by varying tax rates and the level of its expenditures, government can affect the size of the flows in the flow channels—that is, the level of economic activity. Figure 3–3 may be viewed as representing a capitalistic, mixed economy.

fits provided by public assistance programs. Transfers also include tax refunds. Transfer payments are viewed as income by the households receiving them.

In order to help finance its operations, the government must collect taxes from households in the form of income taxes, property taxes, and sales taxes. These tax payments by households to government are represented by the clockwise arrow running from households to government and labeled "income and other taxes." The government also collects taxes from businesses in the form of corporate profits taxes, property taxes, and sales taxes. These tax payments to government are represented by the clockwise arrow running from businesses to government and labeled "business taxes." There is yet one other way in which government can finance its operations. That is by issuing and selling new government bonds in the financial markets. The money proceeds from such sales can be used in the same ways as tax proceeds. (The flow channel between government and the financial markets is not shown in Figure 3–3.)

The government uses receipts from bond sales along with the tax receipts from businesses and households in part to make the transfer and factor payments to households already mentioned. The government also uses these receipts to purchase goods and services from businesses. These include anything from paper clips and staples to jet bombers, space rockets, and the construction of dams, highways, and buildings by private contractors. The payments for these items are represented by the clockwise arrow running from government to businesses and labeled "payments for goods and services." The provision of goods and services in exchange for these payments is indicated by the counterclockwise arrow running from businesses to government and labeled "goods and services."

GOVERNMENT AFFECTS
RESOURCE ALLOCATION
AND INCOME DISTRIBUTION

The taxes paid by businesses must come out of their sales revenue, while those paid by households must come out of their income. By increasing or decreasing the amount of these taxes, government can divert a larger or smaller share of the sales revenue of businesses and the income receipts of households into activities determined by government expenditures, as opposed to the market activities determined by business and household expenditures. This is an obvious way in which government affects resource allocation. Similarly, it can be seen how the government affects income distribution through the redistribution of tax proceeds to households in the form of transfer payments.

GOVERNMENT AFFECTS
LEVEL OF ECONOMIC ACTIVITY

By changing its expenditure and tax policies, government can affect the level of overall economic activity as represented by the flows in Figure 3–3. Consider two extreme examples. Suppose government increases income taxes on

households, but does not spend the increased tax proceeds. This obviously takes income from households that would otherwise have been spent on goods and services or saved and put in the financial markets where it could have ultimately been used by some borrower to buy goods and services. Hence, the volume in the lower two flow channels of Figure 3–3 would be reduced. This would lead to a drop in sales by businesses and a consequent drop in some or all of the categories of business saving, business taxes, and income earned by households, as measured by businesses' money payments of wages, rent, interest, and profit in the upper flow channel of Figure 3–3. Alternatively, suppose government increased expenditures on goods and services but did not raise taxes to finance these expenditures. Suppose, instead, that it financed them by simply printing money. The result would be that businesses would experience an increase in the dollar volume of sales. This would lead to an increase in some or all of the categories—business saving, business taxes, and income earned by households. Changes in the expenditure plans of businesses and households can also lead to changes in economic activity as represented by the flows in Figure 3–3. Government stabilization policy is aimed at changing all or some combination of government expenditures, tax rates, and the money supply in such a way as to offset undesirable changes in the level of economic activity that may result from changes in business and household expenditure plans.

The flow diagrams are very simplified pictures of the economy. Much detail is omitted. Nonetheless, they give some idea how the mixed economy's various decision-making units—business, households, and government—are linked together to form an interlocking, interdependent system.

SUMMARY

1. Individuals have different abilities for performing different tasks. Because of this, individuals have an incentive to specialize in production and to trade the surplus of their output in excess of their own need for the other goods they want but don't produce themselves. This incentive stems from the

fact that specialization and trade make possible a larger output of goods and services than is possible if each individual tries to be self-sufficient—that is, if there is no specialization and trade.

2. There is an incentive to use money as a medium of exchange because it eliminates the need for the coincidence of wants, which is necessary for trade to take place in a barter economy. Because of this, money promotes specialization and trade, and hence makes possible a larger output of goods and services than is possible within the context of a barter system of trade.

3. A firm's costs are all those payments it must make to all resource suppliers in order to bid resources away from use in alternative lines of production of goods. Among the resources used by the firm are financial capital and entrepreneurial skills. When they are being compensated just enough to keep them from leaving and going into some other line of productive activity, we say they are earning a normal profit.

4. Above-normal profits will draw resources to those areas of the economy where they are most in demand. Below-normal profits in one area of the economy will cause entrepreneurial skills and financial capital to move out of that line of productive activity and into those where they can earn their opportunity cost.

5. At a minimum in any economy, government typically has basic responsibility for maintaining law and order, providing for the nation's money supply, its national defense, the judicial system, and a uniform standard of time, weight, and measurement. In mixed economies government reallocates resources in instances where it is felt the market mechanism gives unacceptable or undesirable outcomes; often strives to maintain competitive conditions in markets not naturally conducive to them; redistributes income in accordance with some norm of equity and concern for those who can't work or earn a minimally adequate income; attempts to maintain economic stability with reasonably full employment of resources.

6. There are several reasons why the government is not a very efficient producer of goods and services. Government bureaucracies have a weak incentive structure due to the difficulty of measuring their output and judging their performance. Politicians often support special interest legislation because it wins them votes from special interest groups without losing the votes of an often ill-informed public. A voting citizen must choose from a limited number of candidates, each representing a particular bundle of goods and services that typically does not accurately match the voter's preferences. Politicians are subject to an incentive structure biased toward the adoption of projects and programs with highly visible immediate benefits and well-hidden costs.

7. A mixed economy and the basic economic links between its three groups of decision-making units—businesses, households, and government—can be given a skeletal representation in a flow diagram. Such a diagram can show the flow of resources, and goods and services in exchange for money, flows of savings into the financial markets where they are loaned to borrowers and spent on goods and services, and the flows of taxes, transfers, and expenditures linking the government to businesses and households.

KEY TERMS AND CONCEPTS

barter economy
coincidence of wants
depreciation allowance
exclusion principle
financial markets
normal profit
public assistance programs
public goods
retained earnings
specialization of labor

QUESTIONS AND PROBLEMS

1. We have discussed specialization in terms of its economic advantages. From the laborer's standpoint, what are some of the disadvantages of specialization often heard about in the modern industrialized world?

2. We have noted that it might be possible that someone who has sandals to trade, but no need for chopped wood, might nonetheless accept the chopped wood and trade it for something else. In a situation such as this, where there is a lack of coincidence of wants, do you think the sandalmaker would be more, or less, willing to accept strawberries than chopped wood (given that the sandalmaker wants neither and must trade them for something he or she does want)? Why? Compared to a situation where there is a coincidence of wants between woodchopper and sandalmaker, how do you think the terms of the exchange (the amount of wood needed to purchase a pair of sandals) would be different if the woodchopper wanted sandals but the sandalmaker didn't want chopped wood?

3. Elaborate on the following statement: "Profits can, of course, be immoral—if they are exploitive, for example, or result from price-fixing schemes or monopolies. But most profits . . . are an essential and beneficial ingredient in the workings of a free-market economy."

4. Describe the nature of the role of profit which the author of the following statement must have in mind. "Today profits, far from being too high, are still too low to ensure the nation's continued economic health. Among the top 20 industrialized countries, the United States in recent years has fared badly in terms of new industrial investment per capita . . ."

5. A perhaps overly cynical view of government is that the function of government is to distribute money, that the effectiveness of government is measured by the sums dispensed, and that the worth of politicians is weighted by how much they are able to get the federal government to spend in their districts. It is illegal for a politician to slip a derelict $5 for a vote, but a politician can buy office by legislating billions of dollars. As a result of this situation, a number of critics of Congress claim there is much more government spending than can be justified on objective economic grounds.

One suggested way of dealing with this problem is to require that Congress establish some sort of total spending ceiling at the beginning of each new term.

a. Why might this force congressmen to make more economic choices?

b. Why might this put a curb on the "you vote for my pet project and I'll vote for yours" type of logrolling among congressmen? Why is it such logrolling leads to ever expanding levels of government spending?

6. "Despite general agreement about the need for tremendous amounts of new capital, there is no consensus about how the money should be raised. Liberal economists generally favor more generous individual tax cuts . . . to stimulate consumer buying, which, in turn, creates heightened economic activity. Conservative economists . . . would prefer federal policies that would enable companies to keep more of their earnings either through higher depreciation allowances for the purchase of new equipment or a further lowering of the corporate tax rate."

In Figure 3-3, where would liberal economists' policies affect the flow diagram as contrasted with those of conservative economists?

4

SUPPLY, DEMAND, AND PRICE DETERMINATION

SUPPLY, DEMAND, PAPER BAGS, AND THINGS

ST. LOUIS, March 15—The Great Toilet Paper Shortage scare is over. Rumormongers need not fret, however. There are many more opportunities for shortage scares still under wraps in the paper industry.

While shortages of tickets, shopping bags, and writing tablets aren't serious, the fact is that their supplies are extremely tight. The same is true for toilet paper. This explains why the gentle nudge of a rumor recently circulated by television and the press was enough to tip the scales and temporarily create a real shortage.

Rumors don't have a corner on shortage creation, however. Paper supply is so gingerly balanced against rising demand these days that the slightest touch by some external force can topple the market into temporary shortage. All kinds of problems—from foul weather, strikes, and fuel shortages to rumors—have upset the balance lately and could do it again.

"It's practically impossible to keep up with demand," says a representative for one paper company currently behind in its production efforts. The supply side of the situation is also plagued by an abnormal coincidence of events. The aftermath of strikes at newsprint mills six months ago is still making life miserable for newspapers. A shortage of railroad cars and the truckers' tie-ups have done the same recently. Fuel supplies are low because of the energy crisis. Logging has been a lot harder because of heavy snows in the North, heavy rains in the South, and floods in the West.

Paper people say all this shuffling in the paper market would cease if the industry added more papermaking capacity. The country's current plants, running full tilt this past year, managed to raise output 5 percent. That still wasn't nearly enough. However, the industry is reluctant to build plants because it claims price controls prevent an adequate return on the investment.

This article is but one example of the way supply and demand affect our everyday lives, frequently with an impact that is newsworthy. It is true that many markets and the way they function receive little attention from the press from one year to the next. But like the squeaky wheel, it is typically the market that is disrupted or apparently "out of order" that gets the attention. Prolonged shortages or surpluses of any resources, service, or product that significantly affects the public's standard of living will usually make headlines.

In this chapter we will focus on the laws of demand and supply. We will examine in some detail the notion of the demand curve and the supply curve. And we will consider how demand and supply interact to determine the equilibrium price at which the quantity of a good or resource supplied is just sufficient to satisfy demand for it. We will see how all of this is necessary for a better understanding of how markets work and how prices function to allocate resources.

DEMAND AND DEMAND CURVES

You have already met the notion of demand and its graphical representation, called the demand curve, in Chapter 1. There it was presented as an example of an economic theory or law. Here we want to examine in more detail the law of demand and how the demand curve is determined. We will see how individual demand curves can be combined to give the aggregate demand curve representing the entire market demand for a particular product, resource, or service. Finally, we will examine the very important distinction between shifts in the position of a demand curve and movements along it.

Law of Demand

As we saw in Chapter 1, the **law of demand** is a theory about the relationship between the amount of a good a buyer both desires and is able to purchase per unit of time and the price charged for it. Notice that we emphasize the ability to pay for the good as well as the desire to have it. Your ability to pay is as important as your desire for the good, because in economics we are interested in explaining and predicting actual behavior in the marketplace. Your *unlimited* desires for goods can never be observed in the marketplace because you can't buy more than you are *able* to pay for. (People who try to, by writing bad checks, printing counterfeit money, or by other fraudulent schemes, usually end up in jail.) At a given price for a good, we are only interested in the buyer's demand for that good which can effectively be backed by a purchase.

The law of demand hypothesized that the lower the price charged for a product, resource, or service, the larger will be the quantity demanded per unit of time. Conversely, the higher the price charged, the smaller will be the quantity demanded per unit of time—all other things remaining the same. For example, the law of demand predicts that the lower the price of steak, the more steak you will desire and be able to purchase per year—all other things remaining the same. As we noted in Chapter 1, the law of demand is confirmed again and again by observed behavior in the marketplace. Businesses have sales (cut prices), and the amount of goods they sell per period increases. If the price of steak goes up, the amount purchased per unit of time decreases. Why is this? For most goods there are other goods that may be used to satisfy very nearly the same desires. When the price of steak goes up, if the price of pork chops, lamb chops, and hamburger remains unchanged, then all of these kinds of meats are now relatively cheaper compared to steak. Hence, buyers will purchase more of them and less of steak. These kinds of meats are *substitutes* for steak. Although not exactly the same as steak, they are another kind of meat that will do.

Individual Demand

The inverse relationship between the price of a good and the quantity of the good demanded per unit of time can be depicted graphically as we demonstrated in Chapter 1. Suppose we consider an individual's demand for high-grade typing paper. Table 4-1 shows the number of packs of such paper that the individual will demand per month at each of several different prices. (Assume there are 25 sheets in a pack.) Note that the higher the price, the smaller the number of packs demanded per month. Conversely, the lower the price, the greater the number of packs that will be demanded per month. Why? Again, because the higher the price of high-grade paper, the greater the incentive to cut back on its use and use other kinds of paper instead—assuming their prices and all other things remain the same. *Relative* to high-grade paper, other kinds of paper simply become cheaper to use as the price of high-grade paper rises. Conversely, more high-grade paper will be demanded when successively lower prices are charged for it because it will become less and less expensive relative to other kinds of paper.

If we plot the price and quantity combinations listed in Table 4-1 on a graph, we obtain the **demand curve** *DD* shown in Figure 4-1. (If you need to brush up on how to plot data on a graph, refer back to pp. 10-12.) Economists almost always represent the demand for a good, resource, or service by use of a demand curve. Verbal descriptions or tabular descriptions such as Table 4-1, while useful, are not typically as readily understood. This is an instance where a picture is worth a thousand words.

Demand Determinants: The Other Things That Remain the Same

When we draw a demand curve such as that in Figure 4-1, we emphasize the way in which the price charged for a good determines the quantity of it demanded. The price of the good is thereby singled out as the determining factor, and all other things are said to be equal, or remain the same. (If you prefer Latin, you may say *ceteris paribus*.) The important point is that *movement along the demand curve means that*

After reading this chapter, you will be able to:
1. Formulate and explain the law of demand and construct its graphical representation, the demand curve.
2. Enumerate the determinants of demand.
3. Demonstrate the significance of, and recognize the difference between, shifts in the position of a demand curve and movements along a fixed demand curve.
4. Formulate and explain the law of supply and construct its graphical representation, the supply curve.
5. Enumerate the determinants of supply.
6. Show how supply and demand interact to mutually determine equilibrium price and quantity (also called market equilibrium).
7. Demonstrate how changes in the determinants of supply and demand disturb the existing market equilibrium and result in the establishment of a new market equilibrium.

TABLE 4-1 AN INDIVIDUAL'S DEMAND FOR HIGH-GRADE TYPING PAPER (Hypothetical Data)

Price per Pack	Quantity Demanded (Number of Packs per Month)
$.50	10
.40	20
.30	30
.20	45
.10	65

only the price of the good and the quantity of it demanded change. All other things are assumed to be constant or unchanged. What are these other things? They are: (1) the prices of all other goods, (2) the individual's income, (3) the individual's expectations about the future, and (4) the individual's tastes. A change in one or more of these other things will change the data in Table 4-1. Therefore the position of the demand curve in Figure 4-1 will be shifted. Such a shift in the demand curve is called a *change in demand.* A movement along a fixed demand curve is referred to as a *change in the quantity demanded.*

PRICES OF ALL OTHER GOODS

We may classify all other goods according to their relationship to the good for which the demand curve is drawn, call it good X, say. Other goods are either substitutes for X, complements of X, or basically unrelated to X.

Substitute good: *A good is a substitute for X to the extent that it can satisfy similar needs or desires as X.* Different substitute goods will, of course, vary in the extent to which they satisfy the needs or desires that X does. T-bone steak is a closer substitute for sirloin steak than are lamb chops, although both T-bone steak and lamb chops typically would be regarded as substitutes for sirloin steak. *When the price of a substitute good for good X rises, the demand curve for good X will shift rightward.* This is so because when the price of the substitute *rises,* it becomes cheaper to use X instead of the substitute good.

For example, suppose initially the demand curve for high-grade typing paper is *DD* in Figure 4-2. Now suppose the price of a substitute, super-grade typing paper, rises. This will cause the individual's demand curve to shift rightward from *DD* to D_1D_1. This means that at *any* given price of high-grade typing paper (measured on the vertical axis of Figure 4-2), the quantity of high-grade typing paper demanded (measured on the horizontal axis) will now be larger as a result of the increase in the price of super-grade typing paper.

The opposite of the above is also true—*when the price of a substitute for good X falls, the demand curve for good X will shift leftward.* This happens because when the price of the substitute *falls* it becomes relatively more expensive to use X instead of the substitute good. For example, a fall in the price of super-grade typing paper causes a leftward shift of the demand curve in Figure 4-2, such as from *DD* to D_2D_2.

Complementary good: *A good is a complement, or complementary good, to good X to the extent it is used jointly with good X.* For example, gasoline and tires are complements to one another. So are football shoes and football helmets, records and phonographs, and salad dressing and lettuce. *When the price of a good which is a complement to good X falls, the demand curve for good X will shift rightward.* This happens because the complementary good is now less expensive to use and therefore more of it will be demanded. More of good X will be demanded as well, because it is used jointly with the complement. For example, a complementary good to high-grade typewriter paper is a typewriter. If the price of a typewriter falls, the cost of typing will be less. This will cause the demand curve *DD* for high-grade typing paper to shift to the right in Figure 4-2—to a position such as D_1D_1 for instance. At *any* given price of high-grade typing paper, the quantity of this paper demanded will be greater.

The opposite is also true. *When the price of a good which is complementary to good X rises, the demand curve for good X will shift leftward.* The complementary good is now more expensive to use and therefore less of it will be demanded. Less of good X will be demanded because,

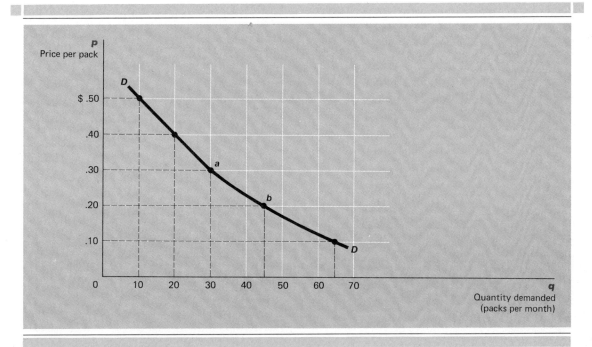

FIGURE 4-1 AN INDIVIDUAL'S DEMAND CURVE FOR HIGH-GRADE TYPING PAPER

The individual's demand curve for high-grade typing paper is plotted here using the data from Table 4–1. It slopes downward from left to right reflecting the inverse relationship between the quantity demanded and the price of the good. It illustrates the law of demand, which says that individuals will demand more of a good the lower is its price. A change in the price of the good causes a change in the quantity demanded, and is represented by a movement along the demand curve. For example, if price changes from $.30 per package to $.20 per pack, the quantity demanded increases from 30 to 45 packs per month. This is represented by the movement from a to b along the demand curve DD.

again, it is used jointly with the complement. In Figure 4–2 a rise in the price of a typewriter will cause DD to shift leftward to a position such as D_2D_2.

Finally, some goods are basically *unrelated* to good X in that it would be very difficult to classify them as either substitutes or complements for X. In this sense toothpaste seems basically unrelated to garden clippers, or pears to combs, or tennis balls to ballpoint pens.

INCOME
Another thing assumed equal or constant when we move along an individual's demand curve is the individual's money income.

How does a change in the individual's income affect the individual's demand curve for a particular good? The answer depends on the nature of the good. Basically we may distinguish between two types of goods in this respect: normal goods, and inferior goods.

Normal good: A normal good is one that most people typically want more of as their income goes up. Such things as food, clothing, and medical services are examples. *An individual's demand curve for a normal good will shift rightward when the individual's income rises. Conversely, when the individual's income falls the demand curve will shift leftward.*

Inferior good: An inferior good is one that an

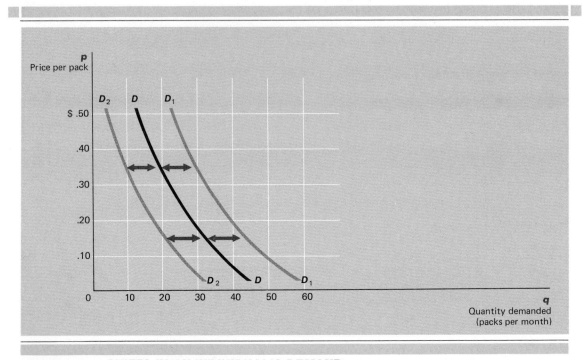

FIGURE 4-2 SHIFTS IN AN INDIVIDUAL'S DEMAND FOR HIGH-GRADE TYPING PAPER

The position of the demand curve is given by the determinants of demand. These are the prices of all other goods, the individual's money income, the individual's expectations about the future, and the individual's tastes. Changes in any of these will cause a change in demand, which is represented by a shift in the demand curve either rightward or leftward. A shift of the demand curve to the right represents an increase in demand. A shift of the demand curve to the left represents a decrease in demand. *Warning:* Do not confuse the concept of a *change in demand,* represented by a shift in the demand curve, with the concept of a *change in the quantity demanded,* represented by movement along a fixed demand curve such as that described by the movement from *a* to *b* in Figure 4-1.

individual will want more of at lower income levels than at higher income levels. For example, it has been observed that poor people tend to eat more potatoes and bread than do people in higher income brackets. Evidence suggests that people tend to cut back on their consumption of such foods as their income rises above a certain level. *An individual's demand curve for an inferior good will shift rightward as income rises only at very low levels of income, and then shift leftward as income rises to higher levels.* Conversely, as an individual's income falls, the individual's demand curve for an inferior good will shift rightward until income reaches some low

level of income at which point a further fall in income will cause the demand curve to shift leftward.

Suppose the individual in Figure 4-2 is a student, and that high-grade typing paper is a normal good. If the student's income were to rise as a result of an increase in a scholarship stipend, the student's demand curve for high-grade typing paper would rise from DD to D_1D_1, say.

EXPECTATIONS

Among the other things assumed equal or constant when we move along an individual's demand curve are the individual's expectations about all things relevant to the individual's economic situation. For example, suppose there is suddenly an upward revision of what the individual expects the price of typing paper to be in the future, and the individual therefore wants to buy more now to avoid paying a higher price for it later. As a result the demand curve DD shifts rightward to a position such as D_1D_1 in Figure 4-2.

This is just the sort of change in expectations that led to the increase in the demand for toilet paper reported in the news item at the beginning of this chapter.

TASTES

Tastes are another thing assumed equal or constant when we move along an individual's demand curve. If a person suddenly develops a sweet tooth, that person's tastes have changed. This will be reflected in a rightward shift in that person's demand curve for candy. Conversely, several painful sessions at the dentist might cause you to lose your taste for candy. In that event your demand curve for candy would shift leftward.

Market Demand:
The Sum of Individual Demands

The **market demand curve** for a good is obtained by summing up all the individual demand curves for that good. To illustrate in the simplest possible case, suppose there are only two individuals who have a demand for high-grade typing paper. The first individual's demand is that given in Table 4-1. These numbers are repeated in Table 4-2, along with the second individual's demand for this kind of paper at each of the five prices listed. The market demand, or total demand, for high-grade typing paper is the sum of the quantities demanded by each individual at every price. The sums obtained in this way at each of five of these prices are shown in the last column of Table 4-2. Using the data from Table 4-2, we construct the individual demand curves in Figure 4-3, along with the market demand curve, which is the summation of these individual demand curves.

Because market demand curves are the sum of individual demand curves, they are subject to the same determinants and affected in the same

way by changes in those determinants as the individual curves. There is one additional determinant of a market demand curve, however, and that is the number of individual demand curves or buyers that enter into the summation. *An increase in the number of buyers in the market will cause the market demand curve to shift rightward. Conversely, a decrease will cause it to shift leftward.* In sum, the other things that are assumed to remain the same as we move along a market demand curve are: (1) prices of all other goods, (2) money income, (3) expectations, (4) tastes, and (5) the number of buyers.

Changes in Quantity
Demanded Versus Shifts in Demand

Warning: One of the most common areas of confusion in economics concerns the distinction between movement along a demand curve versus shifts in the position of the demand curve.

Movement along a demand curve represents a change in the price of the good under consideration and the associated change in the quantity of the good demanded, and nothing else. All other determinants of demand are assumed to remain the same. For example, when the price of high-grade typing paper is changed from $.30 to $.20 in Figure 4-1, the quantity of that paper demanded increases from 30 packs to 45 packs per month. This is represented by the movement from point *a* to point *b* along the demand curve *DD*. By convention, when we simply refer to *a change in the quantity of a good demanded,* we mean *a movement along a fixed demand curve,* such as that from *a* to *b* in Figure 4-1, unless we say otherwise.

In contrast, a change in one or more of the five determinants of demand discussed above will cause the position of the demand curve to change in the manner shown in Figure 4-2. By convention, when we simply refer to a *change in demand* we mean a *shift in the position of the demand curve,* unless we say otherwise. *When the demand curve for a good shifts rightward, more of that good will be demanded at every possible price. When the demand for a good shifts leftward, less of that good will be demanded at every possible price. A change in demand results from a change in one or more of the five determinants of demand.*

**TABLE 4-2 THE MARKET DEMAND FOR HIGH-GRADE
TYPING PAPER: TWO INDIVIDUAL BUYERS** (Hypothetical Data)

Price per Pack	Quantity Demanded per Month					
	First Individual's Demand		Second Individual's Demand		Total Market Demand	
$.50	10	+	5	=	15	
.40	20	+	15	=	35	
.30	30	+	25	=	55	
.20	45	+	35	=	80	
.10	65	+	45	=	110	

CHECKPOINT 4-1

If the price of peas were to rise, what do you think this would do to the demand curve for lima beans? If the price of pretzels were to fall, what do you think this would do to the demand curve for beer? What would it do to the demand curve for pretzels? Would we say there is a change in the demand for pretzels or a change in the quantity of pretzels demanded? If the price of typewriters went up, what do you think this would do to the demand curve for high-grade typing paper?

SUPPLY AND SUPPLY CURVES

Given that there are demands for goods, what is the nature of the process that determines how those demands will be met? To answer this question we must have an understanding of the law of supply and the concept of a supply curve and its determinants.

Law of Supply

The law of supply is a statement about the relationship between the amount of a good a supplier is willing and able to supply and offer

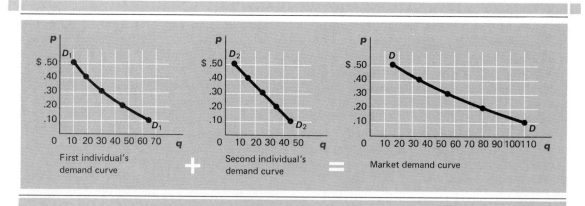

**FIGURE 4-3 THE SUM OF THE INDIVIDUAL
DEMAND CURVES GIVES THE MARKET DEMAND CURVE**

The first individual's demand curve $D_1 D_1$ and the second individual's demand curve $D_2 D_2$ are constructed from their individual demand data of Table 4–2. The market demand curve DD is equal to the sum of the individual demand curves and is constructed from the total market demand data of Table 4–2.

for sale per unit of time and each of the different possible prices at which that good might be sold. That is, if we said to the supplier, "Suppose the good can be sold at a price of such and such dollars per unit. How many units of the good would you be willing and able to produce and offer for sale per unit of time?" We write down the answer along with the price we quoted to the supplier. Then we repeat the question exactly *except* that now we quote a somewhat higher price. We observe that the higher the price, the larger the quantity the supplier is willing and able to supply for sale per unit of time. And, of course, the lower the price, the smaller the quantity that is offered. This observed relationship is the **law of supply**, which *says that suppliers will supply larger quantities of a good at higher prices than at lower prices.*

The Supply Curve

Suppose the supplier whom we have been questioning produces high-grade typing paper. Table 4-3 lists some of the answers that the supplier gave in response to our questions. If we plot the data of Table 4-3 on a graph, we obtain this supplier's supply curve. As in Figure 4-1, we measure the price per unit (a pack) on the vertical axis and the number of units (packs) on the horizontal axis. The resulting curve *SS* is shown in Figure 4-4. We have plotted only the five price-quantity combinations. At all the possible prices in between, we presumably could have filled in the whole curve as shown by the solid line connecting the five plotted points. You may view the **supply curve** in different ways. *It indicates the amount of the good the supplier is willing to provide per unit of time at different possible prices.* Or alternatively, you may say *it shows what prices are necessary in order to give the supplier the incentive to provide various quantities of the good per unit of time.*

The shape of the supply curve clearly shows that as the price of the good rises the supplier supplies more of the good; as the price falls the supplier supplies less of the good. Just as with a demand curve, *such movement along a supply curve always assumes that all other things will remain the same.* Among other things, the prices of all other resources and goods are assumed to remain the same. This assumption and the fact

that resources can be used in a variety of ways to produce a variety of goods are the basic reasons why a supply curve slopes upward to the right.

In general, if resources are to be shifted from producing good Y to producing good Z it is necessary to pay them more for producing Z than what they are paid for producing Y. In order to draw more resources into the activity of producing and supplying more of good Z, it is necessary to pay them more than what they can earn in alternative production activities supplying other goods. For example, consider the individual producer's supply curve for high-grade typing paper shown in Figure 4-4. Assuming the prices of all other resources and goods are constant, if the price per pack is raised from $.10 to $.20, it becomes relatively more profitable to produce this paper. More resources will therefore be induced away from other activities and employed in the production of high-grade typing paper. In this instance, the price increase is just sufficient to make it worthwhile to employ enough more resources in this activity to increase production from 200 packs per month to 600 packs per month. This is indicated by the move from point *a* to point *b* on the supply curve. Similarly, successively higher prices make it even more profitable to produce typing paper and more resources will be drawn into the production of this paper.

Suppose that there are 100 producers of high-grade typing paper, each of whom has a supply curve identical to that of Figure 4-4. At each price per pack listed in Table 4-3, the quantity of high-grade typing paper supplied by the sum of all producers is simply 100 times the amount supplied by one producer. Using this data, Figure 4-5 shows the market or industry supply curve *SS* for high-grade typing paper. Note that the units on the horizontal axis of Figure 4-5 are a hundred times larger than those on the horizontal axis of Figure 4-4.

Supply Determinants: The Other Things That Remain the Same

When we draw a supply curve such as *SS* in Figure 4-5, we emphasize the way in which the price of the good determines the quantity of it supplied. As with a demand curve, the price of

TABLE 4-3 AN INDIVIDUAL PRODUCER'S SUPPLY OF HIGH-GRADE TYPING PAPER
(Hypothetical Data)

Price per Pack	Quantity Supplied (Number of Packs per Month)
$.50	1,200
.40	1,100
.30	900
.20	600
.10	200

the good is singled out as the determining factor and all other things are assumed to be unchanging. These other things are: (1) the prices of resources and other factors of production, (2) technology, (3) the prices of other goods, (4) the number of suppliers, and (5) the suppliers' expectations. If one or more of these things changes, the supply curve will shift.

1. PRICES OF RESOURCES
As we saw in Chapter 1, all production processes require inputs of labor services, raw materials, fuels, and other resources and goods. These inputs to a production process are fre-

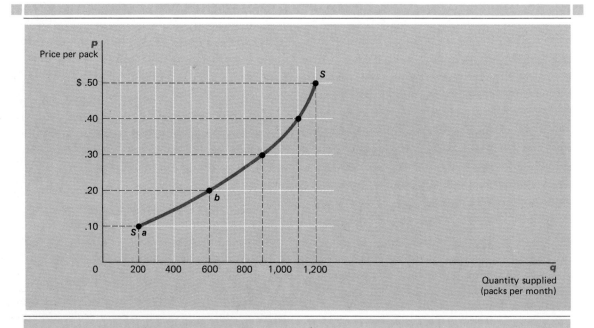

FIGURE 4-4 AN INDIVIDUAL PRODUCER'S SUPPLY OF HIGH-GRADE TYPING PAPER

An individual producer's supply curve for high-grade typing paper is plotted here using the data from Table 4-3. It slopes upward from left to right reflecting a direct relationship between the quantity of the good supplied and the price of the good. It illustrates the law of supply, which says that suppliers will supply more of a good the higher is its price. A change in the price of the good causes a change in the quantity supplied, and is represented by a movement along the supply curve. For example, if price changes from $.10 per pack to $.20 per pack, the quantity supplied increases from 200 packs per month to 600 packs per month. This is represented by the movement from a to b along the supply curve SS.

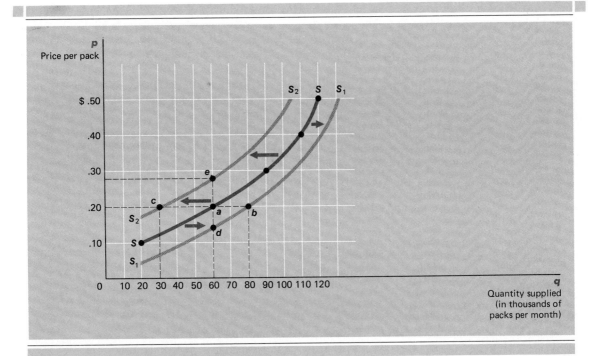

FIGURE 4-5 SHIFTS IN THE MARKET SUPPLY CURVE FOR HIGH-GRADE TYPING PAPER

The position of the supply curve is established by the determinants of supply. These are the prices of factors of production, technology, the prices of other goods, the number of suppliers, and the suppliers' expectations about the future. Changes in any of these will cause a change in supply, which is represented by a rightward or leftward shift in the supply curve. A rightward shift represents an increase in supply. A leftward shift represents a decrease in supply. *Warning:* Do not confuse the concept of a *change in supply,* represented by a shift in the supply curve, with the concept of a *change in the quantity supplied,* represented by movement along a fixed supply curve such as that described by the movement from *a* to *b* in Figure 4-4.

quently referred to as the **factors of production**. The supplier of a good has to purchase these factors in order to produce the good. *In order for suppliers to be willing to produce a certain amount of a good, it is necessary that the price received per unit of the good be sufficiently high to cover all the costs of the factor inputs used in the production of the good.* As we discussed in Chapter 3, such costs also include an allowance for normal profits.

Suppose now that the price of one or more of the factors of production should fall—that is, one or more of the input prices that were as-

sumed to be constant when we drew SS now changes to a lower level. Hence at each possible price of the good suppliers will find it profitable to produce a larger amount of the good than they were previously willing to supply. The supply curve will therefore shift rightward to a position such as S_1S_1 in Figure 4-5. Conversely, if one or more of the input prices should rise, the cost of production will now be higher and producers will not be willing to supply as much at each possible price of the good. The supply curve will therefore shift leftward to a position such as S_2S_2 in Figure 4-5.

For example, if producers could sell high-grade typing paper for $.20 a pack, they would be willing to supply 60,000 packs of this paper per month. This price-supply combination is represented by point a on the industry supply curve SS in Figure 4-5. At this price and level of production, the costs of all factors of production plus an allowance for normal profit are just covered. Suppose that the price of one or more inputs falls so that the industry supply curve shifts rightward to S_1S_1. Now when suppliers are producing 60,000 packs of paper per month, a price of $.15 per pack is sufficient to cover all costs plus an allowance for normal profit, as indicated by point d on S_1S_1. Because they are receiving $.20 per pack, however, they are earning more than a normal profit. This leads them to expand output until they have moved up the supply curve S_1S_1 from point d to point b. Here they are producing 80,000 packs per month. At point b, the price of $.20 per pack is once again just sufficient to cover all costs plus allowance for a normal profit.

Alternatively, suppose the price of one or more inputs should rise so that the supply curve shifts leftward from SS to S_2S_2. Now when suppliers are producing 60,000 packs of paper per month, a price of $.28 per pack is necessary to cover all costs plus an allowance for normal profit, as indicated by point e on S_2S_2. However, if they are receiving only $.20 per pack, they are suffering losses. Therefore, they will reduce output until they have moved back down the supply curve S_2S_2 from point e to point c, where they will produce 30,000 packs per month. Once again, at point c the price of $.20 per pack is just sufficient to cover all costs plus allowance for a normal profit.

In the news item on the paper shortage, a number of difficulties afflicting the industry were mentioned. In particular, it was noted that the "supply side of the situation" is "plagued by an abnormal coincidence of events." Among these events it was noted that past "strikes at newsprint mills" were "making life miserable for newspapers." What does this mean in terms of the supply curve of newsprint? It means that the strike caused that supply curve to shift leftward. It will now cost newspapers more to obtain any given quantity of newsprint. The other sources of supply difficulties mentioned in the news item have the same kind of effect on the supply curve. Each causes it to shift leftward.

2. PRICES OF OTHER GOODS

Along a fixed supply curve, it is also assumed that the prices of other goods are unchanged. Why do we distinguish between the prices of other goods and the prices of factors of production? The prices of factors of production refer only to the goods used in the production of the good for which the supply curve is drawn. The prices of other goods we now refer to are all the other goods not used in the production of the good for which the supply curve is drawn.

As we saw earlier, factors of production are attracted to those production activities where they are paid the highest prices. The higher the price the producer gets for the good produced with those inputs, the greater his or her willingness to pay high prices for those factors. Hence, if the price of beef rises relative to the price of milk, farmers will use less of their pasture land for grazing dairy cattle in order to make it available to graze beef cattle. The opportunity cost of using pasture to produce milk has effectively risen because the value of that pasture in its alternative use of producing beef has risen. Factors must be paid their opportunity cost if they are to be used in a particular productive activity. That is, the price that must be paid a factor input must be at least as high as what it could earn in an alternative activity. Since the price of pasture land will go up because of its increased value in beef production, the cost of using it in milk production will rise. The supply curve for milk will then shift leftward. To induce milk producers to supply any given quantity of milk, the price of a gallon of milk will have to be higher. Why? To cover the increased cost of pasture land, which is now more expensive to use because of its increased value in beef production due to the rise in the price of beef. Again we are reminded that the economic problem is how to allocate scarce resources to alternative uses.

Suppose the price of super-grade typing paper were to fall relative to the price of high-grade typing paper. Exactly the same principle would apply as in the example of beef and milk. Many of the same resources used to produce the super-grade typing paper are used in the production of high-grade typing paper. Because their value in producing super-grade typing paper now would be less, it is less expensive to use them in high-grade typing paper production. Consequently, the supply curve for high-grade typing paper in Figure 4-5 would shift rightward from SS to a position such as S_1S_1. At every level of output the price which producers must receive to induce them to produce that output is now lower because the cost of some of the inputs to the production process are lower.

3. TECHNOLOGY

Any production process uses some form of technology, whether it involves tending a rice paddy with a handmade sickle in southeast Asia or making synthetic fibers in a large plant in Wilmington, Delaware. *The term* **technology** *refers to the methods used to combine resources of all kinds, including labor, to produce goods and services.* The history of the human race has been in no small way a history of the advancement of technology.

This advancement has been characterized by an increase in man's ability to produce goods and services—that is, by an increase in productivity. Often productivity is measured as output produced per labor hour used in the production process. Increases in productivity are then taken to mean increases in output per labor hour. *Because technological advance increases productivity, it lowers the cost of producing goods.* Suppose for example that there is a technological advance in the technique used to produce high-grade typing paper. This lowers the cost of producing the paper. Suppose the position of the supply curve in Figure 4-5 is at SS before the advance. The technological advance will cause the supply curve to shift rightward to a position such as S_1S_1. At every level of output the price necessary to cover all costs including an allowance for a normal profit will now be lower— lower, because costs will be lower.

Circumstances that reduce productivity can arise as well. A drought will reduce the produc-

tivity of land and cause crop yields to be less. Such adverse developments essentially require the application of additional production techniques if output levels are to be maintained— the construction of irrigation ditches, for example. But these new techniques add to the cost of production. If the crop were corn, a rise in the cost of production would cause the supply curve for corn to shift leftward.

In the news item, some of the supply problems in the paper industry are reported to stem from the increased difficulty of logging the timber used to make paper. Logging has been "a lot harder because of heavy snows in the North, heavy rains in the South, and floods in the West." Such circumstances reduce logging productivity. If output levels are to be maintained, additional equipment will be required to overcome these adverse elements. But this equipment will raise the cost of producing paper. Again, this will cause the supply curve of high-grade typing paper to shift leftward from SS to a position such as S_2S_2 in Figure 4-5. To induce suppliers to produce any given level of output, a higher price per pack will be required.

Remember that whenever we speak of movement along a fixed supply curve, the state of technology is assumed to be unchanged.

4. NUMBER OF SUPPLIERS

When we constructed the market or industry supply curve SS in Figure 4-5, we did it by assuming there were a hundred identical individual suppliers, each with a supply curve like that shown in Figure 4-4. Summing the individual supply curves horizontally gave us the market supply curve SS. If there had been more suppliers, the market supply curve would have been further to the right at a position such as S_1S_1. It follows from these observations that when more suppliers enter the industry the aggregate supply curve will shift to the right. When suppliers leave the industry, it will shift to the left. When we speak of movement along an aggregate supply curve, it is assumed that the number of suppliers does not change.

5. SUPPLIERS' EXPECTATIONS

This term refers to the expectations suppliers

have about anything that they think affects their economic situation. For example, if garment manufacturers expect a strike to stop their production in a few months, they may attempt to supply more now so that stores can build up their inventories to tide them over. If suppliers of a good expect its price to be higher in a few months, they may hold back supply now in order to sell it at higher prices later. Changes in expectations can cause the supply curve to shift in either direction depending on the particular situation. However, for any movement along a supply curve, expectations are assumed to remain unchanged.

In sum, the other things that are assumed to remain unchanged when we move along a supply curve are: (1) the prices of resources and other factors of production, (2) technology, (3) the prices of other goods, (4) the number of suppliers, (5) the suppliers' expectations. When one or more of these things change, the supply curve shifts.

Changes in Quantity Supplied Versus Shifts in Supply

Warning: Along with our earlier warning about the demand curve, another common confusion in economics concerns the distinction between movement along a supply curve versus shifts in the supply curve.

Movement along a supply curve represents a change in the price of the good under consideration and the associated change in the quantity of the good supplied. All other things are assumed to be unchanged. By convention, when we simply refer to a *change in the quantity of a good supplied* we mean a *movement along a fixed supply curve,* such as that from *d* to *b* in Figure 4–5, unless we say otherwise.

A change in one or more of the five determinants of supply discussed above will cause the supply curve to shift in the manner shown in Figure 4–5. By contrast, movement along a fixed supply curve always assumes these five things remain unchanged. By convention, when we simply refer to *a change in supply* we mean *a shift in the position of the supply curve,* unless we say otherwise. *When the supply curve for a good shifts rightward, more of that good will be sup-*

plied at every price. When the supply curve shifts leftward, less of that good will be supplied at every price. A change in supply results from a change in one or more of the five determinants of supply.

■CHECKPOINT 4-2

If wages go up, what effect will this have on the supply curve *SS* in Figure 4–5? If someone develops an improved process for treating wood to be used in paper production, what effect will this have on the supply curve *SS* in Figure 4–5? Suppose the price of medium-grade typing paper were to rise. Would we refer to the effect of this on *SS* in Figure 4–5 as a "change in the supply" or a "change in the quantity supplied" of high-grade typing paper? Explain the economic process by which farm land used to produce corn becomes converted to factory property for the production of CB radios.

MARKET EQUILIBRIUM: INTERACTION OF SUPPLY AND DEMAND

As any armchair economist knows, supply and demand are what economics is all about. Like the blades of a scissors, supply and demand interact to determine the terms of trade between buyers and sellers. That is, supply and demand mutually determine the price at which sellers are willing to supply just the amount of a good that buyers want to buy. The market for every good has a demand curve and a supply curve that determine this price and quantity. When this price and quantity are established, the market is said to be in equilibrium. In equilibrium there is no tendency for price and quantity to change.

Equilibrium Price and Quantity

In order to see how equilibrium price and quantity are determined in a market, consider again our hypothetical example of the market demand and supply for high-grade typing paper. Table 4–4 contains the market supply data (usually called the market **supply schedule**) on which the market supply curve *SS* of Figure

TABLE 4-4 MARKET SUPPLY AND DEMAND FOR HIGH-GRADE TYPING PAPER (Hypothetical Data)

(1)	(2)	−	(3)	=	(4)	(5)
Price per Pack	Total Number of Packs Supplied per Month		Total Number of Packs Demanded per Month		Surplus (+) or Shortage (−)	Price Change Required to Establish Equilibrium
$.50	120,000	−	20,000	=	+ 100,000	decrease
.40	110,000	−	40,000	=	+ 70,000	decrease
.30	90,000	−	60,000	=	+ 30,000	decrease
.25	78,000	−	78,000	=	0	no change
.20	60,000	−	90,000	=	− 30,000	increase
.10	20,000	−	130,000	=	− 110,000	increase

4-5 is based. It also contains the market demand data (usually called the market **demand schedule**) that determines the market demand curve for high-grade typing paper. In this case, the market demand schedule has been obtained by supposing that there are 2,000 individual buyers in the market. Each of these buyers is assumed to have an individual demand schedule like that given in Table 4-1. (That table contained the data for the individual demand curve of Figure 4-1.) The market quantity demand data of Table 4-4 thus equals 2,000 times the individual quantity demand data given in Table 4-1.

MARKET ADJUSTMENT
WHEN PRICE IS ABOVE
THE EQUILIBRIUM PRICE

Observe in Table 4-4 that at a price of $.50 per pack suppliers would supply the market 120,000 packs of paper per month (column 2). Buyers, however, would only demand 20,000 packs per month (column 3). At this price, there is an excess of supply over demand, or a *surplus* of 100,000 packs of paper (column 4). A price of $.50 per pack serves as a relatively strong incentive to suppliers on the one hand, and a relatively high barrier to buyers on the other. If suppliers should produce the 120,000 packs, they will find they can sell only 20,000 of them. They will be stuck with 100,000 packs. This sur-

plus will serve notice to suppliers that $.50 per pack is too high a price to charge. They will realize that price must be lowered if they want to sell more paper (column 5), as the law of demand would predict. If they continue to produce 120,000 packs per month in the belief that they can sell that much for $.50 per pack, unwanted inventories will grow due to the continuing surplus. Competition among suppliers will cause the price to be bid down as each tries to underprice the other in order to sell their individual surpluses.

As a result of suppliers' attempts to correct this undesirable situation through competitive price cutting, the price eventually falls to $.40 per pack. Now suppliers will produce a lower total quantity of paper, 110,000 packs per month (column 2), and buyers will increase quantity demanded to 40,000 packs per month (column 3). At this price, the quantity supplied will still exceed the quantity demanded, however. Though smaller, the surplus amounts to 70,000 packs of paper per month (column 4). Again, if suppliers continue to produce 110,000 packs per month in the belief that they can sell that much for $.40 per pack, unwanted inventories will continue to grow due to the continuing surplus. This situation will cause individual suppliers to continue to try to underprice each other in their competitive attempts to get rid of their individual surpluses. The price in the mar-

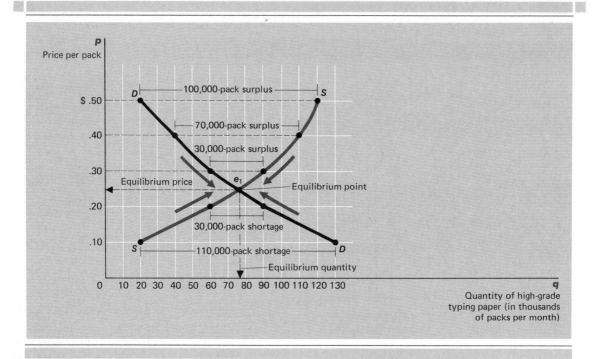

FIGURE 4-6 THE MARKET DEMAND AND SUPPLY DETERMINE THE EQUILIBRIUM PRICE AND QUANTITY FOR HIGH-GRADE TYPING PAPER

The determination of the equilibrium price and quantity is indicated by the intersection of the market demand curve *DD* and the market supply curve *SS* at e_1. The equilibrium price is $.25 per pack and the equilibrium quantity is 78,000 packs. At prices above the equilibrium price, there will be surpluses as indicated. These surpluses will cause a competitive bidding down of price, thereby reducing the quantity supplied and increasing the quantity demanded until they are equal and equilibrium is achieved. At prices below the equilibrium price, there will be shortages as indicated. These shortages will cause a competitive bidding up of price, thereby increasing the quantity supplied and decreasing the quantity demanded until they are equal and equilibrium is achieved.

ket will therefore continue to fall (column 5).

At $.30 per pack, the quantity supplied will still exceed the quantity demanded, but the surplus which cannot be sold will have fallen to 30,000 packs of paper (column 4). Nonetheless, this will still signal that price must fall further (column 5). Only when price has been reduced to $.25 per pack by the competition among suppliers will they be induced to produce and supply a quantity that is just equal to the quantity that will be demanded at that price, 78,000 packs per month (columns 2 and 3). No unsold surplus will be produced (column 4), and there will be no incentive to change price any further (column 5). Market equilibrium will prevail. **Market equilibrium** *is established at the price where the quantity of the good buyers demand and purchase is just equal to the quantity suppliers supply and sell. The price and quantity at which this occurs are called the* **equilibrium price** *and* **equilibrium quantity**. In equilibrium the forces of supply and demand are in balance. Price and quantity will have no tendency to change. They are at rest.

ECONOMIC THINKERS

ALFRED MARSHALL
1847–1924

Marshall was probably the greatest name in economics in the latter part of the nineteenth and the first half of the twentieth century. As a teacher for many years at Cambridge University and as a writer, he influenced several generations of younger economists. His textbook, *Principles of Economics* (1890), was used for many years throughout the world.

In his writing, Marshall introduced numerous concepts that have become basic to the study of economics. Among these was the idea of the *representative firm,* a "typical" enterprise faced with the problems of selling its goods in the market at a profit. Using this representative firm as a laboratory model, Marshall was able to analyze the impact of various economic stimuli on the firm.

Marshall also introduced the dimension of time into the process of economic analysis. He broke time down into three periods: the *market period,* in which all factors were fixed; the *short run,* during which at least one input was fixed; and the *long run,* during which all factors may be varied.

Another Marshallian concept was *consumer surplus,* by which Marshall meant the gain accruing to the buyer who is able to obtain a good at a price lower than that which he would have been willing to pay. (The discriminating monopolist can appropriate this surplus by charging various prices for different portions of his or her sales.)

In his writing, Marshall made use of powerful analogies to explain how economic phenomena worked. Perhaps the most famous of these was his likening of the emergence of market price from the interaction of supply and demand to the working of a pair of scissors. Supply is one blade and demand the other. Both must work together and jointly determine price. Marshall also showed that cost and

utility were key influences on supply and demand and refined the concept of elasticity.

Although highly adept at mathematics, Marshall tended to downplay the technical side of his analysis and maintain a narrative style so that his books would be widely read by noneconomists. He saw his major function as that of a synthesizer, drawing together and refining the thoughts of the various schools of economics of the past. For Marshall, economics was not a body of truth but "an engine to discover the truth."

FOR FURTHER READING
Marshall, Alfred. *Principles of Economics.* 8th ed. London: Macmillan, 1920.

The process just described and the equilibrium achieved are readily visualized with the aid of a market demand curve and a market supply curve. Using the supply and demand schedule data given in Table 4-4, the market supply curve and demand curve for high-grade typing paper are constructed in Figure 4-6. This is done in exactly the same manner used to obtain the demand and supply curves drawn in the previous figures in this chapter. Indeed the supply curve *SS* in Figure 4-6 is the same one shown in Figure 4-5 as *SS.* Both the quantity demanded and the quantity supplied are measured on the horizontal axis in Figure 4-6. Equilibrium occurs at the point where the market demand and supply curves intersect. The equilibrium point corresponds to the equilibrium price of $.25 and the equilibrium quantity of 78,000 packs of paper bought and sold per month. It is readily apparent from the diagram that at prices above $.25 supply exceeds demand. Competition among suppliers attempting to underprice one another in order to get rid of their surpluses will cause price to be bid down. This price cutting will cease when the equilibrium price is reached—the price at which quantity demanded equals quantity supplied.

MARKET ADJUSTMENT WHEN PRICE IS BELOW THE EQUILIBRIUM PRICE

Suppose that we consider an initial price below the equilibrium price, say $.10 per pack. The situation in the market for high-grade typing paper is now reversed. The price inducement for suppliers to produce the paper is relatively low, and so they produce relatively little. Because the price barrier to buyers is relatively low, the quantity demand is relatively high. From Table 4-4 the total quantity supplied is 20,000 packs per month (column 2), while the total quantity demanded is 130,000 packs per month (column 3). Hence there is now an excess demand for high-grade typing paper. Buyers cannot purchase as much as they want at this price. The shortage amounts to 110,000 packs (column 4).

There are not enough packs of paper "to go around" at $.10 per pack. Buyers begin to bid up price (column 5) as they compete with each other by letting suppliers know they are willing to pay more to get the inadequate supply produced. As the price of the paper is bid up, suppliers are encouraged by above normal profits to devote more resources to the production of paper, in accordance with the law of supply. At the same time, as price rises, buyers will begin to reduce the quantity of high-grade typing paper that they demand, in accordance with the law of demand. When price has risen to $.20 per pack, suppliers will be encouraged to increase production to 60,000 packs per month (column 2). The quantity demanded will be reduced to 90,000 packs per month (column 3). The quantity demanded still exceeds the quantity supplied, but the shortage has been reduced considerably—to 30,000 packs (column 4). Nonetheless, there is still a shortage. Buyers will

continue to bid price up (column 5) as they compete with one another for a supply of output inadequate to satisfy demand. Only when price has been bid up to $.25 per pack will the quantity demanded be equal to the quantity supplied—78,000 packs per month (columns 2 and 3). Market equilibrium will prevail. The shortage has been eliminated. All buyers who demand high-grade typing paper at $.25 per pack will be able to get it. All suppliers who are willing to supply it at $.25 per pack will find they can sell exactly the quantity they desire to supply. There will be no further incentive for price to be changed.

This process of adjustment to equilibrium is illustrated in Figure 4-6. At prices below $.25 per pack, quantity demanded clearly exceeds quantity supplied and a shortage will exist. Competitive bidding by buyers attempting to secure some of the inadequate supply will cause price to rise. As price rises suppliers are induced to buy more inputs and produce more paper. The quantity demanded on the other hand will fall as buyers are increasingly discouraged from purchasing paper as the price rises. Again, this process will eventually lead to the equilibrium point where the demand and supply curves intersect to determine the equilibrium price and quantity.

THE NATURE OF MARKET EQUILIBRIUM

Whether price is initially above or below the equilibrium level, market forces operate to cause adjustment to the same equilibrium point. If the process starts from above the equilibrium price level, we may envision buyers moving down the demand curve DD and suppliers moving down the supply curve SS as adjustment takes place. If the process starts from below the equilibrium price level, buyers move up DD and suppliers up SS. There is only one price at which the quantity supplied is equal to the quantity demanded. At that price every buyer will be able to buy exactly the quantity each demands, and every supplier will be able to sell exactly the quantity each desires to supply. *At the equilibrium price the demand intentions of buyers are consistent with the supply intentions of suppliers.* When these intentions are actually carried out in the form of buyers' bids to pur-

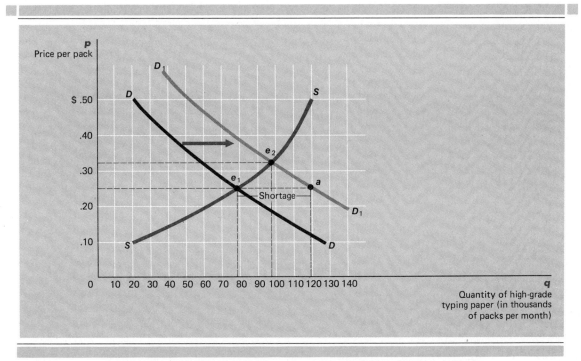

FIGURE 4-7 AN INCREASE IN DEMAND FOR HIGH-GRADE TYPING PAPER

The market is initially in equilibrium where market demand curve *DD* intersects market supply curve *SS* at e_1. At this point, the equilibrium price is $.25 per pack and the equilibrium quantity is 78,000 packs. The increase in demand is indicated by the rightward shift of the market demand curve from *DD* to D_1D_1. This initially gives rise to the shortage of 41,000 packs indicated. Competitive bidding among frustrated buyers pushes the price up until market equilibrium is established at e_2. The new equilibrium price is $.32 per pack and the new equilibrium quantity is 97,000 packs.

chase and suppliers' offers to sell, they mesh perfectly. *In equilibrium, the decisions of buyers are not frustrated by shortages and the decisions of sellers are not frustrated by surpluses.* Since shortages lead to price rises and surpluses to price reductions, *the absence of shortage or surplus will mean price will neither rise nor fall.* The market is in equilibrium.

Changes in Supply and Demand

Let's analyze the news item on the paper shortage in terms of the interaction of the demand and supply concepts we have developed. In particular, let's continue to focus on the market for high-grade typing paper. Suppose it is initially in the equilibrium position depicted by the intersection of the demand and supply

curves shown in Figure 4-6. These curves are reproduced as *DD* and *SS* in Figure 4-7. We know from our discussion of the determinants of supply and demand that any change in one or more of these determinants will cause either the supply curve or the demand curve or both to shift. Such a shift will undo the existing market equilibrium at e_1 and set forces in motion to establish a new equilibrium position in the market.

A CHANGE IN DEMAND

Consider first the effect of the rumor that there is a paper shortage. We noted above in our discussion of the determinants of demand that such a rumor typically affects expectations. The paper-shortage rumor would very likely

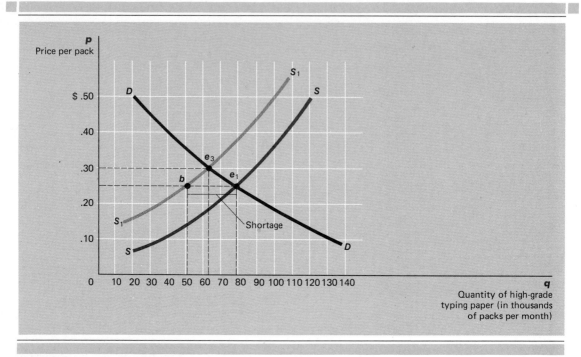

FIGURE 4-8 A DECREASE
IN THE SUPPLY OF HIGH-GRADE TYPING PAPER

The market is initially in equilibrium where market demand curve *DD* intersects market supply curve *SS* at e_1. This gives an equilibrium price of $.25 per pack and an equilibrium quantity of 78,000 packs. The decrease in supply is indicated by the leftward shift of the market supply curve from *SS* to S_1S_1. This initially gives rise to the indicated shortage of 28,000 packs, represented by the distance between points *b* and e_1. Competitive bidding among frustrated buyers pushes the price up until market equilibrium is established at e_3. The new equilibrium price is $.30 per pack, and the new equilibrium quantity is 62,000 packs per month.

cause people to change their expectations about the future price and availability of high-grade typing paper. In particular, people are now likely to expect that the price of this paper will be higher in the future as a result of the shortage. Therefore, they will want to buy more paper now and "stock up" on it in order to avoid paying a higher price for it later. Hence the market demand curve for the paper will shift rightward to D_1D_1 as shown in Figure 4-7. At every possible price the quantity demanded is now larger.

In particular, at the initial equilibrium price of $.25 per pack the quantity demanded will in-

crease from 78,000 to 119,000 packs per month. At this price the quantity demanded will now exceed the quantity suppliers are willing to provide. Specifically, there is now a shortage amounting to 41,000 packs of paper. This shortage is the difference between point *a* on D_1D_1 and the initial equilibrium point e_1 on the supply curve *SS* in Figure 4-7. As a result of this shortage, buyers will tell sellers they are willing to pay a higher price for high-grade typing paper in order to get some. When price is eventually bid up high enough, equilibrium will once again be established. Now, equilibrium is found at point e_2 where the demand curve D_1D_1 intersects the supply curve *SS*. The new equilibrium price is $.32 per pack, and the new equilibrium quantity bought and sold is 97,000 packs per month. Hence *an increase in demand, represented by a rightward shift in the demand curve, will increase both price and quantity assuming other things remain the same.* (Supply is one of the things that remains unchanged as represented by the unchanged position of the supply curve.)

It is interesting to note that the rumor of a paper shortage is in fact sufficient to cause an actual shortage. Eventually price rises enough to ration or cut back the quantity demanded (a movement from a to e_2 along D_1D_1) while at the same time causing an increase in the quantity supplied (a movement from e_1 to e_2 along *SS*). This increase in quantity supplied is sufficient to restore equilibrium in the market and eliminate the shortage.

A CHANGE IN SUPPLY

For the moment set aside the paper-shortage rumor's effect on the market and consider the effect of the other problems mentioned in the news item. In our discussion of the determinants of the supply curve, we noted that adverse weather conditions cause the supply curve to shift leftward. The truckers' tie-ups and railroad car shortages will also have this same effect. In addition the news item pointed out that "fuel supplies are low because of the energy crisis." This shortage of fuel, as we might have predicted, led to an increase in the price of fuel, which is a necessary input to paper production. From our earlier discussion we know that such an increase in price for an input will also cause the supply curve to shift leftward. Again consider the initial equilibrium before the onset of these difficulties as shown in Figure 4-8. (The demand curve *DD* and the supply curve *SS* are in exactly the same position as *DD* and *SS* in Figure 4-7.) The onset of bad weather, the truckers' tie-ups, the railroad car shortages, and the fuel shortages all conspire to reduce supply or shift the market supply curve leftward from *SS* to S_1S_1. At every possible price, suppliers will now reduce the quantity of high-grade typing paper they are willing to supply. In particular, at the initial equilibrium price of $.25 per

pack, they are now only willing to supply 50,000 packs of paper per month. At this price buyers will continue to demand 78,000 packs per month, however. The quantity demanded therefore exceeds the quantity supplied and there is now a shortage amounting to 28,000 packs, represented by the distance between points b and e_1. Again this causes the price to be bid up. When the price reaches $.30 per pack, the quantity demanded will again equal the quantity supplied. Equilibrium in the market will once more be restored. The equilibrium point is now at the intersection of *DD* and S_1S_1 indicated by e_3. At the new equilibrium price of $.30 per pack, the equilibrium quantity bought and sold is 62,000 packs per month. Hence *a decrease in supply, represented by a leftward shift in the supply curve, will increase price and decrease quantity assuming other things remain the same.* (Demand is one of the things that remains the same, as represented by the unchanged position of the demand curve.)

BOTH SUPPLY AND DEMAND CHANGE

The news item reports that in fact the rumor affecting paper demand and the events affecting paper supply unfortunately have all occurred at about the same time. To analyze what actually happened we must consider the rightward shift in the demand curve of Figure 4-7 together with the leftward shift in the supply curve of Figure 4-8. This combination of shifts is shown in Figure 4-9. Again the market supply curve *SS* and the market demand curve *DD* are the same as shown in Figures 4-7 and 4-8, and the initial equilibrium point determined by their intersection is again shown as e_1. The rightward shift in the demand curve from *DD* to D_1D_1 caused by the shortage rumor is exactly the same as that shown in Figure 4-7. The leftward shift in the supply curve from *SS* to S_1S_1 caused by the several events already noted is exactly the same as that shown in Figure 4-8. At the initial equilibrium price of $.25 per pack the quantity demanded increases from 78,000 to 119,000 packs per month. At the same time, quantity suppliers are willing to supply falls from 78,000 to 50,000 packs per month. The shortage now is equal to the sum of the short-

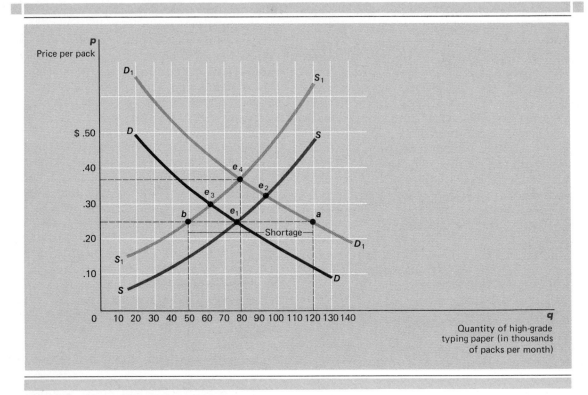

FIGURE 4-9 COMBINED EFFECTS OF AN INCREASE IN DEMAND AND A DECREASE IN SUPPLY FOR HIGH-GRADE TYPING PAPER

The combined effects of the increase in demand in Figure 4–7 and the decrease in supply of Figure 4–8 are shown here. Starting from the initial equilibrium determined by the intersection of *DD* and *SS* at e_1, the market demand curve shifts rightward to D_1D_1 while the market supply curve shifts leftward to S_1S_1. The initial shortage amounts to 69,000 packs, the sum of the initial shortages indicated in Figures 4–7 and 4–8. Competitive bidding among frustrated buyers pushes the price up until market equilibrium is established at e_4. At that point, the new equilibrium price is $.37 per pack, and the new equilibrium quantity is 80,000 packs per month. Notice that the new equilibrium price is higher than that established when either the increase in demand or decrease in supply was considered separately, as in Figures 4–7 and 4–8. The new equilibrium quantity is larger given the relative sizes of the demand and supply curve shifts shown here. Had the leftward shift of the supply curve been larger or the rightward shift of the demand curve been smaller, or both, the new equilibrium quantity could have been smaller than the initial equilibrium quantity at e_1.

ages shown in Figures 4-7 and 4-8. Specifically, there is now a shortage amounting to 69,000 packs of high-grade typing paper, the difference between point *a* on D_1D_1 and point *b* on S_1S_1. To restore equilibrium, price will have to be bid up until the quantity of paper demanded once again equals the quantity suppliers are willing to provide. This occurs where the demand curve D_1D_1 intersects the supply curve S_1S_1 at e_4. The new equilibrium price is $.37 per pack, and the equilibrium quantity bought and sold is now 80,000 packs of paper per month.

Note that when the leftward shift of the supply curve is considered together with the rightward shift of the demand curve in Figure 4-9, the resulting rise in price is greater than when either shift is considered alone, as in Figures 4-7 and 4-8. This is readily apparent from Figure 4-9. When only the demand shift was considered, the new equilibrium point was e_2. When just the supply shift was considered, the new equilibrium point was e_3. When the effect of both shifts is considered, the new equilibrium point is e_4, which occurs at a higher price than at either e_2 or e_3.

In general, when demand increases and supply decreases, as in Figure 4-9, it is possible for the new equilibrium quantity bought and sold to be either larger or smaller than that of the initial equilibrium position. Whether it is larger or smaller depends on the relative size of the shifts in the two curves. In the hypothetical example of Figure 4-9, the relative sizes of these shifts are such that the new equilibrium quantity associated with e_4 is slightly larger than the initial equilibrium quantity associated with e_1. If the leftward shift of the supply curve had been somewhat larger, or the rightward shift of the demand curve somewhat smaller, or both, the new equilibrium quantity might have been somewhat less than the initial equilibrium quantity. Since the main theme of the news item is shortage, at the time it was written the adjustment process accompanying the shortage was no doubt still in progress.

■ CHECKPOINT 4-3

If the price of medium-grade typing paper should fall, what do you predict would happen to the equilibrium price and quantity of high-grade typing paper? If the price of typewriters falls and the wage rate which producers of high-grade typing paper must pay labor also falls, what do you predict would happen to the equilibrium price and quantity of high-grade typing paper? If the price of typewriter ribbon rises and the rent rate for office space used by the producers of high-grade typing paper also rises, what do you predict would happen to the equilibrium price and quantity of high-grade typing paper? If someone told you that the price of high-grade typing paper had risen, but gave you no other information, what would you be able to say about the quantity of it bought and sold? If you were told that the price of shoes had increased and the quantity bought and sold had decreased, what would you make of a newspaper story that claimed consumers' income was increasing? (*Hint:* What do you think an increase in consumers' income would do to shoe demand?)

SUMMARY

1. The law of demand asserts that the lower (higher) is the price charged for a good, the larger (smaller) will be the quantity demanded—all other things remaining the same. This law may be represented graphically by a demand curve that slopes downward left to right on a graph with price measured on the vertical axis and quantity measured on the horizontal. Any point on a demand curve tells us the quantity of a good buyer's desire to purchase per some specified unit of time at the price associated with that point.

2. In addition to the price of the good for which the market demand curve is drawn, the other determinants of market demand are: (1) the prices of all other goods, (2) money income, (3) expectations, (4) tastes, and (5) the number of buyers in the market. A change in one or more of these determinants will cause the market demand curve to shift either rightward (an increase in demand) or leftward (a decrease in demand). A shift in the demand curve is referred to as a change in demand. It is to be distinguished from a change in the quantity demanded, which refers to a movement along a fixed demand curve. The latter can only occur because of a change in the price of the good for which the demand curve is drawn.

3. The law of supply asserts that suppliers will supply larger quantities of a good at higher prices for that good than at lower prices—all other things remaining the same. This law may be represented graphically by a supply

curve which slopes upward left to right on a graph with price measured on the vertical axis and quantity measured on the horizontal axis. Any point on a supply curve tells us the quantity of a good suppliers are willing to produce and desire to sell per some specified unit of time at the price associated with that point.

4. Along with the price of the good for which the supply curve is drawn, the other determinants of supply are: (1) the prices of resources and other factors of production, (2) technology, (3) the prices of other goods, (4) the number of suppliers, and (5) the suppliers' expectations. A change in any of these determinants will cause the supply curve to shift either rightward (an increase in supply) or leftward (a decrease in supply). Such a change is called a change in supply. It is to be distinguished from a change in the quantity supplied, which is a movement along a fixed supply curve due to a change in the price of the good for which the supply curve is drawn.

5. Supply and demand interact to adjust price until that price is found where the quantity of the good demanded is just equal to the quantity supplied. This is the equilibrium price and quantity, which is determined by the intersection of the supply and demand curve. When this point of intersection is established, we have market equilibrium.

6. Changes in supply and demand, represented by shifts in the supply and demand curves, will upset equilibrium and cause either shortages or surpluses. This will set in motion competitive price bidding among buyers and sellers that will ultimately restore market equilibrium, most typically at new levels of equilibrium price and quantity.

7. An increase (decrease) in demand will lead to an increase (decrease) in equilibrium price and quantity—other things remaining the same. An increase (decrease) in supply will lead to a decrease (increase) in equilibrium price and an increase (decrease) in equilibrium quantity—other things remaining the same. When both supply and demand change, the effect on equilibrium price and quantity depends on the particular case.

KEY TERMS AND CONCEPTS
complementary good
demand curve
demand schedule
equilibrium price
equilibrium quantity
factors of production
inferior good
law of demand
law of supply
market demand curve
market equilibrium
normal good
substitute good
supply curve
supply schedule
technology

QUESTIONS AND PROBLEMS

1. Classify each of the following goods according to whether *in your opinion* it is a normal (essential) or inferior good: shoes, beer, leather gloves, life insurance, auto insurance, stereo equipment, pet dog, four-ply tires.

2. Classify each of the following pairs of goods according to whether you think they are substitutes, complements, or basically unrelated to one another: ham and eggs, meat and potatoes, Fords and Chevrolets, ice skaters and swim suits, coffee and tea, butter and margarine, apples and oranges, knives and forks, salt shakers and hats.

3. Suppose today's weather forecast states that chances are 9 out of 10 that there will be rain all during the coming week. What effect do you think this will have on the demand curve for each of the following: umbrellas, baseball tickets, electricity, taxi rides, parking space in shopping centers, camping equipment, books, and aspirin?

4. What do you predict would happen to the market demand curve for oranges in the United States as a result of the following:
a. a rise in average income;
b. an increase in the birth rate;
c. an intensive advertising campaign that convinces most people of the importance of a daily quota of natural vitamin C;
d. a fall in the price of orange juice;
e. a fall in the price of grapefruit juice?

5. What will happen to the supply of cars if each of the following should occur? Explain your answers.

a. an increase in the price of trucks;

b. a fall in the price of steel;

c. introduction of a better assembly line technique;

d. an increase in the desire of auto manufacturers to be highly esteemed by the nation, rather than to earn as much money as possible;

e. an increase in the price of cars.

6. If goods are expensive because they are scarce, why aren't rotten eggs high priced?

7. What will be the effect on the supply curve of hogs of a fall in the price of corn? What will be the effect on the supply curve of corn of a fall in the price of hogs?

8. What effect do you think an advertising campaign for coffee would have on each of the following—other things remaining the same: the price of coffee, the price of tea, the quantity of sugar bought and sold, the price of doughnuts, the quantity of sleeping pills bought and sold, the price of television advertising time on the late show?

9. Suppose you read in the paper that the price of gasoline is rising along with increased sales of gasoline. Does this contradict the law of demand or not? Explain.

10. Suppose there is a strike in the steel industry. Other things remaining the same, what do you predict will happen to: the price of steel, the price of automobiles, the quantity sold and the price of aluminum, the price of aluminum wire, the price and quantity of copper wire sold, and the price of electricity? At each step of this chain spell out your answer in terms of the relevant shift in a demand or supply curve. What do you think of the characterization of the economy as a chain of interconnected markets?

11. Suppose we were to look at some industry data on the buggy whip industry collected at about the time the automobile industry was rapidly moving out of its infancy. What would you make of the finding that many buggy whip manufacturers were getting out of the business, yet the price of buggy whips was not falling? Demonstrate your analysis diagrammatically.

12. During the energy crisis of late 1973 and early 1974 it was not uncommon to see automobiles lined up for blocks waiting to buy gas.

a. Demonstrate diagrammatically what happened in the gasoline market when the energy crisis hit.

b. Given the long lines of cars observed waiting to buy gas, do you think the equilibrium price of gas was established at that time?

c. If gasoline prices haven't risen that dramatically since early 1974, what would explain the disappearance of the lines of waiting motorists at gasoline stations since that time?

TWO

AGGREGATE INCOME, EMPLOYMENT, AND FISCAL POLICY

5

MEASURING NATIONAL INCOME AND PRODUCT

**DATA INDICATE STEADY,
UNSPECTACULAR ECONOMIC GROWTH FOR NEXT YEAR**

WASHINGTON, Dec. 19—Latest signals from government economic statistics indicate steady but unspectacular growth next year. "We will go into next year in good shape," concluded the Commerce Department's chief economist Courtenay Slater.

The new data "point to a fourth quarter [economic growth rate] that looks strong in terms of final sales and less strong in terms of final GNP," she said. Mrs. Slater is referring to "real" gross national product, the total output of the nation's goods and services, adjusted for inflation. The Commerce Department reported a 4.7 percent third quarter growth rate, although Mrs. Slater noted that that number will be revised soon. She also pointed out that though the fourth quarter growth rate probably won't exceed the third quarter's, "the composition will be better" as more growth will come from personal consumption and less from inventory accumulation. Building permits for single-family homes reached record levels, according to the Commerce Department, suggesting continued brisk homebuilding activity. Work was started on new homes at a seasonally adjusted annual rate of 2,105,000 units.

Mrs. Slater termed the November rise in personal income "moderately strong." Contributing to this rise, total private wages and salaries advanced at a $5.7 billion annual rate in the past month. The federal employee pay raise accounted for $600 million of the personal income increase in November. Farm owners' income in November increased at a $4 billion annual rate. Personal interest income increased at the same $1.8 billion rate as in October. Dividend income rose at a $200 million November pace. Transfer payments, which include social security, welfare, unemployment, and veterans' benefits, rose at a $1.2 billion pace.

Business inventories rose a relatively small $1.19 billion in October, reflecting business's desires to trim fat stocks that piled up during the slow summer and fall sales months.

This news item is typical of many accounts of the economy's condition reported in the press and over radio and television. Despite the frequency of such accounts, the average person usually has only a vague idea of the meaning of such terms as GNP, personal income, and personal consumption. Like the various flows depicted in the flow diagrams of Chapter 3, in Part One of this book, these are all aggregate measures of what is happening in the economy. The measurement of those flows and the analysis of their determinants and how they are interrelated will be the subject of Part Two.

In this chapter we will focus on national income accounting, which enables us to measure the economy's performance. You will then be better able to understand what is being described in news items like the one at the beginning of this chapter. In Chapter 6 we will examine the historical record of the American economy in order to gain some perspective and feel for the way the economy has behaved according to various national income accounting measures. Chapters 7, 8, and 9 will focus on explaining how the economy's level of production is determined, the reasons why the economy does not always operate at full capacity (full employment), and the nature of public policies aimed at correcting this recurrent problem.

WHY IS NATIONAL INCOME ACCOUNTING IMPORTANT?

When you drive your car you usually keep an eye on the speedometer to see how fast you are going. You check the fuel gauge before starting out to make sure you have enough gas to reach your destination. The temperature gauge warns you about engine overheating before serious damage is done (the radiator boils over or the radiator hose breaks). Without the information these gauges provide, you could find yourself in a dangerous situation. The same is true with respect to the performance of our economy.

When our economy plunged into the Great Depression of the 1930s, the general lack of any timely, systematic measurements of what was happening became painfully apparent. This experience spurred the government to develop today's national income accounting procedures. Armed with relatively recent statistical measurements of the economy's performance, such as those mentioned in the news item, businesses, households, and government policy makers are better informed about what has been happening in the economy and where it appears to be headed. Businesses and households are therefore in a better position to make economic plans. Government policy makers need this kind of information to assess the economy's performance in order to implement timely policies to improve that performance. Shy of this lofty ambition, policy makers need such information at least to avoid policy actions which may harm the economy's performance.

WHAT IS GROSS NATIONAL PRODUCT (GNP)?

Probably the most cited measure of the economy's overall performance is its **gross national product (GNP)**. In short, *GNP is the market value of all final goods and services produced by the economy during a year.* GNP has several important characteristics. First, it is a flow concept. Second, it is measured in money terms. Third, it only includes goods and services bought for final use, not unfinished goods in the intermediate stages of production that are purchased for further processing and resale. Fourth, GNP has two sides—it may be viewed from the income side or from the expenditure side.

GNP Is a Flow

A **flow** *is a quantity per unit of time,* such as so many gallons of water running through a pipe per minute. By contrast, a stock is a quantity measured without respect to time, such as the number of gallons of water in a tub. GNP is a flow measured as the quantity of final goods and services produced by the economy per year. It is a flow that is measured at an annual rate.

We could measure GNP by giving a complete listing of all final goods and services produced per year—the number of automobiles, haircuts, toothbrushes, car washes, and so forth. (We couldn't add the quantities of these different goods together to get one number—you can't add apples and shirts.) This obviously would be a rather cumbersome list, probably about the size of a large city's telephone directory, depending on how fine a breakdown of product description is desired. It is far easier and less awkward to simply summarize all this information by adding up the dollar values of all these goods. Hence the dollar value of GNP is given as the sum of the price of an automobile times the number of automobiles per year plus the price of a haircut times the number of haircuts per year plus the price of a toothbrush times the number of toothbrushes per year plus the price of a car wash times the number of car washes per year plus . . . , and so forth. *GNP may be viewed either as a flow of numbers of units of final goods and services produced per year, or as a flow of the dollar value of these final goods and services produced per year.*

The importance of distinguishing between final goods and services produced this year and those produced in other years cannot be overemphasized. Only those produced this year are to be counted in this year's GNP. Those produced in other years are counted in GNP for the years in which they were produced.

The measurement of GNP requires that we add up all the market transactions representing the purchase and sale of final goods and services. Such transactions measure the dollar value of productive activity that actually went into the production of final goods and services this year. However, there are many market transactions in our economy that do not involve the purchase and sale of final goods and services produced this year. For the purpose of measuring GNP, these are nonproductive transactions, and care must be taken not to include them in the measurement of GNP. In addition, it should be recognized that some productive activities that should be included in GNP do not always show up as market transactions.

PRODUCTIVE VERSUS NONPRODUCTIVE TRANSACTIONS

Many market transactions that occur in our economy do not represent the production of a good. Therefore, we don't want to count them in GNP.

The purchase and sale of *used goods* is an example of such a transaction. If A buys B's 2-year-old stereo set for $300, this transaction

---

After reading this chapter, you will be able to:
1. Define the concept of GNP and list the kinds of economic transactions that are and are not included in this measure.
2. Explain the difference between current dollar or money GNP and constant dollar or real GNP.
3. State some of the deficiencies of GNP as a measure of the economy's welfare.
4. Explain how, for purposes of national income accounting, GNP may be viewed from two sides—the expenditure side and the income side.
5. State the relationship between gross national product, net national product, national income, personal income, and disposable income.

does not involve the purchase of a final good produced *this year*. When the set was purchased new two years ago, its purchase price was included in GNP for that year. What about a set produced and purchased in February this year and then resold by the initial buyer a month later? The purchase of the set by the *initial* buyer would be included in GNP for this year because it was produced this year. However, it would not be correct to include the resale transaction in GNP because this would amount to counting the production of the set more than once. *The resale of a used good is a transaction that merely represents the transfer of ownership of a previously produced good—it does not represent the production of a new good.* Always remember that GNP is a measure of productive activity. You and I could buy and sell the same car back and forth daily, but we have not produced any new cars.

There are also certain types of *financial transactions* in our economy that do not represent any productive activity that adds to the output of final goods and services. Therefore, they are not included in GNP. Such transactions include: (1) the trading of stocks, bonds, and other kinds of securities in financial markets; and (2) private and public transfer payments.

1. The trading in stocks and bonds in financial markets amounts to several tens of trillions of dollars per year. None of this is counted in GNP, however, because it only represents the trading of paper assets. True, businesses and government often issue new stocks and bonds to raise funds to spend on currently produced final goods and services. But this only amounts to a minute fraction of the total yearly purchases and sales of securities. Funds raised and used to purchase final goods and services are included in GNP when they appear in business firms' accounts recording such sales.

2. Private and public **transfer payments** are transactions in which the recipient is neither expected nor required to make any contribution to GNP in return. The transfer of funds from one individual to another, either as a gift, a bequest, or a charitable donation, constitutes a private transfer payment not included in GNP. Also included under private transfer payments are payments out of private pension funds. Public transfer payments are made to some groups in the economy by the government. The news item at the beginning of this chapter refers to such payments, "which include social security, welfare, unemployment, and veterans' benefits." While these payments are not included in GNP, the national income accounts do keep a record of them, as we shall see.

PRODUCTIVE NONMARKET TRANSACTIONS

If GNP is to measure the economy's production of final goods and services, it is necessary to recognize that not all such productive activities show up as market transactions on the business accounting statements used to construct an estimate of GNP. Therefore, it is necessary to impute a dollar value to productive activities not represented by a market transaction and to include this dollar value in the calculation of GNP.

For example, people who live in their own home do not write themselves a rent check every month. However, those who do not own their home must make such an explicit rent payment. Both groups receive a currently produced service—the shelter provided by their dwellings—yet only the payments made by renters to landlords show up as a market transaction. The rent on owner-occupied homes must be imputed as the rent payments the owners would have to make if they rented their homes from landlords. These payments could also be looked at as the amount of rent owners could receive if they were to rent their home to somebody else. Such an imputed rent on owner-occupied homes is included in GNP, along with the rent payments made to landlords. Similarly, the value of the food that farm families produce and consume themselves must be imputed and included in GNP.

However, there are a number of productive nonmarket transactions that are not included in GNP. The productive services of homemakers—cooking, laundering, housecleaning—are not included despite the fact this constitutes a sizeable amount of productive activity. (If you're not convinced, just check the want ads to

ECONOMIC THINKERS

SIMON S. KUZNETS
1901-

Kuznets, born in Russia, came to the United States as a youth. He was associated with a number of universities and retired from Harvard in 1971, winning the Nobel Prize in the same year.

Early in his career, Kuznets embarked on a line of research that he has followed for nearly half a century. More than any other person, he pioneered in the area of national income analysis. Today it is difficult to imagine the shortage of aggregate economic data that existed in the United States before Kuznets and others did their work. Without data no reasonable conclusions could be drawn, nor intelligent recommendations made. Under the auspices of the National Bureau of Economics Research, Kuznets set about to correct what he has called a "scandal." The first fruit of his work was harvested in 1934 when a Senate document was published estimating U.S. National Income 1929–1932. Of course, this pioneer document had numerous imperfections of which Kuznets was well aware.

Later Kuznets became interested in economic growth and set himself the task of reviewing the aggregate, structural, and international characteristics of economic growth in the modern world. His interest in growth has centered on the past two centuries, which he considered to be a particularly meaningful period. In his view the era is "a relatively long period (extending well over a century) possessing distinctive characteristics that give it unity and differentiate it from the epochs that precede or follow it." Kuznets sees the interplay of technological and institutional changes as the essence of economic growth taking place within the framework of innovation.

Combining all these macroeconomic and microeconomic factors is a huge task, obviously beyond the power of a single individual, but Kuznets has made great progress. Very few scholars have undertaken such long range projects of such immense public value. Even now some five decades after he began, the ultimate contribution of his efforts is difficult to gauge.

FOR FURTHER READING
Simon Kuznets, *National Income and Its Composition.* New York: National Bureau of Economics Research, 1941.

---

see what it would cost you to hire a cook and a housekeeper.) Many people repair and remodel their own homes, cars, and a host of other items. Yet the productive services of the do-it-yourselfers are not included in GNP, largely because it is so difficult to estimate and keep track of the total value of such activities in our economy.

Value Added: Don't Double Count
We have stressed that GNP only includes goods and services bought for final use. It does not include the unfinished goods in the intermediate stages of production that are purchased by one firm from another for further processing and resale. The market value of a final good is the full value of the good in that it already includes the **value added** at each stage of the production process. If we also counted the purchases of the component parts of the good each time they were sold by a firm at one stage of the production process to a firm at the next stage, we would end up counting the market value of the final good more than once. For example, we don't want to count the sale of Firestone tires to the Ford Motor Company because the cost of the tires will be included in the price of the cars

TABLE 5-1 SALE RECEIPTS, COST OF INTERMEDIATE PRODUCTS, AND VALUE ADDED AT EACH STAGE OF PRODUCTION OF NOTEBOOK PAPER (Cents per Pad of Paper)

	(1) Production Stage	(2) Product	(3) Sale Price of Product	(4) Cost of Intermediate Product		(5) Value Added (Wages, Interest, Rent, and Profit)
Firm 1	Tree farm	Trees	$.15	− $.00	=	$.15
Firm 2	Logging company	Logs	.20	− .15	=	.05
Firm 3	Pulpwood mill	Pulpwood	.30	− .20	=	.10
Firm 4	Paper manufacturer	Notebook paper	.45	− .30	=	.15
Firm 5	Retail store	Retailing service	.50	− .45	=	.05
Final Sale						$.50 (Final sale price = sum of value added)

that Ford sells to final customers. If we did include the sale of tires from Firestone to Ford, the tires would be double counted in GNP.

These points are illustrated by the example in Table 5-1. Suppose it costs you $.50 to buy a pad of notebook paper in your local retail store. This pad is a final product since you intend to use the paper yourself, not to transform it into another product and resell it. The market value of the final product, $.50, equals the sum of the values added at each stage of the production process.

How does this work? Firm 5, the retail store that sells the pad of paper to you, must pay $.45 of the $.50 it receives (columns 3 and 4) to Firm 4, the paper manufacturer that provides Firm 5 with the paper. Firm 5 pays out the remaining $.05 in wages, rent, interest, and profit to the factors of production used by Firm 5 to provide the retailing service. This $.05 constitutes the value added (column 5) to the final product by Firm 5 through its provision of these services. Firm 4 must pay $.30 of the $.45 received from Firm 5 to Firm 3, the pulpwood mill, for the

pulpwood Firm 4 processes into notebook paper. Firm 4 pays out the remaining $.15 in wages, rent, interest, and profit to the factors of production it uses to process pulpwood into paper. This $.15 is the value added to the final product by the paper manufacturer. Proceeding back through each stage of production, the pulpwood mill adds value to the final product by processing the logs it buys from the logging company. And the logging company adds value to the final product by making logs out of the trees it buys from the tree farm.

The value added to the final product at each stage of production is the difference between what the firm sells its product for and what it pays for the intermediate materials or good it processes at that production stage. This difference is paid out in wages, interest, rent, and profit to all the factors of production that provide the productive services which add value to the product at that stage of production. The sum of the values added at each stage of production equals the sale price of the final good or service.

In the example of Table 5-1, the $.50 sale

price of the final good, a pad of notebook paper, equals the sum of the value-added figures of column 5. If, instead, we added up the sales figures in column 3 we would get $1.60. This figure overstates the value of the final good because it counts the value added by Firm 1 five times, that of Firm 2 four times, Firm 3 three times, and Firm 4 two times. In order to avoid this double, or multiple, counting, it is necessary to subtract out the purchase price of intermediate products to be processed at each stage of production, as indicated by the arrows. This leaves the value-added figures of column 5, the sum of which equals the correct value of the final product. For this reason this is the only figure we want to include in GNP. We do not add in the sales transactions between the first four firms.

■ CHECKPOINT 5-1

While the purchase and sale of used cars is not included in GNP, the sales commissions earned by used-car dealers are. Similarly, the purchase and sale of stock on the New York Stock Exchange is not included in GNP, but the sales commissions earned by stockbrokers are. Why are the sales commissions generated from these activities included in GNP while the sales themselves are not? During the last 30 years or so the proportion of working wives in the labor force has increased considerably. What effect does this have on GNP? Construct a hypothetical value added table like Table 5–1 for the production and sale of a loaf of bread.

MONEY GNP VERSUS REAL GNP

The news item at the beginning of this chapter points out that the Commerce Department's chief economist "is referring to 'real' gross national product, the total output of the nation's goods and services, adjusted for inflation." It is important to understand what this means.

Adjusting GNP for Price Change: A Simple Example

Suppose, for simplicity, that the entire economy produced only one kind of good. Let's say

that good is widgets. In any given year the economy's money GNP would be calculated as the total current dollar value of the widget sales reported on the accounting statements of business firms. It would be equal to the current price of a widget multiplied by the number of widgets produced during the year. Any change in money GNP from one year to the next could therefore be due to a change in price or a change in quantity or both. However, we typically are only interested in GNP to the extent that it measures the quantity of output produced.

For instance, suppose the economy has a dollar GNP of $1,000 in 1980, which results from the sale of 1,000 widgets at a price of $1 per widget. It will be no better or worse off in 1990 with a dollar GNP of $2,000, if that GNP again results from the sale of 1,000 widgets, at a price of $2 per widget. When prices rise over time in this way we have **inflation**—a decrease in the purchasing power of a dollar. It takes $2 to buy one widget in 1990 that could have been purchased for $1 in 1980. Similarly, if prices decline over time we have **deflation**, an increase in the purchasing power of a dollar. The task is to somehow adjust the dollar GNP figure so that it only reflects changes in quantity of output produced and not price changes—not inflation or deflation.

Table 5-2 illustrates the way in which national income accountants would make this adjustment for our simple widget economy. Suppose that over a five-year period the current price p of widgets rises, as shown in column 2. Suppose also that the quantity Q of widgets produced each year is increasing at a rate of 10 percent per year, as shown in column 3. The money GNP for each year equals the current price p times Q, as shown in column 4. Clearly the increase in money GNP (or GNP in current prices) from year to year is much greater than the yearly increase in the physical quantity of widgets produced, due to the increases in the current price of widgets. Since these money GNP figures are inflated over time by the rising current price of widgets (column 2), it is necessary to adjust them so that they only reflect changes in quantities of output produced, and not price changes.

TABLE 5-2 ADJUSTING MONEY GNP FOR PRICE LEVEL CHANGES TO OBTAIN REAL GNP: A SIMPLE EXAMPLE

(1)	(2)	(3)	(4)	(5)	(6)
Year	Price per Widget (p)	Number of Units (Widgets) of Output per Year (Q)	Money GNP or GNP in Current Prices	Price Index	Real GNP or GNP in Constant Prices or Dollars
			$p \times Q = (2) \times (3)$	(2) ÷ Price in Year 3	(4) ÷ (5)
1	$ 2	1,000	$ 2,000	$\frac{2}{5}$ = $ .40 or 40 percent	$5,000
2	3	1,100	3,300	$\frac{3}{5}$ = .60 or 60 percent	5,500
3 = base year	5	1,210	6,050	$\frac{5}{5}$ = 1.00 or 100 percent	6,050
4	7	1,331	9,317	$\frac{7}{5}$ = 1.40 or 140 percent	6,655
5	10	1,464	14,640	$\frac{10}{5}$ = 2.00 or 200 percent	7,380

This adjustment is made by constructing a **price index**. A price index expresses the current price of widgets in each year as a ratio relative to the current price in some base or benchmark year. This base year may be chosen arbitrarily. In Table 5-2, the base year is the third year. The price index constructed in this way is shown in column 5. For example, the price of a widget in year 1 is two-fifths or 40 percent of the price of a widget in year 3 ($2 ÷ $5). Hence, if we want to adjust the money GNP of year 1 (column 4) to obtain output in terms of year 3 prices, we must multiply the money GNP of year 1 by $\frac{5}{2}$ or, equivalently, divide it by .40, the value of the price index in year 1. Year 1 GNP expressed in year 3 prices is $5,000 (column 6). By the same procedure the money GNP of each of the other four years may be expressed in terms of year 3 prices to give real GNP, or GNP in constant dollars or prices (column 6). The GNP figures in column 6 are 'real' in the sense that their year-to-year change accurately reflects the year-to-year change in the quantity of widgets produced in the economy (column 3). The figures in both columns increase at a rate of 10 percent per year. It also may be said that the GNP figures of column 6 are stated in constant dollars or prices in the sense that they are all expressed in terms of the year 3 price of widgets.

In sum, **money GNP**, *or GNP in current prices or dollars, measures the dollar value of final goods and services produced in a given year at the prices at which they actually sold in that year.* **Real GNP**, *or GNP in constant prices or dollars, measures the dollar value of final goods and services sold in a given year in terms of the prices at which those goods sold in some base, or benchmark, year.*

MONEY AND REAL GNP IN THE UNITED STATES

Our widget economy example greatly oversimplifies the problem of transforming money GNP into real GNP, yet the basic principle of adjustment carries over to the real world. The essential difference, of course, is that a real world economy typically produces a multitude of different goods, not just widgets. This means that there are many different prices that may change over time so that the price index used must be constructed as an average (usually a weighted average) of all these prices.

Such a price index (called the GNP deflator) for the United States economy is shown for selected years in column 3 of Table 5-3. The base

**TABLE 5-3 MONEY GNP AND REAL GNP
IN UNITED STATES, SELECTED YEARS** (in Billions of Dollars)

(1)	(2)	(3)	(4)
Year	Money GNP (Current Dollars)	Price Index:[a] Base Year 1972	Real GNP (Constant 1972 Dollars)
			(2) ÷ (3)
1950	$ 286	.54	$ 534
1955	399	.61	655
1960	506	.69	737
1965	688	.74	926
1970	982	.91	1,075
1972	1,171	1.00	1,171
1975	1,529	1.27	1,202
1978	2,107	1.52	1,385

SOURCE: U.S. Department of Commerce.

[a] GNP deflator.

year is 1972. This column tells us, among other things, that the general level of prices rose 52 percent from 1972 to 1978, that the general level of prices in 1950 was 54 percent of that prevailing in 1972, and that prices roughly tripled between 1950 and 1978. Money GNP—GNP in current prices or dollars—is shown in column 2. Using exactly the same procedure as in Table 5-2, the money GNP figures in column 2 of Table 5-3 are divided by the price index for the corresponding year in column 3 to give real GNP in column 4. This real GNP is thus expressed in constant 1972 prices or dollars. The behavior of real GNP in column 4 indicates that the *quantity* of final goods and services produced by the economy nearly tripled between 1950 and 1978. Column 2 indicates that money GNP, the quantity of final goods and services evaluated in current prices, increased somewhat more than sevenfold over this period. This reflects the fact that prices have roughly tripled, as indicated in column 3. Clearly, if we want a more accurate measure of the economy's productive performance, we must use real GNP—GNP measured in constant dollars (column 4).

The difference in the behavior of money GNP (GNP in current dollars) and real GNP

for the years since 1960 is shown graphically in Figure 5-1. While GNP in current dollars rises continuously throughout these years, largely reflecting the inflation in prices during this period, GNP in constant (1972) dollars generally grows more slowly and even declines in some years (1970, 1974, and 1975). We can see now why the news item at the beginning of this chapter is careful to point out that the Commerce Department's chief economist "is referring to 'real' gross national product, the total output of the nation's goods and services, adjusted for inflation."

■ CHECKPOINT 5-2

Using Table 5-2, calculate real GNP in terms of constant year 2 dollars. It is sometimes said that calculating real GNP "inflates" the money GNP data for years before the base year and "deflates" it for years after the base year. In what sense is this so?

What GNP Does Not Measure

It is easy, and tempting, to look at GNP as a measure of society's well-being. Yet it was never intended to be a measure of social welfare. It is simply an accounting measure of economic ac-

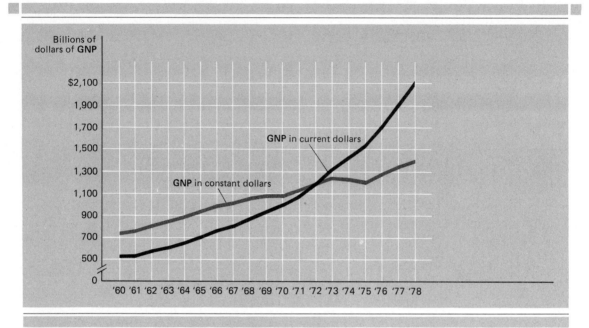

FIGURE 5-1 GROSS NATIONAL PRODUCT (GNP) IN CURRENT AND CONSTANT 1972 DOLLARS: 1960–1978

Since 1960 GNP in current dollars (money GNP) has grown continuously. However, GNP in constant 1972 dollars (real GNP) reveals that growth in the economy's production of final goods and services has not been as rapid or continuous. While real GNP declined in 1970, 1974, and 1975, GNP in current dollars increased, reflecting the general inflation in prices.

tivity. While there is certainly reason to believe that an economy is "better off" if it has a large real GNP—more goods and services for all— this is not *necessarily* so. On the other hand, a society may become better off in a variety of ways that GNP simply does not measure. Let's consider some of the "goods" and "bads" that GNP does not measure.

PRODUCT QUALITY

A generation ago, even a multimillionaire couldn't buy the kinds of medicines commonly available to the person of average means today. Yesteryear's automobiles didn't have four-wheel brakes, automatic transmissions, and a host of safety features commonly built into today's cars. Suppose you were given a Sears catalog for 1950 and a copy of today's Sears catalog with the prices in each listed in the same constant dollars. From which one would you rather buy kitchen appliances, sports equipment, tv sets, adding machines (calculators), and air conditioners? *Because GNP is a quantitative rather than a qualitative measure, it does not measure product improvement and the development of new kinds of goods.* The GNP in 1950 did not include the kind of goods that are included in today's GNP. But when their value is measured in dollars alone, yesterday's products are indistinguishable from today's.

COSTS NOT MEASURED: POLLUTION

GNP does not measure many of the by-products associated with producing the goods and services that are measured by GNP. And many of these by-products are "bads"—smoke, noise, polluted rivers and lakes, garbage dumps, and junkyards. The costs of health problems (both physical and mental) caused by such environmental blight are either not measured at all, or do not show up until years after the production of the GNP that caused them. These undesirable by-products tend to increase right along with growth in GNP. If the costs of these bads were subtracted from GNP, the resulting GNP would not appear as large or grow as fast. It would also be a more accurate measure of society's true well-being.

LEISURE AND GNP

For most people a certain amount of leisure is desirable. When people take more of it, less working time is devoted to producing goods and services. This means GNP will be smaller than it otherwise might be. However, this increase in leisure must add to people's sense of well-being more than enough to offset the forgone output, or else people wouldn't have chosen to take it. Therefore it would be completely misleading to interpret the reduction in GNP that results from increased leisure as a reduction in society's well-being. For example, the length of the average work week has been roughly cut in half over the last century. Workers have chosen to take more leisure, and as a result GNP is not as large as it would be if workers put in as many work hours as they typically did a hundred years ago. However, it would be erroneous to conclude that society is worse off because GNP is not as large as it could be. Why? Because more leisure has been chosen in *preference* to the additional output.

PER CAPITA GNP AND
THE DISTRIBUTION OF OUTPUT

If we divide up a side of beef among five people, each individual will certainly be better off than if we have to divide it up among ten people. Similarly in order to assess how well off a nation is, we need to know more than just the size of its annual output, its real GNP. We also need to know how that output is divided among its citizens. If it were divided equally among them, then we would simply divide the nation's GNP by its population. This gives **per capita GNP**.

While there is in fact no economy where GNP is distributed equally among its citizens, per capita GNP gives a simple measure of how well off an economy would be *if* its GNP were divided up in this fashion. For example, in 1973 the GNP of Bangladesh was approximately $7.7 billion, while that of Chile was about $7.6 billion. However, Bangladesh had a population roughly eight times as large as Chile's. Consequently, per capita GNP in Bangladesh was about $100, while in Chile it was $777. Hence, despite the fact that both nations had about the same level of GNP, Chilean citizens would appear to be much better off than those of Bangladesh.

Because an economy's GNP is typically distributed unequally among its citizens, it is necessary to study this distribution in more detail in order to get a more accurate assessment than that provided by per capita GNP.

COMPOSITION OF GNP

The kinds of goods produced by an economy are completely hidden from view by a GNP figure. One economy could have a $100 billion GNP composed entirely of weapons for war, and another could have a $100 billion GNP composed entirely of sports cars, steak dinners, and fine clothes. These economies would clearly have different kinds of living standards, though you could never tell it from GNP data. GNP alone tells nothing about the composition of the economy's output.

The Two Sides of GNP

Envision a sales counter in any store or business. On one side stands the customer paying out money in exchange for the good or service that the store provides. On the other side stands the proprietor, giving the customer the good or service in exchange for the customer's money. Corresponding to every purchase, there is a sale since there are always two sides to every transaction. We know from our discussion of value added that all the money received on the seller's side of the counter ultimately is paid out in wages, rent, interest, and profit as compensation to the owners of the factors of production used to produce and distribute the product. Therefore all the money received on the seller's side of the counter is income to all the owners of the factors of production—land, labor, and capital.

We may think of all such counters in the

economy across which all final goods and services flow as one big sales counter. The total of all the money flowing across the counter in exchange for all the final goods and services produced in a year is the money GNP. When we view GNP from the buyer's side of the counter, where expenditures are made and goods are taken off the counter, we are viewing GNP from the expenditure, or output, side. This viewpoint is often referred to as the *expenditure, or output, approach* to GNP. On the other hand, if we look at GNP from the seller's side of the counter, where all the income is received and ultimately distributed to the owners of productive factors, we are viewing GNP from the income, or earnings, or allocations side—often called the *income approach* to GNP. These two sides of GNP may be summarized by the following equation which is *always* valid:

$$\left\{\begin{array}{l}\text{Total}\\\text{expenditures}\\\text{on final goods}\\\text{and services}\end{array}\right\} = \text{GNP} = \left\{\begin{array}{l}\text{Total income}\\\text{from production}\\\text{and distribution}\\\text{of final output}\end{array}\right.$$

The left side of this equation may be thought of as representing the lower flow channel in Figure 3-2 of Chapter 3, and the right side as representing the upper flow channel.

To understand the elements that go into national income accounting and the basic concepts used in much macroeconomic analysis, we need to look at both ways of viewing GNP in more detail. In fact, this is necessary even if you only want to make some sense out of an everyday news item like the one at the beginning of this chapter.

THE EXPENDITURE SIDE OF GNP

The economy can be divided into four distinct sectors: the household, business, government, and foreign sectors. Total expenditure on GNP can be divided up according to which of these sectors makes the expenditure. Personal consumption expenditures are made by households; private domestic investment expenditures by businesses; government expenditures by state, local, and federal government; net exports reflect our trade with foreigners.

Personal Consumption Expenditure (*C*)

Personal consumption expenditures by households are often simply termed *consumption,* or designated *C.* These are household expenditures on consumer durables such as cars and household appliances, consumer nondurables such as food and clothing, and services such as medical care, shelter, beauty treatments, haircuts, and dry cleaning. Also included are imputed household expenditures, such as the value of food which farm families produce and consume themselves. In the news item Mrs. Slater is optimistic about the growth in personal consumption as a stimulant to the economy.

Gross Private Domestic Investment (*I*)

Recall the distinction we made in Chapter 1 between the common usage of the term "investment" and that used by economists. In common usage people often speak of investing money in stocks and bonds, for example. However, these are only financial transactions representing the purchase of titles of ownership. When economists and national income accountants use the term **investment,** they are referring primarily to business firms' expenditures on new capital goods—goods that are used to produce other goods and services.

The term "private" means we are referring to expenditures by private business firms, as opposed to government agencies, while the term "domestic" means we are speaking of investment expenditures in the United States. The term "gross" will be explained below. **Gross private domestic investment,** often designated *I,* includes all final purchases of new tools and machines by business firms, all construction (residential as well as business), and changes in inventories. Several clarifying remarks are in order.

1. Only *new* tools and machines are included because, as we have already stressed, purchases of secondhand goods are not included in GNP.

2. Residential construction of owner-occupied dwellings is included along with factories and apartment buildings. These dwellings are income-producing assets in the sense that they produce a service, shelter, that could be rented

out—just like an apartment or other commercial structure. (You might wonder why cars and furniture, which can also be rented, are included in consumption, since the line of reasoning we've been using suggests that they could be included in investment. The fact that they are included under consumption simply illustrates that there is a certain arbitrariness in national income accounting conventions.) The news item cites the "record levels" of building permits issued as an indication that this part of investment spending will increase.

3. Why are changes in business inventories included in gross private domestic investment? First of all, inventories are included in investment because they are a necessary part of the productive process just like any other capital good. Inventories consist of stocks of raw materials and other inputs, goods in various stages of completion, and finished goods not yet sold. The firm has money invested in inventories just as it has money invested in other capital goods. The basic reason for taking account of inventory changes is that GNP is supposed to measure the economy's output of goods and services during a year. But what do inventory changes have to do with this?

Suppose that the economy's production of output for the year exceeds the quantity of output actually sold during the year. The amount of output not sold must go into **inventories**, stocks of unsold goods. Inventories at the beginning of the year consist of goods produced in previous years (and therefore not included in this year's GNP). Therefore, inventories at the end of the year will be larger by the amount of output produced but not sold this year. Therefore, in order to correctly measure *this year's* total output or GNP, we must add this increase in inventories to this year's sales of final goods and services.

Alternatively, suppose the quantity of output sold during the year exceeds the quantity of output produced by the economy. Since this excess of sales over production can only occur by selling goods out of inventories, inventories will be lower at the end of the year than at the beginning. Since inventories at the beginning of the year consist of goods produced in previous years, the sale of those goods should not be included in this year's GNP. Hence, the decrease in inventories must be subtracted from this year's total sales of final goods and services in order to correctly measure *this year's* total output or GNP.

The news item refers to "business's desire to trim fat stocks" of inventories that "piled up during the slow summer and fall sales months." This reflects the fact that inventories consist of goods not yet sold to the final customer. If final sales are not brisk enough, firms will find more and more of their production piling up in inventories. This is a signal to them that their current production is outstripping sales. By cutting the rate of current production below the rate of sales, inventories will be decreased, or "trimmed."

GROSS VERSUS NET
INVESTMENT: DEPRECIATION

Capital goods wear out and get "used up" during the course of producing other goods—they are subject to **capital depreciation**. Machines, tools, and equipment need to be repaired or replaced. Factories and buildings require maintenance. That part of gross private domestic investment expenditures that goes toward these replacement activities simply maintains the economy's existing stock of capital. What is left over represents a net addition to the economy's capital stock and is therefore called **net private domestic investment.** *Gross private domestic investment* equals replacement investment plus net private domestic investment.

For example, in 1978 gross private domestic investment in the United States was about $345 billion. Of this amount about $217 billion was replacement investment, or what national income accountants call capital consumption allowances. This means that there was roughly $128 billion ($345 billion minus $217 billion) worth of net addition to the capital stock in the United States in 1978.

INVESTMENT AND CAPITAL FORMATION

To a large extent, the economy's ability to produce goods and services depends on its stock of capital goods. (Land and labor are its other important factors of production.) Growth in the

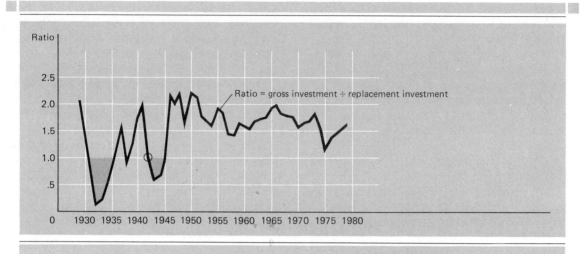

FIGURE 5-2   THE RATIO OF GROSS PRIVATE DOMESTIC INVESTMENT TO REPLACEMENT INVESTMENT IN THE UNITED STATES SINCE 1929

When the ratio of gross investment to replacement investment is greater than one, net investment is positive and the economy's capital stock is growing. This has been true in every year since the end of World War II. When the ratio equals one, net investment is zero and the capital stock remains unchanged, as was the case in 1942. When the ratio of gross investment to replacement investment is less than one, net investment is negative. This means that the capital stock is wearing out or being used up faster than it is being replaced. This was true during the Great Depression of the 1930s and for several years during World War II, as indicated by the shaded areas.

economy's capital stock is therefore important because it contributes to growth in the economy's GNP. When gross investment is greater than replacement investment, net investment is positive and there is growth in the capital stock. When gross investment equals replacement investment, net investment is zero and there is no growth in the capital stock. If gross investment is less than replacement investment, net investment is negative and the economy's capital stock is wearing out faster than it is being replaced.

The relationship between gross investment, replacement investment, and net investment since 1929 is summarized in Figure 5-2, which plots the ratio of gross investment to replacement investment. When this ratio is greater than one, gross investment is greater than replacement investment. This means that net investment is positive and the capital stock is growing. Figure 5-2 shows us that this has been the case for every year since the end of World

War II in 1945. In only one year, 1942, did gross investment just equal replacement investment so that their ratio equaled one and the economy's capital stock remained unchanged— net investment was zero. During the Great Depression of the 1930s, gross investment was less than replacement investment from 1931 through 1935 and also in 1938. The ratio is therefore less than one for these years, as Figure 5-2 shows. The same is true for the war years 1943, 1944, and 1945. Therefore during the Great Depression and World War II, there were years (the shaded areas in Figure 5-2) when net investment was negative and the economy's capital stock, and hence its productive capacity, was actually declining.

Government Spending (*G*)

Government spending, often designated *G*, includes spending on final goods and services by government at all levels—federal, state, local. Expenditures on services include wages paid to all government employees, civilian and military. We have already noted that government transfer payments are not included in GNP because they are not purchases of current production. These payments are not included in government expenditures for the same reason they are not included in GNP.

Net Exports (X)

The total expenditures on final goods and services in our economy include those made by foreigners on our output as well as those made by our own citizens on foreign goods and services. Foreign purchases of our output are **exports**. Our purchases of foreign output are **imports**. Since GNP is supposed to be a measure of productive activity in our economy, it should only measure the output actually produced domestically. Imports are already counted in C, I, and G. Imports must therefore be subtracted from total expenditures on final goods and services when measuring GNP. Exports are not included in C, I, and G. Since exports represent goods produced domestically they must be added in. National income accountants do this by simply adding in exports and subtracting out imports. That is, they add in the difference between exports and imports, or **net exports**, which are designated X.

$$X = \text{net exports} = \text{exports} - \text{imports}$$

Net exports can be either positive or negative depending on whether exports are larger or smaller than imports.

Summary of the Expenditure Side of GNP

When GNP is viewed from the expenditure side it is equal to the sum of personal consumption expenditures C, gross private domestic investment I, government expenditures G, and net exports X. In brief, from the expenditure side:

$$GNP = C + I + G + X$$

■ CHECKPOINT 5-3

In the news item at the beginning of this chapter, the Commerce Department's chief economist is reported to have made the following observation about GNP growth:

"... though the fourth quarter growth rate probably won't exceed the third quarter's, 'the composition will be better' as more growth will come from personal consumption and less from inventory accumulation." Why do you think she feels this particular composition of growth in the fourth quarter is better than that of the third quarter?

THE INCOME SIDE OF GNP

Now let's consider GNP from the seller's side of the counter. Viewed from this vantage point, GNP is distributed as payments or income to the owners of all the inputs that contribute to its production. These payments consist of wages, interest, rent, and profit. In addition, a certain amount goes to pay indirect business taxes and a portion is provided for capital consumption allowances. We will consider the last two items first.

Indirect Business Taxes

Indirect business taxes consist of sales and excise taxes and business property taxes. Because sales and excise taxes are levied on the goods and services businesses produce, and not on the businesses themselves, the term *indirect* is used to describe them.

Since indirect business taxes are paid to the government, they are not a payment or earned income to a factor directly used by the firm to produce a product, as is the case for wages, interest, rent, and profit. Nonetheless, indirect business taxes must be paid out of the sales price of the product. For example, suppose a business firm must receive $10 per unit of a good to cover the costs of all factors used to produce it. If the government levies a 7 percent sales tax, the firm must charge a price of $10.70 to cover both its factor costs and the $.70 it owes the government. Since $10.70 is what must be spent to get a unit of the product (the expenditure side of GNP), the $.70 indirect business tax must be included on the income side of GNP if the two sides are to be equal. This is necessary even though the sales tax is not an item of earned income for any factor of production.

Capital Consumption Allowances: Depreciation

We have already discussed the concept of depreciation, or capital consumption allowances—the difference between gross investment and net investment. When the economy produces its annual output of final goods and services, part of its capital stock or productive capacity is worn out, or used up. If you produce ten hammers but wear out two hammers in the process, it would be misleading to say that you are ten hammers ahead. Similarly, after deducting indirect business taxes from GNP, it would be misleading to say that *all* of the remainder is income earned by the factors of production in the form of wages, interest, rent, and profit. An allowance must first be made for the capital stock that was worn out in the process—the depreciation of machines, tools, commercial and residential buildings. Therefore, *when GNP is viewed from the income side, in addition to deducting indirect business taxes, it is also necessary to deduct depreciation or capital consumption allowances before we may view the remainder as income earned in the form of wages, interest, rent, and profit.*

Wages

Wages, or employee compensation, consists of all payments to employees for labor services of any kind. Hourly wages, salaries, bonuses, and tips come immediately to mind. Also included, however, are employer contributions to the social security system, to private pension and health insurance plans, as well as employer payments in kind—the personal use of a company car or plane, for example. These so-called supplemental benefits to wages and salaries are viewed as part of the necessary wage payments that employers must make to obtain the labor services they want.

Interest

Consistent with the notion that earned income is the payment for the use of productive factors, interest is the payment made by businesses for the use of financial capital. It is calculated as the difference between interest payments made by the business sector and the interest payments it receives from all other sec-tors, plus the difference between interest payments to other countries and those received from them. Interest payments within sectors—business, consumer, or government—are not included because they have a zero net effect on the sector. Interest payments made by the government and consumer sectors, to each other or to the business sector, are not included because they are not regarded as payment for the use of a productive factor. Payments within the business and the consumer sectors are shown as transfer payments in the national income accounts.

Rent

In the national income accounts rent includes the income earned by households for the use of their real property holdings such as land and buildings of all kinds. It also includes the imputed net rent of owner-occupied dwellings, as noted previously. In addition it embraces income payments received by households from copyrights, patent rights, and royalties from the use of things such as a famous name or an endorsement by a famous person.

Profit

National income accounts break profit into two categories: proprietors' income and corporate profits.

PROPRIETORS' INCOME

Proprietors' income is the income earned by the owners of unincorporated businesses. Doctors, lawyers, farmers, and many other small businesses are not incorporated. After these owner-operated businesses have paid wages, rent, and interest to all the factors of production they hire, what remains out of their total sales revenue is income or profit to the owners—proprietors' income.

CORPORATE PROFITS

The profits of corporations, or incorporated businesses, are, of course, derived in the same way. Corporate profits are subject to different tax laws than proprietors' income however. Proprietors' income is subject to income taxes just like wages and salaries. Corporate profits are subject to a corporate profits tax. What is left of corporate profits after this tax may be paid out

TABLE 5-4 THE EXPENDITURE SIDE AND THE INCOME SIDE OF GNP: 1978 (in Billions of Dollars)

Expenditure or Output Side of GNP		Income or Allocation Side of GNP	
Personal consumption	$1,339.7	$ 189.8	Indirect business taxes
		216.9	Capital consumption allowances
Gross private domestic investment	344.5	1,301.2	Wages (compensation of employees including supplements)
	GNP = $2,106.6 =	106.1	Interest
		23.4	Rental income
Government spending	434.2	112.9	Proprietors' income
		160.0	Corporate profits
Net exports	−11.8	−3.7	Miscellaneous adjustments

SOURCE: U.S. Department of Commerce. Figures may not add to total GNP because of rounding.

entirely or in part as dividends to stockholders—the owners of the corporation. That part of after-tax corporate profits which the corporation does not pay out in dividends is called undistributed corporate profits, or retained earnings. These are used by the corporation either to invest in capital or to pay off debt obligations of the firm.

Summary of the Two Sides of GNP

Table 5-4 summarizes our discussion of the two sides of GNP. The items on the expenditure or output side are on the left, while the items on the income or allocation side are on the right. Data for the United States economy for 1978 are given to illustrate how the sum of the expenditure items on the lefthand side of the table add up to the sum of the income items on the righthand side of the table. Each side of course sums up to GNP.

■ CHECKPOINT 5-4

Go over the news item at the beginning of this chapter and group the items mentioned according to whether they pertain to the expenditure or to the income side of GNP. What other expenditure and income items would you like to know more about if you were trying to assess the economy's performance?

RELATED NATIONAL INCOME ACCOUNTING CONCEPTS

There are four other important and related national income accounting concepts needed for a complete picture of the basics of national income accounting. These are: net national product, national income, personal income, and disposable income. Each may be viewed as a link between the total sales of final goods and services, or GNP, and the amount of those total sales receipts that households receive.

Net National Product (NNP): GNP Minus Depreciation

We noted above that if you wear out two hammers while producing ten hammers you are eight hammers "better off," not ten. True, ten hammers were produced and that quantity is a measure of total productive activity over some period of time. But in order to assess what that productive activity has actually provided, it is necessary to deduct the two hammers used up to get the *net* product of our efforts.

Similarly, GNP is a measure of the economy's total productive activity. But it makes no adjustment to account for the quantity of the year's output that must be used to replace the goods used up in producing this year's output. To do so we *subtract the annual depreciation of the economy's capital stock, or capital consump-*

TABLE 5-5 DERIVING NET NATIONAL PRODUCT, NATIONAL INCOME, PERSONAL INCOME, AND DISPOSABLE PERSONAL INCOME FROM GNP: 1978 (in Billions of Dollars)

Gross National Product (GNP)	$2,106.6
Less: Capital consumption allowance	−216.9
Equals: Net National Product (NNP)	1,889.7
Less: Indirect business taxes	−189.8
Equals: National Income (NI)	1,699.9
Less: Corporate income taxes	−84.1
Less: Undistributed corporate profits	−69.1
Less: Social security contributions	−164.3
Plus: Transfer payments	321.2
Equals: Personal Income (PI)	1,703.6
Less: Personal taxes	−256.2
Equals: Disposable Income (DI)	$1,447.4

SOURCE: U.S. Department of Commerce.

tion allowance, from GNP to get the economy's **net national product (NNP)**. *Net national product measures the dollar value of the economy's annual output of final goods and services after adjustment is made for the quantity of the year's output needed to replace goods used up in producing that output.*

Net national product may be obtained by deducting the capital consumption allowance of $216.9 billion from both the righthand side and the lefthand side of Table 5-4. On the lefthand side we may view it as being deducted from gross private domestic investment to give net investment. The subtraction of capital consumption allowances from GNP to give NNP for our economy in 1978 is shown in Table 5-5.

National Income (NI): NNP Minus Indirect Business Taxes

We have already noted that when GNP is viewed from the income side, we are basically interested in how the income earned from the sale of the economy's output is paid out to the owners of the productive factors that produced it. Net national product contains one item that does not represent payment to a factor of production—namely, indirect business taxes. These go to government. In order *to arrive at a figure for the total wage, interest, rent, and profit income earned in the economy during a year, it is necessary to subtract indirect business taxes from net national product to get national income.* **National income (NI)** *measures the income earned by the suppliers of all factors of production used to produce the economy's total output of final goods and services for the year.*

National income may be calculated by adding up all the items on the right side of Table 5-4 except capital consumption allowances and indirect business taxes. The subtraction of indirect business taxes from net national product to arrive at national income is shown in Table 5-5.

Personal Income (PI): Income Received

While national income measures the income earned by factors of production, it does not represent *income actually received by households,* or what is called **personal income (PI)**. That part of national income earned but not received consists of corporate income (or profits) taxes, undistributed corporate profits, and social security contributions (collected by the government in the form of payroll taxes). On the other hand, some income received by households is not earned currently and some is not really earned at all. This income is represented by public and private transfer payments. As noted in the news item, transfer payments consist of such things as social security, welfare, unemployment, and veterans' benefits. Also included are the interest payments on government debt and interest paid by consumers.

To move from income currently earned by households, national income, to income actually received, personal income, it is necessary to subtract from national income the three types of income not received and to add transfer payments. Hence, *personal income equals national income plus transfer payments minus corporate*

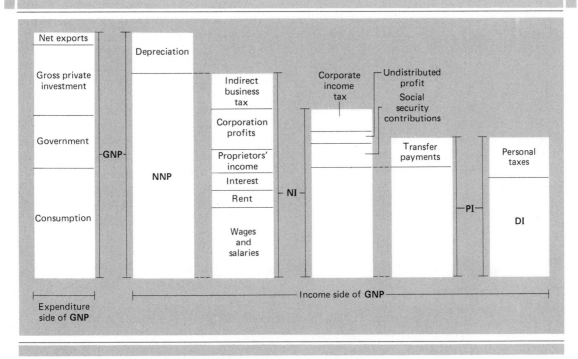

FIGURE 5-3 SUMMARY OF EXPENDITURE AND INCOME SIDE OF GNP, AND RELATIONSHIP BETWEEN GNP, NNP, NI, PI, AND DI

income taxes, undistributed corporate profits, and social security contributions. This calculation is illustrated in Table 5-5.

Disposable Income (DI): PI Minus Personal Taxes

Disposable income (DI) *equals personal income minus personal taxes.* Personal taxes consist of inheritance taxes, property taxes, and personal income taxes, which are by far the largest of the three as well as the most familiar to the typical working person. After paying personal taxes out of personal income, what is left is literally disposable in the sense that households may use it any way they wish. The largest part of disposable income is typically spent; this constitutes the personal consumption expenditures which we have already discussed. The relationship between personal income and disposable income is illustrated in Table 5-5.

At this point you should examine Table 5-5 from top to bottom. It summarizes the relationship between five important accounting measures: (1) gross national product (GNP); (2) net national product (NNP); (3) national income (NI); (4) personal income (PI); and (5) disposable income (DI). Figure 5-3 summarizes our discussion of the expenditure side and the income side of GNP, as well as the relationship between GNP, NNP, NI, PI, and DI.

■ CHECKPOINT 5-5

Use Figure 5-3 to interpret the second to last paragraph of the news item at the beginning of this chapter.

SUMMARY

1. Gross national product (GNP) is the market value of the economy's total output of final goods and services produced during a year.
2. GNP does not include so-called nonproductive transactions, such as the purchase and sale of used goods, the trading of stocks and

bonds in financial markets, and private and public transfer payments. Certain productive nonmarket activities are included, such as the imputed rent on owner-occupied housing and the value of food produced and consumed by farm families. However, other activities are not included, such as the services performed by homemakers, and the myriad of tasks performed by do-it-yourselfers.

3. Money GNP, or GNP in current prices or dollars, measures the dollar value of GNP in a given year in terms of the prices at which final goods and services actually were sold in that year. Real GNP, or GNP in constant prices or dollars, measures the dollar value of GNP in a given year in terms of the prices at which final goods and services sold for in some base, or benchmark, year.

4. When calculating GNP care must be taken to avoid double, or multiple, counting of intermediate goods.

5. GNP is an accounting measure and was never intended to be a welfare measure. GNP does not reflect changes in product quality or in the composition of output, nor does it take account of the costs of pollution or the benefits of leisure. Per capita GNP is a better indicator of an economy's welfare than GNP alone, but neither really tells us anything about the true distribution of an economy's output among its citizens.

6. When GNP is viewed from the expenditure, or output side, it equals the sum of personal consumption expenditures, made by households; gross private domestic investment expenditures, made by business firms; government expenditures, made by federal, state, and local governments; and net exports, the difference between foreign purchases of our goods and our purchases of foreign goods.

7. When GNP is viewed from the income side, it appears as payments, or income, in the form of wages, interest, rent, and profit to the owners of all the inputs that contribute to its production. In addition, a certain amount goes to pay indirect business taxes and a portion is provided for capital consumption allowances.

8. In addition to GNP, there are four other important and interrelated national income accounting concepts: (1) net national product, which equals gross national product minus capital consumption allowances or depreciation; (2) national income, which equals net national product minus indirect business taxes; (3) personal income, which equals national income minus income earned but not received (corporate income or profits taxes, undistributed corporate profits, social security contributions) plus income received but not currently or necessarily earned (public and private transfer payments); and (4) disposable income, which equals personal income minus personal taxes.

KEY TERMS AND CONCEPTS
capital depreciation
deflation
disposable income (DI)
exports
flow
gross private domestic investment
gross national product (GNP)
imports
indirect business taxes
inflation
inventory
investment
money GNP
national income (NI)
net exports
net private domestic investment
net national product (NNP)
per capita GNP
personal consumption
personal income (PI)
price index
proprietors' income
real GNP
transfer payments
value added

QUESTIONS AND PROBLEMS
1. Why is GNP a flow and inventory not a flow?

2. When we measure GNP, why is the problem of productive versus nonproductive transactions never an issue in the case of services (as distinct from goods)?

3. How is a transfer payment different from the purchase of a final good? Why is Christmas so "good for business" if gifts are merely private transfer payments?

4. Home milk delivery service used to be more common a generation ago than it is today, yet milk consumption per capita has not changed all that much in the meantime. What effect do you think the gradual decrease in home milk delivery has had on GNP and why?

5. For a number of years during the last third of the nineteenth century in the United States the general level of prices fell. Suppose you were told that GNP in current prices tripled over this period of time.

a. What would you be able to conjecture about the change in real GNP? (We do not in fact have GNP figures and price indices for this period which are of the quality of those constructed for the years since 1930.)

b. In 1870 the population of the United States was roughly 38.5 million, and by 1900 it was approximately 76 million. What would you be able to conjecture about the change in per capita real GNP over this period of time?

6. When measuring GNP what similarity do you see between the problem of double, or multiple, counting and the problem of nonproductive market transactions?

7. It has been argued that the production of goods often gives rise to bad by-products, such as polluted rivers and air, whose costs to society are not included in the price of the final good. Suppose the average price of an automobile is $6,000. Suppose it would cost $1,000 to clean up the air and water pollution associated with the production of an automobile but that neither the auto company nor the buyer of the car has to pay the cost—the "mess" is simply not cleaned up. If the company were forced to clean up the mess, what would be the effect on money GNP? What would be the effect on real GNP? What do you think of the contention that GNP is such a "silly" measure that if allowance is

made for the cost of bads, GNP actually would go up?

8. GNP is supposed to measure the economy's output of final goods and services. But in what way and to what extent could it also be said to be a measure of the value of the services of productive factors?

9. The following national income accounting data are for the United States in the year 1929 (in billions of dollars), the last year before the onset of the Great Depression of the 1930s.

Transfer payments	$ 4.0
Gross private domestic investment	16.2
Indirect business taxes	7.0
Personal taxes	2.6
Net exports of goods and services	1.1
Undistributed corporate profits	2.8
Capital consumption allowances	7.9
Personal consumption expenditures	77.2
Corporate income taxes	1.4
Interest paid by consumers	1.5
Contributions for social insurance	.2
Government purchases of goods and services	8.5

Use the above data to answer the following questions about the year 1929. Show your work.

a. How much was GNP?

b. What was the amount of personal saving?

c. What was the amount of income earned but not received?

d. What was the amount of income earned by factors of production?

e. What was the amount of personal income?

f. Show two different ways of arriving at the amount of disposable personal income.

g. What was the amount of the addition to the nation's stock of capital?

h. What was national income?

i. Could dividends have been larger?

j. What was net national product?

k. What amount of income was available to households for saving?

l. By how much would you say the economy came out ahead as the result of the year's production?

m. What was the amount of income earned in the form of interest, wages, rent, and profit?

■NEWS ITEM FOR YOUR ANALYSIS

GNP GREW AT 5.1 PERCENT YEARLY RATE, INFLATION AT 4.8 PERCENT IN THIRD PERIOD, REVISIONS SHOW

WASHINGTON, Dec. 21—The nation's real GNP grew in the third quarter at an upward revised 5.1 percent annual rate and inflation ran at a downward revised 4.8 percent pace, the Commerce Department said.

After-tax corporate profits were at a seasonally adjusted $103.6 billion annual rate, down .7 percent from the second quarter. The previous estimate put third quarter profits at a $103.7 billion adjusted pace, down .6 percent.

The latest upward revision for GNP totaled $1 billion, before adjustment for inflation. Consumer purchases were revised upward $2 billion, business fixed investment $800 million, inventory investment $500 million, and net exports $100 million. Those changes were offset by a $2.4 billion downward revision in government expenditures at all levels. The brightest signs in the report were the reduction in the inflation rate and the spurt in business fixed investment in this analyst's view.

After the revisions, third quarter real GNP ran at a $1.347 trillion adjusted annual rate, up from the second quarter's $1.33 trillion. Real GNP grew at a 6.2 percent annual rate in this year's second quarter and at a 7.5 percent clip in the first quarter.

QUESTIONS

1. What impression do you get from this article regarding the accuracy of national income accounting data when it is initially made known to the public?

2. What was the percent rate of growth of money GNP in the third quarter?

3. How much information does this news item provide you about the income side of GNP?

4. What are you told about the expenditure side of GNP? Do the alleged revisions on the expenditure side fit together as reported?

6

ECONOMIC FLUCTUATIONS, UNEMPLOYMENT, AND INFLATION

BUSINESS STRENGTHENS, BUT WORRIES GROW ABOUT LATER THIS YEAR

NEW YORK, January 31—To the surprise of both economists and business people, the economy is picking up steam. Yet at the same time there are doubts about the outlook for later this year. The surge in business has led most economists to raise their forecasts of gains in inflation-adjusted GNP. At the same time there is a growing concern that the good news can't last. Moreover, some analysts think that the swifter pace of current business almost guarantees an acceleration of inflation later this year.

While the recent quarter year's expansion has been most apparent in retail sales, it has benefited a wide range of industries. On a seasonally adjusted basis retail sales in December were down .7 percent from November. However, some economists suggest that consumers have been doing relatively more Christmas shopping in October and November—a trend that the seasonal adjustment process hasn't accounted for yet. But the ambivalent attitude toward the economy shows up in some polls. The Conference Board reported that its measure of business confidence in the future, based on a scale of zero to 100, declined to 52 in the fourth quarter from 59 in the previous three months. The University of Michigan's Survey Research Center said consumer confidence has dropped to its lowest level in nearly two years.

On the other hand, the unemployment rate is looking markedly better, having fallen from 7 percent to 6.4 percent over the last three months. And the stronger economy is further increasing demand for labor. "Unless there are major layoffs or a speedup in labor-force growth, the unemployment rate could fall to around 6 percent or even less by midyear," says Jerry L. Jordan, senior vice-president of Pittsburgh National Bank. The Commerce Department's annual survey of business people indicated that they intend to increase capital outlays this year at a 10.1 percent rate.

The pace of economic growth always is uneven, of course. "The economy has been moving upward in fits and starts," a General Electric Company economist says, "climbing a cliff and then resting on a plateau before climbing another cliff."

Economic fluctuations have been a major problem for our economy throughout its history, and unemployment and inflation are major costs associated with that problem. In this chapter we will concern ourselves with the nature of business cycles and the interrelated problems of unemployment and inflation. Much of our discussion in the following chapters will focus on trying to understand the causes of economic fluctuations, unemployment, and inflation. We will also look at various policies aimed at eliminating or at least reducing these problems.

HOW THE ECONOMY MOVES

Even the most casual observer of our economy is aware that it seems to move by "fits and starts." Periods of rapid growth alternate with periods of slower growth or even contraction. These economic fluctuations, often referred to as business cycles, are most commonly recognized by their effects on unemployment, sales, and the behavior of prices—in particular the rate of inflation. Of course, as the news item suggests, the business cycle is reflected in many other measures of economic activity as well.

Growth and Fluctuations

Some idea of the way the economy moves is conveyed in part a of Figure 6-1 by the graph of real GNP (1972 dollars) since 1929. Two things are obvious. The economy grows over time, but there are irregular fluctuations in its rate of growth from one year to the next. The size of these fluctuations is further illustrated by the graph of the annual percentage changes in real GNP over this period of time, part b of Figure 6-1. Since World War II these fluctuations have been less violent than those of the 1930s or the 1940s. The size of the fluctuations

during the 1930s was a reflection of unstable conditions resulting from the Great Depression. Those of the 1940s came about when the economy was converted to wartime during the first half of the decade and then reconverted to peacetime during the second half. It is easy to see from part a of Figure 6-1 why the GE economist in the news item depicts the economy as "climbing a cliff and then resting on a plateau before climbing another cliff."

The Business Cycle

The fluctuations in real GNP that are so clearly shown in part b of Figure 6-1 are often called **business cycles**. Comparing parts a and b of Figure 6-1, we can see that business cycles are a phenomenon quite separate from the growth trend in this aggregate measure of economic activity. The growth trend (of roughly 3.5 percent over this period) is represented by the horizontal broken line in the bottom graph. The business cycles during this period are represented by irregular but recurrent up-and-down movement of the saw-toothed solid line about this trend. In general, *business cycles are irregular but recurrent patterns of fluctuations in economic activity. They are apparent in aggregate measures of sales, output, income, employment, and a host of other measures over a period of years, quite apart from any long-run trends in these series.*

PHASES OF THE BUSINESS CYCLE

A hypothetical, idealized version of the business cycle, measured in terms of real GNP, is shown in Figure 6-2. The cycle may be viewed as having four phases: the peak, the recession, the trough, and the expansion. The **recession** phase corresponds to the contraction or slowing down of economic activity. During this phase unemployment rises while sales, income, and investment all fall. An unusually severe recession is sometimes called a **depression**, such as the Great Depression of the 1930s which is so noticeable in Figure 6-1. The lower turning point of the business cycle is often called the **trough**. At this point economic conditions are at a low ebb. This is followed by an upturn in economic activity, or the **expansion** phase of the cycle. During this phase unemployment falls and sales, income, output, and capital formation all rise. This phase and the subsequent upper turning point or **peak** phase of the cycle are sometimes referred to as a "boom." Output, income, sales, and capital formation reach their highest levels while unemployment falls to its lowest level. Business and consumer optimism about the future typically rises throughout the expansion phase of the cycle and falls during the recession phase.

Comparison of the real world of Figure 6-1 with the hypothetical one of Figure 6-2 indicates that actual business cycles are not nearly as regular or periodic as the idealized picture presented in Figure 6-2. This is the reason why real world business cycles are often more accurately called business fluctuations—no two are ever quite alike. Furthermore, it is not always very clear when the economy is passing into another phase of the business cycle. This is evident from the news item, which reports that, despite the generally robust signs of economic expansion, business confidence and consumer confidence appear to be weakening.

SEASONAL VARIATION

To get a clearer picture of business cycles, we have seen that it is helpful to abstract from any long-run trend that may be in the data. This is

essentially what we did in part b of Figure 6-1. In addition, it is also helpful to adjust the data for **seasonal variation**. For example, general retail sales are typically high in December because of the Christmas holidays. On the other hand, sales of a particular good, air conditioners, are typically low at that time of the year but high during the summer months. From the standpoint of the business cycle we need to know how sales look after allowing for their typical seasonal behavior. "Raw" retail sales data typically rise from November to December in a given year. When we allow for the usual seasonal rise in these data at that time of year, we might find that retail sales have risen less than normally—for example, because the economy is in a recession.

How do statisticians adjust data to remove seasonal variation? Suppose past monthly sales data for air conditioners indicate that, on average, air conditioner sales in August are 1.9 times as high as average monthly sales over the course of a year. Similarly, suppose air conditioner sales in February are only .7 times as large as average monthly sales over the course of a year. To remove the seasonal variation from the data, the statistician would divide the August sales figures by 1.9 and the February sales figures by .7. In similar fashion the sales figures for each month would be adjusted by such seasonal adjustment factors. The resulting sales figures are said to be "seasonally adjusted."

One of the difficulties with seasonal adjustment is that seasonal variation patterns often change over time. Given that the seasonal adjustment factors are necessarily derived from past data, they are not able to account for these changes in the most recent data. Thus seasonal

---

After reading this chapter, you will be able to:
1. Describe the way the economy moves over time.
2. Explain how the structure of the economy affects the business cycle.
3. Define the concepts of fictional, structural, and cyclical unemployment, and the concept of full employment.
4. Describe the United States' recent experience with inflation.
5. Distinguish between anticipated and unanticipated inflation and explain who gains and who loses when inflation is unanticipated.

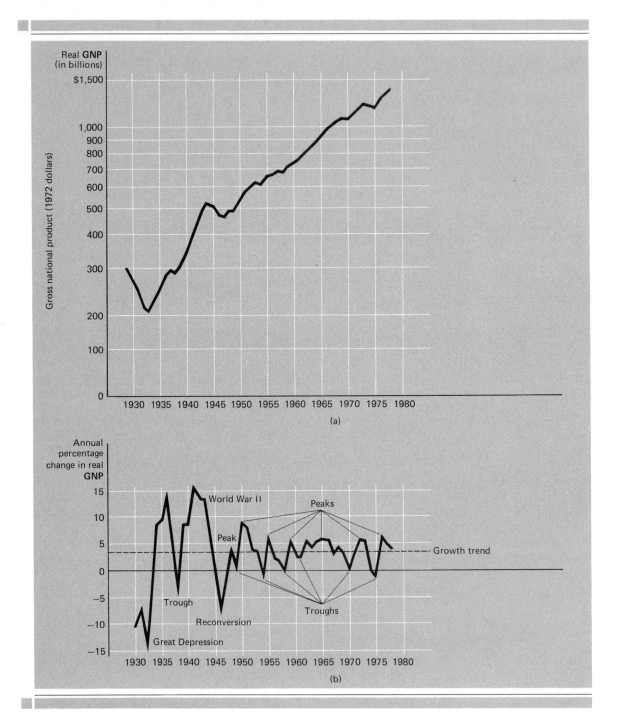

adjustment may not accurately remove the seasonal variation from these data. This is a concern expressed in the news item in regard to the meaning of the .7 percent drop in seasonally adjusted retail sales between November and December. In this instance some economists are concerned that the seasonal variation pattern has changed in such a way that consumers are

FIGURE 6-1 REAL GNP FLUCTUATES ABOUT A LONG-TERM GROWTH TREND

Part a shows real GNP (1972 dollars) since 1929. It fluctuates about a long-term growth trend.

Note that the vertical axis in part a is a logarithmic or ratio scale on which equal distances represent an increase of 100 percent. (Convince yourself, by measuring, that the distance from 600 to 900 equals that from 1,000 to 1,500.) If real GNP were plotted on an ordinary arithmetic scale, its plot would curve sharply upward because a given percentage change in a small number would be represented by a smaller distance than the same percentage change in a larger number.

The plot of the annual percentage changes in real GNP shown in part b gives a more vivid picture of the fluctuations in real GNP. These fluctuations are the so-called business cycles with their peaks and troughs. These fluctuations have been milder since the early 1950s by comparison with the decade of the 1930s and the turbulent war and postwar years of the 1940s.

"doing relatively more Christmas shopping in October and November—a trend that the seasonal adjustment process hasn't accounted for yet."

DURATION OF CYCLES

The ups and downs of the United States economy have been traced by the National Bureau of Economic Research all the way back to

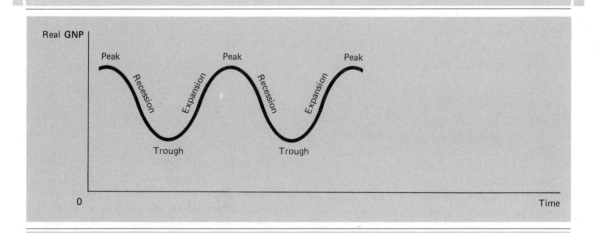

FIGURE 6-2 PHASES OF THE BUSINESS CYCLE

The two hypothetical business cycles shown here (measured in terms of real GNP) are idealizations. Actual business fluctuations are never quite this regular or periodic, and no two are ever quite this similar to one another.

The recession phase of the cycle corresponds to the contraction or slowing down of economic activity. During this phase unemployment rises while sales, income, output, and investment all fall, along with business and consumer optimism. The lower turning point is the trough of the cycle. Here economic activity is at its lowest ebb. In the ensuing expansion phase of the cycle sales, income, output, and investment all rise while unemployment falls. Business and consumer optimism are also on the rise throughout this phase. Finally the expansion loses steam at the upper turning point, or peak, and the cycle then repeats itself.

TABLE 6-1 AVERAGE DURATION OF BUSINESS CYCLES, PRE-WORLD WAR II PERIOD (1854–1945) AND POSTWAR PERIOD
(in Months)

	Pre–World War II 1854–1945	Post–World War II 1945–1975
Number of Cycles	22	6
Average Duration (Trough to Trough)	49.5	59.1
Length of Longest Cycle	99 (1870–1879)	118 (1961–1970)
Length of Shortest Cycle	28 (1919–1921)	34 (1958–1961)
Average Length of Expansions	28.9	47.3
Length of Shortest Expansion	10 (1919–1920)	25 (1960–1961)
Length of Longest Expansion	80 (1938–1945)	106 (1961–1969)
Average Length of Recessions	20.6	11.8
Length of Shortest Recession	7 (1918–1919)	9 (1957–1958, 1960–1961)
Length of Longest Recession	65 (1873–1879)	17 (1973–1975)

1854. From that date to the end of World War II, the National Bureau recognizes a total of 22 cycles. Characteristics of the duration of these cycles are summarized in Table 6-1. Measured from trough to trough the average duration was 49.5 months. The average length of the expansion phase was 28.9 months while the average length of the recession phase was 20.6 months. On average the expansion phases of these cycles were about 1.5 times as long as the recession phases.

The six cycles from the end of World War II up through 1975 had an average duration of 59.1 months. The average length of the expansion phase of these cycles was 47.3 months, and the average length of the recession phase was 11.8 months. The expansion phases of these cycles were somewhat more than four times as long as the recession phases on average.

While business cycles represent recurring patterns of expansion and recession, the sizeable differences shown in Table 6-1 between the shortest and longest indicate a significant degree of variability in their duration.

■ CHECKPOINT 6-1

When we look at the graph in part a of Figure 6–1, it appears that the expansion phase of business cycles is a great deal longer than the recession phase. Would you agree with this assessment? Why or why not? What do you think the monthly seasonal adjustment factors for textbook sales would look like over the course of a year?

Determinants of the Business Cycle

The characteristics of the business cycles of an economy will depend on the shocks that hit it and the way it is "put together"—the nature of its products, the structure of its markets, and the interconnecting relationships between its industries.

PRODUCT CHARACTERISTICS— DURABLES AND NONDURABLES

Industries that produce durable goods—steel, machinery, motor vehicles, construction, consumer appliances, and so forth—experience much larger fluctuations in employment, production, and sales over the course of the business cycle than do industries that produce nondurable goods—textiles, food products, agricultural commodities, and so forth. The major reason for this lies precisely in the difference in the nature of durable and nondurable goods.

When the economy goes into a recession unemployment rises. Businesses find themselves with idle productive capacity in the face of lagging sales as consumer and business optimism about the future declines. Consumers tend to make the old car or refrigerator last another year, particularly if they are unemployed or faced with increasing job uncertainty. Similarly, businesses make do with existing plants and equipment, especially since some of it is idled by the slowdown in sales and the accompanying buildup of unsold inventories. In short, when times are bad and a cloud of uncertainty shrouds the future, durable goods purchases will tend to be postponed. This is possible precisely because durable goods are durable. This, of course, means that a recession hits the durable goods industries especially hard.

By contrast, nondurable goods purchases cannot be put off nearly as long. People can't postpone eating, brushing their teeth, being sick, or heating their homes. They also seem very reluctant to cut back on smoking and other personal consumption habits. As a result history shows that during recessions nondurable goods industries do not experience nearly as severe a decline in employment, production, and sales as do the durable goods industries.

On the other hand, during business cycle expansions, durable goods purchases previously postponed are now carried out. Rising sales put increasing demands on productive capacity and businesses have a greater incentive to buy new equipment and expand plant size. Similarly, consumers have more job certainty, employment and paychecks rise, and more households are willing to replace the old car or refrigerator

with new ones. As a result, durable goods purchases pick up at a faster rate than purchases of nondurables.

MARKET STRUCTURE

Markets in which there are numerous firms competing with one another in the production and sale of a product tend to reduce prices more sharply in the face of declining demand than do markets dominated by a few large firms that have monopoly-type power. On the other hand, monopoly-type markets tend to reduce output and employment more sharply than do markets with numerous competing firms. In short, over the course of the business cycle, monopoly-type markets adjust to changing demand largely by changing production rather than by changing price. Highly competitive markets with numerous firms adjust largely by changing price rather than by changing output.

Monopoly-type market structures tend to prevail in the durable goods industries such as steel, oil, electrical machinery, appliances, and automobiles. Each of these industries is dominated by less than ten firms. (The auto industry is dominated by the well-known Big Three.) On the other hand, competitive market structures tend to prevail in nondurable goods industries such as agriculture and wearing apparel. There are literally tens of thousands of farmers, for example.

THE ACCELERATOR PRINCIPLE: AN INSIGHT

We have argued that one reason why durable goods industries experience more severe fluctuations than nondurable goods industries is that durable goods purchases can be put off more easily than nondurable goods purchases. The so-called **accelerator principle** provides yet another insight into the causes of this greater variability in durable goods industries.

An Example. The way the accelerator principle works is perhaps best illustrated by an example. Suppose we consider the relationship between shoe sales by the shoe industry (a nondurable or semidurable goods industry) and the sale of shoemaking machines by the shoe machinery industry (a durable goods industry).

TABLE 6-2 THE ACCELERATOR PRINCIPLE: RETAIL SHOE SALES AND SHOE MACHINE SALES
(Hypothetical Data in Millions of Dollars)

	Shoe Industry			Shoe Machine Industry
	(1)	(2)	(3)	(4)
	Annual Retail Shoe Sales	Stock of Capital: Shoe Machines[a]	NI = Net Investment in Shoe Machines	Sale of Shoe Machines = NI + Replacement
Year 1	$10	$20	$ 0	$ 0 + $2 = $ 2
Year 2	13	26	6	6 + 2 = 8
Year 3	20	40	14	14 + 2 = 16
Year 4	27	54	14	14 + 2 = 16
Year 5	31	62	8	8 + 2 = 10
Year 6	31	62	0	0 + 2 = 2

[a] Assumes that $2 worth of shoe machinery is needed to produce every $1 worth of shoes.

We will assume that in order to produce $1,000 worth of shoes the shoe industry needs to have roughly $2,000 worth of shoe machinery. In other words, the production of $1 worth of the nondurable good requires the aid of approximately $2 worth of the durable good. What does this say about the relationship between changes in the year-to-year level of shoe sales and the changes in the year-to-year level of the sales of shoe machines?

An answer to this question is given by the data in Table 6-2. In year 1, retail shoe sales are $10 million (column 1). The shoe industry uses $20 million worth of shoe machinery (column 2) to produce this quantity of shoes. We will assume that it has this stock of shoe machinery on hand at the beginning of year 1 so that it does not need to *add* to its capital stock of shoe machines during year 1. Net investment in shoe machinery is therefore zero (column 3). Suppose, however, that $2 million worth of shoe machines wear out every year. The shoe industry must therefore buy $2 million of shoe machines from the shoe machine industry for replacement (column 4). Hence in year 1, shoe industry output and sales are $10 million (column 1), while the shoe machine industry's output and sales are $2 million (column 4).

Now suppose that in year 2 annual retail shoe sales increase by 30 percent to $13 million (col-

umn 1). The shoe industry now needs $26 million worth of shoe machines (column 2) to produce this amount of shoes. Hence, the additional $3 million of shoe production means the industry must add $6 million worth of new shoe machinery (column 3) to its stock of shoe machines. This plus the annual replacement of $2 million worth of shoe machinery brings total shoe machine sales to $8 million (column 4). The upshot is that a 30 percent increase in shoe industry sales between years 1 and 2 causes a 300 percent increase in the sales of the shoe machine industry. In other words, there is an accelerator effect.

When shoe sales rise by 54 percent to $20 million in year 3 (column 1), the shoe industry needs $40 million worth of shoe machinery (column 2). Therefore net investment in shoe machinery rises to $14 million (column 3). This plus replacement expenditures causes total shoe machine sales to rise to $16 million (column 4). Hence a $7 million, or 54 percent, increase in shoe sales between years 2 and 3 (column 1) causes an $8 million, or 100 percent, increase in shoe machine sales (column 4). Again we see an accelerator effect.

But now suppose the increase in shoe sales between years 3 and 4 is again $7 million, the same as it was between years 2 and 3 (column 1). The shoe industry now needs $54 million of shoe machines (column 2). Net investment in shoe machines is once again $14 million (column 3). This plus the annual $2 million replacement expenditure means that shoe machine sales (column 4) are once again $16 million. The startling conclusion is that shoe sales must keep growing at $7 million per year if shoe machine sales are just to stay the same!

When shoe sales increase by only $4 million between years 4 and 5 to $31 million (column 1), the shoe industry's net investment in shoe machines declines to $8 million (column 3). This plus the annual $2 million for replacement means that total shoe machine sales are now only $10 million (column 4), down from the $16 million of the previous year—this despite the fact that annual shoe sales still increased! Suppose that in year 6 shoe sales don't increase at all (column 1). There is now no need for the shoe industry to increase its stock of shoe machines (column 2), so net investment in shoe machines falls to zero (column 3). The shoe machine industry's total sales fall to $2 million (column 4), the annual replacement requirement of the shoe industry. If shoe sales fall in subsequent years, the shoe industry might even cut back on these replacement expenditures.

The annual shoe sales (column 1) and the annual shoe machine sales (column 4) are plotted in Figure 6-3 to give a graphic illustration of the accelerator principle. In general, *the accelerator principle says that ever larger increases in the level of retail sales are needed in order for net investment in capital or durable goods to rise. For net investment to remain constant, retail sales must increase by a constant amount every year. When the expansion of retail sales begins to slow down, the level of net investment will actually fall.* Table 6-2 and Figure 6-3 clearly show that due to the accelerator principle the mere expansion and subsequent leveling off of retail shoe sales caused an expansion, peak, and recession in the sale of shoe machinery—a complete business cycle in the shoe machinery industry.

Qualifications and Extensions. Capital goods—goods used to produce other goods—make up a large part of the output of the economy's durable goods industries. (Consumer durables, such as passenger cars, also account for a

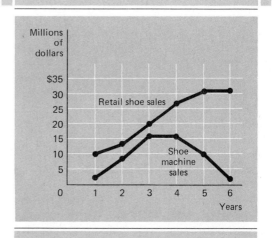

FIGURE 6-3 THE ACCELERATOR PRINCIPLE: RETAIL SHOE SALES AND SHOE MACHINE SALES
(Hypothetical Data)

The graph of retail shoe sales is plotted from the data in column 1 of Table 6-2, while that for shoe machine sales is plotted from the data in column 4.

The ever larger increases in shoe sales between years 1 and 2 and 2 and 3 cause an even more pronounced rise in the sale of shoe machines over this time span. This is known as the accelerator effect. When the rise in shoe sales between years 3 and 4 is the same as that between years 2 and 3, shoe machine sales flatten out. When the expansion of shoe sales slows down between years 4 and 5, shoe machine sales actually decline—a downward accelerator effect. When the sale of shoes flattens out between years 5 and 6, the resulting decline in shoe machine sales is even greater. Hence, the expansion and subsequent flattening out of shoe sales results in an expansion, peak, and recession in shoe machine sales—a complete business cycle in the shoe machine industry. This is an example of the accelerator principle in action.

sizeable portion.) While other factors also affect investment in capital goods, the accelerator principle would seem to provide a key insight into the relatively large fluctuations in the behavior of capital investment in our economy. However, two qualifications on the way the accelerator principle works should be noted. First, if the economy is in the early stages of an expansion, there may be excess capacity in nondurable goods industries so that expansion can occur with no increase in capital goods. Second, in the later stages of an expansion, there may be no excess capacity in capital goods industries so that nondurable goods industries cannot get more capital.

The accelerator principle is also relevant to inventory investment, both in durable and nondurable goods. For example, suppose that for every $1 worth of sales of canned goods grocers desire to keep $2 worth of canned goods in inventory. Table 6-2 and Figure 6-3 could then represent canned goods sales (column 1); the desired inventory of canned goods (column 2); net inventory investment in canned goods (column 3); and gross inventory investment in canned goods, which would include the replacement expenditure due to damaged canned goods (column 4).

CAUSES OF BUSINESS CYCLES

We have briefly examined a few of the important aspects of the economy's internal, or endogenous, structure that determine how it moves when it is subjected to external shocks. The nature of its products (durable versus nondurable), the structure of its markets (competitive versus monopolistic), and the interconnecting relationships between its industries (the operation of the accelerator principle between nondurable and durable goods sales is an example) are all important internal determinants of the economy's motion. In subsequent chapters we will examine other characteristics of the economy's internal structure that are also important determinants of the way it moves. These determinants affect the economy just as weight, size, and center of gravity affect the way a rocking horse moves when given a shove.

Now we will briefly describe a few frequently cited explanatory factors underlying business cycles that are generally regarded as external or exogenous causes, like the shove or kick applied to a rocking horse. Among these factors are changes in population growth rates and migration trends; new inventions and technological developments; the discovery of new mineral deposits and energy sources; the opening up of new land frontiers; political events and social upheavals, such as wars and revolutions.

Most of these factors are thought of as external to the workings of the economy—like the kick to the rocking horse. But it is often difficult to make a clear-cut distinction on this score. For example, increases in the population growth rate seem to be encouraged by economic expansion and dampened by recessions. However, this is a two-way street. Increases in the population growth rate tend to stimulate economic expansion, while decreases tend to slow down the growth of demand for goods and services. The same sort of two-way influences may exist for any of the so-called external factors listed above. Unstable economic conditions in post–World War I Germany may have contributed to the rise of Hitler and the advent of World War II, which in turn pulled the United States economy out of the depression years of the 1930s. On the other hand, the hike in oil prices by the Arab oil exporting countries in 1973–1974 is viewed by many economists as an external shock to the U.S. economy that helped trigger the 1974–1975 recession—the most severe recession in the postwar period.

Finally, the ebb and tide of optimism or confidence about the future—what Lord Keynes called "animal spirits"—is often cited as a crucial factor in the business cycle. For example, it is sometimes argued that optimism lost touch with reality in the late 1920s. This allegedly led to excessive speculation in land and stocks, and overinvestment in plant, equipment, and apartment and office buildings, far beyond what demand warranted. When sober judgment finally set in, the economy was plunged into the deepest and longest depression in our history, and a mood of deep pessimism prevailed. At its depth in 1932 Franklin Roosevelt may have measured the main problem very well when he said "the only thing we have to fear is fear itself."

■ CHECKPOINT 6-2

Gardner Means did a study of the percentage drop in product price and the percentage drop in production in each of ten industries during the onset and downturn of the Great Depression of the 1930s. These industries

ECONOMIC THINKERS

WESLEY C. MITCHELL
1874–1948

Born in Illinois, Mitchell spent the greatest portion of his career at Columbia University and the National Bureau of Economic Research, of which he was the founder. He was also a founder of the New School for Social Research. An institutional economist, Mitchell is generally thought of in connection with his work on business cycles.

While many economists had interested themselves in the business cycle, Mitchell was one of the first to recognize that a great deal of solid data were needed to obtain meaningful results. To this end he organized the National Bureau of Economic Research to collect and process large amounts of information.

Mitchell began his major work with a survey of existing interpretations of the cycle, regarding each as a partial explanation and disregarding none until it had failed to pass muster. He tested the comparability of various indices of business cycles by comparing the five whose time coverage was the most comprehensive (about half a century for the three best). There were, he found, many points of similarity, namely, their sawtooth pattern, their amplitude of month-to-month changes, timing of peaks, duration, and so forth. There were to be sure many dissimilar characteristics, but Mitchell's results helped to establish some validity in the soundness of his procedures.

As he relied on the resources of the National Bureau, Mitchell also relied on a host of willing workers to aid his efforts and his results reflect the wisdom of his approach. Among his close associates was the economist Arthur F. Burns, later chairman of the Council of Economic Advisors in the Eisenhower administration and of the Federal Reserve System's Board of Governors during the Nixon and Ford administrations.

Mitchell, though he had great regard for hard data, did not believe that quantitative economics (at least as it existed in his day) could by itself be much of an aid in economic analysis. The problem of economics would in his view have to be recast in new form in order to be treated statistically. "In the course of this reformulation, of its problems, economic theory will change not merely its complexion but also its content."

Though most notable as a student of the business cycle, Mitchell made many other contributions. He did work in economic history and in money and banking, his first book being *A History of the Greenbacks* (1903). He also made contributions to public service, serving on President Hoover's Committee on Social Trends, and wrote a book on the use of index numbers for the Labor Department.

FOR FURTHER READING
W. C. Mitchell and Arthur F. Burns, *Measuring Business Cycles.* New York: National Bureau of Economic Research, 1946.

---

were textile products, agricultural implements, agricultural commodities, petroleum, motor vehicles, leather, cement, food products, iron and steel, and automobile tires. How do you think they ranked: (1) in terms of the degree of price reduction he observed in each of them; and (2) in terms of the degree of output reduction?

Using the same sales figures in column 1 of Table 6–2, suppose the shoe industry needed roughly $3 worth of shoe machinery for each $1 of shoes produced and sold. How would this affect the behavior of shoe

machine sales in column 4? What insight does this give you into the role of capital intensity (the amount of capital required to produce a dollar's worth of output) as a factor in the behavior of business cycles?

UNEMPLOYMENT AND EMPLOYMENT

The economy's **labor force** *includes all persons over the age of 16 who are employed plus all those who are unemployed but actively looking for work.* The labor force in our economy amounts to more than half of the population over 16. While the labor force includes people in the military, unemployment is a problem that only afflicts the civilian labor force. Our discussion of unemployment and employment therefore focuses on the civilian labor force. In the discussion that follows, we will consider such questions as, Are there different types of unemployment? Is there such a thing as a normal level of unemployment, or what is full employment? What are the costs of unemployment?

Types of Unemployment

A worker may become unemployed in three basically different ways: (1) The worker may quit his or her current job to look for a better job, giving rise to what is called frictional unemployment. (2) The worker's current job may be permanently eliminated—the plight of buggy-whip makers at the turn of the century—possibly causing so-called structural unemployment. (3) The worker's current job may be temporarily eliminated by a recession, thus giving rise to cyclical unemployment. Let's look more closely at each of these types of unemployment.

FRICTIONAL UNEMPLOYMENT

Many times, workers quit jobs to look for ones that pay better, or are more attractive in some other way. In the meantime they are often unemployed for short periods of time while they are between jobs. Suppose, for example, that each worker in the labor force changed jobs once a year and was unemployed for a two-week period while in transition. Suppose also that the number of workers changing jobs at any one time is spread evenly over the year. At any time during the year $2/52$, or 3.8 percent, of the labor force is thus unemployed, if there are no other causes of unemployment. If only half of the labor force switched jobs in this manner, the unemployment rate would be 1.9 percent.

Other forms of frictional unemployment are due to seasonal layoffs, such as those that affect farm workers and construction workers. New entrants into the labor force with marketable job skills are also frequently unemployed for a brief period of time before finding a job.

STRUCTURAL UNEMPLOYMENT

As the term structural implies, this kind of unemployment is due to fundamental changes in the structure of labor demand—specifically, the kinds of jobs that the economy offers. Technological change, the development of new industries and the demise of old ones, the changing economic role of different regions in the country, all mean that new kinds of jobs need to be done while many old ones cease to exist. The new jobs often require different skills and educational backgrounds than the old ones and are frequently located in different geographic regions.

Workers often find themselves displaced by these structural changes. They may lack the required skills and training needed to gain employment in other areas of the economy. Often they are dismayed by the prospect of having to move away from old friends and familiar neighborhoods. As a result, they end up among the ranks of the long-term and hard-core unemployed. This is a particular problem among older workers, unskilled workers in declining economic regions such as Appalachia, and many unskilled, mostly black, youths trapped in decaying inner cities and depressed rural areas. In general, *the basic characteristic of the structurally unemployed is their lack of marketable skills.*

CYCLICAL UNEMPLOYMENT

Cyclical unemployment is caused by the business cycle. When the economy's total demand for goods and services rises during the expansion phase of the cycle, employment rises and unemployment falls. During the recession phase of the cycle, total demand for goods and services falls, causing unemployment to rise and employment to fall. Cyclical unemployment looms large in the movement of the unemployment rate. The news item at the beginning of the chapter focuses on cyclical unemployment when it notes that "the unemployment rate is looking markedly better, having fallen from 7 percent to 6.4 percent over the last three months," and that "the stronger economy is further increasing demand for labor."

Normal Unemployment— or, What Is Full Employment?

It is clear from our discussion of frictional unemployment that full employment cannot mean that there is a zero rate of unemployment. *The general view among economists is that the existence of frictional unemployment and a certain amount of structural unemployment constitutes a normal level of unemployment.* Full employment is the level of employment associated with a normal level of unemployment. In the early 1960s economists generally felt that full employment roughly corresponded to a 4 percent unemployment rate—what might be called the normal unemployment rate. Since that time the level of the normal unemployment rate has been revised upward. In recent years a number of economists have come to think that it may be somewhat more than 5 percent. Why is this? Should we be concerned? How we measure unemployment, and the nature of the relationship between population growth and labor force growth, have a lot to do with the answers to these questions.

MEASURING UNEMPLOYMENT

The most commonly used definition of **unemployment** *states that to be considered unemployed you must be out of work, looking for a job, and available to take one immediately.*

Some think this definition is too broad because it doesn't distinguish between those who need jobs to support themselves and their families, and those who don't. Hence, critics say this measure overstates unemployment distress. They point out that a full-time student seeking part-time work, or a job-seeking teenager living at home with two working parents, counts just as much in this measure of unemployment as

does a jobless head of household out of work for weeks. However, others argue that this measure understates unemployment because it doesn't include "discouraged" workers who have dropped out of the labor force after a prolonged, unsuccessful search for a job, nor does it include part-time workers who are looking for a full-time job.

In fact, the U.S. Labor Department publishes six different measures of the unemployment rate, including the common definition which is the one policy makers and the news media tend to focus on. The narrowest measure counts only those out of work 15 weeks or longer as unemployed. The broadest measure counts all those included in the common measure, plus jobless people discouraged from looking for work and part-time workers seeking full-time jobs. The difference between the three measures is significant. For example, in the third quarter of 1977 the unemployment rate according to the narrowest measure was 1.9 percent, according to the common measure it was 7 percent, and by the broadest measure it was 9.7 percent.

POPULATION AND LABOR FORCE GROWTH

Longer-run changes in the size of the labor force relative to the size of the total population have implications for the unemployment rate and the percent of the working-age population employed. So do longer-run changes in the age and sex makeup of the labor force.

If the size of the total population grows faster than the size of the labor force, the number of people demanding goods and services will grow faster than the number of people who want jobs. Other things remaining the same, this should tend to lower the unemployment rate. On the other hand, if the size of the labor force grows more rapidly than the size of the total population, the number of people wanting jobs increases faster than the number demanding goods and services. This will tend to increase the unemployment rate, other things remaining the same.

Throughout the latter half of the 1960s and the 1970s, the U.S. economy has had to cope with a labor force that has grown faster than the total population. In part this has been due to maturing post–World War II "baby boom" that has swelled the growth of the working-age population during these years. In addition, the proportion of working-age women who have moved into the labor force has increased dramatically. While only about 33 percent of the country's population of adult females was in the labor force in the early years after World War II, about 50 percent now work or are seeking work. Despite this, the economy has done quite well providing jobs for these people. In the decade 1966–1976 total employment in the United States was up 21 percent while population was up 10 percent. In other words, total employment grew twice as fast as the total population. Job creation during the 1966–1976 decade has resulted in a growth in employment nearly double that of the decades 1947–1957 and 1956–1966. Employment increased 12.3 percent in 1947–1957, 14.3 percent in 1956–1966, and 21.2 percent in 1966–1976.

On the negative side, many economists feel that the more rapid rate of growth of the labor force relative to that of the total population has contributed to a rise in the level of what should be considered the normal unemployment rate (the rate that corresponds to so-called full employment). They believe that the unusually large increase in the number of new job seekers relative to the growth in the population pushes the level of frictional unemployment higher. As noted before, this is so because new entrants into the labor force are frequently unemployed for a brief period of time before finding a job, assuming they have marketable job skills. Another possible factor in a higher normal unemployment rate is the increased flow into the public's pockets of nonpaycheck money—unemployment compensation, welfare money, and so on. This may well cause people who are really not trying very hard to get employed to list themselves as unemployed.

What is the meaning of all this for our interpretation of the unemployment rate? It is often assumed that an economy with an unemployment rate of 3 percent is healthier than one with an unemployment rate of 6 percent. Is this necessarily so? In early 1953 the U.S. unemployment rate was only 2.5 percent while the per-

cent of the working-age population (everyone over 16) employed was about 55 percent. In December 1977 the unemployment rate was 6.4 percent, but the percent of the working-age population employed was 58 percent. When the percent of the working-age population employed is considered along with the unemployment rate, the difference in the health of our economy (at least from the standpoint of jobs) between these two periods does not appear as great as when we compare the unemployment rates alone. Some economists say that an undue emphasis on the unemployment rate, at the expense of attention to the percent employed among the working-age population, may place the economy's health in an excessively gloomy light. This may cause government policy makers to try to solve the problem by following excessively stimulative monetary and fiscal policies that cause inflationary pressures. However, others feel that a sound economy should be able to supply work to people seeking it, and therefore that the government should focus on the unemployment rate.

The Costs of Unemployment

Labor is an essential factor of production in our economy. Consequently, the greater the total demand for goods and services, the greater the total demand for labor needed to produce them. The greater the total demand for labor, the higher the level of employment and the lower the level of unemployment, given the available labor supply. Recall from Chapter 2 that unemployment exists whenever any available factors of production are idle. The term available is important. *Unemployment exists among laborers whenever there are laborers who make themselves available for work by actively looking for a job, but are unable to find one.* For society as a whole, unemployment means fewer goods and services are produced, and a smaller pie means there is less available for all. This is the economic cost of unemployment. As a matter of public policy, unemployment is of particular concern because it also represents hardship for those unemployed. How might we measure these costs and hardships?

ECONOMIC COST: THE GNP GAP

How can we measure the economic cost of unemployment to society? First we might estimate the economy's **potential GNP**, or what GNP would be if the economy were "fully" employed. We would then subtract actual GNP from potential GNP to get the GNP gap. *The* **GNP gap** *is the dollar value of final goods and services not produced because there is unemployment. The GNP gap is therefore a measure of the cost of unemployment.*

Government economists have attempted to measure the GNP gap. Their measure (in constant 1972 dollars) of potential GNP and the associated GNP gap, equal to the difference between potential and actual GNP, is shown in Figure 6-4, part b. Immediately below, the unemployment rate is shown in Figure 6-4, part c. We can see by comparing the two graphs how the GNP gap widens when the unemployment rate rises, and narrows when the unemployment rate falls. Indeed during 1952 and 1953 (the Korean War years), and from 1966 through 1969 (the Vietnam War years), the unemployment rate was at its lowest levels and actual GNP exceeded potential GNP (the GNP gap was negative). This reflects the fact that the potential GNP does not represent the *maximum* GNP the economy can produce, but rather that which it can produce at what is considered the normal level of unemployment. At the normal level of unemployment, the economy is considered to be operating at full employment. When the economy produces above its potential level, productive facilities are being utilized beyond their most efficient capacity levels and there is much overtime employment. The unemployment rate is squeezed below what is considered its normal level.

The GNP gap for the years in which the economy operated below its potential is indicated by the shaded areas in Figure 6-4, part b. These areas represent the economic costs of unemployment, measured in constant 1972 dollars. For 1954 these costs amounted to $16 billion. For the years through 1964 the cumulative GNP gap amounted to $237 billion. From 1970 through 1972 it amounted to $83.9 billion, and from 1974 through 1976 it amounted to $281.5

billion. The large costs of the latter years reflect the deepest recession and highest unemployment rates of the postwar years.

OTHER COSTS
OF UNEMPLOYMENT

The burden of unemployment is obviously more severe if you happen to be one of the unemployed than if you are not. And different groups in the labor force tend to have a higher incidence of unemployment than others. For example in 1975, when our economy experienced its highest rate of unemployment since World War II, the overall unemployment rate for the civilian labor force was 8.5 percent. Yet among whites the unemployment rate was 7.8 percent, while among blacks it was 13.9 percent. For blue-collar workers it was 11.7 percent, but for white-collar workers it was only 4.7 percent. Among teenagers, the newest entrants to the labor force, it was a whopping 19.9 percent.

Aside from those aspects of unemployment which can be quantified, there is a social pathology associated with unemployment that is more difficult to measure. The unemployed worker often suffers a loss of self-esteem. Medical researchers have reported findings that suggest that anxiety among unemployed workers leads to health problems and family squabbles. Severely prolonged unemployment among family breadwinners often leads to broken homes and desertion. History suggests that high unemployment rates tend to spawn political and social unrest, and that more than one social order has been upset for want of jobs. The high unemployment rates among black teenagers in our cities has had a lot to do with the sense of hopelessness, desperation, and anger that leads to high crime rates in city streets, and occasionally to the looting and burning of whole neighborhoods.

■ CHECKPOINT 6-3

In the news item at the beginning of this chapter, how does Mr. Jordan acknowledge a relationship between the employment rate and the unemployment rate? Comparing

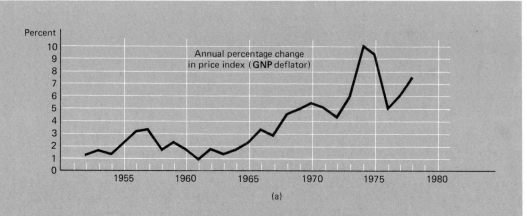

(a)

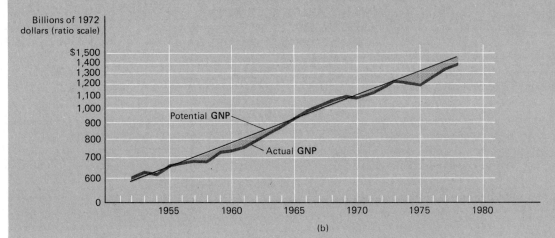

(b)

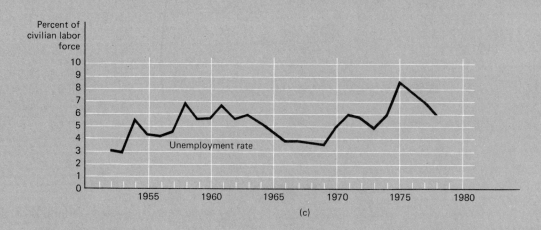

(c)

FIGURE 6-4 THE GNP GAP, THE UNEMPLOYMENT RATE, AND THE CHANGING GENERAL PRICE LEVEL SINCE 1952

Potential GNP is the estimated total dollar amount of final goods and services the economy could produce in a given year if it operated at full employment, the level of employment associated with a normal level of unemployment. The difference between potential and actual GNP since 1952 is the GNP gap shown in part b, expressed in constant 1972 dollars. This gap is a measure of the dollar value of final goods and services not produced because there is unemployment. In this sense it is a measure of the cost of unemployment.

The unemployment rate since 1952 is shown in part c. Comparison of the behavior of the unemployment rate with that of the GNP gap indicates how the unemployment rate rises when the GNP gap widens, and falls when the GNP gap narrows. During 1952 and 1953, the Korean War years, and from 1966 through 1969, the Vietnam War years, the unemployment rate was at its lowest levels and actual GNP exceeded potential GNP (the GNP gap was negative). This reflects the fact that the potential GNP does not represent the maximum GNP the economy can produce, but that which it can produce at some normal level of unemployment.

The annual percentage change of the general price level (the GNP deflator) in the United States is shown in part a for the years since 1952. Up through 1971 the percentage rise in the general price level tended to be larger when the GNP gap narrowed and the unemployment rate fell, and smaller when the GNP gap widened and the unemployment rate rose. By contrast there was a dramatic jump in the percentage rise in the general price level in 1973, 1974, and 1975, accompanied by an unprecedented widening in the GNP gap.

parts b and c of Figure 6–4, what appears to be the level of the normal unemployment rate on which the estimate of potential GNP, the full employment level of GNP, is based?

PRICE CHANGE AND INFLATION

The burden of unemployment falls most heavily and obviously on those who are unemployed. Inflation, while often more subtle, affects virtually everybody. This happens because **inflation** *is a pervasive rise in the general level of prices of all goods and services. Inflation, therefore, reduces the purchasing power of money.* The term inflation is not used when the prices of just a few goods rise. Rather, inflation refers to a situation in which the average of all prices rises. (Deflation is just the opposite of inflation—the average of all prices falls during a deflation.) When we discussed the difference between money GNP and real GNP in the previous chapter, we saw that inflation means that a dollar will purchase fewer goods tomorrow than it does today.

Recent Experience with Inflation

The annual percentage change in a measure of the general price level (the GNP deflator) for the years since 1952 is shown in Figure 6-4, part a. Note that the general price level has gone up, though at different rates, in virtually every year over this period.

It is interesting to compare the size of these percentage increases with the changes in the size of the GNP gap, Figure 6-4, part b, and the unemployment rate, Figure 6-4, part c. Roughly speaking, up through 1971 the percentage rise in the general price level tended to be smaller when the GNP gap widened and the unemployment rate rose—when the economy had more excess capacity. This has long been regarded as the conventional pattern in the relationship between inflation, the GNP gap, and the unemployment rate.

Since 1971 these comparisons reveal a considerably different pattern, however. Most notable is the dramatic jump in the percentage rise in the general price level in 1973, 1974, and 1975. This was accompanied by an unprecedented degree of widening in the GNP gap. In other words the economy experienced its most severe period of inflation during its deepest recession in the postwar period! This unconventional combination of events has given rise to the term stagflation, which means the occurrence of economic stagnation combined with high rates of inflation. In subsequent chapters we will examine explanations of the conventional pattern of the relationship between inflation and unemployment, as well as explanations of the more recent pattern known as stagflation.

Anticipated Versus Unanticipated Inflation

Inflation is sometimes said to be the most effective, continuously operating thief. It steals the purchasing power of your money whether you hold it in your hand, your wallet, your checking account, or even in the vault of a bank. Nothing stops it. People have an incentive to protect themselves from inflation just as they have an incentive to protect themselves from theft of any kind. And they will attempt to do so if they anticipate or expect inflation. It is when they fail to anticipate inflation that they are most often hurt by it.

ANTICIPATED INFLATION AND CONTRACTS

The terms of a great many economic transactions are stated in dollars and are spelled out in a contract to which all parties to the transaction agree. Labor unions and management agree to a labor contract stipulating the hourly wage rate to be paid, along with other conditions of employment—length of work week, amount of paid vacation, and so on. Loan contracts set out the terms of the loan mutually agreed to by borrowers and lenders. These terms include the amount of the loan, the interest rate to be paid by the borrower, and the rights of each party in the event of default. Pension plans, insurance policies, rent leases, construction contracts, and contracts to produce and deliver goods to a customer by a certain date at a certain price are all examples of such contracts.

When one or both parties anticipate inflation, they will attempt to account for it explicitly in the terms of the contract. If it is a labor contract and the union anticipates inflation, it may press to have a cost-of-living clause in the contract. Such a clause might stipulate that if the general price level rises by x percent then the hourly wage rate must be increased by x percent as well. Suppose the union fails to anticipate inflation and agrees to a $5 per hour money wage rate over the next two years. The onset of a 10 percent rate of inflation would mean that the real, or constant dollar, wage would fall to $4.50 by the end of the first year. In other words, the money wage of $5 would only have 90 percent of the purchasing power it did at the beginning of the contract. At the end of two years the money wage of $5 would only have roughly 81 percent of its original purchasing power. If the union had insisted on a cost-of-living clause in the contract, the money wage at the end of the first year would be $5.50. At the end of the second year it would be roughly $6.05. The real wage would then remain $5—5 constant dollars.

In sum, *it is not only money (cash and checking accounts) that is robbed of purchasing power by inflation, but any contract that is stated in terms of dollars. If the inflation is anticipated, the terms of the contract can be set to protect its real value from the erosion of inflation.*

GAINERS AND LOSERS FROM UNANTICIPATED INFLATION

We can see that if inflation is correctly anticipated people can try to take steps to protect themselves against it. Unfortunately, the world is an uncertain place. What is anticipated is often different from what occurs. *The amount of inflation that occurs that is unexpected is* **unanticipated inflation**. *Whenever there is unanticipated inflation, there are both gainers and losers.* Who are they?

1. *Creditors versus debtors.* Suppose A, the creditor or lender, lends $100 to B, the debtor or borrower, at a 10 percent rate of interest for one year. We will assume that A entered into this loan agreement anticipating that there would be no inflation over the year. This means that A,

the creditor, was induced to lend $100 of purchasing power by the prospect of getting back $110 of purchasing power one year from now. Conversely, B, the debtor, is willing to agree to pay A $110 of purchasing power one year from now in order to get $100 of purchasing power today.

Suppose that over the course of the year there actually is a 20 percent rise in the general price level—a 20 percent rate of inflation—that was completely unanticipated by A. Now when B pays $110 at the end of the year, as stipulated by the loan agreement, this $110 has only about 90 percent of the purchasing power of the original $100 that A lent B. The 20 percent rate of inflation more than offsets the 10 percent rate of interest on the loan. As it turns out, A has given up more purchasing power than A actually gets back. Due to unanticipated inflation, A has suffered a loss. B, on the other hand, ends up paying back less purchasing power than was originally received. Because of unanticipated inflation, B has gained. B's gain in purchasing power is just equal to A's loss. A would never have entered into the loan agreement with B had A known that this was going to be the outcome. B in effect has ended up getting a loan on much more favorable terms than would have been possible had A correctly anticipated the inflation.

Whenever there is unanticipated inflation, there is a redistribution of wealth from creditors to debtors that would not occur if the inflation had been anticipated.

2. *Fixed-income groups.* We have noted how a labor union anticipating inflation would like to get a cost-of-living clause in its union contract. Indeed all those anticipating inflation would want to ensure that their real income would not be reduced by inflation. For example, many retired people have found that their pension plans do not have a provision for this. The dollar incomes they receive do not rise with inflation and their real incomes therefore fall. The same thing can happen to any group in our economy that fails to anticipate inflation, or fails to anticipate it sufficiently. People with fixed-dollar incomes lose ground relative to those whose dollar incomes rise right along with any increase in the general price level. The fixed-dollar income group's claim on a share of the economy's total pie falls relative to those whose dollar incomes keep pace with inflation.

3. *Fixed-dollar versus variable-dollar assets.* We have seen that if you lend out money (enter into a loan contract) but fail to anticipate a rise in the general price level, you can end up getting back a smaller amount of purchasing power than you initially bargained for. There are a number of assets that have fixed-dollar values which give them this property.

If you put $100 into a savings account at your local bank, you can subsequently withdraw the $100 plus the initially stipulated rate of interest at any time. If in the meantime there is an unanticipated rate of inflation, you will not get back the amount of purchasing power you had counted on. There are several kinds of **fixed-dollar assets**—money, bonds, bank loans to businesses and consumers, and in general *any kind of asset that guarantees a repayment of the initial dollar amount invested plus some stipulated rate of interest* (zero in the case of money). Parties who make these kinds of investments, without anticipating inflation, end up recovering an amount of purchasing power less than they had bargained for.

On the other hand, there are many assets, **variable-dollar assets**, that *do not guarantee the owner any fixed-dollar value that may be recovered.* Such assets are also frequently called real assets. If you buy a piece of land you can get rid of it any time, but only at what you can sell it for. The same is true of a share of stock in a corporation (an indirect ownership of a real asset), a painting, an automobile, a house, or an antique. When there is an inflation, these assets can frequently (but not always) be sold at prices that are higher than their original purchase price by an amount that reflects the increase in the general price level. People owning these kinds of assets do not necessarily lose purchasing power as do those holding fixed-dollar assets such as money, savings accounts, and bonds. Consequently *an unanticipated inflation will result in a loss of wealth on holdings of fixed-dollar* *assets, and often little or no loss of wealth on variable-dollar assets.* Fixed-dollar asset holders may thus lose relative to variable-dollar asset holders. Since many people own some of each kind, whether they are net gainers or losers will depend largely on the relative proportions of their total assets they hold in each.

UNANTICIPATED INFLATION AND UNCERTAINTY

It is often argued that inflation isn't necessarily bad provided that it occurs at a constant rate that everyone comes to anticipate. Then all parties can make their plans and enter into economic transactions on terms that fully take account of the inflation. There will be no gainers and losers, no unplanned redistributions of income and wealth such as occur when there is unanticipated inflation.

When there is uncertainty about what the rate of inflation may be, fear of the consequences of unanticipated inflation make it harder for businesses and consumers to make plans. This puts a damper on the economy's ability to operate at a full-employment level—to close the GNP gap. Therefore, one of the major goals of economic policy is price stability.

In sum, *price stability is one of the major goals of economic policy because: (1) it is necessary in order to avoid the arbitrary redistribution of wealth that results from unanticipated inflation; (2) by reducing uncertainty about inflation it enhances the economy's ability to operate at its full-employment potential.*

▪ CHECKPOINT 6-4

Deflation is the opposite of inflation. Explain how an unanticipated deflation would affect the distribution of wealth between creditors and debtors, and between fixed income groups and nonfixed income groups. If inflation "steals" money, what does deflation do? When you look at parts a and b of Figure 6-4 for the years 1972–1976, can you think of a possible reason for the severity of the 1973–1974 recession based on inflationary considerations?

WHERE DO WE GO FROM HERE?

We noted at the outset that the business cycle, unemployment, and inflation are all more or less interrelated problems. In the following chapters, we will examine how modern economics attempts to analyze their causes. This will require that we become more familiar with the institutional structure of the economy as well as with some tools of economic analysis. Ultimately, we want to grapple with the following sorts of issues: Can monetary and fiscal policy effectively put a damper on business fluctuations? Is there a trade-off between inflation and unemployment? (That is, can we reduce the amount of one of them only if we are willing to have more of the other?) Why is it in recent years that our economy has been plagued with recessions, and their accompanying high unemployment, while suffering from inflation at the same time—the so-called problem of stagflation (the simultaneous existence of stagnation and inflation)?

SUMMARY

1. The economy grows through time but exhibits fluctuations around its growth trend called business cycles. The four phases of the business cycle—recession, trough, expansion, peak—may vary considerably in magnitude and duration from one cycle to the next, and no two cycles are ever exactly alike.

2. The business cycle affects different industries and segments of the economy in varying degrees. Durable goods industries tend to experience larger fluctuations than nondurable goods industries. These are usually industries with a few large, dominant (monopoly-type) firms which tend to have larger fluctuations in output and employment than in product price. Industries with many small competitive firms tend to show larger fluctuations in product price than in output and employment—typically these are nondurable goods industries. The accelerator principle provides an insight as to why investment is one of the most volatile expenditure components of GNP.

3. While many determinants of the business cycle reflect the internal structure of the

economy, others are considered exogenous (external). The distinction is not always clear-cut, however.

4. Three basic types of unemployment may be identified: frictional, structural, and cyclical. There are several measures of unemployment along with considerable controversy over which is the most appropriate one. There is reason to believe that the economy's so-called normal level of unemployment has risen since World War II.

5. The greater the economy's total demand for goods and services, the greater the total demand for labor needed to produce them. As a result, the level of employment is higher and the level of unemployment is lower. One measure of the cost of unemployment is the GNP gap, the dollar value of the goods and services not produced when there is idle labor. Though often hard to measure, there are also psychological and social costs associated with unemployment. Moreover, the burden of unemployment is quite unevenly distributed among different groups in our economy.

6. Inflation is a rise in the general level of prices of all goods and services. Inflation reduces the purchasing power of money. The effects of anticipated inflation will be accounted for in the terms of economic contracts of all kinds.

7. Unanticipated inflation will result in a loss of purchasing power (wealth and income) among creditors, fixed-dollar income groups, and fixed-dollar asset holders. It results in an arbitrary redistribution of income and wealth. Uncertainty about inflation breeds a fear of these consequences of unanticipated inflation, and this inhibits the economy's ability to perform at its full-employment potential. For these reasons price stability is a major goal of economic policy.

KEY TERMS AND CONCEPTS

accelerator principle
business cycles
depression
expansion
fixed-dollar assets
GNP gap
inflation
labor force
peak
potential GNP
recession
seasonal variation
trough
unanticipated inflation
unemployment
variable-dollar asset

QUESTIONS AND PROBLEMS

1. Can you think of reasons why the average length of business cycle expansions should be longer than the average length of recessions, as indicated in Table 6-1?

2. Do you think that the effect of the accelerator principle on investment expenditures is the same during the expansion phase of the business cycle as during the recession phase? Why or why not?

3. How do you think changes in the size of the armed forces affect potential GNP? How do you think the failure to take account of this manifests itself in Figure 6-4, part b?

4. Think of yourself as an interviewer in an unemployment office. As a practical matter, how would you distinguish the frictionally unemployed from the cyclically unemployed from the structurally unemployed?

5. Since the early 1960s the growth rate of the total population has been considerably lower than it was during the 1950s and late 1940s—the years of the so-called baby boom. Assuming that the population growth rate remains constant at its present lower level, what are the implications for unemployment in the early part of the twenty-first century?

6. In the event of an unanticipated inflation, which of the following assets would you prefer to own: a stamp collection, savings bonds, cash, a collection of old English coins, common stock, a fast-food restaurant, a contract to deliver towels and linen to a hotel chain, a deposit in a savings and loan bank, a mortgage on your neighbor's house?

7. How does inflation affect fixed-dollar income groups? What does it do to their share of real GNP?

■ NEWS ITEM FOR YOUR ANALYSIS ■

BENEFICIAL RIPPLES OF 1977 HOUSING
BOOM ARE EXPECTED TO LAST WELL INTO NEW YEAR

WASHINGTON, January 17—Many businesses benefit substantially from new housing starts. But it is completions, not starts, that make the payoff for companies providing home furnishings and other finishing touches. Ethan Allen, Inc., of Danbury, Conn., forecasts a 10 percent-plus surge in furniture sales this year, despite the fact that housing starts may weaken a little.

While housing starts are expected to dip to about 1.8 million this year from nearly 2 million last year, the National Association of Home Builders estimates that completions of privately owned homes will climb to 1,638,000 from 1,623,000. In addition, the impact of many completions during last year's housing boom will carry over to this year. "The impact of a housing start spreads way beyond just the construction of the house itself," says Michael Sumichrast, chief economist for the home builder's association. "It takes a year before the impact is felt by many industries, but it goes like a snowball and picks up velocity."

This snowball picks up an array of companies ranging from furniture and appliance businesses to makers of locks, lighting fixtures and bathroom hardware. But the economic ripples from housing completions spread beyond home accessories. New housing developments breed shopping centers, playgrounds, and other community facilities, so suppliers of products like cash registers and seesaws also benefit. Carrier Corp. of Syracuse, New York, figures the new shopping centers will need Carrier's commercial air-conditioning equipment if they intend to draw customers in July.

Some industry observers pay closer attention to broad economic trends than to housing completions because home-furnishing purchases are so postponable. "Frankly I think housing is overrated as a variable in furniture sales," says Michael Sherman, director of economic and market research for the National Association of Manufacturers. "I place more emphasis on disposable income than housing starts." Similarly, new residential construction doesn't make or break the carpet industry; its business consists largely of replacement sales, according to Frank E. Masland III, president of the Carpet and Rug Institute, a trade group.

On the other hand, flooring, basic appliances, and locks are essential, and makers of such goods say they can count on sales as soon as a house is occupied. A Shreveport, Louisiana, mailbox maker attributes 60 percent of his sales to new housing, since mailboxes don't wear out with any great regularity.

New homes aren't the only factor in the bullish outlook for the home-furnishings industry. Several older homes change hands when one new house is built. One economist says the market for household products created by older home sales "must be at least double that created by new-home building."

QUESTIONS

1. Draw a diagram which measures time on the horizontal axis and dollars on the vertical axis. Sketch in a hypothetical cycle of construction expenditure on new housing.

a. In the same diagram sketch in where you think the associated cycle in expenditures on furniture and household appliances would go.

b. Again, in the same diagram, sketch in the associated cycle for expenditure on community facilities such as schools and playgrounds.

c. In what sense are there "economic ripples," as the news item suggests?

2. Expenditures on some of the products mentioned are postponable. Others are more subject to the operation of the accelerator principle—they are of necessity quite closely tied to expenditures on housing construction. While the distinction is not always clear-cut, which products do you think are more subject to the operation of the accelerator principle?

3. Think of the chain of houses that might be sold as the result of the purchase of one new house. Assume each of these houses sells for the same price. Is the resulting contribution to GNP equal to the number of these houses times this price, some portion of this, or what? Why? How will this affect the household moving business?

4. Suppose an unanticipated inflation besets the economy. How will this affect the distribution of income and wealth as between renters and landlords?

5. Suppose there was no inflation and suddenly people came to anticipate one. What effect do you think this would have on the level of residential construction? What chain of events would this set in motion?

7

BUILDING BLOCKS OF INCOME AND EMPLOYMENT THEORY: CONSUMPTION, SAVING, AND INVESTMENT

EYEING THE CONSUMER

NEW YORK, Sept. 13—For nearly a year the current economic expansion was carried on the back of the consumer, alone and unaided. Then businesses became convinced that the expansion was real and started adding to inventories instead of reducing them. More recently companies have stepped up spending on new plants and equipment. In the meantime consumer spending has slowed rather dramatically, and that's not good news for the expansion. After all, personal consumption expenditures account for more than 60 percent of the nation's GNP. Moreover, if the consumer really is opting out, businesses will have second thoughts about inventory and capital spending.

What is wrong with the consumer? "The consumer is certainly unhappy about something," says Michael K. Evans, president of Chase Econometric Associates. "Personal income continues to grow handsomely, credit conditions remain unusually easy, and the consumer price index rose at only a 4.4 percent annual rate during the first half of the year. Yet retail sales from March to July declined even in current-dollar terms."

Perhaps the consumer is worried about the recent rise in the unemployment rate, even though it seems this was due to an unusual summer increase in the size of the labor force. In fact, the basic job situation has improved and total employment continues to increase.

Mr. Evans thinks consumer spending will pick up this month, or next, as income continues to rise faster than inflation. However, one thesis that most analysts accept is that consumers now are much more price sensitive than they were a few years ago. Inflation has lasted so long and been so severe that consumers now equate it with bad times.

Finally, this is an election year. Jay Schniedeskamp, director of the University of Michigan's survey of consumer sentiment, notes that in the past consumers have tended to turn more hopeful in election years. This tendency may be based to some extent on the habit that incumbent presidents have of stimulating the economy in an election year.

In Chapter 5 we saw how we keep tabs on the economy's performance by the use of national income accounting. Chapter 6 introduced some of the characteristics of that performance, along with two problem areas of major concern—unemployment and inflation. However, in order to grasp more fully the implications of a news item such as the one that opens this chapter, or to better understand aggregate economic activity in general, we need to become familiar with the building blocks of modern income and employment theory.

Our journey begins in this chapter. First off we will examine why many economists from the time of Adam Smith up through the 1930s believed that capitalistic, market-oriented economies naturally tended to operate at full employment. By examining their reasoning, we will be better able to understand why and how the Great Depression of the 1930s forced a major rethinking on this issue. This rethinking gave rise to the major building blocks of modern income and employment theory that we will examine in this chapter. In Chapter 8 we will see how these may be used to determine an equilibrium level of output and employment—levels that do not necessarily correspond to full employment. Government expenditure and tax effects will be introduced into this framework in Chapter 9, but not until then. At that point we will examine the rationale for using fiscal policy (government's management of its spending and taxing authority) to ensure that the economy achieves its full-employment output level.

THE CLASSICAL VIEW OF INCOME AND EMPLOYMENT

Why was it that so many economists subscribed to the notion that capitalistic, market-oriented economies naturally tended to operate at full-employment output levels? Occasional bouts of unemployment were explained away as the result of some unusual event such as a war, crop losses due to bad weather, or some other interference with the self-regulating, free-working forces of the marketplace. But as long as prices are free to adjust to clear markets (to equate supply and demand), it was considered illogical to think that the economy would not operate at full employment. The classical economist's faith in this point of view was based on Say's Law,[1] an appealing, yet deceptive argument.

Say's Law

Simply put, **Say's Law** *states that supply creates its own demand.* According to Say's Law, people only work to produce and supply goods and services because they want to acquire the income to buy goods and services. Therefore, supply creates its own demand. People work to produce and sell the dollar amount of goods and services that is just equal to the dollar amount of goods and services they want to buy. Full employment corresponds to the production of this dollar amount of goods and services. A level of total dollar spending insufficient to purchase the full-employment output of goods and services would be a logical contradiction. According to Say's Law it wasn't possible because the total income earned from the production of the economy's total full-employment output would be spent to purchase that output. There might be occasional unemployment, but only because of some unusual event that temporarily interferes with the self-regulating, free-working forces of the marketplace.

Classical economists subscribed to two funda-

[1] Initially put forth by the French economist Jean Baptiste Say (1767–1832).

mental assumptions about how the economy worked—two assumptions essential to a belief in Say's Law. First, prices and wages always adjust quickly to clear markets. Second, the interest rate always adjusts to equate saving and investment.

PRICES AND WAGES
ADJUST TO CLEAR MARKETS

The classical economists argued that if the economy's total demand for goods and services declined, flexible prices and wages would quickly adjust downward until the total quantity of goods and services demanded was once again restored to the initial full-employment total output level. Let's examine their argument in more detail.

A typical product market in the economy is shown in Figure 7-1. This could be the market for wheat or shoes or dresses or you name it. The economy is composed of many such product markets. Our discussion of the one shown in Figure 7-1 applies to each of them. Suppose that when the economy is operating at full employment (part a), the equilibrium price and quantity in the typical product market are p_1 and Q_0 respectively, as determined by the intersection of the product market demand curve D and supply curve S. A decline in the economy's total demand would be reflected in leftward shifts in the demand curves in each of the economy's many product markets. In the typical product market, suppose the demand curve shifts to the position D_a, as shown in part b. As long as price is flexible, the price in this market will fall to p_2, corresponding to the intersection of D_a and S. This occurs because competing

firms in this market will lower their prices to get rid of surpluses resulting from falling demand. Output will fall from Q_0 to Q_j. Similar shifts and adjustments occur in each of the economy's other product markets.

The adjustment cannot stop here, however. It is not only product prices that must fall. The wages firms pay labor and the prices they pay for inputs must fall as well. Indeed, at this stage of the adjustment, it is precisely the fact that product prices have fallen and wages and input prices have not that makes firms reduce output. Caught between the squeeze of falling product prices and the as yet unchanged level of wages and input prices, firms cannot afford to buy as many inputs, hire as much labor, and produce as much output as before the fall in demand. Unless wages and input prices fall, firms will continue to produce at reduced output levels, buy smaller quantities of inputs, and employ less labor. In particular, there will now be **involuntary unemployment**. Laborers who were previously employed will now be out of work despite the fact that they are willing to work at the as yet unchanged wage rates. Along with this, the fall in output in each product market means that the economy's total output is also less.

However, classical economists argued that at worst this would be a quickly passing stage in the adjustment process. Unemployed laborers would offer their services at lower wage rates, competing with each other as well as with employed workers for the available supply of jobs. Because the firms' demand curve for labor is downward sloping, firms will hire more and more workers as wages are bid down in this process. Similarly, suppliers of all other inputs will

---

After reading this chapter, you will be able to:

1. State the reasons why classical economists thought a capitalistic, laissez faire economy would automatically tend to operate at a full-employment equilibrium.
2. Evaluate critically the classical argument and understand why the economy might not achieve a full-employment equilibrium.
3. Explain the concepts of the consumption function and the saving function, and the determinants of consumption and saving.
4. Explain the nature of investment expenditures and their determinants.

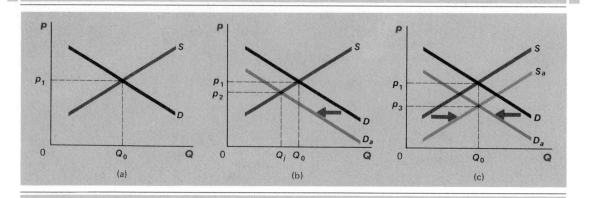

FIGURE 7-1 THE CLASSICAL VIEW OF HOW PRODUCT MARKETS ADJUST WHEN WAGES AND PRICES ARE FLEXIBLE

Equilibrium in a typical product market, of which there are many in the economy, is shown in part a. The intersection of the product demand curve D and the product supply curve S determines the equilibrium price p_1 and the equilibrium output Q_0 in this product market.

A fall in the economy's total demand is reflected in a leftward shift in product market demand curves throughout the economy. Such a shift is illustrated in part b, where the product demand curve D shifts leftward to the position D_a. The equilibrium price falls from p_1 to p_2 and the equilibrium output from Q_0 to Q_j. This also occurs in each of the other product markets in the economy. It reflects the fact that when product demand falls firms are caught in a squeeze between falling product price and the as yet unchanged wage rates and input prices. Consequently, they cut back output and reduce their employment of labor and the purchase of other inputs.

The idled laborers are involuntarily unemployed because they are willing to work at the as yet unchanged wage rates. They therefore compete for the available jobs by bidding down wages. Similarly, suppliers of inputs lower input prices to get rid of their mounting surpluses. The lowering of wages and input prices causes product market supply curves to shift rightward. This process continues until the initial output levels in product markets are restored and all available labor is once again fully employed. Now our typical product market appears as in part c, where the product market supply curve has shifted from S to the position S_a. The initial output Q_0 is restored, but at a lower equilibrium price p_3, determined by the intersection of D_a and S_a.

The economy is once again operating at its full-employment, total output level. Flexible wages and prices would always assure this result according to the classical economists.

compete with each other to get rid of their surpluses. Input prices will be bid down and firms will purchase more inputs—again because the firms' demand curve for inputs is also downward sloping.

These wage rates and input prices are costs to the firms in the product markets. Hence, as wage rates and input prices are bid down, product market supply curves will shift rightward. Classical economists argued that this process would continue until all available labor is once again employed. At this point product market supply curves will have shifted to the point at which equilibrium in each product market again occurs at the output level prevailing before the decrease in product demand.

This final stage of adjustment is illustrated in part c of Figure 7-1. Wage rates and input prices have finally fallen far enough to shift the product market supply curve to the position S_a.

The product price has fallen to p_3 and the quantity of the product produced and sold is once again Q_0, determined by the intersection of D_a and S_a. This adjustment occurs in every product market in the economy, so that each is again producing and selling the same quantity of output that prevailed before the initial decrease in each product demand curve. Therefore, the economy is once again producing the same level of total output that it did before the downward adjustment of all wages and prices.

SAVING AND THE
INCOME-EXPENDITURE FLOW

Our examination of the circular flow diagrams of the economy in Chapter 3, and our discussion in Chapter 5 of how GNP may be viewed either from the expenditure side or the income side, both indicated that:

$$\left.\begin{array}{l}\text{total expenditure}\\ \text{on final goods}\\ \text{and services}\end{array}\right\} = \left\{\begin{array}{l}\text{total income from}\\ \text{the production and}\\ \text{sale of final output}\end{array}\right.$$

For the purpose of simplifying our discussion of this relationship, we will assume there is no government expenditure or taxation. In addition, although we know that total saving is the sum of business saving and personal saving, we will assume that all saving is personal saving. Furthermore, we will assume that capital depreciation is zero. These assumptions mean that gross national product (GNP), net national product (NNP), national income (NI), personal income (PI), and disposable income (DI) are all the same. This is so because it is depreciation (capital consumption allowances), government taxes and transfer payments, and the different components of business saving that distinguish these national income accounting measures from one another.

Consideration of the total-expenditure-equals-total-income relationship immediately suggests a possible problem for a believer in Say's Law. While it is undeniably true that every dollar of expenditure on goods and services creates a dollar of income, it does not follow that the person receiving the income spends all of it. What happens when households save some of their income? Doesn't this mean that some-

thing is "leaking" out of the ongoing flow of total expenditures? And won't this mean that total dollar expenditures on goods and services, and hence total dollar output and income, will fall? And as long as there is a saving leakage from total dollar income, won't total dollar expenditure and total dollar output and income continue to get smaller and smaller? The answer to all of these questions is yes.

The continuing fall in total demand that results when households do not spend all their income means there will be increasing unemployment unless wages and prices fall. In fact, wages and prices would have to fall continually in order to maintain full employment and ensure that the economy's total physical output (as opposed to dollar output) doesn't fall. Even the firmest believer in Say's Law couldn't feel comfortable with the idea that the maintenance of full employment would require continually falling wages and prices—hardly a realistic state of affairs!

THE INTEREST RATE
EQUATES SAVING AND INVESTMENT

But classical economists had an answer to the problem posed by the saving leakage from the income-expenditure flow and the resulting deficiency in total demand. Investment expenditures by businesses would offset the saving by households (their refraining from spending) so there would be no fall in the ongoing level of total expenditure. After all, not all of the economy's income comes from the sale of goods and services to consumers. Some of it results from sales to businesses buying capital goods—investment expenditures. Therefore, if that part of total income which is saved is just matched by an equivalent amount of investment expenditure, there will be no decline in the economy's total expenditures, output, and total income. It might be said that the leakage from the income-expenditure flow that results from saving is offset by the injection of investment into that flow.

But how do we know that the amount of investment expenditures businesses intend to make—planned investment—will be equal to the amount of saving that households intend to do—planned saving? If the level of planned investment is always less than the level of planned saving, there will still be leakage from the income-expenditure flow. Consequently wages and prices will still have to fall continually in order to eliminate the deficiency in total demand and maintain the economy at its full-employment output level. Classical economists also had an answer for this potential problem—namely, the **interest rate**. They contended that in a capitalist economy the interest rate would always adjust—like the price in any other market—to ensure that total planned investment in the economy would equal total planned saving.

Why would a market adjustment in the interest rate be able to do this? Classical economists argued that businesses that want to buy new plant and equipment need to borrow funds to do so. If the interest rate is viewed as the price of borrowing, businesses will demand more borrowed funds for investment at low interest rates than at high rates. Therefore, the investment curve for the economy must slope downward (like any demand curve), as shown in Figure 7-2. On the other hand, classical economists argued that saving out of income involves a sacrifice by households—namely, the forgone consumption they could have enjoyed. Therefore, in order to induce households to save and lend dollars out of income, it is necessary to pay them an interest rate that will compensate them for their sacrifice. The more they save out of a given level of income, the greater is the sacrifice. Therefore, households will be induced to save more at high interest rates than at low rates. Hence, the saving curve for the economy—the supply of dollars available to be loaned out of total income—is upward sloping (like any supply curve), as shown in Figure 7-2.

The intersection of the saving and investment curves in Figure 7-2 corresponds to the equilibrium level of the interest rate, i_e. At i_e the demand for dollars for investment expenditures by businesses is just equal to the supply of dollars that households are willing to save out of income. As in any other market, if the price (interest rate) is above this level, the supply of dollars to loan (saving) exceeds the demand for dollars to invest (investment) and price will be bid down to i_e. Similarly, if the price (interest rate) is below this level, demand exceeds supply,

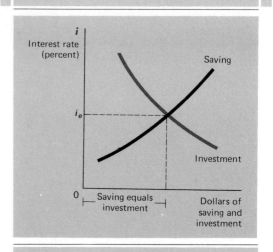

FIGURE 7-2 CLASSICAL ECONOMISTS ARGUED THAT THE INTEREST RATE WOULD MAKE SAVING AND INVESTMENT EQUAL

For businesses, the interest rate is the price of borrowing. Consequently, they will demand more borrowed funds for investment at low interest rates than at high rates. Thus the investment curve slopes downward.

Classical economists contended that saving out of income by households is a sacrifice in the form of forgone consumption. Therefore households can be induced to save more only by paying them a higher interest rate. Hence, the saving curve slopes upward.

The equilibrium interest rate, i_e, equates the quantity of dollars demanded for investment by businesses with the quantity of dollars households are willing to save. According to classical economists, this equality ensured that the economy would operate at full employment.

and price will be bid up to i_e. Because of this market adjustment of the interest rate, classical economists argued that the savings plans of households would always be equal to the investment plans of businesses.

Therefore, classical economists maintained that the economy would operate at its full-employment output level without the need for continually falling wages and prices. *Say's Law assumed that the unfettered forces of free markets and laissez faire capitalism would guarantee full*

ECONOMIC THINKERS

JEAN BAPTISTE SAY
1767-1832

Among other things, Say has the distinction of being the first person on the European continent to hold an academic appointment as professor of political economy.

For a period Say followed (quite successfully) a business career, but in 1816 he joined the faculty of the Conservatoire National Arts et Métiers, and from 1830 until his death, was a professor of political economy at the Collège de France. Say became acquainted with the work of Adam Smith, thought very highly of it, and translated it into French.

While Say admired Smith's work and is regarded as the principal interpreter of Smith's ideas on the continent, he was troubled by Smith's lack of logical organization. His efforts to improve it resulted in the publication of his own book, *A Treatise on Political Economy*, in 1803. This work went through many editions, was published in numerous languages, and found one of its most lucrative markets in the United States where it was used for decades as a standard text in such economics courses as existed.

Say much improved and systematized Smith's work and though known mainly as an interpreter and systematizer, he is due some credit in his own right. Say regarded economics as a positive science and was to some degree a bridge between the classical economists and the early mathematical economists.

Say pushed the cost of production theory of value into the background and adopted a psychological value theory based on human wants as the origin of value. Following this lead, he deduced further the fact that the value of the means of production stems from the value of the end product to which each contributes. Since the prices of all factors depend on

the prices of their products, in the final analysis, factor prices depend upon consumer demand.

Perhaps his most durable contribution was what has come to be known as Say's Law of Markets. Say held that overproduction was impossible since no one produced goods except to sell them and in doing so automatically created markets for other products.

It is worthwhile to remark that a product is no sooner created than it, from that instant, affords a market for other products to the full extent of its own value. When the producer has put the finishing hand to his product, he is most anxious to sell it immediately, lest its value should vanish in his hands. Nor is he less anxious to dispose of the money he may get for it; for the value of money is also perishable. But the only way of getting rid of money is in the purchase of some product or other. Thus, the mere circumstances of one product immediately opens a vent for other products.

---

employment with price stability. If there were disturbances that caused investment or saving curves to shift, or shifts in demand and supply curves in any other market, adjustments in wages, prices, and the interest rate would always return the economy to a position of full-employment equilibrium.

■ CHECKPOINT 7-1

Suppose the economy is operating at full-employment equilibrium. Assume the classical economists' point of view that wages and prices are perfectly flexible. Describe the adjustment process that would occur in product markets in response to an increase in the economy's total demand. When equilibrium is once again restored, will wages and prices be higher, lower, or unchanged? Suppose the economy is operating at full employment equilibrium and that we take account of the role of saving and investment as envisioned by the classical economists. Suppose the

investment curve in Figure 7–2 shifts leftward, but that for some reason the interest rate cannot fall below the level i_e. Will wages and prices rise, fall, or stay the same? Explain your answer.

THE GREAT DEPRESSION AND THE KEYNESIAN REVOLUTION

The Great Depression of the 1930s shook the faith in the inevitability of full employment to its very foundations. Classical economists had always acknowledged that capitalistic, market-oriented economies would experience occasional, temporary bouts of unemployment. These might be caused by rapid shifts in the composition of demand, or by such things as wars, crop failures, and other events that require rapid adjustments in the economy's markets. However, classical economists had always felt somewhat more uncomfortable about the problem of recurring, sometimes embarrassingly long, periods of unemployment associated with the business cycle. It has been said that a small problem often endures because it is never disturbing enough to demand an explanation. Such seems to have been the case with the classical economists' shaky explanation for unemployment. But then came the 1930s. The small problem grew up. A prolonged depression—the Great Depression—gripped the capitalist, market-oriented economies of the world. The gap between theory and fact was now too great to ignore.

In the United States alone, the unemployment rate was never lower than 14.3 percent in the years from 1931 through 1940. Indeed, from 1932 through 1935, it hovered between 20 and 25 percent. In almost any city, long lines of unemployed workers could be seen seeking a free meal or some sort of assistance for their impoverished families. Somehow it all seemed like a paradox. Why was it that able-bodied workers, who wanted nothing so much as a job in order to buy badly needed food and other goods, could not find work producing these products? Wouldn't the income they would earn give rise to the demand that would justify the production that would give them employment? Couldn't failing businesses see the connection between the lack of customers at the front door and the long line of unemployed workers seeking jobs at the back door? How could this situation go on for so long? These riddles led to a growing fear. Had Karl Marx been right all along—would capitalism fall by its own weight? What was the matter?

Many economists of the day, schooled in the classical tradition, argued that the problem lay in a number of markets where wages and prices were "sticky." They contended that in some product markets large monopoly-type firms were not willing to lower product prices as rapidly as was necessary in the face of declining product demand. Similarly, they argued that many unemployed workers were too reluctant to accept lower, or low enough, wages to gain employment. Hence, these economists concluded that classical wage and price flexibility was not allowed to work to bring the economy back to a full-employment equilibrium. Some of these same economists, and others as well, also argued that government interference in banking and financial markets was keeping the interest rate from adjusting properly to equate saving and investment plans.

Meanwhile in England, a group of Cambridge University economists led by John Maynard Keynes thought the problem required an explanation that went beyond the bounds of the classical framework. In 1936 Keynes published his analysis—*The General Theory of Employment, Interest, and Money*—a book about as readable as the Bhagavad Gita in the original Sanskrit. Keynes argued that the inevitability of full-employment equilibrium was an unlikely proposition at best, and simply wrong in general. His assault on the classical economists' arguments in support of Say's Law was telling. The analytical framework he erected in its place provided the basic building blocks of modern income and employment theory. The impact of Keynes's general theory so drastically changed economic thinking about the way income and employment are determined that it is often referred to as the Keynesian revolution. Few books, perhaps none, since the publication of Adam Smith's *Wealth of Nations* (1776) have had such a profound effect on economic theory and policy as Keynes's *General Theory*.

In order better to understand what motivated Keynes and subsequent economists to develop the basic tools of modern income and employment theory, we should briefly examine some of the pitfalls in the classical economists' line of reasoning.

Wage and Price Flexibility

As noted, many economists of the day argued that sticky wages and prices were a major cause of the Great Depression. However, few of them doubted the classical belief that downward wage and price flexibility would cure the problem as long as saving and investment plans matched.

But recall again the argument made by classical economists in connection with the typical product market of Figure 7-1. The initial fall in the economy's total demand causes product market demand curves to shift leftward from positions such as D to those such as D_a in part b. They then argued that downward adjustments in flexible wages and input prices, caused by unemployment and excess input supplies, would cause product market supply curves to shift rightward from positions such as S to those such as S_a in part c. They contended that this adjustment process restored the initial output levels, such as Q_0, and full employment in each product market—hence full employment for the whole economy. End of story.

But wait a minute. If wages and input prices must fall throughout the economy, is it reasonable to assume that product demand curves will remain unchanged at positions such as D_a in each and every product market? With all labor and input suppliers' incomes falling, these demand curves are likely to shift leftward again. There is no assurance that repeating this process over and over will ever result in the achievement of full employment. In Chapter 4, we learned that when we examine the demand and supply curves in a particular market, like that of Figure 7-1, movements *along* such curves assume all other things remain the same. When the supply curves in every product market in the economy are shifting at the same time, such as from S to S_a along product demand curves like D_a (part c), all other things are hardly remaining the same. What is true of the adjust-

ment in a particular market if the rest of the economy is unchanged, is very likely completely different when all markets adjust at once. The classical argument that wage and price flexibility ensure full employment is thus flawed by the fallacy of composition. This fact makes it suspect at best, however plausible it may sound at first.

Furthermore, is it not irrelevant whether complete wage and price flexibility would assure full employment if *in fact* wages and prices are slow to adjust in the real world? During the Great Depression economists were quick to note that this was the case in a number of markets. Wage rates in particular adjusted downward quite slowly. Keynes and his followers incorporated these facts about wage and price behavior into the building blocks of modern income and employment theory. In the post–World War II years, wage rates and prices in a host of markets show a pronounced tendency to rise much more readily than to fall. A theory that ignores these facts is likely to be of little practical use to economic policy makers and others interested in analyzing and forecasting the economy's behavior.

Can the Interest Rate Match Saving and Investment Plans?

Perhaps the weakest link in the classical argument was the idea that interest rate adjustment would ensure the equality of saving and investment plans.

MANY THINGS AFFECT SAVING

The classical economists' argument that households are induced to save more at high interest rates than at low rates raises some questions. Even if the assertion is true, it may take large changes in interest rates to really affect the level of saving much at all, other things remaining the same. Indeed, many of the "other things" may be much more important determinants of saving plans than the interest rate is.

For example, much household saving is directed toward accumulating the funds needed to make some future purchase—a house, an automobile, a college education, a vacation, and so forth. Saving may also be aimed at providing a "nest egg" for unforeseen emergencies such as job loss, illness, or simply a general sense of security. Saving can also provide for retirement years. Some people may simply want to accumulate enough wealth to be able to live off the interest it can earn. The last motive has an interesting implication. The higher the interest rate, the less wealth it takes to earn a given level of income. If the interest rate is 5 percent, it takes $10,000 to earn $500 per year. At an interest rate of 10 percent, it takes half that amount, or $5,000, to earn $500 per year. Therefore, if people save in order to accumulate just enough wealth to be able to earn a certain income level from it, the higher the interest rate the less will be the amount of saving necessary to achieve their goal. Of course, this is just the opposite of the classical proposition that saving will increase when the interest rate increases.

Given any of the above objectives of household saving, Keynes argued that the most important determinant of the amount of saving is the level of the household's income. He asserted that the higher the income level, the larger the amount of saving—if for no other reason, simply because when the household has more income, it is easier for it to save. This relationship between income and saving has become a cornerstone of the theory of income and employment determination, as we shall see.

INVESTMENT—HOW IMPORTANT IS THE INTEREST RATE?

During the Great Depression capital consumption, or depreciation of the economy's capital stock, was actually larger than the amount of gross investment in each of the years from 1931 through 1935! In other words, net investment was negative. Many economists question whether interest rates lower than those that actually prevailed would have substantially increased investment expenditures in those years. A host of other factors are generally considered to be more important determinants of the level of investment.

For example, our discussion of the accelerator principle in the previous chapter indicated that the behavior of retail or final sales is extremely important. Since total income is just the receipts from total sales of the economy's total output of final goods and services, the accelera-

tor principle suggests that the economy's total investment will be strongly affected by the behavior of total income. The fact that money GNP fell by roughly 50 percent between 1929 and 1933 would seem to have some bearing on the fact that gross investment fell by over 90 percent during this same period of time. No matter how low the rate of interest, dramatically falling sales would hardly seem likely to encourage businesses to invest in new plant and equipment, or more inventories.

Later in this chapter we will consider some of the other important characteristics and determinants of investment behavior. Regarding the interest rate, Keynes argued that there might well be a lower limit (above zero) to how far it could fall. Without getting into the complexity of his argument, this meant that the interest rate might not be able to fall low enough to match saving and investment plans and ensure full employment. Keynes also noted that even if the interest rate fell to zero, investment plans might still be less than saving plans. The leakage from saving would then lead to a continuing fall in total demand.

INVESTORS AND SAVERS ARE DIFFERENT GROUPS

The idea that dollars from saving must somehow flow from the hands of savers into the hands of investors in order for investment expenditures to be able to occur is misleading. It is certainly true that there will be a leakage from the income expenditure flow if households desire to save more than businesses want to invest. But households may bury their unspent dollars in the backyard if they wish. In a modern economy the banking system is able to create money (we shall see how in a later chapter) and lend it to businesses that want to invest in plant, equipment, and inventories. As long as the amount of money banks lend to businesses in this way is equal to the amount households desire to save, investment plans will continue to equal saving plans and there need be no interruption in the income-expenditure flow.

The fact that dollars do not literally have to flow from the hands of savers into those of investors illustrates how much the motives and decisions of savers may be disconnected from those of investors. It also highlights an important point. If households put their savings in sugar bowls and mattresses, or bury it in the backyard, investment will have to be financed by the banking system or out of business saving. If the economy's prospects look shaky, as they may in the depths of a depression, there may be a lower limit to the interest rate at which bankers are willing to lend. Keynes argued that this lower limit on the interest rate may not be low enough to match saving and investment plans and ensure full employment.

In sum, *the Great Depression and the work of Keynes and his followers raised serious doubts about any automatic tendency for the economy to maintain a full-employment output level. Flexible wages and prices, together with interest rate adjustment to match saving and investment plans, do not seem likely in reality, nor sufficient in theory, to guarantee the inevitability of such an outcome.*

■ CHECKPOINT 7-2

How would you describe the way saving and investment plans were matched for Robinson Crusoe in his one-man island economy? Could he have an unemployment problem? How well would Say's Law describe the way his economy worked? What is it about modern industrialized economies, as compared to Robinson Crusoe's, that leads to difficulties for Say's Law?

Total Demand and Employment: The Modern View

Largely as the result of the Keynesian revolution, it is no longer assumed that the economy automatically tends to operate at full employment. The modern view takes the position that the level of total income, output, and employment is largely determined by total demand. If total demand is low, then income, output, and employment will be low and unemployment can be a persistent phenomenon—not a temporary, quickly passing thing as the classical economists argued. Of course, if total demand is large enough, the economy can achieve a full-employment position, but such a position is not considered inevitable or even a natural state.

It is almost as if the modern view has taken Say's Law and turned it upside down. Instead of assuming, as Say's Law would have it, that supply creates demand, the modern view is closer to the assertion that demand creates supply. Total income, output, and employment vary directly with total demand. In the remainder of this chapter we will examine two of the key components of total demand from the modern point of view. These are consumption and investment, two of the main categories on the expenditure side of GNP that we discussed in Chapter 5.

In keeping with the real-world observation that wages and prices are sticky, we will assume throughout our discussion that wages and prices are unchanging, unless we say otherwise. This is, of course, the opposite extreme from assuming perfect flexibility of wages and prices. But it is an extreme that seems closer to reality. After we have developed the basic framework of the modern view of income and employment determination, we will be in a better position to examine in later chapters what happens when wages and prices change.

THE PROPENSITY TO CONSUME AND TO SAVE

The news item at the beginning of this chapter conveys some idea of the importance of consumption expenditures in our economy. ("After all, personal consumption expenditures account for more than 60 percent of the nation's GNP.") *Consumption is the portion of their disposable income that households spend on goods and services. Personal saving is the remaining part, the portion of disposable income that households refrain from spending.* Therefore, whatever explains consumption behavior must also explain personal saving behavior.

Consumption and Saving Depend on Income

Keynes contended that the single most important determinant of consumption expenditure and personal saving is the household's disposable income. If you think about the amount of your own expenditures on goods and ser-

TABLE 7-1 THE CONSUMPTION AND SAVING SCHEDULES, THE MARGINAL PROPENSITY TO CONSUME, AND THE MARGINAL PROPENSITY TO SAVE (Hypothetical Data in Billions of Dollars)

(1) Disposable Income (DI)	(2) Change in DI (ΔDI)	(3) Con-sumption (C)	(4) Change in C (ΔC)	(5) Saving (S)	(6) Change in S (ΔS)	(7) Marginal Propensity to Consume (MPC)	(8) Marginal Propensity to Save (MPS)
				$S = (1) - (3)$		$MPC = \dfrac{(4)}{(2)}$	$MPS = \dfrac{(6)}{(2)}$
300		320		−20			
	25		15		10	.60	.40
325		335		−10			
	25		15		10	.60	.40
350		350		0			
	25		15		10	.60	.40
375		365		10			
	25		15		10	.60	.40
400		380		20			
	25		15		10	.60	.40
425		395		30			
	25		15		10	.60	.40
450		410		40			
	25		15		10	.60	.40
475		425		50			
	25		15		10	.60	.40
500		440		60			

vices, you would probably agree that your disposable, or after-tax, income is the single most important determinant of the amount you spend.[2]

True, the amount of a household's expenditures is also affected by such things as family size, the ages and sex of family members, the assets it owns, and the job security and future income prospects of its working members. But statistical studies tend to bear out the claim that the amount of disposable income is the single most important determining. factor of the amount of consumption and saving.

This suggests that if we want to know the to-

[2] All of us know the exact amount of our after-tax or take-home monthly or weekly paycheck. Few of us probably know the amount of our monthly or weekly before-tax pay without looking it up. Why should we? That amount simply isn't at our disposal to spend.

tal amount of consumption expenditure that the economy's households plan or desire to make over some short period of time (a year or less, say) we would be greatly aided by knowing the level of disposable income. Not surprisingly, real-world data show that the level of consumption expenditure in the economy increases with the level of disposable income.

Using hypothetical data, Table 7-1 shows the total amount of consumption (column 3) that the economy's households would plan to do at different levels of disposable income (column 1). The difference between disposable income and consumption is the amount of saving (column 5). This is the amount that households refrain from spending at each level of disposable income. Note that as income increases so do both consumption and saving. All other factors that affect consumption are assumed to be given—that is, they are fixed and unchanging.

THE CONSUMPTION FUNCTION: GRAPHICAL REPRESENTATION

The income-consumption relationship may be represented graphically by measuring consumption expenditures on the vertical axis and disposable income on the horizontal axis. In Figure 7-3, part a, both axes are measured in the same units, billions of dollars. The consumption data from column 3 of Table 7-1 and the disposable income data from column 1 are plotted in Figure 7-3, part a, to give the consumption curve C. This curve represents the theoretical relationship between consumption expenditures and disposable income that Keynes hypothesized. When actual levels of the economy's consumption expenditures are plotted against the associated levels of the economy's disposable income, economists have found a relationship that looks very much like the consumption curve C shown in part a.

Note the 45° line that has been added to the diagram. This line bisects the 90° angle formed by the horizontal and vertical axes of the diagram. Any point on the 45° line lies equidistant from the two axes. This line serves as a very useful reference line for interpreting the relationship between disposable income, consumption, and saving. At any given level of disposable income, the vertical distance between the corresponding point on the consumption curve C and the 45° line represents the amount of saving, or the amount of that disposable income that households refrain from spending. For example, at a disposable income level of $450 billion (horizontal axis) the vertical distance to the corresponding point on the consumption curve measures the $410 billion of consumption spending (vertical axis) that takes place at that disposable income level. The vertical distance from that point on the consumption curve up to the 45° line measures the $40 billion of saving that takes place when disposable income is $450 billion.

The point d where the consumption curve intersects the 45° line corresponds to a level of disposable income equal to $350 billion. The entire $350 billion of disposable income goes into consumption expenditure—saving is zero. At disposable income levels greater than $350 billion, consumption is less than disposable in-come. This is represented by the fact that to the right of point d the consumption curve lies below the 45° line. In other words, at disposable income levels greater than $350 billion, saving is positive and is equal to the vertical distance between the 45° line and the consumption curve.

At disposable income levels less than $350 billion, the economy's households spend more than the amount of disposable income. This is represented by the fact that the consumption curve lies above the 45° line. Households are able to spend more than disposable income either by drawing on wealth accumulated in the past or by borrowing. This amounts to negative saving, or what may be called dissaving. For example, at a disposable income level of $300 billion, the economy's households are dissaving by an amount equal to $20 billion. We can also say that they are saving a negative $20 billion.

The relationship between the level of disposable income and the level of consumption, represented by the consumption curve C, is called the **consumption function**. The term *function* is used here because the level of consumption expenditure is determined by (is a function of) the level of disposable income. *The consumption function shows that as disposable income increases, consumption also increases, but by a smaller amount. Movement along the consumption function is caused by a change in disposable income, while all other things that affect consumption are assumed to remain unchanged.*

THE SAVING FUNCTION: GRAPHICAL REPRESENTATION

What households don't consume out of income they save. Since consumption depends on income, so does saving. We have observed that when income increases consumption also increases, but by a smaller amount. It increases by a smaller amount precisely because part of any increase in income goes into saving. This is reflected by the fact that the consumption function C in part a of Figure 7-3 is less steeply sloped than the 45° line. Therefore, the vertical distance between the consumption function C and the 45° line represents saving. And saving obviously gets larger as income increases.

Part a of Figure 7-3 is just one way of representing graphically the relationship between dis-

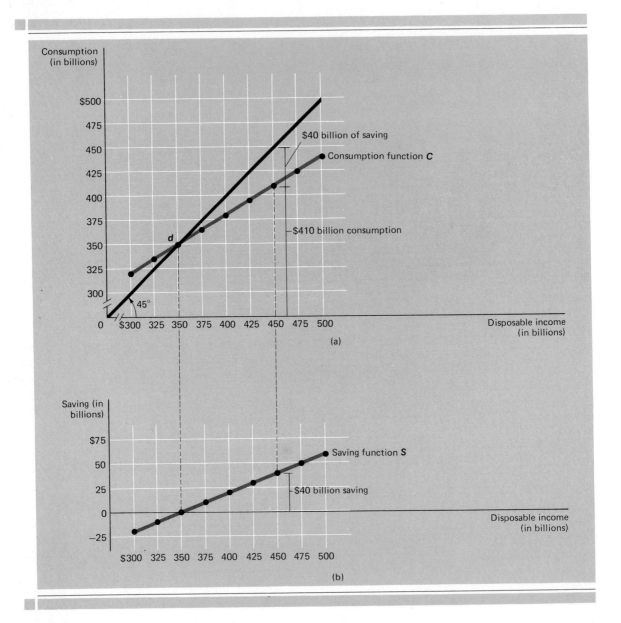

posable income and saving. Another very useful representation is shown in part b of Figure 7–3. The axes are drawn to exactly the same scale as those in part a of Figure 7–3, except that saving is measured on the vertical axis. The horizontal axis in part b measures disposable income and is exactly the same as the horizontal axis of part a. The saving function S is plotted from the data in columns 1 and 5 of Table 7–1.

The vertical distance between the saving function and the horizontal axis represents the amount of saving that the economy's households would desire to do at each income level. At any given income level the vertical distance between the saving function and the horizontal axis in part b is the same as the vertical distance between the consumption function and the 45° line in part a. This correspondence is pointed

FIGURE 7-3 **THE CONSUMPTION FUNCTION AND THE SAVING FUNCTION**

The consumption function C in part a is plotted from the data in columns 1 and 3 of Table 7–1. The term *function* is used because the level of consumption expenditure (vertical axis) depends on the level of disposable income (horizontal axis). Note that as disposable income increases, consumption also increases, but by a smaller amount. Movement along the consumption function is caused by a change in disposable income, while all other things that affect consumption are assumed to remain unchanged.

The amount of saving at any disposable income level is represented by the vertical distance between the consumption function and the 45° line in part a. In other words, what households don't consume they save.

Using the data from columns 1 and 5 in Table 7–1, saving may be plotted against disposable income as shown in part b to give the saving function S. At any given disposable income level, saving is represented by the vertical distance between the consumption function and the 45° line (in part a). The saving function slopes upward, reflecting the fact that the level of planned saving rises as disposable income rises.

out at the $450 billion disposable income level, for example, and is also obvious at the break-even point.

The **saving function** *shows the relationship between the economy's level of disposable income and the level of desired or planned saving. It slopes upward, reflecting the fact that the level of planned saving rises as income rises.*

Marginal and Average Propensities to Consume and to Save

Students often confuse the concepts of marginal and average. The distinction between them is vitally important to our understanding of the consumption and saving functions and their role in the theory of income and employment determination, as we shall see.

MARGINAL PROPENSITY TO CONSUME AND TO SAVE

The marginal propensity to consume (MPC) is the fraction or proportion of any *change* in disposable income that is consumed:

$$MPC = \frac{\text{change in consumption}}{\text{change in disposable income}}$$

The term *marginal* refers to the fact that we are interested *only* in the *change* in the level of consumption brought about by a *change* in the level of disposable income. Similarly, the **marginal propensity to save (MPS)** is the fraction or proportion of any *change* in disposable income that

is saved:

$$MPS = \frac{\text{change in saving}}{\text{change in disposable income}}$$

These concepts are shown in Table 7–1. As we move from one level of disposable income to the next in column 1, the *change* (Δ) in the level of disposable income ΔDI is given in column 2. The associated *change* in the level of consumption ΔC brought about by the *change* in disposable income ΔDI is given in column 4. The associated marginal propensity to consume, *MPC*, is shown in column 7. In this case, *MPC* (which is ΔC ÷ ΔDI), equals .60. Similarly, the change ΔS in the level of saving brought about by the *change* ΔDI in disposable income is given in column 6. The associated marginal propensity to save, *MPS*, is given in column 8. In this case, the *MPS* (which is ΔS ÷ ΔDI) equals .40.

Suppose, for example, that disposable income rises from $450 billion to $475 billion, an increase of $25 billion. What do households do with this increase? According to Table 7–1, they consume .60 of it, which is $15 billion, and save .40 of it, which is $10 billion. These are the only two things households can do with the increase—consume part of it and save the rest. By definition, then, the fraction of the increase in disposable income consumed, *MPC*, plus the fraction saved, *MPS*, when added together are equal to the whole increase in disposable in-

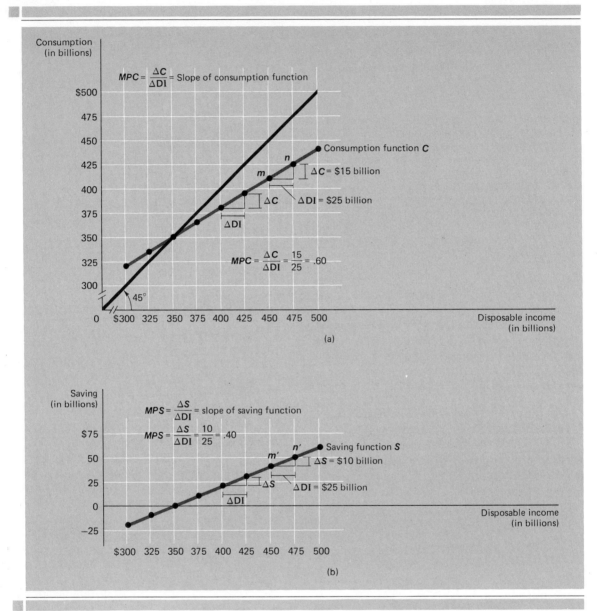

(a)

(b)

come. Therefore, *the sum of MPC and MPS must always equal one:*

$$MPC + MPS = 1$$

The data in Table 7-1 show us that this is true, since

$$.60 + .40 = 1$$

The marginal propensity to consume is represented graphically by the slope of the consumption *function,* as shown in Figure 7-4, part a. (Figure 7-4 is the same as Figure 7-3.) The slope of any line is the ratio of the amount of vertical change in the line to the associated amount of horizontal change. For the consumption function, the vertical change ΔC is associated with the horizontal change ΔDI. Similarly, *the marginal propensity to save is represented graphically by the slope of the saving function* as shown in Figure 7-4, part b.

FIGURE 7-4 THE MARGINAL PROPENSITY TO CONSUME AND THE MARGINAL PROPENSITY TO SAVE

The slope of a line is the ratio of the amount of vertical change in the line to the associated amount of horizontal change.

For the consumption function, the vertical change ΔC is associated with the horizontal change ΔDI, as shown in part a. Hence, the slope of the consumption function is $\Delta C \div \Delta DI$, which is the marginal propensity to consume, MPC. Similarly, the slope of the saving function is $\Delta S \div \Delta DI$, which is the marginal propensity to save, MPS, as shown in part b.

Both of these functions are straight lines. Therefore, the marginal propensity to consume is the same no matter where it is measured along the consumption function. The same is true of the marginal propensity to save measured anywhere along the saving function. In the examples shown here, which are based on the data in Table 7-1, the MPC equals .60 and the MPS equals .40.

If the consumption function is a straight line, then so is the saving function. When the consumption function is a straight line, its slope (*MPC*) has the same value at every point along the line. The same is true of the slope (*MPS*) of the straight-line saving function. The consumption and saving functions of Figure 7-4 are both straight lines. If, however, the consumption function were a curve that was less steeply sloped at higher disposable income levels, then the saving function would be a curve that gets more steeply sloped at higher disposable income levels. In that case the *MPC* would be smaller at higher income levels and the *MPS* would be larger. Draw such consumption and saving functions and illustrate these characteristics.

AVERAGE PROPENSITIES TO CONSUME AND TO SAVE

The **average propensity to consume (*APC*)** is the fraction or proportion of *total* disposable income that is consumed:

$$APC = \frac{\text{consumption}}{\text{disposable income}}$$

Note that whereas the *MPC* is the ratio of the *change* in consumption to the *change* in disposable income, the *APC* is the ratio of the *level* of consumption to the *level* of disposable income. The *APC* and the *MPC* are therefore two distinctly different concepts.

Table 7-2 shows the same data in columns 1, 2, and 3 for DI, C, and S as in columns 1, 3, and 5 of Table 7-1. The average propensity to consume for each level of disposable income (column 1), and its associated level of consumption (column 2), is shown in column 4. *APC* equals $C \div DI$, which is the consumption data in column 2 divided by the disposable income data in column 1. Note that unlike the *MPC* (column 7 of Table 7-1), the *APC* (column 4 of Table 7-2) declines as disposable income increases.

The **average propensity to save (*APS*)** is the fraction or proportion of *total* disposable income that is saved:

$$APS = \frac{\text{saving}}{\text{disposable income}}$$

Again, the *APS* and the *MPS* are distinctly different concepts. While the *MPS* is the ratio of *change* in saving to the *change* in disposable income, the *APS* is the ratio of the *level* of saving to the *level* of disposable income.

The *APS* of our example is shown in column 5 of Table 7-2. Note that while *APC* (column 4) falls as disposable income increases, the *APS* (column 5), increases. In other words, if the fraction of total disposable income consumed gets smaller at higher disposable income levels, it follows that the fraction of total disposable income saved must get larger. Since all disposable income is either consumed or saved, it also follows that

$$APC + APS = 1$$

Movements Versus Shifts in Consumption and Saving

In Chapter 4 we discussed the difference between movement along a good's demand curve

TABLE 7-2 THE CONSUMPTION AND SAVING SCHEDULES, THE AVERAGE PROPENSITY TO CONSUME, AND THE AVERAGE PROPENSITY TO SAVE (Hypothetical Data in Billions of Dollars)

(1)	(2)	(3)	(4)	(5)
Disposable Income (DI)	Consumption (C)	Saving (S)	Average Propensity to Consume (APC)	Average Propensity to Save (APS)
		$S = (1) - (2)$	$APC = \frac{(2)}{(1)}$	$APS = \frac{(3)}{(1)}$
300	320	−20	1.07	−.07
325	335	−10	1.03	−.03
350	350	0	1.00	.00
375	365	10	.97	.03
400	380	20	.95	.05
425	395	30	.93	.07
450	410	40	.91	.09
475	425	50	.89	.11
500	440	60	.88	.12

and shifts in the position of its demand curve. Remember that movement along a demand curve can only result from a change in the price of the good itself, all other things remaining the same. If any of the other things change, this causes a shift in the demand curve. A similar distinction must be made between movement along a consumption function or a saving function and shifts in these functions.

MOVEMENTS ALONG THE CONSUMPTION AND SAVING FUNCTIONS

We have stressed that movement along a consumption function can only be caused by a change in disposable income. All other things that affect consumption are assumed to remain unchanged. Of course, for any movement along a consumption function, there is a corresponding movement along the associated saving function. For example, in Figure 7-4, part a, if disposable income rises from $450 to $475 billion, there is a movement along the consumption function from point *m* to point *n*. Corresponding to this, of course, there is a movement along the saving function, part b, from point *m'* to point *n'*.

SHIFTS IN THE CONSUMPTION AND SAVING FUNCTIONS

When any of the other things (besides disposable income) that affect consumption change, there is a shift in the consumption and saving functions. For example, suppose the consumption function is initially in the position C_0, as shown in part a of Figure 7-5. The associated saving function is S_0, as shown in part b. If the consumption function shifts downward from C_0 to C_1, the saving function then shifts upward from S_0 to S_1. At any given disposable income level, households now consume less and save more. On the other hand, if the consumption function shifts upward from C_0 to C_2, the saving function then shifts downward from S_0 to S_2. In this case households now consume more and save less at any given disposable income level.

Other Determinants of Consumption and Saving

What are some of the "other things" that can change and thereby cause shifts in the consumption and saving functions? The news item at the beginning of this chapter provides several examples. The main point of the news item is

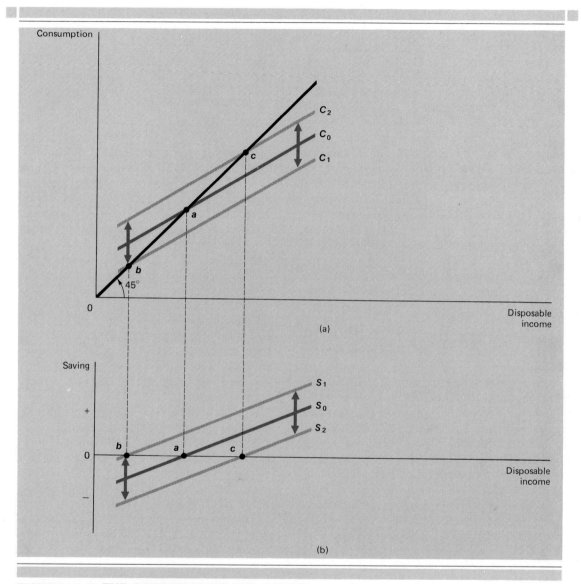

FIGURE 7-5 THE CONSUMPTION AND SAVING FUNCTIONS SHIFT WHEN THE "OTHER THINGS" CHANGE

Movement along the consumption function or the saving function is due to changes in disposable income. All other things that affect consumption are assumed to be unchanged. When any of these other things change, they cause a shift in the consumption and saving functions.

Suppose the consumption function is initially C_0 (part a) and the associated saving function is S_0 (part b). If the consumption function shifts downward from C_0 to C_1, the saving function then shifts upward from S_0 to S_1. At any given income level, households now consume less and save more. Similarly, if the consumption function shifts upward from C_0 to C_2, the saving function then shifts downward from S_0 to S_2. Households consume more and save less at any given disposable income level.

that consumption expenditure has slowed down. Michael Evans notes that this has happened despite the fact that "personal income continues to grow handsomely." Assuming that disposable income increases as personal income increases, this means that consumption expenditures should increase due to a movement along the consumption function—*other things remaining the same.* Yet Evans notes that "retail sales from March to July declined even in current-dollar terms." Obviously other things appear to have changed in such a way as to offset to some extent any movement out along the consumption function that results from an increase in disposable income. In particular, the other things that would cause the consumption function to shift downward appear to have outweighed those that would cause it to shift upward. Among these other things, the following appear to be important.

CREDIT CONDITIONS

Evans notes that "credit conditions remain unusually easy." The easier it is for consumers to obtain credit, the more likely they are to borrow from banks and other financial institutions to buy cars, household appliances, and other goods on credit. This would tend to shift the consumption function upward (and the saving function downward). While not specifically mentioned in the news item, it may well be that consumers were already carrying quite a bit of *indebtedness* at the time of the news story. Therefore, they were concerned about going further into debt. This would have a depressing effect on their willingness to spend, and would cause the consumption function to shift downward.

EXPECTATIONS ABOUT
EMPLOYMENT, PRICES, AND INCOME

Consumer expectations about the course of the economy play a crucial role in their willingness to spend. The news item notes that "the consumer is certainly unhappy about something." This puts a damper on consumer optimism, perhaps causing many of them to consume less out of a given level of disposable income in order to save more for the possible rainy days ahead. Even those not afraid of un-

employment may come to expect a lower level of future disposable income. The result is a downward shift in the consumption function (and an upward shift in the saving function).

It is also noted in the news item that consumers "are much more price sensitive than they were a few years ago. Inflation has lasted so long and been so severe that consumers now equate it with bad times." As we discussed in the last chapter, unanticipated inflation hurts many groups in the economy. Fear of inflation at some as yet unknown rate may well put a damper on consumer enthusiasm and result in a downward shift in the consumption function (and an upward shift in the saving function). (Some economists would suggest just the opposite, arguing that fear of inflation may lead to increased expenditures now as consumers try to avoid paying higher prices later.) However, "Mr. Evans thinks consumer spending will pick up this month, or next, as income continues to rise faster than inflation." In essence he is saying that consumers' real disposable income will rise and there will be movement out along the consumption function, thereby increasing consumer spending.

This news item reports on events in an election year. Specifically, it is reported that the director of the University of Michigan's consumer survey points out that "in the past consumers have tended to turn more hopeful in election years." If he is right, this hopefulness would tend to shift the consumption function upward.

There are several other things that determine the position of the consumption function. Among some of the more important are the size and composition of the stocks of assets owned by consumers (how wealthy do they feel?), the condition of the consumer durable goods they own (are appliances, cars, etc., in good working order, or are replacements badly needed?), and so forth.

■ CHECKPOINT 7-3

Show graphically how the consumption function would have to look if its *MPC* and *APC* are always equal to one another, no matter what the disposable income level. What would be true of the relationship

between the *MPS* and the *APS* of the saving function in this case, and what would the saving function look like? How would the consumption function have to shift for the *APC* to increase and the *MPC* to remain unchanged? Show what would happen to the saving function in this case.

INVESTMENT AND ITS DETERMINANTS

Among the three major categories on the expenditure side of GNP—consumption, investment, and government—investment expenditures vary the most. This is evident from the graphic representation of these three categories in Figure 7-6. It is often said that consumption expenditure is more "passive" than investment expenditure because it reflects the ongoing, everyday needs of households. As long as households are employed and have a steady source of income, consumption varies very little, growing rather steadily through time with the growth of the economy. By contrast, investment grows by fits and starts, often contracting sharply and then rebounding just as abruptly. Government expenditure, while not quite as steady as consumption, has certainly been less variable than investment. What are the main determinants of investment expenditure, and what accounts for its variable behavior?

Investment and Profit

What motivates businesses to make expenditures on plant, equipment, and inventories— that is, to invest in goods used to produce other goods? The answer is profit, or the anticipation of profit. If businesses anticipate that revenue from the sale of goods and services produced with the aid of capital goods will more than cover all costs of production, so that there is a profit, they will invest in the capital goods. Otherwise they won't.

A major underlying reason why investment is so variable (as illustrated in Figure 7-6) is the fact that the decision whether or not to invest in capital goods depends on business expectations about future profits. And investment in many kinds of capital can only be justified if their prospective profitability seems reasonably assured

for a good many future years. Many factors enter into the formation of expectations about a future whose horizon is so distant.

FORECASTING FUTURE PROFIT

Put yourself in the shoes of an investment decision maker. In order to forecast prospective profits in any meaningful way, you have to forecast the magnitudes of all of the ingredients that will enter into the calculation of profit. What do you think the market for your product will be over the next several years—how large will sales revenues be? What will be the levels of your costs, such as wage rates, rents, interest rates, materials prices, utilities payments? How much will you have to pay in various taxes and how might tax rates change? Based on your forecasts of all these items, together with your guesses about changes in the general political and social environment, you will come up with your "best" forecast of the future profits (or losses) likely to result from any investment currently undertaken. Given all these forecasts, you will make your decision whether or not to invest in capital. Clearly, there are a lot of factors that are relevant. And all are uncertain because they pertain to the future.

CHANGING EXPECTATIONS

Quite obviously profit forecasts are dependent on the current expectations held by businesses about the future. Changes in these expectations cause changes in profit forecasts, which in turn lead to changes in the amount of investment businesses want to do. Expectations can be very volatile, buffeted by continually changing information about markets, government policies, political events, the weather, and the ebb and tide of what Keynes called "the animal spirits." In his words

> . . . individual initiative will only be adequate when reasonable calculation is supplemented and supported by animal spirits, so that the thought of ultimate loss which often overtakes pioneers, as experience tells both us and them, is put aside as a healthy man puts aside the expectation of death.
>
> This means, unfortunately, not only that slumps and depressions are exaggerated in degree, but that economic prosperity is

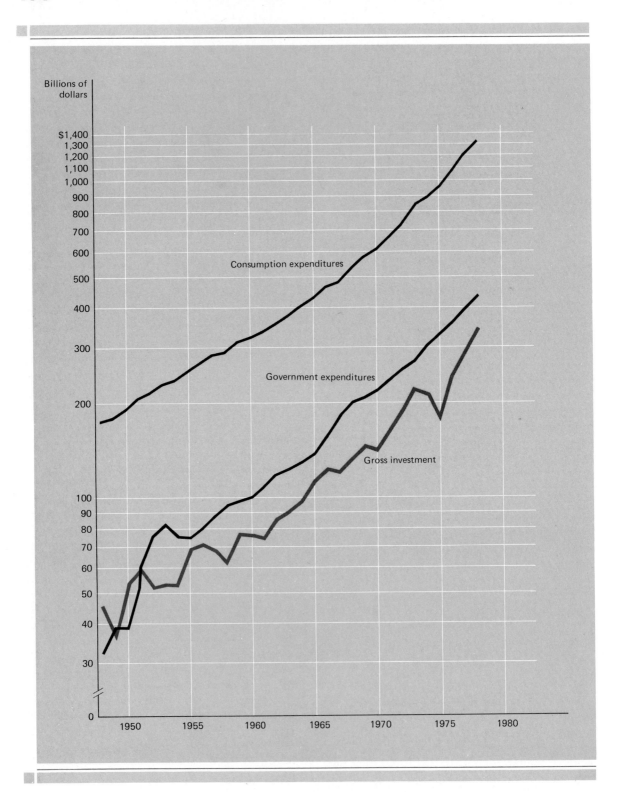

Billions of dollars

Consumption expenditures

Government expenditures

Gross investment

FIGURE 7-6 INVESTMENT VARIES MORE THAN CONSUMPTION AND GOVERNMENT EXPENDITURES

Shown here are consumption, gross investment, and government expenditures over the post–World War II period. (Note that the vertical axis is a logarithmic or ratio-scale on which equal distances represent equal percentage changes.) Investment expenditures have been the most variable of these major components of the expenditure side of GNP during this period.

excessively dependent on a political and social atmosphere which is congenial to the average businessman. . . . In estimating the prospects of investment, we must have regard, therefore, to the nerves and hysteria and even the digestions and reactions to the weather of those upon whose spontaneous activity it largely depends.[3]

The Investment Schedule and Its Determinants

When we develop the basic theory of how the economy's level of total income and employment are determined in the next chapter, we will need to add the consumption plans of households to the investment plans of businesses. In order to do this we will need to relate the level of businesses' investment spending plans to income, just as consumption spending plans are related to income by the consumption function. (Remember we are making no distinction between DI, PI, NI, NNP, and GNP in this chapter, because we are ignoring all those things that differentiate these measures from one another.) The relationship between income and planned investment is represented by the investment schedule I shown in Figure 7-7, part a. The economy's total dollar income, or total output, is measured on the horizontal axis, and its gross investment expenditures are measured on the vertical axis. As drawn, the investment schedule I shows that businesses in aggregate plan to spend an amount equal to I_0 on plant, equipment, and inventories no matter what the level of income in the economy—*all other things remaining the same.* Therefore, the investment schedule I is perfectly horizontal at the level I_0. Our discussion of the determinants of investment, the "other things," will indicate what de-

termines the position of the I schedule, and how it may be shifted by changes in these determinants. Remember that the question of what determines investment expenditure in our economy is basically one of what determines the prospects for profit. Let us consider some of the more important determinants.

1. VARIATION IN TOTAL INCOME

We have already noted how the accelerator principle suggests that investment expenditures will be affected by the economy's total sales of final goods and services. Equivalently, we can say that investment expenditures will be affected by the economy's total income. In addition, it seems reasonable to believe that the higher the level of current economic activity as measured by the level of total income, the more optimistic businesses will be about prospects for future profits. This optimism may well encourage them to invest more at higher income levels. If so, the investment schedule I may slope upward as shown in Figure 7-7, part b. In this case, if the level of total income is Y_1, then the total amount of investment businesses will desire to make is I_1. At the higher income level Y_2, they would want to invest the larger amount I_2. The events reported in the news item at the beginning of this chapter may to some extent reflect this type of effect of the level of economic activity on investment. It notes how the "current economic expansion was carried on the back of the consumer . . ." until "businesses became convinced that the expansion was real and started adding to inventories . . . [and] stepped up spending on new plants and equipment. . . ." In a similar vein the news item goes on to say that "if the consumer really is opting out, businesses will have second thoughts about inventory and capital spending."

[3] J. M. Keynes, *The General Theory of Employment, Interest, and Money* (New York: Harcourt Brace Jovanovich, 1936), p. 162.

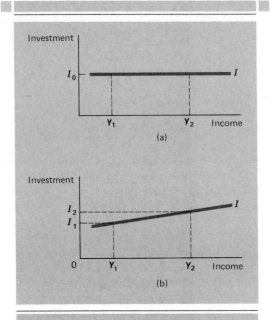

FIGURE 7-7 THE INVESTMENT SCHEDULE

In these diagrams the amount of investment expenditure in the economy is measured on the vertical axis and the economy's total income on the horizontal axis. The investment schedule *I* shows the total amount of investment businesses desire to make at each level of the economy's total income, all other things remaining the same.

The investment schedule in part a is perfectly horizontal. This means that desired investment expenditure in the economy equals I_0 no matter what the level of total income.

The investment schedule in part b slopes upward on the assumption that businesses will be more optimistic about profit prospects the higher is the current level of economic activity as measured by total income. Therefore, desired investment will be larger at higher income levels. For example, desired investment will equal I_1 at income level Y_1, and the larger amount I_2 at the higher income level Y_2.

2. THE INTEREST RATE

The funds that businesses use to make investment expenditures on capital goods must either be borrowed from outside the firm or they must

be generated internally in the form of the firm's business saving (also called retained earnings). If they are borrowed from outside the firm, the cost of borrowing is the interest rate that must be paid to the lender. If they are generated internally, the cost to the firm is the forgone interest the firm could have earned if it had lent the funds to someone else. In either case the interest rate is the cost of the funds invested in capital goods. The higher the interest rate, the more this cost cuts into profit and reduces the incentive to invest in capital goods. Conversely, the lower the interest rate, the larger the profit and the greater the incentive to make investment expenditures.

Since the interest rate is among the "other things" assumed unchanged for any *movement along* the investment schedule, a change in the interest rate will cause the *I* schedule to shift, as shown in Figure 7-8. If the interest rate goes up—increasing cost and reducing profit prospects—the desired amount of investment will fall. This fall is reflected in a downward shift in the investment schedule from I_0 to a lower level such as I_1. Whatever the level of income, the level of desired investment would now be lower. If on the other hand the interest rate were to fall—reducing costs and increasing profit prospects—the desired amount of investment would rise. This rise is reflected in an upward shift in the investment schedule from I_0 to a position such as I_2. The desired level of investment would then be higher at any income level.

In sum, *increases in the interest rate shift the investment schedule downward and decreases in the interest rate shift it upward.*

3. TECHNOLOGICAL CHANGE AND NEW PRODUCTS

Technological change often makes existing capital equipment obsolete. Even though it is still in perfectly good working condition, it may no longer represent the lowest-cost way to produce goods. Firms that fail to invest in capital goods that feature the latest technological breakthrough will find themselves at a competitive disadvantage relative to those that do. Their profit prospects will be lessened or even eliminated. Those that acquire the latest capital first will get a competitive jump on rivals and

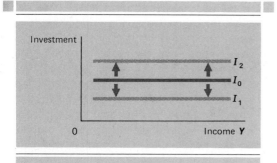

FIGURE 7-8 SHIFTS IN THE INVESTMENT SCHEDULE

The investment schedule shows the total amount of investment businesses desire to do at each level of income, all other things that affect investment remaining the same. If one or more of these other things should change, it will cause the investment schedule to shift, either upward from I_0 to a position such as I_2, or downward to a position such as I_1. Among the other things that can cause such shifts are changes in the interest rate, technology, expectations about prospective profits, and the development of new products.

therefore increase their profit prospects. Given these carrot-and-stick incentives, technological change often results in an upward shift in the investment schedule. Such a shift, from I_0 to I_2, is shown in Figure 7-8.

The development of new products opens up new markets. Lured by the resulting profit opportunities, firms will want to invest in the capital goods necessary to produce these new products. This too will cause an upward shift in the investment schedule.

4. REPLACEMENT AND DURABILITY

The purchase of durable goods, such as capital goods, is postponable. Businesses can make do with older plant and equipment until they are really convinced that the economic outlook and the prospect for profits provide good reasons for investment in new plant and equipment. *The expansion phase of the business cycle may give rise to expectations of higher profits and thus encourage long postponed replacement expenditures on capital goods, causing an upward shift in the investment schedule. Conversely, the*

recession phase of the cycle discourages replacement expenditures on capital goods, causing a downward shift in the investment schedule.

5. THE AMOUNT OF EXISTING CAPITAL

In general, the greater the amount of capital already in place, the lower the profit prospects associated with any investment in new plant and equipment, and the less inclined businesses are to invest. Therefore, *other things remaining the same, the more capital businesses have on hand, the lower will be the investment schedule.*

■ **CHECKPOINT 7-4**

How would an increase in the prices of new capital goods affect the investment schedule? How do you think the investment schedule would be affected if labor unions and management in major industries throughout the country successfully negotiate new labor contracts without resorting to strikes?

SUMMARY

1. Classical economists argued that a capitalistic, laissez faire economy would automatically tend to operate at a full-employment equilibrium. This contention was based on Say's Law, which states that supply creates its own demand.

2. The classical argument held that, if wages and prices were perfectly flexible, a drop in total demand would result in a downward adjustment in wages and prices sufficient to reestablish a full-employment level of total output. In addition, the leakage from the income-expenditure flow due to saving would create no problem because the interest rate would adjust to ensure that saving plans always equal investment plans.

3. The Great Depression of the 1930s led to a critical reexamination of the classical position. It became obvious that in a number of markets, prices and particularly wages were sticky, or slow to adjust downward. Furthermore, the theoretical argument that downward adjustment in wages and prices would eliminate any deficiency in total demand was flawed by the fallacy of composition—what might be true for one market

alone does not hold when all are taken together.

4. The notion that saving and investment plans could be equated by interest rate adjustments alone was abandoned. Basically, savers and investors are different groups, each motivated by different factors often more influential than the interest rate.

5. The Keynesian revolution led to the development of modern income and employment theory and its basic building blocks—the consumption function, the saving function, and the investment schedule. The consumption function shows the amount households want to consume (spend) and the saving function the amount they want to save (not spend) at each disposable income level. The investment schedule shows the amount businesses want to invest at each income level.

6. The marginal propensity to consume (*MPC*) is the fraction of any change in disposable income that is consumed—represented graphically by the slope of the consumption function. The marginal propensity to save (*MPS*) is the fraction of any change in disposable income that is saved—represented graphically by the slope of the saving function. The sum of the *MPS* and the *MPC* always equals one.

7. The average propensity to consume (*APC*) is the fraction of disposable income that is consumed, and the average propensity to save (*APS*) is the fraction of disposable income that is saved. The sum of the *APC* and the *APS* always equals one.

8. Movements along the consumption and saving functions are caused by changes in disposable income, all other things that influence consumption and saving remaining the same. Changes in one or more of the other things will cause shifts in the consumption and saving functions. Important among these other things are: credit conditions; household indebtedness; household expectations about unemployment, prices, and income; the size and composition of the stock of consumer assets; the amount and condition of the stocks of consumer durables.

9. Investment expenditures are more variable than the other two major components of the expenditure side of GNP, consumption and government expenditures. The expectation of profit is what determines the level of desired investment expenditure. The variability of investment expenditure results from the difficulty and complexity of forecasting prospective profits combined with the sensitivity of expectations to changes in the economic, political, and social environment.

10. The investment schedule represents the relationships between the level of planned investment and the level of total income. There are several important determinants of profit prospects that can cause shifts in the investment schedule: interest rate changes; technological change; the development of new products; the need for replacement; the amount of existing capital.

KEY TERMS AND CONCEPTS
average propensity to consume (*APC*)
average propensity to save (*APS*)
consumption function
interest rate
involuntary unemployment
marginal propensity to consume (*MPC*)
marginal propensity to save (*MPS*)
saving function
Say's Law

QUESTIONS AND PROBLEMS
1. According to Say's Law supply creates demand. Why couldn't this law be stated the other way around, namely, that demand creates supply?

2. Suppose you were a completely self-sufficient farmer and trapper living in the wilderness. What would be the relationship between your saving and investment decisions? What would be the significance of the notion of involuntary unemployment?

3. Explain why wage and price flexibility are not sufficient to restore a full-employment equilibrium subsequent to a fall in total demand. What role does the fallacy of composition play in the classical argument that wage and price flexibility would assure full employment?

4. Using a diagram like Figure 7–2, illustrate

what would happen if there were no positive level of the interest rate that would equate saving and investment plans. Describe what would be happening in the economy in this situation.

5. How do you think the following would affect the consumption and saving functions and why?

a. Employer-subsidized pension plans for employees are set up throughout the economy.

b. There is a decline in the stock market.

c. The government announces that gasoline will be rationed to consumers starting three months from now.

d. Households anticipate that the rate of inflation is going to rise from 5 percent per year to 15 percent per year during the next six months.

e. Households begin to doubt the financial soundness of the social security system, causing concern about the level of future retirement benefits that the system will be able to pay them.

6. Show what happens to the consumption and saving functions as a result of the following:

a. The *MPS* decreases.

b. The *APC* increases.

c. The *APC* decreases and the *MPS* increases.

d. The *APS* and the *MPS* decrease.

e. The *APC* and the *MPC* increase.

f. The *APC* decreases and the *MPC* increases.

7. What do you think would be the effect on prospective profit of each of the following and how would the investment schedule shift as a result?

a. Unions demand that employers make larger contributions to employee pension plans.

b. New sources of natural gas are discovered.

c. Congress passes a law allowing larger tax write-offs for research and development costs.

d. Congress passes a law mandating stiffer controls on the disposal of industrial waste.

e. War breaks out in the Middle East threatening the destruction of oil fields in the area.

f. The president calls for price ceilings on final products and an increase in social security taxes.

8. Compare and contrast the way businesses decide to invest with the way households decide how much to consume, and explain why investment is more variable than consumption.

■ NEWS ITEM FOR YOUR ANALYSIS ■

INDUSTRY INVESTS MORE IN
CAPITAL EQUIPMENT, BUT ECONOMISTS FRET

CLEVELAND, March 8—Has the widely publicized "lag" in capital spending been overemphasized?

Business is picking up according to producers of machinery, aircraft, railroad cars and a host of other items. They are hiring more workers, buying more materials and subcontracting more work to outside shops. In short, capital spending is stimulating the economy.

You'd never guess it from the pessimistic analyses of many economists, or the laments of businesses seeking tax cuts to stimulate more plant and equipment investment. They're still talking about the "lag." Nonetheless, most machinery makers are reasonably content with the gradual business pickup they're experiencing. They claim that it has allowed them to hold costs in line, avoiding excessive overtime and premium prices for scarce materials and parts that accompanied the 1973–1974 boom.

"The old idea of a capital-spending boom may be a retired myth," says Patrick S. Parker, chairman of Parker Hannifin Corp. in Cleveland, "and that may be good." The reason? "Companies aren't going out and ordering extra machines because they see delivery times lengthening and prices going up, as they did five years ago," he says. "But that probably means they won't be cancelling orders for machines either, if their business falls off a little."

Currently most corporate investment is going to improve existing facilities, rather than into brand new plants, with a few exceptions like the auto industry, aircraft manufacturers, and makers of office equipment from copiers to computers. In part, this is because demand currently doesn't require more capacity. The Federal Reserve Board's index of plant utilization has been hovering around 82 and 83 percent of capacity, well below the 1973 high of 88 percent. In addition, with the economic recovery relatively mature, many businesses feel that a leveling off or downturn in demand is more likely than a sudden upsurge. Also, the cost of new plants is so high that it seldom pays to tear down an old plant and build a new one.

One particular bright spot is the automobile business. "There's a boom in specialized manufacturing systems for the automotive industry," says W. Paul Cooper, president of Acme-Cleveland Corp. "The downsizing of autos is causing the auto people, under considerable time pressure, to reengineer their systems for producing engine blocks, transmissions, and the whole drive chain."

In general though, many executives don't want to risk the high investment for a new plant given the current uncertain economic and political environment. Questions about the availability and cost of energy, inflation, and possible price controls, import competition, and regulations governing pollution and employee health and safety have been added to the old uncertainty about ups and downs in demand for the output of a new plant.

QUESTIONS

1. If the "businesses seeking tax cuts" get their way, how will it affect those machinery makers who "are reasonably content with the general business pickup they're experiencing"? How do you think the tax cuts would affect the investment schedule initially and why? How do you think the possible problems the machinery makers point out might affect the investment schedule and why?

2. According to this news item, in what way are each of the following factors affecting the investment schedule?

a. total income or demand;
b. the amount of existing capital;
c. the price of new capital;
d. technological change and product change;
e. expectations.

3. Explain how each of the factors listed in the last paragraph of the news item enter into profit forecasts—that is, which factors affect the cost side of the profit calculation and which affect the product or sales side?

8

DETERMINING TOTAL INCOME, OUTPUT, AND EMPLOYMENT

CONSUMER OUTLAYS SLACKEN, CAPITAL SPENDING ON THE RISE

ANN ARBOR, Mich., May 12—American consumers, whose spending underlies whatever zing the economic recovery has shown so far, appear fatigued.

Many analysts who keep track of consumer spending patterns predict the expenditure level is likely to keep rising in coming months, but only modestly. The reason, they explain, is that consumers have spent so heavily in recent months that their savings have dwindled and their indebtedness has soared. It is estimated that the expected spending slowdown would be much more severe were it not for an improving job market and sharply climbing pay rates.

"We're witnessing an end to consumer leadership in the current economic recovery," says Thomas Juster, director of the University of Michigan Survey Research Center. He adds that if the recovery is to be brisk in the months ahead, "the impetus will have to come from other business sectors," such as capital spending.

Most forecasters expect capital spending to take up much of the slack. Corporate outlays for new plant and equipment rose only modestly during much of last year. However, analysts foresee an impressive turnabout this year.

With other economic sectors showing increased strength, some forecasters say that the expected slowing in consumer outlays will actually be beneficial. They claim that if consumer outlays keep roaring ahead and other sectors of the economy also accelerate, inflationary pressures could mount dangerously later this year.

In the last chapter, we examined the basic building blocks of modern income and employment theory—the consumption and saving functions and the investment schedule. Now we will see how these concepts combine to explain how the economy's equilibrium level of total income, output, and employment is determined. Once we understand how equilibrium is determined, we will be able to see how the economy's equilibrium levels of income, output, and employment are affected by changes in consumption and investment expenditures such as those discussed in the news item above. We will also see how the economy's aggregate supply curve interacts with total demand to generate the "inflationary pressures" mentioned in the news item.

We will continue to make no distinction between GNP, NNP, NI, PI, and DI because, as in the last chapter, we assume there is no government expenditure or taxation, that all saving is personal saving, and that capital depreciation is zero. Until the last part of this chapter, we will also continue to assume that wages and prices are unchanging. Then we will discuss the relationship between total demand, aggregate supply, and price changes. These assumptions simplify the analysis without interfering with the learning objectives of this chapter in any way. Government expenditure and tax effects will be introduced into this framework in the next chapter.

TOTAL DEMAND
AND TOTAL INCOME:
DETERMINING EQUILIBRIUM

In Chapter 4 we saw how demand and supply interact to determine the equilibrium price and quantity of a good bought and sold in a particular market. The equilibrium price is the one price, among all possible prices, at which the quantity of the good demanded by buyers is just equal to the quantity of the good that suppliers are willing to supply. The concept of the equilibrium income level for the economy is similar to the concept of the equilibrium price in an individual market. *The* **equilibrium income level** *is the one income level, among all possible income levels, at which the dollar value of the economy's total demand for output is just equal to the dollar value of total output that the firms in the economy desire to produce. It is also the level of total income that will be sustained once it is achieved.* Let's see how it is determined.

Total Demand Equals Consumption Plus Intended Investment

In the last chapter, we examined how the level of consumption expenditure in the economy depends on the level of total income as represented by the consumption function. We also examined several of the crucial determinants of the level of desired or intended investment expenditures, as represented by the investment schedule. We saw that both of these components could be shown in a graph with the income level measured on the horizontal axis and desired consumption expenditures (Figure 7-3, part a) or intended investment expenditures (Figure 7-7) measured on the vertical axis. We may now combine these two components to form the economy's total spending or *total demand schedule.* In this chapter we assume that the only components of total demand are consumption and investment.[1]

[1] Government expenditures will be introduced in the next chapter, and net exports, a minor component of total demand in our economy, will be ignored until we discuss international trade in a later chapter.

The hypothetical example of Table 8-1, which is shown graphically in Figure 8-1, shows how this is done. At each level of total income, column 1 of Table 8-1, the economy's households wish to spend an amount given by the associated level of consumption expenditures *C* shown in column 2. This component of total demand is represented in Figure 8-1 by the data for total income in column 1 of Table 8-1 (measured on the horizontal axis) and the associated levels of consumption expenditure from column 2 of Table 8-1 (measured on the vertical axis).

Column 3 of Table 8-1 shows the level of intended or planned investment expenditures *I* for the entire economy associated with each level of total income in column 1. Our example assumes that the amount of intended investment is the same ($300 billion) no matter what the level of total income. (This pattern of investment could be represented by a horizontal investment schedule like that shown in Figure 7-7, part a.)

The level of total spending or total demand associated with each level of total income, column 1, is shown in column 4 of Table 8-1. The total demand level is obtained by adding the level of consumption expenditures (column 2) to the intended investment expenditures (column 3). It is represented in Figure 8-1 by the line drawn parallel to the consumption function and lying above it by a vertical distance equal to $300 billion, the amount of intended investment. This line is the economy's *total demand schedule D,* which is equal to *C* plus *I*.

The economy's total demand schedule represents the amount of total spending on final goods and services that the economy's households and businesses desire to make at each possible level of total income.

Total Income Equals Expected Total Spending

Given that total demand depends on the level of the economy's total income, the next question is what determines the level of total income? The answer is the level of expected total spending. Why?

Two important characteristics of total income bear on the answer to this question. First, income is a flow measured as so many dollars per period of time—a year for example. Second, total income is the sum of all payments received by the suppliers of all productive factors—land, labor, capital, and all other inputs—used in the production of the economy's total output per period of time.

The economy's business firms buy, hire, and employ these factors in *anticipation* of being able to sell the resulting output. The way this occurs may be thought of as having two steps. First, each of the economy's business firms forms an expectation of what it thinks its level of sales will be during the coming time period. The sum of all these expectations is the dollar value of total sales that the economy's business firms *expect* during the coming time period. In other words, this sum represents the level of *expected total spending* on final goods and services. Second, the economy's business firms buy, hire, and employ just that quantity of productive factors that is needed to produce a dollar value of

---

After reading this chapter, you will be able to:
1. Explain how the equilibrium level of total income is determined.
2. Distinguish between realized and intended investment, and explain their relationship to saving and equilibrium.
3. Define the multiplier and illustrate why shifts in the components of total demand have multiplier effects.
4. Describe and explain the paradox of thrift.
5. State the relationship between total demand and supply.
6. Explain the concept of the inflationary zone, and state its implications for the relationship between inflation and unemployment.

TABLE 8-1 TOTAL DEMAND EQUALS CONSUMPTION PLUS INTENDED INVESTMENT (Hypothetical Data in Billions of Dollars)

(1)	(2)	(3)	(4)
Total Income	Consumption Expenditure (C)	Intended Investment (I)	Total Demand (D) or Total Spending
			D = (2) + (3)
$ 200	$ 300 +	$300 =	$ 600
400	400 +	300 =	700
600	500 +	300 =	800
800	600 +	300 =	900
1,000	700 +	300 =	1,000
1,200	800 +	300 =	1,100
1,400	900 +	300 =	1,200
1,600	1,000 +	300 =	1,300
1,800	1,100 +	300 =	1,400

total output that is equal to expected total spending. But the dollar value of this total output is nothing more or less than the total of all the payments for the factors used to produce it. And this total is the economy's total income. Therefore, it follows that the economy's total income over any time period is equal to the level of expected total spending over that time period.

This concept is represented graphically in Figure 8-2. The axes in this figure are the same as those in Figure 8-1. Expected total spending is measured on the vertical axis and total income on the horizontal axis. Since total income (horizontal axis) is always equal to expected total spending (vertical axis), this relationship may be represented by the already familiar 45° line. Why? Because any point on this line corresponds to a dollar magnitude on either axis that is exactly equal to the corresponding dollar magnitude on the other axis.

For example, suppose the economy's business firms expect total spending to be $1,000 billion (vertical axis), which corresponds to point e on the 45° line. They will then proceed to produce $1,000 billion of total output, an amount just sufficient to satisfy expected total spending. Since this $1,000 billion is the total of all payments for the factors used to produce the total output, it is the level of total income in the

economy. Measured on the horizontal axis, a total income level of $1,000 billion also corresponds to point e on the 45° line.

Determining the Equilibrium Level of Total Income

We can now see how the economy's equilibrium level of total income is determined. This is the level of total income which will be sustained once it is achieved. To do this we combine the economy's total demand schedule D from Figure 8-1 with the 45° line from Figure 8-2 that represents the relationship between expected total spending and total income. This combination is shown in Figure 8-3, which is based on the hypothetical data of Table 8-2. First we will consider two possible nonequilibrium levels of total income. It will then be readily apparent why the equilibrium level of total income occurs where the total demand schedule D intersects the 45° line at point e.

UNINTENDED INVENTORY REDUCTION

Let us suppose that the economy's business firms *expect* total spending (vertical axis) to be $600 billion during the coming period. This corresponds to point a on the 45° line of Figure 8-3. Acting on the basis of this expectation, they produce $600 billion worth of total output. Since this represents $600 billion of payments to

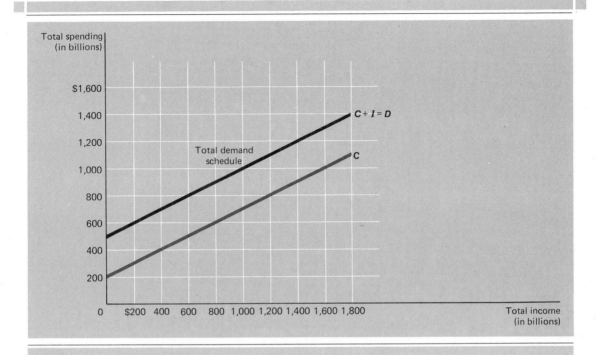

FIGURE 8-1 THE ECONOMY'S TOTAL DEMAND SCHEDULE EQUALS THE SUM OF CONSUMPTION AND INTENDED INVESTMENT AT EACH POSSIBLE LEVEL OF TOTAL INCOME

The consumption function C shown here is constructed from the numbers in columns 1 and 2 of Table 8-1. It shows the level of consumption expenditures (vertical axis) that the economy's households will want to make at each possible level of total income (horizontal axis).

The economy's total demand schedule D is obtained by adding the level of intended investment expenditures I, column 3 of Table 8-1, to the level of consumption expenditures at each level of total income. In this case the level of intended investment expenditures is $300 billion no matter what the level of total income. Consequently, the total demand schedule D is parallel to the consumption function C and lies above it by a distance equal to $300 billion.

The economy's total demand schedule D represents the amount of total spending on final goods and services (measured on the vertical axis) that the economy's households and businesses desire to make at each possible level of total income (measured on the horizontal axis).

all the factors used to produce this total output, the economy's total income level (horizontal axis) is $600 billion, which also corresponds to point a on the 45° line. However, with a total income level of $600 billion, the *actual* level of total spending in the economy will turn out to be $800 billion, which corresponds to point a' on the economy's total demand schedule D. But the economy only produced $600 billion worth

of total output during the period. Consequently, the only way the total demand of $800 billion can be satisfied is for businesses to sell $200 billion of goods from inventories. That is, they must draw from stocks of goods produced and accumulated during *past* periods. The amount of this *unintended inventory reduction* is represented by the vertical distance between point a' on the economy's total demand schedule D and

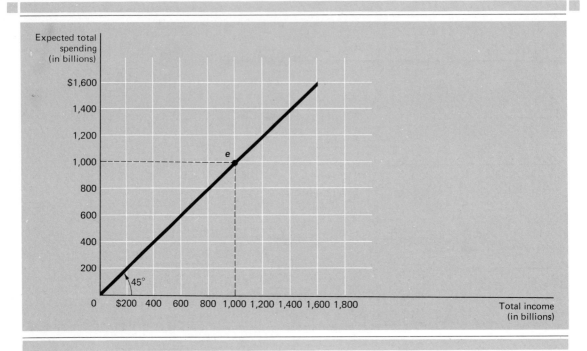

FIGURE 8-2 TOTAL INCOME EQUALS THE LEVEL OF EXPECTED TOTAL SPENDING

The economy's expected total spending is measured on the vertical axis and its total income on the horizontal axis.

The economy's business firms buy and hire just the quantity of productive factors needed to produce a dollar value of total output sufficient to satisfy expected total spending. The dollar value of total output represents the total of all the payments for the factors used to produce it. This is the economy's total income. Consequently total income (horizontal axis) equals expected total spending (vertical axis). This is represented by the 45° line because any dollar magnitude on either axis corresponds to an exactly equal dollar magnitude on the other. For example, expected total spending of $1,000 billion is reflected from the vertical axis to point e on the 45° line and down to the horizontal axis to give $1,000 billion of total income.

point *a* on the 45° line. It is an *unintended* reduction precisely because the economy's business firms underestimated what the level of total spending in the economy was going to be. They expected total spending to amount to $600 billion during the period and therefore they produced that dollar value of output. They had not intended to satisfy sales by selling off stocks of goods, or inventories, produced and accumulated during past periods.

Despite the fact that total spending turned out to be $800 billion during the period, the economy's total income is only $600 billion. That was all that was earned by, and paid to, the economy's productive factors for producing output during the period. The $200 billion sold from inventories during the period represents the value of goods produced in past periods. It was already counted as income earned during those periods.

The fact that the economy's business firms have to sell from inventories to meet total demand tells them that they underestimated total spending. If they were to continue doing this, unintended inventory reduction would also continue. Eventually, perhaps quickly, this will cause them to revise their expectations of total spending upward. The dollar value of total output produced, and hence the level of the economy's total income, will rise accordingly. This adjustment process will continue as long as there is any unintended reduction of inventories.

When and where will the adjustment stop? When unintended inventory reduction ceases— at the income level at which the level of total spending is just equal to that expected. In Figure 8-3 this occurs at a total income of $1,000 billion, corresponding to the intersection of the total demand schedule D with the 45° line at point e. Here the economy's business firms expect total spending (vertical axis) to be $1,000 billion and therefore produce $1,000 billion of total output, which gives rise to $1,000 billion of total income. This total income in turn leads to $1,000 billion of actual total spending—just the amount business firms expect and therefore produce to meet during the period. There is no unintended change in inventories. There is no reason for businesses to revise their expectations and produce a different level of output. Hence, the level of total income will no longer change once this level has been attained. It is therefore the equilibrium level of total income.

Starting from any level of expected total spending—and hence total income—less than $1,000 billion, total income will tend to rise until the equilibrium level is reached and there is no longer any unintended reduction of inventories. This is illustrated in Table 8-2. You should check the numbers shown there and relate them to Figure 8-3.

UNINTENDED INVENTORY INCREASE

Consider what happens at total income levels greater than the equilibrium level. Suppose the economy's business firms expect total spending (vertical axis) to be $1,400 billion, corresponding to point b on the 45° line in Figure 8-3. Therefore, they produce that amount of total output and the economy's total income (horizontal axis) is $1,400 billion. But at that total income level, actual total demand (vertical axis)

will turn out to be only $1,200 billion, point b' on the economy's total demand schedule D. This means that $200 billion of the economy's total output will go unsold and therefore end up as an unintended inventory increase. This increase is represented by the vertical distance between points b and b' in Figure 8-3.

The $1,400 billion level of total income will not be sustained. Why? Business firms will not go on producing more output than they can sell, thereby increasing their unsold inventory. Instead, they will revise their expectations of total spending downward and produce less. As a result, total income will fall until the level of total spending they expect finally turns out to be correct—that is, equal to the level of total spending that actually takes place. At this point, there is no unintended inventory increase and no reason for them to revise their expectation of the level of total spending downward still further. This, of course, is the equilibrium total income level of $1,000 billion, which corresponds to the intersection of the economy's total demand schedule D and the 45° line at point e in Figure 8-3. We can now see that, starting from any level of total income greater than the equilibrium level, total income will tend to fall to the equilibrium level. Again this is illustrated in Table 8-2. You should check out the numbers in this table and relate them to Figure 8-3.

In sum, *the economy's equilibrium level of total income gives rise to a level of total spending or demand that just purchases the total output that the economy's businesses desire to produce. In equilibrium there is no change in inventories because total spending just matches the dollar value of total output.*

EQUILIBRIUM
WITHOUT FULL EMPLOYMENT

Recall that we are assuming that wages and prices remain unchanged when total spending and total income change. Suppose we think of the dollar value of the economy's total output as $p \times Q$—the product of a general price index p multiplied by the quantity of the total output Q, where Q is the number of actual physical units of output. If p remains unchanged when total spending and total income change, the entire

TABLE 8-2 HOW THE ECONOMY'S EQUILIBRIUM TOTAL INCOME LEVEL IS DETERMINED (Hypothetical Data in Billions of Dollars)

(1)	(2)	(3)	(4)	(5)
Expected Total Spending	Total Income	Total Spending or Total Demand (D)	Change in Inventories	Total Income Will Tend to
$ 200	$ 200	$ 600	$ -400	rise
400	400	700	-300	rise
600	600	800	-200	rise
800	800	900	-100	rise
1,000	1,000	1,000	0	equilibrium
1,200	1,200	1,100	+100	fall
1,400	1,400	1,200	+200	fall
1,600	1,600	1,300	+300	fall
1,800	1,800	1,400	+400	fall

change in $p \times Q$ is due to a change in Q. And in order to change Q, it is necessary to change the amount of labor used in production. In other words, the economy's level of total employment must change. Consequently, every level of total income on the horizontal axis of Figure 8-3 corresponds to a different level of total employment. Furthermore, the higher the total income level, the higher the level of total employment.

These considerations, together with our analysis of the determination of the equilibrium level of total income in Figure 8-3 and Table 8-2, have a very significant implication. Namely, *it is entirely possible that the level of employment associated with the equilibrium level of total income will not correspond to full employment.* For example, suppose that the labor force will be fully employed only when the economy produces the level of total output associated with a total income level equal to $1,400 billion. However, we have already seen that if the economy's total demand schedule is D (Figure 8-3), total spending is not sufficient to sustain this level of total income. The sustainable or equilibrium level of total income is only $1,000 billion. Consequently, some of the labor force will be unemployed. In general, the lower the equilibrium level of total income the higher the unemployment rate.

■ CHECKPOINT 8-1

Give the explanation of what happens in the economy starting at any level of expected total spending and proceeding from column 1 to 2 to 3 to 4 to 5 in Table 8-2. In Table 8-2, suppose the economy's level of total spending or total demand (column 3) is higher by $100 billion at every level of total income (column 2). What would be the new equilibrium level of total income, and how would columns 4 and 5 be changed? Can you sketch this change in Figure 8-3? Why is it that the unintended inventory increase, represented by the vertical distance between b and b′ in Figure 8-3, is included in total income, while the unintended inventory reduction, which is equal to the vertical distance between a′ and a, is not?

EQUILIBRIUM AND REALIZED VERSUS INTENDED INVESTMENT

So far, our discussion of how the equilibrium level of total income is determined has focused on the total demand schedule D and its relationship to the 45° line. Now let's look at this relationship more closely. First, we will explicitly recognize that the total demand schedule D is equal to the sum of consumption and the level

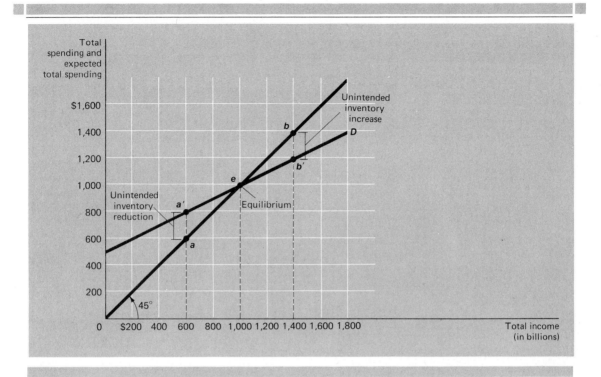

FIGURE 8-3 DETERMINING THE EQUILIBRIUM LEVEL OF TOTAL INCOME

The economy's total demand schedule *D* from Figure 8-1 is combined with the 45° line of
Figure 8-2. The equilibrium level of total income, which equals $1,000 billion, corresponds
to their intersection at point *e*. This level of total income gives rise to a level of total
spending or demand that just equals the total output the economy's businesses desire to
produce. Thus, there are no changes in inventories.

At total income levels lower than the equilibrium level, total demand is greater than total
output. Therefore, unintended inventory reduction is necessary in order to satisfy the
excess of total spending over total output. This will lead the economy's businesses to
increase total output, causing total income to rise toward the equilibrium level.

At total income levels greater than the equilibrium level, total demand is less than total
output. There are unintended inventory increases equal to the excess of total output over
total spending. Therefore, the economy's businesses will decrease total output causing
total income to fall toward the equilibrium level.

The data on which Figure 8-3 is based are shown in Table 8-2.

of intended or desired investment, as shown in
Figure 8-1. Then we will explicitly recognize
the relationship between total income and consumption (the consumption function) and total
income and saving (the saving function). These
relationships were shown in Figure 7-3 of the
previous chapter.

Continuing with our hypothetical example,
the data from Tables 8-1 and 8-2 are shown
again in columns 1, 2, 4, 5, and 6 of Table 8-3.
Also shown is the level of saving (column 3)
which is equal to the difference between total
income and consumption (column 1 minus column 2). Realized investment, which is equal to

TABLE 8-3 DETERMINATION OF THE EQUILIBRIUM LEVEL OF TOTAL INCOME, AND THE RELATIONSHIP BETWEEN INTENDED INVESTMENT, REALIZED INVESTMENT, AND SAVING
(Hypothetical Data in Billions of Dollars)

(1)	(2)	(3)	(4)	(5)	(6)	(7)
Total Income and Output	Con- sumption Expenditure (C)	Saving (S)	Intended Investment (I)	Total Demand (D) or Total Spending	Unintended Inventory Change Equals Total Output Minus Total Demand	Realized Investment Equals Intended Investment Plus Unintended Inventory Change
		$S = (1) - (2)$		$D = (2) + (4)$	$(1) - (5)$	$(4) + (6)$
$ 200	$ 300	$-100	$300	$600	$-400	$-100
400	400	0	300	700	-300	0
600	500	100	300	800	-200	100
800	600	200	300	900	-100	200
1,000	700	300	300	1,000	0	300
1,200	800	400	300	1,100	100	400
1,400	900	500	300	1,200	200	500
1,600	1,000	600	300	1,300	300	600
1,800	1,100	700	300	1,400	400	700

the sum of columns 4 and 6, is shown in column 7. These relationships are shown in Figure 8-4, which is the same as Figure 8-3 except that the consumption function has been added. This function is the level of consumption expenditure C (column 2) associated with each level of total income (column 1). We will use Figure 8-4 to help us define the concept of realized investment and its relationship to intended investment. We will then examine the relationship between these two types of investment and saving, both when the economy is at its equilibrium income level and when it is not.

Realized Investment Always Equals Saving

In Chapter 5 gross private domestic investment was defined as including all final purchases of new tools and machines by business

firms, all construction expenditures, *and all changes in inventories.*

AT TOTAL INCOME LEVELS BELOW EQUILIBRIUM LEVEL

We have seen that when the economy is at a below-equilibrium level of total income, there is an unintended inventory change. This change is an inventory reduction, which is represented by the vertical distance between the total demand schedule D and the 45° line. For example, when total income is $600 billion (Figure 8-4, part a), there is an unintended inventory reduction of $200 billion, which is represented by the vertical distance between a' and a. The amount of intended investment, or the investment that business firms *desire* to do, is $300 billion, which is represented by the vertical distance a' to a'' between the total demand schedule D and the consumption function *C*. However, this $300 billion investment expenditure when combined with the $500 billion of consumption expenditure (a sum equal to $800 billion), exceeds the $600 billion of total output produced during the period, corresponding to point *a* on the 45° line, by $200 billion. Hence, $200 billion of goods has to be sold from inventory to satisfy this excess of total spending over total production. This $200 billion decrease, or *negative change,* in inventories is an offset to the $300 billion of intended investment. It is often called a disinvestment. Actual or **realized investment** therefore amounts to only $100 billion, which is represented by the vertical distance between point *a* on the 45° line and point *a″* on the consumption function *C*.

Note that this vertical distance between point *a* on the 45° line and point *a″* on the consumption function also represents the amount of saving that households do out of the $600 billion total income. Therefore, it follows that *realized investment is equal to saving.* At any total income level less than the equilibrium level of total income (which is equal to $1,000 billion in our example), intended investment is always greater than realized investment. A comparison of columns 4 and 7 of Table 8–3 for the total income levels (column 1) less than the equilibrium level bears this out. At any of these total income levels, it is also always true that realized investment equals saving (compare columns 3 and 7). You should relate these numbers to Figure 8–4.

AT TOTAL INCOME LEVELS
ABOVE EQUILIBRIUM LEVEL

At total income levels greater than the equilibrium level, we observed that there are unintended inventory increases represented by the vertical distance between the total demand schedule *D* and the 45° line. For instance, at a total income level of $1,400 billion (Figure 8–4, part a), we see a $200 billion unintended inventory increase. This increase is equal to the vertical distance between *b* and *b′*. Once again the amount of intended investment that the economy's business firms desires to do equals $300 billion. This desired investment is represented

by the vertical distance between point *b′* on the total demand schedule *D* and point *b″* on the consumption function *C*. This amount of investment expenditure plus the $900 billion of consumption expenditure gives a total spending level of $1,200 billion. But this level is $200 billion lower than the $1,400 billion level of total output produced during the period (point *b* on the 45° line). As a result, $200 billion of unsold goods remain on shelves and in warehouses as inventory. This $200 billion increase or *positive change* in inventories is unintended investment, an unplanned addition to the $300 billion of intended investment. Therefore, actual or *realized investment* amounts to $500 billion, which is equal to the vertical distance between point *b* on the 45° line and point *b″* on the consumption function *C*.

Again this vertical distance represents the amount of saving, equal to $500 billion, that takes place when the total income level is $1,400 billion. Once more we see that *realized investment is equal to saving.* Indeed, this is true at any total income level greater than the equilibrium level. For example, in Table 8–3 compare columns 3 and 7 for each of the total income levels in column 1 greater than the $1,000 billion equilibrium level. It is also true that at any total income level greater than the equilibrium level, realized investment is always greater than intended investment, as we can see by comparing columns 4 and 7. Again, you should relate these numbers to Figure 8–4.

EQUILIBRIUM LEVEL OF TOTAL INCOME

Now consider the equilibrium level of total income, which is $1,000 billion. It is only here that the level of intended investment is equal to the level of realized investment, in this case $300 billion, which is represented by the vertical distance from *e* to *e′* in Figure 8–4, part a. This reflects the fact that there is no unintended change in inventory because the $1,000 billion level of total demand or spending just equals the $1,000 billion of total output produced. Again observe that realized investment equals saving, just as at all other levels of total income. But only at equilibrium is it also true that intended investment equals saving.

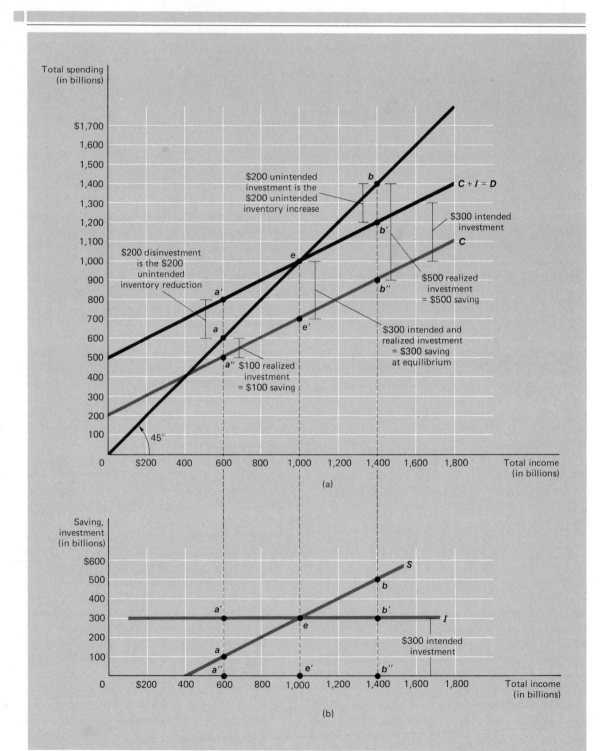

FIGURE 8-4 DETERMINATIONS OF THE EQUILIBRIUM LEVEL OF TOTAL INCOME, AND THE RELATIONSHIP BETWEEN INTENDED INVESTMENT, REALIZED INVESTMENT, AND SAVING

The diagram in part a is the same as that in Figure 8-3 except that the components that make up total demand D, consumption C and intended investment I, are explicitly shown along with the level of saving (which is equal to the difference between consumption C and the 45° line). At total income levels larger than the equilibrium level of $1,000 billion, realized investment exceeds intended investment by the amount of unintended inventory increase. At total income levels less than the equilibrium level, intended investment is greater than realized investment by the amount of unintended inventory reduction. Realized investment always equals saving, no matter what the level of total income. But intended investment equals saving, hence realized investment, only at the equilibrium level of total income.

The diagram in part b shows an alternative but completely equivalent way to represent the determination of the equilibrium level of total income. It combines the saving function S, corresponding to the consumption function in part a, with the investment schedule I, which shows the level of intended investment: the investment schedule I is the same as the vertical distance between the total demand schedule D and the consumption function C in part a. The points corresponding to a, e, b, and so forth in part a are similarly labeled in part b. The vertical distances between these points have exactly the same interpretation in part b as in part a. The equilibrium level of total income is determined by the intersection of the saving function S and the investment schedule I at point e.

By way of summary, we can say that:

1. *Actual or realized investment always equals saving no matter what the level of total income.*

2. *Intended investment equals saving only at the equilibrium level of total income.*

3. *Realized investment and intended investment are equal only at the equilibrium level of total income. At all other levels of total income, they differ by the amount of unintended inventory change.*

Leakages-and-Injections Interpretation of Equilibrium

In Figure 7-3 of the previous chapter, we examined the correspondence between the consumption function and the saving function. The saving function S in Figure 8-4, part b, corresponds to the consumption function C in Figure 8-4, part a, in exactly the same manner. The saving function is based on the data from columns 1 and 3 of Table 8-3. Figure 7-7, part a, of the previous chapter showed us that when the level of intended investment is the same at all income levels it may be represented by a horizontal investment schedule. Hence, the $300 billion level of intended investment represented by the vertical distance between the consumption

function C and the total demand schedule D in Figure 8-4, part a, also can be represented by the investment schedule I in Figure 8-4, part b. This investment schedule is based on the data from columns 1 and 4 of Table 8-3.

The combination of the saving function S and the investment schedule I in Figure 8-4, part b, is an alternative but completely equivalent way to that shown in part a for representing how the equilibrium level of total income is determined. The points corresponding to a, e, b, and so forth in part a are similarly labeled in part b. The vertical distances between these points have exactly the same meaning in part b that they have in part a. However, the combination of the saving function S and the investment schedule I in part b suggests another interesting interpretation of the determination of the equilibrium level of total income. This is the leakages-and-injections interpretation.

THE CIRCULAR FLOW

We anticipated this interpretation in the previous chapter. There we noted that the circular flow nature of the total-spending-equals-total-income relationship suggests that saving is like a leakage from the ongoing flow, while investment is like an injection to that flow. Investment spending by businesses acts as an offset to the saving by households (their refraining from spending out of income), and can prevent a sharp drop in the ongoing level of total spending. This is so because not all of the economy's output is sold to consumers. Some of it is sold to businesses in the form of capital goods; thus, investment spending takes a portion of total output off the market.

What will be the equilibrium, or unchanging, level of the total-spending-equals-total-income circular flow? It will be that level at which the associated amount of leakage due to saving is just exactly offset by the amount of injection due to intended investment. In other words, equilibrium will be reached at the level of total income at which intended investment equals saving. This level is represented in Figure 8-4, part b, by the intersection of the saving function S and the investment schedule I at point e, which corresponds to a total income level of $1,000 billion.

AT TOTAL INCOME LEVELS
ABOVE EQUILIBRIUM LEVEL

At total income levels greater than the equilibrium level, the leakage from saving will be larger than the injection from intended investment. This can be seen by comparing columns 3 and 4 of Table 8-3, and it is also represented by the fact that the saving function S lies above the investment schedule I to the right of point e. For example, at a total income level of $1,400 billion, point b'', the leakage from total income due to saving equals $500 billion, which is represented by the vertical distance from b'' to b. However, the injection due to intended investment is only $500 billion, the vertical distance from b'' to b'. This means that of the $500 billion of total output *not* purchased by consumers only $300 billion is taken off the market through intended investment spending by businesses. The rest, amounting to $200 billion and represented by the vertical distance from b' to b, is left unsold on shelves and in warehouses as an unintended addition to inventory. This addition to inventory will lead the economy's businesses to reduce production of total output and thereby cause the level of total income to fall, as

we discussed earlier in looking at Figure 8-4, part a. Total income will continue to fall until the amount of total output consumers refrain from purchasing—the amount consumers save—equals the amount businesses purchase—their intended investment spending. This equality occurs only at the equilibrium total income level of $1,000 billion, the level at which intended investment and saving both equal $300 billion, as represented by the vertical distance between point e' and e, in Figure 8-4, part b.

AT TOTAL INCOME LEVELS
BELOW THE EQUILIBRIUM LEVEL

At total income levels less than the equilibrium level, the leakage from saving will be less than the injection from intended investment. This may be seen by comparing columns 3 and 4 of Table 8-3. It is also represented by the fact that the saving function lies below the investment schedule to the left of point e, in Figure 8-4, part b. For instance, at a total income level of $600 billion, point a'', the leakage from total income due to saving is only $100 billion, represented by the vertical distance from a'' to a. But the injection from intended investment amounts to $300 billion, which is equal to the distance from a'' to a'. The difference, amounting to $200 billion, is the excess of total demand or spending over total output, which is represented by the vertical distance between a and a'. In order to satisfy this excess demand, producers must sell goods from inventories. But this reduction in inventories will lead the economy's businesses to increase the production of total output. Consequently the economy's total income will rise, as we discussed earlier in connection with part a of Figure 8-4. Total income will continue to rise, and the amount of leakage due to saving will continue to increase until it equals the amount of injection into the circular flow due to intended investment. Again, this equality occurs only at the equilibrium total income level of $1,000 billion, the level at which the saving function S intersects the investment schedule I at point e in Figure 8-4, part b.

EQUILIBRIUM LEVEL OF TOTAL INCOME

Finally, representation of equilibrium in Figure 8-4, part b, as the point at which the saving

ECONOMIC THINKERS

JOHN MAYNARD KEYNES

1883-1946

Keynes, the great British scholar, was doubtless the most influential economist of the first half of the twentieth century.

In 1906, when he graduated from Cambridge, he took the civil service examination and was assigned to the India office, but in 1908 he returned to Cambridge, and was soon elected a fellow of Kings College. He remained at least formally associated with the college for the balance of his life. When World War I began he was appointed to the British delegation at the Versailles Peace Conference. Keynes burst into public view in 1919 with the publication of his small book, *Economic Consequences of the Peace,* which denounced the economic aspects of the Versailles treaty. From that time until his death, he was a public personage.

As the 1930s passed, and Keynes's grim predictions of the results of the treaty came to pass, he gained increasing authority. By the mid-1930s Keynes had published several major books, and was about to make his leading contribution in economics. In 1936 he published *The General Theory of Employment Interest and Money,* a book which had about the same impact on affairs as had been exerted by Adam Smith's *The Wealth of Nations* a century and a half before.

Up to this point Keynes had generally accepted the elements of neoclassical economics as espoused by such great economists as Alfred Marshall, the English economist who had been his teacher at Cambridge. Neoclassical economics assumed that Say's law of markets was valid, that full employment was the natural case when the economy was in equilibrium. Prices and interest rates would be flexible, varying with demand and supply. Free competition would be the normal case. If unemployment occurred, there would be a tendency toward the restoration of full employment. There would at all times be sufficient demand to take the goods produced off the market. Any deviation from this norm would be brief (of course there might be hard times, the business cycle, etc.) but these would be abnormal and largely self-correcting.

Keynes objected to these concepts in whole or in part. He contended that the economy might well be in equilibrium and at the same time at a position of less than full employment. That is, aggregate demand for goods and services might be inadequate to support full employment. Of course there was increasing evidence that prices and wages were often rigid due to monopolistic elements in the economy, unions, price fixing, nonprice competition, and other factors. U.S. economists especially argued that this was in fact most often the case.

However, Keynes's theory did not rest merely on the existence of rigid prices and wage rates. In his view the volume of employment was determined by the level of "effective demand." Even if wages were flexible the same problem might be present because of the possible rigidity of interest rates.

Keynes suggested increased government expenditures to supplement private expenditures for consumption and investment in the event that these expenditures were inadequate to provide full employment, which was often the case.

In the United States some American economists battling the depression advocated Keynesian measures as part of the "New Deal" machinery. These battles were fought throughout the 1930s, but President Roosevelt's advisors were not really active Keynesians until after 1938, and Roosevelt himself was never convinced of the virtue of budget deficits. By the 1950s Keynesian economics had become well integrated into basic theory and was an integral part of economics as taught on the undergraduate level.

FOR FURTHER READING

R. F. Harrod. *The Life of John Maynard Keynes.* New York: Harcourt Brace Jovanovich, 1951.

Hugh S. Norton. *The Employment Act and the Council of Economic Advisers 1946-1976.* Columbia: University of South Carolina Press, 1977.

function S and the investment schedule I intersect reminds us of an important point made by Keynes and his followers. That is, factors that determine saving are quite different from those that affect the decision to invest. This is true because those who save, namely households, are a different group of decision makers with different motives from those who invest, namely businesses. *The equilibrium level of total income, corresponding to the intersection of the saving function S and the investment schedule I, is the only level where the total of the saving plans of the economy's households just matches the total of the investment plans of the economy's businesses. At any other level there will be a discrepancy between the plans of these two groups.*

■ CHECKPOINT 8-2

Explain why realized investment is *always* equal to saving. Explain why it is sometimes said that "this is obvious because that part of total output that is not consumed must go someplace." In the previous chapter, we noted that "if households put their saving in sugar bowls and mattresses, or bury it in the backyard, investment will have to be financed by the banking system." What bearing does this have on the fact that total spending is always greater than total income at levels of total income less than the equilibrium level?

SHIFTS IN TOTAL DEMAND AND THE MULTIPLIER EFFECT

Our examination of the business cycle in Chapter 6 indicated that total output, income, and employment are always "on the move." One of the main reasons for this movement is that total demand frequently shifts. In the simple economy we are considering in this chapter, where government expenditure and taxation are ignored, shifts in total demand can be caused by shifts in either or both of its components—consumption and intended investment. Such shifts are represented by changes in the position of the total demand schedule that are reflected in changes in the equilibrium levels of total income, output, and employment.

Shifts in the consumption and saving functions, the investment schedule, and hence the total demand schedule, are due to causes *other than* changes in the level of total income. Changes in the level of total income cause *movement along* these curves. Changes in all other things—expectations, wealth, interest rates, and so forth—cause *shifts or changes in the position* of these curves. It is extremely important to keep this distinction in mind.

Shifts in total demand, whatever the underlying cause, give rise to even larger changes in total income and output. This is referred to as the multiplier effect. Given the dollar amount of the shift in total demand, the resulting change in total income and output will be several times larger, or some multiple of this amount. This multiple is called the **multiplier**. For instance, if intended investment rises by $10 billion and the resulting change in total income amounts to $30 billion, the multiplier is 3. If the rise in total income is $40 billion, the multiplier is 4. Let's see why there is a multiplier effect, and what determines the size of the multiplier.

Graphical Interpretation of the Multiplier Effect

Suppose the economy's business firms believe that sales are going to pick up in the coming year and that they are going to need more productive capacity to meet this increase. This may be what the analysts cited in the news item at the beginning of the chapter have in mind when they "foresee an impressive turnabout this year" in spending on plant and equipment. What would be the effect on the economy of such an increase? Let's suppose that investment spending increases from $200 billion to $400 billion.

The effect of this increase on total income and output is shown in Figure 8-5. In this figure the economy is initially in equilibrium at a total income level of $800 billion. This is the level at which the total demand schedule D_0 (which equals $C + I$) and the 45° line intersect, point a in part a. Equivalently, it is the point at which the investment schedule I_0 and the saving function S intersect, point a in part b. A $200 billion increase in investment from I_0 to I_1 causes the total demand schedule in part a to shift upward from D_0 (which equals $C_0 + I_0$) to D_1 (which equals $C_0 + I_1$). Equivalently, this is represented in part b by the upward shift in the investment schedule from I_0 to I_1. Each of the diagrams shows that the equilibrium level of total income rises from $800 billion to $1,400 billion—given by the intersection of D_1 and the 45° line at point b in part a, and the intersection of S and I_1 at point b in part b. In other words, the $200 billion increase in investment causes a $600 billion increase in total income and output. This is the multiplier effect. The value of the multiplier is 3 in this hypothetical example.

The multiplier effect also applies for any decrease in the level of investment spending. For example, suppose that the economy is now at the equilibrium total income level of $1,400 billion. Then suppose the economy's business firms' expectations about future sales turn pessimistic, and investment spending shifts downward $200 billion from I_1 to I_0. This is represented in Figure 8-5, part a, by a downward shift in the total demand schedule from D_1 (which equals $C_0 + I_1$) to D_0 (which equals $C_0 + I_0$). Equivalently, it is represented in part b by a $200 billion downward shift in the investment schedule from I_1 to I_0. In either diagram we can see that total income and output fall by $600 billion, from $1,400 billion to $800 billion. Once again, the multiplier effect is at work, and the value of the multiplier is 3.

A Numerical Interpretation of the Multiplier Effect

We can also provide a numerical interpretation of the example of the multiplier effect that is illustrated in Figure 8-5. In this example, the marginal propensity to consume *MPC*, which is the slope of the consumption function, is $2/3$. Hence, the marginal propensity to save *MPS*, the slope of the saving function, is $1/3$. We will see how the *MPC* and the *MPS* play a crucial role in the multiplier effect, and in the determination of the size of the multiplier.

To do so, let's consider the data in Table 8-4. Again, we will assume that the economy is initially in equilibrium at a total income level of $800 billion. The table shows how an increase in investment expenditure of $200 billion has a chain-reaction effect on the economy. The expenditure increase causes an increase in income. Part of this income increase is spent, causing a

further increase in income, part of which is spent, and so on, round after round. At the first round firms react to the increase in total demand by increasing total output by $200 billion. This increased output, of course, is received as increased income (column 1), in the form of wages, rents, interest, and profit by the households who own the factors of production used to produce the increased output. Given an *MPC* of $2/3$, households will spend $133.4 billion of this income increase (column 2), and save $66.6 billion (column 3).

At the second round firms react to this $133.4 billion increase in total demand by increasing total output an equivalent amount. This gives rise to another increase in total demand by increasing total output an equivalent amount. This gives rise to another increase in payments to factors of production and a further rise in total income of $133.4 billion (column 1). In turn, $2/3$ of this, or $89 billion, is spent (column 2), and $44.4 billion is saved (column 3).

At the third round, the $89 billion increase in total demand again causes a like increase in total output, factor payments, and hence income (column 1). Then $2/3$, or $59.4 billion, of this increase is spent at the fourth round, and then $39.6 billion is spent at the fifth round, and so forth until the additions to total income ultimately become so small they are insignificant. Adding up all the round-by-round increases in total income in column 1, the total increase in total income and output is $600 billion. This is the same result we saw in Figure 8-5.

Why does the expansion in total income end here? The reason is that the $600 billion increase in total income gives rise to a $200 billion increase in the amount of saving, or leakage (column 3), that is just enough to offset the initial $200 billion increase in investment, or injection. At this point the economy is once again in equilibrium. Total income has increase by three times the initial increase in investment because the economy's households save $1/3$ of any increase in income. The multiplier is 3, just as it was in Figure 8-5.

The Multiplier and the *MPS* and *MPC*

Our example of the multiplier effect, illustrated in Figure 8-5 and Table 8-4, suggests

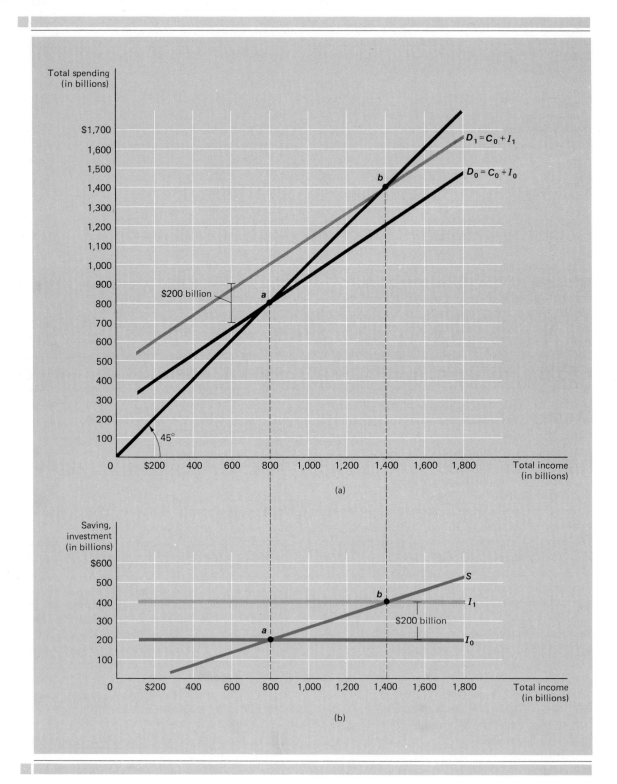

FIGURE 8-5 SHIFTS IN TOTAL DEMAND HAVE A MULTIPLIER EFFECT ON TOTAL INCOME AND OUTPUT

The total demand schedule in part a will be shifted by a shift in either or both of its components, the consumption function (hence the saving function) and the investment schedule. If the investment schedule shifts upward by $200 billion from I_0 to I_1, the total demand schedule will shift upward from D_0 (which equals $C_0 + I_0$) to D_1 ($C_0 + I_1$). Consequently, the equilibrium level of total income and output will rise from $800 billion to $1,400 billion, or by three times the amount of the investment spending increase. This is the multiplier effect. The multiplier equals 3 in this example.

Part b shows an equivalent representation of this shift in terms of the investment schedule and the saving function. This diagram indicates clearly why there is $600 billion increase in total income in response to the $200 billion increase in investment spending. The $600 billion increase in total income gives rise to a $200 billion increase in saving, or leakage, that is just enough to offset the initial $200 billion increase in investment, or injection.

that the size of the multiplier depends on the size of the *MPS* or its complement, the *MPC*. (Remember that *MPS* + *MPC* = 1, always.)

Recall that the *MPS* is represented by the slope of the saving function (see Figure 7-4, part b, of the previous chapter). The *MPS* or slope of the saving function S in Figure 8-5, part b, is ⅓. This means that every $1 increase in saving (vertical movement) corresponds to a $3 increase in total income (horizontal move-

ment). Consequently, when the investment schedule shifts upward by $200 billion from I_0 to I_1, saving likewise rises by $200 billion (vertical axis) and total income rises by $600 billion (horizontal axis). Every $1 of increase in investment spending gives rise to a $3 increase in total income. The multiplier is therefore 3. But this is just the reciprocal of the *MPS*—the value of the *MPS*, which is equal to ⅓, turned upside down.

TABLE 8-4 MULTIPLIER EFFECT OF AN EXPENDITURE INCREASE, ROUND BY ROUND (Hypothetical Data in Billions of Dollars)

Expenditure Round	(1) Change in Income and Output	(2) Change in Consumption MPC = ⅔	(3) Change in Saving MPS = ⅓
First round	$200.0	$133.4	$ 66.6
Second round	133.4	89.0	44.4
Third round	89.0	59.4	29.6
Fourth round	59.4	39.6	19.8
Fifth round	39.6	26.4	13.2
Rest of the rounds	78.6	52.2	26.4
Totals	$600.0	$400.0	$200.0

If the saving function S in Figure 8-5, part b, had an MPS equal $\frac{1}{2}$, it would be more steeply sloped. Then every \$1 of increased investment would result in a \$2 increase in total income. The multiplier would be 2, which is again equal to the reciprocal of the MPS of $\frac{1}{2}$. The \$200 billion increase in investment would result in a \$400 billion increase in total income. On the other hand, if the saving function had an MPS of $\frac{1}{4}$, it would be less steeply sloped and the multiplier would be 4. Total income would increase by \$800 billion in response to the \$200 billion increase in investment. (To convince yourself that this is so, sketch in the saving functions with an MPS of $\frac{1}{2}$ and $\frac{1}{4}$ by pivoting the saving function S in Figure 8-5, part b, about its intersection with the investment schedule I_0.)

When we look at the numerical illustration of our example in Table 8-4, the same conclusion emerges. When the MPS equals $\frac{1}{3}$, every \$1 of increased investment ultimately results in \$3 of increased total income—the \$200 billion increase in investment spending ultimately results in a \$600 billion increase in total income. The multiplier is 3. If the MPS had been $\frac{1}{2}$, the ultimate increase would have been \$400 billion—the multiplier is 2. If the MPS had been $\frac{1}{4}$, the increase would have been \$800 billion—the multiplier is 4.

In sum, for the simple economy of this chapter (no net exports, no government expenditures, no taxation), *the multiplier is equal to the reciprocal of the MPS:*

$$\text{the multiplier} = \frac{1}{MPS}$$

If MPS equals $\frac{1}{3}$, for example, then

$$\text{the multiplier} = \frac{1}{\frac{1}{3}} = 3$$

Note that, because $MPC + MPS = 1$, it is true that $MPS = 1 - MPC$ so that we can also say that

$$\text{the multiplier} = \frac{1}{1 - MPC}$$

Also note that *the smaller is the MPS, and therefore the larger the MPC, the larger the multiplier. Conversely, the larger the MPS, and hence the smaller the MPC, the smaller the multiplier.*

(Convince yourself of this by computing the multiplier first when $MPS = \frac{1}{2}$, hence $MPC = \frac{1}{2}$; and second when $MPS = \frac{1}{4}$, hence $MPC = \frac{3}{4}$.)

TWO IMPORTANT POINTS

Finally, two important points should be made about our discussion of the multiplier effect and the multiplier. First, our example assumed that the multiplier effect was triggered by a shift in investment spending. Exactly the same results would have followed if the trigger had instead been a shift in consumption spending, as represented by a shift in the consumption and saving functions. Second, the multiplier effect and the multiplier are just as applicable to downward shifts in investment or consumption spending as they are to upward shifts.

■CHECKPOINT 8-3

Suppose that the total demand schedule and the investment schedules are D_0 and I_0 in parts a and b respectively in Figure 8-5. Show what the effect would be in both parts a and b if there is a \$200 billion upward shift in the consumption function. Suppose the MPS is $\frac{1}{5}$. Show what the effect of a \$100 billion *downward* shift in consumption would be in a table like Table 8-4. Also, illustrate this effect graphically, using a figure like Figure 8-5, parts a and b. The news item at the beginning of the chapter notes that "consumers have spent so heavily in recent months that their savings have dwindled. . . ." In what sense is the word "savings" used? The news item seems to be talking about both movements along and shifts in the consumption function. Illustrate what is being said in terms of a diagram like Figure 8-5.

THE PARADOX OF THRIFT: WHAT DID BEN FRANKLIN SAY?

You have probably heard the old saw, attributed to Ben Franklin, that "a penny saved is a penny earned." It seems like good advice for a household. But it may not be good for the economy if all households follow it. Here we have a case of the fallacy of composition—what is true

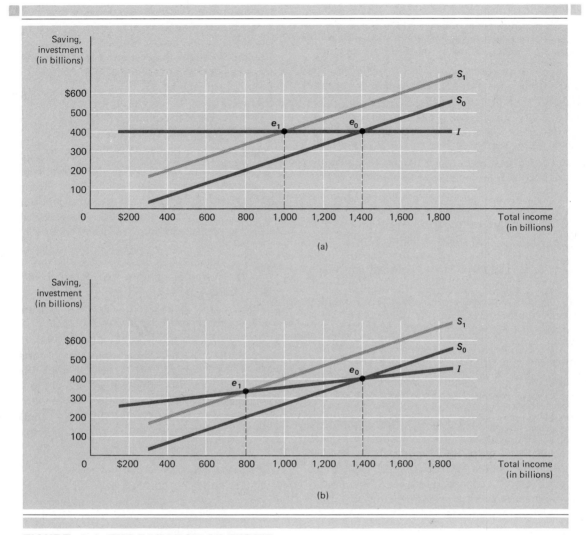

FIGURE 8-6 THE PARADOX OF THRIFT

It may well be good advice for a household to try to save more, but bad for the economy if all households attempt to do so.

Suppose the economy's equilibrium level of total income is initially $1,400 billion, as determined by the intersection of the saving function S_0 and investment schedule I at point e_0. If the economy's households attempt to save more, the saving function will shift up to the position S_1. Given the investment schedule I in part a, total income and output will fall to $1,000 billion and the amount of saving will in fact remain unchanged at $400 billion. If the level of intended investment varies with the level of total income and output, as shown in part b, the attempt to save more actually causes the amount saved to fall!

of the part is not necessarily true of the whole.

Suppose the equilibrium level of total income and output in the economy is $1,400 billion. This level is determined by the intersection of

the saving function S_0 with the investment schedule I at point e_0 in Figure 8-6, part a. The level of saving and investment (vertical axis) is $400 billion. Now suppose the economy's households follow Ben Franklin's advice. They decide to save more at every level of total income. The result would be an upward shift in the saving function from S_0 to S_1. But look what happens! The equilibrium level of total income and output falls from $1,400 billion to $1,000 billion, as determined by the intersection of S_1 and I at e_1. Furthermore, the amount of saving that actually takes place remains unchanged at $400 billion. A penny saved is not a penny earned. Quite the contrary, the *attempt* to save more results in no increase in saving and, worse yet, leads to an actual decline in the total income earned!

This **paradox of thrift** is even more pronounced if the level of intended investment varies with the level of total income, so that the investment schedule I slopes upward as shown in Figure 8-6, part b. Then the same upward shift in the saving function from S_0 to S_1 results in an even greater fall in total income and output, from $1,400 billion to $800 billion, as determined by the intersection of S_1 and I at e_1. Moreover, the amount of saving that actually takes place is now smaller! The attempt by the economy's households to save more leads to the paradoxical result that they end up saving less.

What explains the paradox of thrift? The answer is that the attempt to save more results in a larger leakage from total income. At the initial equilibrium level of total income, $1,400 billion in our example, the leakage exceeds the amount of intended investment spending. Consequently, the level of total income falls as the economy's businesses cut back the production of total output in order to avoid unintended inventory increases. This fall in total output and income continues until the level of saving, or leakage, is once again brought into equality with the level of intended investment, or injection. At this point there is no unintended inventory accumulated and the economy is once again at equilibrium.

■ CHECKPOINT 8-4

Explain the paradox of thrift in terms of what happens if the economy's households attempt to save less. To do so, use Figure 8-6, parts a and b. The news item at the beginning of the chapter suggests that consumers may attempt to rebuild "their savings" that have "dwindled." What do you as an "analyst" think about this? What are the possible implications for auto workers and steelworkers?

TOTAL DEMAND AND SUPPLY: INFLATION AND UNEMPLOYMENT

In a money-using, market-oriented economy like that of the United States, total output and the general price level are jointly determined by the interaction of total demand and aggregate supply. We may think of total demand as total money expenditures on goods and services, and aggregate supply as the economy's total production of goods and services.

So far in this chapter we have assumed that prices and wages are fixed or remain unchanged. This means that any change in the dollar value of total income and output is due entirely to a change in the quantity of real output—so many bushels of wheat, pairs of shoes, tons of steel, and so forth. Now we want to allow for the real-life situations in which wages and prices change. This requires that we bring the analysis of total demand, developed in this chapter, together with the concept of the aggregate supply curve.

The Aggregate Supply Curve

The relationship graphed in parts a and b of Figure 8-7 are two different ways of representing the aggregate supply curve for the economy. In part a, the economy's total quantity of output Q is measured on the horizontal axis. (In our simple example in Chapter 5 of an economy that produced only widgets, Q would be the number of widgets.) The economy's total money expenditure is measured on the vertical axis. It equals the general price level p multiplied by the total physical quantity of output Q, or $p \times Q$. (In the simple widget economy example, p would be the price of widgets.) The aggregate supply curve in part a shows the total quantity of output Q (horizontal axis) that the economy's business firms are willing to produce in response to each possible level of total money expenditure $p \times Q$ (vertical axis). Part b shows the conventional representation of the supply curve, such as that discussed in Chapter 4—price p on the vertical axis and total output Q on the horizontal axis. However, the representation of the aggregate supply curve in part a will be useful in our study of macroeconomics.

RANGE I OF THE AGGREGATE SUPPLY CURVE—NO INFLATION

Suppose that when the economy's total expenditure (vertical axis) is in Range 1 of the aggregate supply curve in Figure 8-7, part a, the economy has much excess capacity and unemployed labor. Profits, income, and employment are low. Therefore over this range any increase in total money expenditure is met entirely by an increase in the supply of total output Q (horizontal axis). That is, there is no increase in the general price level. It remains unchanged at p_0. Hence, the relationship between total money expenditure and total output over this range is represented by the straight, upward-sloping portion of the aggregate supply curve from 0 to point c in Figure 8-7, part a. The relationship between the general price level and total output over this range is further illustrated in Figure 8-7, part b, the conventional representation of the supply curve. As indicated by the horizontal segment $p_0 c$, the general price level (vertical axis) remains unchanged at p_0 for any change in output (horizontal axis) in Range 1. In sum, when total money expenditure increases over Range 1, part a, the price level remains constant at p_0 while total output Q supplied increases—there is no inflation.

RANGE 2 OF THE AGGREGATE SUPPLY CURVE—SOME INFLATION

Suppose that once the economy is producing the output level Q_0 in response to total money expenditure $p_0 \times Q_0$, there is a further increase of total money expenditure into Range 2 (vertical axis, Figure 8-7, part a). Some firms in some industries in the economy would begin to reach the limit of their capacity to produce and to have difficulty acquiring certain kinds of labor and other inputs. This means that further increases in the economy's total output will be accompanied by price increases as well. Hence,

the general price level will begin to rise with further increases in total money expenditure. The relationship between total money expenditure and total output in Range 2 is indicated by the curvilinear line segment from c to d in Figure 8-7, part a. The corresponding relationship between the general price level and total output in Range 2 is shown by the curvilinear line segment from c to d in Figure 8-7, part b. As total money expenditure increases in this range, the increase in the general price level p per each unit increase in total output Q becomes ever larger. The economy experiences inflation. The news item at the beginning of Chapter 6 notes that "some analysts think that the swifter pace of current business almost guarantees an acceleration of inflation later this year." These analysts appear to feel that the economy's total money expenditure is moving ever further into Range 2.

RANGE 3 OF THE AGGREGATE SUPPLY CURVE—ALL INFLATION

When total money expenditure reaches $p_f \times Q_f$ (vertical axis, Figure 8-7, part a) or beyond, the economy reaches full employment. Its productive capacity is fully utilized and it produces its maximum total output Q_f (horizontal axis)—its full-employment output level. Further increases in total money expenditure into Range 3 will only result in an increase in the general price level. Q remains at Q_f, and increases in total money expenditure go dollar for dollar into the rise in the general price level above p_f. This is represented by the vertical line segment above point d in both part a and part b of Figure 8-7.

REAL GNP, MONEY GNP, AND THE AGGREGATE SUPPLY CURVE

In the previous chapter, we explained the distinction between real GNP and money GNP. In terms of Figure 8-7, part a, you may think of money GNP as being measured on the vertical axis and real GNP as being measured on the horizontal axis. In Figure 8-7, part b, the index of current prices measuring the general price level would appear on the vertical axis, and real GNP would again be measured on the horizon-

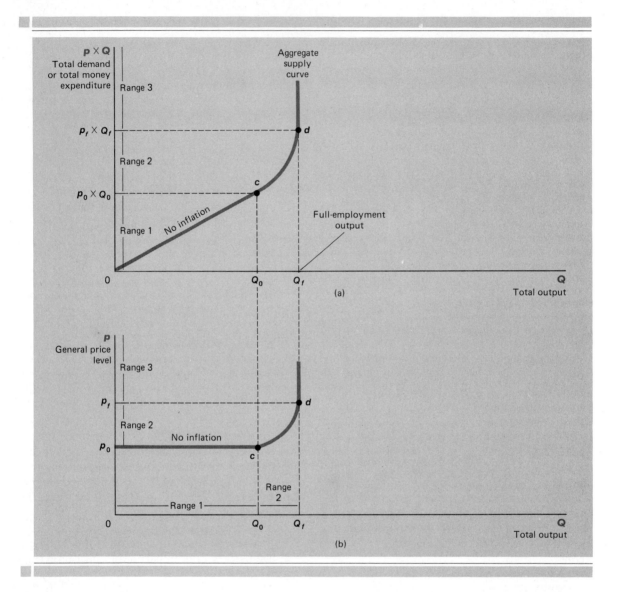

tal axis. Over Range 1, increases in money GNP and real GNP are the same because the general price level is constant. Over Range 2, money GNP increases faster than real GNP because the general price level is rising. Over Range 3, money GNP increases but real GNP remains unchanged.

Relationship Between Total Demand and Aggregate Supply

Figure 8-8 combines the aggregate supply curve, in part b, with total demand, in part a.

The vertical axes in both parts measure the same thing, the dollar amount of the economy's total spending or demand. The horizontal axis in part b measures the real quantity of output Q, the quantity of actual physical units produced by the economy. Total dollar spending (vertical axis) may be thought of as equal to the price p per unit of output multiplied by the quantity of output Q ($p \times Q$).

The economy's aggregate supply curve in part b shows the amount of total output (horizontal axis) that the economy's business firms

FIGURE 8-7 **THE RELATIONSHIP BETWEEN TOTAL MONEY EXPENDITURE, TOTAL OUTPUT, AND THE GENERAL PRICE LEVEL**

The relationship between the economy's total money expenditure and the economy's total output is shown in part a. When total money expenditure (vertical axis) increases in Range 1, there is a corresponding increase in the economy's total output Q (horizontal axis). This happens because in this range the economy has a lot of excess productive capacity. Consequently, the general price level remains unchanged at p_0 for increases in output all the way up to total output level Q_0, as shown in part b.

As total money expenditure increases in Range 2 (vertical axis, part a), the economy begins to encounter capacity limitations. Consequently, total output does not increase as much as total money expenditure, and the general price level begins to rise, as shown in part b.

When total money expenditure increases beyond Range 2 and into Range 3 (vertical axis, part a), the economy's productive capacity becomes fully utilized, and further increases in output beyond Q_f are not possible. Any increase in total money expenditure in Range 3 goes entirely into a rise in the general price level as shown in part b.

The relationships graphed in parts a and b are two different ways of representing the economy's aggregate supply curve. The one shown in part b is the conventional representation—price on the vertical axis and output on the horizontal. The one in part a is useful in macroeconomic analysis.

will produce in response to any given level of total demand or spending (vertical axis). Suppose that the equilibrium total income level in the economy equals $1,300 billion, as determined by the intersection of the total demand schedule D_0 with the 45° line at point e_0 in part a of Figure 8-8. The $1,300 billion of total spending is the level $p_0 \times Q_0$ on the vertical axis of part b—the index of current prices p_0 multiplied by the quantity of total output Q_0. This level of total spending corresponds to point e_0 on the economy's aggregate supply curve. And point e_0 corresponds to Q_0 (horizontal axis), the quantity of total output that the economy's business firms produce in response to this level of total spending.

Inflation and Unemployment

Suppose the economy must produce a level of total output equal to Q_f, in part b of Figure 8-8, in order to fully employ its labor force and other productive facilities. Producing the total output level Q_f does not typically mean that there is no unemployment. Rather, it means that the level of unemployment cannot be squeezed lower. Further increases in total demand simply drive up the price level. This is reflected in the fact that the aggregate supply curve becomes vertical at Q_f.

However, bottlenecks, shortages of one kind or other, and the onset of various kinds of operating inefficiencies will cause production costs to begin to rise well before the economy reaches its full-employment total output level Q_f. In fact, the aggregate supply curve of part b indicates that these difficulties will begin to set in once total spending in the economy reaches a level of $1,300 billion, which is equal to the level $p_0 \times Q_0$ (vertical axis, parts a and b). This corresponds to point e_0 on the aggregate supply curve and a level of total output equal to Q_0 (horizontal axis, part b).

THE INFLATIONARY ZONE AND DEMAND-PULL INFLATION

A less than full-employment equilibrium position will prevail when the total demand schedule of part a is D_0. The total demand schedule, hence total spending, may shift up to this level without causing any increase in the general price level. Up until this level of total demand (D_0) is reached, total spending increases will be matched dollar for dollar by increases in total output, as represented by the straight-line portion of the aggregate supply curve $0e_0$ in Figure 8-8, part b. The price level will remain unchanged at p_0 over this range. All of the increase

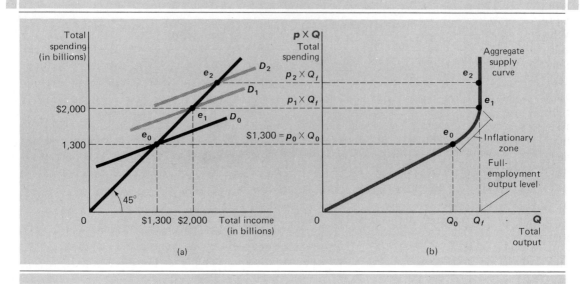

FIGURE 8-8 THE RELATIONSHIP BETWEEN TOTAL DEMAND AND AGGREGATE SUPPLY

The total demand schedule in part a may be combined with the economy's aggregate supply curve in part b to show the relationship between total demand or spending, the general price level p, and the total quantity of real output Q (units of physical output) produced.

When the economy's total demand schedule is D_0 in part a, total spending (vertical axis of parts a and b) is $1,300 billion, which is equal to $p_0 \times Q_0$. This corresponds to point e_0 on the aggregate supply curve and a level of total output Q_0 on the horizontal axis of part b. Shifts in the total demand schedule up to the position D_0 in part a cause no increase in the general price level. Increases in total spending go entirely into increases in Q, as represented by the straight-line segment of the aggregate supply curve from 0 to e_0 in part b, the price level remaining unchanged at p_0.

Shifts in the total demand schedule from D_0 to D_1 in part a cause the economy to produce in the inflationary zone of the aggregate supply curve between points e_0 and e_1 in part b. In this zone, increases in total spending result in ever larger increases in the price level p and ever smaller increases in output Q until the full-employment output level Q_f is reached and the price level has risen from p_0 to p_1.

Further upward shifts in the total demand schedule, such as from D_1 to D_2, will only cause the price level p to rise further, such as from p_1 to p_2. Since the economy is at full employment, total output cannot increase beyond Q_f, as represented by the vertical segment of the aggregate supply curve above Q_f on the horizontal axis. At this point further increases in total demand result in pure demand-pull inflation.

in total spending will be reflected in a rise in Q.

However, suppose the total demand schedule begins to shift up to a position above D_0 in part a. The economy will then move up along the aggregate supply schedule above the point e_0 in part b. While the level of total output (horizontal axis) will rise above Q_0, a larger and larger portion of the increase in total spending will go into a rise in p and an ever smaller portion into increased Q. This is the inflationary zone of the aggregate supply curve, which lies between e_0 and e_1. Once the total demand schedule has risen to the position D_1, in part a, total spending and the equilibrium level of total income will be $2,000 billion. The economy will be at full employment producing a total output of Q_f, and the price level will have risen to p_1 in part b.

Whenever the economy operates in the inflationary zone, further increases in total demand are accompanied by ever larger increases in the general price level. This is a cause of concern to those forecasters reported in the news item (at the beginning of this chapter) as saying that "the expected slowing in consumer outlays will actually be beneficial. They claim that if consumer outlays keep roaring ahead and other sectors of the economy also accelerate, inflationary pressures could mount dangerously later this year."

PURE DEMAND-PULL INFLATION

Once total spending (vertical axis) has reached \$2,000 billion, the level $p_1 \times Q_f$ in part b, further increases in total demand and spending will result in pure demand-pull inflation. For example, suppose the schedule shifts up from D_1 to D_2 in part a. The equilibrium level of total income and spending is now determined by the intersection of D_2 with the 45° line at point e_2 in part a. However, the entire increase in total spending now goes into a rise in the general price level from p_1 to p_2. Total spending rises from $p_1 \times Q_f$ to $p_2 \times Q_f$ on the vertical axis of part b, while total output remains unchanged at Q_f, corresponding to the vertical portion of the aggregate supply curve from e_1 to e_2.

COST-PUSH INFLATION[2]

Demand-pull inflation *originates on the demand side of the economy's markets for goods and services.* **Cost-push inflation** *originates on the supply side.* Cost-push may occur in the labor market where powerful unions coerce firms to pay them higher wages under the threat of a labor walkout or strike. The resulting rise in per unit costs of production is then likely to be passed on by these firms in the form of higher product prices. Similarly, a few large firms in a number of key industries might exercise their market power and try to raise profits by increasing the prices they charge for their products.

[2] The rest of this chapter may be postponed until Chapter 14.

Cost-push inflation may also result from an increase in the price of any vital resource needed to produce a variety of products. The sharp rise in the price of imported oil in 1973–1974 drove up the cost of energy—a necessary ingredient to any production process. The resulting rise in per unit production costs pushed up the prices of almost all products. This was reflected in a dramatic rise in the general price level.

The effect of cost-push inflation on the economy's aggregate supply curve is illustrated in Figure 8-9. (The curves drawn here are just like those of Figure 8-7.) The cost-push may originate in any of the ways just described, but it will always result in pushing up the prices charged for final goods and services. In Figure 8-9, part b, suppose the general price level (vertical axis) associated with any level of total output (horizontal axis) is initially given by the aggregate supply curve p_0s_0. The associated representation of the aggregate supply curve in part a is given by $0S_0$. Now suppose a cost-push occurs. This means that whatever level of total output we consider, it will be sold at a higher general price level than before. This is represented by the upward shift in the aggregate supply curve to p_1s_1 in part b. The associated representation of the shifted aggregate supply curve in part a is $0S_1$.

Before the cost-push occurred, any total output level up to Q_0 would have been sold at the general price level p_0, as indicated in Figure 8-9, part b. Any total output level between Q_0 and Q_f would have been sold at a higher general price level given by the corresponding point on the upward-sloping part of p_0s_0. After the cost-push, any total output level up to Q_0 will now be sold at the higher general price level p_1. Any output level between Q_0 and Q_f will be sold at a yet higher general price level given by the corresponding point on the upward-sloping part of p_1s_1. In terms of the aggregate supply curves of part a, the level of total money expenditure (vertical axis) on any given level of total output (horizontal axis) will have to be higher after the cost-push. This is because the general price level will be higher. For example, at total output level Q_0 total dollar expenditure will be $p_1 \times Q_0$. This is larger than $p_0 \times Q_0$ because at this output level the general price level has been pushed up from p_0 to p_1.

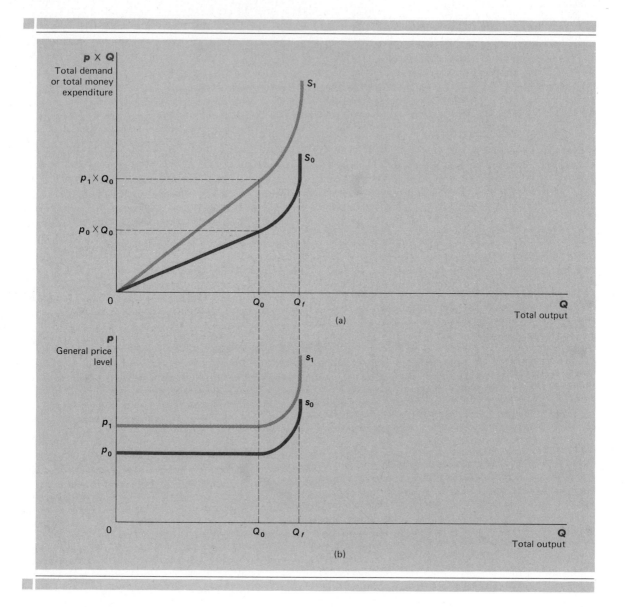

$p \times Q$
Total demand
or total money
expenditure

S_1

S_0

$p_1 \times Q_0$

$p_0 \times Q_0$

0   Q_0 Q_f Q
Total output

(a)

p
General price
level

s_1

s_0

p_1

p_0

0   Q_0 Q_f Q
Total output

(b)

COST-PUSH INFLATION
AND UNEMPLOYMENT

In recent years the economy has experienced periods during which the unemployment rate has risen at the same time that the rate of inflation has increased (during the 1973–1975 recession for example), a phenomenon often referred to as stagflation. We will examine the problem of stagflation more extensively in Chapter 14. However, we can begin to get some insight into

the problem by examining the relationship between cost-push inflation and unemployment at this point.

Consider Figure 8–10. Suppose the total demand schedule D intersects the 45° line at point e to determine an equilibrium level of total spending and income of $2,000 billion, shown in part a. Suppose the economy's aggregate supply curve is initially in the position $0S_1$ in part b. Since the level of total spending equals $2,000

FIGURE 8-9 COST-PUSH INFLATION AND AGGREGATE SUPPLY

Cost-push inflation originates on the supply side of the economy. The aggregate supply curves shown here are just like those in Figure 8–7.

In part b, the general price level (vertical axis) associated with any level of total output (horizontal axis) is initially determined by the aggregate supply curve p_0s_0. The associated representation of the aggregate supply curve in part a is given by $0S_0$.

Suppose a cost-push occurs—possibly due to a wage hike by powerful unions, or price hike by large firms seeking higher profits in key industries, or the rise in price of some resource vital to production. Now whatever the level of total output, it will be sold at a higher general price level than before. This is represented by the upward shift in the aggregate supply curve to p_1s_1 in part b. The associated representation of the shifted aggregate supply curve in part a is $0S_1$.

billion (vertical axis), the economy produces a full-employment level of total output equal to Q_f (horizontal axis), corresponding to point a on the aggregate supply curve $0S_1$. The quantity of total output Q_f is bought and sold at the general price level p_1 so that the total spending of $2,000 billion equals $p_1 \times Q_f$.

Now suppose the economy experienced some sort of cost-push—for example, an increase in the price of imported oil. This will cause costs of production to rise and business firms will now charge higher prices to cover their higher costs. To induce the economy's firms to produce any given level of total output, the general price level will now have to be higher than previously. This is represented by an upward shift in the aggregate supply curve from $0S_1$ to a position such as $0S_2$ in part b. However, given the *unchanged* level of total spending, equal to $2,000 billion as determined in part a, a rise in the general price level means that the quantity of total output produced and sold in the economy must decrease. Hence, the quantity of total output decreases from Q_f to Q_0 while the price level rises from p_1 to p_2. The economy now produces at point b on the aggregate supply curve $0S_2$ in part b. Total spending is still $2,000 billion, as determined in part a, but it equals the product of a higher price level p_2 multiplied by a lower total output level Q_0, or $p_2 \times Q_0$. Since the production of total output is less than the full-employment level, employment is reduced and there is now unemployment. In short, *a cost push results in a rise in the general price level and the unemployment rate.*

CHECKPOINT 8-5

Using a diagram like Figure 8–10, can you explain how the simultaneous occurrence of demand-pull and cost-push inflation might take place without any change in the unemployment rate? Suppose labor unions begin to demand higher wages in order to keep up with a rising cost of living (a rising general price level) caused by upward shifts in the total demand schedule. Using a diagram like Figure 8–10, can you explain how this could give rise to stagflation?

SUMMARY

1. The equilibrium level of total income, output, and employment occurs where the total demand schedule intersects the 45° line. At equilibrium the total income earned from production of the economy's total output corresponds to a level of total spending or demand just sufficient to purchase that total output.

2. At levels of total income less than the equilibrium level, total demand is greater than total output and there is unintended inventory reduction. This leads the economy's business firms to increase total output so that total income and employment rise toward the equilibrium level. At levels of total income greater than the equilibrium level, total demand is less than total output and there are unintended increases in inventories. The economy's business firms then reduce total

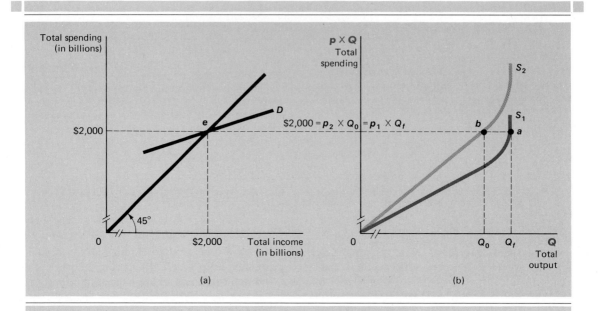

FIGURE 8-10 COST-PUSH INFLATION AND UNEMPLOYMENT

The economy's total demand schedule D determines an equilibrium level of total spending and income equal to $2,000 billion in part a. If the aggregate supply curve is $0S_1$, the economy will be producing the full-employment total output level Q_f, corresponding to point a on $0S_1$ (part b). The quantity of total output Q_f is bought and sold at the general price level p_1 so that the total spending of $2,000 billion equals p_1Q_f.

Suppose there is a cost-push that shifts the aggregate supply curve up to $0S_2$. Since total spending (determined in part a) remains unchanged at $2,000 billion, the economy now produces a lower level of total output Q_0, corresponding to point b on $0S_2$ (part b), and sells it at the higher general price level p_2. The total spending of $2,000 billion now equals $p_2 \times Q_0$. Since total output has declined, employment is reduced and there is now unemployment.

output so that total income and employment tend to fall toward the equilibrium level.

3. Realized investment is always equal to saving. Intended investment equals saving only at the equilibrium level of total income. Therefore, intended investment and realized investment are equal at the equilibrium level of total income, but differ from one another by the amount of unintended inventory change at all other levels of total income.

4. Intended investment may be viewed as an injection into the circular flow of spending and income, while saving may be viewed as a leakage from that flow. At the equilibrium

level of total income, the injection of intended investment is equal to the leakage due to saving. Graphically, this corresponds to the point at which the investment schedule intersects the saving function. At levels of total income greater than the equilibrium level, the leakage due to saving exceeds the injection due to investment, and total income will tend to fall toward the equilibrium level. At less than equilibrium levels of total income the leakage due to saving is less than the injection from intended investment. This inequality causes total income to rise toward the equilibrium level.

5. Spending changes represented by shifts in the total demand schedule cause changes in total income that are several times the size of the initial spending change. This multiplier effect may be triggered by changes in either or both of the components of total demand— the consumption function (and therefore the saving function) and the investment schedule. In the simple economy of this chapter, the multiplier equals the reciprocal of the marginal propensity to save.

6. If households try to save more, the economy's total income will fall and the level of saving will be no higher than it was initially, or it may even be lower. This is the paradox of thrift.

7. The total demand schedule and the aggregate supply curve jointly determine the relationship between the level of total spending in the economy and the level of total real output. As total demand or spending rises into the inflationary zone and the full-employment level of total output is approached, the price level begins to rise. Once the economy reaches full employment, further increases in total demand cause pure demand-pull inflation.

8. Cost-push inflation occurs when suppliers of factors of production increase the prices at which they are willing to sell them. Such increases cause the aggregate supply curve to shift upward. For any given level of total demand or expenditure, this upward shift will cause an increase in the general price level and a reduction in the level of total output and employment.

KEY TERMS AND CONCEPTS
cost-push inflation
demand-pull inflation
equilibrium income level
multiplier
paradox of thrift
realized investment

QUESTIONS AND PROBLEMS
1. How do you think the position of the total demand schedule D in Figure 8-3 would be affected by each of the following?

a. a decline in MPC;
b. a decline in MPS;
c. a reduction in the size of the multiplier;
d. a rise in the interest rate;
e. an increase in the wealth of households;
f. an increase in consumer indebtedness.

2. Why does total income equal expected total spending? In what sense are inventories a buffer against mistakes in forecasting?

3. Why does realized investment always equal saving? When realized investment and intended investment are not equal, why does the level of total income, output, and employment tend to change?

4. When injections exceed leakages what happens to the economy's level of total income? What is the relationship between intended investment and realized investment in this case? If the level of total income is falling, what must be the relationship between saving and intended investment? If the level of total income is rising, what must be the relationship between realized investment and saving?

5. If the saving function shifts downward, what must happen to the investment schedule in order for the total demand schedule to remain unchanged? What will happen to the level of employment in this instance? Why will this happen?

6. What happens to the value of the multiplier if the consumption function becomes steeper? What happens to the value of the multiplier if the saving function shifts downward to a position parallel to its initial position? What is the effect on the level of total income in this case?

7. Explain the paradox of thrift in terms of Figure 8-4, part a. Suppose the marginal propensity to consume MPC decreases because households want to save more out of income so they won't be so hard pressed for funds when Christmas shopping time rolls around. What do you predict this decrease in MPC will do to ease their budget problems come Christmas?

8. Explain the concept of the aggregate supply curve. What happens in the inflationary zone? What happens to the price level over the range from 0 to e_0 of the aggregate supply curve in Figure 8-8, part b?

■NEWS ITEM FOR YOUR ANALYSIS

BUSINESS INVENTORIES AND PERSONAL INCOME INCH UP

WASHINGTON, Feb. 21—Just before the start of the long holiday weekend, the Commerce Department reported that business inventories fell less than a seasonally adjusted .1 percent in December. At the same time the department noted that personal income inched up in January a scant .3 percent, or $4.3 billion at an adjusted annual rate.

QUESTIONS

Note: In this chapter we make no distinction between GNP, NNP, NI, PI, and DI because we ignored all the factors that differentiate these national income accounting measures. Continue to ignore these factors and simply regard PI in the above news item as total income.

1. Using a diagram like Figure 8–3, show where the level of personal income reported in the news item would be in relation to the equilibrium level of total income.

2. Given the facts reported in the news item, does it make sense to you that "personal income inched up in January?" Why or why not?

3. What will determine whether personal income continues to inch up or not?

9

GOVERNMENT SPENDING, TAXATION, AND FISCAL POLICY

SENATE VERSION OF TAX-CUT PLAN HEADS FOR FLOOR VOTE

WASHINGTON, March 22—The Senate Finance Committee finally approved its version of the tax cuts the president says are needed to prod the economy closer to full employment.

Like the House, the Finance Committee provided a $50-a-person rebate on last year's taxes, a permanent increase in the standard deduction, a simpler tax form, and a credit for employers hiring new workers this year and next. In addition, the Finance Committee also voted an extra two percentage points of investment tax credit for companies that buy machinery.

Late next week the bill goes to the Senate floor. Close votes are likely on the $50 rebate, which Republicans want to replace with a permanent tax cut, and on the makeup of tax cuts for business. The measure could also become bogged down on the floor as Senators try to attach a variety of other tax breaks to the bill.

We are now familiar with the basic explanation of why the equilibrium level of total income may be less than the full-employment level. This chapter brings the role of government into the analysis and shows how **fiscal policy**—government's management of its spending and taxing authority—affects the equilibrium level of total income, output, and employment. One of the primary objectives of present-day fiscal policy is to smooth out the ever present fluctuations in economic activity and "prod the economy closer to full-employment" without inflation. While fiscal policy cannot be expected to accomplish such a task alone, it must play a key role.

THE GOVERNMENT BUDGET

Like any budget, *the federal government's budget is an itemized account of expenditures and revenues over some period of time.* In this case, the time period is the fiscal year beginning October 1 and ending September 30 of the following year. The expenditure, or outlay side, of the budget consists mainly of defense expenditures and transfer payments in the form of social security and welfare payments, unemployment compensation, medical payments, and interest on the government debt. Revenues to cover these outlays come largely from corporate and personal income taxes. The next largest source of revenues is social insurance taxes, which are paid into the social security system by employers and employees. These are followed by excise taxes, which are taxes levied on the sale of certain products, such as alcohol and tobacco. Interest on government-managed trust funds and customs duties levied on certain internationally traded goods also provide revenue.

An examination of state and local **government budgets** shows the largest proportion of outlays going to education. Next come expenditures for police and fire protection, the administration of judicial and legislative operations, the development of natural resources, and the establishment and maintenance of recreation programs and facilities. The largest proportion of the remaining expenditures go into highways and roads, hospitals, and health and welfare programs. The major sources of revenue for state and local governments are property taxes (on land and buildings, and sometimes on personal property and financial assets) and retail sales taxes. However, the fastest growing source of state and local revenues in recent years are state and local income taxes.

Since World War II, state and local government tax revenues have increased much more rapidly than federal tax revenues. This reflects the growing economic importance of state and local government activities.

Deficits and Surpluses

A government has a **balanced budget** if total expenditures equal total tax revenues. It has a **budget surplus** if expenditures are less than tax revenues. It has a **budget deficit** if expenditures are greater than tax revenues. The federal budget in our economy has shown a deficit in all but eight years since 1931. The last time there was a budget surplus was 1969, and the last time there were back-to-back surpluses was in 1956 and 1957. During one string of 16 years, 1931 through 1946 (the Great Depression and war years), there was a federal budget deficit virtually every year. In this chapter we will see why budget deficits generally tend to stimulate income, output, and employment, while surpluses have the opposite effect.

Fiscal Policy
and the Employment Act
of 1946

The Great Depression of the 1930s made people fearful that the economy might plunge into another depression when peacetime conditions returned at the end of World War II. This led Congress to pass the Employment Act of 1946, which declared that "it is the continuing policy and responsibility of the Federal Government . . . to coordinate and utilize all its plans, functions, and resources . . . in a manner calculated to foster and promote free competitive enterprise and the general welfare . . . to promote. maximum employment, production, and purchasing power."

This act clearly called for the federal government to use its taxing and spending authority to prevent recessions and inflationary booms. Recent developments in economic theory, due to Keynes and his followers, suggested that the consumption and investment decisions of individual households and businesses could give rise to either too little or too much total demand. The collective effect of private decisions based on self-interest could result in either excessive unemployment or excessive inflation. By contrast, government acting for society as a whole could manage its spending and taxing activities to prevent these unwanted developments. This is the spirit of modern fiscal policy. Let's see how it works in theory and practice.

PRINCIPLES OF
DISCRETIONARY
FISCAL POLICY

Discretionary fiscal policy is the government's deliberate regulation of its spending and taxing activities to attempt to smooth out business fluctuations and ensure maximum employment with as little inflation as possible. Our discussion of discretionary fiscal policy will be simplified by assuming that the only kind of taxes collected by the government are personal income taxes. This means that personal income PI now differs from disposable income DI by the amount of these taxes. We will continue to make no distinction between GNP, NNP, NI, and PI. They are all the same—what we called total income in the previous chapter. From now on we generally will use the term GNP when referring to total income. In our simplified world, then, GNP differs from DI only by the amount of personal income taxes T.

Government
Expenditure and Total Demand

Suppose initially that government spending and taxation are zero. Assume that the equilibrium level of GNP is $1,200 billion as determined by the intersection of the total demand schedule $C + I$ and the 45° line in Figure 9-1, part a. This intersection corresponds to the intersection of the saving function S and the in-

After reading this chapter, you will be able to:

1. Explain how government spending and taxation affect total demand and the equilibrium level of GNP.
2. Explain the practical limitations of discretionary fiscal policy.
3. Describe how automatic stabilizers work to moderate the cyclical swings in our economy.
4. Outline the major views of budget policy and be able to explain the concept of the high-employment budget.
5. Explain the financing effects of budget surpluses and deficits.
6. Describe the differences between public and private debt and the nature of the possible burdens of the government debt.

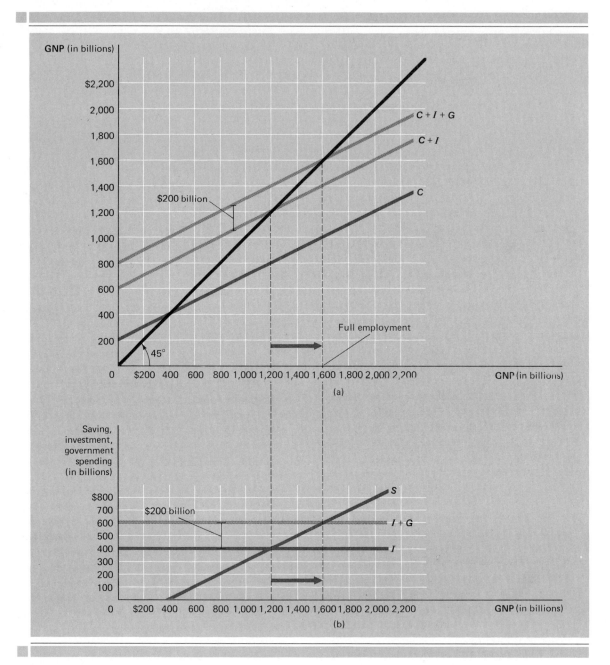

GNP (in billions)

$2,200
2,000
1,800
1,600
1,400
1,200
1,000
800
600
400
200

$200 billion

C + I + G
C + I
C

45°

Full employment

0    $200 400   600   800 1,000 1,200 1,400 1,600 1,800 2,000 2,200   GNP (in billions)

(a)

Saving,
investment,
government
spending
(in billions)

$800
700
600
500
400
300
200
100

$200 billion

S
I + G
I

0    $200 400   600   800 1,000 1,200 1,400 1,600 1,800 2,000 2,200   GNP (in billions)

(b)

vestment schedule I in Figure 9-1, part b. If the full-employment level of GNP is $1,600 billion, the economy is plagued by a considerable amount of unemployment when GNP is only $1,200 billion.

The economy can be pushed to full employment if the government spends $200 billion on goods and services. Suppose the government were to do this no matter what the level of GNP. This amount of government spending G then adds another layer onto the total demand schedule, pushing it vertically upward by $200 billion to the position $C + I + G$ in Figure 9-1, part a. Given that the MPC is assumed to equal

FIGURE 9-1 EFFECT OF GOVERNMENT SPENDING ON EQUILIBRIUM GNP

Government spending of $200 billion causes the total demand schedule to shift upward from $C + I$ to $C + I + G$ in part a. The equilibrium level of GNP is thereby increased from $1,200 billion, corresponding to the intersection of $C + I$ and the 45° line, to $1,600 billion, corresponding to the intersection of $C + I + G$ and the 45° line.

This can be shown equivalently in terms of leakages and injections in part b. The $200 billion of government expenditure adds another layer G onto the investment schedule I to give the $I + G$ schedule. The new equilibrium level of GNP at $1,600 billion corresponds to the intersection of the saving function S and the $I + G$ schedule. Here the $600 billion leakage from saving is exactly offset by the injections equal to the sum of the $400 billion of intended investment I and the $200 billion of government spending G.

$\frac{1}{2}$ (hence the MPS equals $\frac{1}{2}$), the multiplier is 2. Therefore, GNP increases by $400 billion from $1,200 billion to $1,600 billion, corresponding to the intersection of the total demand schedule $C + I + G$ with the 45° line.

This also may be shown in terms of Figure 9-1, part b. Here the $200 billion of government spending G adds another layer onto the investment schedule I to give the schedule $I + G$. The intersection of $I + G$ with the saving function S is the point at which the leakage from saving, equal to $600 billion, is just offset by the sum of the injections from intended investment I, equal to $400 billion, and government spending, equal to $200 billion. When we bring government spending into the picture, we see that it is no longer necessary for intended investment to equal saving at equilibrium. What is important is that the leakages from income equal the injections into it, or that $S = I + G$, in this case. (Note that the government expenditures do not need to be financed by taxes, although they may be, as we shall see below.)

Of course, a decline in G will cause the total demand schedule (part a) and the $I + G$ schedule (part b) to shift downward and the equilibrium level of GNP to fall. In sum, *increases in the level of government spending will cause increases in the level of GNP, just like upward shifts in the level of intended investment and consumption. Decreases in government spending will cause decreases in GNP.*

Taxation and Total Demand

Government spending is one side of fiscal policy. Taxation is the other. Suppose the government decides to finance its $200 billion expenditure by levying a lump-sum tax of $200 billion. This is a lump-sum tax in the sense that government will collect $200 billion in taxes no matter what the level of GNP. How will this affect the equilibrium level of GNP?

Figure 9-2 demonstrates what will happen. The equilibrium of Figure 9-1, part a, determined by the total demand schedule $C + I + G$, is shown again in this figure. Initially GNP equals DI. When the government imposes the lump-sum tax, a wedge equal to $200 billion will be driven between GNP and disposable income DI at every level of GNP. Since part of every dollar of DI is consumed and the rest saved, it follows that the reduction in DI will be reflected partly in a reduction in consumption and partly in a reduction in saving. The degree of reduction in each category is determined by the size of the MPC and the MPS. The MPC and MPS are each equal to $\frac{1}{2}$ in this case. Therefore, the $200 billion tax will cause a $100 billion reduction in consumption and a $100 billion reduction in saving at every level of GNP. The consumption function is the only component of the total demand schedule affected by the tax. It is shifted down by $100 billion from C to C_1 at every level of GNP. Consequently, the total demand schedule is shifted downward by $100 billion from $C + I + G$ to $C_1 + I + G$, as shown in Figure 9-2, part a. The equilibrium level of GNP therefore declines from $1,600 billion, the full-employment level, to $1,400 billion. This $200 billion change is the result of the multiplier effect.

We get the same result if we take the leakages-injections point of view. The equilibrium of Figure 9-1, part b, determined by the inter-

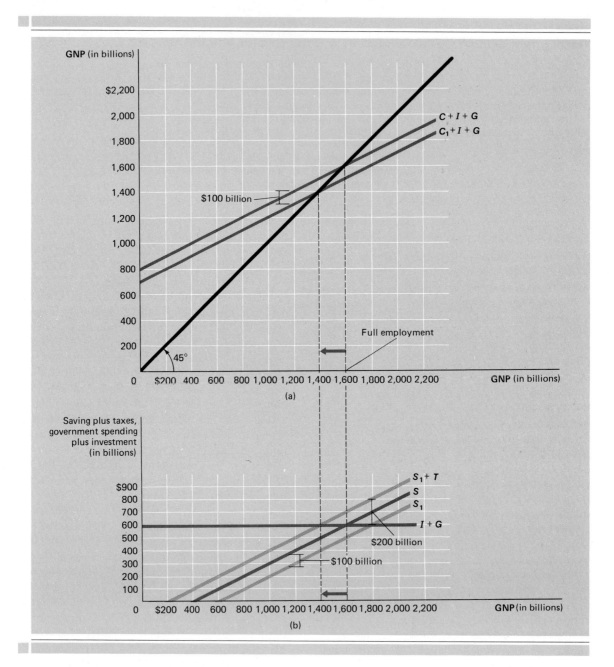

(a)

(b)

section of the saving function S and the $I + G$ schedule, is shown again in Figure 9-2, part b. When the $200 billion lump-sum tax is imposed, DI is reduced by this amount at every level of GNP. With an MPS of $\frac{1}{2}$ this means that saving is reduced by $100 billion at every level of GNP so that the saving function shifts down-

ward from S to S_1. In addition to the leakage from GNP due to saving, now there is also a $200 billion leakage due to taxes at every level of GNP. Adding this to the saving function gives us the total leakage function $S_1 + T$. The equilibrium level of GNP is now $1,400 billion, determined by the intersection of $S_1 + T$ and

FIGURE 9-2 EFFECT OF GOVERNMENT TAXATION ON EQUILIBRIUM GNP

Suppose the government imposes a lump-sum tax of $200 billion. This means that DI will be $200 billion less at every level of GNP.

Assuming that the *MPC* equals ½, and therefore, that the *MPS* is also ½, consumption will be $100 billion less at every level of GNP. The consumption function will be shifted downward by this amount. The total demand schedule will therefore shift downward by this amount, from $C + I + G$ to $C_1 + I + G$ in part a. The equilibrium level of GNP will fall from $1,600 billion to $1,400 billion.

In terms of the leakages-injections approach of part b, with an *MPS* of ½, the $200 billion reduction in DI will cause saving to be $100 billion less at every level of GNP. Hence, the saving function will be shifted downward by this amount, from S to S_1. The $200 billion tax leakage must be added to the saving leakage at every level of GNP to give the total leakage function $S_1 + T$. The new equilibrium level of GNP is $1,400 billion, determined by the intersection of the $I + G$ schedule and the $S_1 + T$ function. At this level the leakage, which equals saving plus taxes, is just offset by the injections, which equal intended investment plus government spending. At this level $S_1 + T = I + G$.

$I + G$ in Figure 9-2, part b. Here the sum of the leakages from GNP, which is equal to saving plus taxes, is just offset by the sum of the injections, which is equal to intended investment plus government spending. At equilibrium, $S_1 + T = I + G$.

Whether we look at it from the total demand schedule vantage point of part a or from the leakages-injection vantage point of part b, we see that imposing a tax will cause the equilibrium level of GNP to fall. Similarly, removing the tax would cause the total demand schedule to rise or, equivalently, the $S + T$ function to fall, so that the equilibrium level of GNP would increase. In sum, *increases in taxes will cause decreases in GNP. Decreases in taxes will cause increases in GNP.*

The Balanced Budget Multiplier

Note that the $200 billion of government spending alone *increases* the equilibrium level of GNP from $1,200 billion to $1,600 billion (Figure 9-1). However, the $200 billion lump-sum tax collected to finance the spending *decreases* the equilibrium level of GNP from $1,600 billion to $1,400 billion (Figure 9-2). The net increase in the equilibrium level of GNP—from $1,200 billion to $1,400 billion—is therefore $200 billion. In short, a $200 billion increase in government spending, financed by a $200 billion increase in taxes, results in a $200 billion increase in GNP.

This illustrates the **balanced budget multiplier**: *a government expenditure increase balanced by an equivalent increase in taxes will result in an increase in GNP of exactly the same size. The balanced budget multiplier equals 1.* The increase in GNP is equal to 1 times the amount of the government expenditure increase, or 1 times the amount of the government tax increase. Similarly, a government expenditure decrease balanced by an equivalent decrease in taxes will result in a decrease in GNP of exactly the same size. The balanced budget multiplier equals 1 no matter what the size of *MPS* and *MPC*.

What explains the operation of the balanced budget multiplier? Consider our example again. The government expenditure increase of $200 billion is in part offset by the $200 billion increase in taxes. Why? Because with an *MPC* of ½, and therefore an *MPS* of ½, the tax increase causes a $100 billion decrease in consumption spending. The net result is an increase in total spending of $100 billion—the difference between the $200 billion increase in government spending and the $100 billion reduction in consumption spending. This is only the initial effect however. The $100 billion net increase in total spending times the multiplier 2 ultimately gives a net increase in GNP of $200 billion.

In the example shown in Figures 9-1 and 9-2, GNP must equal $1,600 billion if there is to be full employment. Starting from a GNP level of $1,200 billion, the balanced budget multiplier tells us that a $200 billion increase in government spending, financed by a $200 billion increase in taxes, will only increase GNP to $1,400 billion. This is what we found in Figure 9-2. Assuming that we want a balanced government budget, how much would government spending and taxes have to be increased in order to raise GNP from $1,200 billion to $1,600 billion? According to the balanced budget multiplier, both government spending and taxes would have to be raised by $400 billion.

Discretionary
Fiscal Policy in Practice

Our analysis of the effects of government expenditure and taxation on the equilibrium level of GNP indicates how discretionary fiscal policy might be used to combat recessions and overheated, inflationary booms.

Reductions in government expenditures or increases in taxes or both may be used to reduce the level of total demand when economic expansions create excessive inflationary pressures. If the government budget is in deficit to begin with, a reduction in the deficit or possibly its replacement with a surplus will be required to reduce total demand. If the budget is balanced to begin with, the creation of a budget surplus will be required to reduce total demand. If a surplus exists initially, an even larger surplus will be required.

When the economy is slipping into a recession, increases in government expenditures or reductions in taxes or both may be used to increase total demand. If the government budget is initially in deficit, these actions will give rise to an even larger deficit. If the budget is balanced to begin with, a deficit will result. And if a surplus exists initially, the surplus will be reduced or replaced by a deficit.

These prescriptions for the ideal exercise of discretionary fiscal policy are not so easy to carry out in practice. Let's see why.

POLITICS AND PRIORITIES

Federal government expenditure and tax programs are ultimately formulated and passed by Congress. This political process is affected by many different special interest groups and lobbies, each with a list of priorities that often conflict with the goals of discretionary fiscal policy. For example, suppose prudent fiscal policy calls for a reduction in government expenditures to reduce inflationary pressures. But nobody wants government expenditures that affect his or her region to be cut back. The other alternative is to increase taxes. But which taxes, and who shall pay them? Neither politicians nor the public ever like increasing taxes.

The news item at the beginning of this chapter is a typical example of the controversy surrounding a tax cut. And tax cuts are popular! Here the president is trying to get Congress to exercise some discretionary fiscal policy "to prod the economy closer to full employment." As always, the question is whether Congress will resolve the various issues associated with the bill and pass it in time to counteract a possible recession.

FORECASTING,
RECOGNITION, AND TIMING

The sluggishness of the democratic political process is not the only thing that can throw off the timing of fiscal actions. This problem aside, it is necessary to be able to forecast the future course of the economy fairly accurately. Otherwise, it is not possible to take appropriately timed fiscal actions to head off expected recessions or curb inflationary booms. Forecasting is still more an art than a science, despite the development of large economic (that is, statistical or econometric) models of the economy. The record of economic forecasters, both in government and out, is mixed at best.

It is not only difficult to forecast where the economy is going. Often it is almost as hard to recognize where the economy is. Frequently the economy has been in a recession for several months before economists, policy makers, and other observers recognize and agree that this is the case. Part of the problem is the fact that many important measurements of the economy's performance are only available some time after the events that they measure have occurred. For instance, statistics on GNP become available every quarter year. The first measurement of GNP for the third quarter of the year (July through September) may not be available

ECONOMIC THINKERS

PAUL SAMUELSON
1915-

If Professor John Kenneth Galbraith is the economist most widely known among noneconomists, Samuelson is probably the best known among his professional peers and some would argue the greatest contemporary American economist.

Samuelson was awarded a Ph.D. degree at Harvard in 1941, and his dissertation (*Foundations of Economic Analysis*) became a landmark book. To cap this performance, Samuelson became a full professor at the Massachusetts Institute of Technology at 32, and in 1970 he won the first Nobel Prize ever awarded to an American economist.

Samuelson's great contribution has been twofold. First, he pioneered the use of mathematics in economics, as illustrated by his dissertation and countless articles in professional journals. He thus broke new ground in making economics more precise and scientific. Second, he was instrumental in reorganizing the teaching of undergraduate economics along Keynesian lines. His *Principles of Economics,* first published in 1947, has gone through ten editions, a most unusual performance, and sold millions of copies.

Samuelson has been compared to Alfred Marshall, who was anxious to meld the best work of diverse schools. Marshall meshed the work of the classical writers with that of the marginalist school. Samuelson did much the same with Keynesian economics and the classics, putting the synthesis into logical and readable form.

Samuelson, however, made a definite break with Marshall's neoclassical approach. Marshall, like most economists of his day, had regarded mathematics as a secondary route to the approach to economics and had warned his fellow economists about the waste of time which arose from putting literary propositions into mathematical form. Samuelson, reversing this warning, noted that the waste arises when essentially mathematical propositions are put into literary form, involving "mental gymnastics of a peculiarly depraved form."

Samuelson has done so much it is impossible to

do him justice in a brief sketch. Although his forte is theory and he is essentially an academician (he rejected an offer from President Kennedy to be chairman of the Council of Economic Advisers), he has also been a commentator on economic affairs and writes a column in *Newsweek.* Although he has avoided any official status, he was an informal Kennedy advisor and is credited with the authorship of a preelection task force report which largely set the tone of JFK's economic policy.

FOR FURTHER READING

Samuelson, Paul A. *Foundations of Economic Analysis.* New York: Atheneum Press, 1965. Originally published by Harvard University Press, Harvard Economics Studies, no. 80, 1947.

———. *Collected Papers.* Vols. 1 and 2. Edited by Joseph Stiglitz. Cambridge: The M.I.T. Press, 1966.

———. *Collected Papers.* Vol. 3. Edited by Robert C. Merton. Cambridge: The M.I.T. Press, 1972.

———. *Collected Papers.* Vol. 4. Edited by Hiroaki Nagatani and Kate Crowley. Cambridge: The M.I.T. Press, 1978.

until some time in November, for example. In general, what is the result of this recognition lag? It is that discretionary fiscal policy tends to be more of a reaction to past developments in the economy rather than an anticipation of those to come.

In practice, the forecasting and recognition problems combine with political considerations and the sluggishness of democratic decision making to create serious timing problems for discretionary fiscal policy. In addition, even when a change in government spending or taxes finally takes place, there is often a considerable time lag before its full effect on the economy is realized. Given all these considerations, it is not hard to see how a government spending increase—or a tax cut—intended to offset a recession might be badly timed. Such actions could end up taking place in the expansion phase of the business cycle, *after* the trough of the recession has passed. Rather than reducing the depth of the recession, these actions would simply add inflationary pressures to the expansion phase of the cycle that follows. Similarly, a government spending decrease—or a tax increase—intended to offset inflationary pressures during a boom in the economy could end up taking place after the boom has passed. Such actions could actually cause or worsen the next recession. To this extent, *the timing problems associated with discretionary fiscal policy can make economic fluctuations worse.*

STATE AND LOCAL GOVERNMENTS

Discretionary fiscal policy might be more effective if it represented a coordinated effort of federal, state, and local governments. However, the Employment Act of 1946 applies only to the federal government. If anything, state and local governments tend to conduct their fiscal activities in ways that contribute to, rather than smooth out, the fluctuations of the business cycle. This happens largely because state and local governments are under more pressure to balance their budgets than is the federal government. Their ability to tax and raise money to finance expenditures rises and falls with the business cycle. Therefore, they tend to spend more heavily on postponable projects like schools and highways during periods of general economic prosperity, rather than during recessions.

THE VARIETY OF TAXES
AND THEIR EFFECTS ON SPENDING

There are a variety of different taxes—income taxes, sales taxes, corporate profit taxes, property taxes, and so forth. All of them have one thing in common. They take spending power away from those taxed. However, beyond this, these taxes differ in the burden each places on different groups in the economy.

Roughly speaking, a particular tax is said to be *progressive* if it takes a larger percentage out of a high income rather than a low income. The personal income tax is an example of a progressive tax. (We will define this term in more detail shortly.) A sales tax on Rolls Royces is another progressive tax because typically only people with high incomes buy them. A particular tax is said to be a **regressive tax** if it takes a smaller percentage out of a high income than a low income. For example, a sales tax on food is considered regressive because the percentage of income spent on food by a low-income household is usually larger than that spent by a high-income household. Therefore, the amount of food sales tax paid by the low-income household, measured as a percentage of its income, is larger than the corresponding percentage for a high-income household.

A given amount of tax revenue could be collected by using progressive taxes or regressive taxes or some combination of both. However, it is not clear in general whether progressive or regressive taxes have a more depressing effect on total income and expenditures. Some economists argue that progressive taxes on personal and business income reduce the incentive to work and depress investment spending. Therefore, they feel progressive taxes depress total demand more than regressive taxes. Other economists claim that regressive taxes depress total demand more because of their effect on consumption. They argue that low-income groups consume more of their income than high-income groups. Since regressive taxes fall heaviest on low-income groups, these economists contend that consumption spending is more depressed by regressive taxes.

Such considerations indicate that raising or lowering taxes to bring about a *given size change in GNP* is far more difficult than was suggested by our discussion of Figure 9-2. In the real world Congress has to decide which of a wide variety of taxes to change, as we can see from the news item. Often there is only the vaguest idea of what the effects on GNP will be.

■ CHECKPOINT 9-1
Consider again the example of Figures 9-1 and 9-2, and suppose that the MPS is ¼ and

the *MPC* is ¾. Explain how the total demand schedule is now affected by a $100 billion increase in government expenditures financed entirely by a $100 billion increase in lump-sum taxes. Give an explanation in terms of the leakages-injections approach. Explain why the balanced budget multiplier equals 1 no matter what the value of *MPC* and *MPS*.

AUTOMATIC STABILIZERS: NONDISCRETIONARY FISCAL POLICY

Discretionary fiscal policy requires deliberate action by Congress. The decisions to change the level of government spending, taxation, or both must be made on a case-by-case basis. However, our economy also contains automatic stabilizers. **Automatic stabilizers** *are built-in features of the economy that operate continuously without human intervention to smooth out the peaks and troughs of business cycles.* They are comparable to the automatic pilot that keeps an airplane on course. Like an automatic pilot, the economy's automatic stabilizers don't eliminate the need for deliberate action. But they do reduce it. Let's look at some of the more important built-in stabilizers and how they work.

Tax Structure

Up to now we have used only lump-sum taxes in our analysis, so that the amount of tax revenue is the same no matter what the level of GNP. In reality, the tax structure of the U.S. economy is such that the amount of tax revenue rises when GNP increases and falls when GNP declines. The significance of this for economic stability is illustrated in Figure 9-3. There it is assumed that the level of government and intended investment expenditures is the same at all levels of GNP—the $I + G$ schedule is flat.

Part a of Figure 9-3 shows the lump-sum tax case with which we are already familiar. Suppose that the sum of investment and government expenditure is initially $300 billion, as represented by the $I_0 + G$ schedule. The equilibrium level of GNP is $1,200 billion, determined by the intersection of $S + T$ and $I_0 + G$. If investment spending increases by $100 billion

from I_0 to I_1, the $I_0 + G$ schedule shifts up to $I_1 + G$ and the equilibrium level of GNP increases by $400 billion, from $1,200 billion to $1,600 billion. If at this point investment were to decrease by $100 billion, the $I_1 + G$ schedule would shift back down to $I_0 + G$. GNP would decrease by $400 billion, from $1,600 billion to $1,200 billion, in response to a $100 billion fluctuation in investment.

PROPORTIONAL TAXES

Now consider the effect of the same fluctuation in investment, given the same saving function S, when the economy's tax structure is such that tax revenues rise and fall *proportionally* with GNP. This situation is shown in part b of Figure 9-2. The tax revenue at each level of GNP is represented by the vertical distance between the saving function S and the saving plus tax function $S + T$. This distance gets proportionally larger as GNP increases. *With a* **proportional tax,** *an X percent rise (or fall) in GNP always results in an X percent rise (or fall) in tax revenues.* For example, suppose the proportional tax rate is .2. If GNP increases by 10 percent, from $1,000 billion to $1,100 billion, tax revenues will increase by $20 billion from $200 billion (.2 × $1,000 billion) to $220 billion (.2 × $1,100 billion). That is, tax revenues also increase by 10 percent. Given the position of the saving function S, the larger (smaller) is the proportional tax rate, the steeper (flatter) will be the $S + T$ function in part b.

When the $I + G$ schedule is in the position $I_0 + G$, the equilibrium level of GNP is $1,300 billion. When the $100 billion increase in investment shifts the schedule up to $I_1 + G$, the equilibrium level of GNP increases by $200 billion to $1,500 billion. Similarly, a $100 billion fall in investment pushing the $I + G$ schedule down from $I_1 + G$ to $I_0 + G$ would cause a $200 billion fall in GNP, from $1,500 billion to $1,300 billion. In short, the same $100 billion fluctuation in investment causes a smaller fluctuation in GNP under a proportional tax structure than under a lump-sum tax structure—a $200 billion versus a $400 billion GNP fluctuation. Why is this?

Recall that taxes, like saving, are a leakage that drains off potential spending on goods and

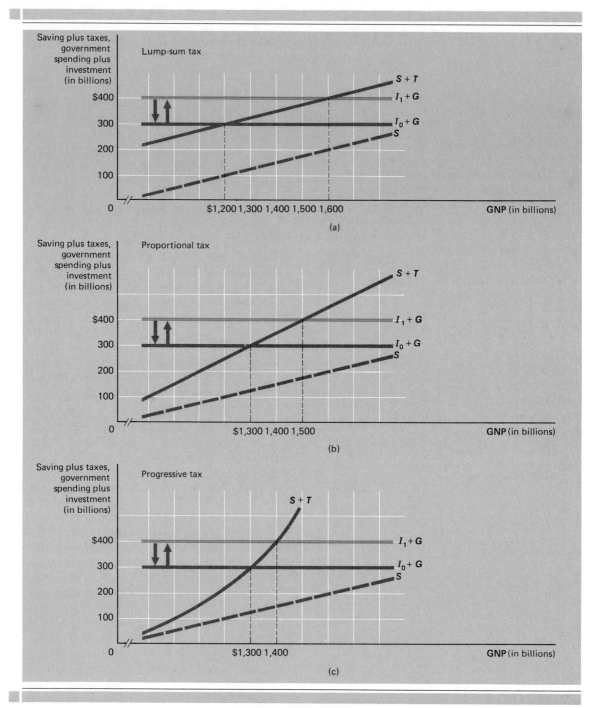

(a)

(b)

(c)

services. With a lump-sum tax the tax leakage does not change with changes in GNP. But with a proportional tax the leakage increases as GNP increases and has an *even greater* braking effect on further rises in GNP. Hence, a rise in injections due to increased investment or government spending or both is more quickly offset by an increase in leakages under a proportional tax

FIGURE 9-3 THE TAX STRUCTURE AS AN AUTOMATIC STABILIZER

Proportional taxes and progressive taxes act as automatic stabilizers because they increase leakages when GNP rises and decrease leakages when GNP falls.

The leakages-injections diagrams of parts a, b, and c all have the same saving function and the same $100 billion $I + G$ schedule shifts. The only difference between the diagrams is that they each assume different tax structures. When taxes are lump sum (part a), the leakage due to taxes is the same no matter what the level of GNP. A $100 billion shift in the $I + G$ schedule, from $I_0 + G$ to $I_1 + G$, or vice versa, causes a $400 billion change in GNP. By comparison, the same shifts in the $I + G$ schedule under a proportional tax structure (part b) cause a smaller change (equal to $200 billion) in GNP. The same shifts under a progressive tax structure result in a still smaller change (equal to $100 billion) in GNP.

structure than under a lump-sum tax structure. Similarly, a fall in the level of injections results in a more rapid decline in leakages under a proportional tax structure. Therefore, GNP does not have to decline as far to reestablish the equality between injections and leakages.

The stabilizing effect of the proportional tax structure is greater the larger is the proportional tax rate or the percent of GNP that is collected in taxes. An increase in the proportional tax rate makes the $S + T$ function in part b steeper. This means that the shift in the $I_0 + G$ schedule to $I_1 + G$, or from $I_1 + G$ to $I_0 + G$, will cause an even smaller change in GNP. Hence, the economy is more stable in that it is less sensitive to such a disturbance.

PROGRESSIVE TAXES

In reality, tax revenues in our economy tend to rise and fall more than proportionally with increases and decreases in GNP. This happens largely because personal and business income is subject to a progressive tax. *A* **progressive tax** *on income imposes successively higher tax rates on additional dollars of income as income rises.* For example, the first $10,000 of an individual's income might be subject to a 20 percent tax rate, the second $10,000 to a 30 percent rate, the third to a 40 percent rate, and so forth. This means that the fraction of total income taxed away gets larger as total income rises. If the individual in our example makes $10,000, then 20 percent or one-fifth of it goes to taxes; if the individual's income is $20,000, then 25 percent (equal to the average of 20 percent and 30 percent) or one-fourth of it goes to taxes, and so

forth. By contrast, with a proportional tax rate the fraction of total income taxed away is the same no matter what the level of total income.

The effect of a progressive tax structure on the economy's stability is illustrated in Figure 9-3, part c. The saving function S is the same as in parts a and b. However, the $S + T$ function now curves upward, reflecting the fact that taxes rise more than proportionally with increases in GNP and fall more than proportionally with decreases. Now the same $100 billion fluctuation in investment considered in parts a and b results in an even smaller fluctuation in GNP. When $I_0 + G$ shifts up to $I_1 + G$, there is only a $100 billion increase in GNP, from $1,300 billion to $1,400 billion. By comparison, under the proportional tax rate of part b, this shift resulted in a $200 billion increase in GNP. With the lump-sum tax of part a, there was a $400 billion increase.

In general, *the progressive nature of the U.S. economy's tax structure acts as a built-in stabilizer by automatically increasing tax leakages more than proportionally as GNP rises, and reducing such leakages more than proportionally as GNP falls. This is generally desirable because anything that increases leakages during an inflationary expansion will have a dampening effect on the economy. Conversely, anything that decreases leakages during a recession will tend to buoy up spending.*

Unemployment Compensation

Since the 1930s **unemployment compensation** has become an increasingly important automatic stabilizer in our economy. Recessions swell the ranks of the unemployed. Without some form of assistance, laid off workers must cut back their spending drastically. This only makes the recession worse. Paying laid off workers unemployment benefits enables them to better sustain their consumption spending and thus cushions the downturn. These unemployment benefits are paid out of unemployment trust funds which are built up with unemployment taxes during periods of economic expansion. These taxes constitute an increase in leakages during boom periods. As such, they help to curb excessive inflationary expansions. In sum, during recessions injections into the economy from unemployment benefits tend to exceed the leakages due to unemployment taxes, and the economy is stimulated on balance. During expansionary periods leakages due to unemployment taxes tend to exceed injections from unemployment benefits and the net effect is to curb inflationary pressures.

Other Automatic Stabilizers

Other automatic stabilizers in our economy include family assistance programs, price-support programs for agriculture, and a tendency for older workers laid off during recessions to start claiming their social security retirement benefits. Let's briefly look at each of these.

Not surprisingly, during recessions many families find themselves forced into financial straits that make them eligible for certain forms of family assistance. This aids them to sustain their otherwise sagging purchasing power.

Farm product prices tend to fall during recessions. Government price-support programs keep them from falling below a certain level and thus prop up farm family incomes and spending.

After older workers have been laid off for a certain period of time, their prospects for reemployment often diminish rapidly. Once they have used up the amount of unemployment benefits to which they are entitled, they frequently retire and claim social security retirement benefits. These benefits thus pick up where unemployment benefits leave off for this group of workers. To this extent social security retirement benefits tend to automatically cushion recessions in the same way as unemployment compensation.

Automatic Stabilizers Are a Double-edged Sword

The same characteristics of automatic stabilizers that make them desirable can also be a curse under certain circumstances. For example, the tendency of the U.S. tax structure to increase leakages when GNP rises helps to curb inflationary pressures when the economy is near full employment. However, if the economy is coming out of the depths of a recession, the same tendency for leakages to rise acts as a drag on economic recovery.

This can be seen with the aid of Figure 9-3, parts b and c. Suppose the full-employment level of GNP is \$1,500 billion but that the $I + G$ schedule is in the position $I_0 + G$. The equilibrium level of GNP is now \$1,300 billion, and the economy is operating at considerably less than full employment. As we have already seen, the automatic stabilizing tendency of the progressive tax structure (part c) is stronger than that of the proportional tax structure (part b). This makes it more difficult to reach full-employment GNP in part c than in part b. Why? Suppose investment spending recovers and increases by \$100 billion, as represented by the upward shift of $I_0 + G$ to $I_1 + G$ in parts b and c. This increase is enough to raise GNP to the \$1,500 billion full-employment level in part b. But the faster rise in leakages under the progressive tax structure of part c stops the rise in GNP at \$1,400 billion, \$100 billion short of the full-employment level of GNP.

Discretionary and Nondiscretionary Expenditures

While automatic stabilizers tend to smooth out the peaks and troughs of business cycles, they will not eliminate them entirely. Research on the matter suggests that the amplitude of business cycles (the difference in GNP from trough to peak) may be reduced by anywhere from one-third to one-half as a result of the presence of automatic stabilizers. This means there is still a role for well-timed discretionary fiscal policy in eliminating that part of the business cycle not smoothed out by the automatic stabilizers.

Discretionary fiscal policy expenditures usually have a different impact on the economy than do the expenditures arising from nondiscretionary fiscal policy. Discretionary government expenditures are typically for goods and services—roads, buildings, trucks, research grants, and so forth. Nondiscretionary government spending usually takes the form of transfer payments, such as unemployment compensation, welfare benefits, and interest on the government debt. Hidden behind a given dollar figure for government expenditure is a variety of decisions about the role of government in our economy.

Viewed only in terms of the expansionary impact on the economy, however, most economists regard government spending on goods and services as more expansionary than transfer payments. For example, suppose the multiplier equals 2, and that the economy is not operating at full employment. Government spending of $20 billion on goods and services will cause the economy to produce $40 billion of additional output—$20 billion to meet government purchases and $20 billion to meet increased consumer spending as a consequence of the multiplier effect. Alternatively, if the government paid out the $20 billion in unemployment compensation benefits, no increase in output would be needed to satisfy government purchase orders. The government would simply hand unemployed workers $20 billion. The unemployed will spend half of this on goods and services (because a multiplier of 2 implies an *MPC* of $\frac{1}{2}$), or $10 billion. The operation of the multiplier effect on this $10 billion expenditure means that the economy's total output increases $20 billion. In sum, a $20 billion government expenditure on goods and services causes the economy's total output to increase $40 billion. But a $20 billion transfer payment causes total output to rise only $20 billion.

■ CHECKPOINT 9-2

Does the "$50-a-person rebate on last year's taxes" mentioned in the news item act like a reduction in a lump-sum tax, a proportional tax, or a progressive tax? Suppose the government spending component of the *I* + *G* schedules in Figure 9–3 is always equal to $200 billion, whatever the level of GNP. For each of the three cases shown in parts a, b, and c of Figure 9–3, explain how the government budget changes as a result of the $100 billion change in investment, both when it represents an increase from I_0 to I_1, and when it represents a decrease from I_1 to I_0. That is, for each case, does the budget remain balanced, go from surplus to deficit or from deficit to surplus, or what? In light of your findings, how might you state the way the automatic stabilization effect works in terms of the government budget?

BUDGET POLICY

Government budget policy is the joint result of government spending and tax policy. Budget policy makers have to consider such questions as: When and how often should the budget be balanced? When should it be in surplus, when in deficit? How should deficits be financed—by printing money or issuing bonds? And what should be done with surpluses? These questions have always provoked controversy.

Different Views on Budget Policy

The following represent three of the most often heard views on budget policy. Now that we are familiar with how government spending and taxation affect the economy, we can consider the economic implications of each of them.

CLASSICAL VIEW:
BALANCE THE BUDGET ANNUALLY

The classical economists generally believed that government expenditures should be matched by government tax revenues every fiscal year—that is, that the budget should be balanced annually. As a result of the Great Depression of the 1930s, and the loss of faith in the classical theory of full employment, few economists subscribe to this view today. Yet, there are still politicians and others who believe that the government budget should be balanced annually. Generally, they view the government budget in the same way as that of a household or business firm. Households and businesses that have budget deficits often go bankrupt.

However, if the government budget is balanced every year, fiscal policy will add to economic instability rather than reduce it. For example, suppose the economy is in the expansionary phase of a business cycle. As GNP rises tax revenues rise even faster because of a progressive tax structure. Given the level of government expenditures, the increase in tax revenues may well give rise to a budget surplus. In order to keep the budget balanced, the government will have to cut taxes or increase government expenditures or both. However, we have seen that increases in government expenditure, as well as reductions in taxes, push up total demand. This will add to the economic expansion.

On the other hand, suppose the economy is entering a recession. As GNP declines, tax revenues will fall. Given the level of government expenditure, this may result in a budget deficit. In order to keep the budget balanced, the government will have to increase taxes or reduce government spending or both. But such actions will reduce total demand even further and make the recession worse.

Thus, the annually balanced budget would make the expansion phase of the business cycle larger, and the recession phase deeper. Business cycles would be more severe.

BALANCE THE BUDGET CYCLICALLY

Another point of view argues that the budget should be balanced over the course of the business cycle. That is, the budget should be balanced over whatever period of time it takes for a complete business cycle, measured from either trough to trough or peak to peak. Those who favor this approach contend that balancing the budget in this way will at the same time permit the exercise of a stabilizing fiscal policy. During a recession the government would run a budget deficit by increasing spending and reducing taxes to stimulate the economy. During the expansion and boom phase of the cycle, the government would run a surplus by cutting back its spending and increasing taxes in order to curb inflationary pressures. Ideally, the size of the deficit that occurs in the recession is just matched by the size of the surplus during the boom. The budget is therefore balanced over the business cycle.

In reality, it is very difficult to do this because

recessions and expansions typically differ from one another in length and magnitude. Therefore, the size of the deficit incurred while fighting the recession is not likely to be the same as the size of the surplus generated by attempts to curb an inflationary expansion.

FUNCTIONAL FINANCE

The functional finance point of view contends that the goals of economic stabilization and full employment without inflation should come ahead of any concern about balancing the budget. This means that the budget may have to run in deficit over a period of several years in order to keep employment high, or in surplus to curb inflation. Proponents of functional finance argue that whatever difficulties are associated with ongoing deficits or surpluses are far outweighed by the benefits of high employment without inflation.

Critics of the functional finance approach argue that it throws away the fiscal discipline imposed by a balanced budget objective. Generally, the critics do not argue for slavish pursuit of a balanced budget. Rather, they believe that it should be a rough guideline used to keep inflationary deficit spending under control.

The High-Employment Budget

Each of the viewpoints on budget policy we have just mentioned has obvious drawbacks. The annually balanced budget is destabilizing. Balancing the budget over the business cycle is very difficult if not impossible. Functional finance seems to lack any standard for evaluating budget policy performance. Another budget concept—the high-employment budget—has gained popularity among economists and policy makers because it provides a way of judging to what extent fiscal policy is pushing the economy toward a high-employment level of GNP. (A high-employment level might be deemed to be a level of GNP where the unemployment rate is 5 percent, for example.)

THE ACTUAL BUDGET AND THE HIGH-EMPLOYMENT BUDGET

The *actual* government budget surplus or deficit is equal to the difference between *actual* government expenditures and *actual* tax revenues. Suppose actual GNP is less than the high-employment level of GNP. Given that the tax structure is progressive, the actual tax revenues are less than the amount that would be collected at the high-employment GNP level. The actual government budget might well show a deficit, as prudent fiscal policy would say it should during a recession. Injections from government spending exceed tax leakages (there is a net injection). But is this actual budget deficit large enough to combat the recession? How can we tell?

Suppose we compare this actual level of government spending with the amount of tax revenue that would be collected *if* GNP were at the high-employment level. It might turn out that the high-employment level of tax revenue would exceed actual government spending. In other words, if the economy were at the high-employment level of GNP, there would be a budget surplus. And this means that actual fiscal policy would be a force tending to push GNP down and away from the high-employment level! Clearly, the *actual* budget deficit is not as large as it should be if fiscal policy is to be oriented toward pushing GNP up to the high-employment level of GNP.

We conclude that, *compared to the actual budget deficit or surplus, a more meaningful measure of the impact of fiscal policy is the difference between the actual level of government spending and the level of tax revenue that would be collected if the economy were operating at a high-employment level of GNP. This is the* **high-employment budget**. If actual GNP is below the high-employment level of GNP, and there is a high-employment budget deficit, fiscal policy may be viewed as a force favorable to the achievement of a high-employment level of GNP. On the other hand, if under these same circumstances there is a high-employment budget surplus, fiscal policy may be viewed as not sufficiently expansionary for the purpose of achieving a high-employment level of GNP. If actual GNP is above the high-employment level of GNP, the existence of a high-employment budget deficit would suggest that fiscal policy is overly expansionary and is contributing to inflationary pressures. However, if under these same circumstances there is a high-employment budget surplus, fiscal policy

may be viewed as a force favorable to curbing excessive expansion.

Finally, note carefully the following point. Even if the high-employment budget (deficit or surplus) indicates that the current stance of fiscal policy is favorable to the achievement of a high-employment level of GNP, it is no guarantee that this goal will be realized. Consumption and investment spending may be either so expansionary or so contractionary that a high-employment equilibrium level of GNP cannot be reached or maintained. Put another way, even though the high-employment budget may be favorable to the achievement of a high-employment level of GNP, the *size* of the high-employment budget (deficit or surplus) may not be large enough given the existing level of consumption and investment spending.

RECENT BUDGET EXPERIENCE

Figure 9-4 compares the difference between actual government spending and actual tax revenues (the actual budget deficit or surplus) with the difference between actual government spending and high-employment GNP tax revenues (the high-employment budget deficit or surplus) for the years since 1968. Observe that in most of these years the actual budget deficit was much greater than the high-employment budget deficit. If one only looked at the actual budget deficit, the expansionary impact of fiscal policy would appear more pronounced than is indicated by the high-employment budget deficits. Nonetheless, the high-employment budget was in deficit for a substantial number of these years, indicating that fiscal policy was often expansionary over this period. Largely due to the automatic stabilizers, it was particularly expansionary, as was desirable, during the latter stages of the severe recession that reached its trough at the end of the first quarter of 1975.

Effects of Deficit
Financing on the Economy

By definition, a budget deficit means that tax revenues are less than government expenditures. How and where does the government get the funds to finance the difference? There are two ways in which the government can obtain the needed funds: (1) It can borrow the money from

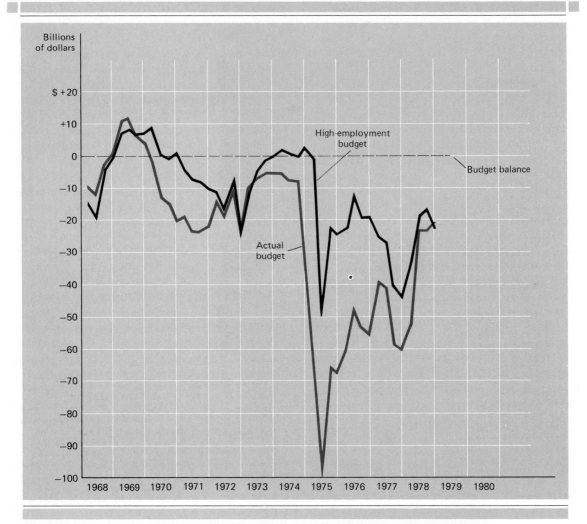

FIGURE 9-4 THE ACTUAL BUDGET AND THE HIGH-EMPLOYMENT BUDGET SINCE 1968

The actual budget deficit or surplus equals the difference between actual government spending and actual tax revenues. The high-employment budget deficit or surplus equals the difference between actual government spending and the level of tax revenues that would be collected at the high-employment GNP level. The high-employment budget deficit or surplus is a better indicator of how well the government is managing fiscal policy.

For most of the periods shown here both the actual budget and the high-employment budget have shown a deficit. But the actual budget deficit has been greater than the high-employment budget deficit because actual GNP has been below the high-employment level of GNP for much of this period. The fact that the high-employment budget was in deficit throughout most of this period indicates that fiscal policy was geared toward pushing the economy to the high-employment level of GNP.

SOURCE: Federal Reserve Bank of St. Louis.

the public by selling government bonds; or (2) it can print the money. It can also do some combination of both. The expansionary effect on the economy of a budget deficit varies, depending on which method is used to finance the deficit.

BOND FINANCING

Like any other bond, a government bond is a contract whereby the borrower (the government) agrees to pay back the lender (the buyer of the bond) the amount lent plus some rate of interest after some specified period of time. For example, consider a $1,000 government bond that pays a 5 percent rate of interest and promises to pay back the lender after one year. At the end of one year the lender or bond buyer gets back $1,050 (the original $1,000 plus 5 percent of $1,000, or $50) from the government, the bond seller. As with any bond, the only way the government can sell the bond (borrow the $1,000) is by paying a high enough rate of interest to induce people to buy it (lend the $1,000).

The government must sell its bonds in the bond market, in competition with bonds sold by businesses that are trying to borrow funds to finance their investment spending. In order to induce the public to buy these government bonds instead of those issued by the business sector, the government will have to pay an interest rate high enough to make their bonds relatively more attractive. This competition between the financing needs of the government and those of the business sector will push up the rate of interest. We know from our discussion in Chapter 7 (see Figure 7–8) that this interest rate rise will cause the level of investment spending to fall, as represented by a downward shift in the investment schedule. Therefore, *when a government deficit is financed by selling government bonds, the expansionary effect of the deficit on the economy is somewhat offset by a downward shift in investment spending.*

PRINTING MONEY

The other way in which the government can finance the deficit is to create the needed money. We will be able to describe the way this is done in a modern economy after we have studied how the banking system works in Chapters 10 through 12. For the moment, we will simply assume that the government cranks money out with a printing press. Using this method means that there is no longer a need to issue bonds and, hence, there is no rise in the interest rate that depresses investment spending. It follows that *when the government finances a deficit by creating new money, the expansionary effect of the deficit on the economy will be greater than when the deficit is financed by borrowing (issuing bonds).*

What to Do with a Budget Surplus

The government may collect more tax revenue than it spends (have a budget surplus) in the boom phase of an expansion. (Note, however, that budget surpluses have been rare.) The budget surplus is desirable at this phase of the business cycle because it is antiinflationary, meaning that it dampens inflationary pressures. But the extent of this dampening effect depends on what the government does with the surplus. There are two possibilities. The government can use the surplus to retire some of the outstanding government debt by paying back bond holders. Alternatively, the government can simply hold on to the surplus as idle funds. This amounts to withdrawing the money from the economy.

Suppose the surplus is used to retire outstanding debt. Think of the surplus as the net leakage—the excess of the leakage due to taxes over the injections of government spending. Returning the surplus to the economy by retiring debt offsets this net leakage to the extent that it puts money back into the hands of the public, which then spends it. Debt retirement thereby reduces the antiinflationary effect of the budget surplus. However, if the government simply holds the surplus as idle funds, there is no offset to reduce this net leakage. We conclude that the *antiinflationary effect of a government budget surplus is greater when the surplus funds are held idle than when they are used to retire government debt.*[1]

[1] Note that retiring government debt removes government bonds from the bond market and thus reduces competition with private bonds. This tends to reduce the interest rate and thereby stimulate investment spending. This is another source of stimulus to the economy that occurs when there is debt retirement.

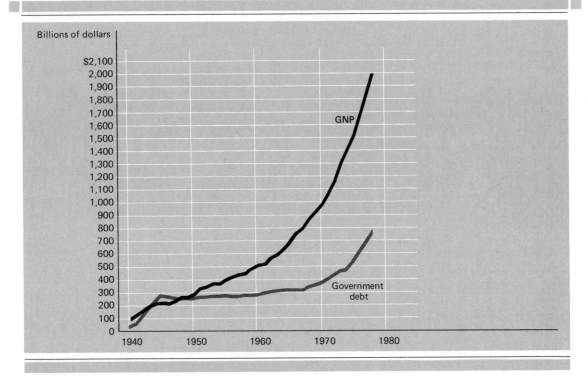

FIGURE 9-5 GOVERNMENT DEBT AND THE GNP

One measure of the burden of the government debt is its size relative to that of GNP. Since World War II, when the debt grew dramatically, GNP has grown faster than the debt. In the immediate postwar years, the debt was larger than GNP. This has changed so that now GNP is roughly three times larger than the debt. To the extent GNP represents the tax capacity to pay off the debt as well as to pay interest on it, the burden of the debt on the economy has declined.

■ **CHECKPOINT 9-3**

Compare Figure 9–4 with Figure 6–4, part b, and describe how well fiscal policy has performed in view of the behavior of the GNP gap since 1968. What are the implications for the high-employment budget concept of the fact that the expansionary impact of a deficit depends on how it is financed? Similarly, what are the implications for this concept of the different ways of disposing of a surplus?

THE GOVERNMENT DEBT

The government debt is a subject of controversy and a source of concern to many people.

Should we be concerned about it? Who owes what to whom? How can we tell whether the debt is too big or not? What are the burdens of the debt? Almost every citizen worries about these questions from time to time.

What Is the Government Debt?

Since the beginning of World War II government budget deficits have far outnumbered surpluses. Financing these deficits by selling government bonds has resulted in a large increase in the stock of bonds outstanding—the size of the government debt. Figure 9-5 shows that much of this increase was concentrated in the war years, 1941-1945, and in the years since 1967.

Public Versus Private Debt

Most of us are accustomed to thinking in terms of private debt, the personal debt people incur when they borrow money to buy a car, a house, or a college education. The chief fear is that of not being able to pay the debt off as repayments come due. If you can't, your assets—the car, the house, the furniture—may be seized by those who have lent you money. They may even be able to put a lien on your paycheck. This is a legal claim that allows them to take a part of every paycheck (direct from your employer) until they have been paid back the amount originally lent to you. In short, a private debt is what one party, the debtor, owes another, the creditor. Failure by the debtor to repay the creditor on time can result in severe hardship and loss for the debtor. Of course, the creditor is made poorer as well, possibly losing all that was originally loaned.

The government or public debt is different from a private debt in certain important respects, though it is similar in others. Consider the following hypothetical example. Suppose the government's debt is held entirely by its own citizens, and that each citizen owns the same number of government bonds as every other citizen. Since it is the citizens' government, the government debt is the citizens' debt, or what the citizens owe themselves! Suppose the government decided to pay off the entire debt by levying and collecting a tax of the same size from each citizen. The amount of taxes that each citizen would pay the government would be just equal to the amount of money each would receive from the government for the government bonds that each holds. It is the same as if each citizen were to take X dollars out of his or her left pocket and put the X dollars back into the right pocket.

What about interest payments on a government's debt held entirely by and distributed equally among its own citizens? Again, suppose the government levies and collects a tax of the same size from every citizen to pay the interest on the debt. Each citizen would then pay an amount of tax exactly equal to the interest payment received on the government bond he or she holds. Again, what each citizen takes out of the left pocket matches what is put back into the right pocket.

Obviously, in our hypothetical example the existence and size of the government debt is of no consequence whatsoever. The example shows how different a government or public debt can be from a private debt.

The Burden of the Government Debt

Our hypothetical example served another important purpose. It suggests that any cause for concern about the government debt lies in the fact that certain of the example's assumptions don't hold in reality. Because of this, the government debt imposes certain burdens similar to those of a private debt.

DISTRIBUTION EFFECTS

First of all, government bonds outstanding are not distributed equally among the nation's citizens. Some people hold none and others own a great number. However, any attempt to retire some or all of the debt would have to be financed out of taxes which are paid by all citizens (except those who somehow avoid paying taxes). This large transfer payment would result in a redistribution of income. Some citizens would end up paying out an amount of taxes larger than their holdings of government bonds. These citizens would be net losers since they would pay out more than they would get back. Others would be net gainers in this transfer. Their tax payment toward the debt retirement effort would be less than their holdings of government bonds.[2]

Interest payments on the government debt have the same distribution effects. These interest payments are transfer payments, financed by taxes on the general population and paid to those holding government bonds. A citizen is a net gainer if the amount received in interest payments exceeds his or her share of the tax payments used to pay interest on the debt. Otherwise the citizen is a net loser in this transfer.

[2] Many government bonds are held by trust funds, banks, insurance companies, and other businesses. A multitude of citizens either own or have claims on these institutions and therefore own government bonds indirectly. This makes no difference to our argument.

In sum, the issue of public debt burden may be viewed in terms of the distribution effects of the transfer payments used to retire the debt or pay interest on it. It is a burden to those citizens who are net losers in this transfer. *For them the burden is similar to that of a private debt.*

RELATIVE SIZE
OF PUBLIC DEBT AND GNP

It is difficult to give an accurate statistical measure of the burden created by redistribution effects. Whatever they are, the economy's ability either to retire the public debt or to pay interest on it is all relative to the economy's capacity to pay taxes. A reasonable measure of this ability is the size of the GNP relative to the size of the debt and to the amount of the interest payments that must be paid on it.

Figure 9-5 indicates that, since World War II, GNP has become much larger relative to the size of the government debt. In the immediate postwar years, 1945–1947, the debt was actually larger than GNP. Since then, however, GNP has grown until it is roughly three times as large as the government debt. By this criterion the burden of the public debt has declined over time.

What about the size of GNP relative to the amount of the interest payments on the debt? From the end of World War II up through the middle 1960s, these payments amounted to between 1.5 and 2 percent of GNP. In recent years they have increased somewhat, representing about 3.5 percent of GNP. Nonetheless, this still seems a small fraction of total GNP.

EXTERNAL VERSUS INTERNAL DEBT

Government debt (bonds) held by U.S. citizens is what these citizens collectively owe to themselves. The redistribution effects associated with taxation and transfer payments only redistribute the economy's total output domestically. As a nation there is no loss in total output. That part of government debt held by foreigners is another matter. Interest payments on such debt, as well as the retirement of that debt, amounts to a transfer of purchasing power from a nation's citizens to foreigners. In other words, a part of the nation's output must be given up to

another nation. It is like private debt in that one party loses purchasing power by virtue of the obligation to pay another.

In the United States the portion of government debt held by foreigners has increased in recent years. In the late 1960s foreigners held anywhere from 3 to 5 percent of the total government debt. During the 1970s this figure increased to around 12 to 14 percent. While this is still a small portion of the total debt, the trend is somewhat disturbing. Some say it reflects the fact that political turmoil abroad has caused foreign investors in general to seek the relatively safe haven provided by U.S. government bonds. Others point particularly to the influx of Arab investors seeking a safe investment for their swollen oil revenues.

GOVERNMENT BANKRUPTCY?

It is extremely unlikely that the government debt could cause government bankruptcy in the United States. Figure 9-5 strongly suggests that, if anything, the government debt is much less of a burden today than at any time since World War II. Furthermore, most of that debt is what U.S. citizens owe themselves. In addition, the transfer payments necessary to pay interest on the debt amount to but a tiny fraction of GNP. And don't forget, these are only a burden to the extent that they cause redistribution of income among U.S. citizens. Moreover, it is not even clear that this redistribution is from lower to higher income groups in the economy. Finally, you may have wondered how the government pays off bondholders when their bonds mature. Typically the government simply sells new bonds and uses the proceeds to pay off the old bonds.

WHEN IS DEBT CREATION
A BURDEN, AND WHEN NOT?

It is sometimes argued that government debt creation imposes a burden on future generations. Is this true? Yes, and no.

Debt creation does saddle future generations with the redistribution effects associated with the taxes and transfer payments needed to make ongoing interest payments on the debt. To the extent that taxpayers and bondholders are not necessarily the same people, this redistribution of income will be a burden to some members of future generations.

The creation of public debt during times when the economy is operating at full employment *may* represent a burden to future generations, but not necessarily. New government bonds may "crowd out" bonds being issued by businesses when the economy is producing at maximum capacity. To this extent business may have to cut back on capital expansion for lack of funds. The government gets the funds and uses the resources otherwise going to businesses for something else. Suppose the government spends the funds from its bond sales inefficiently or on something society doesn't want—fighter planes that don't fly or fancy inaugural dances. Present and future generations are *burdened* because of the forgone capital that would have allowed the economy to produce more now and tomorrow. Note, however, that the government might have raised taxes instead of selling bonds to get the funds for those foolish expenditures. *Only* if selling bonds was easier than raising taxes (due to political considerations, say) is it true that creating government debt is a cause of the burden. Even then the real cause is poor fiscal policy.

Creation of public debt can be a blessing under certain conditions. Suppose the economy is in a recession. Prudent fiscal policy would call for increased government spending and reduced taxes—in short, a deficit. And creating this deficit requires the creation of more government debt.[3] If the government didn't take these actions, the economy would have a longer and deeper recession than otherwise. Goods and services, including capital goods, that otherwise could be produced would not be. This year's forgone production would be forever lost to society. Society would be saddled with *the burden of doing without goods it could have had*—now and in the future.

[3] Even if the government financed the deficit by creating more money ("printing" it), it would be necessary to create more bonds under modern central banking arrangements, the subject of Chapters 10 through 12.

CHECKPOINT 9-4

Suppose half of the nation's citizens each hold an equal share of the government debt, and that all citizens each pay an equal share of the taxes used to pay interest on the debt. Given this, how large do you think the total debt could be in relation to GNP before serious unrest might develop? What would government bankruptcy mean in this case?

SUMMARY

1. The government budget is an itemized account of government expenditures and revenues over the course of a year. The budget is said to be balanced, in surplus, or in deficit depending, respectively, on whether government spending equals, is less than, or is greater than government tax revenues. The Employment Act of 1946 gives the government responsibility for maintaining full employment. Achieving this goal must therefore be a major concern of budget policy.

2. The equilibrium GNP can be raised by increasing government expenditures or by lowering taxes or by doing both. Conversely, the equilibrium GNP can be lowered by decreasing government expenditures or by raising taxes or by doing both. According to the balanced budget multiplier, a simultaneous increase in government expenditures and taxes of a matched or balanced amount will result in an increase in GNP equal to the increase in government spending. The converse is true of a decrease.

3. During a recession a suitable discretionary fiscal policy calls for Congress deliberately to increase government spending and reduce taxes. An inflationary expansion would call for a decrease in government spending and an increase in taxes. In practice, discretionary fiscal policy is hampered by: the difficulty of forecasting the future; timing problems due to the politics and sluggishness of democratic processes, and to lags in recognizing the current state of the economy; the tendency of fiscal actions by state and local government to accentuate contractions and expansions; the variety of taxes that Con-

gress may change, each having a quantitative impact that is difficult to assess.

4. Nondiscretionary fiscal policy relies on the economy's built-in automatic stabilizers. Chief among these are a progressive tax structure and unemployment compensation programs, which cause tax revenues to vary more than proportionally with changes in GNP. These automatically tend to generate expansionary budget deficits during recessions and budget surpluses that dampen inflationary pressures during expansions. Automatic stabilizers reduce but do not eliminate the need for discretionary fiscal policy. Sometimes they pose a problem, for they can slow down the recovery from a recession and, to this extent, hinder rather than help the economy.

5. Annually balanced budgets tend to accentuate the business cycle. A cyclically balanced budget policy is difficult to follow because the expansion phase of a business cycle typically differs in length and magnitude from the recession phase. Consequently, functional finance is the budget policy most often followed.

6. Given the actual level of government spending, the high-employment budget measures what the budget deficit or surplus would be if GNP were continually at the full-employment level. The high-employment budget deficit or surplus is a more accurate measure of the impact of fiscal policy than is the actual budget deficit or surplus.

7. A budget deficit has a more expansionary impact on the economy if it is financed by creating new money than if it is financed by borrowing. A budget surplus has less of a contractionary impact on the economy if the surplus is used to retire debt outstanding than if it is simply left to accumulate in the government treasury.

8. The government debt, or stock of government bonds outstanding, was larger than GNP in the immediate post–World War II years. Since then GNP has grown faster than the debt so that GNP today is roughly three times the size of the debt. By this criterion the debt has become less of a burden over time.

9. The government debt may be a burden to the extent that the taxes and transfer payments needed to make interest payments on the debt cause a redistribution of income among citizens; to the extent that the debt is held by foreigners; to the extent that debt creation allows the financing of unproductive or unnecessary government spending.

KEY TERMS AND CONCEPTS
automatic stabilizers
balanced budget
balanced budget multiplier
budget deficit
budget surplus
fiscal policy
government budget
high-employment budget
progressive tax
proportional tax
regressive tax
unemployment compensation

QUESTIONS AND PROBLEMS
1. Suppose the government budget is balanced and that the economy is experiencing an inflationary boom. Assuming the economy's *MPC* is $\frac{4}{5}$, compare and contrast each of the following discretionary fiscal actions in terms of their effectiveness in dealing with this situation:
a. increase lump-sum taxes by $10 billion;
b. decrease government spending by $10 billion;
c. decrease both government spending and lump-sum taxes by $10 billion;
d. decrease government spending by $16 billion and lump-sum taxes by $20 billion.

2. From 1931 through 1940 the unemployment rate never fell below 14.3 percent (1937), and yet the government had a budget deficit in every one of these years. If deficits are expansionary, what were the possible problems? Use a leakages-injections diagram to illustrate your answer. (Any of the diagrams from Figure 9–3, parts a, b, or c will do, but show both the government spending schedule and the investment schedule separately, as well as their sum.)

3. Assume a $100 billion downward shift in consumption spending. Using the diagrams in parts a and b of Figure 9–3, what would be the difference in the discretionary change in government spending required to keep the equilibrium GNP from changing, comparing the lump-sum tax case with the proportional tax case? What does this illustrate about the relationship between the role of automatic stabilizers and the need for discretionary fiscal action?

4. A number of economists have argued that discretionary fiscal policy is not well suited to deal with the relatively brief recessions that the United States has experienced since World War II. They contend that it is necessary to rely more on the built-in stabilizers to deal with such recessions. On the other hand, they argue that the relative importance of discretionary versus nondiscretionary fiscal policy is just the reverse in a depression like that of the 1930s. Explain why you would agree or disagree with these economists.

5. It has been argued by some economists that financing government deficits by borrowing may actually result in completely offsetting the expansionary effect of the deficit. What must they be assuming about the degree of difficulty of inducing the public to buy government bonds and the degree of sensitivity of investment spending to interest rate changes? These economists would refer to this as a situation of "complete crowding out" where the real issue is one of *who* will decide how resources are to be used—the government or the private market. Explain.

6. Relative to other views on budget policy, it has been said that "functional finance isn't so much a deliberate budget policy as a rationalization for what actually happens." Considering all the difficulties associated with discretionary fiscal policy, as well as the difficulties of pursuing the other budget policies, give an assessment of this statement.

7. In what sense is the public debt "what we owe ourselves"? In what sense, and why, might this not be true from the standpoint of an individual taxpayer? Why do foreign holdings of our nation's government debt put us in a position like that of an individual who is in debt?

■ NEWS ITEM FOR YOUR ANALYSIS ■

THE PROGRESSIVE INCOME TAX STRUCTURE AND INFLATION

WASHINGTON, June 28—The idea of correcting tax rates for inflation—indexing—should not be forgotten as long as we have inflation. An indexing amendment to the tax reform bill now before the Senate deserves serious consideration.

The measure calls for the first inflation adjustment of the income tax brackets, personal exemptions, and standard deductions. It would correct for the average price increase in the Consumer Price Index in the year beginning July 1 of this year over the average CPI in the previous year.

For example, if the increase in the CPI works out to 6 percent, the personal exemption and standard deduction would be multiplied by 1.06. Similarly, so would each income threshold from one bracket to the next. A worker who pays 14 percent on his or her first $1,000 of taxable income and 15 percent in the next bracket would now stay in the lower bracket up to $1,060 before getting clipped at the higher rate.

Without such adjustment, the workers whose wage increase just makes up for the 6 percent inflation is pushed into a higher tax bracket. Therefore, just to keep even, the worker's wages must rise faster than the cost of living. So Senator Taft, sponsor of the amendment, is quite correct in arguing that the inflation penalty is "one of the basic causes for inflationary wage demands, since a worker must receive a wage increase in excess of the cost-of-living increase simply to maintain the real value of his or her take-home pay."

Why has official Washington been cool to indexing? It seems politicians of every stripe like the inflation tax because they don't have to vote for it. It goes up automatically with inflation. Liberals think it provides more revenues for social spending; conservatives think it helps balance the budget.

The chairman of the Senate Finance Committee argues that inflation also pushes up the cost of government. Therefore, he claims, it is reasonable to allow the inflation tax to support those increased costs. His argument would be valid if the income tax were purely proportional. But, in fact, inflation takes two bites out of income, once through proportionality and once through progressivity.

For instance, if national income were 100 and the tax was a proportional 25 percent, revenues would be 25. If national income were inflated to 200, the tax would produce revenues of 50, sufficient to pay for the inflated cost of government. But because the tax is progressive, when national income goes from 100 to 200 tax revenues go from 25 to, say, 75.

These unscheduled, unplanned, unlegislated taxes constitute taxation without representation in a very real sense.

QUESTIONS

1. What are the implications of the inflation tax for the high-employment budget?

2. In late 1973 the rate of inflation picked up sharply, spurred in large part by the sudden jump in the price of oil. The economy had its worst recession since the 1930s, starting in November 1973 and reaching its trough in March 1975. What possible light does this news item shed on the events of that period?

3. It is sometimes said that the inflation tax provides a "fiscal dividend" to the government but is a "fiscal drag" on the economy. What do you think is meant by this?

4. How does the inflation tax affect the economy's aggregate supply curve?

5. Why might the inflation tax be viewed as an antiinflation tool?

THREE

MONEY, BANKING, AND MONETARY POLICY

10

THE NATURE AND FUNCTIONS OF MONEY AND BANKING

A HISTORY LESSON—ON INFLATION AND MONEY

PHILADELPHIA, July 1—On October 20, 1774, the Continental Congress decreed that "all manufactures of this country be sold at reasonable prices," and that "vendors of goods or merchandise will not take advantage of the scarcity of goods . . . but will sell the same at rates we have been respectively accustomed to do for 12 months last past."

The years that followed saw both the states and Congress print reams of paper money (about $400 million) and an equivalent volume of price-control legislation—two activities that always seem to go together. The Revolutionary War was mainly financed by printing money. By November 1776, commodity prices were 480 percent above the prewar average, and the Continental Congress announced that "any person who shall hereafter be so lost to all virtue and regard for his country as to refuse [Continental currency] in payment, or obstruct and discourage the currency or circulation thereof . . . shall be deemed . . . an enemy of his country."

Public jawboning, private threats, ostracism, boycotts, fines—all proved useless against the flood of paper money. In Boston the price of common labor, fixed at 3 shillings a day in 1777, had risen to 60 shillings by mid-1779. George Washington complained in April 1779 that "a wagonload of money will scarcely purchase a wagonload of provisions." When the Continental Congress again endorsed price controls in 1779, the request was for state laws limiting wage and price increases "not to exceed twentyfold the levels of 1774." However, not even that modest goal was attainable, and Congress allowed controls to expire when it met again in February 1780.

Early in 1781, Virginia tried to fix the price of a cavalry horse at $150,000 in Continental currency. An index of wholesale prices rose from 78 in 1775 to 10,544 in 1780. The phrase "not worth a Continental" survives.

It has been said that money is "the oil that lubricates the wheels of trade." When the economy's monetary system is functioning well, this seems an apt analogy. However, history shows that money and the closely related activity of banking are often the source of economic instability, inflation, and unemployment. The historical sketch above indicates that providing for the economy's money supply was not the least of our country's birth pangs. Indeed, monetary problems have frequently plagued our economy throughout its history.

This chapter focuses on the basic nature and functions of money and banking. In addition, we will see how and why the Federal Reserve System was developed to provide the basic structure for money and banking in our economy. Chapter 11 will study in detail the way our banking system affects the size of the economy's money supply. Chapter 12 will focus on how the money supply affects the level of total demand for goods and services, and the role that money plays in determining the economy's equilibrium level of total output and employment.

THE NATURE OF MONEY

What does money do? What are the different kinds of money? What determines the value of money?

What Money Does

Essentially, money does three things. It functions as a medium of exchange, a unit of account, and a store of value.

MONEY AS A MEDIUM OF EXCHANGE

Without money people would have to carry on trade by *barter*—the swapping of goods for goods. In Chapter 3 we saw that for trade to take place in a barter economy there must be a *coincidence of wants* between individuals. If I have good X to trade and I want to get good Y, I must find someone who not only wants to get good X but also coincidentally has good Y to give in exchange. The difficulties involved in finding a coincidence of wants tend to discourage and inhibit specialization and trade in a barter economy (recall the discussion in Chapter 3). Because of this, the gains from specialization and trade cannot be fully realized and therefore the total output of the economy is less than it otherwise might be. However, if money is used to carry on trade I can sell good X to whoever wants it and accept money in exchange. Whether the purchaser has the good Y that I want is now irrelevant. I can use the money to buy good Y from whoever has it, regardless of whether or not they want good X. Trade is now easier because **money** *is something that is generally acceptable to everyone as payment for anything.*

The existence of money eliminates the need for a coincidence of wants. Therefore when goods are bought and sold using money as the medium of exchange, the economy is able to be more productive. Its production possibilities frontier is shifted outward.

MONEY AS A UNIT OF ACCOUNT

In a barter economy, comparing the relative values of different goods and services is much more complicated than in a money-using economy. For example, to get an idea of the cost of an orange in a barter economy would require a knowledge of the rate at which oranges exchange for apples, shoes, tea, bread, haircuts, and so forth. A shopping trip would entail numerous cross comparisons of the exchange rates between widely different goods and services.

"Let's see, if 3 oranges will buy 8 apples, and 5 apples will buy 2 pears, that must mean . . . ah . . . 15 oranges will buy 16 pears." There is no need for such complex calculations if everything is valued in terms of the same unit of account, money. Then in the above example the price of an orange is $.16, an apple $.06, and a pear $.15.

Money provides a common unit of account for expressing the market values of widely different goods and services. The existence of this common unit of account greatly reduces the time and effort needed to make intelligent economic decisions. As a result, more time and effort are available for use in other productive activities. This is another reason why money shifts the economy's production possibilities frontier outward.

MONEY AS A STORE OF VALUE

You can hold wealth in many forms: houses, yachts, stocks, bonds, jewelry, and so on. But, *no form of wealth is as readily convertible into other goods and services as money is. This ready convertibility, or* **liquidity**, *makes money an attractive store of value, or source of purchasing power.*

If you had to sell your new wristwatch within the next five minutes to get money to make purchases, you would probably only get a fraction of what you paid for it. If you had paid $50 for it, you might only be able to get $20—a loss of $30. If instead you had $50, you could easily make $50 worth of purchases within five minutes. In general, you can rank assets on a scale from the most liquid to the least liquid according to the amount of loss, including **transaction costs** (such as brokerage fees, advertising costs, time and effort searching for a buyer), that would result if they had to be converted into money *within a short period of time.* Money of course heads the list. A car, a house, a painting, or a piece of land might be at or near the bottom.

Kinds of Money

Throughout history money has taken many forms. Many of the oldest kinds of money are still used today, while new kinds continue to be developed. In order of their historical evolution, the principal kinds of money are commodity money, coins, paper money, and demand deposits. All these different kinds of money share one common characteristic that is the essence of "moneyness." Namely, money is something that is generally acceptable to everyone as payment for anything.

COMMODITY MONEY

The earliest forms of money were commodities that often had other uses besides serving as money. Hides, furs, jewelry, precious stones and metals, and livestock are but a few examples. Even today these items often serve as money in some economically underdeveloped regions of the world. When the German deutsche mark became worthless as a result of the German

---

After reading this chapter, you will be able to:

1. Explain the nature and functions of money.
2. Describe the differences between commodity money, fiat money, bank money or demand deposits, and near money.
3. State the nature of the relationship between the supply of money, prices, and the value of money.
4. Explain how banks evolved from a mere safekeeping function to a fractional reserve banking operation, creating money through their lending activities.
5. Describe the purposes, organization, and functions of the Federal Reserve System.
6. Describe the role of the commercial bank and how it is different from and yet similar to other types of banks.

hyperinflation in the early 1920s, Germans used cognac and cigarettes as money.

Some commodities are better suited for use as money than others. The ideal commodity money does not suffer from handling and time—it wears well. Eggs and other perishables won't do. It should be valuable enough that small amounts, easily carried, are sufficient to buy a week's groceries. Anything requiring a wheelbarrow instead of a pocketbook is out. The ideal commodity money is easily divisible to make change and small purchases. Diamonds, the most durable commodity, are too difficult to split. Finally, the market rate of exchange of the commodity money with other goods should be relatively stable.

Historically the precious metals, gold and silver, have been the most continuously used forms of commodity money. Small amounts are quite valuable so that as a commodity money they are easy to carry. Both are attractive metals and interact little with other substances, though silver does tarnish and gold is soft.

COINS

Coins were a natural outgrowth of the use of precious metals as commodity money. Using gold dust in bulk form meant that every merchant needed a scale to carry on business. Every transaction, however small, required careful and time-consuming weighing. The first coins were made by kings or rulers who weighed out an amount of precious metal and made a coin out of it. The coin had the amount of precious metal it contained stamped on it (its "face value") along with the ruler's seal as a guarantee of the weight. This made trading easier as long as the ruler was honest and the citizens didn't tinker with the coins to "clip" or remove precious metal from them. Monarchs and those they ruled being human (despite the monarchs' frequent claim to the contrary), the debasement of the coin of the realm was common.

Another problem with coins is that they often disappear from circulation whenever the market value of the precious metal they contain exceeds the amount of the face value stamped on them. Suppose a 25-cent piece contains $.30 worth of silver. Eventually circulation will bring them into the hands of someone who will melt them

down for the $.30 worth of silver rather than use each coin for purchasing $.25 worth of goods, the face value stamped on the coin.

To avoid this problem governments now issue **token coins**—coins that contain an amount of metal that is worth much less than the face value of the coin. Such coins are **fiat money**—*money that the government declares by law to be legal tender for the settlement of debts.* This means that if you owe somebody $.25 and you offer them a quarter coin to pay off the debt, they must accept it. If they don't, they no longer have a legal claim on you. This illustrates an important characteristic of fiat money. *Fiat money is money that is not backed by or convertible into gold or any other precious metal. It is acceptable because the government declares it to be acceptable, not because of the value of the materials contained in it. It is acceptable not as a commodity itself, but rather because people know that it can be used to buy goods and services.*

PAPER MONEY

Paper money, the bills in your wallet, is also money in today's economy. It too illustrates that money is acceptable because it will buy goods. The value of the bills themselves as a commodity is next to nothing. Indeed, the materials needed to make a $1 bill, or a $10,000 bill, cost but a tiny fraction of a cent. Today all paper money in the United States is issued by the Federal Reserve System (which we shall look at shortly) in the form of Federal Reserve notes. At one time the Treasury used to issue paper money, but no longer. There is very little Treasury currency left in circulation today.

DEMAND DEPOSITS

If you place currency (coins and paper money) in a **demand deposit** at a commercial bank, the bank is legally obligated to give that money back to you the moment you ask for it—that is, on demand. Demand deposits are also called checking accounts because you can write checks against them.

A check is nothing more than a slip of paper, a standardized form, on which you write the bank an order to withdraw funds from your checking account and pay them either to someone else or to yourself. The check is a convenience that makes it unnecessary for you to go to your bank and withdraw currency from your demand deposit every time you need money to make a purchase or pay a bill. You simply write on the check the exact amount of the purchase or bill payment, the name of the party to whom your bank is to give the funds, and sign your name. You can either hand the check directly to that party or mail it. The receiving party (an individual, business, or other institution) has only to sign or endorse the check to receive the funds from your bank out of your demand deposit. Often the party receiving the check will simply endorse and deposit it in his or her own checking account, frequently in a different bank. The banks conveniently handle the transfer of funds from your checking account to that of the receiving party.

Demand deposits function as money by virtue of the check-writing privilege. Compared to currency they have several advantages. Lost or stolen currency is almost impossible to recover. Lost or stolen checks are much more difficult for another party to use, so that a demand deposit is relatively secure from such mishaps. Checks may be sent through the mail much more readily and safely than currency. Checks therefore make trade possible between parties separated by great distances. They also provide a convenient record of completed transactions. Given these advantages, it is not surprising that in terms of dollar value checks account for by far the largest amount of transactions in our economy.

Today almost all economists regard demand deposits as money because they can be converted into currency on demand, and because checks are such a widely used medium of exchange. At present the most widely accepted definition of money is that it is the sum of currency and demand deposits, or what is called M_1:

$$M_1 = \text{currency} + \text{demand deposits}^1$$

[1] More accurately, M_1 equals the sum of: currency outside of the U.S. Treasury, Federal Reserve banks (to be described later in this and subsequent chapters), and vaults of commercial banks; demand deposits at commercial banks (to be described in the next chapter), other than those demand deposits owned by another commercial bank; and foreign demand deposits at Federal Reserve banks.

NEAR MONEY

Currency and demand deposits are regarded as money because they seem to perform all three functions of money (as a medium of exchange, a unit of account, and a store of value) better than any other asset. But there are several other kinds of assets that fulfill the unit of account and store of value functions at least as well. In addition, they can be converted rather easily into currency or demand deposits. These assets are often called **near money**—they are like money except that they are not usually regarded as a medium of exchange.

1. *Savings Deposits.* Various kinds of savings deposits fit the description of near money. Unlike demand deposits, most cannot be transferred by check nor are they legally subject to withdrawal on demand, but require prior notice (though this is rarely enforced). These include deposit shares at savings and loan associations, mutual savings banks, and credit unions, as well as time **certificates of deposit (CDs)** at commercial banks. CDs differ from other kinds of savings deposits in that CDs require that the depositor deposit a specified amount of money (such as $1,000, $5,000, etc.) for a certain length of time (such as for six months, a year, etc.). In return, the depositor is guaranteed a specified rate of interest on the deposit for that length of time. However, if the depositor withdraws the money before that length of time has expired, the depositor incurs a penalty—typically in the form of a lower rate of interest received on the deposit. Many would argue that savings deposits are a better store of value than money because they typically earn interest while currency and demand deposits do not. However, it takes time and effort (a trip to the bank) to convert savings deposits into demand deposits or currency whenever the medium of exchange function is needed. But the higher the interest rate on savings deposits, the more worthwhile it is to hold funds in that form—the return makes up for the inconvenience of shifting to currency and demand deposits when necessary.

2. *Time Deposits at Commercial Banks.* Until recently, **time deposits** at commercial banks were like other kinds of savings deposits

in that they could not serve as a medium of exchange. On November 1, 1978, new federal regulations took effect that allow commercial banks to transfer funds automatically from a depositor's interest-bearing time deposit to his or her checking account as needed. This change has blurred the distinction between demand deposits (checking accounts) and time deposits. In effect, time deposits at commercial banks can now serve as a medium of exchange, and checking accounts (demand deposits) effectively can earn interest like a time deposit.

3. *NOW Accounts.* In recent years some savings banks have taken steps to make it easier for depositors to shift back and forth between savings deposits and demand deposits. (This can be done by mail or in some instances by phone or other rapid communication.) Currently the use of the **negotiable order of withdrawal (NOW)** account, is being pushed in some regions of the country. Such accounts are savings deposits from which the depositor may have funds transferred to a designated party by simply sending the savings bank a checklike form, the NOW. This effectively means that in the future savings accounts may become more of a medium of exchange like checking accounts and time deposits at commercial banks.

4. *Short-Term Government Bonds.* Some argue that short-term government bonds, such as **Treasury bills**, that mature one, three, or six months after the day they are issued, are also near money. These are less liquid than savings deposits because their prices fluctuate with changes in the interest rate between the day they are issued and the day they mature. Therefore, unlike a savings deposit, one cannot be sure of the amount of purchasing power that can be realized from the sale of a short-term government bond from one day to the next. While the price may be higher than the original purchase price, it may also be lower. Hence, there is some uncertainty about the store of value of a bond on all days except the maturity date. In addition, a brokerage fee must be paid when buying or selling a bond. Moreover, it is not possible to buy fractions of a bond and this

"lumpiness" makes them less attractive to individuals than they are to large businesses and other institutions. (Treasury bills are not usually issued in denominations of less than $10,000.) Nonetheless, large corporations, banks, and other financial institutions (pension funds, trust funds, and insurance companies) find short-term government bonds a convenient form of near money.

5. *Negotiable Certificates of Deposit.* For similar reasons, the large **negotiable certificates of deposit** (CDs with a minimum denomination of $100,000) issued by commercial banks are also attractive to large investors. Unlike the CDs described earlier (often called nonnegotiable CDs), negotiable CDs may be bought and sold at any time just like a bond. Hence, their price also fluctuates on a day-to-day basis just like that of a bond.

BROADER DEFINITIONS OF MONEY

Because of the near-money nature of the different kinds of savings deposits and certificates of deposit, broader definitions of money to include these items have gained increased attention in recent years. The basic argument for including these near-money assets in the broader definitions is that the near moneys are almost as liquid as currency and demand deposits. Most savings deposits are less liquid than currency and demand deposits only because of the transactions costs (a trip to the bank, a postage stamp, or a phone call) incurred when they are transferred into currency and demand deposits. As we have already noted, new federal regulations have effectively made time deposits at commercial banks as liquid as demand deposits. As already noted, M_1 is defined as the sum of currency and demand deposits. The broader definitions of money are defined as follows. M_2 *is defined as M_1 plus time deposits at commercial banks. M_3 is equal to M_2 plus deposits at thrift institutions* (mutual savings banks, savings and loan associations, and credit unions). *M_4 and M_5 include large negotiable CDs: M_4 equals M_2 plus large negotiable CDs; M_5 equals M_3 plus large negotiable CDs.* Table 10-1 provides an idea of the sizes of M_1, M_2, M_3, M_4, and M_5,

TABLE 10-1 MEASURES OF MONEY IN THE UNITED STATES: M_1, M_2, M_3, M_4, M_5
(Seasonally Adjusted, Billions of Dollars, February 1979)

		Percentage of				
		M_1	M_2	M_3	M_4	M_5
Currency	$ 98.9	27.6	11.2	6.5	10.1	6.1
Plus: Demand deposits (at commercial banks)	259.9	72.4	29.6	17.2	26.5	16.1
Equals:						
M_1	358.8	100.0				
Plus: Time deposits[a] (at commercial banks)	518.3		59.1	34.3	52.9	32.1
Equals:						
M_2	877.1		100.0			
Plus: Deposits at nonbank thrift institutions	632.9			41.9		39.2
Equals:						
M_3	1,510.0			100.0		
M_2	877.1					
Plus: Large negotiable CDs	102.1				10.4	
Equals:						
M_4	979.2				100.0	
M_3	1,510.0					
Plus: Large negotiable CDs	102.1					6.3
Equals:						
M_5	1,612.2					100.0

SOURCE: *Federal Reserve Bulletin*, April 1979.

[a] Excludes negotiable time certificates of deposit in denominations of $100,000 or more.

along with the relative importance of the various components that make up each of these definitions of money.

CREDIT CARDS AND TRADE CREDIT

A near money is often just as good a store of value as currency and demand deposits. But a near money is not a medium of exchange, though it can be readily converted to one. Credit cards and trade credit have very much the opposite properties of near money. They cannot serve as a store of value, but they are a medium of exchange.

If a business will sell you goods and services without requiring your immediate payment in the form of cash or a check, we say the business has extended you credit. If you carry a recognized credit card, many businesses will sell goods and services to you, on the spot, in exchange for nothing more than your signature on a credit slip bearing your credit card number. This allows you to defer payment by cash or check for some period of time. The credit card essentially serves as a short-term medium of exchange, a substitute for a check or cash. It is short term because the business ultimately expects to receive either currency or a check.

Businesses often extend credit to other businesses that are regular customers—a wholesaler supplying a retailer for example. Such credit is called **trade credit**. It allows one business to buy goods from another without making immediate full payment by check or with currency. Trade credit is usually extended on the basis of past dealings that have convinced the seller that the buyer is financially sound and reliable—that the buyer will ultimately "pay up" with currency or a check. Like the credit card, trade credit serves as a short-term medium of exchange even though it is not a store of value.

Credit cards and trade credit reduce the need for currency and demand deposits as mediums of exchange. They cannot replace currency and demand deposits, however, because such credit is not a store of value.

What Determines the Value of Money?

Money in our economy today is neither backed by nor convertible into gold or any other precious metal. Coins contain an amount of metal that is worth much less than their face value. Paper money is just that—pieces of paper. Both coins and paper money are money because the government declares it so—they are fiat money. Demand deposits or checking accounts are just bookkeeping entries. Indeed, the government has not even declared demand deposits to be money, which only shows that general acceptability in exchange is more important than a government declaration. If coins, currency, and demand deposits are not backed by gold or any other precious metal, and if they have no value in and of themselves, then what determines their purchasing power or real value? The value of money is determined by supply and demand, just like the value of anything else. Let's see why.

MONEY DEMAND AND SUPPLY

Money's value derives from its scarcity relative to its usefulness in providing a unique service. The unique service lies in the fact that money can be readily exchanged for goods and services. The economy's demand for money derives from its demand for this service. Therefore, the economy's demand for money is largely determined by the total dollar volume of its current transactions as well as its desire to hold money for possible future transactions.

What determines the supply of money? In the next chapter we will see how our economy's commercial banks as a whole can create money in the form of demand deposits. We will also see how the government, through the Federal Reserve System, can promote, or limit, this kind of money creation. Therefore, not only is the government in a position to control the supply of fiat money (coins and paper money), it is also able to regulate the supply of money more broadly defined.

MONEY DEMAND AND SUPPLY DETERMINE MONEY'S VALUE

The value of a unit of money (such as a dollar) is its purchasing power, or the amount of goods and services that it will buy. The higher the economy's price level, the smaller the quantity of goods and services that a unit of money will buy. Conversely, the lower the price level, the larger the quantity of goods and services a unit of money will buy.

If you are going to the grocery store to buy four loaves of bread and the price of bread is $.50 per loaf, then you will need $2 of money to exchange for bread. However, if the price of a loaf of bread is $1 per loaf, you will need $4 of money. There is obviously a relationship between the total quantity of such transactions in the economy, the prices at which they take place, and the economy's demand (need) for money. Oversimplifying somewhat, the following tends to be true. Given the economy's total quantity of transactions (such as the number of bread loaves purchased) and its demand for money needed to execute these transactions, the greater the supply of money, the higher the price level at which these transactions will tend to take place. Conversely, the smaller the supply of money, the lower the price level at which these transactions will tend to take place. Hence, the supply of money and the demand for it play an important role in determining the price level in the economy. Therefore, it follows that the supply and demand for money play an important role in determining the purchasing power, or value, of a unit of money.

In sum, *given the demand for money, the larger the supply of money, the higher the price level will tend to be and, hence, the less the purchasing power, or value, of a unit of money. Conversely, the smaller the supply of money, the lower the price level will tend to be and, thus, the greater the purchasing power, or value, of a unit of money.*

MONEY AND PRICES

The news item at the beginning of this chapter provides an interesting historical illustration of the relationship between the amount of money supplied to the economy, the price level, and the value of a unit of money—in this case the continental dollar. (You should reread the news item at this point.)

During the Revolutionary War in our country, it was very difficult for the government to raise sufficient revenue through taxation to finance military operations. Consequently, both the states and the Continental Congress resorted to printing money to pay for supplies, weapons, and troops. As a result, the supply of paper money in the economy increased by an enormous amount between 1774 and 1781. This increase in the supply of paper money greatly exceeded the growth in the economy's capacity to produce goods and services. Hence, the growth in the money supply was much larger than the growth in the quantity of transactions involving the purchase and sale of goods and services. As a result, the prices at which these transactions took place rose rapidly, and the purchasing power of a unit of paper currency fell accordingly. State laws passed in an effort to control the rapid rise in the price level and the deteriorating value of the dollar were fruitless because they attacked the symptom, the hyperinflation, rather than the cause of the problem, the tremendous increase in the money supply. "Public jawboning, private threats, ostracism, boycotts, fines—all proved useless against the flood of paper money."

A more recent example of hyperinflation occurred in Germany between 1921 and 1923. The German government increased the supply of currency to such an extent that the wholesale price index rose to a level in November 1923 that was 30 billion times higher than it was in January 1921! By this point the deutsche mark's value as money had been destroyed. An item purchased for a mark in 1921 cost 30 billion marks in 1923. Cases of hyperinflation like these are relatively rare. But many governments, particularly in underdeveloped countries, regularly print fiat money to finance their expenditures. Inflation rates on the order of 50 to 200 percent per year are not uncommon in such countries.

The tendency for the general level of prices and the money supply to move together is illustrated in Figure 10-1. In this figure, money, defined as M_1 and M_2, is plotted along with the Consumer Price Index (CPI) for the years since 1905. The data are plotted on a ratio scale so that equal vertical distances represent equal percentage changes.

■ CHECKPOINT 10-1

What would you rather use for money, $10 worth of aluminum or $10 worth of steel? Why? Rank the following in terms of their liquidity: a savings deposit, a $100,000 negotiable CD, a $10 bill, a 90-day Treasury bill, a stamp collection, a $1,000 bill, a demand deposit, a Master Charge credit card, a lot in a suburb. Rank each of the above items as a store of value, given that there is a 10 percent rate of inflation. Explain this quote: "Money is acceptable because it is acceptable." Using the information in Figure 10-1, evaluate how a dollar bill has served as a store of value over the period since 1905.

THE DEVELOPMENT OF BANKING

An examination of the nature and development of early banking practices will enable us better to understand how modern commercial banks function. It will also reveal why it was felt necessary to create the Federal Reserve System in order to put commercial banking on a sounder footing. In addition, we will gain fur-

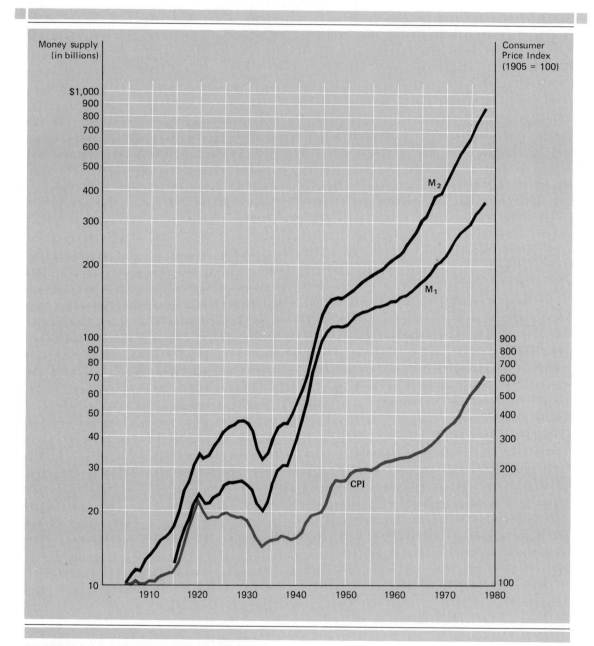

FIGURE 10-1 MONEY AND CONSUMER PRICES IN THE UNITED STATES SINCE 1905

The general level of consumer prices and the money supply tend to move together. This is illustrated by the behavior of the Consumer Price Index (CPI) and the money supply, defined either as M_1 or M_2. The data are plotted on a ratio scale so that equal vertical distances represent equal percentage changes.

TABLE 10-2 BALANCE SHEET OF AN EARLY COMMERCIAL BANK

Assets			Liabilities	
Ounces of gold	1,000		Ounces of gold receipts	1,000
Ounces of total assets	1,000	=	Ounces of total liabilities	1,000

ther insight into the nature of money and how it functions.

Primary Functions of Banks

Modern commercial banks have three primary functions: (1) they provide safekeeping services for all kinds of assets, not just money; (2) they make loans; and (3) as a group they create money. Originally the provision of safekeeping services was their only function. The functions of lending and money creation developed later, although today these functions represent by far the most important role of commercial banks in our economy.

SAFEKEEPING—
THE OLDEST BANKING FUNCTION

Goldsmiths were the forerunners of early banks. They had to have strong safes in order to protect and keep gold. Aware of this, people would often bring their own gold to the goldsmith for deposit in the safe. Usually the goldsmith received a fee for this safekeeping service. The depositor received a receipt designating the amount of gold deposited and attesting to the depositor's right to withdraw the gold on demand upon presentation of the receipt. When gold depositors needed their gold to purchase goods and services, they simply presented their receipts to the goldsmith who then gave them back their gold. Perhaps the closest counterpart of the goldsmith's safe in modern commercial bank is the safe-deposit box you rent from the bank for an annual fee.

LENDING—
THE FIRST COMMERCIAL BANKS

We might think of early commercial banking as evolving from the original safekeeping activities of goldsmiths. Suppose such a bank opens and accepts 1,000 ounces of gold from depositors. The depositors in turn receive receipts—

their legal claim to the gold. The bank's balance sheet is shown in Table 10-2. Like any balance sheet, the left-hand side shows the assets of the bank, or what it has in its possession. In this case, the bank's assets consist of the 1,000 ounces of gold. The right-hand side shows the bank's liabilities—the claims on the bank's assets, or who owns them. In this case the liabilities consist of the depositor's receipts, which are their proof of legal ownership, or claim to the gold. Like all balance sheets, total assets must equal total liabilities—assets amounting to 1,000 ounces of gold are balanced by liabilities or receipts laying claim to 1,000 ounces of gold.

On a typical day the quantity of receipts turned in at the bank's deposit window by depositors wishing to withdraw their gold amounts to only a small fraction of the total 1,000 ounces of gold. Moreover, these withdrawals are often approximately offset by new deposits of gold with the bank. As a consequence, our early banker observes that there is usually a sizeable amount of gold standing idle in the safe. It occurs to the banker that in addition to the fees earned for providing safekeeping services, there is another possible money-making activity. Why not lend out some of this idle gold to people who are willing to pay the banker interest to borrow it? As long as the banker keeps enough gold in the safe to meet withdrawal demands of depositors, the depositors never even need to know that some of their gold is being lent to other people. Even if they do know, they won't care as long as they can always get their gold back on demand.[2]

Suppose the banker observes that depositors

[2] One ounce of gold is indistinguishable from any other. Depositors are therefore only concerned about being able to get back the number of ounces of gold deposited, not the exact same particles of gold they deposited.

TABLE 10-3 EARLY COMMERCIAL BANK'S BALANCE SHEET AFTER LOANING OUT 800 OUNCES OF GOLD

Assets			Liabilities	
Ounces of gold (reserves)	200		Ounces of gold receipts	1,000
Ounces of gold in IOUs	800			
Ounces of total assets	1,000	=	Ounces of total liabilities	1,000

never withdraw more than 15 percent of the gold in the safe on any one day. The banker therefore decides it is safe to loan out about 80 percent, or 800 ounces, of the gold. This leaves 20 percent, or 200 ounces, in the safe as a reserve to satisfy depositors' withdrawal demands, somewhat more than the banker's experience suggests is necessary. The banker receives an IOU from each party that borrows gold. This note, a contract signed by the borrower, states the amount of gold owed to the bank, the date it must be paid back, and the interest rate that the borrower must pay the banker for the loan. The bank's balance sheet now appears as shown in Table 10-3. Comparing this balance sheet with that in Table 10-2, we see that for assets the bank now has 200 ounces of gold plus a number of pieces of paper, the IOUs, stating that various borrowers owe the bank 800 ounces of gold. For liabilities the bank still has obligations to give depositors 1,000 ounces of gold on demand, represented by paper gold receipts in the hands of depositors.

The bank will have no difficulties as long as depositor's demands for withdrawal do not exceed 200 ounces of gold in any one day. Should this happen, the bank would be unable to honor its commitment to give depositors their gold on demand.

MONEY CREATION AND THE EARLY COMMERCIAL BANKS

Now that we have looked at the principle behind the way in which early banks evolved to combine safekeeping and lending functions, it is not difficult to see how they became creators of money as well.

It takes time and effort for depositors to go to the bank to withdraw gold every time they need it to make purchases of goods and services. In the community in which our early bank operates, suppose merchants know customers fairly well and that the bank has a sound reputation. Merchants are therefore willing to sell goods in exchange for customers' gold receipts. The customer simply signs the paper gold receipt and specifies that its ownership has been transferred to the merchant. The merchant can either take the receipt to the bank to claim gold, or use it to make purchases from someone else, transferring its ownership once again in the same manner. The receipt itself is now used as money. It is acceptable in trade because people know it can be redeemed for gold on demand at the bank. It is used as money because it eliminates the need for frequent trips to the bank. And receipts are also easier to carry.

Expanding the Bank's Lending Activities. Once the gold receipts are being used as money, the banker sees a way to expand the bank's lending activity. At present the banker has to keep only a fraction of the gold as reserves—the rest is loaned out. Specifically, 200 ounces is kept in the safe and 800 ounces leaves the bank on loan. But if gold receipts are now acceptable as money, why not just give borrowers paper gold receipts rather than actual gold in exchange for their IOUs? The borrower can use the receipts just as readily as the gold to make purchases. The banker previously felt that it was necessary to keep only 200 ounces of actual gold on hand (asset side of Table 10-3) when there were gold receipts outstanding amounting to claims on 1,000 ounces (liability side of Table 10-3). If this was workable, wouldn't 1,000

**TABLE 10-4 EARLY COMMERCIAL BANK'S BALANCE SHEET
AFTER LOANING OUT GOLD RECEIPTS FOR 4,000 OUNCES OF GOLD**

Assets			Liabilities	
Ounces of gold (reserves)	1,000		Ounces of gold receipts	5,000
Ounces of gold in IOUs	4,000			
Ounces of total assets	5,000	=	Ounces of total liabilities	5,000

ounces of gold in the safe be adequate if there were gold receipts outstanding amounting to claims on 5,000 ounces? There would still be gold receipt claims on 5 ounces for every 1 ounce of actual gold, just as before.

As a consequence of the fact that gold receipts are acceptable as money, the banker can now keep all 1,000 ounces of deposited gold in the safe and print up and loan out gold receipts amounting to claims on 4,000 ounces of gold. Now the banker can earn interest on 5 times as many IOUs, generated by the lending of 4,000 ounces of gold as represented by the gold receipts given to borrowers (previously the banker earned interest on IOUs for 800 ounces of gold). These receipts will have the same claim on the gold in the safe as the receipts received by the original gold depositors. Our early commercial bank's balance sheet now looks as shown in Table 10-4. All 5,000 ounces worth of gold receipts are not circulating in the economy as money. Note however that there are only 1,000 ounces of actual gold.

As in the case depicted by Table 10-3, it is also true here that if all holders of these gold receipts brought them into the bank at one time and demanded gold, they could not be satisfied. The bank would not be able to honor its commitments to give out gold on demand. However, as long as no more than 20 percent of the gold receipts are presented for payment at one time, there is no problem.

**BANK NOTES AND
FRACTIONAL RESERVE BANKING**

It is now easy to see how banks got into the business of issuing paper money in the form of **bank notes**. The gold receipts of our hypotheti-

cal early commercial bank are but a short step removed from the status of these notes. To take this short step all the bank has to do is give a gold depositor bank notes instead of a receipt with the depositor's name on it.

Suppose the bank decides to print up a bank note that says "one dollar" across the front of it and, in smaller letters below this, "this note is redeemable for one ounce of gold on demand." Now the note could have just as well been called "one John," "one Sue," "one Kleebop," or "one Mark." The dollar was chosen as the basic unit of account in the United States by the Coinage Act of 1792.[3] As far as the money-using public was concerned, the important thing was that the bank note could be converted into gold at the bank on demand. Our hypothetical early commercial bank's balance sheet now appears as shown in Table 10-5. Compare this with Table 10-4.

During much of the nineteenth century, each bank in the United States could issue its own uniquely engraved bank note or currency. Through their lending activity such banks typically ended up issuing an amount of bank notes considerably larger than the amount of gold they had to back up the notes. That is, the bank notes had only fractional backing, thus giving rise to the term **fractional reserve banking**. There was usually nothing wrong with this if a bank used good judgment and didn't issue "too many" bank notes. But the main difficulty with

[3] The name derives from an old German word *thal* meaning "valley." Its early origin stems from coins used in the valley of Saint Joachim in Bohemia as early as 1519. These coins were first called *Joachimsthaler,* then *thaler,* which in English became "dollar."

TABLE 10-5 EARLY COMMERCIAL BANK'S BALANCE SHEET AFTER ONE-DOLLAR BANK NOTES REPLACE GOLD RECEIPTS
(Hypothetically, $1 = 1 Ounce of Gold)

Assets			Liabilities	
Gold reserves (1,000 ounces)	$1,000		Bank notes	$5,000
IOUs	4,000			
Total assets	$5,000	=	Total liabilities	$5,000

a system that combined fractional reserve banking with a convertible currency (convertible into gold) was that even a well-managed bank could get caught short. Banks frequently found themselves confronted with demands to exchange gold for their bank notes that exceeded the amount of gold in their safes. When this happened a bank would be forced to close its doors. People left holding that bank's currency were really holding only worthless pieces of paper.

Fractional reserve banking of this kind typified the so-called wildcat period of banking in the United States from 1836 to 1864. A large number of note-issuing private and state banks came into existence during this time. The term *wildcat bank* was used to describe many of these banks because they often issued bank notes far in excess of the amount of gold they had on hand. And they would locate in remote regions (where the wildcats were) to discourage people from trying to turn the bank notes in for gold. By 1863, there were roughly 1,600 different kinds of bank notes in circulation in the United States. To correct the excesses of the wildcat period, Congress passed the National Bank Acts of 1863 and 1864. These acts provided for a national currency and created national banks which were allowed to issue bank notes.

Bank Panics and Economic Instability

The National Bank Acts did not put an end to the nation's monetary and banking problems. Just as the banks had created bank notes when they made loans, they could also create demand deposits. When they granted a loan and received an IOU, they simply credited the amount of the loan to a demand deposit in the borrow-

er's name. Banks now came to use national currency as reserves, either keeping them in their own safe or possibly on deposit at another bank. Again the reserves typically amounted to only a fraction of the amount of their demand deposit liabilities. As a typical example, the asset side of the balance sheet in Table 10-5 would now have $1,000 of national currency as reserves and, as before, the $4,000 of IOUs. The liability side would have $5,000 of demand deposits.

THE NATURE OF BANK PANICS

The problem, as before, was that if too many depositors attempted to withdraw currency from their demand deposits, the bank might not have enough reserves to satisfy their demands. Because of this, bank panics and financial crises were still frequent. Even a rumor that a bank had made some bad loans (an IOU that some borrower wasn't meeting interest payments on or couldn't pay off) could cause people holding deposits at the bank to panic. There would then be a "run on the bank" as depositors rushed to withdraw currency from their accounts—"to get their money out." Even if the rumor were false, the bank might be forced to close because the sudden increase in demand for deposit withdrawals could exceed the amount of currency in its safe. Paradox: the rumor of possible bankruptcy could cause bankruptcy.

In general, bank failures caused by runs on banks could be triggered by an adverse turn of events anywhere in the economy. Once banks started to fail, a chain reaction could set in, causing a recession throughout the economy. One of the most common causes of these financial crises was the growth of the economy itself as the United States developed into an industrial power in the last third of the nineteenth century. Let's see why.

LIMITS TO MONEY SUPPLY EXPANSION

Commercial banks themselves could not increase the total amount of the national currency available in the economy. They could of course provide credit (make loans) to feed economic expansion. The increase in deposits created by this loan expansion meant that the amount of demand deposits would get ever larger relative to the amount of currency available for bank reserves. Compounding the problem was the fact that more currency was also needed to serve as a medium of exchange in an expanding economy. The result was that bank reserves would become an ever smaller fraction of deposit liabilities, and banks would become more susceptible to a sudden surge of deposit withdrawals. Inevitably this would happen. The bank caught short might scramble to withdraw currency from its deposit at another bank, setting off a chain of bank failures and a general financial crisis. Consumers and businesses who dealt with these banks would suffer financial losses. This would cause a general decline in consumption and investment expenditures—that is, a decline in total demand. GNP would fall, unemployment would rise, and the economy would be plunged into recession.

It was clear that the nation's monetary system, its money-creating mechanism, was not responsive enough to the economy's ever growing need for money. In short, the money supply mechanism was not "elastic" enough. The money supply could not readily "stretch out" to meet the increasing demand for money caused by economic expansion. This was so often the case in nineteenth-century America that recessions were typically referred to as financial crises or panics. After the financial crises of 1907, Congress set up a National Monetary Commission to study the problem. The commission's recommendations resulted in the Federal Reserve Act of 1913.

■CHECKPOINT 10-2
Why might a bank note be said to be like an IOU? When currency is convertible into gold,

how does the amount of gold in the economy put a limit on the amount of money in the economy? Describe how you think people's opinions about the soundness of banks at any particular time would affect the upper limit to the amount of the economy's money, defined as currency plus demand deposits. If bankers become cautious about the business outlook, how do you think this would affect the amount of IOUs on their balance sheets, and why and how would this affect the amount of money in the economy? How do you think this would affect total demand for goods and services?

THE FEDERAL RESERVE SYSTEM: ORGANIZATION AND FUNCTIONS

The basic recommendation of the National Monetary Commission was that control over the economy's money supply and the nation's commercial banks should be centralized. This control was to be vested in a central bank, an arm of the federal government, that would deliberately manage the money supply to foster economic stability with maximum output and employment and as little inflation as possible. (Indeed, several other nations already had central banks.) The Federal Reserve Act of 1913 gave life to this concept by forming the Federal Reserve System.

Organization of the Federal Reserve System
Rather than having one central bank as in most countries, the United States has 12, each representing and serving one of the 12 districts into which the country is divided by the Federal Reserve System.[4] All are under the control of a central policy-making body called the Board of Governors of the Federal Reserve System, often referred to as the Federal Reserve Board, located in Washington, D.C. The Board of Governors has the responsibility and authority for

[4] The Federal Reserve banks are located in Boston, New York, Philadelphia, Cleveland, Richmond, Atlanta, Chicago, Saint Louis, Minneapolis, Kansas City, Dallas, and San Francisco.

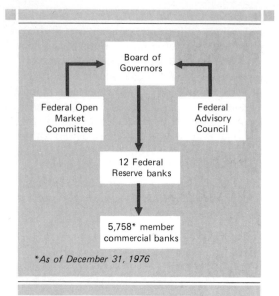

| |
| Board of Governors |
| Federal Open Market Committee |
| Federal Advisory Council |
| 12 Federal Reserve banks |
| 5,758* member commercial banks |

*As of December 31, 1976

FIGURE 10-2 ORGANIZATION OF THE FEDERAL RESERVE SYSTEM

The Board of Governors, assisted by the Federal Open Market Committee and advised by the Federal Advisory Council, is responsible for the formulation of the nation's monetary policy and the regulation of the member commercial banks. The 12 Federal Reserve banks are responsible for implementing the Board's policies and regulating the member commercial banks in their respective regions of the country.

the administration of the Federal Reserve System and the nation's monetary policy.

Each Federal Reserve bank is responsible for carrying out board policy as directed by the Board of Governors. And each does so by virtue of its authority over the commercial banks in its region that are members of the Federal Reserve System. The Board of Governors is assisted in its policy making by the Federal Open Market Committee (FOMC) and, to a lesser degree, by the advice of the Federal Advisory Council. This broad organizational outline of the Federal Reserve System is shown in Figure 10-2.

THE BOARD OF GOVERNORS

There are seven governors on the board, each appointed by the president and subject to con-

firmation by the Senate. Each governor serves for a term of 14 years and the terms are staggered so that one governor is appointed every two years. This gives the board stability and a certain degree of independence from political pressures. Otherwise, the political party in power might be able to pressure the board to pursue partisan objectives rather than goals that are consistent with the best interests of the economy as a whole. The president appoints one governor to serve as chairman of the board for a four-year term.

The board, assisted by the Federal Open Market Committee (FOMC), is charged with controlling and regulating the nation's money supply and commercial banking system to promote economic stability and maximum output and employment with minimum inflation. To accomplish this: (1) it can conduct open market operations; (2) it can establish reserve requirements for the commercial banks; and (3) it can set the level of the discount rate. The board also has the power to impose selective controls on stock market purchases, on interest rates paid by commercial banks on time deposits, and on certain kinds of consumer credit. We will discuss the three main tools of monetary policy along with other powers in greater detail in the next two chapters.

The Federal Open Market Committee (FOMC). The FOMC is composed of the seven Federal Reserve Board governors plus five presidents of member Federal Reserve banks. The president of the New York Federal Reserve bank is a permanent member of the committee, like the governors, while the other four positions are rotated on a regular basis among the other 11 Federal Reserve bank presidents. The FOMC meets once a month in Washington, D.C., to evaluate the economy's current condition and where it appears to be headed. In light of this evaluation, the FOMC decides what monetary policy should be during the coming month in order to best promote the achievement and maintenance of maximum output and employment with a minimum of inflation. In short, the FOMC is responsible for the formulation of monetary policy.

The Federal Advisory Council. The Federal Advisory Council is made up of 12 commercial bankers, one selected from each Federal Reserve district by the district's Federal Reserve bank. Though the Council meets periodically with the board, it is only an advisory body to the board and has no policy-making powers.

THE FEDERAL RESERVE BANKS

There are 12 regional Federal Reserve banks rather than one central bank because it was originally felt that this arrangement would make the Federal Reserve System more sensitive to particular regional needs.

Each Federal Reserve bank is technically "owned" by the member commercial banks in its respective district. However, ownership of Federal Reserve bank stock is in the nature of an obligation of membership in the Federal Reserve System. It does not carry with it the rights of control and financial interest ordinarily attached to stock ownership in corporations that are operated for profit. Moreover, the policies followed by the Federal Reserve banks are dictated by the governmentally appointed and controlled Board of Governors, not the member commercial banks. The objective of the board is not to make profit for the Federal Reserve banks but rather to foster prosperity for the economy as a whole.

The Federal Reserve banks do not deal with the public directly. They operate as banker to the commercial banks. Just as commercial banks hold the deposits of households and businesses, the Federal Reserve banks hold deposits of commercial banks. Just as commercial banks make loans to the public, Federal Reserve banks make loans to member commercial banks. In addition, the Federal Reserve banks are given the authority under the Federal Reserve Act to issue currency in the form of Federal Reserve notes. Commercial banks are no longer allowed to issue currency, or bank notes, as they were in the nineteenth century.

The Member Commercial Banks

There are approximately 14,000 commercial banks in the United States, of which roughly 5,700 are members of the Federal Reserve Sys-

tem. However, in terms of the dollar value of deposits, member banks account for about 70 percent of total deposits at commercial banks.

Commercial banks may be divided into two classes—**state banks** and **national banks**. About one-third of all commercial banks are national banks, the rest being state banks. National banks are chartered by the federal government, state banks by state governments. All national banks are required by law to be members of the Federal Reserve System. State banks may become members of the Federal Reserve System if they wish, and if they meet certain requirements. However, only about 10 percent of all state banks have chosen to join the system. This small percentage is largely due to the severe restrictions that would be placed on their operating procedures if they became system members.

ADVANTAGES AND
OBLIGATIONS OF SYSTEM MEMBERSHIP

A commercial bank realizes several advantages from system membership. Membership lends an image of financial soundness to the bank which may help attract depositors. Membership also entitles the bank to borrow funds for short periods from its regional Federal Reserve bank. In principle this is an important advantage. Recall that in the nineteenth century banks were frequently forced to close because of a lack of reserves to satisfy depositors' withdrawal demands. The member bank borrowing privilege of the Federal Reserve System was intended to make it possible for a bank with otherwise sound assets to borrow whatever reserves were needed to meet a sudden surge of deposit withdrawals. In practice, many economists feel that this borrowing privilege has not always been granted when it should have been, citing especially experiences during the Great Depression.

What are the obligations of bank membership in the system? First of all, to become a member a bank must purchase stock in its regional Federal Reserve bank. A member bank must hold an amount of reserves (in its vault or on deposit or both, at its regional Federal Reserve bank) equal to no less than a certain stipulated fraction of the amount of its deposits. A member bank must also abide by the laws of membership and submit to periodic, sometimes unannounced, examination of its books and operations by Federal Reserve bank examiners.

THE MONEY SUPPLY
AND COMMERCIAL BANKS

We have seen how a commercial bank can make a loan by accepting the debt instrument, or IOU, of an individual or business and crediting a demand deposit in the borrower's name for the amount of the loan. The asset side of the bank's balance sheet is increased by the dollar amount of the IOU, and the liability side is increased by the same amount in the form of a demand deposit held in the name of the borrower. The borrower or depositor may then write checks against this demand deposit (also called a checking account) and the bank is obliged to honor these checks. Hence, **commercial banks** *can do something that no other type of financial institution can do; namely, they can create money by extending credit in the form of loans to businesses and households.* We will investigate this process in more detail in the next chapter.

The amount of money supplied to the economy through demand deposit creation is limited only by the amount of reserves that commercial banks have. And the Fed (the abbreviated expression often used when referring to the Federal Reserve System) can control the amount of reserves through its open market operations, its setting of legal reserve requirements, and its willingness to lend reserves to the member banks. Hence, *it is the control over commercial bank reserves that gives the Fed the ability to influence the size of the economy's money supply and thereby affect the level of total demand for goods and services in the economy. It is through this mechanism that the Board of Governors must try to implement monetary policy.* We will examine this process in more detail in the next three chapters.

COMMERCIAL BANKS
AS FINANCIAL INTERMEDIARIES

Commercial banks are financial intermediaries, just like a number of other kinds of banks and financial institutions in our economy. *A* **financial intermediary** *is a business that acts as a middleman (intermediary) by taking the funds of lenders and making them available to borrowers. A financial intermediary tries to cover its costs and make a profit on the difference between the interest it charges borrowers and the interest it must pay to attract the funds of lenders.* When a financial intermediary accepts a lender's funds, it issues an obligation against itself, a liability, to pay the lender back. When the intermediary in turn lends these funds to a borrower, it takes on an asset in the form of the borrower's IOU, or obligation, to pay the funds back.

The liabilities that a commercial bank issues are in the form of demand deposits and time deposits. Time deposits are either in the form of passbook saving accounts, tailored to small depositors, or in the form of large negotiable certificates of deposit (CDs) that are usually issued in denominations of $100,000. CDs are much like short-term bonds and are tailored to the needs of large businesses and other institutions seeking to earn interest on the large amounts of funds they have at their disposal from time to time. In addition to creating demand deposits through their lending activities, commercial banks also receive funds deposited in demand deposits which they can then lend out.

The Role of Financial Intermediaries. What special services and advantages do financial intermediaries provide for our economy? Basically, there are three.

1. *Financial intermediaries have expertise as credit analysts. They have the ability and experience to evaluate and compare the risk and return, or credit worthiness, of different kinds of loan opportunities.* Imagine trying prudently to loan out your money by doing this in your spare time, after performing a day's work as a carpenter or doctor or whatever. Credit analysts do this full time for a living, just as carpenters and doctors work full time. Credit analysis is just another area of specialization in a modern, industrialized economy.

2. *Financial intermediaries take the many different-sized amounts of funds that households, businesses, and other institutions want to lend and package them into the typically different-sized*

amounts that individual borrowers want to borrow. For example, many small depositors at a commercial bank can indirectly make a $50,000 loan to a business.

3. *Financial intermediaries provide an opportunity for small lenders with small amounts of money to participate in risk-reducing diversification.* By depositing a small amount of money in a financial intermediary, a depositor in effect takes a proportional share of every loan the intermediary makes. Simply stated, the depositor has not put all of his or her eggs in one basket. The likelihood of loss is therefore reduced.

4. *Other financial intermediaries.* Other kinds of financial intermediaries in our economy include savings and loan associations, mutual savings banks, credit unions, and insurance companies. Savings and loan associations, mutual savings banks, and credit unions issue liabilities against themselves that are much like the time deposits of commercial banks. Savings and loan associations and mutual savings banks make loans mostly to people buying homes and other real estate, thereby acquiring mortgages as assets. Credit unions acquire assets in the form of claims against people to whom they make consumer loans. Insurance companies issue liabilities in the form of insurance policies. The premiums they collect from policyholders are used to acquire assets like mortgages, various kinds of bonds, and corporate securities.

Further Functions
of the Federal Reserve System

The Fed's most important and most difficult task is to attempt to manage the economy's money supply in a manner that avoids inflation while at the same time promoting the achievement and maintenance of a high-employment level of GNP. However, in addition to this and its other functions already mentioned, there are several rather routine but nonetheless important functions that are indispensable to the smooth operation of our monetary system.

1. *The Federal Reserve banks serve as clearinghouses for the collection of checks.* Recall that a check is simply a standardized form on which you write your bank an order to withdraw funds from your checking account and pay them to

another party. If the other party deposits the check in his or her checking account, and that account happens to be in the same bank as yours, your bank can simply draw down (debit) your account by the amount of the check and increase (credit) the account of the other party by this amount. However, the other party is more likely to have an account at a different bank, perhaps in another part of the country. In that case the Federal Reserve banks will collect the funds from your account and deposit them in the account of the party to whom you wrote the check. We will examine the mechanics of this process in more detail in the next chapter.

2. *The Federal Reserve banks serve as the bankers for the federal government.* The checking accounts of the U.S. Treasury are for the most part kept at Federal Reserve banks. Federal government bond sales and redemptions, as well as tax collections, are also handled by these banks. In short, the Federal Reserve banks are the government's fiscal agents.

3. *The Federal Reserve banks provide the economy's paper money.* When people need more cash, they typically withdraw it from their deposits at commercial banks. The commercial banks can provide this cash from their vaults. However, if they do not have adequate funds, they can get cash by drawing on their accounts at the Federal Reserve banks, the bankers' banks, in the same way that people write checks to draw cash out of their checking accounts at commercial banks. The Federal Reserve banks can print more cash, in the form of Federal Reserve notes, to supply member commercial banks' demand for cash if need be. Conversely, if depositors deposit a lot of cash in their deposits at commercial banks, the commercial banks can in turn deposit at the Federal Reserve banks what they don't want to keep in their vaults.

Promoting Sound Banking
and Protecting Depositors

A long history of bank failures and truly tragic stories of depositors "losing their money" has led to the establishment of a number of ways for government to supervise banks. Every state has banking commissions that regulate state-chartered banks. At the federal level, the Federal Reserve banks continually examine the operations and practices of member banks and enforce correction of irregularities where necessary. The U.S. Comptroller of the Currency has supervisory authority over all national banks, a power granted under the National Bank Acts of 1863 and 1864.

One of the most significant pieces of banking legislation in U.S. history was the Banking Act of 1933 which created the Federal Deposit Insurance Corporation (FDIC). The FDIC is probably the most important protection provided to depositors. It insures deposits at commercial banks and savings banks against loss up to $40,000 in the event of bank failure. This greatly forestalls runs on banks by panicking depositors—the rumor of trouble that itself often causes the most trouble. The very existence of deposit insurance puts depositors at ease. If the bank fails, they still get their money back. It has the same effect as the "ounce of prevention" that forestalls the need for "the pound of cure."

The FDIC also has the power to examine the loans made by insured banks because, of course, deposits are no safer than loans into which depositor's funds are put. All national banks are required to be insured by the FDIC. State banks may be covered if they choose. In fact, almost every bank carries federal deposit insurance, paying insurance premiums to the FDIC that are proportional to the total amount of their deposits.

Similar deposit insurance is provided for savings and loan associations by the Federal Savings and Loan Association, and for credit unions (federally chartered) by the National Credit Union Administration.

Where Do We Go from Here?

In the next chapter, we will examine in more detail the nature of the modern commercial bank and how it works. We will also study how the whole banking system functions to create money and how this process is influenced by the Fed. In Chapter 12, we will examine how the money supply affects the level of total demand for goods and services, and the role that money plays in determining the economy's equilibrium level of total output and employment.

■CHECKPOINT 10-3

How does the Federal Reserve System give "elasticity" to the money supply? Why do you suppose the Fed is sometimes referred to as the "lender of last resort"? How are commercial banks different from other financial intermediaries? How are they similar? Some say deposit insurance is more effective in dealing with the problem of bank panics than is the member bank's privilege of borrowing from the Federal Reserve banks. Why?

SUMMARY

1. Money is anything that functions as a medium of exchange, a store of value, and a unit of account. Money is the most liquid of all assets.

2. The basic kinds of money are commodity money, currency (fiat money consisting of coin and paper money), and demand deposits (checking accounts). A near money can function as a unit of account and store of value like money, but not as a medium of exchange—though it is readily convertible into money.

3. Money in our economy is neither backed by nor convertible into gold. It has value because of the goods and services it will buy due to its acceptability in trade. The purchasing power of money depends on the price level. And this in turn depends on the government's management of the money supply.

4. Banks evolved from the safekeeping service provided by goldsmiths to become lenders as well. After gold receipts began circulating as money, banks were able to create money (bank notes) through the expansion of their lending activities. This eventually gave rise to present-day fractional reserve banking, with demand deposits serving as money by virtue of the check-writing privilege.

5. The Federal Reserve System was established to provide the economy with a more elastic money supply so that the bank panics and financial crises that plagued nineteenth-century America might be avoided. The Federal Reserve System consists of the Board of

Governors of the Federal Reserve System and the 12 regional Federal Reserve banks.

6. The Board of Governors of the Federal Reserve System has responsibility for the supervision of the economy's commercial banking system and the management of the economy's monetary policy. The board's policy orders are carried out by the 12 Federal Reserve banks. They serve as central banks, dealing directly with, and serving as bankers to the member commercial banks. The Federal Reserve banks are owned by the member commercial banks but are controlled and directed by the board.

7. The economy's commercial banks function as financial intermediaries, accepting deposits and making loans. However, unlike other kinds of financial intermediaries, commercial banks can create money. They do this by creating demand deposits through their lending activities. Because of the Fed's control over commercial bank reserves, the Fed has the ability to influence the size of the economy's money supply and, hence, the level of total demand for goods and services in the economy.

8. The Federal Reserve System also serves as a clearinghouse for the collection of checks, and as the banker for the federal government, provides the economy's paper money, and supervises and regulates the banking practices of member banks. The Federal Reserve System's supervisory activity is supplemented and augmented by a number of other government agencies. These include state banking commissions, the U.S. Comptroller of the Currency, and the Federal Deposit Insurance Corporation, which provides deposit insurance.

KEY TERMS AND CONCEPTS
bank note
certificate of deposit (CD)
commercial bank
demand deposit
fiat money
financial intermediary
fractional reserve banking
liquidity

M_1
M_2
M_3
M_4
M_5
money
national bank
near money
negotiable certificates of deposit
negotiable order of withdrawal (NOW)
state bank
time deposit
token coins
trade credit
transactions costs
Treasury bill

QUESTIONS AND PROBLEMS

1. What are the differences between inflation and deflation in terms of their effects on the three basic functions of money?

2. Compare and rank the different definitions of money—M_1, M_2, M_3, M_4, and M_5—in terms of their relative merits: (1) as mediums of exchange and (2) as stores of value. What difference would it make for your answer to (2) if: (a) there was an inflation, (b) there was a deflation, (c) there were neither inflation nor deflation?

3. Our money is no longer backed by nor convertible into gold or any other precious metal. Why is it still valuable?

4. The following item appeared in the *Wall Street Journal,* June 12, 1978.

> The Treasury revoked 1974 rules that prohibited exporting, melting or otherwise treating or processing pennies. The ban was imposed in April 1974 because high copper prices made it profitable to melt the coins for their metal content or to export them. Because of stabilized prices, the prohibitions aren't necessary any longer, the agency said.

Explain this news item, taking care to distinguish between commodity money and fiat money.

5. Why might fractional reserve banking be described as the "swapping of one debt obligation for another?"

6. The U.S. economy was largely agricultural in the nineteenth century. In the spring, banks would make many loans to farmers who needed money to plant crops. It was anticipated that once the crops were harvested and sold, the farmers would be able to pay off their loans to the banks in the late summer and early autumn. Describe the likely chain of events resulting from a drought. Suppose you were the banker in a farm community, and in the middle of the summer farmers came to you requesting loans so that they could construct irrigation ditches in their fields. What would you do? Why? What role might rumor play in all of this, depending on the *likely* outcome of your decision on these loan requests?

7. Why and how might central banking (the existence of the Federal Reserve System) have greatly reduced bank panics in the nineteenth century? Why might deposit insurance also have helped?

8. Describe how the basic functions of the Federal Reserve System are supposed to contribute to economic stability?

9. Why and how is financial intermediation important to our economy?

■ NEWS ITEM FOR YOUR ANALYSIS ■

INTEREST ON CHECKING,
STARTED BY MOST BANKS, IS OFFSET BY FEE RISES

NEW YORK, Dec. 6—"I'm going to make a scene," the woman at the Charleston, W. Va., bank said. Whereupon, the story goes, the customer produced a pair of scissors and snipped her checkbook into pieces. "That's what I think of your service charge," she reportedly said as she stalked out. What was the woman's problem?

On November 1 new federal regulations made it legal for commercial banks to transfer funds automatically from a customer's interest-bearing savings account to his or her checking account as needed—in effect allowing customers to earn interest on checking account balances. What the woman discovered, like other bank customers, is that the ballyhooed interest on checking is being accompanied by unballyhooed increases in bank fees for checking account service. The charges in many cases more than offset gains for the customers from the new interest rate payments.

According to bankers, the fees are necessary to meet the costs of services. By one estimate, it costs a medium-sized bank $5.27 a month to service a checking account on which 20 checks a month are written. The bank can offset some costs by investing the deposits. But an average balance of $666 is said to be needed in the account for the bank to break even without charging fees if it invests the funds at $9\frac{1}{2}$ percent interest.

In any event, the new automatic-transfer accounts are not what they seem for many bank depositors. The charges levied by the banks to protect their profits are such that only those customers relatively flush with funds are likely to come out ahead by using the new service.

QUESTIONS

1. It has often been argued that the automatic transfer of customer's funds from interest-earning savings accounts to demand deposits (checking accounts) as needed would make savings accounts more like near money. What light does the news item shed on this argument?

2. Before the new federal regulations made it legal for commercial banks to automatically transfer funds from a customer's savings account to his or her demand deposit, customers were not paying the fees mentioned in the news item. Also, before the legislation it was simply not possible, in effect, to receive interest on checking accounts. But the news item clearly indicates that it has always cost a bank money to service a checking account. Why do you suppose customers were not previously charged service fees on checking accounts?

3. What are the implications of the news item for the distinction between M_1 and M_2?

11

BANKS, MONEY CREATION, AND THE ROLE OF THE FEDERAL RESERVE SYSTEM

FED SEEN RAISING DISCOUNT RATE,
POSSIBLY BOOSTING RESERVE REQUIREMENTS ON BANK DEPOSITS

NEW YORK, June 26—The Federal Reserve System may have to dig deeper into its bag of credit-tightening tricks to stem the sharp rise in the nation's money supply.

This is the view of a growing number of analysts who closely watch Federal Reserve policy and its impact on money creation. They say that a boost from 7 to 7½ percent in the discount rate is almost certain. They also suggest that the Fed may decide to raise reserve requirements on specific types of deposits at banks.

The discount rate, the fee the Fed charges on loans to member commercial banks, has been at 7 percent since early May. At a 7 percent rate, discount borrowings represent a bargain for banks. For example, federal funds, the uncommitted reserves banks lend one another, are currently commanding rates of about 7¾ percent. According to David M. Jones, an economist for Aubrey G. Lanston and Co., "Banks are becoming more sensitive than usual" to the differences in the two rates.

Such sensitivity was apparent in member bank borrowing figures released by the Fed Thursday. These revealed that bank borrowings from the Fed averaged $1.07 billion in the week ended Wednesday, up from $688 million the previous week. It was on Wednesday that the Fed indicated it had raised its federal funds target rate from 7½ to 7¾ percent.

The Fed may have to take a look at a more basic tool of monetary authorities: the amount of reserves banks are required to keep idle behind customers' deposits. The Fed hasn't changed those requirements in about two years. At that time the effect was to lower required reserves. Since loans are made by the creation of deposits, stiffer reserve requirements normally will temper the banking systems' lending ability.

This news item describes some of the basic tools used by the Federal Reserve System (the Fed) to carry out monetary policy. You need to be able to understand a news item like this in order to evaluate intelligently the likely impact of the Fed's actions on our banking system, the money supply, and the level of economic activity in general. To achieve this level of understanding requires that in this chapter we first look more closely at the way commercial banks operate. We will then examine the process by which our commercial banking system as a whole is able to expand and contract the total amount of demand deposits, a principle component of the money supply. Finally, we will examine the tools and methods that the Fed uses to control this process and thereby pursue its monetary policy objectives.

THE COMMERCIAL BANKS

The previous chapter described the origins and basic nature of commercial banks and the way they function. We saw that a bank is a business seeking to make a profit, just like any other kind of business. But we also saw that banks are a unique kind of financial intermediary because they create money in the process of extending credit through their loan-making activity, their principal source of earnings.

Our discussion was aided by the use of a highly simplified version of a bank's balance sheet. In order to understand better how modern commercial banks operate, we need to look at the bank balance sheet in more detail. We also need to consider the distinction between actual, excess, and required reserves in order to understand the deposit expansion (or contraction) process by which our commercial banking system increases (or decreases) the economy's money supply. The commercial bank's need for

liquidity on the one hand, and its desire to make a profit on the other, bears closely on how this deposit expansion (or contraction) process works. With this in mind, we will also consider how commercial banks juggle the often conflicting goals of liquidity and profitability.

The Balance Sheet: Assets and Liabilities

Our discussion of how a bank gets started and the way in which it manages its assets and liabilities will be conducted in terms of the bank's balance sheet.

STARTING A BANK

Suppose a group of people decide to start a commercial bank, calling it Citizens' Bank. Say they put $100,000 of their own money into the business and receive in exchange shares of capital stock—paper certificates indicating their ownership of the bank. The owners' $100,000 of capital stock is the equity, or net worth, of the bank. Part of the $100,000, say $85,000, is used to buy a building and other equipment needed to operate a bank. Assume that the remaining $15,000 is needed to buy stock in the district Federal Reserve bank to establish Citizens' Bank's membership in the Federal Reserve System. At this point Citizens' Bank's balance sheet is as shown in Table 11-1. The left, or asset, side of the balance sheet shows what the bank owns. The right, or liability and equity, side of the balance sheet shows the claims against the bank. The bank's total assets equal its total liabilities and equity, of course, because everything the bank possesses is claimed by someone.

THE BANK OPENS ITS DOORS

The bank is now ready for business. When its doors open suppose that customers deposit $1,000,000 in currency. The bank now adds

TABLE 11-1 BALANCE SHEET OF CITIZENS' BANK

Assets		Liabilities and Equity	
Stock in Federal Reserve bank	$ 15,000		
Building and equipment	85,000	Equity (stock certificates of Citizens' Bank)	$100,000
Total assets	$100,000 =	Total liabilities and equity	$100,000

$1,000,000 in demand deposits to the liability and equity side of its balance sheet and $1,000,000 cash to the asset side. Its balance sheet now appears as shown in Table 11-2. Those who have claims on the bank, represented on the liability and equity side of the balance sheet, are divided into two groups—the owners of the bank and the nonowners. The claims of the owners represent the bank's equity, or net *worth,* amounting to $100,000 (the value of the stock certificates issued by Citizens' Bank). The claims of the nonowners are represented by the $1,000,000 of demand deposits. The nonowners' claims constitute the bank's liabilities. Hence, **equity** (*or* **net worth**) *equals the difference between total assets and total liabilities.*

REQUIRED RESERVES, ACTUAL RESERVES, AND EXCESS RESERVES

Suppose the legal **required reserves** imposed by the Fed on member banks is 20 percent. This means that a member bank is required by law to hold an amount of reserves equal to 20 percent of the total amount of its demand deposits. *The ratio of required reserves to the total amount of demand deposits is the* **required reserve ratio.** *The law defines* **reserves** *as cash held in the bank's vault and the deposits of the bank at its district Federal Reserve bank.* Since the Citizens' Bank has $1,000,000 of demand deposits, it must hold at least $200,000 (20 percent of $1,000,000) in the form of reserves. Suppose it deposits $200,000 of its $1,000,000 of cash in its account at the Federal Reserve bank. The Citizens' Bank's balance sheet now appears as shown in Table 11-3. While its legally required reserves amount to $200,000, its total reserves actually amount to $1,000,000—$200,000 on deposit at its district Federal Reserve bank and $800,000 in the form of cash in its vault. Citizens' Bank's total reserves now exceed its required reserves by $800,000. This amount is called its **excess reserves.**

In sum, total (or actual) reserves are equal to required reserves plus excess reserves. Required reserves are the reserves that a bank is legally

---

After reading this chapter, you will be able to:

1. Explain the nature of the balance sheet of a commercial bank.
2. Describe the conflict between the commercial bank's desire to make profits and its need for liquidity and security.
3. Characterize the differences and similarities between the operation of an individual bank in a system of many banks, and the operation of the banking system considered as a whole.
4. Describe how deposit expansion and money creation takes place in our banking system.
5. Explain and describe the three main tools used by the Federal Reserve System to affect the economy's money supply.
6. Describe the nature of the federal funds market and how the Fed uses it to implement monetary policy.

TABLE 11-2 BALANCE SHEET OF CITIZENS' BANK

Assets		Liabilities and Equity	
Cash	$1,000,000	Demand deposits	$1,000,000
Stock in Federal Reserve bank	15,000		
Building and equipment	85,000	Equity (stock certificates of Citizens' Bank)	100,000
Total assets	$1,100,000 =	Total liabilities and equity	$1,100,000

required to hold against demand deposits. Required reserves are equal to the amount of demand deposits multiplied by the required reserve ratio. Excess reserves are the reserves held above and beyond the amount needed for required reserves. Excess reserves are equal to total reserves minus required reserves.

LOANING OUT EXCESS RESERVES

At this point Citizens' Bank has excess reserves of $800,000. A bank's largest potential source of earnings is the interest it can earn by making loans and buying and holding various kinds of bonds and securities. Citizens' Bank therefore will want to put these excess reserves to work rather than hold "idle" cash which earns no interest at all.

Suppose it loans out $300,000 to consumers who want to buy cars, household appliances, and perhaps bonds and stocks. Suppose $200,000 is loaned to businesses that need money to stock inventories of goods and raw materials, and to buy equipment. The bank holds IOUs from these consumers and businesses in

the form of notes (typically IOUs of consumers and small businesses) and commercial paper (the IOUs of large corporations). Suppose the bank also purchases $100,000 worth of U.S. government securities and $100,000 of other securities, such as corporate bonds and state and local government bonds. As a precautionary measure, Citizens' Bank elects to keep $100,000 of its cash as excess reserves—to meet sudden withdrawal demands by depositors or to be able to provide credit to a regular loan customer on short notice. Citizens' Bank's balance sheet now appears as shown in Table 11-4.

REAL-WORLD BANK BALANCE SHEET

The stages of development of our hypothetical Citizens' Bank, illustrated in Tables 11-1 through 11-4, are like those of a real-world commercial bank. The Citizens' Bank balance sheet shown in Table 11-4 is now very similar to the balance sheet of a typical commercial bank in our economy.

Consider, for example, the consolidated balance sheet of all the U.S. commercial banks

TABLE 11-3 BALANCE SHEET OF CITIZENS' BANK

Assets		Liabilities and Equity	
Reserves	$1,000,000	Demand deposits	$1,000,000
On deposit at Federal Reserve bank	200,000		
Cash	800,000		
Stock in Federal Reserve bank	15,000		
Building and equipment	85,000	Equity (stock certificates of Citizens' Bank)	100,000
Total assets	$1,100,000 =	Total liabilities and equity	$1,100,000

TABLE 11-4 BALANCE SHEET OF CITIZENS' BANK AFTER LOANING OUT EXCESS RESERVES

Assets		Liabilities and Equity	
Reserves	$ 300,000	Demand deposits	$1,000,000
On deposit at Federal Reserve bank	200,000		
Cash	100,000		
Consumer loans	300,000		
Business loans	200,000		
Government securities	100,000		
Other securities	100,000		
Stock in Federal Reserve bank	15,000		
Building and equipment	85,000	Equity (stock certificates of Citizens' Bank)	100,000
Total assets	$1,100,000 =	Total liabilities and equity	$1,100,000

shown in Table 11-5. This consolidated balance sheet is obtained by adding together the assets and liabilities of all the individual commercial banks in the economy. The distribution of assets and liabilities in Table 11-5 is fairly representative of that of a typical commercial bank. We can see that the asset side of the balance sheet of our hypothetical Citizens' Bank in Table 11-4 is similar to the asset side of this consolidated balance sheet.

A comparison of the liability and equity sides of these two balance sheets reveals an important item that we didn't introduce in our Citizens' Bank example—namely, time deposits (the savings deposits at commercial banks discussed in the previous chapter). The Fed imposes a legal reserve requirement on time deposits at member banks just like that imposed on demand deposits. The required reserve ratio on time deposits is lower than that on demand deposits however. The total amount of time deposits at commercial banks is larger than the amount of demand deposits in Table 11-5.

Liquidity and Security Versus Profit: Bank Portfolio Management

As a financial intermediary, a commercial bank primarily engages in making short-term

TABLE 11-5 CONSOLIDATE BALANCE SHEET OF ALL U.S. COMMERCIAL BANKS, MARCH 29, 1978 (in Billions of Dollars)

Assets		Liabilities and Equity	
Reserves: cash assets including reserves with Federal Reserve banks	$ 131.4	Demand deposits	$ 321.8
Loans	677.2	Time deposits	570.6
U.S. government securities	97.9	Other liabilities	159.0
Other securities	159.2		
Other assets: bank premises and other property	68.8	Capital accounts: includes equity	83.2
Total assets	$1,134.6 =	Total liabilities and equity	$1,134.6

SOURCE: *Federal Reserve Bulletin,* April 1978.

loans to businesses and households, as well as purchasing and holding bonds and other securities. *The bank's income-earning assets—its loans, bonds, and securities—together with its excess reserves constitute the bank's portfolio.* A commercial bank manages its portfolio by adjusting the relative proportions of the different income-earning assets it holds in such a way as to satisfy two often conflicting objectives: (1) the maintenance of liquidity and security and (2) the realization of profit.

MAINTENANCE OF LIQUIDITY AND SECURITY

In the previous chapter, we saw how banks could fail if they didn't have adequate reserves to meet depositors' demands to withdraw their funds. It is clear from Table 11-5 that modern commercial banks hold an amount of reserves equal to only a fraction of their deposit liabilities. Moreover, the largest part of a bank's reserves typically are held to satisfy the legal reserve requirement, and the bank can't really use these to satisfy depositors' withdrawals. (We shall see shortly that the main purpose of required reserves is to give the Fed control over the banking system's money creation process.) Hence, in practice a bank will have to use its excess reserves to meet any sudden surge of deposit withdrawals. And if these excess reserves are not adequate, it will then have to liquidate some of its income-earning assets—that is, convert them into funds that can be used to meet deposit withdrawals.

A commercial bank therefore needs to restrict itself to holding income-earning assets that are relatively liquid and secure. As we saw in the previous chapter, *the more liquid an asset is, the easier it is to convert into money without loss. The security of an asset refers to the degree of likelihood that the contracted obligations of the asset will be met.* For example, a bond is a contract stipulating that the borrower, the bond issuer, will pay the lender or bondholder a certain amount of interest on specified dates and return the amount of money borrowed (the principal) on the maturity date of the bond. U.S. Treasury bonds are the most secure asset a bank can hold. Loans made to consumers and households

are less secure and, of course, the degree of security will vary from one consumer or business to the next.

It is important to recognize that liquidity and security, though related, are not the same thing. For example, a U.S. Treasury bill that matures in 90 days is for all intents and purposes just as secure as a U.S. Treasury bond that matures in 5 years. Yet the market value or price of the 5-year Treasury bond will tend to fluctuate more on a day-to-day basis than that of the 90-day Treasury bill. The Treasury bill is, therefore, considered more liquid. (A simple, but not complete, explanation why is that a Treasury bill is typically closer to its maturity date—the date when its price is guaranteed.) This is true in general of shorter-term bonds as compared to longer-term bonds.

In the case of loans to consumers and businesses, represented by financial paper and notes (IOUs of businesses and consumers), and in the case of bonds issued by corporations and local governments, the shorter the term to maturity, the greater the degree of security generally associated with such assets. This is so because there is more certainty about the likely financial situation of the borrowers in the short run than in the long run. In general, a commercial bank restricts its holdings of earning assets to shorter-term loans, bonds, and securities because of the relatively higher degree of liquidity and security associated with these assets. This restriction is dictated by the large amount of deposit liabilities subject to withdrawal on demand.

BALANCING PROFIT AGAINST LIQUIDITY AND SECURITY

A commercial bank is like any other business in that it wants to maximize the profits realized by its owners, the stockholders. First and foremost, however, the bank is obliged to meet deposit withdrawals on demand. Whenever it is unable to do this the bank is out of business.

Obviously, if a bank held nothing in its portfolio but vault cash, it would maximize liquidity and security. It would never have any problem satisfying demands for deposit withdrawal. But without any earning assets in its portfolio the bank wouldn't be very profitable either. At the other extreme, if a bank holds no excess reserves and tries to hold only those earning assets which yield the highest return, it may earn large profits. But the bank will run a high risk that it will not be able to meet a sudden surge of deposit withdrawals. Clearly, *there is a conflict between the maintenance of liquidity and security on the one hand, and the realization of profit on the other. The main task of bank portfolio management is to strike a balance between these conflicting objectives.*

Borrowers whose ability to repay loans is questionable typically must pay higher interest rates to obtain loans. Similarly, the lower the probability that the contractual obligations of a bond or security will be met, the higher is the interest it must yield to get a lender to buy it. In short, the less security an earning asset offers, the greater the return that can usually be realized from holding it. The higher return is compensation for the higher probability that the asset holder, or lender, may suffer a sizeable loss if the asset does not meet its contractual obligations (the borrower fails to make interest payments or pay the loan or principal back or both). Obviously, there is a temptation to acquire earning assets that offer less security but higher returns in order to increase bank profits, hoping of course to avoid the possible losses.

It is also tempting for a bank to hold longer-term bonds because their market value fluctuates more than that of short-term bonds. Consequently, if the portfolio manager can purchase a long-term bond when its market value is low and sell it when its value rises, sizeable profits can be realized. Of course, if the bank needs money to meet a sudden surge of deposit withdrawals on a given day, it might be forced to sell some of its long-term bonds for considerably less than it paid for them. In short, the greater profits that can possibly be realized on long-term bonds must be weighed against the fact that they are less liquid than short-term bonds.

The balance between the need for liquidity and security and the desire for profit is reflected in the consolidated balance sheet for all U.S. commercial banks, Table 11-5:

1. The banks' *reserves* are of course their most liquid and secure assets. However, reserves (vault cash and deposits at Federal Reserve banks) earn no interest.

2. Among the income-earning assets, holdings of *U.S. government securities* consist mostly of short-term U.S. Treasury bills, which are highly liquid and just as secure as vault cash or deposits at the Federal Reserve banks. These are sometimes referred to as secondary reserves.

3. *Loans to businesses and consumers* represent by far the largest portion of the income-earning assets. Their degree of security is considerably less than that of reserves and U.S. Treasury bills, but they yield much higher rates of return and are the main source of commercial bank earnings. The loans are predominantly short term, some for periods less than a month but few for a period longer than five to ten years. The loans are represented by notes (typically the IOUs of consumers and small businesses) and commercial paper (the IOUs of large corporations) of varying degrees of liquidity.

4. *Other securities* consist mostly of longer-term federal and state and local government bonds. Most of these generally yield a higher rate of return than U.S. Treasury bills, but a lower return than loans to businesses and consumers. This difference is largely a reflection of the fact that their degree of security is greater than that of such loans.

The relative proportions of these four categories of assets in commercial bank portfolios reflect each individual bank's choice of balance between liquidity, security, and profitability. However, these proportions also reflect certain legal limitations on the kinds of assets commercial banks are allowed to hold in their portfolios. For example, they are generally not allowed to hold common stocks.

■ CHECKPOINT 11-1

From 1933 through 1940 commercial banks kept a considerably larger portion of their assets in the form of excess reserves than is the case today. Why do you suppose they did this?

TABLE 11-6a BALANCE SHEET OF CITIZENS' BANK

Assets		Liabilities and Equity	
Reserves	$1,000,000	Demand deposits	$1,000,000
Required reserves	200,000		
Excess reserves	800,000		
Stock in Federal Reserve bank	15,000		
Building and equipment	85,000	Equity	100,000
Total assets	$1,100,000 =	Total liabilities and equity	$1,100,000

DEPOSIT EXPANSION AND THE BANKING SYSTEM

In the previous chapter we saw how a commercial bank can make a loan by accepting the IOU of an individual or business and crediting a demand deposit in the borrower's name for the amount of the loan. The asset side of the bank's balance sheet is increased by the amount of the IOU, and the liability side is increased by the same amount in the form of a demand deposit held in the name of the borrower. The borrower may then write checks against this demand deposit and the bank is obliged to honor these checks. We will now examine how the banking system as a whole, consisting of many such banks, creates money through this process.

First we will consider the position of an individual bank in a system of many banks. We will then examine how the process of money creation would work if there were just one large commercial bank, a monopoly bank, serving the whole economy. We will then examine the process under the much more realistic assumption that there are a large number of commercial banks in the economy.

The Individual Bank in a System of Many Banks

Consider once again the Citizens' Bank when it is in the position shown by its balance sheet in Table 11-3, reproduced here as Table 11-6a. It has $1,000,000 in demand deposit liabilities and holds $1,000,000 of reserves. Again assuming that the legal reserve requirement is 20 percent, the required reserves amount to $200,000. Therefore, the bank has $800,000 of excess reserves and is in a position to make loans by creating demand deposits.

What amount of loans and, hence, demand deposits will the Citizens' Bank create? It cannot create more than $800,000 worth. At this stage Citizens' Bank's balance sheet appears as in Table 11-6b. The bank cannot lend out more than $800,000 because borrowers will most likely immediately spend these funds by writing

TABLE 11-6b BALANCE SHEET OF CITIZENS' BANK, AFTER MAKING LOANS OF $800,000 BUT BEFORE CHECKS ARE WRITTEN AGAINST BANK

Assets		Liabilities and Equity	
Reserves	$1,000,000	Demand deposits	$1,800,000
IOUs: loans to businesses, to consumers	800,000		
Stock in Federal Reserve bank	15,000		
Building and equipment	85,000	Equity	100,000
Total assets	$1,900,000 =	Total liabilities and equity	$1,900,000

**TABLE 11-7 BALANCE SHEET OF CITIZENS' BANK,
AFTER CHECKS FOR $800,000 ARE WRITTEN AGAINST BANK**

Assets		Liabilities and Equity	
Reserves	$ 200,000	Demand deposits	$1,000,000
IOUs: loans to businesses and consumers	800,000		
Stock in Federal Reserve bank	15,000		
Building and equipment	85,000	Equity	100,000
Total assets	$1,100,000 =	Total liabilities and equity	$1,100,000

checks against the $800,000 of demand deposits that the bank has credited to them. Since the Citizens' Bank is just one among thousands of banks in the banking system, it is highly likely that these checks will be made payable to parties who deposit their money in these other banks. Therefore, when all of these checks are presented to the Citizens' Bank for collection of payment, Citizens' Bank will have to pay out its $800,000 of excess reserves to satisfy the checks which are orders to withdraw the $800,000 of deposits on demand. Assume that this happens. Citizens' Bank's balance sheet will now appear as in Table 11–7.

Note that the bank is now "fully loaned up." It has just the amount of reserves on hand to meet the legal reserve requirement—$200,000 of reserves held against $1,000,000 of demand deposits. There are no excess reserves. While the Citizens' Bank now has the same amount of demand deposits it had in the beginning, it has created $800,000 more money in the economy. That money is now deposited in other commercial banks. Although unlikely, it could have happened that all of the checks written against the $800,000 of demand deposits created by Citizens' Bank in Table 11-6b were paid to parties who redeposited them at Citizens' Bank. The deposits of those who wrote the checks would then be reduced by $800,000, while the deposits of those who received the checks would be increased by $800,000. The total amount of demand deposit liabilities at Citizens' Bank would remain unchanged at $1,000,000. Also unlikely, but possible, the $800,000 of demand deposits created in Table 11-6b might be with-

drawn by the borrowers in the form of currency, so that the final position of the bank would be as shown in Table 11-7.

In general, *a single bank in a banking system composed of many banks cannot lend more than the amount of its excess reserves. This is so because borrowers will most likely write checks against the deposits that will cause the bank to lose these excess reserves, along with the deposits, to other banks.* This means that the single bank cannot permanently increase the amount of its demand deposit liabilities (by making loans) beyond the amount it had to begin with.

Monopoly Bank: One Commercial Bank Serving the Whole Economy

Suppose now that the entire economy is served by just one giant commercial bank—a monopoly bank. While this assumption is clearly unrealistic, it will help us better to understand how money creation takes place when there are many commercial banks, such as is the case in the U.S. economy.

Suppose that the balance sheet of our Monopoly Bank is initially as shown in Table 11-8. The bank holds the same assets and has the same liabilities and equity, and in the same proportions, as was the case for our Citizens' Bank in Table 11-3. The only difference is that the assets, liabilities, and equity of Monopoly Bank are a thousand times larger than those of the Citizens' Bank. Note that the Monopoly Bank is a member of the Federal Reserve System, as indicated by the fact that $15 million of its assets consist of stock in a Federal Reserve bank.

**TABLE 11-8 THE MONOPOLY
BANK'S BALANCE SHEET** (in Millions of Dollars)

Assets		Liabilities and Equity	
Reserves	$1,000	Demand deposits	$1,000
Required reserves	200		
Excess reserves	800		
Stock in Federal Reserve bank	15		
Building and equipment	85	Equity	100
Total assets	$1,100 =	Total liabilities and equity	$1,100

MONEY CREATION

Suppose again that the legal reserve requirement is 20 percent. The Monopoly Bank is therefore required to hold $200 million of reserves against its $1 billion of demand deposits. But since it is holding $1 billion of reserves, the Monopoly Bank clearly has $800 million of excess reserves. It is obviously in a position to make loans and create more demand deposits in the process.

What amount of demand deposits can it create? Since the Monopoly Bank is legally required to hold $1 of reserves for every $5 of demand deposits (because the legal reserve requirement is 20 percent), its $800 million of excess reserves can be used to support another $4 billion of demand deposits. How can this be? How is it that the Monopoly Bank can make an amount of demand deposits that is five times greater than the amount of its excess reserves? It can do so because it is the only bank in the economy. When borrowers write checks against their newly created deposits to buy goods and services, the sellers receiving the checks can only deposit these checks in the Monopoly Bank. The bank simply reduces or debits the deposits against which the checks are drawn and increases (or credits) the deposits of the recipients by a like amount. The Monopoly Bank's total amount of deposit liabilities therefore remains unchanged. There are no other banks to whom the Monopoly Bank can lose deposits and reserves.

The asset side of the Monopoly Bank's balance sheet now has $4 billion more assets in the form of IOUs (the promissory notes of businesses and consumers), and the liability side has $4 billion more liabilities in the form of demand deposits. This new situation is shown in Table 11-9. The bank is now "loaned up"—required reserves are $1 billion, and it has no excess reserves. The bank's $1 billion of reserves are able to support $5 billion of demand deposits and no more.

DEPOSIT EXPANSION IS MULTIPLE OF EXCESS RESERVES

Note that when the Monopoly Bank is fully loaned up, the number of dollars of demand deposits is five times the number of dollars of reserves. This multiple of 5 is the reciprocal of the legally required reserve ratio of .20 (20 percent). That is, 5 is the number you get when you divide 1 by .20. If the legally required reserve ratio had been .10 (10 percent), then the fully loaned-up monopoly bank would have been able to support $10 billion of demand deposits with $1 billion of reserves. The multiple of 10 is the reciprocal of .10. Moreover, *since demand deposits are money, whenever the Monopoly Bank has excess reserves, it is able to create an amount of money through lending that is equal to a multiple of its excess reserves. And that multiple is equal to the reciprocal of its legally required reserve ratio.* In the case of our Monopoly Bank, its $800 million of excess reserves allows it to create 5 times (1 divided by .20) this amount of demand deposits, or $4 billion (Table 11-9).

REVERSIBILITY OF THE MONEY CREATION PROCESS

This process of money creation is also reversible. Suppose, for example, that the Monopoly Bank is fully loaned up in the position shown in

TABLE 11-9 THE MONOPOLY BANK'S BALANCE SHEET, AFTER MAKING $4 BILLION OF LOANS BY CREATING $4 BILLION OF DEMAND DEPOSITS (in Millions of Dollars)

Assets		Liabilities and Equity	
Reserves	$1,000	Demand deposits	$5,000
IOUs in loans to businesses and consumers	4,000		
Stock in Federal Reserve bank	15		
Building and equipment	85	Equity	100
Total assets	$5,100 =	Total liabilities and equity	$5,100

Table 11-9. What would happen if the Fed were to increase the required reserve ratio from .20 to .40? With $5 billion of demand deposit liabilities, the Monopoly Bank now must hold $2 billion of reserves to satisfy the legal reserve requirement. It only has $1 billion of reserves and is therefore short $1 billion. The Monopoly Bank would have to reduce the amount of its loans by $2.5 billion, thereby eliminating $2.5 billion of demand deposits. Its $1 billion of reserves are sufficient to satisfy the legal reserve requirement against its remaining $2.5 billion of demand deposits.

MONEY CREATION
BY SECURITY PURCHASES

Throughout our discussion of the Monopoly Bank, we have assumed that demand deposit expansion would take place in exactly the same way if the Monopoly Bank acquired assets in the form of securities, such as government or corporate bonds. Starting from a position in which it had excess reserves, as in Table 11-8, the bank could purchase securities by creating demand deposits in the name of the sellers equal to the amount of the purchases. The amount of money that could be created in this way would be the same multiple (the reciprocal of the required reserve ratio) of excess reserves as before.

Banking System of Many Banks

We have seen that a single bank in a banking system of many banks cannot lend out more than the amount of its excess reserves. At the other extreme, we have seen that if the banking system consists of just one bank, the Monopoly Bank, such a bank can make loans and create an amount of demand deposits worth several times the amount of its excess reserves. We will now see that a banking system made up of many banks can also make loans and create demand deposits equal to several times the amount of total excess reserves in the system. This is exactly the same result as in the case of the Monopoly Bank.

Why is this so? Recall that a single bank in a banking system of many banks cannot permanently increase the amount of its demand deposits because the demand deposits it creates by lending are transferred by check-writing borrowers to other banks. As a result, the demand deposits of other banks are increased. Therefore, the amount of demand deposits in the *whole* banking system is increased because the banking system considered as a whole operates just like the Monopoly Bank. Reserves and deposits cannot be lost to other banks outside the banking system because there are no other banks outside the system. Let's now explore in more detail lending and deposit creation in a banking system consisting of many banks. We will see why the amount of money created is the same multiple of the total amount of excess reserves as in the case of the Monopoly Bank.

MONEY CREATION IN A
BANKING SYSTEM OF MANY BANKS

Suppose somebody deposits $1,000 of currency in a demand deposit at Bank A. Assume that the legally required reserve ratio is 10 percent, or .10, and that the bank was fully loaned up prior to the time of the $1,000 deposit. Bank A now has $1,000 more demand deposits as liabilities and $1,000 more reserves as assets, of which $100 are required reserves and $900 are excess reserves. (In the discussion to follow, we will ignore all items on the bank's balance sheet but those that change as a result of deposit expansion.) Bank A's balance sheet changes as follows:

BANK A
(Bank A receives $1,000 in demand deposits.)

Assets			Liabilities		
Reserves	+	$1,000	Demand deposits	+	$1,000
Required reserves	+	100			
Excess reserves	+	900			
Assets +		$1,000	Liabilities +		$1,000

Bank A, as an individual bank, can now lend out $900 by creating $900 of new demand deposits, an amount equal to its excess reserves. At this point Bank A's balance sheet changes like this:

BANK A
(Bank A makes $900 of loans,
increasing demand deposits by $900.)

Assets			Liabilities		
Reserves		$1,000	Demand deposits		$1,000
Loans	+	900	Demand deposits	+	900
Assets		$1,900	Liabilities		$1,900

Presumably, the party borrowing the $900, in whose name Bank A creates the $900 demand deposit, will soon spend that $900 by writing a check against the deposit for that amount. That is, the borrower will use the money to pay for some good or service. Suppose the recipient of that check deposits the check in another bank, Bank B. Since the check is drawn against Bank A, $900 of reserves will be transferred from

Bank A to Bank B. After all this, the change in Bank A's balance sheet is the following:

BANK A
(Bank A loses $900 of reserves and
deposits after check is written against it.)

Assets			Liabilities		
Reserves ($1,000 − $900)	+	$ 100	Demand deposits ($1,900 − $900)	+	$1,000
Loans	+	900			
Assets +		$1,000	Liabilities +		$1,000

Bank A is now fully loaned up. It has $1,000 of demand deposits and holds $100 of reserves, just the amount required by law, given that the required reserve ratio is .10. It has no excess reserves.

When the $900 check drawn on Bank A is deposited in Bank B, and $900 of reserves are transferred from Bank A to Bank B, the following changes are made in Bank B's balance sheet:

BANK B
(Bank B receives $900 deposit from Bank A,
and $900 of reserves are transferred to Bank B.)

Assets			Liabilities		
Reserves	+	$900	Demand deposits	+	$900
Required reserves	+	90			
Excess reserves	+	810			
Assets	+	$900	Liabilities +		$900

Bank B's demand deposits and reserves are each increased by $900. With a required reserve ratio of .10, the increase in the amount of its legally required reserves amounts to $90, while the increase in its excess reserves amounts to $810.

Suppose that Bank B now creates demand deposits by lending out $810, an amount equal to its excess reserves. Bank B's balance sheet will now change as follows:

BANK B
(Bank B makes $810 of loans, increasing demand deposits by $810.)

Assets			Liabilities		
Reserves	$	900	Demand deposits	$	900
Loans	+	810	Demand deposits	+	810
Assets	+	$1,710	Liabilities	+	$1,710

Now suppose the borrower writes a check for $810 against this newly created demand deposit. If the recipient of the check deposits it in another bank, Bank C, $810 of reserves will then be transferred from Bank B to Bank C. The change in Bank B's balance sheet appears as follows:

BANK B
(Bank B loses $810 of reserves and deposits after check is written against it.)

Assets			Liabilities		
Reserves ($900 − $810)	+	$ 90	Demand deposits ($1,710 − $810)	+	$900
Loans	+	810			
Assets	+	$900	Liabilities	+	$900

Now Bank B has $900 of demand deposits and $90 of reserves. The reserves are equal to 10 percent of the amount of demand deposits, just the amount it is legally required to hold. Bank B is fully loaned up—it has no excess reserves.

The Pattern of Lending and Deposit Creation.
There is a pattern to this process of lending and deposit creation. Bank A's excess reserves allow it to make loans and create new demand deposits equal to the amount of its excess reserves, which are then transferred by check-writing borrowers to Bank B. Bank B acquires all of Bank A's excess reserves in this process. Bank B is required to hold a fraction (equal to the legally required reserve ratio) of these new reserves against its newly acquired demand de-

posits. The remainder are excess reserves that allow B to make loans and create new demand deposits, which are in turn transferred by check-writing borrowers to Bank C, and so on. After borrowers write checks transferring Bank C's newly created demand deposits, along with its excess reserves, to Bank D, the change in Bank C's balance sheet will be as follows:

BANK C

Assets			Liabilities		
Reserves	+	$ 81	Demand deposits	+	$810
Loans	+	729			
Assets	+	$810	Liabilities	+	$810

And repeating the same pattern another step further, the change in Bank D's balance sheet would appear as follows:

BANK D

Assets			Liabilities		
Reserves	+	$ 73	Demand deposits	+	$729
Loans	+	656			
Assets	+	$729	Liabilities	+	$729

And similarly, for Bank E the change is:

BANK E

Assets			Liabilities		
Reserves	+	$ 66	Demand deposits	+	$656
Loans	+	590			
Assets	+	$656	Liabilities	+	$656

The complete process of demand deposit expansion throughout the banking system is summarized in Table 11-10. Starting with the initial demand deposit of $1,000 at Bank A (column 1), follow the arrows and notice that the successive increases in demand deposits at Banks B, C, D, and so on, become smaller and smaller. This reflects the fact that when a bank receives de-

TABLE 11-10 EXPANSION OF THE MONEY SUPPLY BY LENDING AND DEPOSIT CREATION BY THE BANKING SYSTEM (Legally Required Reserve Ratio Is .10)

Bank	(1) New Reserves and Demand Deposits	(2) Excess Reserves Equal to the Amount Bank Can Lend, Equal to New Money Created (1) − (3)	(3) Required Reserves (1) × required reserve ratio of .1
A	$ 1,000	$ 900	$ 100
B	900	810	90
C	810	729	81
D	729	656	73
E	656	590	66
F	590	531	59
G	531	478	53
H	478	430	48
All remaining banks	4,306	3,876	430
Total	$10,000	$9,000	$1,000

mand deposits and reserves from another bank, only a portion of these reserves, the excess reserves (column 2), can be passed on to yet another bank through lending and the creation of new demand deposits. The other portion must be kept as required reserves (column 3). If we want to know the total amount of new demand deposits that this process creates—the total amount of money creation—we must add up all the deposit increases throughout the banking system, as shown in column 1.

The Process of Deposit Creation Completed. When the entire process of deposit expansion is complete, all banks in the banking system are fully loaned up—there are no excess reserves anywhere in the banking system. The initial $1,000 increase in reserves is totally tied up as required reserves (column 3). Including the initial increase in demand deposits of $1,000 at Bank A, the total increase in demand deposits and, therefore, money for the whole banking system amounts to $10,000. That is, the total increase in demand deposits (column 1), is ten times the initial $1,000 increase in reserves at Bank A. This multiple of 10 is the reciprocal of the required reserve ratio of .10. Note that these are exactly the same results we got for our Monopoly Bank when the required reserve ratio is .10. Similarly, viewed in terms of the initial increase in excess reserves of $900 at Bank A, the total amount of new money created by the expansion process is $9,000 (column 2). Again, the multiple is 10, just as in the case of the Monopoly Bank.

In sum, *a single bank in a banking system can-*

*not permanently increase the amount of its de-
mand deposits by lending out its excess reserves.
But when each individual bank in the system lends
out its excess reserves, the banking system considered as a whole is just like one giant monopoly
bank. That is, the total expansion in demand deposits throughout the entire banking system is
equal to a multiple of any increase in reserves.
The multiple is equal to the reciprocal of the required reserve ratio.*

DEPOSIT CONTRACTION:
DESTRUCTION OF MONEY
BY THE BANKING SYSTEM

The deposit expansion or money creation
process is also reversible. Suppose the banking
system is fully loaned up and a depositor at
Bank A decides to withdraw $1,000 of currency.
In essence this leads to a reversal of the process
summarized in Table 11-10—think of the direction of the arrows as now being reversed.

Initially Bank A loses $1,000 of reserves in
the form of cash (column 1). Since it has $1,000
less demand deposits, it no longer needs to hold
the $100 in required reserves (column 3) against
these deposits. But since Bank A was fully
loaned up to begin with, it is now short $900 of
the amount of required reserves it must hold
against its remaining deposits. Consequently,
Bank A will have to get rid of $900 of other
assets in its portfolio (column 2) to replenish its
reserves. Suppose it does this by selling $900 of
government bonds to someone who holds demand deposits in Bank B. This party writes a
check against Bank B for $900 (column 1) pay-
able to Bank A. Bank A deposits this $900
check in its deposit at its district Federal Reserve bank. Since deposits at the Fed count as
reserves, Bank A now has just the amount of
reserves needed to satisfy its legal reserve requirement.

However, when Bank A's account at the Fed
is marked up, or credited, $900, Bank B's ac-
count at the Fed is drawn down, or debited,
$900. While Bank B no longer needs to hold $90
of required reserves (column 3) because it has
lost $900 of demand deposits (column 1), it is
now short $810 of the amount of required re-
serves it must hold against its remaining deposits. Therefore, Bank B sells $810 of government

bonds to someone who holds demand deposits
in Bank C. This party writes a check against
Bank C for $810 (column 1) payable to Bank B.
Bank C then loses deposits and finds itself short
of required reserves, and the whole contraction
process is repeated over and over with respect to
Banks D, E, F, and so forth. In the end, the
total reduction in demand deposits for the
whole banking system amounts to $10,000 (col-
umn 1). Hence, the initial decrease in demand
deposits and, therefore, reserves of $1,000 re-
sults in a total reduction in the amount of demand deposits which is 10 times greater. Note
again that this multiple is the reciprocal of the
required reserve ratio, $\frac{1}{10}$ or .10.

In sum, *the process of multiple contraction of
demand deposits is just the reverse of the process
of multiple expansion of deposits.*

Determining the Deposit Multiplier

We have seen that any initial increase in reserves can result in an increase in the total
amount of demand deposits, or new money,
that is equal to a multiple of the amount of increase in reserves. This was equally true for
both our Monopoly Bank and the banking system consisting of many banks, provided they
were fully loaned up. In both cases the multiple
equals the reciprocal of the required reserve ratio r, or $1/_r$. This reciprocal is often called the
deposit multiplier:

$$\text{deposit multiplier} = \frac{1}{r}$$

If the required reserve ratio is 20 percent, or
.20, the deposit multiplier $1/_r$ equals $1/_{.20}$, or 5. If
the required reserve ratio were 10 percent, or
.10, then the deposit multiplier would equal
$1/_{.10}$, or 10. In this case, for example, the maximum increase in the dollar amount of new demand deposits resulting from a $10 increase in
reserves would be $100. We can express this
through the following equation:

$$\$10 \times \frac{1}{r} = \$10 \times 10 = \$100$$

In general, if E is the change in reserves and D
is the maximum increase in demand deposits,
then

$$D = E \times \frac{1}{r}$$

Of course, the deposit multiplier is applicable to a decrease in reserves as well as to an increase. That is, if reserves are removed from the banking system when it is fully loaned up, there will be a contraction in the amount of demand deposits in the system that is equal to the amount of reserves removed multiplied by the deposit multiplier $1/_r$. For example, in our discussion of multiple deposit contraction, the legally required reserve ratio was .10. The deposit multiplier was therefore 10. Assuming that the banking system was fully loaned up, we saw that an initial $1,000 reduction in reserves resulted in a total loss of demand deposits amounting to $10,000 for the whole banking system ($1,000 × 10).

Other Determinants of the Size of the Deposit Multiplier

By now you have probably been struck by the similarity between the deposit multiplier and the income or expenditure multiplier discussed in Chapter 8. Indeed, the deposit expansion process of Table 11-10 looks very similar to the income expansion process of Table 8-4. Just as the deposit expansion multiplier is equal to the reciprocal of the required reserve ratio, the expenditure multiplier is equal to the reciprocal of the marginal propensity to save. Just as the expenditure multiplier reflects the fact that expenditure by one party is income for another, the deposit multiplier reflects the fact that reserves and deposits lost by one bank are reserves and deposits gained by another. The size of the expenditure multiplier is determined by the amount of leakage into saving at each round of expenditure, as determined by the size of the *MPS*. Similarly, the size of the deposit multiplier is determined by the amount of leakage of reserves into required reserves at each round of the deposit expansion process.

The similarity between the two multipliers ends here however. This is so because the expenditure multiplier deals with a flow, income, while the deposit multiplier deals with a stock, the money supply. Moreover, money and income are completely different concepts. Nonetheless, the leakage concept is very useful to our understanding of the other determinants of the size of the deposit multiplier.

LEAKAGES INTO EXCESS RESERVES

Up to this point in our discussion of the deposit multiplier, we have assumed that leakage into required reserves is the *only* type of leakage from the deposit expansion process. In other words, we have assumed that banks are always fully loaned up. In reality, this is not always the case.

For example, as part of their portfolio management policy banks may want to keep a certain amount of excess reserves on hand for liquidity purposes. This constitutes another source of leakage from the deposit expansion process in addition to the leakage into required reserves. This means that a greater portion of the reserves one bank receives from another is set aside at each round of deposit expansion—part to satisfy legal reserve requirements, and part to be held as excess reserves to satisfy the liquidity objectives of a bank's self-imposed portfolio management policy. In short, a smaller amount of reserves is now passed on from one bank to the next and, therefore, the full amount of deposit expansion will be less. This makes the deposit multiplier smaller. For example, if the legal reserve requirement is 10 percent, and in addition banks set aside as excess reserves another 10 percent of any reserves received, the deposit multiplier is equal to 1 ÷ .20 (the sum of .10 and .10), or 5.

Similarly, the deposit multiplier for the deposit contraction process will be smaller if banks choose to keep excess reserves on hand for liquidity purposes. Why? Each bank will be able to meet deposit withdrawals out of excess reserves before it needs to start selling off assets, which would lead to further deposit withdrawals at other banks, in the manner we have already described.

LEAKAGES DUE TO CASH WITHDRAWAL

Another source of leakage from the deposit expansion process is cash withdrawal. In our discussion it was assumed that when a check was written against a deposit at one bank, the recipient deposited the entire amount in another bank. In reality, the recipient may deposit only part of the amount of the check and hold the rest in cash. Since cash in banks constitutes reserves, this means that a smaller amount of reserves ends up being transferred from one bank to the next, and the full amount of the deposit expansion process is reduced accordingly. For example, suppose that in addition to the 10 percent leakage into excess reserves, there is another 10 percent leakage due to cash withdrawals by the public at each step of the deposit expansion process. The deposit expansion multiplier will now be equal to $1 \div .30$ (the sum of .10, .10, and .10), or 3.3.

VARIATION IN WILLINGNESS TO LEND AND BORROW

Finally, the willingness of banks to lend and the eagerness of businesses and consumers to borrow tends to vary with economic conditions. At one extreme, if there is no lending and borrowing, there will be no deposit expansion at all. At the other extreme, when banks are fully loaned up there is the maximum possible amount of deposit expansion. The amount of deposit expansion usually lies somewhere between these two extremes, depending on the banks' willingness to lend and the demand for loans by borrowers. Generally, banks are more cautious and eager borrowers less numerous when the economy is in the contraction phase of a business cycle. Obviously, therefore, the amount of excess reserves banks hold will tend to vary over the course of the business cycle. Consequently, so will the size of the deposit multiplier.

In sum, *the theoretical deposit multiplier calculated as the reciprocal of the required reserve ratio assumes that banks are fully loaned up. It tells us the maximum amount of deposit expansion or contraction that can take place in response to a change in excess reserves. In reality, banks are not always fully loaned up and there are also leakages due to cash withdrawal by the public. Consequently, the size of the actual deposit multiplier is typically variable as well as smaller than the theoretical deposit multiplier.*

■ CHECKPOINT 11-2

Change the required reserve ratio in Table 11-10 to .25 and show how the deposit expansion process will look as a result. How might the actions of one bank or one depositor put a stop to this expansion process? Suppose bankers' willingness to lend increases. Describe how and why this will affect the economy's money supply. With a required reserve ratio of .25, what will be the maximum possible effect on the economy's money supply if you decide to withdraw $100 in cash from your bank? Under what conditions will your withdrawal have the least possible effect on the money supply? (Define the money supply as M_1— demand deposits plus currency held *outside* of banks.)

THE ROLE OF THE FEDERAL RESERVE SYSTEM

The Board of Governors of the Federal Reserve System, the "Fed" is responsible for the conduct of *monetary policy* in our economy. *Monetary policy is deliberate action taken to affect the size of the economy's money supply for the purpose of promoting economic stability and maximum output and employment with a minimum of inflation.*

The Fed is able to affect the size of the economy's money supply by controlling the quantity of reserves in the commercial banking system. If the Fed increases the quantity of reserves, money creation takes place through the process of deposit expansion. If the Fed decreases the quantity of reserves, the amount of money in the economy is reduced through the process of deposit contraction. In this section we will examine the tools the Fed actually uses to conduct monetary policy. We will also look at the so-called federal funds market and its relationship to the way in which the Fed conducts monetary policy. Finally, we will examine the "minor" tools of monetary policy.

The Three Major Tools of Monetary Policy

There are three major tools which the Fed can use to conduct monetary policy: (1) open market operations, (2) setting reserve requirements for member commercial banks, and (3) setting the level of the discount rate—the interest rate it charges member commercial banks when it lends them reserves. We will consider each of these tools in turn.

OPEN MARKET OPERATIONS

The Fed can directly affect the amount of member bank reserves by buying or selling government securities, such as U.S. Treasury bills, in the open market where these securities are traded. Such transactions are called **open market operations**. Open market operations are the Fed's most important tool for carrying out monetary policy. *When the Fed conducts open market purchases, it buys government bonds and puts reserves into the banking system, causing an expansion of demand deposits or an increase in the economy's money supply. When the Fed conducts open market sales, it sells government bonds and takes reserves out of the banking system, causing a contraction of demand deposits or a decrease in the economy's money supply.* Let's consider how each of these operations works in more detail.

1. ***Open Market Purchases.*** Suppose the Fed buys $100,000 of Treasury bills in the open market and that the seller is a member commercial bank. (We will focus only on those items in the Fed's and the member bank's balance sheet that are affected by this transaction.) The Fed pays the member bank by increasing (crediting) the member bank's reserve account at its district Federal Reserve bank by the amount of the purchase, or $100,000. Hence, the Fed has $100,000 more assets in the form of Treasury bills and $100,000 more liabilities in the form of member bank reserve deposits at the Fed. The changes in the Federal Reserve bank's balance sheet look like this:

FEDERAL RESERVE BANK

Assets		Liabilities	
Treasury bills	+ $100,000	Member bank reserve deposits	+ $100,000

The member bank now has lost $100,000 of assets in the form of Treasury bills sold to the Fed, but it has gained $100,000 of assets in the form of reserves—deposits at the Fed. The changes in the member bank's balance sheet therefore look like this:

MEMBER BANK

Assets	
Reserves: deposits at the Fed	+ $100,000
Treasury bills	− $100,000

Note that while the total amount of the member bank's assets have not changed, the member bank now has more reserves. If the member bank previously was fully loaned up, it now has $100,000 of excess reserves. It is now in a position to make new loans by creating demand deposits if it wishes. We have seen how this can lead to deposit expansion, or money creation, throughout the banking system.

Suppose the Fed buys $100,000 of Treasury bills in the open market, but that the seller is one individual or a business other than a bank. The Fed simply makes out a check for $100,000 drawn against a Federal Reserve bank and payable to the seller of the Treasury bills. The check most likely will be deposited in a member bank by the seller. The member bank then presents the check to its district Federal Reserve bank for collection, and the member bank's reserve account at the Federal Reserve bank is increased (credited) $100,000. The changes in the Federal Reserve bank's balance sheet are as follows:

FEDERAL RESERVE BANK

Assets		Liabilities	
Treasury bills	+ $100,000	Member bank reserve deposits	+ $100,000

Again, the Fed has $100,000 more assets in the form of Treasury bills and $100,000 more liabilities in the form of member bank reserve deposits.

The member bank now has $100,000 more liabilities in the form of demand deposits and $100,000 more assets in the form of reserves represented by deposits at its Federal Reserve bank. These changes in the member bank's balance sheet look like this:

MEMBER BANK

Assets		Liabilities	
Reserves: deposits at the Fed	+ $100,000	Demand deposits	+ $100,000

Again, we see that member bank reserves are increased by the amount of the open market purchase. Assuming that the member bank was initially loaned up, it now has excess reserves because it is only required to hold a fraction of its new reserves against its newly acquired $100,000 of demand deposits. Deposit expansion and money creation can take place just as before.

In sum, member bank reserves are increased by the amount of Federal Reserve open market purchases no matter whether the seller of the securities is a bank or a nonbank.

2. **Open Market Sales.** Suppose the Fed sells $100,000 of Treasury bills in the open market and that the buyer is a member commercial bank. The Fed takes payment from the member bank by reducing the member bank's reserve deposit with its Federal Reserve bank by $100,000. In other words, the Fed's liability to the member bank is reduced by $100,000, while its assets are reduced to the extent of the $100,000 of Treasury bills it sells. The changes in the Federal Reserve bank's balance sheet look like this:

FEDERAL RESERVE BANK

Assets		Liabilities	
Treasury bills	− $100,000	Member bank reserve deposits	− $100,000

The member bank has gained $100,000 of assets in the form of Treasury bills purchased from the Fed. But, at the same time, it has had to give up $100,000 of its reserve deposits at its Federal Reserve bank to pay the Fed for these Treasury bills. The changes in the member bank's balance sheet look like this:

MEMBER BANK

Assets	
Reserves: deposits at the Fed	− $100,000
Treasury bills	+ $100,000

While the total amount of the member bank's assets has not been changed by these transactions, the member bank now has less reserves. This can set in motion the deposit contraction process, or reduction in the money supply, we have already discussed.

What if the buyer of the $100,000 of Treasury bills sold by the Fed is an individual or business other than a bank? Payment would typically be made to the Fed with a check drawn against the buyer's deposit at a member bank. When the Fed receives the check, it decreases (or debits) the member bank's reserve deposits at its Federal Reserve bank by $100,000. Once again, payment to the Fed is represented by a reduction of a Federal Reserve bank's liability to a member bank. The change in the Federal Reserve bank's balance sheet looks like this:

FEDERAL RESERVE BANK

Assets		Liabilities	
Treasury bills	− $100,000	Member bank reserve deposits	− $100,000

The member bank's demand deposit liabilities are reduced by $100,000 because of the check written by its depositor, the buyer of the Treasury bills. The member bank's assets are likewise reduced $100,000 by the reduction in its reserve deposits at the Federal Reserve bank which takes place when its depositor's check clears. The member bank's balance sheet is changed as follows:

MEMBER BANK

Assets		Liabilities	
Reserves: deposits at the Fed	− $100,000	Demand deposits	− $100,000

Again, we see that $100,000 of member bank reserves are removed from the banking system by the Fed's open market sale of $100,000 of Treasury bills.

In sum, member bank reserves are decreased by the amount of Federal Reserve open market sales, regardless of whether the buyer is a bank or a nonbank.

LEGAL RESERVE REQUIREMENTS

The news item at the beginning of this chapter reported that the Fed "may have to dig deeper into its bag of credit-tightening tricks to stem the sharp rise in the nation's money supply." It suggested that the Fed may resort to an increase in legal reserve requirements because "stiffer reserve requirements normally will temper the banking system's lending ability." Let's see why this is so.

The Fed has the authority to set the required reserve ratios within limits established by Congress. (The minimum limit is 7 percent and the maximum is 22 percent.) Recall that the required reserve ratio establishes the minimum amount of reserves that member banks must hold against demand deposit liabilities. These reserves may take the form of vault cash or deposits at a Federal Reserve bank or both. How does the Fed affect the economy's money supply by changing member bank reserve requirements?

Suppose that all banks in the banking system are fully loaned up and that the required reserve ratio is .10. None of the banks has any excess reserves. The balance sheet of a typical member bank would look like this (only its reserves and demand deposits are shown):

TYPICAL MEMBER BANK

Assets		Liabilities	
Reserves	$100,000	Demand deposits	$1,000,000

The member bank has $100,000 of reserves, which is just equal to 10 percent of its demand deposit liabilities of $1,000,000.

Increase in the Legal Reserve Requirement. Suppose that the Fed wants to tighten up the economy's money supply, or bring about a "credit tightening," as it is put in the news item. This means that the Fed wants to force the banks in the banking system to reduce their lending activity or their holdings of other earning assets. This will cause a deposit contraction throughout the banking system and, hence, a reduction in the money supply.

To bring this about, suppose the Fed increases the legal reserve requirement from 10 percent to 12 percent. Our typical member bank is now required to hold $120,000 of reserves against its $1,000,000 of demand deposits (.12 × $1,000,000). Since it only has $100,000 of reserves, it is $20,000 short. In order to make up this deficiency, the member bank must reduce its loans or sell off $20,000 of its other earning assets (or do some combination of both totaling $20,000). This will set in motion the deposit contraction process, or the reduction in the money supply, we have discussed before.

Decrease in the Legal Reserve Requirement. On the other hand, if the Fed wants to ease up on credit, or increase the money supply, it can reduce the reserve requirement. Suppose, for example, that it reduces the required reserve ratio from .10 to .08 (from a 10 percent reserve requirement to an 8 percent reserve requirement). Our typical member bank is now required to hold only $80,000 of reserves against its $1 million of demand deposits. Therefore, it has $20,000 of excess reserves. If it loans this out, deposit expansion, or money creation, can take place throughout the banking system in the manner we have already discussed.

In sum, *an increase in the required reserve ratio will force a deposit contraction, or money supply reduction, if member banks are fully loaned up. This contraction will be less pronounced to the extent that member banks have excess reserves. A decrease in the required reserve ratio increases the amount of excess reserves, encouraging banks to increase lending and deposit expansion, thereby increasing the money supply.*

As the news item notes, in practice the Fed does not change reserve requirements very often. This is so largely because reserve requirement changes of even a half of a point (from 15 percent to 15.5 percent, for example) can require quite an abrupt adjustment throughout the banking system.

SETTING THE DISCOUNT RATE

In the previous chapter, we noted that, just as commercial banks make loans to the public, Federal Reserve banks make loans to member commercial banks. *The interest rate that the Fed charges member banks who borrow reserves from the Federal Reserve banks is called the* **discount rate**. As a figure of speech, it is often said that a member bank borrows at the **discount window** when it borrows reserves from its Federal Reserve bank.

The Federal Reserve bank lends the member bank reserves by increasing (crediting) the member bank's reserve deposit with the Federal Reserve bank by the amount of the loan. When member banks borrow from the Fed, these additional reserves enable them to make more loans and create more deposits. Therefore, borrowing at the discount window allows more deposit expansion and money creation to take place throughout the banking system than would otherwise be possible.

Member banks naturally find it attractive to borrow from the discount window whenever the interest rates they can earn from making loans to businesses and consumers, or by purchasing securities, are greater than the discount rate. And the greater the difference, the greater the inducements for member banks to borrow. On the other hand, when the discount rate is higher than these interest rates, member banks are discouraged from borrowing at the discount window. It follows that *another possible way for the Fed to affect the amount of reserves in the banking system is by its setting of the discount rate. If the Fed raises the discount rate, member bank borrowing is reduced and the amount of reserves in the banking system falls. This tends to cause deposit contraction and a reduction in the size of the money supply. If the Fed lowers the discount rate, member bank borrowing rises, causing an increase in reserves and deposit expansion and, hence, an increase in the money supply.*

The Federal Funds Market and Monetary Policy

Another way that individual banks in the banking system can increase their reserves is to borrow from other banks in the system. On any given day some banks may find themselves temporarily with excess reserves that they would prefer to earn interest on if they could. At the same time, there usually are other banks who find themselves temporarily low on reserves. Rather than borrow reserves from the Fed, the banks caught short on reserves can borrow reserves from those banks that have undesired excess reserves. The market in which this borrowing and lending of reserves between commercial banks takes place is called the **federal funds market**. The **federal funds rate** is the interest rate that borrowing banks must pay the banks that lend them these reserves, which are often called **federal funds**.

While an individual bank in the banking system can borrow (federal funds) from another bank, the total amount of reserves in the banking system as a whole is controlled by the Fed. When the demand for federal funds by borrowing banks rises relative to the supply of such funds provided by lending banks, the federal funds rate is bid up. This tends to happen when the demand for loans from banks by businesses, consumers, and state and local governments increases. The excess reserves in the banking system decline as more and more banks become fully loaned up. When this process pushes the federal funds rate above the discount rate, banks find it cheaper to borrow reserves from the Federal Reserve banks. More reserves flow into the banking system to support the lending activity and the associated deposit expansion and money creation of the commercial banks.

THE FEDERAL FUNDS RATE TARGET

Reread the news item at this point. Note the reference to the fact "that the Fed indicated it had raised its federal funds target rate from $7\frac{1}{2}$ to $7\frac{3}{4}$ percent." Through its open market operations the Fed affects the amount of reserves in the banking system. Open market purchases increase reserves and reduce the demand for borrowing relative to the supply of lending in the federal funds market, causing the funds rate to fall. Open market sales have just the opposite effect and cause the federal funds rate to rise. Because of this the Fed views the federal funds rate as an indicator of the "ease" or "tightness" of money in the economy. The higher the funds rate, the tighter is money; the lower the funds rate, the easier. The tighter is money, the more fully loaned up are banks; the easier, the less fully loaned up. Hence, the Federal Open Market Committee, the Fed's policy-making authority, implements monetary policy by deciding each month what the target level of the federal funds rate should be in order to be consistent with the objectives of monetary policy. The Fed then conducts open market operations on a day-to-day basis that are aimed at setting the federal funds rate at the targeted level.

COORDINATING THE
TOOLS OF MONETARY POLICY

From the news item we can see why the Fed must coordinate the use of its three tools: open market operations, reserve requirements, and the setting of the discount rate. Having decided to target the federal funds rate at $7\frac{3}{4}$ percent, the Fed can not very well leave the discount rate at 7 percent. Why? Because member banks will find it attractive to borrow reserves from the Fed. The increased reserves flowing into the banking system through the discount window will put downward pressure on the federal funds rate. This will work against the Fed's efforts to keep the funds rate at $7\frac{3}{4}$ percent through its open market operations. In fact, it will have to make continuous open market sales to "sop up" the reserves flowing in through the discount window. To avoid this the Fed will have to raise

the discount rate, or else these two tools in its arsenal will be working at cross purposes. This is why the news item reports that a growing number of analysts "say that a boost from 7 to $7\frac{1}{2}$ percent in the discount rate is almost certain."

Why doesn't the Fed drop the targeted level of the funds rate instead? Because then it would have to put more reserves into the banking system. This would tend to increase the money supply. But according to the news item, the Fed is trying "to stem the sharp rise in the nation's money supply."

Minor Tools of Monetary Policy

In addition to the three major tools of monetary policy we have discussed, the Fed also has the power to regulate lending for stock market purchases, to put ceilings on the interest rates that commercial banks pay on time deposits, and regulate certain kinds of credit during emergencies, such as wartime.

STOCK MARKET CREDIT
AND MARGIN REQUIREMENTS

The Fed has the authority to set margin requirements on stock market purchases. The **margin requirement** is the minimum percentage of a stock purchase that must be paid for with the purchaser's own funds. For example, if the margin requirement is 70 percent, a minimum of 70 percent of the price of the stock must be paid for with the purchaser's own money, while the remainder may be financed with borrowed funds. Congress originally gave the Fed the power to set the margin requirement so that the Fed would be able to control the amount of stock "speculation" financed with borrowed funds. It was felt that excessive stock market speculation financed with credit was a major cause of the disastrous stock market crash of 1929. When the prices of stocks began to fall, people who had purchased them at higher prices with borrowed funds were often able to pay back only a small part of the original loan. The very attempt to recover their funds by selling out their stock holdings caused stock prices to "crash." When the Fed (specifically, the Board of Governors) feels that stock market speculation is increasing, it can put a damper on

ECONOMIC THINKERS

JAMES TOBIN
1918-

Tobin, born in Illinois, received his Ph.D. from Harvard in 1947. His career has been marked by service in both academic economics and the public sector. He served on the Council of Economic Advisers under President Kennedy and returned to Yale at the end of his service in 1962. Tobin, well grounded in quantitative economics, also combines skill in varying methodological approaches and is at home in empirical research. His interest has been largely in the macroeconomic analysis of national income and in the policy implications which stem from his conclusions.

Tobin developed a technique for measuring the demand for money using what he called the "portfolio balance approach," in which, as in the Keynesian model, saving is largely determined by income, but the types of assets in which savings are held are determined by the relative certainty of equivalent yields of these assets.

Tobin recognized two possible sources of liquidity preference: (1) the inelasticity of expectations of future interest rates and (2) the uncertainty of the future of interest rates. His risk aversion theory of liquidity preference was designed to explain diversification by a single individual investor between cash and bonds. This contrasts with Keynesian liquidity preference theory, which holds that each investor will hold only one or the other of these assets. Tobin thus laid the foundation for modern theories of portfolio selection in which the average return and risk are separately considered.

Tobin has also had a great impact at Yale through the Cowles Foundation. Large sums of money were made available for research purposes, and this effort resulted in many dissertations and research projects. Tobin thus became responsible for enhancing a substantial number of graduate careers. The range of his thinking is well illustrated by his volume *National Economic Policy* (1966), which contains 18 essays ranging from international economic policy to the work of academic economists in Washington, of which Tobin was one. Tobin represents the younger economists of the period following World War II. He is pragmatic, at home both in theory and practice. Like many economists, Tobin is slightly less sanguine now than he was a decade ago about the usefulness of economic policy to solve problems. A brief quotation from the selection "Academic Economics in Washington" is worth noting:

> The Council of Economic Advisers is sometimes criticized for being "political" and "partisan" for compromising the purity and objectivity of academic learning. But economics has always been a policy-oriented subject. Unless it is applied to the urgent policy issues of the day, it will become a sterile exercise, without use or interest. Those who fear that economics will be discredited if it is applied remind me of a football coach who never plays his star back for fear he might be injured.

Tobin won the John Bates Clark medal in 1955 and was president of the American Economic Association in 1971.

FOR FURTHER READING

Among Tobin's major publications are: *Essays in Economics* (1971), *National Economic Policy* (1966), *Financial Markets and Economic Activity* (1967), and *The New Economics One Decade Older* (1974).

---

such activity by increasing the margin requirement. This is intended to prevent the development of conditions that might lead to a rapid fall in stock prices.

CEILINGS ON TIME-DEPOSIT INTEREST RATES: REGULATION Q

Congress established **Regulation Q** during the 1930s. It gives the Fed the authority to put a ceiling on the interest rates that member banks can pay on time deposits. Suppose interest rates on savings deposits at other financial institutions, such as mutual saving banks and savings and loan associations, and on securities in general, rise above the Regulation Q ceiling rate. Commercial banks will tend to experience time-deposit withdrawals as depositors move funds to these other assets, now relatively more attractive because of their higher interest rates. By setting appropriate Regulation Q levels, the Fed can channel funds either into or away from commercial banks. Since these other financial institutions tend to specialize in financing residential construction, whereas commercial banks tend to do more short-term lending to businesses and consumers, changes in the Regulation Q ceiling will cause changes in the allocation of funds and, hence, the availability of financing for these different activities. Since the 1960s commercial banks have increasingly been able to get around the constraints of Regulation Q by issuing large negotiable certificates of deposit, or CDs, that are not subject to Regulation Q.

CREDIT REGULATION DURING WARTIME

During wartime Congress often has given the Fed the authority to regulate the availability of credit for financing various kinds of consumer and business spending that threatens to direct resources and productive activity away from the war effort. The Fed does this by establishing stringent minimum downpayment requirements and fairly short repayment periods for the financing of such purchases.

■ CHECKPOINT 11-3

It has been argued by a number of economists that the discount window and the setting of the discount rate is no longer a very useful tool for monetary policy. They claim, in fact, that it really reduces the Fed's control over the money supply. Why do you think this might be true? On the other hand, some economists argue that the existence of the discount window provides the banking system some protection against an unnecessarily restrictive monetary policy.

How do you think the argument supporting this point of view might go? Describe how Regulation Q might be used by the Fed to affect the amount of residential construction in the economy.

SUMMARY

1. The composition of the typical commercial bank's portfolio of earning assets reflects a compromise between two often conflicting objectives: (a) the maintenance of liquidity and security and (b) the realization of profit.

2. A commercial bank generally restricts its holdings of earning assets to short-term loans, bonds, and securities because of their relatively high degree of liquidity and security. This restriction is dictated by the large amount of commercial bank deposit liabilities which are subject to withdrawal on demand.

3. In general, the amount of demand deposits, or money, that a single commercial bank can create through lending cannot exceed the amount of its excess reserves. This is so because borrowers will most likely write checks against these newly created deposits which the check recipients will deposit in other banks.

4. By contrast, a monopoly bank is able to create an amount of demand deposits, or money, through lending that is equal to a multiple of its excess reserves. This is so because the recipients of checks written by borrowers against these deposits have no alternative but to deposit them at the monopoly bank—there are no other banks. The multiple of excess reserves by which deposit expansion or money creation can occur is the reciprocal of the required reserve ratio.

5. A commercial banking system considered as a whole is just like a monopoly bank. When each individual bank in the banking system lends out its excess reserves, the banking system as a whole can create an amount of demand deposits, or money, which is a multiple of the total amount of excess reserves in the system. While individ-

ual banks in the banking system can lose reserves and deposits to other banks in the system, their system as a whole cannot.

6. As in the case of the monopoly bank, the multiple for the banking system as a whole is the reciprocal of the required reserve ratio. This multiple is called the deposit multiplier. It also applies to deposit contraction, which is just the reverse of the deposit expansion process.

7. The three major tools used by the Fed to conduct monetary policy are: (a) open market operations, (b) the setting of reverse requirements for member commercial banks, and (c) the setting of the level of the discount rate.

8. Open market operations refer to the Fed's buying and selling of government securities in the open market. When the Fed buys government securities, it puts reserves into the banking system, causing an expansion of demand deposits or an increase in the economy's money supply. When the Fed sells government bonds, it takes reserves out of the banking system, causing a contraction of demand deposits, or a decrease in the economy's money supply.

9. An increase in the required reserve ratio will force a deposit contraction, or money supply reduction. The extent of reduction will depend on the amount of excess reserves in the banking system. A decrease in the required reserve ratio increases the amount of excess reserves, encouraging banks to increase lending and deposit expansion, thereby increasing the money supply.

10. When the Fed raises the discount rate, member bank borrowing is discouraged. The amount of reserves in the banking system falls, and this tends to cause deposit contraction and a reduction in the size of money supply. If the Fed lowers the discount rate, member bank borrowing tends to rise, resulting in an increase in reserves and deposit expansion and an increase in the money supply.

11. Commercial banks borrow and lend their excess reserves to one another in the federal funds market at a rate of interest called the federal funds rate. Through its open market operations the Fed is able to set the federal funds rate at a target level. The target is chosen to be consistent with the objectives of monetary policy.

12. Minor tools that the Fed can use to affect lending in the economy include: (a) the setting of margin requirements on the purchase of stocks, (b) the use of Regulation Q to set interest rate ceilings on time deposits at member banks, and (c) the authority granted the Fed by Congress during wartime to regulate the lending for various kinds of consumer and business spending.

KEY TERMS AND CONCEPTS
deposit multiplier
discount rate
discount window
equity
excess reserves
federal funds
federal funds market
federal funds rate
margin requirement
net worth
open market operations
Regulation Q
required reserve ratio
required reserves
reserves

QUESTIONS AND PROBLEMS

1. Consider the consolidated bank balance sheet of Table 11-5 and suppose that the required reserve ratio for time deposits is 10 percent (.10), while that for demand deposits is 20 percent (.20). Does the banking system have excess reserves and, if so, how much? What is the amount of new loans and demand deposits that could be created? Alternatively, what is the amount of government securities that could be purchased?

2. Consider the balance sheet of the following individual bank, Bank X, in a banking system of many banks:

BANK X

Assets		Liabilities and Equity	
Reserves	$ 220,000	Demand deposits	$ 950,000
Loans, securities, and other assets	780,000	Equity	50,000
Total assets	$1,000,000 =	Total liabilities and equity	$1,000,000

Assume the required reserve ratio is 20 percent (.20).

a. How much excess reserves does Bank X have?

b. Suppose Bank X creates an amount of demand deposits through lending that equals the amount of its excess reserves multiplied by the deposit multiplier. What will be the amount of the new loans it has created? What will Bank X's balance sheet look like before any checks have been written against the new deposits?

c. Given your answer to part b, suppose now that borrowers write checks against the newly created demand deposits and that the recipients of these checks deposit them in other banks. What will happen to the level of reserves in Bank X? What now will be the level of excess reserves in Bank X?

d. Given your answers to part c, describe what Bank X must do to get its house in order. Once it has done so, how will its balance sheet look?

e. What does this example tell us about the difference between an individual bank and the banking system as a whole?

f. Starting again with the answer to part a, if you were running Bank X, describe what you would do at this point. How would Bank X's balance sheet now look after your management strategy had been carried out?

3. It is sometimes said that there is a "trade-off" between bank profits, on the one hand, and liquidity and security, on the other. Describe what is meant by this and why it is so. How does this trade-off affect the size of the deposit multiplier?

4. Suppose Bank A's balance sheet looks as follows and that the required reserve ratio is 15 percent (.15):

BANK A

Assets		Liabilities and Equity	
Reserves	$ 200,000	Demand deposits	$ 900,000
Loans, securities, and other assets	800,000	Equity	100,000
Total assets	$1,000,000 =	Total liabilities and equity	$1,000,000

a. What would be the maximum amount of cash that depositors could withdraw before Bank A would be forced to do something about the amount of loans, securities, and other assets it holds?

b. Suppose Bank A decides to make loans by creating demand deposits. Assume that Bank A and all other commercial banks in the banking system expect that 5 percent of any loans they make will be withdrawn immediately in the form of cash. What will be the maximum amount of deposit expansion, or money creation, that will take place throughout the banking system as a whole?

c. Show the deposit expansion process of part b in a table like Table 11–10.

5. What is the effect on the size of the actual deposit multiplier of increases and decreases in the public's desire to hold currency? If the public's desire to hold currency rises during recessions and falls during the expansionary phase of the business cycle, over the course of the business cycle how does this affect the Fed's ability to change the money supply per dollar of any open market purchase of sale?

6. Of the three major tools of monetary policy, which one do you think is probably the least effective for controlling the amount of reserves in the banking system? Why?

7. It has been said that the Fed can be much

more effective when it wants to contract the money supply than when it wants to expand the supply. Why might this be so? Explain in terms of each of the three major tools of monetary policy.

8. What role do Federal Reserve bank liabilities to member commercial banks play in the way that open market operations affect the economy's money supply?

9. Describe the federal funds market and explain why the Fed tries to maintain a target level for the federal funds rate. Describe how and why open market operations affect the federal funds rate.

■ NEWS ITEM FOR YOUR ANALYSIS ■

FEDERAL RESERVE AGAIN TIGHTENS CREDIT; BASIC MONEY SUPPLY ROSE IN LATEST WEEK

NEW YORK, June 26—The Federal Reserve System escalated its war on inflation by tightening its credit reins for the second time in little over a week.

In the latest action, the Fed boosted to $7\frac{1}{4}$ percent from 7 percent its target interest rate on federal funds, the uncommitted reserves banks lend one another. Only a little more than a month ago, the federal funds rate target was $6\frac{3}{4}$ percent. The Fed signaled the tightening by allowing the federal funds rate to rise to $7\frac{5}{16}$ percent yesterday before finally taking offsetting action at 1:30 PM EST.

The interest rate on federal funds (the funds rate) is an indicator of the availability of reserves in the banking system. Therefore, the Fed uses it as a guide in carrying out monetary policy. The funds rate is also a kind of base from which most other interest rates are scaled upward. Therefore, analysts said that the recent rise in the funds rate will most likely soon lead to a boost in both the discount rate and the prime rate, the minimum interest banks charge on corporate loans.

"It will probably trigger a substantial increase in member bank borrowing from the Fed and result in a boost in the discount rate," said one economist. He noted that at $6\frac{1}{2}$ percent the discount rate is well below the federal funds rate, and banks will likely take advantage of this bargain at the Fed's discount window.

Statistics released yesterday by the Fed also showed underlying strength in loan demand at commercial banks. Nationally, last week commercial loans surged $766 million. In addition, commercial paper outstanding in the previous week soared $1.3 billion. Other figures showed that the basic money supply, M_1, has grown at a 13 percent annual rate in the past four weeks in contrast to its sluggish behavior earlier in the year. M_2's recent four-week growth rate was a more modest 9 percent.

In response to the Fed's policy, the short-term interest rates on 90-day and six-month Treasury bills have gone up. These rates are now well above the maximum interest fees that banks and savings and loan associations are able to pay on deposits. It is feared that this will hurt the availability of mortgage money for housing because such securities will attract increasing amounts of funds away from thrift institutions.

QUESTIONS

1. What would be the "offsetting action" which the news item claims the Fed took when the funds rate rose to $7\frac{5}{16}$ percent? Explain how this "offsetting action" works to affect the level of the funds rate.

2. What is meant by the remark that "banks will likely take advantage of this bargain at the Fed's discount window"—what is the bargain?

3. What is the nature of the relationship between the rise in the funds rate, the "underlying strength in loan demand at commercial banks," and the reported surge in the growth rate of M_1?

4. Why can't the rise in interest rates on Treasury bills be matched by a rise in the interest rates on commercial bank time deposits?

12

THE ROLE OF MONEY IN INCOME DETERMINATION

FEDERAL RESERVE CUTS RISE
IN MONEY SUPPLY, WORRIES SOME ANALYSTS

WASHINGTON, March 3—The Federal Reserve System has slammed the brakes on the growth of the nation's money supply. If this slow growth continues, many analysts expect an easing of inflationary pressures. But they also expect a drop in economic growth and possibly even a recession before the end of the year.

Some economists think the monetary slowdown has been partly accidental and will be short-lived. However, others stress that a climbing inflation rate, together with a declining unemployment rate, have increased the odds that the Fed will continue to pursue a restrictive policy.

When G. William Miller, chairman of the Federal Reserve Board, appeared before the House Banking Committee earlier this month, he forecast a "continued expansion in economic activity" this year. But he also told the legislators that he was "more concerned today" about inflation than he had been in the past. When testifying before the Senate Budget Committee Wednesday, Mr. Miller took an even tougher line. "I hope we have the courage to make inflation our highest priority for domestic economic policy," he said.

This news item testifies to the key role that the Federal Reserve System plays in our economy through its authority to regulate the money supply. In the last chapter we examined how the Fed is able to change the level of commercial bank reserves and thereby cause the economy's money supply to expand or contract. But how and why do changes in the economy's money supply affect the general level of economic activity? In this chapter we will focus on this question. More specifically, we will examine the basic role that money plays in the determination of the level of total income and employment in an economy such as that of the United States.

We should note at the outset that economists are not in complete agreement on just how and to what extent money affects the economy. In this chapter we will focus on the Keynesian view by introducing money into the Keynesian analysis of income determination we developed in Chapters 8 and 9. In the next chapter, we will compare the Keynesian interpretation with the monetarist point of view which has gained increased recognition in recent years. There we will be particularly concerned with the different implications each point of view has for the Federal Reserve's ability to carry out the objectives of monetary policy.

MONEY DEMAND
AND SUPPLY AND
THE INTEREST RATE

The demand for money interacts with the supply of money to determine the rate of interest in what is often referred to as the *money market*. And it is the interest rate that provides the primary link between money and the rest of the economy in the Keynesian analysis of in-

come determination. We have seen how the Federal Reserve System regulates the supply of money. Now let's examine the determinants of the demand for money. We will then put these pieces—demand and supply—together and examine the nature of equilibrium in the money market.

Transactions and
Precautionary Demands for Money

Part of the demand for money stems from the service it provides as a medium of exchange. In short, money is needed to transact the purchase and sale of goods and services. This need is referred to as the **transactions demand** for money. What determines the size of this demand? The amount of transactions taking place in the economy, of course. One rough measure of the amount of such transactions is the level of total income, as represented by the level of money GNP for example. *When total income rises, the transactions demand for money increases; and when total income declines, the transactions demand decreases.*

Money is also needed for precautionary purposes. Hence, there is a **precautionary demand** for money. Unforeseen events or emergencies often require immediate expenditures. Money is the most liquid asset and, therefore, ideally suited to meet such contingencies. For this reason most of us carry a little more currency with us than is needed to cover anticipated transactions for such things as lunch and bus fare. Some people even keep sizeable amounts of currency in safes and safe-deposit boxes just in case some of their other assets cannot be readily liquidated. It is probably generally true that the precautionary demand for money in the economy varies with the level of total income, as does the transactions demand.

Money Demand and the Interest Rate

The level of total income is an important determinant of money demand primarily because of its relationship to the transactions and precautionary motives for holding money. The interest rate is also regarded as an important influence on the demand for money, particularly in the Keynesian analysis. Why is this so?

THE INTEREST RATE: AN OPPORTUNITY COST

It has been said that "money is barren." Money, in the form of currency or demand deposits, is barren because such assets do not earn interest. The opportunity cost of holding money (whether for transactions, precautionary, or any other purposes) is the forgone interest that could be earned on other assets—such as savings deposits or bonds, for example. Therefore, the interest rate may be thought of as the price of holding money. As with any good or service, people will demand less money when its price is high than when it is low, all other things remaining the same. That is, the higher the interest rate, the lower the quantity of money demanded; and the lower the interest rate, the greater the quantity demanded. This inverse relationship between the demand for money and the interest rate is illustrated by the demand curve for money L shown in Figure 12-1. (The letter L is used to designate the demand curve for money simply as a reminder that money is the most liquid asset—the demand for money is the demand for liquidity.)

THE INTEREST RATE AND BONDS

Keynesian analysis argues that the interest rate is an important determinant of the demand for money because people also desire to hold money for speculative purposes (in addition to the desire to hold money for transactions and precautionary purposes). However, before considering the speculative demand for money, it is necessary to understand why interest rates and bond prices always move in opposite directions.

A bond is a promissory certificate issued by borrowers (typically businesses and governments) in exchange for funds provided to them by lenders. The bond represents the borrower's promise to pay back to the lender (the bondholder) the amount of money borrowed (the principal) at the end of a certain number of years (the maturity date). The bond also promises that the borrower will make payments (coupon payments) of a set number of dollars to the lender at regular intervals (annually, for example). The coupon payments represent the rate of return or the interest rate that induces the lender to loan money to the borrower.

Consider a bond that promises to make coupon payments of $10 per year, year in and year out, forever. (Such bonds, called consols, are issued by the British government, for example.) If you purchased (invested in) such a bond for $100, you would earn a 10 percent rate of interest—the $10 coupon payment divided by the $100 purchase price, expressed as a percentage. If you paid $200 for the bond you would earn a 5 percent rate of interest—$10 divided by $200, expressed as a percentage. Obviously, the higher

---

After reading this chapter, you will be able to:

1. Define the major determinants of the demand for money.
2. Explain how money demand and money supply interact to determine the equilibrium level of the interest rate in the money market.
3. Explain why the interest rate is a determinant of the level of investment spending.
4. Describe how the money market, the level of investment spending, and the total demand for final goods and services interact to jointly determine the economy's equilibrium level of total income.
5. Distinguish between general equilibrium and partial equilibrium analysis.

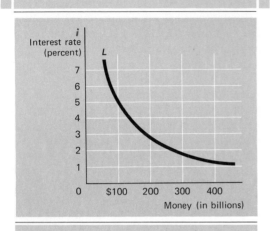

FIGURE 12-1 THE DEMAND FOR MONEY IS INVERSELY RELATED TO THE INTEREST RATE

The demand curve for money slopes downward left to right for two reasons.

First, the interest rate represents the opportunity cost of holding money either in the form of currency or of demand deposits since neither of these assets earns interest. Therefore, a smaller quantity of money is demanded at a high than at a low interest rate.

Second, the nature of the speculative demand for money suggests that people will desire to hold more money and fewer bonds when the interest rate is below what is considered its normal level. This is so because bond prices are then above their normal levels, and it is thought likely that they will once again decline to those levels, resulting in losses to bondholders. On the other hand, if the interest rate is above its normal level, bond prices are below their normal levels. People will desire to hold less money and more bonds because it will be thought likely that bond prices will rise to their normal levels, and bondholders will realize gains. In sum, the speculative demand for money also suggests that a smaller quantity of money is demanded at a high than at a low interest rate.

the price you pay for the bond, the lower the interest rate you receive. Conversely, the lower the price paid, the higher the interest rate. Calculation of the interest rate earned on a bond with a set maturity date is more complicated,

but the link between the interest rate realized on the bond and the price of the bond is the same. *The price of a bond and its interest rate always move in opposite directions.*

THE SPECULATIVE DEMAND FOR MONEY

Suppose people believe that there is some average, or "normal," level for the interest rate, a level determined by their observation of the interest rate in the past. Because bond prices and the interest rate are linked, this means there is also some normal level of bond prices.

If the interest rate is currently above its normal level, bond prices will be below their normal level. People will tend to believe that the interest rate is likely to fall and, therefore, that bond prices will rise. People will therefore prefer to hold more bonds and less money because of the gains they will realize if the likely rise in bond prices occurs. On the other hand, if the interest rate is currently below its normal level, bond prices will be above their normal level. People will tend to believe the interest rate is likely to rise and bond prices to fall. They will want to hold more money and fewer bonds because of the losses on bonds that would result if the likely fall in bond prices occurs. Thus, the **speculative demand** for money provides another reason why less money is demanded at a high than at a low interest rate.

The demand curve for money in Figure 12-1 slopes downward left to right not only because of the opportunity cost of holding money, represented by the interest rate, but also because of the speculative demand for money arising from the fact that interest rates and bond prices fluctuate.

Changes in the Demand for Money

A change in the quantity of money demanded is represented by movement along the money demand curve of Figure 12-1. This movement occurs when the interest rate changes, all other things remaining the same. A change in the demand for money is represented by a shift in the position of the money demand curve. Such a change occurs when one or more of the other things changes. (Recall the distinction made in Chapter 4 between a change in quantity demanded and a change in demand.)

Among the other things that can change, the

economy's total money income (or money GNP) is a particularly important determinant of the transactions demand for money. It also influences the demand for money for precautionary purposes. (Recall the distinction between money GNP and real GNP made in Chapter 5. Hereafter, the term total income is always taken to mean total money income.) If total income increases, both the transactions and the precautionary demand for money rise. A decline in total income has the opposite effect. Therefore, a rise in total income will increase the demand for money and cause the demand curve for money to shift rightward, such as from L_0 to L_1 in Figure 12-2. A decline in total income would cause a leftward shift, such as from L_1 to L_0.

The Money Supply

In the previous chapter we examined how the Fed is able to control the quantity of member bank reserves by the use of open market operations and the setting of the discount rate. Through its control over bank reserves and the setting of reserve requirements, we saw how the Fed affects the deposit expansion or contraction process and the creation or destruction of money. In short, we saw how the Fed controls the economy's money supply.

At any given time, the supply or stock of money available to satisfy the demand for money is fixed. The fixed supply of money may be represented by a vertical supply curve such as M_0 in Figure 12-3. (The vertical supply curve means that the money supply is unresponsive to the interest rate.) M_0 represents a stock of money equal to $200 billion. If the Fed were to increase the money supply by $100 billion, the money supply curve would be shifted rightward from M_0 to M_1, as shown in Figure 12-3. A decrease in the money supply would be represented by a leftward shift in the money supply curve.

The Money Market: The Interaction of Supply and Demand

Now we are ready to bring money demand and money supply together to form the money market. At the outset we should remind our-

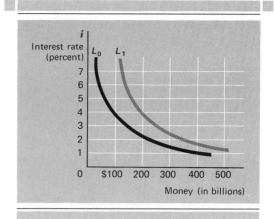

FIGURE 12-2 CHANGES IN THE DEMAND FOR MONEY: SHIFTS IN THE MONEY DEMAND CURVE

Changes in the demand for money are represented by shifts in the money demand curve, such as from L_0 to L_1. Shifts are caused by changes in one or more of the other things assumed constant when we move along a demand curve. Among these other things, the economy's total income is particularly important because when total income rises, it increases the transactions demand and the precautionary demand for money, and has the opposite effect when it declines. Therefore, an increase in total income shifts the demand curve for money rightward, such as from L_0 to L_1. A decline in total income would shift it leftward, such as from L_1 to L_0.

Changes in the quantity of money demanded are represented by movement along a fixed money demand curve. Such movement occurs when the interest rate changes, all other things remaining the same.

selves that the supply of money and the demand for money are measured as stocks, not flows.

EQUILIBRIUM AND DISEQUILIBRIUM

Suppose that money demand and supply are represented by the demand curve L and supply curve M shown in Figure 12-4. The supply or stock of money made available by the Federal Reserve System amounts to $300 billion. Given the demand curve L, the quantity of money demanded will equal $300 billion only if the interest rate equals 6 percent, corresponding to the

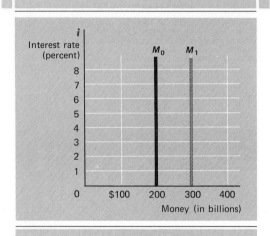

FIGURE 12-3 THE MONEY SUPPLY CURVE

The fixed supply or stock of money available to satisfy demand may be represented by a vertical supply curve. (The fact that the supply curve is vertical means that the money supply is unresponsive to the interest rate.)

For example, M_0 represents a stock of money equal to $200 billion. If the Fed were to increase the money supply by $100 billion, the money supply curve would be shifted rightward from M_0 to M_1. A decrease in the money supply would be represented by a leftward shift in the money supply curve, such as from M_1 to M_0.

intersection of L and M at point e. Hence, 6 percent is the equilibrium level of the interest rate. If the interest rate were higher or lower than this, the money market would be in disequilibrium, and market forces would move the interest rate back to the 6 percent equilibrium level.

Interest Rate Below the Equilibrium Level. For example, if the interest rate were 4 percent, the quantity of money demanded would equal $500 billion, represented by point d on the demand curve. At this interest rate, there would be an excess demand for money of $200 billion (equal to the $500 billion demanded minus the $300 billion supplied). This excess demand is represented by the distance between c and d in Figure 12-4. In their attempts to obtain more

money people try to convert other assets, such as bonds, into money by selling them. While each individual thinks he or she will be able to get more money in this way, obviously society as a whole cannot increase the amount of money it has. A seller of securities gains the money balances that the buyer of the securities loses, so the total money supply is unaltered. The total amount of money available is fixed at $300 billion, and every bit of this is always held by somebody.

Consequently, as people try to sell bonds for money, they only succeed in pushing bond prices down. This means that the interest rate will rise. When the interest rate rises, the quantity of money demanded declines (as represented by the movement up along the demand curve away from point d), and the amount by which money demand exceeds money supply gets smaller. When will this process stop? When bond prices have fallen far enough to raise the interest rate level to 6 percent. At this point people will demand, or be satisfied to hold, just that quantity of money that is supplied (as represented by the intersection at point e of the money demand curve D and the money supply curve M).

Interest Rate Above the Equilibrium Level. Alternatively, what if the interest rate is above the equilibrium level of 6 percent? Suppose it is 9 percent. At this level, the quantity of money demanded equals $100 billion (represented by point a in Figure 12-4). There is an excess supply of money amounting to $200 billion (equal to the $300 billion supplied minus the $100 billion demanded), represented by the distance between points a and b. Of course, every bit of the $300 billion of money supplied would be held by people. But at an interest rate of 9 percent, this is more than people desire to hold. Consequently, people will try to convert their excess money holdings into other assets, such as bonds. The attempts to buy bonds will cause bond prices to rise and the interest rate to fall. As the interest rate falls, the quantity of money demanded increases (represented by the movement down along the demand curve away from point a), and the excess supply of money gets smaller. Finally, when bond prices have risen

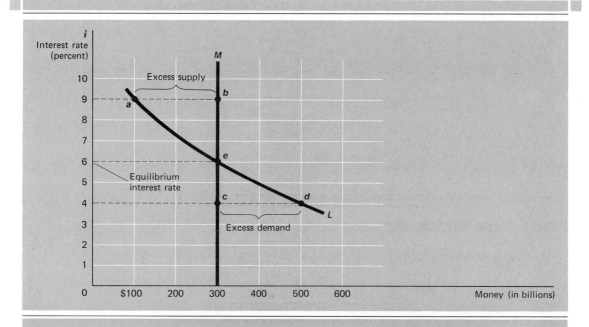

FIGURE 12-4 THE MONEY MARKET: EQUILIBRIUM AND DISEQUILIBRIUM

Money market equilibrium occurs at that interest rate at which the money demand curve L intersects the money supply curve M at point e, corresponding to a 6 percent interest rate in this case.

At interest rates below the equilibrium level, there is an excess demand for money. For example, at a 4 percent interest rate the excess demand for money amounts to $200 billion, which is represented by the distance between c and d. In their attempts to get more money people will try to sell bonds, pushing bond prices down and the interest rate up until it reaches the 6 percent equilibrium level.

At interest rates above the equilibrium level, there is an excess supply of money. For example, at a 9 percent interest rate the excess supply of money amounts to $200 billion, which is represented by the distance between a and b. In their attempts to reduce their holdings of money people will try to buy bonds, pushing bond prices up and the interest rate down until it reaches 6 percent, the equilibrium level.

far enough to lower the interest rate level to 6 percent, the money market will be in equilibrium. At a 6 percent interest rate, the $300 billion money supply is just the amount people desire to hold.

CHANGES IN THE MONEY SUPPLY

What happens when there is a change in the money supply? Suppose the Federal Reserve buys government bonds in the open market and that the increase in bank reserves gives rise to the deposit expansion and money creation process described in the last chapter. Suppose the

resulting increase in the money supply amounts to $200 billion—an increase from $300 billion to $500 billion, as represented by the rightward shift in the money supply curve from M_0 to M_1 in Figure 12-5.

Before the money supply increase, the equilibrium interest rate in the money market was 6 percent, determined by the intersection of the money supply curve M_0 and the money demand curve L at point e. However, once the money supply curve has shifted rightward to M_1, an interest rate of 6 percent will produce an excess supply of money equal to $200 billion. This ex-

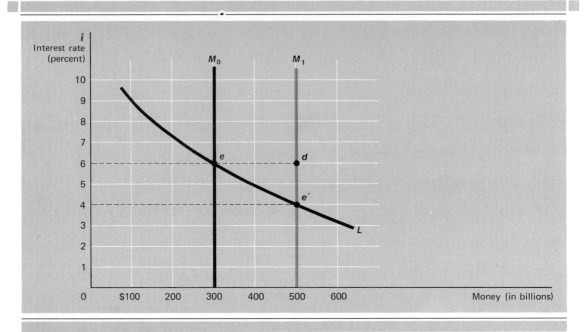

FIGURE 12-5 A CHANGE IN THE MONEY SUPPLY

An increase in the money supply is represented by a rightward shift in the money supply curve, a decrease by a leftward shift.

A $200 billion dollar increase in the money supply is represented here by the rightward shift in the money supply curve from M_0 to M_1. Initially the equilibrium interest rate is 6 percent, determined by the intersection at point e of the money supply curve M_0 and money demand curve L. However, after the increase there is an excess supply of money represented by the distance between e and d. Bond prices are pushed up as people attempt to convert their excess money holdings into bonds. This process continues until bond prices have risen far enough to lower the interest rate to 4 percent, the rate at which money demand and supply are once again equal. This new equilibrium is represented by the intersection of the money supply curve M_1 and money demand curve L at point e'.

Now you should be able to explain what happens if the initial equilibrium is given by the intersection of M_1 and L at e' and there is a reduction in the money supply, represented by a leftward shift in the money supply curve from M_1 to M_0.

cess supply is represented by the distance between e and d. It will lead to a rise in bond prices and a fall in the interest rate in exactly the manner we have already examined. Equilibrium in the money market will be restored when the interest rate has fallen to 4 percent, determined by the intersection at point e' of the money supply curve M_1 and the money demand curve L. (Starting from this position, describe the reverse process that would occur if the money supply were reduced $200 billion, represent-ed by a leftward shift in the money supply curve from M_1 to M_0.)

CHANGES IN THE DEMAND FOR MONEY

Now let's consider the effect on the money market of a shift in the money demand curve. We have already seen that a change in total income can cause such a shift. Suppose the money market is initially in the equilibrium position determined by the intersection of the money demand curve L_0 and the money supply

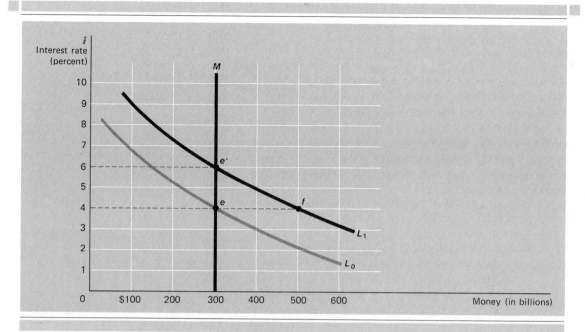

FIGURE 12-6 A CHANGE IN MONEY DEMAND

An increase in money demand is represented by a rightward shift in the money demand curve from L_0 to L_1. Initially the equilibrium interest rate is 4 percent, determined by the intersection at point e of the money supply curve M and the money demand curve L_0. However, after the increase there is an excess demand for money represented by the distance between e and f. Bond prices are pushed down as people sell them to obtain more money. This process continues until bond prices have fallen far enough to raise the interest rate to 6 percent, where money demand and supply are once again equal. This new equilibrium is represented by the intersection of the money supply curve M and money demand curve L_1 at point e'.

Now you should be able to explain what happens if the initial equilibrium is given by the intersection of M and L_1 at e' and there is a reduction in money demand, represented by a leftward shift in the money demand curve from L_1 to L_0.

curve M at point e in Figure 12–6. The quantity of money is $300 billion, and the equilibrium interest rate is 4 percent.

Now suppose that total income increases. This causes an increase in the demand for money, due to an increase in the transactions and precautionary demands for money. The money demand curve shifts rightward from L_0 to L_1. At the initial 4 percent interest rate, there is now an excess demand for money amounting to $200 billion, represented by the distance between e and f. As people try to obtain money they sell bonds, pushing bond prices down and the inter-

est rate up. This process continues until the interest rate has risen to 6 percent, represented by the intersection of the demand curve L_1 and the money supply curve M at e'. Here the supply and demand for money are once again equal. (Starting from this position, you should be able to describe the reverse process that would occur if total income were to decline sufficiently to shift the demand curve leftward from L_1 to L_0.)

While the precautionary demand for money is influenced by changes in total income, it is also affected by changes in people's general sense of security. If people become less secure and, therefore, more cautious, the precautionary demand for money increases, causing a rightward shift in the demand curve for money, such as that shown in Figure 12-6. A decline in cautiousness has the opposite effect.

Summary: Money Demand and Supply and the Interest Rate

In sum, *the Keynesian view argues that there are three basic sources of money demand: the transactions demand, the precautionary demand, and the speculative demand. These three combined make up the demand for money as represented by the demand curve for money. The money supply is determined by the Federal Reserve System. The demand for money together with the supply of money jointly determine the equilibrium rate of interest in the money market.*

■ CHECKPOINT 12-1

Which of the following would have the greatest effect on the interest rate: (a) an increase in money demand accompanied by an increase in money supply, (b) an increase in money demand alone, (c) an increase in money demand accompanied by a decrease in money supply? Illustrate each of these cases—(a), (b), and (c)—graphically. How do you think the demand curve for money would be affected if people were to revise upward their notions of the normal level of the interest rate? How do you think the demand curve for money would be affected if people became more uncertain about their jobs, say, as the result of the onset of a recession? Why?

ROLE OF THE MONEY MARKET IN TOTAL INCOME DETERMINATION

We are now ready to combine our understanding of the workings of the money market with the Keynesian analysis of income determination that we developed in Chapters 8 and 9. We will then be able to examine the role of money in the determination of total income, output, employment, and the price level. We will also have a better understanding of the reasoning behind monetary policy—the Federal Reserve System's regulation of the economy's money supply for the purpose of promoting economic stability and maximum output and employment with a minimum of inflation.

Our first step in putting the pieces together is to show the relationship between the money market, the interest rate, and the level of investment expenditures in the economy. We will then be able to examine the relationship between the money market and the economy's total demand for goods and services and, hence, the relationship between the money supply provided by the Fed and the level of total spending and income in the economy.

Money, Interest, and Investment

What is the relationship between the money market and investment expenditures? To answer this we first recall the relationship between the interest rate and investment expenditures discussed in Chapter 7. We will then see how the interest rate serves to link the money market and the level of investment expenditures.

INVESTMENT AND THE INTEREST RATE

In Chapter 7 we argued that the interest rate is the cost to the firm of funds invested in capital goods. If such funds are borrowed from outside the firm, the cost of borrowing is the interest rate that must be paid to lenders. If the funds are generated internally, the cost is the forgone interest the firm could have earned by lending the funds to someone else.

Interest Rate Versus Expected Rate of Return. When a firm considers whether or not to purchase or invest in a capital good, it must compare its expected rate of return on the capital good with the interest rate. If the firm is going to use its own funds, the two relevant choices are either to lend the funds to some other party or to invest them in the capital good. If the expected rate of return is higher than the interest rate, the firm can earn more by investing internally generated funds in the capital good than by lending them out. The firm will earn the difference between the expected rate of return on the capital good and the interest rate. Similarly, if the firm borrows outside funds to

ECONOMIC THINKERS

MILTON FRIEDMAN
1912–

Friedman, along with John Kenneth Galbraith and Paul Samuelson, is one of the best-known contemporary United States economists. He was awarded the Nobel Prize for Economics in 1976. Friedman has spent most of his career at the University of Chicago, where he is Paul Snowden Russell Distinguished Service Professor Emeritus.

Friedman is perhaps best known to the public for his "monetarist" views, which put emphasis on the importance of the money supply in the economy, and for his view that the role of government should be severely limited. He thinks that, in recent years, monetary policy has been given less attention than it deserves. Fiscal (Keynesian) policy is, in his view, less effective than monetary policy, which influences the amount of money in circulation.

Friedman maintains that the general prosperity since World War II has not been due to "fine tuning" by the Council of Economic Advisers and others, or to various countercyclical devices, but to the fact that the great economic errors of the interwar period were largely avoided, especially severe reductions in the stock of money. Friedman holds that neither monetary nor fiscal policy will eliminate minor business fluctuations. Consequently, an automatic policy designed to increase the money supply by some given figure each year would be far superior to actions of the Fed, or to policies devised by the Council. This automatic policy would work much more effectively if accompanied by meaningful efforts to reduce price rigidity stemming from monopolistic elements in the economy. Furthermore, he believes, a modest but steady increase in the money supply is the best way to try to maintain effective demand at the level of full employment.

Friedman's other claim to fame is his frequent questioning of most governmental policies designed to stimulate or regulate economic activity. Friedman would largely confine the government to the role of rule maker and umpire. Under capitalism, government must provide a stable framework within which economic arrangements can be carried on.

Friedman sees these "rules" as having to do largely with property rights, contracts, and the provision of the money supply. The role of umpire is played by the police, the courts, and the monetary authorities.

Friedman accepts three cases in which government power can be reasonably used: (1) in cases of "technical monopoly," such as telephone or power companies, where it is clearly impracticable or inefficient to rely on a number of competing smaller firms to control prices; (2) to control "neighborhood effects," that is, external diseconomies which arise from the action of one party which damages others, such as smoke, pollution, and so forth, since the traditional framework of capitalism has no mechanism to solve this problem; (3) and in cases of mental incompetence or immaturity. In the last instance, Friedman recognizes that voluntary action would be preferable, but cannot be relied upon.

FOR FURTHER READING
Among Friedman's major works are: *Price Theory: A Provisional Text* (1962), *A Monetary History of the United States* (co-authored with Anna J. Schwartz, 1963), *The Optimum Quantity of Money and Other Essays* (1969), *A Theory of the Consumption Function* (1957), and *Essays in Positive Economics* (1953).

---

invest in the capital good, it will earn exactly the same difference—the difference between the expected rate of return on the capital good and the interest rate that must be paid on the borrowed funds. However, if the expected rate of return on the capital good is less than the interest rate, it will not pay to invest in the capital good.

Expected Rate of Return on a Capital Good.
What is the expected rate of return? *The ex-pected rate of return is the amount of money a firm expects to earn per year on funds invested in a capital good expressed as a percent of the funds invested.*

What determines the expected rate of return on a capital good? Profit, or the anticipation of profit—as noted in Chapter 7. For example, suppose that the annual revenue anticipated from the sale of goods and services produced with the aid of a capital good amounts to $500. Suppose that the anticipated annual costs of production, *excluding* the interest rate cost of the funds invested in the capital good, equals $400. The difference, in this case $100, is the amount of money the firm expects to earn per year on the funds invested in the capital good. If the price of the capital good is $1,000, the expected rate of return on the $1,000 investment in the capital good is 10 percent—$100 ÷ $1,000, expressed as a percentage.

If the interest rate is 9 percent, the firm could borrow the $1,000 at a cost of $90 per year. Alternatively, $1,000 of internal funds could earn $90 per year if lent out at 9 percent. Either way the firm will come out ahead $10 per year if it invests in the capital good. The capital good is therefore a profitable investment, and the firm should buy it. If on the other hand the interest rate is 11 percent, the same calculations show that the firm will lose $10 per year if it invests $1,000 in the capital good. The good will not be a profitable investment, and the firm should not buy it. In sum, *a firm will invest in a capital good if its expected rate of return is higher than the interest rate. It will not invest if the expected rate of return is less than the interest rate.*

Inverse Relationship Between Interest Rate and Investment Spending. At any given time a typical firm has a number of investment projects it could undertake—build a new plant, buy a new fleet of trucks, build a new loading dock, and so on. The firm forms an expectation of what the rate of return would be for each of these projects. The lower the interest rate, the larger is the number of these projects having expected rates of return higher than the interest

rate. Hence, the lower the interest rate, the greater the amount of investment expenditure by the firm. Of course, the higher the interest rate, the smaller the number of projects with expected rates of return above the interest rate—therefore, the smaller the amount of investment expenditure by the firm.

If we consider all the firms in the economy, the total amount of investment spending will increase as the interest rate decreases. This inverse, or negative, relationship between the interest rate and investment is illustrated by the downward-sloping investment demand curve I_d in Figure 12-7. *The investment demand curve shows the total dollar amount of investment projects, or capital goods formation, that the economy's firms will demand or desire to do at each interest rate.* The investment demand curve is just another way of representing the relationship between the interest rate and investment spending that we discussed in Chapter 7 (Figure 7-8).

THE MONEY MARKET AND THE LEVEL OF INVESTMENT

Now we can see how the money market and the level of investment spending in the economy are related. The connecting link between them is the interest rate. This is illustrated in Figure 12-8, where the money market is shown in part a, and the investment demand curve is shown in part b.

Suppose initially that the money supply provided by the Federal Reserve System amounts to roughly $215 billion, represented by the money supply curve M_0 in part a. Given the money demand curve L, the equilibrium interest rate in the money market is 7 percent, determined by the intersection of M_0 and L at point a. The number of investment projects with expected rates of return greater than 7 percent is such that there will be $300 billion of investment spending when the interest rate is at that level, corresponding to point a' on the investment demand curve I_d in part b.

Suppose the Fed increases the money supply (by open market purchases or by lowering reserve requirements or by lowering the discount rate or some combination of these) from $215

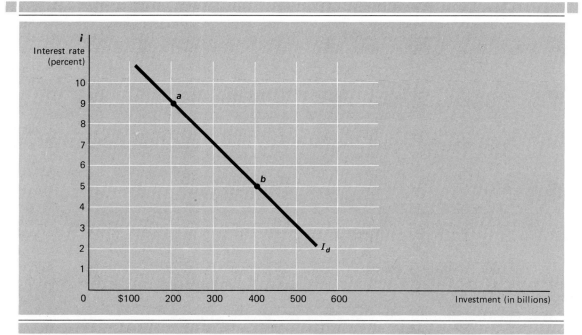

FIGURE 12-7 THE INVESTMENT DEMAND CURVE: INVESTMENT SPENDING VARIES INVERSELY WITH THE INTEREST RATE

The investment demand curve I_d is downward sloping, reflecting the inverse, or negative, relationship between the level of the interest rate and the amount of investment expenditure in the economy. For instance, if the interest rate were 9 percent, there would be $200 billion of investment spending, corresponding to point a on the investment demand curve I_d. At a lower interest rate, such as 5 percent, the amount of investment spending would be larger, equal to $400 billion, corresponding to point b.

The reason for the inverse relationship between the interest rate and investment is that the lower the interest rate, the larger the number of investment projects that have an expected rate of return greater than the interest rate. The economy's firms will invest in all those projects that are profitable, as represented by the fact that their expected rates of return are higher than the interest rate.

billion to $300 billion. This increase is represented by the rightward shift in the money supply curve from M_0 to M_1 in part a. At the original 7 percent interest rate, there is now an excess supply of money. As people attempt to convert this excess into other assets such as bonds, bond prices rise and the interest rate falls to 6 percent. This is the new equilibrium interest rate represented by the intersection of M_1 and L at point b. The drop in the interest rate from 7 to 6 percent increases the amount of investment spending in the economy by $50 billion to $350 billion, corresponding to point b' on the invest-

ment demand curve I_d. This happens because investment projects with expected rates of return between 6 and 7 percent now become profitable. Therefore, they are undertaken in addition to all those having expected rates of return greater than 7 percent.

In sum, *the Fed can influence the amount of investment spending in the economy through its control over the money supply*. Increases in the money supply lower the interest rate and cause investment spending to increase. Decreases in the money supply raise the interest rate and cause investment spending to decrease.

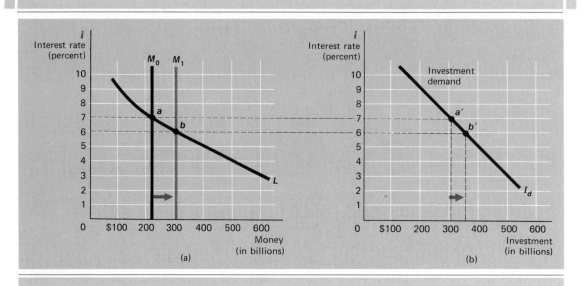

FIGURE 12-8 **THE MONEY MARKET AND INVESTMENT SPENDING ARE LINKED BY THE INTEREST RATE**

The intersection of the money demand and money supply curves in part a determines the equilibrium level of the interest rate. Given the investment demand curve I_d, this interest rate determines the amount of investment spending in part b.

Suppose the money supply provided by the Federal Reserve System amounts to $215 billion, represented by the money supply curve M_0 in part a. The equilibrium interest rate is then 7 percent, determined by the intersection of the money demand curve L and the money supply curve M_0 at point a. The 7 percent interest rate will give rise to $300 billion of investment spending, corresponding to point a' on the investment demand curve I_d in part b.

Suppose the Fed increases the money supply from $215 billion to $300 billion, represented by the rightward shift in the money supply curve from M_0 to M_1 in part a. The interest rate will then fall to a new equilibrium level of 6 percent, determined by the intersection of the money demand curve L and the money supply curve M_1 at point b. This drop in the interest rate will cause an increase in investment spending to $350 billion, corresponding to point b' on the investment demand curve I_d in part b.

Interaction of Money, Total Demand, and Total Income

We know from our discussion in Chapter 8 that investment spending is an important part of total spending in the economy. We saw that it plays a crucial role in determining the level of total demand, which in turn determines the equilibrium level of total income. And we learned that changes in investment spending cause even larger changes in total income because of the multiplier effect. We are now in a position to introduce the money market into that analysis of income determination and see

how money market equilibrium and the level of total income are jointly determined to give general equilibrium in the whole economy.

GENERAL EQUILIBRIUM

Recall that the level of total income in the economy is a major determinant of money demand and, hence, the position of the money demand curve. The money supply (determined by the Fed) and money demand curves determine the level of the interest rate, which in turn determines the level of investment spending, as shown in Figure 12-8. However, we know that the level of investment spending determines the level of total income via the multiplier (Chapter 8). This level of total income in turn determines the position of the money demand curve in the money market, which in turn determines the interest rate. We have come full circle—we are back to where we started. We see that the interest rate and the total income level are mutually interdependent. The level of one is interconnected with the level of the other.

Interconnecting Links Between Money Market, Investment, and Income. These interconnecting links between the money market, the level of investment, and the level of total income are illustrated in Figure 12-9. Parts a and b of Figure 12-9 are the same as parts a and b of Figure 12-8. Part c shows the economy's total demand schedule for goods and services. Recall that this demand schedule is obtained by adding the level of consumption expenditures C that would take place at each level of total income to the level of investment expenditures I. The level of investment expenditures is determined by the interest rate in part b. The economy's equilibrium level of total income is determined by the intersection of the total demand schedule with the 45° line in part c. And this level of total income determines the position of the money demand curve in part a.

For the whole economy to be in general equilibrium the following must be true: the level of the interest rate determined in part a determines a certain level of investment in part b. That level of investment will in turn determine a certain level of total income in part c. And that level of total income will determine a position of the money demand curve in part a that combines with the money supply curve to give the interest rate that we started with. In Figure 12-9 the equilibrium level of the interest rate is 6 percent (part a). A 6 percent interest rate determines a level of investment I of $350 billion (part b). This amount of investment gives rise to a total demand schedule D = C + I (part c) that determines a total income level of $1,500 billion. This level of total income determines the position of the money demand curve shown in part a of Figure 12-9. This money demand curve combined with the money supply curve (deter-

mined by the Fed) determines an interest rate level equal to 6 percent.

The Uniqueness of General Equilibrium. *The combination of interest rate and total income that give rise to general equilibrium in the economy is unique.* For example, in Figure 12-9 general equilibrium occurs only when the interest rate is 6 percent and the level of total income is $1,500 billion. To convince ourselves of this, suppose we start with a lower interest rate in part a, such as 5 percent. A 5 percent interest rate in part b would mean that investment spending would now be larger, $400 billion instead of $350 billion. But a higher level of investment spending would mean that the total demand schedule in part c would be shifted upward. This upward shift would give rise to a level of total income greater than $1,500 billion. But a level of total income higher than $1,500 would shift the money demand curve in part a rightward, giving rise to an interest rate greater than 6 percent. We have obviously not come back to the interest rate level of 5 percent that we started with. We would find the same thing to be true whatever level of interest rate below 6 percent we consider.

Suppose we start with a higher interest rate in part a, such as 7 percent. A 7 percent interest rate in part b would mean that investment spending would now be lower, $300 billion instead of $350 billion. A lower level of investment spending would shift the total demand schedule in part c downward. Total income would now be less than $1,500 billion. A level of total income less than $1,500 billion means that the money demand curve in part a would be shifted leftward so that the interest rate would be less than 6 percent. We have come back to an interest rate lower than the 7 percent level we started with. We would find the same problem at any interest rate we consider above 6 percent.

We conclude that general equilibrium prevails in the economy of Figure 12-9 only when the interest rate equals 6 percent and the level of total income is $1,500 billion.

In sum, *the interest rate determines, and is determined by, the level of total income. Or, equivalently, the level of total income determines, and is*

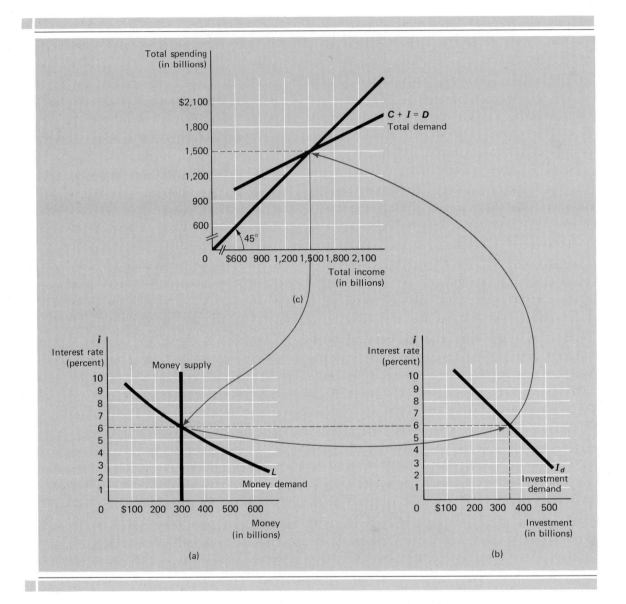

determined by, the interest rate. General equilibrium requires that interest rate that will determine a level of total income that will in turn determine just that level of the interest rate.

CHANGE IN THE MONEY SUPPLY: PARTIAL VERSUS GENERAL EQUILIBRIUM

We have seen how the money market and the determination of the level of total income fit to-gether to give general equilibrium. Using this framework, we can now get a better idea of how the Federal Reserve can affect the economy by changing the money supply. In the process we can also examine the nature of the distinction between partial and general equilibrium analysis.

The general equilibrium position of the economy shown in Figure 12-9 is reproduced in the upper half of Figure 12-10. The money supply

FIGURE 12-9 TOTAL INCOME AND THE INTEREST RATE ARE JOINTLY DETERMINED IN GENERAL EQUILIBRIUM

For the whole economy to be in general equilibrium the following must be true: the level of the interest rate (6 percent) determined in the money market in part a will determine a certain level of investment ($350 billion), given the investment demand curve in part b. That level of investment will in turn determine the position of the total demand schedule ($C + I$) in part c, which in turn will determine a certain level of total income ($1,200 billion). And that level of total income will determine a position of the money demand curve in part a that combines with the money supply curve (determined by the Fed) to give the interest rate (6 percent) that we started with.

If we start with any other level of the interest rate in part a, and follow through the interconnecting links indicated by the arrows, we will not come back to the interest rate from which we started. Hence, the combination of the interest rate and total income corresponding to general equilibrium is unique.

curve M_0 (representing a money supply of $300 billion) and money demand curve L_0 (corresponding to a total income of $1,500 billion) determine a 6 percent interest rate. Given the position of the investment demand curve, this interest rate in turn gives rise to a level of investment of $350 billion. This amount of investment spending determines the position of the total demand schedule $C + I$, which in turn determines the equilibrium level of total income of $1,500 billion. This level of total income determines the position of the money demand curve L_0, which together with M_0 determines the 6 percent interest rate.

Partial Equilibrium Analysis. Now suppose the Fed increases the money supply by $200 billion (from $300 billion to $500 billion), represented by the rightward shift in the money supply curve from M_0 to M_1. At the initial interest rate of 6 percent, there would now be an excess supply of money. This excess causes the interest rate to fall from 6 percent to 4 percent, determined by the intersection of M_1 and L_0. The decline in the interest rate from 6 percent to 4 percent means that there would be an increase in the number of investment projects having expected rates of return greater than the interest rate. The resulting increase in investment spending ΔI (change in I) would amount to $100 billion (a rise from $350 billion to $450 billion). This increase would cause the total demand schedule to rise from $C + I$ to

$C + I + \Delta I$, and total income to increase from $1,500 billion to $1,700 billion.

This is only a partial equilibrium analysis however. *In* **partial equilibrium analysis** *we focus on a change in one market and its consequences for that market, and possibly a few others. All other markets are assumed to be unchanged. In* **general equilibrium analysis** *we consider the adjustments that a change in one market may cause in each and every other market.*

Our analysis of the consequences of a money supply change in the upper half of Figure 12–10 is a partial equilibrium analysis because it does not take into account the effect the rise in total income will have on the money demand curve and hence on the interest rate. A general equilibrium analysis of the consequences of the $200 billion increase in the money supply from M_0 to M_1 must take account of this effect.

General Equilibrium Analysis. The general equilibrium analysis is shown in the lower half of Figure 12–10. As the interest rate falls and increased investment causes a rise in total income, the rise in total income causes the money demand curve to shift rightward at the same time. This shift in the money demand curve keeps the interest rate from falling as far as it does when the shift is ignored, as in the partial equilibrium analysis in the upper half of Figure 12–10. Consequently the rise in investment $\Delta I'$ is now less, amounting to only $50 billion.

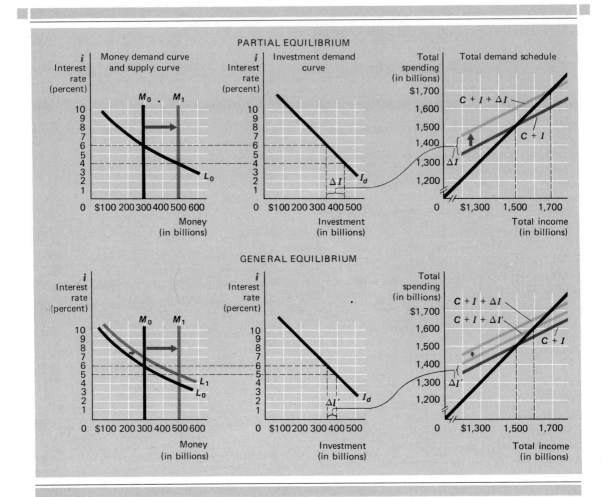

FIGURE 12-10 MONEY SUPPLY CHANGE: PARTIAL VERSUS GENERAL EQUILIBRIUM ANALYSIS

The top half of the figure shows the partial equilibrium analysis of the effects of a $200 billion increase in the money supply. The interest rate falls from 6 percent to 4 percent, causing a rise in investment ΔI of $100 billion, which in turn causes the total demand schedule to shift upward from $C + I$ to $C + I + \Delta I$. This upward shift in turn causes total income to rise from $1,500 billion to $1,700 billion. This analysis is partial because it doesn't allow for the effect of the rise in total income on money demand and hence on the interest rate.

The bottom half of the figure shows the general equilibrium analysis of the effects of the same $200 billion money supply increase. Now the interest rate falls a smaller amount, from 6 percent to 5 percent, because of allowance for the fact that the rise in total income causes the money demand curve to shift rightward from L_0 to L_1. Because of this, the rise in investment $\Delta I'$ of $50 billion is smaller. Hence, the total demand schedule shifts upward a smaller amount, from $C + I$ to $C + I + \Delta I'$, and therefore the rise in total income is less, from $1,500 billion to $1,600 billion.

The resulting upward shift in the total demand schedule is now smaller—from $C + I$ to $C + I + \Delta I'$. The rise in total income is therefore smaller—from \$1,500 billion to \$1,600 billion. The position of the money demand curve at L_1 corresponds to (is determined by) the \$1,600 billion total income level. In the general equilibrium analysis, the level of the interest rate falls to 5 percent, a higher level than the 4 percent of the partial equilibrium analysis.

In conclusion, our analysis indicates that *an increase in the money supply causes a decrease in the interest rate and an increase in the level of total income. A decrease in the money supply will have the opposite effect, causing an increase in the interest rate and a decrease in the level of total income.*

Easy Money Versus Tight Money. When the Federal Reserve increases the money supply, it is often said to be following an easy-money policy, or to be "easing credit." This manner of speaking reflects the fact that the fall in the interest rate makes it cheaper to borrow, or to get credit. An easy-money policy stimulates the economy because it leads to a rise in total income. A tight-money policy, or a policy of "credit tightening," refers to the opposite situation—a reduction in the money supply leading to a rise in the interest rate and a decline in total income. This is the type of situation referred to in the news item at the beginning of this chapter. There it is reported that the Fed "has slammed the brakes on the growth of the nation's money supply." If this tight-money policy continues, many analysts worry that there may be "a recession before the end of the year."

■ CHECKPOINT 12-2

Suppose the investment demand curve in Figure 12-8, part b, is pivoted clockwise about point a' so that it is now steeper. Given the increase in the money supply from M_0 to M_1 shown in Figure 12-8, part a, will the resulting increase in investment spending in part b now be larger or smaller than before? Suppose the money demand curve L in part a is pivoted clockwise about point a so that it

is now steeper. Given the money supply increase from M_0 to M_1, will the resulting increase in investment spending (given the original investment demand curve I shown in part b) now be larger or smaller than before? In the lower half of Figure 12-10, if money demand were more sensitive to a change in total income (that is, if the change in the transactions and precautionary demand for money is greater per dollar of change in total income), would the increase in total income resulting from the increase in the money supply from M_0 to M_1 be larger or smaller than before?

SUMMARY

1. In the Keynesian view there are three basic components of the demand for money: the transactions demand, the precautionary demand, and the speculative demand. The transactions and precautionary demands for money vary directly with the level of total income. The speculative demand for money varies inversely (negatively) with the level of the interest rate.

2. Both because of the speculative demand for money and the fact that the interest rate is the opportunity cost of holding money, the money demand curve slopes downward. Because of the transactions and precautionary demands for money, the money demand curve is shifted rightward by an increase in total money income and leftward by a decrease.

3. The money supply curve is vertical, representing the assumption that the Federal Reserve System controls the money supply. The money supply and demand curves jointly determine the equilibrium interest rate in the money market. An increase in the money supply lowers the equilibrium interest rate, a decrease raises it.

4. Businesses will invest in those capital goods having an expected rate of return greater than the interest rate. The lower the interest rate, the larger the amount of investment spending that is profitable by this criterion. Hence, the investment demand curve slopes downward because more investment spend-

ing will take place at low than at high interest rates.

5. The money market is linked to the level of investment spending by the interest rate. The level of investment spending determines the level of total income via the multiplier. The level of total income in turn determines the position of the money demand curve in the money market. Hence, given the money supply, the interest rate determines and is determined by the level of total income in general equilibrium. There is only one value of the interest rate and one level of total income that gives general equilibrium.

6. An increase in the money supply lowers the interest rate. This increases investment spending, which pushes up the total demand schedule, raising the level of total income via the multiplier effect. The rise in total income pushes the money demand curve rightward causing the interest rate to rise, though not enough to offset the full effects of the initial decrease in the interest rate. A partial equilibrium analysis would ignore the effect on the money demand curve of the rise in total income.

7. Increasing the money supply lowers the interest rate and raises the total income level—this is often referred to as an easy-money policy. Decreasing the money supply raises the interest rate and lowers the total income level—this is often called a tight-money policy.

KEY TERMS AND CONCEPTS
expected rate of return
general equilibrium analysis
partial equilibrium analysis
precautionary demand
speculative demand
transactions demand

QUESTIONS AND PROBLEMS

1. How can it be that when there is an excess supply of money, people hold more than they want, yet when equilibrium is restored, they are content to hold the same amount? Where did the excess go? If there is an excess demand for money, what must be true of people's desired holdings of bonds?

2. How would the money demand curve change if people's demand for money became more sensitive to changes in the interest rate? Show how this would affect the money demand curve L passing through point e in Figure 12-5. Would the money supply increase shown in Figure 12-5 now have a larger or smaller effect on the equilibrium level of the interest rate? Consider the same change in the money demand curve passing through point e in Figure 12-6. If the money demand curve shifts rightward by an amount equal to the distance between e and f, would the rise in the interest rate be greater or less than previously?

3. Using a partial equilibrium analysis, start with the initial equilibrium position in the top half of Figure 12-10 (money supply M_0 equal to $300 billion) and trace through the likely effects of each of the following (indicate the direction of changes where it is not possible to measure the precise magnitudes of changes):
a. The Fed increases the discount rate.
b. The Fed reduces the required reserve ratio.
c. The Fed makes an open market sale of bonds.
d. The Fed reduces the money supply by $75 billion.

4. How would your answers to question 3 be affected if full adjustment in all markets is taken into account—that is, how would the answers in each case be different if a general equilibrium analysis were carried out, instead of a partial equilibrium analysis?

5. In Figure 12-10, how would the slopes of the money demand curve L_0 and the investment demand curve I_d have to be different for the $200 billion increase in the money supply to have a larger impact on total income? What implications do the slopes of the money demand and investment demand curves have for the effectiveness of monetary policy?

6. Link up the analysis in the top half of Figure 12-10 with the analysis in Chapter 8 (Figure 8-7), and describe how monetary policy affects the level of real output Q and the general price level p.

■ NEWS ITEM FOR YOUR ANALYSIS ■

FEDERAL RESERVE TIGHTENS CREDIT A NOTCH

NEW YORK, July 21—The Federal Reserve System has tightened its credit reins another notch to try to dampen the economy's persistent inflation and slow the unusually rapid growth of the money supply, money market analysts said.

"I think we can say with a strong degree of assurance that the Fed has tightened by a notch," David M. Jones, vice-president and economist of Aubrey G. Lanston & Co., said. Alan C. Lerner, senior vice-president of Bankers Trust Co., said he believes the Fed "has given some indication that they have moved (the target rate) to 8 percent." Donald E. Maude, vice-president and director of research at Merrill Lynch Government Securities, Inc., notes that borrowings from the Fed's discount window on Wednesday rose to $1.5 billion on a daily average basis, "a level which in the past has proven sufficiently high to warrant a discount rate increase."

In a related development, money market analysts' forecasts of a decline in the nation's money supply for the week ending July 12 proved correct. Figures released yesterday through the Federal Reserve Bank of New York showed M_1, the basic money supply, declined $2 billion in the week.

Merrill Lynch's Mr. Maude claimed the money supply figures "provided credence" to the Fed's tightening move since they showed "only a partial washout" of the unusually large increase in M_1 for the week ended July 5. "This $2 billion decline quite obviously wasn't sufficient enough to bring the M_1 growth rate for the June–July period back within acceptable bounds," he said.

QUESTIONS

1. In terms of a diagram like Figure 12–10, describe the role that the discount window appears to be playing in the events described here—is it contributing to inflationary pressures or not?

2. In terms of a diagram like Figure 12–10, describe the effect that the possible discount rate increase mentioned by Mr. Maude should have on the economy.

3. In terms of a diagram like Figure 12–10, describe the implications of the fact that there has been " 'only a partial washout' of the unusually large increase in M_1 for the week ended July 5."

FOUR

INFLATION, UNEMPLOYMENT, ECONOMIC STABILITY, AND GROWTH

13

MONETARY AND FISCAL POLICY: KEYNESIAN AND MONETARIST VIEWS

**FED CHIEF DENIES THERE'S ACCORD
TO SWAP EASIER CREDIT FOR A TOUGHER FISCAL POLICY**

WASHINGTON, June 8—The Federal Reserve Board doesn't have an agreement with the White House to relax its tight monetary policy in exchange for a tougher fiscal policy, says Fed chairman G. William Miller.

Mr. Miller said that Fed action to relax interest rates "can't be done as a quid pro quo." Speaking before a National Press Club audience, he said, "there isn't any agreement between the White House and the Fed." But he went on to emphasize, as he has before, that "to the extent that there is greater discipline on fiscal policy" there is "less pressure on monetary policy."

Almost since he became Fed chairman, Mr. Miller has stressed that the Fed can't fight inflation without help. The Fed chairman has been credited with helping convince President Carter to pare the budget deficit to a red-ink figure of $53 billion. He may be behind current administration efforts to narrow it even further.

Yesterday, Mr. Miller once again called for a fiscal budget deficit of "$50 billion or less" in the coming fiscal year and a balanced federal budget by fiscal 1982.

We have now developed almost all the tools needed to examine the major views on the effectiveness of monetary and fiscal policy. The basic question is, To what extent can monetary and fiscal policy smooth out economic fluctuations (the so-called business cycle) and prod the economy closer to full employment without excessive inflation?

There is in fact a spectrum of views on this issue, and most economists see this spectrum shading into the Keynesian point of view at one end and the monetarist point of view at the other. In this chapter we will first focus on the basic reasons why these two camps hold differing opinions on the effectiveness of monetary policy. We will then examine why and how they disagree over the merits of fiscal policy. It will be seen that certain kinds of fiscal actions have monetary overtones that make it difficult to distinguish purely fiscal from purely monetary effects. We will then be better able to understand the conflicts, such as those reported in the news item, that often arise between monetary and fiscal policy.

IDEOLOGICAL DIFFERENCES BETWEEN KEYNESIANS AND MONETARISTS

Before beginning our discussion of monetary and fiscal policy, it should be recognized that monetarists and modern-day Keynesians (sometimes called neo-Keynesians) typically have differing political views and opinions on the proper role and size of government in our economy. Monetarists tend to favor a more laissez faire or free-market economy, with government intervening mainly to restrain monopoly and other forms of anticompetitive market practices. They believe that the market system generally does a good job of efficiently allocating resources to answer the basic economic questions of what to produce, how to produce it, and for whom. Those who adhere more to the Keynesian point of view tend to be less satisfied with the results provided by the market mechanism in a number of areas of the economy. They believe that the government can and should play a more effective and active role in correcting the shortcomings of the market mechanism. Monetarists, on the other hand, tend to view government as generally inefficient, bureaucratically cumbersome, and prone to making large mistakes when dealing with problems. Moreover, they generally fear the political implications of increasing government's control over the economy's decision-making process. They argue that increased government control poses a threat to personal freedoms and puts a damper on individual initiative.

In view of these ideological differences, it should not be surprising that monetarists are leery of fiscal policy as a stabilization tool. We have already discussed (in Chapter 9) the timing problems associated with discretionary fiscal policy. Quite aside from this, however, monetarists fear that fiscal policy gives rise to too much direct government intervention in the economy. On the other hand, Keynesians feel government intervention is needed to solve other kinds of social and economic problems. So, why shouldn't the government also use its spending and taxation authority to attack the problems of economic instability, unemployment, and inflation? Besides, Keynesians see the Great Depression of the 1930s as evidence that the self-regulating forces of the marketplace are not sufficient to ensure that the economy will continuously operate near its full-employment capacity. They also argue that monetary policy alone was incapable of coping with such a depression. In contrast, monetarists see regulation of the money supply as a much more powerful tool for affecting the economy. They argue that the Great Depression was so severe largely because the Fed did a particularly bad job of managing monetary policy. Moreover, monetarists feel comfortable using monetary policy to regulate economic activity. It doesn't require the same direct and potentially extensive government intervention in the economy as fiscal policy.

KEYNESIAN VIEW VERSUS MONETARIST VIEW ON THE ROLE OF MONEY

To what extent can the Fed influence economic activity by regulating the size of the money supply? We noted at the beginning of the previous chapter that economists are not in complete agreement on just how and to what extent the supply of money affects the economy.

As a consequence of the publication of Keynes's *General Theory* in 1936, the mainstream of economic thought came to give less importance to the role of money in the economy than had classical economists. True, the *General Theory* had a lot to say about the role of money. But it was Keynes's novel analysis of how total demand determines total income, output, and

employment, and the potentially key role for fiscal policy in this process, that captured the attention of most economists. (We have seen the bare bones of this aspect of the *General Theory* in Chapters 7, 8, and 9.) These theoretical developments seemed to give economists a much better explanation for the Great Depression of the 1930s than classical economic thought had to offer. Moreover, the *General Theory* seemed to make compelling arguments for the use of fiscal policy to avoid such calamities and to smooth out economic fluctuations in general.

The consensus view of monetary policy that emerged with the growing popularity of Keynesian thought was often summed up as follows: Monetary policy could be effective in curbing inflation and cooling down an overheated economy, but it was not an effective tool for getting the economy out of a recession. During inflationary expansions, the effectiveness of monetary policy was likened to pulling on a string; during recessions, to pushing on a string. This view was largely unchallenged up until the 1960s, when a school of thought known as **monetarism** began to assert itself. The monetarists, largely led by Milton Friedman (winner of the 1976 Nobel Prize in Economics), argue that money plays a much more important role in determining the level of economic activity than is granted to it by the Keynesians. We will now consider some of the main differences between

---

After reading this chapter, you will be able to:

1. State the basic ideological differences between Keynesians and monetarists.
2. Explain the difference between the equation of exchange as a definition and as a theory—the quantity theory of money.
3. Explain the difference between Keynesian and monetarist views on the role of money in our economy.
4. Describe the difference between Keynesian and monetarist views on the extent to which money supply changes affect employment, output, and the price level.
5. Explain the different effects on the economy of pure fiscal policy actions as distinguished from those accompanied by money supply changes.
6. Give reasons why it is often difficult to coordinate monetary and fiscal policy.

these two points of view. We will begin by examining the equation of exchange, a notion that goes back to the classical economists. The equation of exchange will provide a common point of reference for making comparisons between the Keynesian and monetarist points of view.

Monetarism and the Equation of Exchange

The dollar value of the purchases of final goods and services produced by the economy during a year is the economy's money GNP—the GNP expressed in terms of the prices at which the goods are actually purchased. (Recall the distinction between real GNP and money GNP made in Chapter 5.) Each purchase typically requires the buyer to give money in exchange for the good or service provided by the seller. The economy's money supply, its total stock of money, is used to transact all these exchanges during the course of a year.

Money GNP, a flow, is usually several times larger than the economy's money stock. This means that the money stock must be used several times during the year to carry out all the transactions represented by the money GNP. In effect, the money stock must go around the circular flow of money exchanged for goods (discussed in Chapter 3) several times during the course of a year. This idea is given expression by the **equation of exchange**, which is written

$$M \times V = p \times Q$$

In this equation $p \times Q$, price times quantity, is money GNP. For example, if the economy produces nothing but widgets, p would be the price per widget and Q the quantity of widgets produced per year. More realistically, for an economy that produces many kinds of goods, Q may be thought of as real GNP and p as an index of current prices (the prices at which goods are currently bought and sold). M is the economy's money supply. V is the number of times the money stock must "turn over" during a year in order to transact all the purchases of final goods and services that add up to money GNP. In other words, V is the number of times a typical dollar of the money stock must go around the circular flow of money exchanged

for final goods and services during a year. For this reason V is called the velocity of circulation of money, or simply the **velocity** of money.

For example, if the economy's money supply M is \$300 billion, and its money GNP is \$1,500 billion, the equation of exchange would be

$$\begin{array}{ccc} M & V & GNP \\ \$300 \times & 5 & = \$1,500 \end{array}$$

The velocity of money V is therefore 5. This means that the money stock must turn over five times per year. A dollar of the money stock typically would be used five times per year in the purchase of final goods and services.

THE EQUATION OF EXCHANGE AS DEFINITION

The equation of exchange as it stands is true simply by definition. If you know the size of the money supply and the level of the money GNP, you can calculate the value of V. By definition V has to take on whatever value is necessary to maintain the equality between the two sides of the equation $M \times V = p \times Q$. However, suppose you took annual money GNP data and money stock data for a series of years in an economy and calculated the value of velocity for each of those years. If the calculated values of velocity didn't change much from year to year, and from the earlier to the later years, your curiosity should be aroused. You should be even more curious if the same calculations for different economies revealed the same kind of regularity for V.

Regularity in any phenomenon is the watchword of science. When Galileo dropped objects of unequal weight from the same height on the leaning tower of Pisa, he discovered that they always reached the ground at the same time. No matter how different the weights, he always found this to be true. He thus discovered the law of falling bodies. Had he found no regularity in the relationship between the time taken for objects of different weights to reach the ground, his experiments would have been of little interest. It is regularity that leads to the formulation of theories—and often to controversy. Galileo's experiments and his formulation of the law of falling bodies went against the then prevailing opinion that heavier bodies fall faster than light ones. This opinion was so strong that he was forced to resign from his position as professor of mathematics at the University of Pisa.

The story of Galileo gives us some perception on the depth of feeling that often characterizes the clash between monetarist and Keynesian viewpoints about the role of money. Here, too, regularity is a large part of the issue. Monetarists argue that velocity V in the equation of exchange is fairly stable or regular. Those leaning toward the Keynesian point of view dispute this contention. You might well ask why not settle the argument by an appeal to facts—the calculations of velocity already mentioned. As in Galileo's time, facts aren't always convincing. Moreover, the facts about velocity are not as clear-cut as those about falling bodies, as we shall see later.

THE EQUATION OF EXCHANGE AS THEORY: THE QUANTITY THEORY OF MONEY

What does it mean to say that velocity V is stable? It means that V is more than just a symbol that takes on whatever value is necessary to ensure equality between the left- and right-hand sides of the equation of exchange. The classical economists contended that V was reasonably stable because it reflected the institutional characteristics of the economy. These characteristics include the frequency with which people are paid, the organization of banking, and the level of development of the transportation and communications system. They argued that these determinants of the economy's payments mechanism were slow to change and therefore that V was stable. This view of the equation of exchange became known as the **quantity theory of money**.

With the assumption that V is stable, the equation of exchange passes from the realm of definition to that of theory because it enables us to predict the consequences of an event, namely a change in the money supply. (You might want to review the discussion of the characteristics of a theory in Chapter 1.) If the money supply is increased by a certain percent, then money GNP will increase by a like percent. In the ex-

ample above where M equals \$300 billion, V equals 5, the money GNP equals \$1,500 billion, suppose the money supply M is increased from \$300 billion to \$400 billion—a 33 percent increase. If V is stable at a value of 5, money GNP will increase 33 percent, from \$1,500 billion to \$2,000 billion.

MONETARIST VIEW OF THE MONEY TRANSMISSION MECHANISM

Monetarism may be viewed as a sophisticated version of the quantity theory of money. Monetarists contend that the effects of money supply changes on the economy are transmitted through a host of channels, not just via the interest rate route which is so strongly emphasized in the Keynesian point of view. In particular, monetarists argue that an increase in the economy's money supply initially increases the money holdings of consumers and businesses. That is, there is an excess supply of money. The excess money holdings are then spent on goods and services, directly pushing up total demand and money GNP (equal $p \times Q$). Conversely, a decrease in the economy's money supply creates an excess demand for money. In an attempt to increase their money holdings, consumers and businesses cut back on their spending. This causes total demand for goods and services to fall and money GNP to decrease.

In sum, *monetarists tend to believe that the cause-effect transmission from changes in the money supply to changes in money GNP are reasonably direct and tight. That is, in terms of the equation of exchange, monetarists believe that V, the velocity of money, is quite stable. Hence, they argue that changes in the money supply have a fairly direct effect on money GNP.*

An extreme version of monetarism would assume that velocity is an unchanging constant—as in the hypothetical example above where velocity was assumed always to equal 5. If this crude version of monetarism were true, monetary policy would indeed be a powerful and reliable tool for affecting the level of money GNP or total income. The Federal Reserve would know that it could change money GNP by any percentage amount it desired simply by changing the economy's money supply by that percentage amount. However, not even the most ardent monetarists subscribe to the view that velocity is constant.

The Keynesian View and the Equation of Exchange

The Keynesian view of the equation of exchange holds that V, the velocity of money, is much less stable than the monetarists contend. Moreover, the Keynesian view argues that velocity V may in fact move in the opposite direction from changes in the money supply M. Hence, attempts to affect the level of money GNP by changing the money supply are largely thwarted by offsetting changes in velocity.

To understand the Keynesian view of velocity it is necessary to interpret the equation of exchange in terms of the Keynesian transmission mechanism presented in the previous chapter. The Keynesian view that velocity is not very stable is consistent with a particular view of the Keynesian transmission mechanism. Namely, that money demand is quite sensitive to changes in the interest rate while investment demand is not. The implications of this view are illustrated in Figure 13-1. (Note that this figure is similar to Figure 12-10.)

EFFECTS OF A MONEY SUPPLY CHANGE ON MONEY GNP

The top half of Figure 13-1 corresponds more closely to the Keynesian view of the interest rate sensitivity of investment demand and money demand than does the bottom half, or alternative view. For instance, the money demand curve L_1 is less steeply sloped than the money demand curve L_2. Hence, money demand as represented by L_1 is more sensitive to a change in the interest rate (the Keynesian view) than is money demand as represented by L_2 (the alternative view). For example, a drop in the interest rate from 8 percent to 7 percent would result in a $100 billion increase in money demand along L_1. But the interest rate would have to drop from 8 percent to 6 percent for there to be a $100 billion increase in money demand along L_2. The investment demand curve I_1 is more steeply sloped than the investment demand curve I_2. Investment demand as repre-

sented by I_2 is, therefore, more sensitive to a change in the interest rate (the alternative view) than is investment demand as represented by I_1 (the Keynesian view). For example, a drop in the interest rate from 8 percent to 7 percent would result in an increase in investment of $50 billion along I_1. Along I_2 such a drop in the interest rate would result in an increase in investment of $100 billion.

Suppose the Fed increases the money supply by $100 billion, represented by the rightward shift in the money supply curve from M_0 to M_1. Let's compare the difference in the effects on total demand and total income which result from the difference between L_1 and L_2 and between I_1 and I_2. (We will ignore the effects of the total income change on the money demand curve because it only complicates our analysis without affecting our comparison of the different points of view.) In the upper half of Figure 13-1 (the Keynesian view), the money supply increase causes the interest rate to fall from 8 percent (the intersection of M_0 and L_1) to 7 percent (the intersection of M_1 and L_1). In the lower half of Figure 13-1 (the alternative view), the same money supply increase results in a larger drop in the interest rate, from 8 percent to 6 percent, because the money demand curve L_2 is steeper than L_1.

The larger drop in the interest rate, combined with the fact that I_2 is not as steep as I_1, results in a larger increase in investment spending in the lower half of Figure 13-1 than in the upper half. The increase in investment spending ΔI, in the upper half of the figure, amounts to $50 billion. This increase in investment shifts the total demand schedule upward by $50 billion from $C + I$ to $C + I + \Delta I$, resulting in a $100 billion increase in total income from $1,400 billion to $1,500 billion in the upper half of Figure 13-1. In the lower half of the figure, the $200 billion increase in investment shifts the total demand schedule upwards by $200 billion from $C + I$ to $C + I + \Delta I'$, causing a $400 billion increase in total income from $1,400 billion to $1,800 billion. Clearly, a $100 billion increase in the money supply would cause us to predict a greater effect on total demand and income if one takes the alternative rather than the Keynesian point of view.

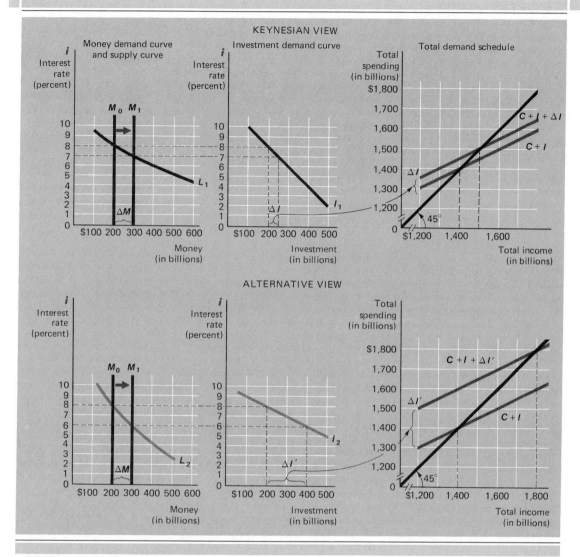

FIGURE 13-1 DIFFERING VIEWS ON THE IMPACT OF A CHANGE IN THE MONEY SUPPLY

An increase in the money supply causes less of a change in total income according to the Keynesian view (top half of figure) than it does according to the alternative view (bottom half of figure). This difference is due to the fact that money demand is more sensitive to interest rate changes in the Keynesian view than in the alternative view, while investment demand is less sensitive to interest rate changes in the Keynesian view than in the alternative view. Comparing the money demand curves, this means that L_1 is less steeply sloped than L_2, while for the investment demand curves I_1 is more steeply sloped than I_2. Consequently, in the alternative view the increase ΔM in the money supply from M_0 to M_1 results in a larger reduction in the interest rate, a larger increase in investment, and, hence, a larger increase in total demand schedule and total income than occurs in the Keynesian view.

CHANGES IN VELOCITY

What do the two points of view expressed in Figure 13-1 imply about the stability of velocity? At the initial equilibrium position in both the upper and lower halves of Figure 13-1, the money supply is $200 billion and total income (or money GNP) is $1,400 billion. In both cases the equation of exchange is

$$\$200 \times V = \$1,400$$

In the initial equilibrium position velocity V therefore equals 7. After the $100 billion increase in the money supply, the equation of exchange at the new equilibrium in the upper half of Figure 13-1 (the Keynesian view) is now

$$\$300 \times V = \$1,500$$

Therefore velocity must now equal 5. In the Keynesian view velocity has fallen from 7 to 5.

At the new equilibrium in the lower half of Figure 13-1 (the alternative view), the equation of exchange is now

$$\$300 \times V = \$1,800$$

Velocity must now equal 6. In the alternative view velocity has fallen from 7 to 6. Therefore, velocity changes by less in the alternative view (from 7 to 6) than in the Keynesian view (from 7 to 5).

In sum, we can now see why *Keynesians argue that the effects of a money supply increase can be largely offset by a movement in velocity in the opposite direction. Monetarists believe such offsetting effects are relatively weak.*

Velocity in the Real World

What do real world data show about the relationship between the money supply and money GNP? How does velocity actually behave?

THE MONEY SUPPLY AND MONEY GNP

Figure 13-2 illustrates the behavior of the money supply (M_1, defined as demand deposits plus currency) and money GNP in the United States for the years since 1946. Monetarists contend that the almost parallel movement shown by the money supply and money GNP reflects a causal relationship running from the money supply to money GNP. *However,* Keynesians re-

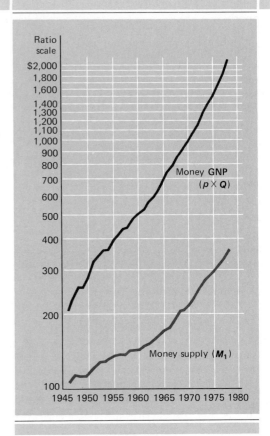

FIGURE 13-2 THE MONEY SUPPLY AND MONEY GNP

There is a striking parallel in the movements of the money supply and money GNP. Monetarists cite this as evidence to support their claim that the money supply is an important causal determinant of money GNP. Keynesians claim that this parallel movement is equally supportive of the view that causation runs in the opposite direction—from money GNP to the money supply. They argue that total demand $C + I + G$ can shift upward for reasons unrelated to money. As total demand shifts upward, consumers and business increase their demand for loans from banks in order to carry out their plans for increased spending. As a result, banks increase loans through the deposit expansion process that gives rise to an increase in the money supply.

ply that the observed relationship is equally supportive of their point of view. They argue that the causality can also run in the other direction—from money GNP to the money supply. They point out that the economy's total demand schedule $C + I + G$ can shift upward for a host of reasons that have nothing to do with money supply changes. Technological change, changes in profit expectations, and the development of new products can cause investment I to rise. Changes in consumer tastes, an increase in consumer optimism, population growth, and so forth can cause the consumption function C to shift upward. Government expenditures G may increase for reasons of national defense or to build more highways, schools, and so forth. Keynesians argue that these so-called autonomous increases in total spending in the economy lead to an increase in the demand for loans from banks as businesses and consumers borrow to finance their spending. Banks *respond* by lending out excess reserves and, thereby, creating money through the deposit expansion process we studied in the previous chapter. Growth in the money supply is, therefore, caused by the increase in the total demand for goods and services, rather than the other way around.

The ongoing debate between monetarists and Keynesians finds both sides enlisting the data of Figure 13-2 as support for their point of view.

THE EVIDENCE ON VELOCITY

Velocity can be calculated from the money supply and money GNP data given in Figure 13-2. We can do this simply by recognizing that the equation of exchange $M \times V = p \times Q$ may also be expressed as

$$V = \frac{p \times Q}{M}$$

Dividing money GNP ($p \times Q$) by money supply data (M) gives us velocity in the United States since 1930, plotted in Figure 13-3, part b. This figure shows us that velocity gradually declined over the 1930-1946 period. But since World War II velocity has climbed steadily upward from a value of about 2 to around 6. In addition to these long-run trends, velocity has also varied on a year-to-year basis. This valu-

ation is illustrated in Figure 13-3, part c, which shows the year-to-year percentage change in the velocity data plotted in part b.

Monetarists believe that the growth in velocity has been reasonably slow and predictable. They suggest that the long-run upward trend in velocity since World War II reflects the increased use of credit cards and the increased availability of short-term credit for consumer purchases. Both of these developments make it possible for individual or business to transact any given amount of purchases of final goods and services with a smaller balance of money on hand. Hence, the economy's money supply turns over more often, or goes around the circular income-expenditure flow more times during the course of a year—velocity increases.

Keynesians acknowledge the impact of these same developments on velocity. But they also note that the long-run rise in velocity has been accompanied by a long-run rise in the interest rate, shown in part a of Figure 13-3. We have already discussed the fact that Keynesians believe both that money demand is quite sensitive and investment demand relatively insensitive to interest rate changes. And we saw how this implied that velocity is more unstable in the Keynesian view as compared to an alternative view in which money demand is less sensitive and investment demand more sensitive to interest rate changes—our discussion of Figure 13-1. In particular, while the interest rate went from 8 percent to 7 percent, velocity changed from 7 to 5 in the Keynesian view (top half of Figure 13-1). By comparison, in the alternative view (bottom half of Figure 13-1), while the interest rate went from 8 percent to 6 percent, velocity only changed from 7 to 6, despite the fact that change in the interest rate was larger. Hence, Keynesians believe velocity is quite sensitive to interest rate changes. And Keynesians claim the long-run rise in the interest rate (Figure 13-3, part a) that accompanies the long-run rise in velocity (Figure 13-3, part b) is consistent with their point of view. As further support for this view, Keynesians also note that the gradual decline in the interest rate from 1930 through 1946 accompanied the decline in velocity over this period.

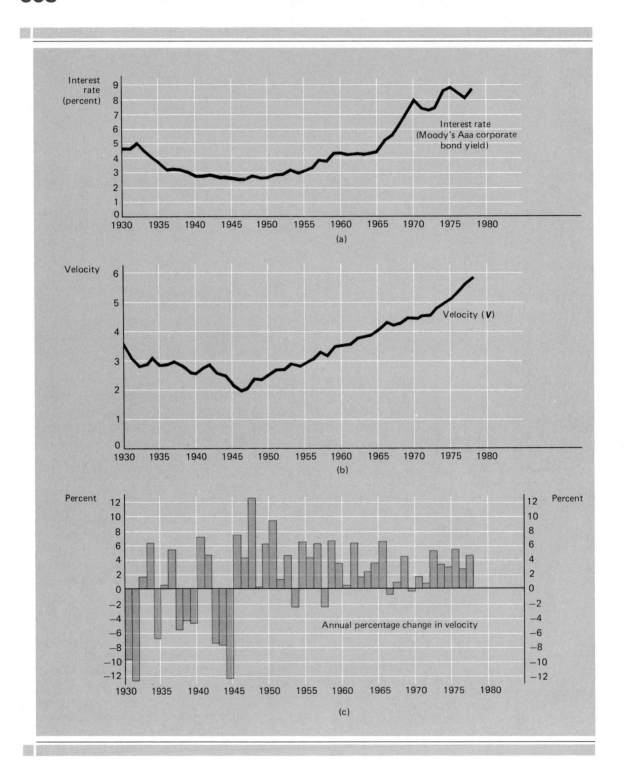

FIGURE 13-3 THE BEHAVIOR OF VELOCITY AND THE INTEREST RATE

Velocity, plotted in part b, is calculated by dividing money GNP by the money supply (M_1). It shows a long-run declining trend from 1930 to 1946 and a long-run rising trend since 1946. The short-run stability of velocity is more easily judged from the year-to-year percentage changes in velocity plotted in part c.

Monetarists believe that the evidence in parts b and c covering the period since the early 1950s shows that velocity is reasonably stable. The more variable behavior of velocity from 1930 through 1951 seems less supportive of this view. It is argued that the long-run rising trend in velocity since 1946 is due to the increased use of credit cards and availability of short-term credit.

Keynesians take special note of the way that the interest rate in part a moves in a parallel manner to velocity in part b. This is consistent with their view that money demand is sensitive to the interest rate. Our discussion of velocity in connection with Figure 13-1 showed how this view implies that velocity is sensitive to the interest rate, rising when the interest rate rises and falling when the interest rate falls.

Since the early 1950s velocity has never increased by more than about 6.5 percent from one year to the next, and it has never decreased by more than about 2.5 percent (Figure 13-3, part c). Monetarists argue that this amount of short-run variability of velocity over this period is consistent with their view that velocity is quite stable. However, Keynesians are quick to point out the relatively greater instability of velocity that is evident during the more turbulent years from 1930 through 1951. For example, consider the 12.8 percent drop in velocity from 1931 to 1932 in the depths of the Great Depression. At the same time, money GNP fell 23.4 percent. In terms of the equation of exchange $M \times V = p \times Q$ this means that more than half of the drop in money GNP ($p \times Q$) reflects the drop in V. Keynesians see this as evidence for their contention that increases in the money supply M aimed at getting the economy out of the Great Depression would have had to overcome the sizeable offsetting effect of a declining V.

A Constant Money Growth Rate

Monetarists believe there is a fairly stable relationship between the money supply and money GNP—in other words, a fairly stable V. But they do not advocate attempts to offset recessions and curb excessive economic expansions by alternately expanding and contracting the money supply. They generally argue that such a discretionary monetary policy is more likely to aggravate economic fluctuations than to minimize them. Why?

TIME LAGS IN MONETARY POLICY

Monetarists contend that changes in the money supply affect the level of economic activity over a long and variable period of time. Yes, a change in the money supply will definitely affect the level of money GNP. But there is a time lag between the point when the money supply change occurs and the point where its effect on money GNP is fully realized. Moreover, monetarists claim that the length of this time lag is quite variable and difficult to predict. Research by the foremost monetarist, Milton Friedman, suggests that the length of this time lag may vary anywhere from roughly a half year to two and a half years. As a result, monetarists argue that it is almost impossible for policy makers to schedule expansions or contractions in the money supply so that they will have their impact on the economy at the desired time. An expansion of the money supply, intended to offset a recession, may have its greatest impact a year or more down the road after the economy has recovered and is already expanding. Hence, the money supply increase may end up adding fuel to a potentially inflationary situation rather than offsetting a recession. Similarly, a contraction of the money supply, intended to curb an overheated economy, may end up having its greatest impact after the economy has already begun to slow down. As a result, the money supply contraction may actually contribute to an ensuing recession.

Most monetarists contend that the historical record since the founding of the Federal Reserve System in 1913 suggests that discretionary monetary policy has in fact tended to destabilize rather than stabilize the economy. Therefore, monetarists claim that monetary policy mismanagement must bear some of the blame for economic instability.

IMPLICATIONS FOR MONETARY POLICY

What is the upshot of the monetarist contentions? Some prominent monetarists, such as Milton Friedman, argue that the most appropriate monetary policy is to avoid discretionary decisions to expand or contract the rate of growth of the money supply. Instead, they recommend *a constant money growth rate rule,* whereby the Fed concentrates on expanding the money supply at a constant rate, year-in and year-out. Monetarists argue that this will automatically tend to smooth out the business cycle. When the economy's rate of growth (the growth rate of money GNP) falls below the constant money supply growth rate, during a recession, the continually increasing money supply will automatically provide a stimulus to get the economy going again. When the economy's growth rate rises above this rate, during a boom, the slower growing money supply will automatically put a curb on the excessive economic expansion.

Keynesians generally regard the constant money growth rule as unnecessarily cautious. They feel that there are definitely times when discretionary changes in the rate of growth of the money supply are obviously called for. This issue continues to be hotly debated by the two camps.

■ CHECKPOINT 13-1

What is the main distinction between the equation of exchange viewed as a definition and as a theory? Consider again the money supply increase discussed in Figure 13–1. Keynesians have argued that the money demand curve becomes flatter at lower interest rate levels. At some very low interest rate, they argue, the curve may become perfectly flat. If the money supply is increased enough to push the interest rate down to this level, Keynesians argue that further increases in the money supply will be completely offset by decreases in velocity V. Can you explain why in terms of a diagram like Figure 13–1?

HOW MONEY AFFECTS OUTPUT, EMPLOYMENT, AND PRICES

We have now seen why monetarists and Keynesians hold differing opinions on how changes in the money supply can affect total income or money GNP, ($p \times Q$). Recall from Chapter 8 that the economy's aggregate supply curve shows how changes in money GNP ($p \times Q$) break down into changes in the price level p and real output Q, as illustrated in Figure 8-7. These changes in real output, of course, mean changes in employment as well. With the aid of the aggregate supply curve, we can ask what do the differences between the monetarist and Keynesian views imply about the Federal Reserve's ability to affect real output, employment (hence, unemployment), and the price level?

Increases in the Money Supply

In the case of money supply increases, this question was answered in part by our discussion of the equation of exchange, and the differences between the monetarist and the Keynesian views on the stability of V, the velocity of money. We saw that a given size money supply increase will cause less of an increase in the total demand for goods and services in the Keynesian view than in the monetarist view. To complete the answer, all we need to do is make use of the relationship between the economy's total demand schedule and its aggregate supply curve, as shown in Figure 8-8 of Chapter 8. That figure is reproduced here as Figure 13-4.

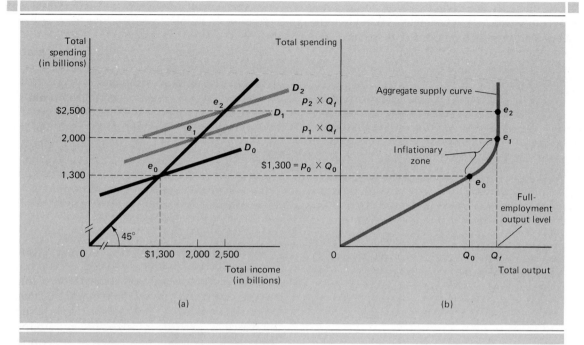

FIGURE 13-4 RELATIONSHIP BETWEEN TOTAL SPENDING, THE PRICE LEVEL, AND TOTAL OUTPUT

Increases in the money supply push up the total demand schedule D (part a), increasing total spending and total income $p \times Q$ in the economy. The increase in total spending causes changes in the economy's price level p and total output level Q. The relative size of each of these changes is determined by where the economy is on its aggregate supply curve (part b). (This diagram is described in more detail in the caption accompanying Figure 8–7.)

In the example illustrated here, money supply increases that push total spending and income up to as high as the $1,300 billion level increase real output Q without increasing price p. This happens because the economy moves up along the aggregate supply curve in the range from 0 to e_0 (part b). Further increases in the money supply, pushing total spending and income up to as high as $2,000 billion, increase both real output Q and the price level p. This is so because the economy moves up along the inflationary zone of its aggregate supply curve, from e_0 to e_1 (part b). Beyond the $2,000 billion income level, increases in the money supply simply cause the price level to rise because output cannot increase beyond its full-employment level Q_f. The economy is then producing along the vertical range of its aggregate supply curve above point e_1 (part b).

MONEY SUPPLY INCREASES THAT ONLY AFFECT OUTPUT

Recall that when the economy's total demand schedule for final goods and services is at D_0 (part a of Figure 13-4), total spending equals $p_0 \times Q_0$, or $1,300 billion, measured on the vertical axes of both parts of the figure. This level of spending corresponds to point e_0 on the aggregate supply curve and the level of total output Q_0 on the horizontal axis of part b. Increases in the money supply that shift the total demand schedule up to the position D_0 (part a) cause no increase in the general price level. Increases in total spending go entirely into increases in Q as the economy expands production along the straight-line portion of the aggregate supply curve from 0 to e_0 (part b). Throughout this range, the price level remains unchanged at p_0. In terms of the equation of exchange ($M \times V = p \times Q$), over this range, increases in M cause Q to increase while p remains unchanged. A greater portion of any given increase in M would be offset by a fall in V in the Keynesian view than in the monetarist view, as our discussion of velocity in connection with Figure 13-1 indicated. Hence, it would take larger increases in the money supply to get the total demand schedule up to D_0 in the Keynesian view than it would in the monetarist view.

MONEY SUPPLY INCREASES THAT AFFECT BOTH OUTPUT AND THE PRICE LEVEL

Further increases in the money supply that shift the total demand schedule to positions anywhere between D_0 and D_1 (part a) cause the economy to produce in the inflationary zone of the aggregate supply curve between points e_0 and e_1 (part b). In this zone, increases in total spending result in ever larger increases in the price level p and ever smaller increases in output Q until the full-employment output level Q_f is reached, and the price level has risen from p_0 to p_1. In terms of the equation of exchange, increases in M cause both p and Q to increase over this range. V falls more, or less, depending on whether you take a Keynesian view or a monetarist view.

MONEY SUPPLY INCREASES THAT CAUSE PURE INFLATION

Further increases in the money supply that shift the total demand schedule from D_1 to yet higher positions, such as D_2 (part a), will only drive up the price level. This is so because total output cannot increase beyond Q_f, as indicated by the vertical segment of the aggregate supply curve directly above Q_f on the horizontal axis of part b. Once the economy is moving up along the vertical segment of the aggregate supply curve, such as from point e_1 to e_2, the equation of exchange becomes $M \times V = p \times Q_f$. Since full-employment output Q_f is fixed, further increases in M simply cause p to rise, such as from p_1 to p_2.

Summarizing our discussion of Figure 13-4, money supply increases that push total spending and income up to as high as the $1,300 billion level increase real output Q without increasing the price level p. Further increases in the money supply, pushing total spending and income up to as high as $2,000 billion, increase both real output and the price level. A greater share of the increase goes into price level rise as full employment is approached. Past the $2,000 billion income level, increases in the money supply simply cause the price level to rise.

Demand-Pull Inflation and Monetary Restraint

Other factors beside an increase in the money supply can cause the economy's total demand schedule for goods and services to shift upward. Increases in government spending, and upward shifts in the consumption function and investment schedule resulting from so-called autonomous increases in consumption and investment spending, will also have this effect. These increases will cause a rise in the general price level if the economy is producing anywhere along its aggregate supply curve above the point e_0 (part b of Figure 13-4). How effectively can the Federal Reserve restrain such upward shifts in total demand through its control over the money supply? To what extent can it be expected to curb this type of demand-pull inflation? These were the main issues raised by the news item at the beginning of Chapter 12.

We may look at the "continued expansion in economic activity" that was forecast by the Federal Reserve Board chairman in that news item as the upward shift in the total demand schedule pictured in Figure 13-4, part a. As total spending and income rise, the economy moves up along its aggregate supply curve above the point e_0 in part b. More and more of the increase in total spending goes into a rise in the general price level p and less and less into increases in real output Q. This happens because the economy encounters "bottlenecks" and capacity constraints as it approaches the full-employment output level and unemployment falls. It is the reason that some economists "stress that a climbing inflation rate, together with a declining unemployment rate, have increased the odds that the Fed will continue to pursue a restrictive policy," as reported in the Chapter 12 news item.

Both monetarists and Keynesians agree that halting or slowing the growth in the money supply will put a brake on inflation. But monetarists feel that this brake is more powerful than do Keynesians. We can explain this difference of opinion by using concepts we developed in Chapter 12. Recall that increases in the economy's total income cause the money demand curve to shift rightward, as we discussed in connection with Figure 12-2. Our discussion of general equilibrium (Figure 12-10) showed us how this rightward shift in the money demand curve would tend to dampen an expansion in total spending and income.

EFFECTIVENESS OF MONETARY RESTRAINT: KEYNESIAN VERSUS MONETARIST VIEWS

Suppose that when the total demand schedule is in the position D_0 (part a of Figure 13-4), the economy's money supply M is \$300 billion, the equilibrium interest rate is 5 percent, and investment spending equals \$400 billion. The Keynesian view of this equilibrium position is shown in the upper half of Figure 13-5. There the 5 percent interest rate is determined by the intersection of the money demand curve L_1 with the money supply curve M, point a. The \$400 billion level of investment spending is determined by the 5 percent interest rate and the investment demand curve I_1. The monetarist view may be represented as shown in the lower half of Figure 13-5. The intersection of L_2 and M, point a, determines the 5 percent interest rate, which together with I_2 determines the \$400 billion level of investment. The differences in slope between I_1 and I_2, and between L_1 and L_2, reflect the difference between the Keynesian and alternative views discussed earlier in Figure 13-1. Monetarists argue that money supply

changes affect the economy through other channels in addition to the interest rate channel. However, in terms of the interest rate transmission mechanism shown here, the monetarist view is like the alternative view.

Now suppose that the economy's total demand schedule, part a of Figure 13-4, begins to shift upward—because of an upward shift in the consumption function, for example. Suppose also that the Fed decides to hold the money supply fixed at M in Figure 13-5. That is, the Fed attempts to curb the rise in the general price level p that occurs as the economy moves up along the inflationary zone of the aggregate supply curve above point e_0 in part b of Figure 13-4.

For a given increase in total income, there will be a certain amount of rightward shift in the money demand curve, Figure 13-5. L_1 shifts to L_1' (Keynesian view), and L_2 shifts to L_2' (monetarist view). The amount of this shift, equal to the distance between a and b, is of course the same in both cases because both shifts are caused by the same given increase in total income. Note however that in the monetarist view the resulting rise in the interest rate is larger (from 5 to 7 percent) than in the Keynesian view (from 5 to 6 percent). The larger rise in the interest rate, combined with the fact that I_2 has a flatter slope than I_1, results in a larger reduction in investment spending in the monetarist view than in the Keynesian view. The reduction in investment spending works in the opposite direction from the upward shift in the consumption function that is pushing up the total demand schedule in Figure 13-4, part a. And this offsetting effect is obviously greater in the monetarist view than in the Keynesian view.

The result is that the total demand schedule will be able to rise to a position such as D_2 in the Keynesian view, but only to D_1 in the monetarist view, Figure 13-4, part a. Figure 13-4, part b, shows clearly that the increase in total spending and the price level will be less in the monetarist view than in the Keynesian view. Hence, compared to a Keynesian, a monetarist would argue that a tight money policy is more effective in fighting demand-pull inflation.

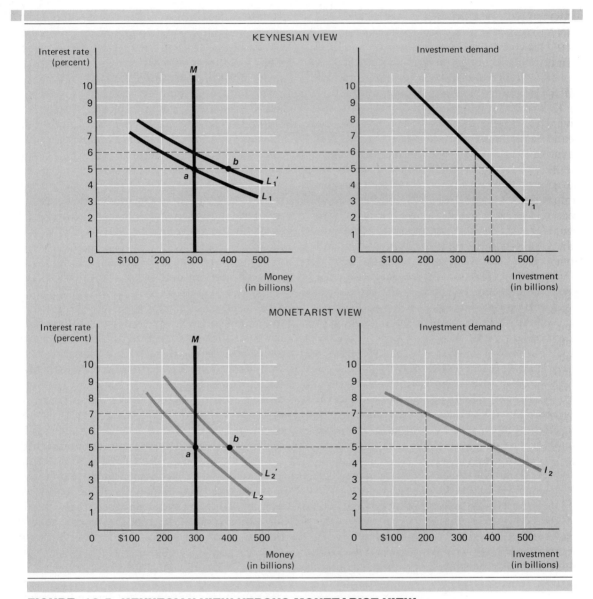

FIGURE 13-5 KEYNESIAN VIEW VERSUS MONETARIST VIEW ON THE EFFECTS OF AN INCREASE IN TOTAL INCOME ON INVESTMENT

A given increase in total income will shift the money demand curve rightward, from L_1 to L_1' in the Keynesian view, and from L_2 to L_2' in the monetarist view. At the initial equilibrium interest rate of 5 percent, the amount of this rightward shift equals the distance from a to b. The money demand curve is more steeply sloped in the monetarist than in the Keynesian view. Therefore, the interest rate rises further in the monetarist view (from 5 to 7 percent) than in the Keynesian view (from 5 to 6 percent). Combined with the fact that the investment demand curve I_2 is less steeply sloped than I_1, this means that investment spending is reduced more in the monetarist than in the Keynesian view.

MONETARY RESTRAINT IN TERMS OF THE EQUATION OF EXCHANGE

In terms of the equation of exchange ($M \times V = p \times Q$), the rise in $p \times Q$ due to the upward shift of the total demand schedule is larger in the Keynesian view than in the monetarist view. Given that the money supply M is constant, this means that velocity V increases more in the Keynesian view than in the monetarist view. We have seen why the Keynesians argue that the instability of velocity makes it difficult to stimulate the economy with a money supply increase. Now we see how this same instability argument makes Keynesians less optimistic than monetarists about the ability of a tight money policy to control demand-pull inflation.

■ CHECKPOINT 13-2

Some have said that monetary policy is like pushing on a string when the Fed is trying to stimulate the economy, and like pulling on a string when the Fed is trying to curb an inflationary expansion. What factors determine the appropriateness of this analogy? If the Fed does a bad job of deciding when and how much to stimulate or to put a brake on the economy, would we be better off if the Keynesian view is correct, or if the monetarist view is correct?

FISCAL POLICY: KEYNESIAN VIEW VERSUS MONETARIST VIEW

Aside from the ideological differences we discussed at the beginning of this chapter, why do Keynesians have more faith than monetarists in the ability of fiscal policy to smooth out the business cycle, foster full employment, and curb inflation? When does fiscal policy have monetary effects? Are fiscal and monetary policy well coordinated or do they frequently work at cross purposes with one another? Let's now consider each of these questions in turn.

Pure Fiscal Policy and Crowding Out

The basic differences between the Keynesian and monetarist views on the effectiveness of fiscal policy are perhaps most clearly illustrated in terms of pure fiscal policy. *Pure fiscal policy* consists of changes in government expenditure or taxation, or both, that do not change the money supply.

Monetarists argue that pure fiscal policy causes very little change in total income and employment. For example, the monetarist view holds that an increase in government expenditure leads to the *crowding out* of private sector expenditure, particularly investment spending. Hence, any expansionary effect on total demand caused by an increase in government spending is largely offset by an accompanying decline in investment spending. In contrast, Keynesians argue that crowding out is not that significant.

WHY THERE IS CROWDING OUT

What is the explanation for the crowding-out effect and the difference in opinion between Keynesians and monetarists regarding its size? The answer hinges on the effect of a rise in total income on money demand, the interest rate, and investment spending, as illustrated earlier in Figure 13-5. There, a given increase in total income caused a rightward shift in the money demand curve. Given the money supply M, the resulting increase in the interest rate and reduction in the level of investment spending was larger in the monetarist view than in the Keynesian.

The crowding-out effect is illustrated in Figure 13-6. Here, the economy's total demand schedule is D_1, which means that the equilibrium level of total income (GNP) is GNP_0 as shown in both the upper and lower half of the figure. Now suppose government spending increases by the amount ΔG. If we momentarily ignore the effects of the resulting rise in total income on money demand, the economy's total demand schedule is shifted up to D_2 (upper and lower half of Figure 13-6). However, if we allow for the effects of the total income rise on money demand, the interest rate, and the level of investment spending, as shown in Figure 13-5, the total demand schedule cannot rise to the position D_2 in Figure 13-6. Why? Because the effect of the rise in government spending will be offset in part by the reduction or crowd-

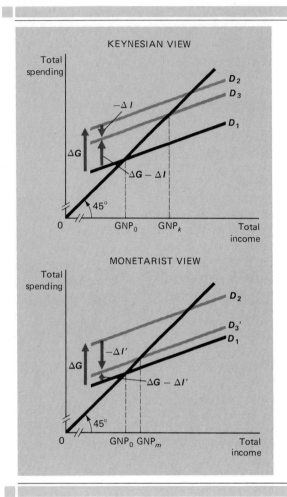

FIGURE 13-6 THE CROWDING-OUT EFFECT OF FISCAL POLICY

An increase in government expenditure ΔG pushes the total demand schedule from D_1 up to D_2 if we momentarily ignore the effects of the rise in total income, or GNP, on money demand, the interest rate, and investment. Taking account of such effects (as illustrated in Figure 13–5), the rise in total income increases the demand for money, which pushes up the interest rate and causes a reduction or crowding out of investment spending.

This crowding out of investment spending is larger according to the monetarist view (bottom half of Figure 13–5) than according to the Keynesian view (top half of Figure 13–5). Consequently, there is a greater offsetting change in investment in the monetarist view, equal to $-\Delta I'$, than in the Keynesian view, equal to $-\Delta I$. As a result, the total demand schedule only rises from D_1 to D_3', increasing GNP from GNP_0 to GNP_m, in the monetarist view. By comparison the exact same increase in government spending, ΔG, increases the total demand schedule from D_1 to D_3, and GNP from GNP_0 to GNP_k, in the Keynesian view.

ing out of investment spending that results from the rise in the interest rate. According to the Keynesian view (upper half of Figure 13-6), the crowding out of investment will equal $-\Delta I$, so that the total demand schedule is shifted up to D_3—or by an amount equal to $\Delta G - \Delta I$. Equilibrium GNP rises from GNP_0 to GNP_k. According to the monetarist view (lower half of Figure 13-6), the crowding out of investment will be larger, equal to $-\Delta I'$. The total demand schedule is shifted up by a smaller amount, equal to $G - \Delta I'$, to D_3', and GNP rises only from GNP_0 to GNP_m.

CROWDING OUT AND TAXATION

Our illustration of the crowding-out effect has assumed that the fiscal action taken was an in-

crease in government spending. But a tax reduction also shifts the total demand schedule upward, as we saw in Chapter 9, and results in the same type of crowding-out effect. Similarly, an increase in government expenditures matched by an increase in taxes (a balanced budget increase) shifts the total demand schedule upward and gives rise to the crowding-out effect. Recall that the balanced budget multiplier of Chapter 9 was equal to 1—the increase in total income equaled the amount of increase in government spending, which was matched by the tax increase. When we take account of the crowding-out effect, the balanced budget multiplier is less than 1.

In sum, *monetarists believe fiscal policy actions have very little effect on the level of total income* and employment because of the offsetting crowd-ing-out effect. The Keynesians view holds that fiscal policy has a sizeable effect on the level of total income and employment because the offsetting crowding-out effect is not considered that significant.

Fiscal and Monetary Effects Combined

Fiscal policy has monetary effects whenever a fiscal action is accompanied by a change in the money supply. This may happen whenever a change in government expenditure or taxation, or both, gives rise to a government budget deficit or surplus.

FINANCING BUDGET DEFICITS WITHOUT A MONEY SUPPLY CHANGE

Recall our discussion of the financing of government budget deficits in Chapter 9. There we noted that whenever government expenditure exceeds tax revenues the government must finance the difference by issuing government bonds. If the public (businesses, individuals, and private institutions) buys the bonds, they typically write checks against their demand deposits. These checks are made payable to the U.S. Treasury for the amount of government bonds purchased. The government then spends this money, putting it right back into the hands of the public. There is no change in the supply of money in the economy when the government deficit is financed in this fashion. Hence, the only question is how much the expansionary effect of the government expenditure increase or tax reduction, or both, is offset by the crowding-out effect—the same issue we discussed in connection with Figure 13-6.

FINANCING BUDGET DEFICITS WITH A MONEY SUPPLY CHANGE: MONETIZING THE GOVERNMENT DEBT

In Chapter 9 we observed that if the government chooses not to finance its deficit by selling bonds to the public, it can "print the money" it needs. Now that we've seen how the Federal Reserve System can create money (Chapters 10 and 11), we can see exactly how this is done.

A Hypothetical Example. The Federal Reserve is the arm of the government that "prints

the money." The following hypothetical example illustrates how this can occur. Rather than sell the deficit-financing government bonds to the public, suppose the U.S. Treasury simply sells them directly to the Fed. How can the Fed pay for the bonds? Since the Fed is the government's banker, suppose it simply credits or adds to the U.S. Treasury's account at the Fed (the government's checking account) the amount of funds necessary to cover the purchase of the bonds. Then the government writes checks against this account when it purchases goods and services in the economy. The check recipients, who provide the goods and services, deposit the checks in their banks and the economy's money supply is increased by this amount. In sum, one arm of the government, the Federal Reserve, creates money for another arm of the government, the U.S. Treasury. The Treasury spends this money, thereby increasing the entire economy's money supply.

"Printing Money" in the Real World. It may have struck you that this process is very similar to what happens when the Federal Reserve makes an open market purchase of government bonds. The major difference is that in our example the Fed buys the bonds directly from the U.S. Treasury rather than from the public. In fact, the direct sale of bonds by the U.S. Treasury to the Fed is illegal. However, in essence this is what happens when the Treasury sells government bonds to the public while at the same time the Fed makes an open market purchase of an equivalent amount of government bonds from the public. In effect, the Fed (one arm of the government) is buying up the government debt issued by the Treasury (another arm of the government) to finance the government deficit. It's a "wash." In essence the government deficit is financed by the government's creation of money. When the Fed finances government deficit spending in this way, it is said to be *monetizing the government debt*—turning newly issued government bonds directly into newly created money. That is, the Fed is "printing money." The Fed may purchase an amount of bonds equal only to a portion of the bonds sold by the Treasury to finance the budget deficit. In that case, only that portion of

the deficit spending is financed by "printing money."

When deficit spending is financed by monetizing the government debt, the money supply is increased. And we know that such an increase will cause an upward shift in the economy's total demand schedule and a rise in the equilibrium level of GNP (Figure 13-1). This shift is an addition to the upward shift in the total demand schedule and the rise in equilibrium GNP that results from the increase in government spending or reduction in taxes, or both (Figure 13-6). In sum, *deficit spending financed by the creation of money—monetizing the government debt—is more expansionary than deficit spending financed only by selling bonds to the public—that is, without the creation of money.*

KEYNESIAN VIEW
VERSUS MONETARIST VIEW
ON DEFICIT FINANCING

Monetarists argue that deficit spending has a pronounced expansionary effect on the economy only to the extent that it is financed by the creation of money. This position is dictated by the monetarist view that money supply increases are very expansionary, while government expenditure increases or tax reductions, or both, are largely offset by crowding out (bottom half of Figure 13-6). The Keynesian view doesn't see money supply increases as nearly so expansionary (top half of Figure 13-1), or the crowding-out effect as nearly so large (top half of Figure 13-6). Consequently, the Keynesian view holds that deficit spending is expansionary largely because of the direct effects of government expenditure or tax reduction, or both, on the economy's total demand schedule for goods and services. Keynesians would agree that deficit spending is more expansionary if it is financed by money creation than by the sale of bonds to the public without money creation. However, they don't think the method of financing makes nearly as much difference as the monetarists do.

Coordinating Fiscal
and Monetary Policy

In principle, the goals of monetary and fiscal policy are the same—to smooth out economic fluctuations, to promote full employment, and to curb inflation. Ideally, therefore, policy makers should coordinate monetary and fiscal actions to achieve these ends. For example, during a recession appropriate fiscal policy should give rise to a deficit, while appropriate monetary policy would increase the rate of expansion of the money supply. On the other hand, suppose the economy is operating close to full employment, and inflationary pressures are increasing. Prudent fiscal policy would generate a budget surplus, and appropriate monetary policy would reduce the rate of expansion of the money supply. In practice, monetary and fiscal policy are not always so well coordinated, as the news item at the beginning of this chapter indicates.

FISCAL POLICY AND
THE POLITICAL PROCESS

A major reason for this lack of coordination is that the size and timing of government expenditure and tax programs are influenced by other considerations in addition to those of economic stabilization. Recall our discussion of this point in Chapter 9. There we noted that expenditure and tax programs are a product of the political processes of Congress. As such, these programs reflect the objectives and priorities of many different special interest groups and regions of the country. Congress must heed many voices. It is not surprising that there is often little regard for the fiscal policy implications of expenditure and tax programs conceived under these conditions.

Fiscal responsibility is shared by 535 senators and representatives, each speaking for the special interests of his or her own constituency. Each one finds it difficult, if not politically unrewarding, to consider actions taken on behalf of constituents in terms of their impact on the overall government budget. A representative or senator who votes for closing down Army bases in his or her district because the Army no longer needs them risks defeat at the polls. It may be true that the base closings will help trim the federal government's budget and relieve inflationary pressures in the economy. But local voters will be more concerned about the adverse impact of the base closings on the local economy. With the responsibility for overall fiscal policy in principle in the hands of so many, it may often end up in practice being the responsibility of no one.

In principle, the executive branch of the federal government is in a better position to have a broader perspective on fiscal policy. Moreover, the president is typically held accountable by voters for the overall state of the economy. Nonetheless, the president still must deal with Congress in order to have fiscal policy actions approved. A concerned president, seeking to avoid a recession by initiating a tax cut or a spending program, may be stymied by congressional politics. Or, a president, seeking to curb inflation and an overheated economy, may have to resort to the exercise of presidential veto power over expansionary expenditure and tax programs passed by Congress. Even then, if the president vetoes a spending program or tax cut considered inflationary, Congress can override such a veto by passing the legislation again by a two-thirds majority of both houses.

The question is not whether or not to have fiscal policy. Whenever decisions are made about government spending and taxation, for whatever reasons, the resulting government expenditure and tax actions unavoidably affect total income, output, employment, and the level of prices. All such actions amount to a fiscal policy, even when they are taken primarily in pursuit of other objectives unrelated to maintaining economic stability, reasonably full employment, and a rein on inflation. *A basic difficulty with fiscal policy as a stabilization tool is that there are so many other objectives that often take precedence in the determination of government spending and tax policy. It is largely for this reason that fiscal policy often conflicts with monetary policy.*

THE PROCESS OF MONETARY POLICY

Unlike fiscal policy, monetary policy is made by a relatively small group of people: the Federal Open Market Committee (FOMC), consisting of the seven governors of the Federal Reserve Board plus five Federal Reserve bank presidents. The FOMC meets once a month in a closed-door session to hammer out monetary policy. The minutes of these secret meetings are not available to the public until two months after each meeting. Furthermore, the public does not have direct ballot box control or influence over FOMC members as it does with members of Congress. Indeed, the general public hardly knows what the Federal Reserve System is, let alone that monetary policy is made by the members of the FOMC. Hence, compared to members of Congress, FOMC members are sheltered from, and largely unaccountable to, public pressures.

Because of these institutional differences, FOMC members are relatively more free to pursue economic stabilization objectives than are members of Congress. When the 12-member FOMC decides on a course of monetary action at its monthly meeting, it issues a directive to the open market desk at the Federal Reserve bank of New York. The directive essentially implements the monetary policy decisions of the FOMC over the coming month. If a more rapid expansion of the money supply is called for, the open market desk will make open market purchases of government securities during the month. If the directive dictates monetary contraction, the open market desk will be engaged for the most part in making open market sales.

In sum, compared to fiscal policy, the process of making and carrying out monetary policy is more organized. It is also easier for monetary policy to focus more continuously on the pursuit of economic stabilization goals since, compared to fiscal policy, it is relatively less hampered by other considerations and the more direct political pressures that often dominate Congress. Nonetheless, between presidential jawboning and Congressional oversight, the Fed may not be as independent as it sometimes appears.

IS FISCAL POLICY
A BURDEN ON MONETARY POLICY?

Because of the unwieldy nature of the fiscal policy process, it often appears that monetary policy is left with the larger share of the burden of pursuing economic stabilization goals. This has seemed particularly so since the late 1960s. The government budget has had continually large deficits throughout the 1970s. At the same time, the economy has been plagued by uncomfortably high rates of inflation. This combination flies in the face of conventional fiscal policy wisdom, which dictates that the government budget should be in surplus during periods of reasonably full employment and persistent inflation.

This is the background to the position taken by former Federal Reserve Board chairman G. William Miller, reported in the news item at the beginning of this chapter. There, the Fed chairman states "to the extent that there is greater discipline on fiscal policy" there is "less pressure on monetary policy." The article adds, "Almost since he became Fed chairman, Mr. Miller has stressed that the Fed can't fight inflation without help."

■ CHECKPOINT 13-3

From the news item it appears that the president would like the Fed to take action to lower the interest rate. But the Fed seems concerned about fighting inflation, and that fiscal policy is not helping in this fight. Describe the nature of the conflict in terms of Figures 13-4, 13-5, and 13-6, and show why the interest rate is being driven up. Suppose the Fed accedes to the president's wishes. What could it do to lower the interest rate? What would be the consequences of this action for inflation? Describe your answer in terms of Figures 13-4, 13-5, and 13-6. Also, in terms of these figures, describe how "greater discipline on fiscal policy" would put "less pressure on monetary policy."

SUMMARY

1. Keynesians tend to favor government intervention in the economy because they see shortcomings in the way the market system answers the basic economic questions of what to produce, how, and for whom. They are also doubtful that markets have the self-regulating ability to assure economic stability and full employment without the aid of an active fiscal policy. Monetarists tend to see government intervention as an unnecessary and harmful interference with the market system, as a threat to individual freedom, and as a dampener on individual initiative.

2. The equation of exchange, $M \times V = p \times Q$, is a definitional relationship between the economy's money stock M and the economy's total money income, or money GNP, which is equal to the price level p times the quantity of real output Q. V is the velocity of circulation of money. When V is regarded as stable—a reflection of institutional characteristics of the economy—the equation of exchange becomes the expression for the quantity theory of money.

3. Monetarism may be regarded as a sophisticated version of the quantity theory of money. Monetarists argue that the cause-effect transmission from changes in the money supply to changes in money GNP are reasonably direct and tight. They argue that the effects of a money supply change are transmitted through a host of channels, not just the interest rate channel so strongly emphasized by the Keynesian view. While monetarists regard velocity as stable, Keynesians believe the velocity of money is unstable, consistent with their view that money demand is sensitive and investment demand relatively insensitive to interest rate changes.

4. Keynesians favor discretionary monetary policy. Monetarists argue that such a policy is likely to aggravate the business cycle rather than diminish it. Therefore, some prominent monetarists argue for a constant money growth rate rule.

5. Compared to monetarists, Keynesians believe it is harder for money supply increases to stimulate real output and employment because of offsetting changes in velocity. Similarly, compared to monetarists, Keynesians also believe it is more difficult for monetary policy to restrain demand-pull inflation caused by autonomous expenditure increases.

6. Keynesians argue that fiscal policy is a more powerful economic stabilization tool than monetary policy. Disagreeing, monetarists claim that pure fiscal policy actions have little effect on total income and employment because of offsetting crowding-out effects on private spending, particularly investment. Keynesians, on the other hand, do not believe the crowding-out effect is that significant. Monetarists argue that deficit spending stimulates the economy only to the extent it is financed by money creation.

7. It is often difficult to coordinate fiscal and monetary policy in order to achieve economic stability and reasonably full employment with a minimum amount of inflation. A major reason is that many other considerations and political pressures affect government expenditure and tax programs, and these often take priority over economic stabilization objectives. By contrast, the monetary policy-making process is more organized, relatively more sheltered from political pressure, and, therefore, more easily and continuously focussed on economic stabilization goals.

KEY TERMS AND CONCEPTS

equation of exchange
monetarism
quantity theory of money
velocity

QUESTIONS AND PROBLEMS

1. Suppose the Fed is prone to making mistakes in its exercise of discretionary monetary policy. According to which view, Keynesian or monetarist, would the resulting fluctuations in money GNP be the greatest? Why? What bearing does this have on the Keynesian view versus the monetarist view about discretionary monetary policy?

2. Assume the Fed decides to implement monetary policy by always keeping the interest rate at the same target level. For instance, if the interest rate falls below the target level, the Fed conducts open market sales to push it back up, while if the interest rate rises above the target level, the Fed conducts open market purchases to push it back down. Suppose there are autonomous changes in spending, such as those discussed in connection with the total demand schedule of Figure 13-4. Do you think the Fed's constant interest rate policy would tend to stabilize or destabilize the economy? Why?

3. What problems does discretionary monetary policy share with discretionary fiscal policy? (Recall the discussion of discretionary fiscal policy in Chapter 9.) In what ways would the exercise of discretionary monetary policy differ from the exercise of discretionary fiscal policy?

4. How are Federal Reserve open market purchases similar to the financing of government deficits through money creation? How are they different?

5. It is often said that the extent of the crowding-out effect that results from a pure fiscal policy action is different when the economy is in a recession than when it is operating close to full-employment capacity. Explain why this might be so. Suppose a deficit is financed entirely by money creation. Can there still be a crowding out? Explain.

6. Suppose the economy is in a deep depression like the Great Depression of the 1930s. Suppose also that the money demand curve becomes very flat at a low level of the interest rate, and suppose that the equilibrium interest rate is at this low level. Would a pure fiscal policy action, such as a balanced budget government expenditure and tax increase, have a crowding-out effect? Under these conditions, would it make any difference whether the government resorts to a pure fiscal policy action as opposed to deficit spending financed by money creation?

■ NEWS ITEM FOR YOUR ANALYSIS

FED MAY BE ABLE TO EASE MONETARY POLICY BEFORE LONG, FED CHAIRMAN INDICATES

HOT SPRINGS, Va., Sept. 4—Federal Reserve Board chairman G. William Miller, appearing at a Business Council meeting here, indicated that the Fed may be able to relax monetary policy before long. The Fed chairman applauded the president's recent decision to push antiinflation efforts by trimming his proposed tax cuts as well as to delay them another three months.

"The more discipline we have in fiscal policy, the more pressure we take off monetary policy, and the more probability there is that we won't have the need for the same degree of restraint in monetary matters," Mr. Miller said. But he went on to note that economic expansion is currently "unusually strong" and that monetary policy will "need to be very judicious" during the second quarter.

Speaking at a separate Business Council news conference, Treasury secretary Michael Blumenthal indicated that now that the president has pared his tax-cut proposal to narrow the budget deficit, the administration expects the Fed to avoid further increases in interest rates. "I don't think there will be a continual upward pressure on interest rates," he said.

The Business Council, made up of top executives of major corporations, also applauded President Carter's decision to cut budget deficits by trimming and delaying tax cuts. But a number of Business Council executives also argued that the administration should cut federal spending to further foster its antiinflation stand.

QUESTIONS

1. Why should the president's decision to reduce the size of his proposed tax cuts make Fed chairman Miller's job easier? Explain your answer with the aid of diagrams.

2. How would other factors, such as the behavior of autonomous expenditures, give the Fed chairman cause to feel that monetary policy will "need to be very judicious" during the second quarter?

3. How would you explain the justification for the Treasury secretary's statement about interest rates?

4. Explain the logic of the Business Council executives' view that federal spending cuts would also help the administration's antiinflation stand.

14

INFLATION, UNEMPLOYMENT, AND THE DILEMMA OF STAGFLATION

FED CHIEF SAYS STEPS THAT RISK RECESSION
MAY BE NEEDED IF U.S. SPENDING ISN'T CUT

WASHINGTON, May 26—If the government doesn't reduce spending, the Federal Reserve Board may take restrictive actions that could slow the expansion and possibly cause a recession. So warned Fed chairman G. William Miller in testimony before the Senate Banking Committee.

The Fed chairman argued that if only the Fed fights inflation, "then we do run the risk that we'd slow down business expansion and even bring on a recession." Mr. Miller reiterated that only with attempts at fiscal restraint and balancing the budget can there be "prospects for less monetary restraint." He stressed the need to reduce spending at an "ordered pace," claiming that this "would greatly relieve the burden" on the Fed to fight inflation with tight monetary policy.

Mr. Miller went on to point out that "opportunities for lower interest rates" would also result if the government curbed deficit spending. But the Fed chairman also told the committee that inflation may get in the way of easier monetary policy. "If the current annual rate of inflation continues, interest rates just won't come down," he said.

It is conventional to associate a rising rate of inflation with a declining unemployment rate during the expansion phase of the business cycle. Until recent years it was also conventional to expect a declining rate of inflation along with a rising unemployment rate during recessions. However, in the 1960s and 1970s, and even in the late 1950s, inflation declined little if at all during periods of rising unemployment. These experiences have baffled the public and sent perplexed economists scrambling for explanations. These events have even given rise to a new economic term, *stagflation,* which suggests a stagnant economy with high unemployment, underutilized production capacity, and chronically high inflation.

In this chapter we will examine the recent behavior of inflation and unemployment in the United States. We will begin by asking whether there is an inflation-unemployment trade-off, as suggested by a concept known as the Phillips curve. Using tools developed in previous chapters, we will then examine possible explanations for the behavior of inflation and unemployment. We will also examine the nature of the dilemma posed for stabilization policy by the inflation-unemployment problem and stagflation. In addition we will consider the conflicts that often arise between fiscal and monetary policy, and how such conflicts aggravate the inflation-unemployment problem—the underlying theme of the news item. Finally, we will examine the changing nature of the unemployment problem and its implications for inflation.

IS THERE AN INFLATION-UNEMPLOYMENT TRADE-OFF?

Ever since the late 1950s, economists, policy makers, and politicians have speculated and ar-

gued about the existence of a trade-off between inflation and unemployment. Many have claimed that it is possible to reduce unemployment if we are willing to tolerate higher rates of inflation. Conversely it is often claimed that inflation can be reduced only by incurring higher rates of unemployment. The implication is that there exists a trade-off—we can have less unemployment for more inflation, or less inflation for more unemployment.

The graphical representation of this trade-off is known as the **Phillips curve**, after the British economist A. W. Phillips, who in 1958 put forward empirical evidence of such a trade-off for the British economy over the period 1862-1957. Economists have subsequently devoted considerable effort to investigating the possible existence of Phillips curve trade-offs in industrialized countries for the postwar period. The experience with inflation and unemployment during the 1960s and 1970s suggests that such a trade-off is not so simple or straightforward. Indeed, the events of the 1970s have raised serious questions about whether such a trade-off even exists.

The Phillips Curve

Recall our discussion of the inflationary zone of the aggregate supply curve in Figures 8-7 and 13-4. Those figures showed us that up to the point at which the economy reaches full employment, increases in the economy's total demand cause output and employment to increase, unemployment to fall, and the economy to move closer to full employment and full utilization of its productive capacity. However, in the inflationary zone of the aggregate supply curve the economy encounters ever increasing production bottlenecks and supply shortages. Hence, over this region, increases in total demand result in ever larger increases in the general price level and ever smaller increases in employment and the quantity of real output. Similarly, the ever larger increases in the general price level are accompanied by ever smaller reductions in the unemployment rate. This description characterizes the onset of demand-pull inflation as the economy approaches full employment. It suggests that we can only have a lower unemployment rate if we are willing to have a higher rate of inflation. This is the essence of the logic underlying the Phillips curve concept.

GRAPHICAL REPRESENTATION OF THE PHILLIPS CURVE: A MENU OF CHOICES

A hypothetical Phillips curve is shown in Figure 14-1. The annual percentage rate of increase in the price level, the rate of inflation, is measured on the vertical axis, and the unemployment rate is measured on the horizontal axis. The curve slopes downward left to right, a reflection of the fact that a lower unemployment rate can only be achieved by having a higher rate of inflation, and vice versa.

The Phillips curve represents a menu of choices for monetary and fiscal policy. For example, the hypothetical Phillips curve of Figure 14-1 suggests that if policy makers want to keep the rate of inflation at 2 percent or less, they must be willing to settle for an unemployment rate of 7 percent or more, as represented by point *a* on the Phillips curve. On the other hand, if policy makers are willing to tolerate a 4 per-

cent inflation rate, the unemployment rate can be reduced to 5 percent, point *b* on the Phillips curve. The trade-off between inflation and unemployment, represented by the slope of the curve between points *a* and *b*, is a reduction of 2 percentage points in the unemployment rate in exchange for a 2 percentage point increase in the inflation rate. However, the trade-off worsens between points *b* and *c*. If policy makers want to reduce the unemployment rate from 5 percent to 4 percent, they must be willing to settle for an increase in the inflation rate from 4 percent to 8 percent.

The lower right-hand portion of the Phillips curve suggests that to achieve a zero rate of inflation would require an unacceptably high rate of unemployment. Conversely, the upper left-hand portion suggests that a reduction of the unemployment rate below 4 percent would give rise to prohibitively high rates of inflation. The Phillips curve reminds us that economics is a study of choices, and that every choice has an associated cost. For example, choosing point *b* instead of point *a* means choosing a 5 percent instead of a 7 percent unemployment rate, a reduction in unemployment which is considered desirable. However, the cost of this choice is an additional 2 percentage points of inflation, from a rate of 2 percent at point *a* to 4 percent at point *b*—a move that is undesirable but necessary in order to achieve the lower unemployment rate.

It should be emphasized that the Phillips curve shown in Figure 14-1 is strictly a hypo-

After reading this chapter, you will be able to:
1. Explain the concept of the Phillips curve.
2. Describe how cost-push inflation can cause unemployment.
3. Explain how cost-push and demand-pull forces can combine with anticipated inflation to create stagflation.
4. Describe the nature of the stabilization policy dilemma associated with stagflation.
5. Describe how monetary policy and government deficits can combine to give the economy an inflationary bias.
6. Describe how the changing nature of unemployment may aggravate the inflation-unemployment problem.

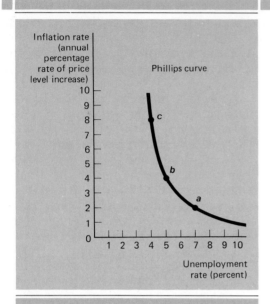

FIGURE 14-1   THE PHILLIPS CURVE: THE INFLATION-UNEMPLOYMENT TRADE-OFF (Hypothetical Example)

The Phillips curve is downward sloping left to right, suggesting that there is a trade-off between inflation (vertical axis) and unemployment (horizontal axis). The curve implies that the economy typically will experience both inflation and unemployment at the same time, and that price stability and full employment are not compatible goals of fiscal and monetary policy. Most economists agree that increases in total demand will lead to higher rates of inflation and lower unemployment rates, a movement up along the curve. However, today most would question whether this process is reversible—namely, that the economy could move back down the *same* curve if there is a decrease in total demand.

IMPLICATIONS OF THE PHILLIPS CURVE: THE REVERSIBILITY ISSUE

One important implication of the Phillips curve is that the economy typically will experience both inflation and unemployment at the same time. In other words, price stability and full employment are not compatible goals of fiscal and monetary policy. Another implication is that the economy can move up along the Phillips curve, reducing the unemployment rate and increasing the rate of inflation. However, the Phillips curve also implies that this process is reversible—that the economy can move back down the curve, as from point *c* to point *b* to point *a*, reducing the rate of inflation and increasing the unemployment rate. This implication is far more questionable and controversial than the others. Why?

It appears to most observers of the U.S. economy that the rate of inflation rises more readily than it falls. Almost all economists would agree that an increase in total demand is likely to lead to an increase in the rate of inflation and a reduction in the unemployment rate, a movement up the Phillips curve. But few would argue that the economy is likely to follow the same path back down the Phillips curve in response to a decrease in total demand. What does the evidence show?

THE EVIDENCE:
IS THERE A STABLE PHILLIPS CURVE?

Figure 14–2 plots the rate of inflation (vertical axis) and the associated unemployment rate (horizontal axis) for the U.S. economy in each year since 1953. The data strongly suggest that there is not a stable Phillips curve relationship.

This figure shows us that periods during which the inflation rate rose and the unemployment rate fell were followed by periods in which the inflation rate fell by less than the previous rise as the unemployment rate increased. Clearly movements up along any alleged Phillips curve are not followed by reverse movements back down the same Phillips curve. Moreover, even more striking are the instances in which both the inflation rate and the unemployment rate rose (1956 to 1957, 1962 to 1963,

thetical example. The curve could lie to the left or right of the position shown. It might conceivably intersect the horizontal axis at a 9 percent unemployment rate. This would suggest that if we were willing to settle for a 9 percent unemployment rate we could have a zero rate of inflation.

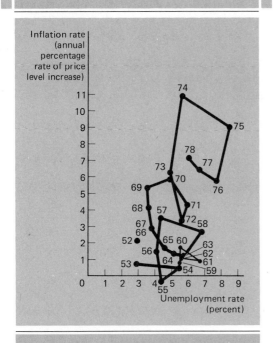

FIGURE 14-2 THE RELATIONSHIP BETWEEN INFLATION AND UNEMPLOYMENT

The relationship between the inflation rate (vertical axis) and the unemployment rate (horizontal axis) in the U.S. economy suggests that the Phillips curve is not stable. Periods of increasing rates of inflation accompanied by reductions in the unemployment rate were followed by periods in which the inflation rate fell by less than the previous rise as the unemployment rate increased. Even more striking are the instances in which both the inflation rate and the unemployment rate rose (1956 to 1957, 1962 to 1963, 1969 to 1970, and 1973 to 1974). Such movements are completely contrary to the alleged shape of the Phillips curve.

Also, on average, the unemployment rate seems to have increased during the 1970s. Much of the rest of this chapter is concerned with possible explanations for the phenomena shown in Figure 14-2.

Cost-Push Inflation and Unemployment

In the Keynesian analysis, the equilibrium levels of total income, output, and employment are determined by demand, as represented by the intersection of the economy's total demand schedule with the 45° line. The concept of the Phillips curve really derives from the notion that increases in total demand tend to increase inflation and reduce unemployment, while decreases in total demand tend to reduce inflation and increase unemployment. However, during the 1970s the U.S. economy suffered a number of severe shocks on the supply side—large increases in the price of imported oil and other fuels, as well as intermittent worldwide food and raw materials shortages. These shocks have led economists to focus more attention on the role of aggregate supply and its interaction with total demand as an explanatory factor underlying the behavior of inflation and unemployment.

AGGREGATE SUPPLY AND TOTAL DEMAND

Recall our discussion in Chapter 8 of cost-push inflation and the way it might be represented in terms of the aggregate supply curve, as illustrated in Figure 8-9. (You may want to re-read that discussion at this point.) There we noted that a cost-push inflation could occur in a number of ways. It might come about because powerful unions force firms to pay higher wages by threatening to strike. These firms then pass on the resulting rise in per unit costs, at least in part, in the form of higher product prices. Cost-push inflation may also result because a few large firms in key industries exercise their market power to raise profits by increasing the prices they charge for their products. Another source of cost-push inflation, common during the 1970s, is increases in the prices of vital re-

1969 to 1970, and 1973 to 1974). These movements are completely contrary to the alleged shape of the Phillips curve. If anything, the data in Figure 14-2 suggest that the economy has experienced an upward spiraling inflation rate associated with a cyclical unemployment rate.

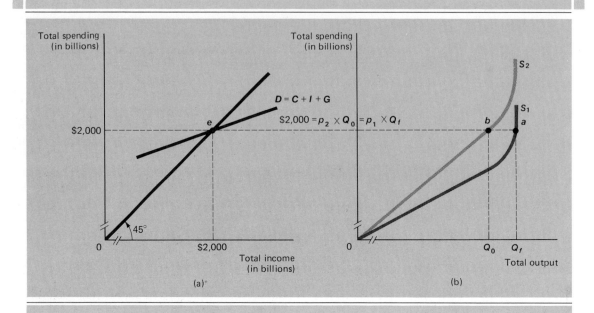

FIGURE 14-3 COST-PUSH INFLATION, TOTAL DEMAND, AND AGGREGATE SUPPLY

The economy's total demand schedule D (equal to $C + I + G$) determines an equilibrium level of total spending and income equal to $2,000 billion (part a). If the aggregate supply curve is $0S_1$, the economy will be producing the full-employment total output level Q_f, corresponding to point a on $0S_1$. The quantity of total output Q_f is bought and sold at the general price level p_1 so that the total spending of $2,000 billion equals $p_1 \times Q_f$.

Suppose there is a cost-push that shifts the aggregate supply curve up to $0S_2$. Since total spending (determined in part a) remains unchanged at $2,000 billion, the economy now produces a lower level of total output Q_0, corresponding to point b on $0S_2$, and sells it at the higher general price level p_2. The total spending of $2,000 billion now equals $p_2 \times Q_0$. Since total output has declined, employment is reduced and there is now unemployment. Hence, given a cost-push, the economy experiences both an increase in the rate of inflation and the unemployment rate.

sources, such as energy and strategic raw materials. Again, such increases cause increases in per unit production costs that push up the prices of almost all goods and services, as reflected by a rise in the general price level. In Figure 8-9 we saw how cost-push inflation is represented by an upward shift of the aggregate supply curve. For example, the aggregate supply curve $0S_0$ in Figure 8-9, part a, shifted upward to $0S_1$.

What is the relationship between cost-push inflation and unemployment? To answer this

question, recall how we combined our analysis of total demand with that of aggregate supply in Chapter 8, Figure 8-10.

This is repeated in Figure 14-3. Suppose the total demand schedule D (equal to $C + I + G$) intersects the 45° line at point e. This determines an equilibrium level of total spending and income of $2,000 billion, as shown in part a. Suppose the economy's aggregate supply curve is initially in the position $0S_1$, as shown in part b of Figure 14-3. With a level of total spending equal to $2,000 billion (vertical axis), the econ-

ECONOMIC THINKERS

A. W. H. PHILLIPS
1914-1975

Phillips, a New Zealander by birth, spent much of his life in England as student and faculty member at the London School of Economics. He was a scholar whose reputation was made by a single paper, published at the right time. This was "The Relationship Between Unemployment and the Rate of Change of Money Wage Rates in the United Kingdom 1861-1957" (1958).

In this paper Phillips suggested a relationship between inflation and unemployment—a great "tradeoff." He illustrated this concept with a curve linking the apparent relationship between unemployment on one axis and changes in money wages on the other. His work indicated that perhaps the economy might progress in one area at the expense of the other. If this were true, economic policy makers were faced with a cruel dilemma. If they were to press for full employment, would it be at the expense of undue price increases and vice versa?

The "Phillips curve" became very widely discussed by economists and policy makers, due in part perhaps to its graphic simplicity and appeal. Many economists were critical of his analysis, especially those engaged in policy making, such as on the Council of Economic Advisers and the Joint Economic Committee. Phillips indicated that data for the period 1948-1957 corresponded rather closely with a curve based on data from the years 1861-1913, but in his paper he offered little explanation of the underlying theory of the relationship, and the factors underlying the location of the curve, or curves. As the curve shifted to the right, the likelihood of finding an acceptable combination of unemployment and price increases became increasingly remote. A vast outpouring of literature has accumulated in the economics journals regarding the location of the curve and how it might be shifted to a more favorable position.

The Phillips curve led to many questions. How is the position of the curve influenced by imperfect competition or lack of knowledge in the labor market? What policies can a modern government undertake to shift the curve into a more desirable position (that is, to the left)? What will be the impact of improving technology which might enable money wage rates to go up without an increase in unemployment? Or what about reductions in agricultural prices which might lower living costs and ease pressure for wage increases?

During the 1960s and 1970s the Phillips curve analysis became embroiled in the argument between those who argued that unemployment was chiefly structural (due to poorly trained workers, geographic shifts in industry, and the like), and those who argued that it was due to lack of aggregate demand and could be cured by large expenditures. Another policy issue to which the curve was central was the argument over "cost-push" or "demand-pull" inflation, that is, did prices rise because of increasing demand, increasing costs of inputs, or some of both? The existence of the Phillips curve has been severely challenged by rapidly changing and unpredictable economic conditions in the 1960s and 1970s.

omy produces a full-employment level of total output equal to Q_f (horizontal axis), corresponding to point a on the aggregate supply curve $0S_1$. The quantity of total output Q is bought and sold at the general price level p_1 so that the total spending of $2,000 billion equals $p_1 \times Q_f$. (If the economy only produced widgets, for example, p_1 would be the price per widget and Q_f

would equal the total quantity of widgets produced at full employment.) Finally, we will assume that the economy has been in this position for some time. That is, the price level has been steady at p_1—the rate of inflation is zero.

INCREASED INFLATION WITH INCREASED UNEMPLOYMENT

Now suppose the economy is subjected to some sort of cost push, such as a sudden rise in the price of imported oil. This will cause the costs of production to rise. Producers will now charge higher prices to cover their higher costs. To induce the economy's firms to produce any given level of total output, the general price level will now have to be higher than previously. This is reflected by an upward shift in the aggregate supply curve from $0S_1$ to a position such as $0S_2$ (part b). However, given the *unchanged* level of total spending, equal to $2,000 billion as determined in part a, an *increase* in the general price level means that the quantity of total output produced and sold in the economy must *decrease*. Hence, the quantity of total output decreases from Q_f to Q_0 while the price level rises from p_1 to p_2. The economy now produces at point *b* on the aggregate supply curve $0S_1$ (part b). Total spending is still $2,000 billion, as determined in part a, but now it is the product of a higher price level p_2 multiplied by a lower total output level Q_0, or $p_2 \times Q_0$. Since the production of total output is less than the full-employment level, employment is reduced and there is now unemployment. In sum, a cost-push has resulted in a rise in both the general price level *and* the unemployment rate. The rate of inflation has increased from zero to some positive amount.

Given a cost-push, the economy can experience an increase in both the rate of inflation and the unemployment rate at the same time. Note that this is contrary to the conventional Phillips curve trade-off. Note also, however, that it does provide an explanation for the simultaneous increases in the rate of inflation and the unemployment rate incurred from 1956 to 1957, from 1962 to 1963, from 1969 to 1970, and from 1973 to 1974, as shown in Figure 14-2.

■ CHECKPOINT 14-1

Suppose the Phillips curve in Figure 14-1 shifts in such a way that unemployment can be reduced with a smaller increase in the rate of inflation. Sketch how the new Phillips curve might look. Suppose the Phillips curve in Figure 14-1 shifts so that the economy can have a zero percent rate of inflation when it has a 9 percent unemployment rate, and yet require larger increases in the inflation rate for each percentage point of reduction in the unemployment rate. Sketch how such a Phillips curve might look. If the Phillips curve represents a menu of choices, is the policy maker's selection of a point on the curve a normative or a positive issue? Why? In Figure 14-3, suppose Q_f equals 1 billion widgets. Given that total spending equals $2,000 billion, what must be the value of p_1? If Q_0 equals 800 million widgets, what must be the value of p_2?

THE DILEMMA OF STABILIZATION POLICY

The data in Figure 14-2 suggest that the rate of inflation has been spiraling upward by progressively larger jumps. At the same time, the fluctuating unemployment rate seems to be drifting to generally higher levels in recent years. This experience seems quite at odds with the conventional Phillips curve. Possible explanations for these unhappy and perplexing developments are currently the subject of much debate and controversy among economists. These developments are also a source of grave concern for stabilization policy, the use of fiscal and monetary policy to smooth out business fluctuations while maintaining reasonably full employment and price stability.

During the 1970s policy makers seemed to have been losing the battle with the rising general price level. At the same time, unemployment rates were generally higher in the second half of the decade than during the first half, a development which combined with worsening inflation has given rise to the term stagflation. Figure 14-4 shows the relationship between the

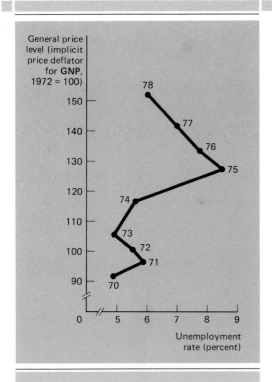

General price level (implicit price deflator for GNP, 1972 = 100)

FIGURE 14-4 THE GENERAL PRICE LEVEL AND THE UNEMPLOYMENT RATE DURING THE 1970s

The general price level is measured on the vertical axis and the unemployment rate on the horizontal axis. As the general price level rose during the first years of the decade (1970–1974), the unemployment rate fluctuated between levels of roughly 5 to 6 percent. While the general price level continued to rise during the second half of the decade, the unemployment rate was pushed up dramatically by the 1973–1975 recession. During the second half of the decade, the unemployment rate never quite decreased to the levels of the first half of the decade.

general price level (vertical axis) and the unemployment rate (horizontal axis) for each of the years during the 1970s. While the general price level increased during the first half of the decade (1970–1974), the unemployment rate fluctu-

ated between levels of roughly 5 to 6 percent. The unemployment rate increased dramatically during the 1973–1975 recession while the general price level continued its rise throughout the second half of the decade. During the second half, the unemployment rate never quite decreased to the levels that prevailed during the first half of the decade. Let's pursue our analysis of the interaction of total demand and aggregate supply to see what light it might shed on the developments shown in Figure 14-4.

The Wage Catch-up and Unemployment: Demand-Pull and Cost-Push Inflation Combined

Suppose the economy is initially in the equilibrium position determined by the total demand schedule D_1 in Figure 14-5, part a. Total spending and income equal $1,800 billion, corresponding to the intersection of D_1 with the 45° line at point e_1. The economy is producing a total output equal to Q_0, corresponding to point a on the aggregate supply curve $0S_1$ in Figure 14-5, part b. The price level is p_0, and the total spending of $1,800 billion equals $p_0 \times Q_0$. There is unemployment because Q_0 is less than the full-employment output level Q_f.

Suppose policy makers want to push the economy toward full employment, thereby reducing the unemployment rate. Suppose they do this by increasing the money supply (or by increasing government spending or reducing taxes, or both) enough to push the total demand schedule from D_1 up to the position D_2 (part a). Total spending and income rise from $1,800 billion to $2,000 billion, corresponding to point e_2 (part a). This causes the economy to move up along the aggregate supply curve $0S_1$ from point a to point b, the inflationary zone of $0S_1$ (part b). Total output increases from Q_0 to Q_f, while the general price level rises from p_0 to p_1, so that the total spending of $2,000 billion equals $p_1 \times Q_f$. Employment increases and unemployment is reduced.

However, while the general price level of final goods and services in the economy has risen, suppose the money wages of the labor force (or some sizeable portion of the labor force) have

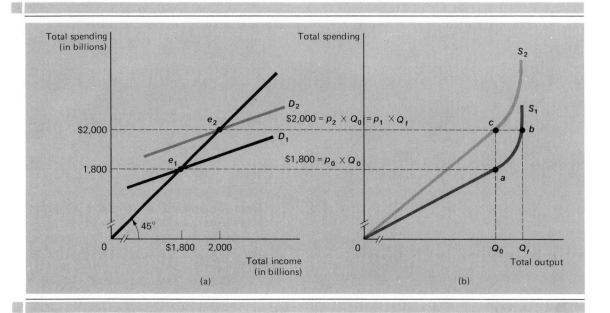

(a)

(b)

remained unchanged.[1] This means that labor's **real wage**, which is equal to the money wage divided by the general price level, has fallen. A worker gets paid the same number of dollars but these dollars buy less. Correctly perceiving themselves as worse off, the labor force demands a higher money wage in order to "catch up" with the rise in the general price level. But this pushes up producers' costs of production.

[1] This is of course only a temporary situation. When total demand increases, businesses are the first to become aware of it. They notice that goods are moving off shelves faster, that inventories are becoming more rapidly depleted, and that there is an increase in their backlogs of unfilled orders. Businesses respond to the increased demand by increasing output. But more and more of them begin to encounter production bottlenecks and capacity constraints. Hence, as the economy moves up along the inflationary zone of its aggregate supply curve, firms begin to increase prices more and output less in response to increased demand. Some kinds of labor in short supply may also get higher wages. But only *after* firms have increased prices do workers in general begin to become aware of the price increases—for example, during the course of their shopping around for various goods and services. Only *after* workers in general have become aware of the rise in the general price level will they begin to demand higher money wages. Then they will want to "catch up" with the rise in the "cost of living."

As a result, producers raise prices to compensate for part or all of their increased labor costs. This gives a cost-push to the aggregate supply curve, causing it to shift upward from $0S_1$ to $0S_2$. Given the unchanged level of total spending of $2,000 billion, determined in part a, total output is reduced from Q_f to Q_0, corresponding to point c on $0S_2$. The general price level is increased from p_1 to p_2. Output falls because the general price level has risen while total spending remains unchanged. Employment falls and unemployment increases.

Consider what has happened. Starting from a position at which the economy was operating at less than full employment, policy makers stimulated total demand by increasing the money supply. This had the desired effect of increasing total output and reducing unemployment, but also the undesirable inflationary effect of increasing the general price level—a demand-pull inflation. The rise in the general price level caused labor to demand catch-up money wage increases, giving rise to increased labor costs. This caused a further increase in the general price level *and* a reduction in total output, hence an increase in unemployment. In sum, policy makers' attempts to reduce unemployment gave rise to a demand-pull inflation followed by a cost-push inflation. The reduction in

FIGURE 14-5 DEMAND-PULL AND COST-PUSH INFLATION COMBINED

In part a the total demand schedule D_1 gives rise to an equilibrium total spending and income level of $1,800 billion. Following the horizontal guideline from point e_1, over to point a on aggregate supply curve $0S_1$, the $1,800 billion of total spending leads the economy's firms to produce the less than full-employment total output Q_0 and to sell it at the general price level p_0—the $1,800 billion of total spending equals $p_0 \times Q_0$.

In order to reduce unemployment, suppose policy makers increase the money supply (or increase government spending or reduce taxes, or both) so that the total demand schedule shifts upward from D_1 to D_2 in part a. Total spending and income rises from $1,800 billion to $2,000 billion. The economy moves up along the inflationary zone of the aggregate supply curve $0S_1$ from point a to b in part b. Total output increases from Q_0 to the full-employment level Q_f, the general price level rises from p_0 to p_1, and unemployment falls. Total spending of $2,000 billion equals $p_1 \times Q_f$.

Assuming labor's money wages have remained unchanged, their real wages have fallen. In an attempt to catch up, labor demands higher money wages. This imparts a cost-push to the aggregate supply curve, causing it to shift up to $0S_2$. Total output falls to Q_0, corresponding to point c on $0S_2$, the general price level rises further to p_2, and unemployment rises. Overall, the policy makers' attempts to reduce unemployment have led to a demand-pull inflation followed by a cost-push inflation. There is still unemployment.

unemployment associated with the demand-pull inflation was temporary since unemployment increased again as a result of the cost-push inflation. Overall, while the general price level has risen, there has been no permanent improvement in the unemployment rate.

The Wage-Price Spiral and Unemployment

Couldn't the process described in Figure 14-5 repeat itself? Yes, indeed. And when it does, the economy will get into an upward wage-price spiral accompanied by a fluctuating unemployment rate. Let's see how.

Parts a and b of Figure 14-5 are reproduced in parts a and b of Figure 14-6. Suppose that the "full-employment" output level Q_f is associated with a 5 percent unemployment rate. That is, policy makers regard this as the closest the economy can reasonably get to full employment before excessive bottlenecks and frictional and structural unemployment (discussed in Chapter 6) cause the aggregate supply curve to become vertical. Suppose when the total output level is Q_0 that the unemployment rate is 7 percent. Associated with the economy's initial position at point a on the aggregate supply curve (part b) is an unemployment rate of 7 percent and a price level of p_0, corresponding to point a in part c of

Figure 14-6. Note that part c shows the relationship between the general price level (vertical axis) and the unemployment rate (horizontal axis) in exactly the same way as Figure 14-4. When policy makers prod the economy to point b on the aggregate supply curve $0S_1$ (part b), the unemployment rate falls to 5 percent and the price level rises to p_1, corresponding to point b in part c. When the ensuing wage increase occurs, the aggregate supply curve is shifted up to $0S_2$, and the economy moves to point c on aggregate supply curve $0S_2$ (part b). The price level rises to p_2, and unemployment again increases to 7 percent, corresponding to point c in part c.

Despite the initial success at reducing unemployment, the unemployment rate has increased again to 7 percent. Suppose policy makers again try to attain their goal of reducing the unemployment rate to 5 percent by increasing the money supply. This pushes the total demand schedule up to D_3, and the equilibrium level of total spending and income rises to $2,200 billion, corresponding to point e_3 in part a. The demand-pull inflation occurs just as before. The economy moves up the aggregate supply curve $0S_2$ from point c to point d (part b), and the unemployment rate is reduced to 5 percent, while the price level rises to p_3, corresponding to point d in part c. Once again labor demands higher money wages to catch up with the rising

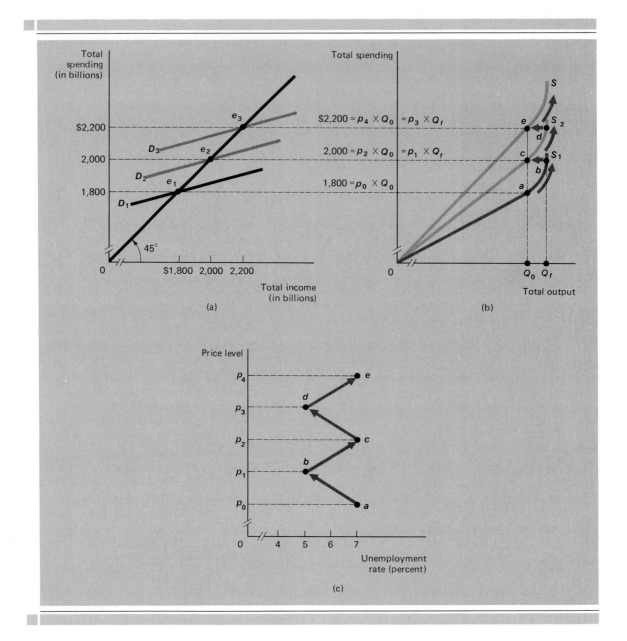

(a)

(b)

(c)

price level. This pushes the aggregate supply curve in part b up to $0S_3$, once again giving rise to cost-push inflation. The economy now produces at point e on $0S_3$ and the price level rises to p_4, while the unemployment rate increases again to 7 percent, point e in part c.

Confronted with the unemployment problem once more, policy makers react again and the upward wage-price spiral continues, with the unemployment rate fluctuating between 7 and 5 percent. Our hypothetical example illustrates how the policy makers' well-intentioned attempts to get the unemployment rate down to more desirable levels can result in an undesirable inflation. Moreover, the unemployment rate reduction proves to be temporary. (We are reminded of the behavior of the general price level and the unemployment rate shown in Fig-

FIGURE 14-6 THE WAGE-PRICE SPIRAL AND UNEMPLOYMENT

Policy makers increase the money supply, thereby shifting the total demand schedule upward from D_1 to D_2 in part a. This causes the economy to move up along its aggregate supply schedule $0S_1$ from point a to b (part b). Corresponding to this, the unemployment rate falls from 7 percent to 5 percent, while the price level rises from p_0 to p_1, the move from a to b in part c. In response to this demand-pull inflation, labor demands a higher wage, which causes the aggregate supply curve to shift up from $0S_1$ to $0S_2$ (part b). Given the unchanged level of total spending, the economy moves to produce at point c on $0S_2$, the output level falls from Q_f to Q_0 and the price level rises from p_1 to p_2—there is a cost-push inflation. Corresponding to the rise in the price level, there is a rise in the unemployment rate, as shown in part c.

Faced again with an unemployment problem, policy makers increase the money supply once more, and total demand shifts upward from D_2 to D_3 (part a). The entire cycle repeats itself again with the economy moving from point c to d to e in parts b and c, and the price level moving ever higher as the unemployment rate fluctuates between 5 and 7 percent.

ure 14-4 when we look at Figure 14-6, part c). Unfortunately, the situation can get worse with the onset of anticipated inflation. Let's see why.

Unemployment and Anticipated Inflation

Assume the process described in Figure 14-6 has repeated itself several times. Both business firms and labor have experienced a general rise in the price level for some time now. Hence, they come to expect, or anticipate, inflation. Laborers will no longer demand higher wages simply to catch up with already realized increases in the price level. Rather than simply reacting in catch-up fashion, they will begin to anticipate such increases and try to stay ahead of, or at least even with, inflation. Similarly, business firms will come to anticipate inflation and the associated increases in their costs. They will begin to pass such cost increases on in the form of higher product prices, in anticipation of rising demand rather than simply in reaction to it.

As business and labor come to anticipate inflation, the upward shifts in the aggregate supply curve take on a life of their own. Suppose this occurs at the point at which the total demand schedule has reached the position D_2, Figure 14-7, part a, and the aggregate supply curve is in the position $0S_2$, part b. The equilibrium level of total spending and income is $2,000 billion (part a), which equals $p_2 \times Q_0$ (part b), corresponding to point c on $0S_2$, and the unemployment rate is 7 percent, point c in

part c. Now as they come to anticipate inflation, business and labor push up wages and prices causing the aggregate supply curve to shift up to $0S_3$ (part b). With total spending still equal to $2,000 billion, determined by D_2 in part a, the price level rises from p_2 to p_3, and output falls to Q_1, corresponding to point d on $0S_3$. As a result, employment falls and the unemployment rate now rises to 9 percent, corresponding to the move from point c to point d (part c).

Now consider what happens when policy makers attempt to reduce the unemployment rate by increasing the money supply and pushing the total demand schedule upward from D_2 to D_3 (part a). If there had been no anticipated inflation, the economy would have moved up along the aggregate supply curve $0S_2$ from point c to point d'. The unemployment rate would have fallen from 7 percent to 5 percent, and the price level would have risen from p_2 to p_3, corresponding to the move from c to d' indicated by the broken line in part c. Instead, however, as the result of the onset of anticipated inflation, the increase in total demand from D_2 to D_3 causes the economy to move up along the aggregate supply curve $0S_3$ from point d to point e (part b). The unemployment rate falls from 9 percent to 7 percent, and the price level rises from p_3 to p_4, as indicated by the move from point d to point e (part c).

In sum, as a result of the onset of anticipated inflation, the price level increase is larger, from p_2 to p_4, and the unemployment rate is higher.

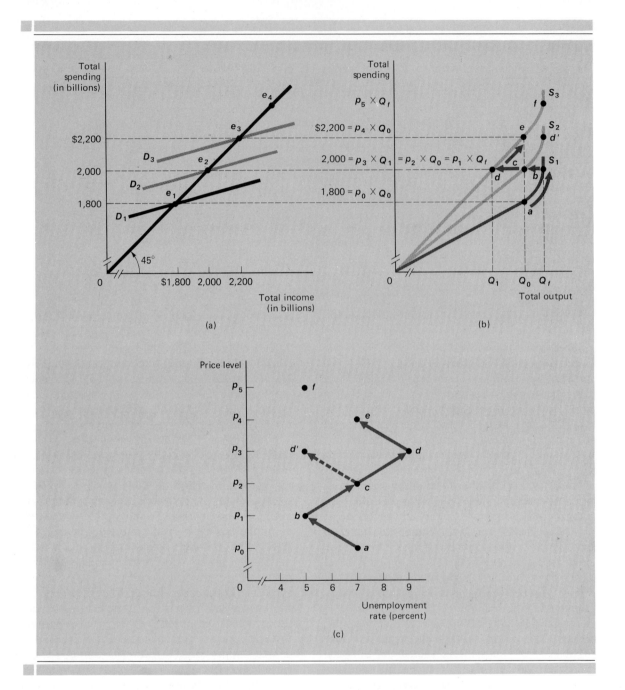

(a)

(b)

(c)

The policy makers' problem has worsened. Again, when we look at Figure 14-7, part c, we are reminded of the behavior of the general price level and the unemployment rate shown in Figure 14-4.

ACCELERATING INFLATION

Starting from point *c* in parts b and c of Figure 14-7, the onset of anticipated inflation combined with the increase in the total demand schedule from D_2 to D_3 (part a) has caused the

FIGURE 14-7 ANTICIPATED INFLATION

When labor and business come to expect inflation, they will begin adjusting wages and prices upward in anticipation of increases in the price level, rather than in reaction to such increases. This will cause the aggregate supply curve to shift upward on its own, instead of only in response to increases in total demand.

Suppose the onset of inflationary expectations occur when total demand is D_2 (part a), and the economy is producing at point c on aggregate supply curve $0S_2$ (part b). The aggregate supply curve shifts up to $0S_3$. The economy moves from point c to d (parts b and c), pushing the price level up from p_2 to p_3 and the unemployment rate up from 7 percent to 9 percent. Now suppose policy makers increase the money supply and push total demand up from D_2 to D_3 (part a). The economy moves up along the aggregate supply curve $0S_3$ from point d to e (part b), and the corresponding change in the price level and the unemployment rate is given by the move from point d to e in part c.

By contrast, had there been no onset of inflationary expectations the same increase in total demand would have caused the economy to move up along the aggregate supply curve $0S_2$ from point c to d'. The corresponding changes in the unemployment rate and the price level are indicated by the movement from point c to d' in part c. Clearly, the onset of anticipated inflation results in a greater rise in the price level and a worsening of the unemployment problem.

price level to rise from p_2 to p_4, corresponding to point e in parts b and c. Without the onset of anticipated inflation, the price level would only have increased from p_2 to p_3, corresponding to point d' in parts b and c. This suggests that the onset of anticipated inflation may cause inflation to accelerate.

For one thing, the greater rise in the price level may cause labor and business to revise their expectations of the rate of inflation upward, leading to even larger upward shifts in the aggregate supply curve. And this itself could contribute to an acceleration of inflation. However, the major impetus to such an acceleration may well come from policy makers' reaction to the rise in the unemployment rate. Let's see why.

The onset of anticipated inflation causes the unemployment rate to rise from 7 percent to 9 percent, corresponding to the movement from point c to d in parts b and c of Figure 14-7. Alarmed by such a high unemployment rate, suppose policy makers try again to reduce the rate back to the 5 percent "full-employment" level. In order to do this, suppose they increase the money supply by the amount necessary to shift the total demand schedule upward from D_2 to a position intersecting the 45° line at e_4 (part

a). Total spending increases until it equals $p_5 \times Q_f$ (part b). The economy responds by increasing total output from Q_1 to Q_f, moving up its aggregate supply curve $0S_3$ from point d to point f (part b). The unemployment rate is reduced to 5 percent, but the price level has now increased to p_5, corresponding to point f (part c).

Had there been no onset of anticipated inflation, starting from point c (parts b and c) policy makers could have reduced the unemployment rate to 5 percent, while increasing the price level only from p_2 to p_3, corresponding to the movement from point c to point d' in part c. However, because of the onset of anticipated inflation, and policy makers' subsequent attempts to reduce the unemployment rate back to 5 percent, the price level rises from p_2 to p_5. Again, this larger rise in the price level may cause an upward revision of inflationary expectations, leading to even larger upward shifts in the aggregate supply curve. Policy makers react even more strongly to the resulting rise in unemployment and the inflation accelerates.

THE POLICY DILEMMA: STAGFLATION
Once inflationary expectations have set in and the aggregate supply curve is shifting upward on its own, policy makers are caught in a

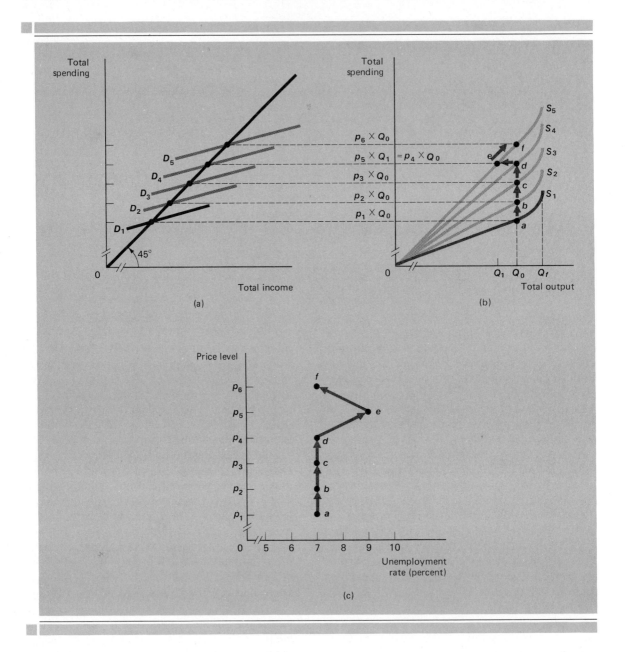

(a)

(b)

(c)

dilemma. The upward shifting aggregate supply curve causes both cost-push inflation and unemployment at the same time. If policy makers try to reduce unemployment by stimulating total demand, inflation tends to accelerate in the manner just described in Figure 14–7. On the other hand, if they try to curb inflation by tight-

ening the reins on total demand, the unemployment rate rises.

The policy makers' dilemma is illustrated in Figure 14–8. Suppose inflationary expectations have set in and the aggregate supply curve is shifting upward (part b). Suppose policy makers are increasing the money supply at a rate suffi-

FIGURE 14-8 STAGFLATION, A POLICY DILEMMA

Stagflation is a situation in which the economy experiences both inflation and excessive unemployment at the same time.

Suppose policy makers increase the money supply at a rate sufficient to keep total demand (part a) rising at the same rate that the aggregate supply curve is shifting upward (part b). The continuing rise in total demand confirms the inflationary expectations and, thereby, causes the rise in the aggregate supply curve to continue.

Total output is stable at Q_0 (part b), and the price level rises from p_1 to p_2 to p_3, and so forth, as total demand rises from D_1 to D_2 to D_3, while aggregate supply increases from $0S_1$ to $0S_2$ to $0S_3$, and so forth. The unemployment rate remains at 7 percent, while the price level rises as shown in part c, from point a to b to c, and so forth, corresponding to points a, b, c, and so forth, in part b. This is stagflation.

If policy makers attempt to curb inflation when the total demand schedule is at D_4 (part a), the economy moves from point d to e (parts b and c). The price level rises from p_4 to p_5, total output falls from Q_0 to Q_1, and the unemployment rate rises from 7 percent to 9 percent. Concern about these recessionary developments will put policy makers under pressure to continue to expand demand, such as from D_4 to D_5, moving the economy from point e to f (parts b and c). The unemployment rate is again 7 percent, and the inflation continues.

cient to keep total demand (part a) rising at the same rate that the aggregate supply curve is shifting upward (part b). Total output is stable at Q_0 (part b), and the price level rises from p_1 to p_2 to p_3, and so forth as total demand rises from D_1 to D_2 to D_3, while aggregate supply increases from $0S_1$ to $0S_2$ to $0S_3$, and so forth. The rise in total demand confirms the inflationary expectations and, thereby, causes the aggregate supply curve to continue to rise. The unemployment rate remains at 7 percent, while the price level rises as shown in part c, from point a, to point b, to point c, and so forth, corresponding to points a, b, c, and so forth, in part b. In short, we have **stagflation**—*a situation in which the economy experiences both inflation and excessive unemployment at the same time.* (By excessive unemployment we mean an unemployment rate that is greater than what is considered the full-employment unemployment rate, here assumed to be 5 percent.)

Suppose that at the point where the total demand schedule has risen to the position D_4 (part a), policy makers try to curb inflation. The economy is producing at point d on the aggregate supply curve $0S_4$ (part b). Now the aggregate supply curve continues to shift up to $0S_5$ (part b) due to anticipated inflation, but the to-

tal demand schedule remains at D_4 (part a). Consequently, total output is reduced to Q_1 as the economy now produces at point e on the aggregate supply curve $0S_5$. The price level rises to p_5, and the unemployment rate rises from 7 percent to 9 percent, corresponding to the move from point d to point e in part c. The policy makers' attempt to halt the rise in the general price level has not succeeded. At the same time, the economy experiences a recession and a rise in the unemployment rate.

It is likely that policy makers will now come under pressure to take action to fight the recession and reduce the unemployment rate. Responding, they increase total demand to D_5 (part a). Total output rises to Q_0 as the economy moves up its aggregate supply curve $0S_5$ from point e to point f (part b). The unemployment rate is reduced from 9 percent to 7 percent, and the price level rises from p_5 to p_6, corresponding to the move from point e to point f (part c).

Of course, spiraling inflation is not inevitable or unavoidable. But once it is underway, the principal question facing policy makers is how deep and long a recession does it take to squeeze inflationary expectations out of the economy? The higher the cost in terms of increased unemployment and reduced output, the more difficult it is to break out of the inflationary spiral. The evidence in Figures 14-2 and 14-4 is not encouraging. After the worst recession (1973-1975) in the postwar period, and unemployment rates of 8.5, 7.7, and 6.6 percent in each of the years 1975, 1976, and 1977, respectively, the rate of inflation's lowest level was 5.8 percent in 1976. This is above its highest point of the 1960s.

SUPPLY SHOCKS AND STAGFLATION

Any shock to the economy that tends to shift the aggregate supply curve upward can aggravate the stagflation problem. For example, in late 1973 the major oil producing countries, the Organization of Petroleum Exporting Countries (OPEC), took actions that caused a fourfold increase in the world price of oil. In addition, crop failures in the Soviet Union and Asia led to large U.S. exports of agricultural products. This reduced domestic supplies and drove up food prices during 1973-1974. Further aggravating the supply side of the economy, a worldwide shortage of certain basic raw materials sharply increased their prices. The impact of these events on the rate of inflation, the general price level, and the unemployment rate in the U.S. economy in the 1973-1975 period is evident in Figures 14-2 and 14-4. The economy experienced its deepest recession since the Great Depression and its highest rates of inflation since the Korean War (see Chapter 6, Figure 6-4).

These supply shocks, combined with anticipated inflation and the wage-price spiral, have led economists to focus increasingly on the interaction of total demand and aggregate supply in the manner we have described. The simplified analysis we have examined gives the flavor of the kind of explanation many economists offer for the recent behavior of the general price level and the unemployment rate shown in Figure 14-4. It should be added that this area of economic analysis is currently the subject of much debate and controversy.

■ CHECKPOINT 14-2

Why is it reasonable to believe that a cost-push inflation cannot continue for long unless there are also increases in total demand? Why is it that the onset of anticipated inflation tends to be a self-fulfilling prophecy? Examine Figure 14-2 again. To what extent do you see evidence of accelerating inflation?

CONFLICTING GOALS AND CHANGING TRADE-OFFS

There are other factors that many economists claim have contributed to the inflationary spiral experienced by the economy in recent years. In the previous chapter we discussed some of the difficulties of coordinating monetary and fiscal policy. We will now focus more specifically on the role that the interest rate plays in the conflict between government deficit financing and the objectives of monetary policy. In particular, we will examine why a number of economists think that this conflict contributes to the inflationary process. Another area of concern is the changing nature of unemployment. In particular, is it possible that the traditional tools of fiscal and monetary policy cannot reduce unemployment without generating higher rates of inflation than was the case in the past? Before considering each of these issues, here again we should stress that we are dealing with some very important, yet very controversial, areas of economic policy and analysis.

Monetary Policy and Government Deficits

In Figures 14-5 through 14-8, we assumed that the increases in the total demand for goods and services were caused by increases in the money supply. Autonomous increases in consumption and investment spending, and increases in government spending or reductions in taxes, or both, can also cause the total demand schedule to shift upward. However, recall from the last chapter that the resulting rise in total income, or GNP, will lead to an increase in the demand for money. This in turn will cause the interest rate to rise. The result is a cutback in investment spending that tends to dampen the rise in total demand, with the extent of the cutback depending on the interest rate sensitivity of investment demand and money demand. (Recall the Keynesian view versus the monetarist view on this issue.) The only way to avoid this interest rate rise is for the Federal Reserve to increase the money supply. Of course, if the economy is already operating at or close to full employment, such a monetary expansion will result in a rise in the price level.

INTEREST RATE
STABILITY AND DEFICIT SPENDING

Over the years critics of the Federal Reserve have frequently claimed that it is overly concerned with maintaining interest rate stability. As a result, such critics allege, the Fed often expands the money supply to keep the interest rate from rising when the rise itself is caused by an inflationary increase in total demand. It would be wiser for the Fed to refrain from increasing the money supply and, thus, allow the interest rate rise to check the expansion of total demand, thereby dampening inflationary pressures. Instead, when the Fed expands the money supply in such a situation, it adds further fuel to the inflationary increase in total demand.

Critics go on to argue that these inflationary implications of the Fed's preoccupation with interest rate stability are of even more concern in the presence of government deficit spending. Why?

Interest Rate and Total Demand. Recall our discussion of government deficit spending in the last chapter. There we observed that a government deficit must be financed by issuing new government bonds. Recall that when these bonds are sold to the public there is no change in the economy's money supply as long as the Federal Reserve doesn't engage in open market purchases (monetize the debt). The money that the public gives to the U.S. Treasury in exchange for the new bonds is returned to the economy when the government spends it. This government spending shifts the total demand schedule upward, increasing GNP and the demand for money. *The interest rate rises* and cuts back investment spending (the crowding-out effect), which tends to dampen the upward shift in the total demand schedule.

However, if the Fed does not want the interest rate to rise, it must engage in open market purchases. That is, as soon as the interest rate

begins to rise, the Fed will carry out open market purchases to keep it down. As we saw in the last chapter, this amounts to financing the government deficit by printing money, or monetizing the government debt. The money supply is increased. Government deficit spending financed in this way causes the economy's total demand schedule to shift upward, both because of the spending increase and because of the increase in the money supply. Clearly, if the Fed does not want the interest rate to rise, the curb on the rise in total demand due to the crowding-out effect is absent and inflationary pressures are greater.

An Inflationary Bias. This is the reason that critics of the Fed contend that a preoccupation with interest rate stability gives monetary policy an inflationary bias that is accentuated by government deficit spending. They claim that this bias has been of particular concern since the middle 1960s. There has been only one government budget surplus (1969) since then. More alarming, however, has been the behavior of the high-employment budget, which economists generally regard as a more accurate measure of the expansionary impact of fiscal policy (see Chapter 9). Critics of the Fed note that the government ran a high-employment budget *surplus* throughout the last half of the 1950s and the first half of the 1960s—fiscal policy was contractionary. Since the beginning of 1966, except for 1969 and 1974, the government has run a high-employment budget *deficit*—fiscal policy has been predominantly expansionary (see Chapter 9, Figure 9-4). To the extent that the Fed has been preoccupied with interest rate stabilization, critics argue that monetary policy and fiscal policy have jointly contributed to the inflationary spiral shown in Figures 14-2 and 14-4.

INFLATION AND THE INTEREST RATE:
REAL VERSUS MONEY INTEREST RATE

There is another important consideration that bears on the issue of interest rate stability and monetary policy: the relationship between inflation and the interest rate. Whenever there is inflation, it is necessary to recognize the existence of two distinct measures of the interest rate: the real interest rate and the money interest rate.

The Real Interest Rate. The **real interest rate** *is the interest rate calculated in terms of its purchasing power over goods and services.* Suppose I agree to lend you $100 for one year at an interest rate of 10 percent. At the end of one year you will pay me back the $100 plus $10, or $110. If there is *no change in the general price level* in the meantime, I give up $100 of purchasing power over goods today in exchange for $110 of purchasing power over goods a year from now. In one year I will get back 10 percent more purchasing power than I originally gave up. Hence, in this example the real interest rate equals 10 percent. The real interest rate is the rate that we would actually see in the market when the general price level is stable—that is, when there is no inflation (or deflation).

The Money Interest Rate. The **money interest rate** *(sometimes called the nominal or market rate) is the interest rate calculated in terms of units of money, not purchasing power over goods.* Only when the general price level is expected to be stable is it true that the money interest rate equals the real interest rate. This is so because under these circumstances the purchasing power of a unit of money remains unchanged. Whenever there is anticipated inflation (or deflation), the money interest rate and the real interest rate will differ from one another by the amount of the anticipated inflation (or deflation). This is so because when there is a change in the general price level the purchasing power of a unit of money changes.

Anticipated Rate of Inflation. The **anticipated rate of inflation** *is the difference between real and money interest rates.* To illustrate the difference between the real interest rate and the money interest rate, consider our $100 loan example again. To be willing to lend you $100, I again insist on getting back 10 percent more purchasing power in one year than I originally gave up. But now suppose both you and I *expect* a 5 percent rate of inflation. This means we both expect the purchasing power of a unit of money, a dollar, to decline by 5 percent over the next year. Therefore, I must charge you an additional 5 percent just to compensate myself for

the anticipated loss in purchasing power on each unit of money, or dollar, that I lend you. Hence, I lend you $100 at a money rate of interest of 15 percent. The 15 percent money rate of interest equals the 10 percent real rate of interest plus the anticipated rate of inflation of 5 percent. This additional 5 percent may be thought of as an inflation premium that is added on to the real rate of interest. You will be willing to pay the 15 percent money rate of interest to borrow the $100 from me. Why? Because you will recognize that you are going to pay me back dollars that have lost 5 percent of their purchasing power due to inflation.

In short, the 15 percent money rate of interest means that I lend you $100 of money now, and in one year you repay me $115 of money. The 10 percent real rate of interest means that I lend you $100 of purchasing power *now,* and in one year you repay me the equivalent amount of purchasing power *plus* another 10 percent of purchasing power.

In summary:

money interest rate = real interest rate + anticipated rate of inflation

If the anticipated rate of inflation is zero, then the money interest rate and the real interest rate are the same. The money interest rate is the one we actually observe in the market for loans and bonds. The real interest rate is unobservable unless the anticipated rate of inflation is zero. In everyday life, the "interest rate" that people talk about is the money interest rate.

Now let's consider the implications of the distinction between the money and the real interest rate for the interest rate stabilization issue.

INTEREST RATE STABILITY AND ANTICIPATED INFLATION

Critics who claim that the Fed is too preoccupied with interest rate stability are referring to the money interest rate, since it is the rate observed in the market. The alleged inflationary bias of such a policy seems even more likely when this fact is recognized.

For example, assume the economy is operating close to full employment, somewhere along the inflationary zone of the aggregate supply curve. Now suppose there is an increase in total demand (possibly due to an increase in government deficit spending or an increase in autonomous investment and consumption spending, or both). The resulting rise in GNP causes money demand to increase, which in turn leads to a rise in the money interest rate. There is also a rise in the price level. Now the Fed reacts by increasing the money supply in order to bring the money interest rate back down (say by making an open market purchase). But this causes a further upward shift in the total demand schedule for goods and services, which means another increase in GNP and the price level. The increases in the price level cause people to begin to anticipate inflation. The onset of anticipated inflation causes the money interest rate to increase more as lenders now add on a larger inflation premium to the real interest rate. But this leads the Fed to again increase the money supply. The increase in the money supply causes another increase in total demand, a further rise in GNP and the price level, another increase in the anticipated rate of inflation and, hence, the money interest rate, and so on for another round.

By trying to stabilize the level of the money interest rate, the Fed actually triggers self-defeating increases in the anticipated rate of inflation which cause the money interest rate to rise even more as inflation gets worse! At some point in this process Fed critics contend that the Fed becomes alarmed at the accelerating inflation and slams the brakes on the growth of the money supply.

By this point the economy may be well into a stagflation situation such as that depicted in Figure 14–8. The brake on monetary expansion occurs at point d (parts b and c of Figure 14–8). The total demand schedule stops rising at D_4 (part a), while anticipated inflation continues to push up the aggregate supply schedule to $0S_5$ (part b). The economy moves to point e in parts b and c. Total output falls from Q_0 to Q_1, the unemployment rate rises, and the economy experiences a recession—while the price level continues to rise! Now the Fed feels compelled to fight the recession above all else. Once again it expands the money supply, total demand shifts

upward from D_4 to D_5, and the economy moves from point e to f (parts b and c of Figure 14–8). The inflationary spiral continues, accompanied by periodic recessions and expansions with fluctuations in the unemployment rate, as the process repeats itself. Again we are reminded of the actual behavior of the rate of inflation, the general price level, and unemployment in the U.S. economy, Figures 14–2 and 14–4. The Fed's alternating between fighting inflation and unemployment has been tagged the "stop-go policy" by critics.

IMPLICATIONS FOR
FISCAL AND MONETARY POLICY

A pattern of conflict among policy goals seems to be a major contributing factor to the inflation-unemployment process we have examined in this chapter. The Fed would like to stabilize the interest rate, but this goal conflicts with its desire to curb inflation. And its desire to curb inflation conflicts with its desire to avoid recession and unemployment. When the fiscal policy stance is one of almost continual budget deficits, particularly full-employment budget deficits, the inflationary bias of a monetary policy oriented toward interest rate stabilization is accentuated by the inflationary bias of fiscal policy.

Many critics of fiscal and monetary policy make the following recommendations: (1) The Federal Reserve should worry less about interest rate stabilization. These critics contend that this would help reduce the Fed's contribution to the inflationary bias jointly shared by fiscal and monetary policy. They claim that if the Fed focused less on interest rate stabilization, it could more effectively restrain demand-pull inflation. This, in turn, would go far to eliminate the Fed's periodic need to tighten the money supply in an attempt to curb an alarming acceleration of inflation, efforts that often bring on recession and unemployment—without the benefit of much relief from inflation. (2) Congress must act more responsibly to curb excessive deficit spending, particularly during those times when the economy is experiencing inflationary expansion. At such times, a reduction or elimination of the high-employment budget deficit would, in turn, make it easier for the Fed to control inflation without causing a recession.

These concerns underlie the news item at the beginning of this chapter. (You should reread the news item at this point.) There the Federal Reserve Board chairman recognizes the Fed's dilemma. In the absence of "attempts at fiscal restraint and balancing the budget," a greater share of the burden for fighting inflation falls on the Fed. Chairman Miller also seems to recognize the conflict between attempts to keep interest rates down and a fiscal policy characterized by continual deficit spending. Note his observation that "if the current annual rate of inflation continues, interest rates just won't come down." This seems a safe bet, given the role that the anticipated rate of inflation plays in determining the level of the money interest rate.

Inflation and the Changing Nature of Unemployment

What level of the unemployment rate corresponds to "full employment"? This is the level that is regarded as the acceptable, or the normal, unemployment rate. Recall our discussion of this question in Chapter 6. (You may want to reread that discussion.) There we observed that many economists believe that since the mid-1960s there has been a definite rise in the *level* of the unemployment rate that corresponds to the normal unemployment rate. What are the implications of this rise for efforts by policy makers to deal with the problems of inflation and unemployment? To answer these questions, let's first consider the changing nature of the unemployment rate, and then the way this change is reflected in the aggregate supply curve.

THE CHANGING NATURE OF UNEMPLOYMENT

In Chapter 6 we noted that the Department of Labor actually publishes six different measures of the unemployment rate. The level of unemployment can appear considerably different depending on which measure we look at. However, the news media, the public, politicians, and policy makers all tend to focus on only one of these. It is considered the official unemployment rate.

The official unemployment rate goes back to the 1930s. Then it was designed to measure unemployment among male adult heads of household. At that time, adult male heads of household did in fact constitute nearly the entire labor force. Over the years, however, the composition of the labor force has changed drastically, so that now the official unemployment rate covers a much more diverse group of people. Today work by male heads of household still accounts for about 67 percent of all hours worked because these men are primarily full-time workers. But now they constitute no more than 40 percent of the labor force. The other 60 percent of the labor force is made up of the following types of workers:

1. About 50 percent of the country's population of adult females now work or are seeking work. The great majority of these are not "heads of household," but "dependents" holding part-time jobs.

2. People who are officially "retired," but available for part-time work up to the point at which their earnings would reduce payments from their social security benefits.

3. Young single adults who maximize their incomes by alternating between periods of full-time employment and periods of official "unemployment," when they draw tax-free "unemployment" compensation.

4. Unemployables registered for "employment" in order to be eligible for welfare checks and food stamps.

5. A sizeable number of full-time students who are available for part-time work only.

In sum, the composition of the labor force has changed over time so that male heads of household represent a smaller portion, while all others (the five categories listed above) represent a larger portion. Many economists argue that a large number of the people in the "all other" portion are in circumstances that do not compel them to find work with the same urgency as the typical adult male head of household. Others in the all other portion are simply not as employable, either because of a lack of marketable job skills or because of disabilities of one form or another. Hence, many economists claim that the growing importance of the all other portion of the labor force means that the

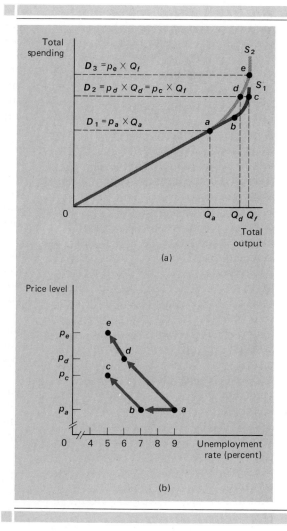

(a)

(b)

FIGURE 14-9 THE CHANGING NATURE OF UNEMPLOYMENT AFFECTS THE AGGREGATE SUPPLY CURVE
(Hypothetical Example)

Many economists argue that the changing nature of unemployment has caused price level increases to be larger when the economy approaches full employment. Such change causes the aggregate supply curve to change shape from $0S_1$ to $0S_2$ (part a).

As a result, when total spending increases from D_1 to D_2, the economy moves up along the aggregate supply curve $0S_2$ from point a to d, and total output increases from Q_a to Q_d. The price level rises from p_a to p_d, and the unemployment rate falls from 9 percent to 6 percent, corresponding to the move from point a to d in part b. Before the change in the nature of unemployment, the same increase in total spending would have caused the economy to move from point a to c on $0S_1$. Total output would have increased more, from Q_a to Q_f. The price level would rise less, from p_a to p_c, while the unemployment rate would be reduced more, from 9 percent to 5 percent, corresponding to the move from point a to c in part b.

To reduce the unemployment rate to 5 percent when the aggregate supply curve is $0S_2$ requires total spending to rise to D_3. This causes a further rise in the price level from p_d to p_e, corresponding to the move from point d to e (parts a and b).

level of the official unemployment rate corresponding to the notion of "full employment" has risen.

Remember from Chapter 6 that another factor that may contribute to this rise in the normal unemployment rate is the more rapid rate of growth of the labor force relative to the rate of growth of the total population. This situation reflects an influx of young workers born in the postwar "baby boom" combined with a sharp drop in the birthrate since the early 1960s. Yet another possible factor in the rise of the normal unemployment rate is the increased flow of nonpaycheck money in the form of more liberal unemployment compensation and welfare

benefits. It is argued that this makes it easier for people to remain unemployed longer while looking for a job, and may lead some to list themselves as unemployed even though they are not trying very hard to find work.

AGGREGATE SUPPLY AND INFLATION: POLICY IMPLICATIONS

The changing nature of unemployment has implications for the aggregate supply curve and the relationship between inflation and unemployment. These implications are illustrated in the hypothetical example of Figure 14-9. Suppose the level of total output Q_f (part a) corresponds to a 5 percent rate of unemployment in the economy. The aggregate supply curve corresponding to the situation *before* the changes in the nature of unemployment just described is $0S_1$, and $0S_2$ is the aggregate supply curve *after* these changes.

Assume that these changes make no difference in the economy's ability to produce any total output level up to the amount Q_a, and that the output level Q_a corresponds to a 9 percent unemployment rate. Therefore, the aggregate supply curves are the same from the origin 0 up to point *a* (part a). However, beyond point *a* the aggregate supply curve $0S_2$ lies above $0S_1$. This reflects the fact that along $0S_2$ beyond point *a*, as compared to $0S_1$, it is harder for the economy's producers to obtain the additional labor needed to increase output without paying higher wages. The more rapid rise in wages along $0S_2$, as compared to $0S_1$, means a more rapid rise in firms' costs. This, in turn, causes a more rapid rise in the prices firms charge for their products. Consequently, for increases in total output beyond point *a*, the economy's price level rises more for any given increase in total output along $0S_2$ than it does for the same increase in total output along $0S_1$.

Implications for Fiscal and Monetary Policy. Consider the implications of this for fiscal and monetary policy. Assume total spending in the economy initially is D_1, so that total output is Q_a, and the price level is p_a. D_1 therefore equals $p_a \times Q_a$. The unemployment rate is 9 percent, which corresponds to point *a* in parts a and b. Suppose policy makers desire to reduce the unemployment rate by stimulating total demand (either by increasing the money supply, or government expenditures, or reducing taxes, or some combination of these) so that total spending eventually rises to D_2 (part a).

If the aggregate supply curve is $0S_1$, the price level doesn't begin to rise until the economy reaches point *b* on the aggregate supply curve. Movement up to this point reduces the unemployment rate from 9 to 7 percent, represented by the move from point *a* to *b* in part b. Once total spending rises to D_2, total output will have risen to Q_f and the price level to p_c, so that $D_2 = p_c \times Q_f$, corresponding to point *c* on $0S_1$ (part a). The unemployment rate will fall fur-

ther, from 7 percent to 5 percent, as the price level rises from p_a to p_c, corresponding to the move from point *b* to point *c* in part b. (Note that the inflationary zone of the aggregate supply curve $0S_1$ corresponds to the segment of the curve between points *b* and *c*, while that for $0S_2$ corresponds to the segment between points *a* and *e*.)

By comparison, suppose the aggregate supply curve is $0S_2$, the curve that reflects the changes in the nature of unemployment we have described. The inflationary zone of $0S_2$ rises more sharply than that of $0S_1$. Now, when total spending increases from D_1 to D_2, the price level begins to rise immediately as the economy moves up along the aggregate supply curve $0S_2$ from point *a* to *d*. Total output rises by less than before, from Q_a to Q_d, while the price level rises by more, from p_a to p_d, so that $D_2 = p_d \times Q_d$ (part a). At the same time, this larger rise in the price level is accompanied by less of a reduction in the unemployment rate, from 9 percent to 6 percent, corresponding to the move from point *a* to *d* (part b). If policy makers are intent on raising total output to Q_f and reducing the unemployment rate to 5 percent, they will have to stimulate aggregate demand even further until total spending rises to D_3. The price level will rise further to p_e so that $D_3 = p_e \times Q_f$, corresponding to point *e* on $0S_2$ (part a). The rise in the price level from p_d to p_e, and the associated reduction in the unemployment rate from 6 percent to 5 percent, corresponds to the move from point *d* to *e* in part b.

Summary of Implications of Changing Nature of Unemployment. In sum, as a result of the changing nature of unemployment, the economy has to incur a larger rise in the price level in order to reduce the unemployment rate. This is another factor which many economists believe has contributed to the inflation-unemployment problem that has plagued the U.S. economy in recent years. Policy makers' attempts to reduce the official unemployment rate to levels considered normal or "acceptable" in the past now seem to generate higher rates of inflation. This is why a number of policy makers and economists have tended to move the "full employment" benchmark of the official unemployment rate figure from around 4 percent up to as much as 6 percent.

Taking account of the effect on the aggregate supply curve of the changing nature of unemployment only worsens the inflation-unemployment problems discussed earlier in connection with Figures 14-6 through 14-8. It is also another factor that may possibly underlie the behavior of the general price level and unemployment in the U.S. economy, as shown in Figure 14-4.

■ CHECKPOINT 14-3

If the general price level declined over a long period of time (as it did in the United States during the latter part of the nineteenth century) so that people came to expect deflation, would the money interest rate be above or below the real interest rate? Why? Starting with the early 1960s, compare the behavior of the money interest rate shown in Figure 13-3, part a, with the annual percentage rate of change of the price level shown in Figure 6-4, part a. How might you explain the relationship between these two measures? Look at the data in Figure 14-2 again. Do you see any pattern in these data which might, at least in part, be attributable to the changing nature of unemployment?

SUMMARY

1. Economists have speculated that there is a trade-off between inflation and unemployment. The trade-off may be represented by the Phillips curve, which indicates that lowering the unemployment rate means accepting more inflation, and that reducing inflation means accepting more unemployment. However, evidence suggests that movements up the Phillips curve (increasing inflation and reducing unemployment) cannot be followed by movements back down the same curve (reducing inflation while increasing unemployment). Data show that the economy has experienced an upward-spiraling inflation rate associated with a cyclical unemployment rate.

2. Increases in the price of inputs to production that are initiated on the supply side of the economy raise production costs and give rise

to cost-push inflation. This is represented by an upward shift of the aggregate supply curve. Given the level of total spending, the price level rises, output declines, and the rate of unemployment increases.

3. When the economy is operating along the inflationary zone of its aggregate supply curve, an increase in total demand will cause a demand-pull inflation along with a reduction in unemployment. Workers whose money wage remains unchanged experience a decline in their real wage and, therefore, demand a catch-up money wage increase. This results in a cost-push inflation and an increase in unemployment. If policy makers increase total demand again in order to reduce unemployment, the process repeats itself, giving rise to a wage-price spiral and fluctuating unemployment.

4. A continually rising price level eventually leads people to anticipate inflation. The onset of anticipated inflation causes the aggregate supply curve to shift upward as labor and business try to stay abreast of inflation rather than merely react in catch-up fashion. This gives further impetus to the wage-price spiral, thus accelerating inflation and accentuating fluctuations in unemployment. This can lead to stagflation, the existence of both a high unemployment rate and a high rate of inflation at the same time.

5. Confronted with stagflation, the dilemma of stabilization policy is that attempts to curb inflation result in yet a higher unemployment rate, while attempts to reduce unemployment accelerate the rate of inflation.

6. A monetary policy that is preoccupied with interest rate stability tends to have an inflationary bias, particularly in the presence of government deficit spending. This bias is accentuated by the onset of anticipated inflation, which causes the money interest rate to be greater than the real interest rate. Critics of such a policy argue that the inflation-unemployment problem would be lessened if monetary policy makers worried less about interest rate stability, and fiscal policy makers avoided high employment budget deficits during periods of inflationary economic expansion.

7. Since World War II the composition of the labor force has changed so that male heads of household represent a declining portion. Many economists argue that this has caused the inflationary zone of the aggregate supply curve to rise more sharply. Consequently, policy makers' attempts to reduce the official unemployment rate to levels considered "acceptable" in the past now cause sharper rises in the general price level, or more inflation. Therefore, a number of economists and policy makers advise that the "full-employment" benchmark of the official unemployment rate should be moved upward in order to avoid excessively inflationary fiscal and monetary policy.

KEY TERMS AND CONCEPTS
money interest rate
Phillips curve
real interest rate
real wage
stagflation

QUESTIONS AND PROBLEMS

1. Which years in Figure 14–2 most strongly suggest the possible existence of a Phillips curve? What is the reversibility issue, and how do the data in Figure 14–2 bear on this issue?

2. Classify each of the following changes according to whether you think they affect the economy's total demand schedule, or the economy's aggregate supply curve, or both. Explain your answer in each case.

a. an increase in personal income taxes;
b. an increase in employers' legally required contribution to employee social security taxes;
c. a worldwide strike by dockworkers;
d. an increase in employee absenteeism;
e. the outbreak of war;
f. a major discovery of oil within the continental United States;
g. a stock market crash;
h. an announced upward revision of the White House's forecast of GNP growth in the coming year.

3. Describe why the onset of anticipated inflation leads to a considerable complication of the policy makers' problems. A number of observers say that the fact that the president and Congress must run for reelection so frequently really worsens these problems. Explain why this might well be true.

4. Many economists argue that the quadrupling of oil prices in 1973 would not have been such a severe shock to the economy were it not for the already present anticipated inflation. How would you explain their position?

5. Consider the interest rate that your local commercial bank is currently paying on savings, or time, deposits. Using the currently reported rate of inflation, calculate what you think is the real rate of interest earned on such deposits. Remember that the money interest rate you earn is taxable income. Taking this into account, what do you think of the real rate of interest you earn on such a deposit?

6. A number of economists claim that the Federal Reserve can push the money interest rate down in the short run. That is, they say that open market purchases have the initial effect of pushing it down but that these same purchases "sow the seeds" leading to a later rise in the interest rate. Explain how and why this might be so.

7. How do you think each of the following would affect the shape of the inflationary zone of the aggregate supply curve and why?

a. increasing unemployment benefits and relaxing the requirements for eligibility;
b. setting up job-market clearinghouses that provide extensive information about job openings across the country;
c. increasing the age at which people become eligible for retirement benefits.

◼ NEWS ITEM FOR YOUR ANALYSIS ◼

SKILLED-LABOR SHORTAGE
PLAGUES MANY FIRMS, DELAYS SOME PROJECTS

LOS ANGELES, October 16—"Hughes Needs Engineers," reads a banner towed through the skies over Los Angeles by a small plane. This illustrates the seriousness of the current shortage of professional and skilled workers.

To attract needed workers some companies are raising salaries, offering bonuses, and hunting further afield for job candidates. Other firms have had to hire less-qualified people, use more temporary help, and step up the use of costly overtime. Nonetheless, some production and delivery schedules are being delayed.

Enough job markets are experiencing labor scarcities "to suggest an economywide shortage," says Kenneth Goldstein, associate economist at the Conference Board, a business research and service organization based in New York. Some economists warn that further expansion of the economy amid a growing shortage of skilled labor could aggravate inflation. Serious shortages are reported in manufacturing, as well as localized difficulties in finding clerical workers, bank tellers, nurses, paralegals, and secretaries.

Labor shortages seem odd in an economy where the unemployment rate is stuck at historically high levels. The seasonally adjusted unemployment rate was 6 percent in September, indicating that about 6 million Americans said they were looking for work and couldn't find it.

However, economists say most of the jobless simply aren't qualified for many of the good jobs available. One major problem is the influx of unskilled women and teenagers into an increasingly technological economy. "The inventory of skills and experience isn't high for the same percentage of unemployment" as in former years, the Conference Board's Mr. Goldstein says. Moreover, the unskilled women and teenagers, stuck in jobs that often pay little more than welfare benefits, tend to move frequently from job to job. They are periodically unemployed during the transitions.

Many companies are simply hiring workers with fewer qualifications. "We are being forced to hire the most qualified from a batch of the least qualified," a spokesperson at Koppers' Baltimore plant says. Companies such as Middlestadt Machine of Baltimore are dismayed at the rate at which skilled workers are being lured away. The concern complains that it has been training mechanics and tool-and-die makers, but losing such workers to companies paying $2 an hour more than its current rate of approximately $7 an hour. At General Dynamics' Convair division in San Diego, Louis M. Whitney, corporate manager for personnel placement, complains, "only 20 to 25 percent [of people responding to job offers] have the qualifications we are looking for."

The current economic expansion seems to have sopped up the supply of skilled workers. The unemployment rate for married adult men, who are more likely to be skilled workers, has fallen to 2.7 percent from 3.3 percent a year ago. Unemployment rates for the less-skilled groups remain substantially higher: 5.6 percent for married adult women and 16.6 percent for teenagers.

QUESTIONS

1. Which observations reported in this news item bear on the level of frictional unemployment? (Frictional unemployment was defined in Chapter 6.)

2. Which observations and facts suggest that the shape of the inflationary zone of the aggregate supply curve has changed *over the years*?

3. If policy makers attempt to reduce the unemployment rate to a level below 6 percent, what effects do you think this will have on business firms' incentives to run training programs aimed at producing more skilled workers?

15

GUIDELINES, CONTROLS, INDEXING, AND JOBS

CAPITOL HILL TALK OF MANDATORY
CONTROLS SEEN SPURRING INFLATION, DEEP RECESSION

WASHINGTON, December 6—A congressional study claims that a debate in Congress over mandatory wage-price controls could trigger accelerating inflation and the arrival of a deep recession. The study concluded that Capitol Hill discussion of mandatory controls would cause business and labor to rush to raise prices and wages prior to the controls period. Moreover, the resulting jump in prices would force the Federal Reserve Board to further tighten the money supply, and "recession will arrive that much sooner and be that much deeper."

The Carter administration, currently pursuing a voluntary wage-price guideline program, has said repeatedly that it doesn't want authority to impose mandatory controls. The administration claims they don't work. "They [controls] very quickly do more harm than good" said Alfred Kahn, chairman of the Council on Wage and Price Stability.

Citing an analysis of the 1971–1974 mandatory controls period, the congressional committee's study found that while controls temporarily halt inflation, the long-run inflation rate wouldn't "have been substantially different in the absence of price controls." The study also said that, once controls are removed, a "price explosion" would follow. The committee's economists went on to say that mandatory controls appear to have "considerable appeal" because policy makers often believe controls can combat inflation "without at the same time necessitating the demand restriction that brings recession."

George Meany, president of the AFL-CIO, said that he favors mandatory controls, but that they must also apply to interest rates, dividends, rents, profits, and other forms of income. The labor leader complained that under the Carter administration's voluntary program, "wages—and wages alone—are targeted for controls."

Policy makers, politicians, and economists have not always been satisfied with attempts to deal with the problems of inflation and unemployment by using the conventional tools of fiscal and monetary policy. Since the late 1960s in particular, increased rates of inflation coupled with high unemployment rates have led to the formulation of other policy measures aimed at dealing with these problems.

Some of these measures have been tried in the past. For example, price controls were imposed during World War II and during 1951 and 1952, Korean War years. Varying degrees of price controls were also imposed by the Nixon administration from 1971 to 1974. Wage-price guidelines were used by the Kennedy and Johnson administrations from 1962 to 1966, as well as by the Carter administration in the late 1970s. Various forms of public works projects and government-sponsored manpower training programs aimed at reducing unemployment trace their origins to the depression-era New Deal legislation of the 1930s. A number of other measures have been proposed and given serious consideration by both Congress and the executive branch of government in recent years. One of these, which we will consider in this chapter, is indexing, a procedure that ties wages, income tax rates, and fixed-dollar assets to the rate of inflation in order to keep their real value (purchasing power) constant.

In this chapter we will consider the pros and cons of several of these measures, both the old and the new, the tried and the untried. Controversy surrounds all of them with respect to their effectiveness and the way they affect different groups in the economy. The different views on mandatory controls expressed in the news item are typical. First we will examine policy measures for dealing with inflation. Then we will turn to policy measures aimed at the problem of unemployment.

POLICIES FOR DEALING WITH INFLATION

Whenever policy makers are either unwilling or unable to conduct monetary and fiscal policy in such a way as to avoid inflation, there is inevitably a hue and cry to do "something" about inflation. Even when inflation is caused by an excessively expansive fiscal and monetary policy, it is always tempting to tackle the symptom—rising prices—rather than the cause. The logic is simple. If prices are rising, grab them and hold them down. *A* **wage-price guidelines** *policy attempts to curb inflation by getting business and labor to refrain voluntarily from increasing wages and prices at rates in excess of some guideline rate specified by the government. If voluntary compliance isn't forthcoming, or is deemed unworkable, government may make compliance mandatory by imposing so-called* **wage-price controls.**

We will now examine guidelines and controls policies. In particular, we want to consider how they are carried out, their workability, and their effectiveness. Along the way we will also look at some of their implications for resource allocation and some of the ways they affect different groups in the economy.

Wage-Price Guidelines

Wage-price guidelines are effective only to the extent that business and labor voluntarily comply with them. When the Carter administration initiated such a program in late 1978, it requested that annual increases in wages and private fringe benefits (health and pension benefits) should not exceed 7 percent. Business firms were asked to limit price increases to one-half of one percentage point below their average annual rate of price increase during 1976 and 1977. Labor was reluctant to comply with the wage guideline because at the time the rate of inflation of the general price level exceeded 7 percent. Labor feared that compliance would mean a loss in the purchasing power of their wages. Many businesses were reluctant to comply because they feared that the prices of inputs and the wages of labor would rise faster than the allowable increases in the prices of their products under the guidelines. In short, they feared that compliance would squeeze profits and possibly even cause losses. The dilemma facing individual workers, unions, and business firms in voluntary compliance is like that of individuals in a crowd standing at a football game. No one can see any better when everyone is standing than when everyone is sitting down. But those who voluntarily sit down are relatively worse off if others remain standing. Hence, no one is willing to sit down.

Since one of the basic problems with a wage-price guidelines policy is that of ensuring voluntary compliance, a number of policies have been proposed or used to provide economic incentives for compliance. Two that have been considered, but as yet not tried, are wage insurance and the so-called tax-based income policy (TIP). Another method is to use moral suasion, or jawboning, backed by thinly veiled threats that the government may take more drastic measures if compliance is not forthcoming.

WAGE INSURANCE

Let's say that the wage guideline is 7 percent—that is, government requests that labor not seek wage increases greater than 7 percent per year. But suppose labor is reluctant to comply with the guideline for fear that consumer prices may rise at a rate greater than 7 percent, thus reducing the purchasing power of a wage that rises only 7 percent. One way to alleviate labor's fear is for the government to offer wage insurance. **Wage insurance** *guarantees that the government will repay labor for the purchasing power that they lose if they comply with the guideline but consumer prices, measured by the consumer price index (CPI), rise faster than the guideline rate for wages.* The repayment would be calculated on the basis of the difference between the annual percentage rate of growth in the CPI and the guideline rate for wages. For example, suppose a worker making $10,000 per year agreed to accept a 7 percent raise (the guideline rate) and the CPI then rose 8 percent over the year. The government's wage insurance program would pay the worker $100, which is 1 percent of $10,000. If the CPI rose 10 percent the worker would get $300, or 3 percent of $10,000.

By providing wage insurance the government hopes to be able to get labor to comply voluntarily with a wage guideline. However, critics contend that those workers who think they can bargain for wage increases greater than the increase in the CPI would still not comply. But suppose all wage and salary workers do comply

---

After reading this chapter, you will be able to:

1. Describe how wage and price guidelines work, and list the pros and cons of incentive programs to induce voluntary compliance with guidelines.
2. Describe how wage and price controls work, how they affect the economy, and why they are difficult to enforce.
3. Outline the experience of the United States with wage and price controls.
4. Explain how indexing may be applied to the U.S. tax structure and to fixed-dollar assets in order to protect purchasing power.
5. Summarize the different views on how indexing affects economic stability.
6. Outline policies, other than conventional fiscal and monetary policy, for dealing with unemployment.

and an overly expansive fiscal and monetary policy causes the CPI to increase at a rate greater than the guideline rate. Critics argue that a wage insurance policy would not only become incredibly expensive, but self-defeating as well. For example, suppose wages and salaries totaled $1 trillion per year. Wage insurance payments would amount to $10 billion for every percentage point of inflation above the guideline rate. Moreover, the wage insurance payments would amount to the government giving everybody the money they had voluntarily refrained from taking in the form of wage increases in the first place. As a result, critics contend that inflation would continue just as if there had never been compliance with the wage guideline.

Critics also point to technical problems that make the workability of a wage insurance program doubtful. For example, should fringe benefits be included in the wage guideline? Suppose they are not included. Unions can take the wage increases they forgo under the guideline in the form of increased fringe benefits instead. They would bargain with employers for higher-cost retirement and health compensation benefits. On the other hand, suppose fringe benefits are included in the wage guideline. How do you place a value on them? For example, the cost of increased pension benefits to be received in the future depends on assumptions about how long the worker lives after retirement, and how long his or her dependent spouse lives. Different assumptions give different answers. The paperwork and labor hours required to set up and enforce answers to these questions can grow rapidly, both for the government and private employers.

TAX-BASED INCOME POLICY (TIP)

There are two basic versions of the **tax-based income policy (TIP)**. Both attempt to provide an economic incentive for compliance with a wage guideline. But one uses the carrot while the other uses the stick.

The Carrot Version. *What we may call the carrot version of TIP rewards with tax credits (reductions in income taxes) those workers who keep their wage increases below the guideline rate.* For

example, suppose the guideline rate for wage increases is 7 percent. A worker earning $10,000 per year who settles for a wage increase of 6 percent, or $600, would get a tax credit of $100 (the difference between 7 percent of $10,000 and 6 percent of $10,000). That is, the worker's income tax bill would be reduced by $100. If the worker had settled for a 7 percent wage increase, the guideline rate, there would be no $100 tax credit. But, of course, the worker would have $100 additional income. However, this extra income would be subject to the income tax. If the tax rate were 20 percent, the worker could keep only $80 of the additional income. This is $20 less than what the worker would have by settling for a 6 percent wage increase and having $100 less taxes to pay. Clearly, the carrot version of TIP gives labor an incentive to settle for wage increases below the guideline rate. However, critics are quick to point out that while this version of TIP would encourage compliance with the guideline, labor's purchasing power would not be reduced. Indeed, it would be slightly greater, and it is argued that this would only add to inflationary pressures—the basic problem guidelines seek to control.

The Stick Version. *What we may call the stick version of TIP is aimed at forcing employers to comply with a wage guideline. The stick version punishes with tax penalties employers who grant wage increases in excess of the guideline rate.* The tax penalties are supposed to stiffen management's resistance to union demands for wage increases larger than the guideline rate.

However, what happens if unions respond by becoming more militant in their wage demands? Is it not possible that more or longer labor strikes will result? If so, then firms may find the higher costs (in terms of lost sales) of more or longer shutdowns greater than the tax penalties incurred by granting wage increases that exceed the guideline rate. In that case, firms would be better off by giving in to the excessive wage increases. Of course, one way to deal with this possible shortcoming would be to make the tax penalties high enough so that the higher costs of more or longer strikes would still be less than the tax penalties. Critics argue that there then would be more or longer shutdowns due to strikes. As a result firms would end up producing less output, giving rise to shortages. Since shortages cause prices to rise, the rate of inflation would increase rather than slow down—just the opposite result of that intended by a wage guideline policy.

According to critics, there is also another reason why the stick version of TIP may cause inflation to increase rather than to decrease. Suppose firms experiencing increased demand for their output want to respond to the increased profit opportunities by expanding production. They may have to increase wages more than the guideline rate in order to hire the additional labor needed to produce more output. Because of the tax penalty they will incur, the size of the prospective profits will be decreased. And this will diminish the incentive for the firms to expand output. Hence, output will increase less in response to the increased demand than it would if there were no tax penalties, and, consequently, prices will increase more. In this situation, the existence of tax penalties curbs wage increases but accentuates product price increases. The more rapidly increasing product prices will in turn cause labor to press even harder for larger increases in wages in order to keep up with the rising cost of living.

JAWBONING AND ARM-TWISTING

One approach frequently used to gain compliance with wage-price guidelines is "jawboning"—government appeals to business and labor's sense of patriotic responsibility. This may take the form of presidential statements to the effect that "every American should do his or her part to help fight inflation." Or if a particular corporation increases its product price by an excessive amount, or if there is a particularly excessive wage settlement in some industry, the president might publicly express "disappointment" and "concern" that more restraint was not used. Corporate executives and union leaders may be contacted directly, or even called to the White House, for a discussion of the matter. The president might request a price "rollback," or very publicly "keep an eye" on the final stages of a particular labor contract negotiation.

When jawboning doesn't work, the government may resort to "arm-twisting." The government simply announces that it is prepared to take actions directly affecting those who don't comply with the guidelines. For example, companies either seeking or holding government contracts (companies selling products to the government under contract) may be required to certify that they are complying with the guidelines. The president may direct government agencies to purchase only from those companies observing the guidelines. The government might also campaign to encourage consumer boycotts of companies that don't comply with the guidelines. Those industries that are sheltered from foreign competition by tariffs (a tax added on to the price of an imported good) and other types of import restrictions may be threatened with removal of those restrictions if they don't comply with the guidelines. Without such restrictions, firms in those industries would be under greater pressure from foreign competition to hold down wage-price increases.

Wage-Price Controls

Experience with wage-price guidelines and voluntary compliance suggests that such a policy has little, if any, effect on inflation. A principal problem is that compliance by business executives and union leaders requires that they voluntarily behave in a manner contrary to their primary responsibilities. Business executives are hired and paid to run companies as efficiently and profitably as possible. Executives who comply with price guidelines at the expense of company profits may well have to answer to angry stockholders and boards of directors. Similarly, union leaders are chosen by the rank-and-file union members to get them the best possible wage settlement. Union leaders who honor the wage guideline instead of rank-and-file goals may be replaced. Another problem is that those firms and unions that do comply voluntarily with wage-price guidelines run the risk of losing economic ground relative to those that don't—the standing-crowd-at-the-football-game problem.

Wage-price controls make compliance with government-specified guidelines mandatory. The limits on the rate of wage-price increases are no longer mere guidelines, but standards—

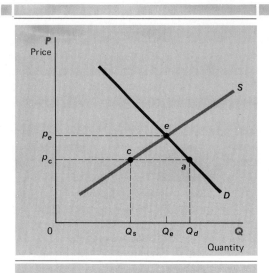

FIGURE 15-1 THE ECONOMIC INCENTIVE TO EVADE PRICE CONTROLS

In a typical freely functioning market, the equilibrium price p_e and quantity Q_e are determined by the intersection of demand curve D and supply curve S at point e. The existence of price controls forbidding suppliers to sell their product at a price higher than p_c would lead them to supply quantity Q_s to the market, corresponding to point c on S. However, buyers would demand the larger amount Q_d, corresponding to point a on D, resulting in a persistent shortage equal to Q_d minus Q_s. The existence of frustrated buyers willing to pay a higher price for the good gives suppliers an economic incentive to evade price controls. Hence, the effectiveness of price controls depends on how intensively the government polices them to detect evasion.

like posted speed limits on highways. To exceed them is to break the law. Like speed limits, wage-price controls require enforcement. And enforcement can be costly and difficult because evasion can take many forms.

ENFORCEMENT AND EVASION

The basic reason why controls are hard to enforce is illustrated in Figure 15-1, which shows the demand curve D and supply curve S for a typical market in the economy. (You may want to review briefly the discussion of market demand and supply in Chapter 4.) If the market were allowed to operate freely, the equilibrium price and quantity would be p_e and Q_e, respectively, corresponding to the intersection of the demand curve D and the supply curve S at point e. However, suppose price controls make it illegal for suppliers in this market to allow the price to rise above p_c. At the price p_c suppliers are only willing to supply the quantity Q_s, corresponding to point c on S, while buyers will demand a quantity Q_d, corresponding to point a on D. Hence, there will be a shortage in the market equal to Q_d minus Q_s. Without controls the price would rise to p_e, eliminating this excess demand. But with the price held down to p_c, there will be a persistent shortage and frustrated buyers who cannot get as much of the good as they want. These buyers are willing to pay a higher price, however, to get more of the good. Hence, there is an economic incentive for suppliers to evade the price controls. To do so, they must run the risk of getting caught breaking the law. Obviously, the effectiveness of price controls will depend on how intensively the government polices them to detect evasion.

The same is true of wage controls. Suppose that employers' demand for labor in a particular labor market is represented by the demand curve D in Figure 15-1, while S is the supply curve of labor. If wage controls prohibit employers from paying a wage higher than p_c, there will be a shortage of labor equal to Q_d minus Q_s. Frustrated employers will be tempted to evade the wage control and pay a higher wage in order to get more labor. And, of course, more workers will be induced to offer their services if they can get a higher wage.

The U.S. economy produces literally millions of different kinds of products varying in complexity from hairpins to 747 jets. To enforce price controls on every one of them would take an army of enforcement agents. We can get some idea of the magnitude of the problem of enforcing wage-price controls by considering a few examples of how such evasion can occur.

Price-Control Evasion Through Product Change. Producers can effectively evade controls by changing the product without changing the price. For example, the typical automobile contains around 15,000 different parts. If the price of automobiles is controlled, the producer can substitute a cheaper plastic part for a metal part here, use a little less or a cheaper grade fabric there, and so on. The outside of the car may look the same but the inside of the car can be changed in numerous ways. While the overall price of the car hasn't increased, the quality and durability of the car that is purchased at that price has been lessened. In a simple product such as a 10-cent pack of gum, the size of the gum sticks could be reduced. Whether the product is simple or complex, changes like these mean that consumers are getting less for their money—and that's inflation, controls or no controls. Such changes mean that reported price data for the consumer price index (CPI) may not rise above control limits. Hence, the rate of inflation measured by the rise in the CPI will appear to slow down as a result of the controls, but product quality changes spurred by the controls make this a false impression. The rate of decline in what you are getting for your money may not have slowed down at all. In truth, properly measured, the upward trend in inflation may be unaffected by controls.

Wage-Control Evasion—Reducing Actual Work Hours. Evasion of wage controls can take place in a similar fashion. An enforcement agent who periodically inspects company payrolls may find that hourly wages are not in violation of wage controls. However, in competing with one another to hire various kinds of labor services, companies may well resort to giving workers longer lunch and coffee breaks, longer paid vacations, and more paid holidays off. While recorded hourly wages may be held in check by the enforcement of wage controls, the amount of hours *actually* worked will be less. Total hours on the job are different than hours actually worked. In effect, the same number of dollars spent on wages is buying fewer hours of actual work. Again, wages per actual hour of work—measured to take account of all these ways of evading controls—would reveal that, in truth, wages are increasing at a rate in excess of that allowed by controls. Like prices, recorded wages may appear to be held in check by con-

trols when, in reality, wages per actual hour worked are rising more rapidly. And the latter is the meaningful measure of inflation. The reported prices and wages can really disguise, even hide altogether, the true rate of inflation.

COST OF ENFORCING CONTROLS

The larger the army of enforcement agents, the more likely it is that the various forms of evasion of wage-price controls will be detected and kept in check. However, the policing activity itself could become very costly.

This point is perhaps best illustrated by an example. Suppose 1 percent of the economy's labor force were lured away from whatever they were doing and employed by the government as enforcement agents for wage-price controls. Each of them can now be assigned to police full time the economic activities of each member of the other 99 percent of the labor force. Employers' attempts to evade price controls by changing product quality, or to evade wage controls by compensating workers with longer coffee breaks and so forth, would be detected more often and prevented, though probably not completely. "Under-the-counter" deals or "middle-of-the-night" trades between consumers and retailers at prices exceeding control limits would also be detected more often and prevented, though again probably not completely.

Note, however, that with 1 percent of the labor force now employed full time as enforcement agents, the goods and services that 1 percent previously produced are no longer available. Only 99 percent of the economy's former output of goods and services can be produced now. The other 1 percent has been replaced with the output of wage-price control enforcement services. The cost, the opportunity cost, of evasion-preventing enforcement is the 1 percent of the GNP that could otherwise have been produced. Moreover, with 99 percent as many goods and services available—that is, with supply reduced—there will be additional upward pressure on prices. The enforcement agents would have their hands full, not only with those they are policing but in limiting their own demand for goods as well. For don't forget, to hire 1 percent of the labor force away from their previous jobs requires that they usually be paid wages that are at least equal to what they previously made. And enforcement agents will spend their wages just like everyone else. The irony is that in an attempt to keep people from having to pay higher prices for goods, we have seen to it that they don't get 1 percent of the goods and services they used to get. Is this cost of enforcement worth it? This is a question that society has to confront when considering the use of controls.

A number of critics of wage-price controls claim that there is another cost of controls that is also very important, although difficult to measure. They worry that enforcement activities pose a threat to individual freedoms and the democratic processes on which our form of government is based. They fear that wage-price controls constitute too much government interference with the rights of individuals to enter into private contracts (agreements to buy and sell) at mutually agreed upon terms.

Effects of Wage-Price Controls on the Economy

Controls affect the way markets allocate the economy's resources. In addition, controls affect different groups in the economy to different degrees, and this raises questions of equity. Moreover, as indicated in the news item, the mere prospect of controls can generate undesirable effects on expectations.

EFFECT OF CONTROLS ON RESOURCE ALLOCATION

In a market-oriented economy, prices provide the signals that determine what to produce, how to produce it, and for whom. Critics argue that wage-price controls (and guidelines as well) interfere with this crucial function, and that, as a result, they give rise to the misallocation of resources (land, labor, and capital). In a dynamic economy there are a multitude of different markets in which supply and demand are continually shifting due to changes in technology, consumer tastes, and a host of other factors. If wages and prices are not free to change to reflect these shifts in supply and demand, there are no effective signals to redirect the use of resources in response to these changes. For exam-

ple, suppose the demand for a particular good increases. If price controls prevent the price of the good from rising, there will be no signal indicating to suppliers society's desire that more resources be devoted to the production of this good. As a result there will be a shortage of the good, such as that shown in Figure 15-1.

In a changing economy with extensive wage-price controls that are effectively enforced, shortages and bottlenecks will occur in many markets as time passes. Buyers will not be able to buy all they want at the controlled price. With controls, markets simply cannot function to equate supply and demand. For example, in a typical market, such as that shown in Figure 15-1, there is a shortage at the controlled price p_c equal to the quantity demanded Q_d minus the quantity supplied Q_s. Since all buyers can't be satisfied, who will decide which buyers get the quantity Q_s of the product and which don't?

One way is simply to sell to those first in line—first come, first served. In many markets, however, sellers will take care of their friends first. The trouble with either of these possibilities is that some buyers get all they want while the rest get none. To many this seems a most unfair and undesirable aspect of a wage-price controls program. One way around the problem is for the government to issue ration coupons to all who want the good. The total amount of these coupons will be just enough to lay claim to the total quantity of the good supplied, which in Figure 15-1 is Q_s. Since each buyer who wants the good at price p_c will be given some of the coupons, all will be assured of getting some of the good. Obviously, some buyers will not be able to get all they would have liked, but this seems more equitable than a situation in which some get none at all. Such a ration coupon system was used during World War II. At that time an extensive system of wage-price controls was imposed and intensively enforced by the government.

No matter how the shortages that result from wage-price controls are handled, economists generally agree on one point. The extent of resource misallocation and the severity of shortages will become more pronounced the longer wage-price controls are imposed.

CONTROLS AND EQUITY

Controls invariably affect different groups in the economy to different degrees. Critics of controls claim that this isn't equitable. The largest business firms and unionized labor tend to be watched more closely for control violations than smaller firms and nonunionized labor. This is partly due to the fact that larger firms and unionized labor are more visible and, hence, easier to watch. Furthermore, it is often argued that large business firms and unions account for such a large share of the economy's output, and represent such a large concentration of economic power, that they serve as a bellwether for wages and prices in the rest of the economy. Some argue, therefore, that it is necessary to make them the focal point of wage-price control efforts.

Labor unions often complain that wage controls tend to be more heavily policed than price controls. This is the opinion expressed by AFL-CIO president George Meany in the news item. Since labor must negotiate wages with management, it is to some extent unavoidable that some of the responsibility for wage controls must be borne by management. This irks labor because it seems to them that an "army" of "patriotic" business executives will help enforce wage controls, but that no comparable army will help enforce price controls.

Many critics share George Meany's other concern, expressed in the news item, that perhaps the greatest inequity of all is that interest rates, dividends, rents, profits, and other forms of income are not usually controlled to the same extent that wages are. Since higher-income groups tend to derive a larger share of their income from these sources than do lower income groups, the inequity favors higher-income groups.

EFFECT OF
CONTROLS ON EXPECTATIONS

The news item reports that the study by economists of Congress's Joint Economic Committee concluded that "Capitol Hill discussion of mandatory controls would cause business and labor to rush to raise prices and wages prior to the controls period." Because wage-price controls have to be legislated by Congress, such a program is unavoidably preceded by a good deal of public debate. It's a little like a football team yelling its next play from the huddle. The other team is then able to anticipate and prepare for what is about to happen. Business and labor react to the congressional debate by initiating price and wage increases they otherwise might not have made until later—better take what they can get while they can. The effect of the debate is to trigger more inflation, the very thing a wage-price control program is intended to prevent.

Some contend that the way to avoid this problem is for Congress to give the president standing authority to impose wage-price controls. It is argued that the president could then simply switch on the controls at any time, thereby reducing business and labor's chance to "jump the gun." Critics of this idea feel uncomfortable about giving the president such unlimited authority. Besides, they claim, when inflation heats up, business and labor would be on the lookout for possible presidential action. As a result, they might mistakenly jump the gun several times, increasing wages and prices even though the president takes no action. Such mistaken anticipation would only add more fuel to inflation.

Despite the jumping-the-gun problem, it is often argued that once wage-price controls are imposed they would tend to dampen inflationary expectations. In the last chapter we saw how inflationary expectations, once established, can create severe problems for fiscal and monetary policy. Once business and labor come to expect inflation, they begin to push up prices and wages in anticipation of future increases in the general price level. They try to stay even with inflation rather than just react to it. But as we saw, this actually contributes to an acceleration of inflation. A number of economists contend that imposing well-enforced wage and price controls for a short period of time could check the rise in wages and prices, thereby causing a downward revision of inflationary expectations and a deceleration of inflation. Others are afraid that controls would have to be imposed for too long a period for this to occur, and that the result would be a serious misallocation of resources.

Controls and Fiscal and Monetary Policy

As reported in the news item, wage-price controls have appealed on occasion to policy makers who think that controls can be used to combat inflation without using restrictive fiscal and monetary policy. Their argument is that controls can be used to curb inflation, thereby freeing fiscal and monetary policy to push the economy toward full employment without fear of the usual inflationary consequences. Indeed, this was the reasoning underlying the controls program imposed by the Nixon administration during the early 1970s.

ARGUMENTS AGAINST CONTROLS AS A SUBSTITUTE FOR RESTRICTIVE FISCAL AND MONETARY POLICY

However, many economists claim that the idea that controls can curb inflation in the face of an expansionary fiscal and monetary policy is simply wishful thinking. In particular, they argue that if the money supply continues to expand at a faster rate than the economy's output of goods and services, there will continue to be upward pressure on prices. A monetary expansion to finance large government deficits as the Federal Reserve monetizes the government debt (as described in the previous chapter) will make it very difficult for wage-price controls to check inflation. If differences in enforcement mean that some prices are more restrained by controls than others, the less restrained prices may very well rise faster than they otherwise would. This happens because shortages will tend to develop where controls are effective, and when consumers with more money in their hands can't get all they want in some markets, they will tend to spend more on goods they can get in other markets. In short, uncontrolled prices will be bid up even more with the funds made available by the increasing money supply. Unless, that is, the controls somehow keep people from spending the additional money, so that the velocity of money V in the equation of exchange ($M \times V = p \times Q$) is reduced. And saving the money in financial institutions such as banks doesn't count, since that money is loaned out and spent. Essentially, it is argued, controls only work if they make people stuff the additional money in mattresses or bury it in the ground.

In sum, these critics contend that in the face of expansionary fiscal and monetary policy, the prices of controlled products may be held down, but those of uncontrolled, or loosely controlled, products will be driven even higher than otherwise. As a result, the average level of all prices, and the overall rate of inflation, will be affected very little by controls. Critics ask how this can possibly justify the numerous shortages and misallocations of resources that controls cause.

ARGUMENTS FOR CONTROLS AS A SUBSTITUTE FOR RESTRICTIVE FISCAL AND MONETARY POLICY

However, there is another school of thought that argues that fiscal and monetary policy cannot be counted on to curb inflation because of the existence of large corporations and unions. Recall our discussion of the stagflation issue in the previous chapter. There we saw that, once business and labor come to expect inflation, the aggregate supply curve takes on a life of its own, shifting upward in anticipation of inflation rather than merely reacting in catch-up fashion. Some economists claim that there is another reason for this cost-push aspect of inflation. That is the existence of large unions and corporations that aggressively push up wages and prices simply because they can exercise so much market power.

Whenever unions and corporations use their market power in this way, the aggregate supply curve shifts upward. This causes the economy's total output to decline and unemployment to rise, as we saw in the previous chapter. Fiscal and monetary policy could allow such recessionary developments to persist until sagging demand deters the large unions and corporations from trying to push up wages and prices still further. However, it is argued that policy makers, fearful of the rise in unemployment, quickly react with expansionary policies that pump up demand. The result is that the big unions and corporations push up wages and prices, and policy makers quickly move to accommodate these increases in order to avoid recessionary developments. Unions and corporations act, and policy makers react, over and over again. The result is inflation, with the unions and corporations calling the tune. Proponents of this version of the inflationary process argue that unless policy makers are willing to take a firmer stance against inflation and worry less about unemployment, wage-price controls are the only policy that will break this vicious cycle.

Experience with
Wage-Price Controls

Most of the U.S. economy's experience with wage-price controls occurred during World War II and then again during the Nixon administration.

WARTIME CONTROLS

Many economists who are otherwise leery of wage-price controls tend to feel that if controls are useful at all, they are useful during wartime, when an economy has to divert a large share of its resources and productive activity away from making peacetime goods and into the production of wartime goods. A strictly enforced system of wage-price controls can help by effectively reducing the quantity of peacetime goods supplied in different markets. Consider again the market shown in Figure 15-1, for example. In the absence of a price control, the equilibrium quantity of the good supplied will be Q_e at the equilibrium price p_e. With the imposition of a price control that prohibits the price from rising above p_c, producers will only be willing to supply the smaller quantity Q_s, corresponding to point c on the supply curve S. Therefore, fewer resources will be devoted to the production of this good. Those no longer used will now be available for use in the production of wartime goods. During wartime, well-policed wage-price controls may also help hold down the inflation that inevitably results from the all-out, full-employment production effort that characterizes a wartime economy.

As we have already noted, wage-price controls were used extensively during World War II. They were enforced by an army of agents, aided by the good intentions of citizens motivated by wartime patriotism. Price controls on a variety of consumer goods, chiefly foods, were reinforced by a coupon-rationing system. Wages were controlled by the so-called Little Steel Formula, which limited the rise in wages to 15 percent above the level of January 1941, with exceptions allowed to remove inequities and to meet special needs. In general, economists believe that the World War II experience with wage-price controls was reasonably successful.

Many point out, however, that the controls program received considerable aid from other government policies aimed at diverting consumer spending away from peacetime goods. Private investment spending was held to a low level by a battery of direct controls. A system of priorities and allocations ensured that scarce materials were used only for activities deemed essential for the war effort. Nonessential building activity was prohibited, and the production of certain types of goods was limited by direct order or forbidden altogether. In addition, saving was stimulated by intensive campaigns to get citizens to buy government savings bonds (often called war bonds) through systematic payroll deduction programs. In addition, the government increased personal income taxes in order to hold down disposable income and, hence, consumption spending.

In sum, it is noteworthy that the largest part of the increase in the wholesale price index during the decade of the 1940s took place before America's entrance into the war in December 1941 and after the war's conclusion in August 1945. No doubt, the wartime wage-price controls created some inequities. Black markets (markets in which goods are sold at prices above the legal limit) flourished for some goods. However, on balance, many economists feel that controls definitely aided the war effort.

PEACETIME CONTROLS

When the Nixon administration took office in January 1969, the economy was experiencing its highest rate of inflation since the end of the Korean War in 1953 (see Figure 6-4, part a). The administration attempted to curb inflation by exercising fiscal and monetary restraint. As a result, the government had an actual budget surplus in 1969 for the first time since 1960, and a high-employment budget surplus for the first time since 1965. But despite the restrictive stance of fiscal policy, the rate of inflation ended up even higher in 1969 than it had been in 1968. Policy makers became even more concerned in 1970, when a slight recession and a rise in the unemployment rate (from 3.5 percent in 1969 to 4.9 percent in 1970) were still accompanied by a high rate of inflation (see Figure 14-2, the years 1968, 1969, and 1970). It seemed that the years of almost continually increasing rates of inflation since 1963 (Figure 14-2) had given rise to firmly entrenched inflationary expectations. By 1971 the outlines of the stagflation problem were becoming apparent.

On the one hand, the Nixon administration wanted to reduce the unemployment rate. On the other hand, the administration feared that a more expansionary fiscal and monetary policy would cause even higher rates of inflation. To get around this policy dilemma, the administration decided to impose wage-price controls to check inflation. The administration hoped this program would permit a more expansionary fiscal and monetary policy to reduce unemployment without at the same time making inflation worse.

Phases I and II of the Nixon Plan. Congress gave President Nixon the authority to impose wage-price controls when it passed the Economic Stabilization Act of 1970. The administration did not use this authority until August 1971. Then it imposed a controls program that went through several phases before the president's authority to use controls expired in April 1974. Phase I lasted two months (August 15, 1971, to November 19, 1971) and imposed a freeze on all wages and prices throughout the economy. Phase II lasted 14 months (November 19, 1971, to January 11, 1973) and represented a relaxation of the controls of Phase I. Under Phase II wage increases were not supposed to exceed 5.5 percent per year, while prices could be raised to cover increased costs—which meant businesses were not allowed to increase profit

margins. While the rate of inflation remained reasonably stable during Phases I and II, the rate of inflation had begun to fall in 1970, considerably before the Phase I freeze (see Figure 14-2). Hence, it is not clear how effective Phases I and II controls actually were. It could be that the drop in the rate of inflation from 1970 to 1972 was really a reflection of the widening gap between potential and actual GNP (the GNP gap) that took place during these years (see Figure 6-4, part b).

Phases III and IV. A further loosening of controls began with the imposition of Phase III, which lasted seven months (January 11, 1973, to August 13, 1973). During this period the economy's total demand for goods and services began to expand sharply and the GNP gap was closed (Figure 6-4, part b). The rate of inflation rose quite sharply (Figure 14-2, the years 1972 and 1973). Because Phase III controls appeared to be losing badly to inflation, Nixon reimposed a complete freeze from August 13 to September 12, 1973—Phase III ½. Phase III ½ briefly checked the rise in the inflation rate, but shortages became such a problem that the cure seemed worse than the inflation. Hence, Phase III ½ gave way to Phase IV, during which decontrol was extended to more and more sectors of the economy until Congress allowed the authority to impose controls to expire in April 1974.

The experience with Phases III and IV did much to confirm the idea that loosely enforced controls are almost useless in the face of a strong expansion of total demand. (The energy crisis that occurred during Phase IV also added to the inflation problem.) And when a freeze, Phase III ½, was imposed during this period, it seemed to bear out the contention that strict controls create severe resource misallocation and shortages. There have been many studies of the effectiveness of the Nixon wage-price controls program. By and large, their conclusions have been very much the same as those of the study of the 1971-1974 mandatory control period reported in the news item at the beginning of this chapter. Namely, that "the long-run inflation rate wouldn't 'have been substantially different in the absence of price controls.'"

■ **CHECKPOINT 15-1**

Some critics of wage-price controls argue that they control wages and prices "artificially," and that, as a result, when controls are removed there is a "price explosion." What do you think these critics mean, and how might you explain their position in terms of Figure 15–1? The study by the Joint Economic Committee concluded, as reported in the news item, that Capitol Hill discussion of mandatory controls would lead to a rush to raise wages and prices prior to the control period, and that the resulting jump in prices would force the Fed to tighten the money supply so that "recession will arrive that much sooner and be that much deeper." Can you explain the study's conclusion in terms of the aggregate supply and total demand framework that we used to discuss stagflation in the previous chapter?

INDEXING—PROTECTING PURCHASING POWER FROM INFLATION

Wage-price guidelines and controls are aimed at curbing inflation. By contrast, **indexing** *is a policy aimed at protecting people against the loss of the dollar's purchasing power that is caused by inflation. Indexing keeps constant the purchasing power of wages, taxes, and fixed-dollar, or nominal, assets by adjusting their dollar-denominated values for the change in the general price level.* (Recall our discussion in Chapter 6.) For example, suppose an employer has agreed to index employees' wages, which currently are $5 per hour. If there is a 10 percent rate of inflation over the coming year, the employer automatically increases the wage to $5.50. Thus, while goods cost 10 percent more, an employee's dollar-denominated wage has also increased 10 percent. The employee is being paid the same amount of purchasing power, or the same real wage, per hour.

Let's examine how the government might use indexing to adjust income taxes, capital gains taxes, and government bonds for the rate of inflation. We will also briefly consider how indexing may be used in the private sector.

Indexing Income Taxes

Personal and business income in the U.S. economy is subject to a progressive tax. Recall from Chapter 9 that a progressive tax on income imposes successively higher tax rates on additional dollars of income as income rises. As a hypothetical example, suppose income tax rates are such that the first $10,000 of an individual's income is subject to a 20 percent tax rate, the second $10,000 to a 30 percent rate, the third to a 40 percent rate, and so forth. This means that as one's total income rises, the fraction of that total income taxed away gets larger. If the individual makes $10,000, 20 percent, or one-fifth, of it goes to taxes; if $20,000, then 25 percent (the average of 20 percent and 30 percent), or one-fourth, of it goes to taxes, and so forth. When there is inflation, a progressive tax structure effectively raises the tax rates on incomes of constant purchasing power (that is, a before-tax income whose purchasing power is unaffected by inflation). Let's see why.

INFLATION AND THE PROGRESSIVE TAX STRUCTURE

The problem with a progressive tax structure is that it is calculated on the basis of fixed-dollar amounts that don't account for changes in the purchasing power of the dollar resulting from inflation. Consequently, even if your dollar income rises at the same rate as the general price level, the quantity of goods you can purchase with the income you have left after paying taxes will decline. This is so because as your dollar income increases, it is subjected to progressively higher rates of taxation.

Consider an example using the hypothetical progressive tax rates mentioned above. Suppose you are making $10,000 per year, which means you are taxed at a 20 percent rate. Your after-tax income is, therefore, $8,000. Now suppose there is a 10 percent rate of inflation but that your dollar income also increases 10 percent, from $10,000 to $11,000, or $1,000. The purchasing power of your before-tax income thus remains unchanged—it is an income of constant purchasing power. While the first $10,000 of your income is taxed at a 20 percent rate, the additional $1,000 is taxed at a 30 percent rate.

Hence your after-tax income is now $8,700 ($11,000 minus the sum of .20 × $10,000 and .30 × $1,000, or $11,000 minus $2,300). Over the year your after-tax dollar income has increased from $8,000 to $8,700, or 8.75 percent. Though your before-tax dollar income increased at the same rate as the general price level (10 percent), your after-tax dollar income has not. The purchasing power of your before-tax income is constant, but you can only purchase goods with what you have left after taxes. And since your after-tax dollar income has not kept up with the increase in the general price level, you now have less purchasing power— you are worse off. Inflation combined with a progressive income tax structure automatically taxes away purchasing power.

HOW INDEXING INCOME TAXES WORKS

It has often been pointed out that this loss of purchasing power amounts to an unlegislated, unvoted, unsigned tax hike, literally "taxation without representation." The basis for this claim is that inflation automatically pushes people into progressively higher tax brackets. These brackets are not adjusted for the fact that the purchasing power of the dollar is reduced by inflation, however. Indexing income taxes would adjust these tax brackets upward at the same rate as the rate of inflation. Indexing would, therefore, prevent the automatic taxing away of purchasing power. Let's see why.

Consider our hypothetical example once more, and assume that the tax brackets are indexed to the rate of inflation. Once again, the first tax bracket is the first $10,000 of income (taxed at a 20 percent rate), the second tax bracket applies to income earned beyond $10,000 up to $20,000 (taxed at a 30 percent rate), the third applies to income beyond $20,000 up to $30,000 (taxed at a 40 percent rate), and so forth. If the rate of inflation over the coming year is 10 percent, each tax bracket will be adjusted upward 10 percent. The first tax bracket now will be the first $11,000 of income, the second bracket will be from $11,000 up to $22,000, the third from $22,000 up to $33,000, and so forth. Now when your dollar income increases 10 percent (the same as the rate of infla-

tion), from $10,000 up to $11,000, this increase doesn't move you into the next tax bracket as before. Therefore, your after-tax dollar income increases from $8,000 to $8,800, also an increase of 10 percent. Since your after-tax income has increased the same percentage amount as the general price level, you still have the same purchasing power.

The indexing of income taxes would prevent inflation from taxing away purchasing power, or real income. And, of course, government's real income tax revenue would no longer increase automatically because of inflation. When developing spending programs Congress could not count on inflation to provide additional financing. It would be forced to vote for tax increases. Proponents of indexing argue that this would make Congress look at its spending activities more carefully and more openly before the public.

INCOME TAX INDEXING AND STABILITY

Opponents of income tax indexing claim it would be destabilizing. They argue that the automatic reduction in purchasing power that occurs when inflation pushes people into higher tax brackets acts to dampen inflationary booms. Proponents of indexing acknowledge this point, but claim that there is another aspect of the stability question that argues even more strongly for indexing. Without indexing, as we discussed above, the after-tax purchasing power of a before-tax income of constant purchasing power declines. Suppose wage and salary earners' before-tax incomes rise at the same rate as the general level of prices. Without indexing, they find themselves worse off because the purchasing power of their after-tax income has declined. To "catch up" they must push for increases in their before-tax wages and salaries that are greater than the rate of inflation. But this will tend to push the rate of inflation even higher as employers pass these wage and salary increases along to the consumer in the form of higher prices. The rate of inflation will accelerate. Even though before-tax wages and salaries may keep pace with inflation, the purchasing power of after-tax wages and salaries will continue to lose ground. The cycle goes faster and faster, like a dog trying to catch its own tail. Proponents claim that income tax indexing is necessary to eliminate this source of accelerating cost-push inflation.

Indexing Capital Gains Taxes

Capital gains taxes *are taxes levied on any gain one realizes from selling an asset at a price greater than the original purchase price.* Many have criticized capital gains taxes because they do not make any distinction between gains that merely reflect an increase in the general level of prices, and those that represent an increase in the asset owner's purchasing power, or a real capital gain.

TAXING PAPER GAINS
INSTEAD OF REAL GAINS

Let's assume capital gains are taxed at a rate of 25 percent. Suppose you bought a piece of land for $10,000 ten years ago. Assume that in the meantime inflation has taken place so that the general level of prices has risen 100 percent, or doubled. Now suppose that you sell your land today for $20,000. Despite the fact that you get twice as many dollars for the land as you originally paid for it, you are still just getting back the same amount of purchasing power that you originally paid. Why? Because the dollar you receive today buys only half what it did ten years ago. However, the capital gains tax does not recognize that fact. You will be taxed 25 percent of the dollar, or paper, gain. That is, you will have to pay the government 25 percent of the difference between the $20,000 sale price and the $10,000 purchase price, or $2,500 (.25 × $10,000). The result is that after tax you keep $17,500. In effect you get back 75 percent more dollars than you originally paid, but since the general level of prices has increased 100 percent you are getting back less purchasing power. In terms of purchasing power, or so-called real terms, you have actually taken a loss. You are only getting back 87.5 percent of the purchasing power ($17,500 ÷ $20,000) originally paid for the land. In real terms you have been taxed 12.5 percent for selling an asset on which there was no real capital gain.

This simple example illustrates how the capi-

tal gains tax collects taxes where there has been no real capital gain at all. Worse yet, suppose the price of an asset rises but at a rate less than the rate of inflation. If the owner sells it, less purchasing power will be received than was paid for it. Adding insult to injury, the capital gains tax will then take some more away! In fact (with a capital gains tax rate of 25 percent), it is necessary for the price of an asset to rise *more* than 25 percent *more* than the rise in the general level of prices for the seller of the asset to realize any real gain after tax at all.

For example, suppose today you sell for $23,333 the land that you paid $10,000 for ten years ago. Again, suppose the general price level has risen 100 percent in the meantime. The price of your land has gone up 33.3 percent more than the rise in the general price level (from $10,000 to $23,333 is a rise of 133.3 percent). The paper gain of $13,333 ($23,333 − $10,000) would be taxed at the 25 percent rate, and you would pay $3,333 in taxes (.25 × $13,333). This effectively taxes away your entire real gain! You are left with $20,000, exactly the amount of purchasing power you paid for the land ten years ago.

Critics conclude that the capital gains tax combined with inflation imposes such severe penalties on the sale of assets that it discourages investment. Why? The prospective return on investment in new assets (machines, buildings, and land) must be quite high to induce people to sell existing assets and incur the capital gains tax. Hence, critics contend that the flow of financial capital out of old assets and into new ones is impeded.

INDEXING—TAXING
ONLY THE REAL GAINS

Many critics point out that capital gains tax laws were originally written when there was little or no inflation. Little thought was given to the way these laws might affect real after-tax gains and losses in an inflationary environment. Tax reformers now argue that capital gains taxes should be indexed to the rate of inflation so that the tax only applies to the real gain, and not the so-called paper gain. The way to do this would be to adjust the original purchase price of the asset upward by the amount of the inflation that has taken place since the asset was originally purchased.

Consider again our initial example in which you paid $10,000 for land ten years ago and sell it for $20,000 today, while the general level of prices has risen 100 percent. With an indexed capital gains tax you would owe no tax at all. Why? Because when we adjust the original purchase price for inflation it becomes $20,000 in terms of the purchasing power of today's dollars. Hence, there is no real capital gain to tax because the inflation-adjusted purchase price is the same as the sale price.

Consider again the case where the price of the asset rises 33 percent more than the rise in the general price level. That is, you sell the land for $23,333 that you paid $10,000 for ten years ago. Again, suppose that the general price level has risen 100 percent in the meantime. If the capital gains tax is indexed, the original purchase price would be calculated as $20,000. In terms of today's dollars (which buy half as much as a dollar did ten years ago), this is exactly the amount of purchasing power that was originally paid for the land. The capital gains tax rate of 25 percent then would be applied to the real gain of $3,333 ($23,333 − $20,000), so that you would pay the government $833.25 (.25 × $3,333) in capital gains taxes. Recall that in this case, when the capital gains tax was not indexed, the entire real gain was taxed away.

Tax reformers contend that indexing the capital gains tax, like indexing the income tax, would deprive the government of another source of "unvoted and unlegislated" tax revenue. It is also alleged that indexing would remove the damper on investment imposed by a nonindexed capital gains tax. A study conducted at the National Bureau of Economic Research by Martin Feldstein and Joel Slemrod measured the total excess taxation in 1973 of corporate shares of stock caused by inflation. They found that the total capital gains taxes paid on dollar (as opposed to real) capital gains by individuals amounted to $1.1 billion. With indexing, the tax liability on the real capital gains would have been only $661 million. Hence, inflation raised tax liabilities by almost

$500 million, roughly doubling the overall effective tax rate on corporate stock capital gains.

Indexing Government Bonds

Recall our discussion of anticipated versus unanticipated inflation in Chapter 6. (You may find it helpful to reread that section at this point.) We saw that whenever there is an unanticipated inflation, there is a redistribution of wealth from lenders to borrowers—borrowers gain at lenders' expense. American citizens have loaned enormous sums to the U.S. government over the years, testified to by the fact that the government debt amounts to about three-quarters of a trillion dollars. To the extent that there is unanticipated inflation, the government gains at citizens' expense. Because bonds are fixed-dollar assets, the government repays citizens the same number of dollars originally borrowed. However, the dollars repaid have less purchasing power due to inflation.

Let's suppose a citizen loans the government $100 for one year by buying a government bond that pays a 5 percent rate of interest. Furthermore, suppose that the citizen buys the bond anticipating that there will be no inflation during the year. Hence, the citizen loans the government $100 of purchasing power because of the prospect of getting back 5 percent more purchasing power in one year, or $105. The citizen assumes that each dollar will have exactly the same purchasing power as that originally loaned. However, suppose that over the course of the year there is a 10 percent rise in the general price level, a 10 percent rate of inflation that was completely unanticipated by the citizen. Now when the government pays the citizen $105 at the end of the year, the $105 has only about 95 percent of the purchasing power of the $100 that the citizen originally loaned the government. The citizen gets back 5 percent more dollars than originally loaned, but each dollar now buys 10 percent less. The 10 percent rate of inflation has more than offset the 5 percent rate of interest. Because the citizen did not anticipate the inflation, the government has gained the purchasing power and the citizen has lost it.

Many feel that when citizens lend to their own government, they should not be subject to the risk of loss due to unanticipated inflation. Since the government controls fiscal and monetary policy, it is in a position to generate an unanticipated inflation and, thereby, reduce in real terms (purchasing power) the amount of the debt it has to pay back. It is highly doubtful that government creates inflation for this reason. However, fiscal and monetary policy makers are not immune from making mistakes that can cause inflation. And as we saw in the last chapter, the complexities that beset fiscal and monetary policy management in today's world can, and have, led to this result. Therefore, many argue that government bonds should be indexed to the rate of inflation to ensure that their real value remains constant.

To see how the indexing of government bonds would work, let's consider our bond example again. Suppose the $100 government bond were indexed to the rate of inflation. Again, suppose there is a 10 percent rate of inflation. At the end of the year, when the bond matures, the bondholder would automatically get back $110, the amount of purchasing power the bondholder loaned to the government initially. In addition, the bondholder receives the 5 percent interest rate on the purchasing power loaned. That is, the bondholder receives an additional $5.50, or 5 percent of $110. Hence, the citizen gets back the amount of purchasing power after one year that was originally anticipated when the bond was purchased.

Other Applications of Indexing

Besides its application to taxes and bonds, there are several other ways that indexing can be used in both the government and the private sectors of the economy.

Corporate bonds, mortgage loans, and savings deposits are fixed-dollar assets just like government bonds. Unanticipated inflation also causes losses for those lenders who put money into these assets. Lenders and borrowers could agree to index such assets in exactly the same way described for government bonds. The indexing of these assets has not yet occurred to any significant extent in the United States, possibly because inflation has not yet been severe enough.

Wages in the United States have been indexed to varying degrees in some areas of the economy. These areas include the wages of certain government workers, as well as those of workers in unions that have wage escalator clauses in their contracts. **Escalator clauses** *effectively index wages to inflation by stipulating that wages must be adjusted upward periodically to keep pace with the rising cost of living, as measured by the consumer price index, for example.*

Congress has legislated the indexing of social security payments and federal retirement benefits. On the other hand, the indexing of retirement pension benefits in the private sector of the economy has not been extensive. If the inflation problem persists, however, the practice of indexing private pension benefits will probably become more widespread.

Indexing and the Fight Against Inflation

Most economists agree that indexing can eliminate many of the arbitrary windfall gains and losses caused by unanticipated inflation. It can protect people's savings in fixed-dollar assets, such as bonds and savings accounts, from losing their real value. It is often argued that middle- and lower-income groups have few alternatives to holding their savings in the form of fixed-dollar assets. Therefore, indexing would reduce the uncertainty they face when making long-run saving plans to buy a house or car, to educate their children, or to provide for old age.

While many agree that indexing can reduce the pain of inflation, far fewer believe that it is a cure for inflation. The reason is that indexing deals with the symptoms of inflation, not its basic causes—such as overly expansive fiscal and monetary policy, and aggregate supply shocks. However, some economists contend that indexing would remove government's incentive to follow such expansionary fiscal and monetary policies. They argue, for example, that if the tax structure were indexed, the government wouldn't be able to collect more tax revenues by using inflation to push people into higher tax brackets. Similarly, the government wouldn't be able to pay off government debt with inflation-depreciated dollars. Supposedly this would make legislators more cautious about generating large bond-financed deficits. Yet other economists contend just the opposite. They argue that if policy makers felt people were protected from inflation by indexing, there would be even less concern about the inflationary consequences of continuous deficit spending.

We have already noted how indexing income taxes might reduce wage-push as a source of inflation. Some economists contend that indexing wages and salaries would also contribute to a reduction of wage-push. They argue that if wages and salaries were indexed, workers could be certain that they wouldn't lose ground to inflation. Hence, they would feel less compelled to push up wages and salaries in anticipation of inflation. They would not be so anxious about getting the jump on inflation out of fear inflation might get the jump on them. This would tend to reduce the upward shift of the aggregate supply curve caused by anticipated inflation that we discussed in the previous chapter. Hence, it might be easier for fiscal and monetary policy to deal with the policy dilemma posed by stagflation.

■ CHECKPOINT 15-2

Between 1968 and 1979 Congress cut taxes on five different occasions. Some say that in part this was done to offset the effects of inflation on taxes, that it was a discretionary form of income tax indexing. From a politician's viewpoint, can you think of two reasons why discretionary tax adjustment might be preferable to the automatic adjustment provided by an indexed income tax? Some people object to indexing government bonds because they claim it might have an adverse effect on the private sector's ability to borrow. Why might this be so? Recently, a high ranking government official said he didn't think much of indexing because it meant "you've given up the fight against inflation." What do you think of this point of view?

DEALING WITH UNEMPLOYMENT

What options are there for dealing with unemployment besides the conventional tools of fiscal and monetary policy? One problem with expansionary fiscal and monetary policy is that it tends to push up demand in all areas of the economy. This increased demand can cause prices to rise in industries already operating at full capacity, and wages to rise where the required kinds of labor are already fully employed or in short supply. The result is more inflation, but little reduction in unemployment. Meanwhile stubborn pockets of unemployment may still persist in certain areas of the economy. Trying to get at those pockets by expanding total demand is a little like trying to paint a picture with an 8-inch wide housepainter's brush. You hit a lot of areas that you don't want to touch.

In an effort to get around this problem, a number of policies have been proposed that focus on unemployment in more specific ways. A few of these have actually been tried while some have only been considered. Their effectiveness is a subject of ongoing debate. Let's consider a few of them—namely, manpower programs, public works projects, and job tax credits.

Manpower Programs

Manpower programs, *also known as job-training programs, are aimed at developing the job skills of the young and unemployed in order to increase their employability.* These programs also attempt to upgrade the job skills of older unemployed workers whose previous jobs have been eliminated by technological change and shifts in product demand. For example, the need for coal miners has been greatly reduced both by the mechanization of coal mining and the increased use of other kinds of fuel since the 1930s. As a result, miners who can no longer find employment will need new skills for use in industries where workers are needed.

CETA AND OTHER PROGRAMS

Several programs were undertaken to upgrade the job skills of low-income groups during the 1960s and early 1970s. Many of these individual programs were brought together under the Comprehensive Employment and Training Act (CETA) in 1973. CETA established a community manpower system to give people training and transitional public-service employment with the aim of enhancing their employability in the private sector. The federal government's role in CETA is to provide support and technical assistance to local programs. The Older American Community Service Employment Act of 1973 subsidizes jobs for older workers. Other federal activities include apprenticeship programs, the Job Corps, and the Work Incentive Program (WIN). The federal government helps support apprenticeship programs run by employers, often jointly with labor unions, to train workers on the job in a skilled trade. The Job Corps trains disadvantaged youth, largely at residential centers, and more recently has conducted nontraditional training for women. The Work Incentive Program provides manpower, placement, and other services to help people receiving Aid to Families with Dependent Children get and keep jobs.

PROGRAM EFFECTIVENESS

Have these programs been very effective at improving employability and helping to reduce the unemployment rate? It is difficult to tell.

Some say that the Job Corps' experience with efforts to train disadvantaged youths, the "hard-core" unemployed among the young, suggests that progress is possible. However, high costs and drop-out rates are a problem. Moreover, Job Corps training, like any job-training program, has little value if there is no job to enter once training is completed. Particularly discouraging is the high unemployment rate among black teenagers. It has climbed with little interruption for over a quarter of a century until now roughly 40 percent are unemployed, as compared to 16.5 percent in 1954. Analysts who monitor this problem offer various explanations. Notably, they say government job programs don't focus enough on inner-city neighborhoods where black teenagers predominate. Also, new jobs are emerging farther from inner-city areas. Many claim that the minimum wage eliminated many jobs that would otherwise be available to unskilled workers. Another factor cited is inadequate educational facilities.

Public-service jobs funded by CETA are intended to reduce hard-core unemployment and provide temporary, entry-level jobs into the economic mainstream for people without much training or work experience. But critics note that local projects often call for workers with sophisticated skills. They also cite some large cities where funds intended for jobs for poor blacks, Hispanics, and welfare mothers are being used to rehire municipal workers laid off in budget cutbacks. Critics also point out that federal public-service money, rather than creating new jobs, is often diverted into supporting activities that state and local governments might have provided from their own budgets.

Public Works Projects

Since the days of the Great Depression, public works projects have been seen as a way to use government expenditures to put the unemployed back to work while meeting important community needs. However, it is not always easy to devise projects that are truly worthwhile on their own merits, and not just excuses to spend money to "make work." During the Great Depression, the Works Progress Administration (WPA) put many unemployed people to work on a variety of projects, such as developing park areas, building roads, constructing dams and public buildings, and so forth. While many of these projects were considered worthwhile, others were of a "make work" nature—leaf raking, construction projects using men and shovels where motorized equipment would have been more efficient, and so on. Today many proponents of public works projects contend that unemployed young people could be employed on such projects as slum clearance and urban rehabilitation. It is argued that these activities would create jobs in inner cities where unemployment among youth, particularly blacks, is highest.

Ideally, it is desirable to locate public works projects in those areas of the country where unemployment rates are highest. This has proved difficult in practice, however. Federal statistics are often not precise enough to identify areas with the highest unemployment. The national jobless rate is based on a monthly survey of 50,000 households, but the sample doesn't produce precise rates for particular geographic areas. Building trades unions, for example, complain that the government seems to have difficulty pinpointing places where their numbers are particularly hard-hit by unemployment. Some states that work up their own figures often seem to underestimate dramatically the number of the long-term, chronically unemployed.

The idea of timing public works projects so that they are initiated and carried out during the recession phases of business cycles has turned out to be largely unworkable. We have already noted in Chapter 6 how the timing of discretionary spending aimed at offsetting recessions is hindered by the uncertainties of forecasting and recognition and the sluggishness of the democratic decision-making process. As a result, slow-starting projects may aggravate inflation later by tightening up labor markets in an improving economy.

Employment Tax Credit

The basic idea behind an employment tax credit is to reduce the cost of labor to business firms so that they will hire more labor. *The em-ployment tax credit allows firms to exclude a certain amount of their income from taxation, an amount equal to some specified percent of the wages they pay labor.* This credit effectively reduces the cost of employing labor, thus encouraging firms to hire more workers than they would otherwise.

Some economists view the employment tax credit as a less inflationary way of stimulating the economy and increasing employment than reductions in personal and corporate income taxes. They contend that cuts in personal and corporate income taxes put extra dollars in the hands of consumers and businesses without initially expanding the supply of goods that will be demanded with these dollars. By contrast, it is argued that an employment tax credit puts extra dollars in circulation through bigger payrolls, while at the same time expanding production through the hiring of additional workers. Proponents also claim that by lowering production costs such a credit encourages businesses to hold down prices.

Some economists think that an employment tax credit is a cheaper, more effective, more permanent way of putting the hard-core unemployed to work than federal spending on public works or public-service jobs. We have noted that public-service jobs, such as those funded by CETA, are intended to provide temporary, entry-level jobs into the economic mainstream for the hard-core unemployed and others without much training or work experience. Those who prefer the employment tax credit approach argue that it puts these people into the economic mainstream immediately, and gives them on-the-job training that is difficult to duplicate in public-service jobs. However, some economists believe that subsidizing wages via the employment tax credit inhibits investment in labor-saving machinery, which is needed to increase productivity. On the other hand, others argue that less emphasis on capital and more on labor is appropriate for a society trying to conserve energy and other natural resources and prevent pollution.

SUMMARY

1. A wage-price guidelines policy attempts to curb inflation by getting business and labor to refrain voluntarily from increasing wages and prices at rates in excess of some guideline rate specified by government.

2. Two measures designed to provide incentives for compliance with wage-price guidelines are wage insurance and the tax-based income policy (TIP). Wage insurance guarantees that the government will repay labor for the purchasing power that they lose if they comply with the guideline and consumer prices rise faster than the guideline rate for wages. The carrot version of TIP rewards with tax credits (reductions in income taxes) those workers who keep their wage increases below the guideline rate for wage increases. The stick version of TIP punishes with tax penalties employers who grant wage increases that exceed the guideline rate.

3. High administration officials usually resort to jawboning and arm-twisting in their attempts to gain voluntary compliance with guidelines.

4. Wage-price controls make it illegal to increase wages and prices beyond limits set by government. Controls are difficult and costly to enforce because they cause short-

ages. Frustrated buyers willing to pay a higher price for the good give suppliers an economic incentive to evade controls. In addition to selling at prices above the legal limit, evasion can take the form of changing product quality and the compensation of labor in ways that effectively reduce the quantity of work actually performed for the same wage.

5. Wage-price controls affect resource allocation because wages and prices are not free to move to reflect shifts in supply and demand in different markets. Controls also raise questions of equity because enforcement efforts tend to focus more heavily on some groups than others, and to control wages and prices more than interest rates, dividends, rents, profits, and other forms of income.

6. The mere expectation that controls are about to be imposed may lead to an acceleration of wage-price increases. Whether or not the existence of wage-price controls dampens inflationary expectations remains a question of debate.

7. Experience suggests that controls have not proven very effective in the face of expansionary fiscal and monetary policy, except when supported by other antiinflationary policies, as they were during World War II.

8. Indexing keeps constant the purchasing power of wages, taxes, and fixed-dollar assets by adjusting their dollar-denominated values for the change in the general price level.

9. Indexing the income tax would prevent inflation from pushing people into progressively higher tax brackets, a process that otherwise increases the tax rate on incomes of constant purchasing power. Indexing the capital gains tax would mean that those selling an asset would be taxed only on their real gain, not dollar gains attributable to inflation. Indexing government bonds, mortgage loans, savings deposits, and other fixed-dollar assets would eliminate many of the arbitrary gains and losses caused by unanticipated inflation.

10. Indexing wages and salaries might elimi-

nate a source of cost-push inflation because workers, insulated from inflation, would feel less compelled to push up wages and salaries in anticipation of inflation. Some economists argue that indexing income taxes and government bonds would also reduce inflation because it would make it harder for government to finance deficit spending. Others disagree, claiming that if policy makers felt people were protected from inflation by indexing, there would be even less concern about curbing an overly expansive fiscal and monetary policy.

11. Conventional fiscal and monetary policy has difficulty reducing stubborn pockets of unemployment without generating inflationary price increases in those parts of the economy already operating at capacity. Policies more specifically focused on dealing with hard-core unemployment problems seem to be necessary.

12. Manpower programs provide job training for the young and hard-core unemployed to increase their employability. Public works projects are often aimed at providing employment while at the same time constructing needed public facilities, such as schools, roads, and parks. An employment tax credit is designed to reduce the cost of labor and encourage employment by giving firms tax credits equal to some specified percent of the wages paid to labor.

KEY TERMS AND CONCEPTS
capital gains taxes
employment tax credit
escalator clause
indexing
manpower programs
tax-based income policy (TIP)
wage-price controls
wage-price guidelines
wage insurance

QUESTIONS AND PROBLEMS
1. Suppose the government institutes a wage-price guidelines policy. If you are running a business, what would determine your willingness to comply with the guidelines?

2. Explain why some economists argue that whether the carrot version of TIP will lead to more, or less, inflation depends on how the government decides to replace the tax revenue lost when workers earn tax credits. How would a combined carrot-and-stick version of TIP affect your analysis of this issue? What advantages might a combined carrot-and-stick version of TIP have over wage insurance?

3. Rank the following industries or markets according to how difficult you think it would be to enforce price controls: antiques; haircuts; steel; gasoline; auto parts; firewood; cosmetics; electric power; airline passenger service; ladies apparel; hockey game tickets. Explain what considerations determined your ranking.

4. It has been said that because controls affect resource allocation, inflation actually takes place even though prices are not allowed to rise. Explain the logic underlying this point of view.

5. "Controls can affect expectations in a variety of ways, some tending to curb and others to aggravate inflation." Elaborate on this statement.

6. Assume the following progressive income tax structure: 15 percent tax on the first $10,000 of income; 17 percent on income between $10,000 and $15,000; 20 percent on income between $15,000 and $20,000; 25 percent on income between $20,000 and $30,000; and 50 percent on all income in excess of $30,000.

a. Suppose your income is indexed (note: your income, not the income tax) to the consumer price index (CPI) by agreement with your employer, and that initially your income is $9,000 per year. Suppose that the CPI increases 140 percent over the next ten years. How will the purchasing power of your after-tax income ten years from now compare with that of your after-tax income today?

b. Alternatively, suppose that initially your income were $14,000 per year. Again, assume it is indexed to the CPI and that the CPI increases by 140 percent. How would the purchasing power of your after-tax income ten years from now compare with that of your after-tax income today?

c. Considering your answers to parts a and b, what do you conclude about the way inflation affects lower- versus middle-income groups, given this tax structure?

d. Suppose your income were $30,000 initially. Again, assuming it is indexed and that the CPI rises 140 percent, how would your after-tax purchasing power be affected? What do you conclude about the way inflation affects upper- versus middle- and lower-income groups, given this tax structure?

e. Show how the tax structure would be changed if it were indexed, and explain how this would affect after-tax purchasing power. How strongly do you think different income groups might feel about income tax indexing?

7. It has been argued that if all wages and salaries as well as all fixed-dollar assets were indexed, the slightest bit of excessive fiscal or monetary expansion would create an inflation that would feed on itself, getting worse and worse, eventually turning into hyperinflation. Explain why you agree or disagree with this point of view.

8. While job-training programs and employment tax credits are both aimed at reducing unemployment, they each have implications for inflation as well. What are the inflationary implications of each? Which do you think might be more inflationary and why?

■ NEWS ITEM FOR YOUR ANALYSIS ■

WAGE-PRICE GUIDELINES GET OFF
TO A SLOW START, WITH SUCCESS IN DOUBT

WASHINGTON, November 21—Announcing the voluntary wage-price guidelines on October 24, Mr. Carter pleaded with Americans to "give this program a chance." He said the plan "can work—but that will take time." Indeed, early evidence suggests that the antiinflation program is getting off to a shaky start.

Labor leaders are outraged by it, and many threaten defiance. Businesses are confused by it, though still pledging cooperation. And Carter administration inflation fighters seem overwhelmed by the huge task of organizing, explaining, and running the program. Some critics are already writing off the wage-price guidelines, arguing that a more restrictive fiscal and monetary policy is a more important antiinflation step.

Administration officials insist that the guidelines policy stresses simplicity and voluntarism. They say that all a company has to do is hold its average annual wage and benefit increases to 7 percent, and keep its average price increases half a percentage point below average increases in 1976–1977. Exceptions are to be made for special situations. But businesses complain that the guidelines, the exceptions, and the 45-page "fact book" outlining formulas for compliance are far from simple. "The formulas have sigma signs and square roots; if you haven't seen them, you haven't lived," says Allan Choka, vice-president of Helene Curtis Industries, Inc.

In fact, the guidelines are not entirely voluntary. Those who don't comply may be disqualified from federal contracts, be exposed to increased competition from imports, and have their workers declared ineligible for certain proposed tax rebates. Fearful of such sanctions, many companies are turning for help in interpreting the guidelines to Washington law firms, some of which are hiring additional lawyers to become guide-line experts.

President Carter is determined to avoid creating a bloated bureaucracy at the wage-price council, the overseer and administrator of the guidelines. He has decided that the guidelines can be managed by building up the council's staff to 135 from its present 35. The aim is to have this slim force focus on monitoring the pricing activity of the nation's 400 largest corporations. Alfred Kahn, head of the council, says that "gives you [coverage of] a big hunk of the economy fast." However, given the complexities of the pricing practices of major corporations and the thousands of products those corporations produce, even this limited task may easily overwhelm the council.

No doubt the council will have its hands full just clarifying how the guidelines apply to different situations. Many sticky questions have already arisen. For instance, are pay increases, promised before the guidelines went into effect, to be granted even though they exceed the guideline rate of increase? How are employees' bonuses and sales commission income to be treated? What if just maintaining the level of hospitalization benefits in current contracts pushes the total package of a new labor contract beyond the wage guideline—does that mean labor's hourly wage must be held to no increase at all? How is deferred compensation of executives to be treated under the guidelines? For example, is compensation earned in past years, but due to be paid this year, subject to the guideline on wages or not? These are but a few of the questions that the council must deal with immediately. A council staffer laments, "if the lid comes off and all prices start moving up, we probably don't have enough people" to do even a minimal job.

QUESTIONS

1. What kinds of questions and problems do you think will arise if it is decided that guidelines should apply to pay increases already promised (but not yet delivered) before the guidelines were established?

2. What kinds of questions and problems do you think will arise if it is decided that guidelines should apply to employees' bonuses and sales commission income? If the guidelines do not apply to these sources of income?

3. How would you resolve the question as to whether or not the guidelines should apply to fringe benefits such as employer-paid health insurance and retirement pensions? Why?

4. What difference do you think it would make whether or not deferred compensation is subject to the guideline, taking into account deferred compensation that is earned now (but not paid until some date in the future) as well as deferred compensation earned in the past (but to be paid now)? What difference does it make in terms of inflation today versus inflation tomorrow?

16

ECONOMIC GROWTH

PERILS OF THE PRODUCTIVITY SAG

WASHINGTON, February 5—Throughout the 1960s, the United States experienced rapid economic growth along with low unemployment and low inflation. By contrast, in the 1970s the economy has been plagued by inadequate expansion, persistently high unemployment, and galloping inflation. Why? While no single factor can take all the blame, it is extremely significant that productivity growth slowed sharply during the 1970s.

During the 1960s, output per labor hour worked increased at an average of 3 percent per year. This healthy pace had been maintained since shortly after World War II. Productivity growth in the 1970s averaged only about half that. Some economists at first thought the slowdown was a cyclical fluke, a product of the recessions of 1970 and 1973–1975 (recessions typically slow productivity growth because companies slow down operations and keep workers on the payroll who do not have much to do). However, the annual report of the Council of Economic Advisors pretty well blew away that theory. It points out that during the past two years of expansion productivity in the private economy rose only 1.6 percent in 1977 and a disappointing .4 percent during 1978. The report pessimistically suggests the United States may be entering a new era in which productivity growth for many years will average no more than 1.5 percent.

The implications of such low productivity growth could be disastrous. Productivity growth is necessary to raise living standards and to control inflation. True, in the short run, low productivity growth can create jobs because more workers will be required to satisfy rising demand. But in the long run, low productivity growth hurts employment. It was believed that in the 1960s the economy could grow 4 percent each year without setting off demand-pull inflation. However, because of the slowdown in productivity growth, the administration now figures the safe-growth ceiling to be 3 percent. The question is, can an economy growing that slowly create enough jobs for all those looking for work?

Our discussion in preceding chapters has dealt mostly with the analysis of income and employment determination in the short run. We have focused on the problem of how to smooth out economic fluctuations and at the same time keep the economy operating close to its full-employment capacity without generating excessive inflation. The framework of modern income and employment analysis that we have used throughout implicitly assumes that there is a given, unchanging, quantity of resources and a given state of technology. That assumption is what makes it a short-run analysis. In the short run, there is a given amount of labor, capital, and land to employ, a given state of technological know-how, and a given population to clothe, house, and feed.

Economic growth takes place because in the long run the quantity of available resources, the state of technology, and the size of the population all change. It is necessary to study economic growth in order to understand how and why the economy's capacity to produce goods and services changes in the long run. As the news item suggests, economic growth (or the absence of it) also has important implications for how well we can handle many of the problems that confront our economy in the short run. Emphasizing the importance of the short run, Keynes once remarked that "in the long run we are all dead." Nonetheless, the long-run phenomenon of economic growth has important consequences for how well we live in the short run.

Our first concern in this chapter will be the definition and measurement of economic growth. Then we will examine the major past and present explanations of why there is economic growth. Finally, we will consider the apparent slowdown in U.S. economic growth mentioned in the news item, the issue of the benefits and costs of economic growth, and the increasing concern about the possible limits to economic growth.

DEFINING AND MEASURING ECONOMIC GROWTH

We can define economic growth in several different, but related, ways. Moreover, how we define economic growth largely determines how we measure it. Definition and measurement are closely related issues.

Defining Economic Growth

Defined quite generally, **economic growth** *is the expansion of an economy's capacity to produce goods and services that takes place over prolonged periods of time, year in and year out, from decade to decade, from one generation to the next, or even over the course of centuries.*

THE EXPANDING PRODUCTION POSSIBILITIES FRONTIER

Recall our discussion of the economy's production possibilities frontier in Chapter 2. Suppose the economy produces two kinds of goods—consumer goods and capital goods. The production possibilities frontier *AA* in Figure 16-1 shows the different maximum possible combinations of quantities of capital and consumer goods that the economy can produce if it fully employs all its available resources of labor, capital, and land, given the existing state of technological know-how. If there is an increase in the quantity or quality of any of these resources, or if there is improvement in the state of technological know-how, the economy's productive possibility frontier will shift outward to a position such as *BB*. As a result, the economy can produce more of both kinds of goods. This gives us an insight into the nature and causes of economic growth. Economic growth may be viewed as the continual shifting outward of the production possibilities frontier, caused by growth in the quantity or quality, or both, of the economy's available resources, by ongoing improvement in the state of technological know-how, or by some combination of both.

STAYING ON THE FRONTIER

When the economy's production possibilities frontier shifts outward, the economy's *capacity* to produce increases. But the economy will not realize the full benefits of this capacity increase unless it is always on its production possibilities frontier. In Chapter 2 we saw that there are two reasons why the economy may operate inside its production possibilities frontier.

First, the economy will not operate on its production possibilities frontier if any of its resources are unemployed. Whenever part of the labor force is unemployed, or whenever there is unused plant capacity, the economy operates inside its production possibilities frontier. In order to remain on the frontier, the economy's total demand for goods and services must grow at a rate sufficient to utilize fully the increased productive capacity provided by economic growth.

Second, the economy will not operate on its production possibilities frontier if any of its resources are underemployed—that is, if there is not efficient resource allocation. Efficient resource allocation requires that resources be employed in those activities for which they are best suited. Only then will the economy be able to realize the maximum possible output with its available resources. (Recall the example in Chapter 2 of the effect on the economy's output of wheat and oranges that results from trying to grow wheat in Florida and oranges in Minnesota.)

In sum, if the economy is to stay on its expanding production possibilities frontier and realize the gains from economic growth, it must avoid both unemployment and underemployment. While it is not possible to eliminate unemployment completely, fiscal and monetary policy must see to it that total demand expands fast enough to utilize the increased productive capacity provided by economic growth. And, in order to minimize underemployment, markets must operate efficiently to allocate resources to those productive activities in which the value of their contribution to total output will be greatest.

THE INTERDEPENDENCE OF DEMAND AND ECONOMIC GROWTH

The rate of increase of total demand for goods and services and the rate of economic growth are interrelated. If total demand doesn't expand fast enough to keep the economy operating on its production possibilities frontier, the resulting unemployment will mean that a certain amount of capital goods that could be produced will not be. Capital goods not produced today will not be available to produce other goods tomorrow. Consequently, the outward expansion of the economy's production possibili-

---

After reading this chapter, you will be able to:

1. Define the concept of economic growth.
2. Describe the ways in which economic growth and its major components are measured.
3. Explain the classical view of economic growth.
4. Summarize the sources of economic growth.
5. Describe the problems underlying the apparent recent slowdown of economic growth in the United States.
6. Explain the controversy over the benefits and costs of economic growth, and the concern about possible limits to economic growth.

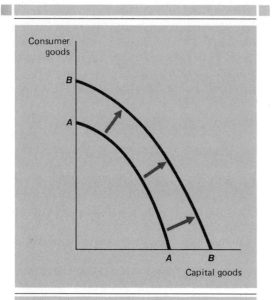

FIGURE 16-1 ECONOMIC GROWTH SHIFTS THE PRODUCTION POSSIBILITIES FRONTIER OUTWARD

Economic growth may be represented by an outward shift of the production possibilities frontier, such as from *AA* to *BB*. The shift is caused by growth in the quantity or quality, or both, of the economy's available resources, by ongoing improvement in the state of technological know-how, or by a combination of both. To realize the full benefits of economic growth, the economy must maintain full employment and avoid inefficient allocation of its resources.

ties frontier will not be as great. There will be less economic growth than otherwise would have been possible had total demand expanded fast enough to keep the economy continually operating on its production possibilities frontier.

For example, during the Great Depression total demand declined so much that the nation's firms actually allowed their capital stock to wear out faster than they replaced it—net investment was negative, as was shown in Figure 5-2. This meant that the economy's capital stock actually declined. One of the major costs of the Great Depression was the enormous quantity of capital goods that the economy nev-

er produced. This lack of capital goods production resulted in a severe decline in the rate of expansion of the economy's productive capacity, hence its rate of economic growth.

Measuring Economic Growth

If economic growth is represented by an outward expansion of the economy's production possibilities frontier, then *one measure of economic growth is the rate of growth of the economy's full-employment level of total output.* This is the level of total output the economy can produce when it is on its production possibilities frontier. The money value of full-employment total output can change because of a change in prices. Since we are only interested in measurements of growth that represent an increase in the output of actual goods and services, economic growth rates must be calculated using constant-dollar, or real, measures of full-employment total output. An example of such a measure is potential, or full-employment, real GNP measured in constant 1972 dollars, as was shown in Figure 6-4, part b.

FULL-EMPLOYMENT REAL GNP

The rate of growth of full-employment real GNP is a measure of the growth in the economy's overall capacity to produce goods and services. But it tells us little about how the economy's standard of living is changing over time. One measure of the economy's standard of living is output per capita, the economy's full-employment total output level divided by the size of its population. We can express this as

$$\text{full-employment real GNP per capita}$$
$$= \frac{\text{full-employment real GNP}}{\text{population}}$$

It is obvious from this expression that growth in full-employment real GNP does not necessarily mean an increase in the standard of living as measured by full-employment real GNP per capita. If full-employment real GNP (the numerator) grows faster than population (the denominator), full-employment real GNP per capita will grow and the economy's standard of living will increase. However, if full-employment real GNP grows at a slower rate than population, full-employment real GNP per capita declines and the standard of living goes down. Remember, however, that full-employment real GNP per capita is an average and, thus, a very rough measure of living standards. Few economists consider it an ideal measure of the economy's standard of living. For example, it doesn't tell us anything about the actual distribution of income in the economy. (At this point you should reread the discussions in Chapter 5 of what GNP does not measure.) Nonetheless, *the rate of growth of output per capita is a measure of economic growth that provides a rough indication of change in the standard of living.*

OUTPUT PER LABOR HOUR

Another important measure closely linked to economic growth is output per labor hour (often referred to as output per man hour). As mentioned in the news item, output per labor hour is the conventional way of measuring **productivity.** It gives us some indication of how efficiently each labor hour combines with the capital stock and the existing state of technology to produce output. Output per labor hour is an appealing measure of productivity because it is a combined reflection of the quality of labor (education, technical skill, motivation), the quantity and quality of capital that labor uses, and the degree of sophistication of the state of technology. *The greater the rate of growth of output per labor hour, the larger the rate of growth of productivity, and this obviously contributes to the rate of economic growth.*

COMPONENTS OF FULL-EMPLOYMENT TOTAL OUTPUT

The economy's full-employment total output Q may be viewed as having four components. The size of the economy's population N (the number of people) is the first component. The second is the fraction of the population that makes up the labor force. This fraction is equal to the number of laborers L divided by the size of the population N. Note that the number of laborers L may be computed as the population N multiplied by the fraction of the population in the labor force:

$$L = N \times \frac{L}{N}$$

The third component is the average number of hours H that each laborer actually works. The total number of labor hours actually worked by the entire labor force therefore equals L multiplied by H. Note that the total number of labor hours $L \times H$ may be expressed as

$$L \times H = N \times \frac{L}{N} \times H$$

The fourth component is productivity, or output per labor hour, which is equal to full-employment total output Q divided by the total number of labor hours $L \times H$:

$$\frac{Q}{L \times H}$$

The economy's full-employment total output Q is equal to the total number of labor hours $L \times H$ multiplied by output per labor hour $Q/(L \times H)$:

$$Q = L \times H \times \frac{Q}{L \times H}$$

Since

$$L \times H = N \times \frac{L}{N} \times H$$

the economy's full-employment total output Q may also be expressed as

$$Q = N \times \frac{L}{N} \times H \times \frac{Q}{L \times H} \qquad (1)$$

Equation 1 shows that the economy's full-employment total output Q may be viewed as being equal to the product of the four components: the size of the population N multiplied by the fraction of the population in the labor force L/N multiplied by the average number of hours each laborer actually works H multiplied by output per labor hour $Q/(L \times H)$. Clearly the growth of the economy's full-employment total output Q will depend on the way each of these four components in equation 1 changes over time. (Note that N, L, and H in the numerator of equation 1 may be cancelled out by the N, L, and H in the denominator of equation 1 to give $Q - Q$ which is true by definition.)

The total output of the U.S. economy, as measured by real GNP (in constant 1972 dol-

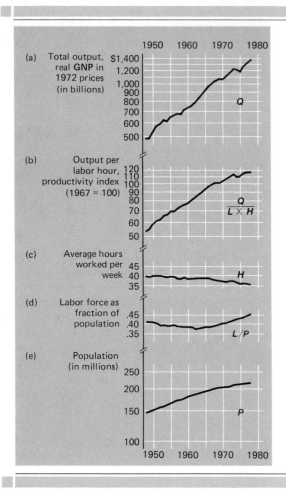

FIGURE 16-2 THE COMPONENTS OF ECONOMIC GROWTH IN THE AMERICAN ECONOMY SINCE 1948

The growth of total output Q, measured by real GNP (part a), is the product of change in four components: population, P; the fraction of the population in the labor force, L/P; the average hours worked per laborer, H; and productivity, or output per labor hour, $Q/(L \times H)$.

Productivity growth (part b) has been the single most important contributor to real GNP growth since 1948. Next in order of importance has been population growth (part e). The decline in the proportion of the population in the labor force (part d) from 1948 to 1962 tended to work against real GNP growth, while the increase in that proportion since 1962 has been favorable to real GNP growth. The decline in average hours worked per week (part c) tended to hold back real GNP growth.

Note that the vertical axis in each diagram is a logarithmic or ratio scale on which equal distances represent equal percentage changes. For example, in part a the distance from 600 to 900 is the same as the distance from 800 to 1,200 since each represents an increase of 50 percent.

---

lars), is shown in part a of Figure 16-2. Since 1948 real GNP has increased roughly threefold. Let's examine the role that each of the four components has played in this growth.

ROLE OF THE COMPONENTS OF TOTAL OUTPUT IN ECONOMIC GROWTH

1. *Population—P.* Population growth contributes to economic growth from both the demand side and the supply side. A growing population means a growing demand for all kinds of goods and services. On the supply side, an increasing population provides the ever larger pool of labor needed to produce the larger quantity of output required to satisfy growing demand.

Throughout its history the United States has experienced steady population growth due to a high birthrate, a declining death rate, and at times (especially during the nineteenth century) substantial immigration. The U.S. population increased from approximately 5 million persons in 1800 to approximately 76 million in 1900. By 1978 it had increased to about 220 million. In recent years the birthrate has declined somewhat, reflecting a trend toward smaller families. (This trend in part may be due to the increasing participation of women in the labor force.) Population experts project the population will grow to somewhere between 245 million and 290 million by the year 2000, the range largely reflecting the difference between assuming a low or a high birthrate. The growth in the postwar

U.S. population since 1948 is illustrated in part e of Figure 16-2. Clearly, population growth has been a contributing factor to the growth in real GNP shown in part a.

2. *Labor force, as a fraction of the population—L/P.* While the population provides the source of the labor pool, it is the proportion or fraction of the population that actually joins the labor force, *L/P,* that determines the size of the labor pool. The larger the fraction, the larger the labor force provided by a given size population and, hence, the greater the productive capacity of the economy.

The behavior of this fraction in the postwar U.S. economy is shown in part d of Figure 16-2. Expressing the fraction *L/P* as a percentage, the percentage of the population in the labor force fell from roughly 41 percent in 1948 to somewhat less than 38 percent in 1962. Since that time it has increased steadily, reaching over 45 percent in the late 1970s. In other words, the labor force has been growing faster than the population. As we observed in Chapter 6, in part this has been due to a maturing post-World War II "baby boom" that swelled the working-age population during the 1960s and 1970s. Another contributing factor has been the increase in the proportion of working-age women that has joined the labor force during these years.

3. *Hours, average hours worked per laborer—H.* In 1890 the length of the average work week was roughly 60 hours. During the early part of the twentieth century, it declined steadily to about 43 hours in 1930. Since then the decline has continued at a more gradual pace (interrupted by an increase during World War II). From 1948 to around 1966 the average work week only declined by about 1 hour, from about 40 hours per week down to about 39 hours, as illustrated in part c of Figure 16-2. Since then it appears to have declined to around 36 hours.

Obviously, a decline in the length of the average work week tends to reduce the rate of economic growth. However, the reduction in hours worked reminds us that economic growth is certainly not the be-all and end-all of the "good life." Most economists argue that the steady decline in the average work week reflects a preference for more leisure, one of the fruits made possible by the higher standard of living provided by economic growth. Indeed, while the length of the average work week today is about 40 percent shorter than it was in 1890, real GNP per capita has increased roughly 500 percent over this time period.

4. *Output per labor hour—Q/(L × H).* Growth in productivity, or output per labor hour, is the principal component in economic growth. In all countries that have experienced sustained increases in their standard of living, productivity growth has been the wellspring. Productivity growth results from increases in the educational and skill levels of the labor force, growth in the quantity and quality of capital, and the steady advancement of the state of technological know-how. Output per labor hour has more than doubled in the U.S. economy since 1948, as shown in Figure 16-2, part b.

Comparing parts b, c, d, and e of Figure 16-2, we can see that productivity growth (part b) has been the single most important contributor to the growth in real GNP (part a) since 1948. Next in order of importance has been population growth (part e). The decline in the proportion of the population in the labor force (part d) from 1948 to 1962 tended to work against economic growth, while the increase in that proportion since 1962 has been favorable to economic growth. The decline in average hours worked per week (part c) has tended to hold back growth in real GNP. However, it should be stressed that, if the shorter work week represents a choice of more leisure in exchange for less growth in the output of goods, it signifies an increase in well-being.

THE SIGNIFICANCE OF GROWTH RATES—THE "RULE OF 72"

What difference does it make whether an economy grows at 3 percent, or 4 percent, or 5 percent? A great deal! A rule-of-thumb calculation known as the "rule of 72" readily shows why. For any growth rate in real GNP, the rule of 72 says that the number of years it will take for real GNP to double in size is roughly equal to 72 divided by the growth rate. For example, if the economy's real GNP grows at a rate of 2 percent, it will take approximately 36 years (72 ÷ 2) for real GNP to double. If it grows at a 3 percent rate, it will take 24 years to double (72 ÷ 3). A 6 percent growth rate would mean real GNP would double in only 12 years (72 ÷ 6)!

Consider the implications of the different growth rates discussed in the news item at the beginning of this chapter. The news item reports that "it was believed that in the 1960s the economy could grow 4 percent each year without setting off demand-pull inflation." However, because of the slowdown in productivity growth during the 1970s, "the administration now figures the safe-growth ceiling to be 3 percent." According to the rule of 72, at a 4 percent growth rate real GNP would double in roughly 18 years (72 ÷ 4). Starting from the year 1982, this doubling would occur at the turn of the century in the year 2000. However, at the "safe-growth" rate of 3 percent needed to avoid excessive inflation, real GNP would not double until approximately the year 2006, which is 24 years from 1982.

Suppose we start with the actual level of real GNP in 1978 and project these two different growth paths into the future, as shown in Figure 16-3. Clearly, the farther into the future we go on these two different paths, the greater the difference in the possible levels of real GNP. In 1980 the difference amounts to about $40 billion. By 1990 real GNP on the 4 percent growth path is about $2,160 billion, while on the 3 percent growth path it is $1,950 billion, a difference of $210 billion. By the year 2000 the difference amounts to about $634 billion! This gives some idea why there is so much concern about the implications of the slowdown in productivity growth reported in the news item.

■ CHECKPOINT 16-1

From 1950 to 1978 productivity in the U.S. economy roughly doubled (Figure 16-2, part b). What does the rule of 72 tell us about the rate of growth of productivity during this time period? According to the news item at the beginning of this chapter, the annual report of the Council of Economic Advisors projects

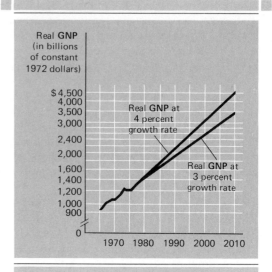

FIGURE 16-3 THE DIFFERENCE BETWEEN A REAL GNP GROWTH RATE OF 4 PERCENT AND A RATE OF 3 PERCENT

Starting from the actual level of real GNP in 1978, the difference between growing at a 3 percent and at a 4 percent rate becomes more pronounced as we proceed into the future. In 1980 the difference amounts to about $40 billion. But by the year 2000 it amounts to roughly $634 billion. (Note that the vertical axis is a logarithmic or ratio scale on which equal distances represent equal percentage changes.)

that productivity growth in the United States may average no more than 1.5 percent per year in coming years. What does this imply about the projected behavior of the other three components of economic growth, given the "safe-growth ceiling" reported in the news item? Compare parts a and e of Figure 16-2 and give a rough estimate of how much real GNP per capita has increased since 1948 in the United States.

EXPLAINING ECONOMIC GROWTH

It has been difficult for economists to come up with a single, comprehensive theory that explains economic growth. How does a country that has experienced a low and unchanging standard of living for centuries transform itself into one that realizes a sustained, decade-by-decade increase in productivity and real GNP per capita? Part of the difficulty economists have with this question is that a good deal of the answer no doubt requires an explanation of the political, cultural, and sociological processes that underlie such a transformation. The classical economists, such as David Ricardo and Thomas Malthus, painted a rather gloomy picture of the prospects for economic growth. Subsequent generations of economists have had the benefit of observing economic growth on a scale that the classical economists had not anticipated. Present-day explanations of economic growth place a great deal of emphasis on such things as capital formation, technological change, and saving.

The Classical View of Economic Growth

During the late eighteenth and early nineteenth centuries the Industrial Revolution in England was just getting under way. Much of the rest of Western Europe remained untouched by this development. Observing the world around them, it is little wonder that classical economists, such as Malthus and Ricardo, argued that a nation's economic growth would inevitably lead to stagnation and a subsistence standard of living. In its simplest form, their argument rested on two basic premises. The first was the law of diminishing returns. The second was the proposition that the population would expand to the point where the economy's limited resources would only provide a subsistence living.

PRODUCTION AND THE LAW OF DIMINISHING RETURNS

The law of diminishing returns is a proposition about the way total output changes when the quantity of one input to a production process is increased while the quantities of all other inputs are held constant. Classical economists applied this law to economic growth. *Given the state of technological know-how, classical econo-mists argued that as a larger and larger population works with a fixed amount of land and other resources, the increase in total output becomes less and less.* In other words, there are diminishing returns in the form of successively smaller additions to total output. As a consequence the average output per capita declines as the population grows.

The law of diminishing returns is illustrated in Figure 16-4 for a hypothetical country. In part a, population P is measured on the horizontal axis and total output Q on the vertical axis. The total output curve TQ shows the relationship between the size of the country's population and the quantity of total output that population can produce, assuming a fixed quantity of resources and a given state of technological know-how. With a population of 1 million the economy is able to produce a total output of 10 million units. If the population increases by 1 million, to a total of 2 million, the level of total output rises by 9 million units to a total of 19 million units. A population increase to 3 million results in an increase in total output from 19 million to 25 million units, or a rise of 7 million units, and so forth. Note that each successive 1 million person increase in the population results in a smaller increase in total output. The successively smaller increases in total output associated with each 1 million person increase in population reflect the law of diminishing returns. Once the population reaches 8 million, further increases in population actually cause total output to fall. That is, the TQ curve bends over and begins to decline beyond a population of 8 million.

The consequences of diminishing returns for average output per capita are shown in Figure 16-4, part b. Average output per capita (vertical axis) is calculated for each population level P (horizontal axis) by dividing the total output Q (from part a) by P. For example, when the population size is 1 million and total output equals 10 million units, corresponding to point c on TQ (part a), average output per capita is 10 units, corresponding to point c' (part b). The average output per capita is calculated and plotted in a similar fashion for each population size to give the average output per capita curve AQ.

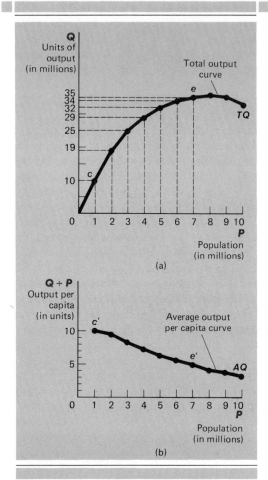

FIGURE 16-4 TOTAL OUTPUT, AVERAGE OUTPUT PER CAPITA, AND THE LAW OF DIMINISHING RETURNS

Given an unchanging state of technology, when a larger and larger population P works with a fixed quantity of land and other resources, total output Q (vertical axis, part a) increases by successively smaller amounts, a reflection of the law of diminishing returns. Thus the TQ curve (part a), which represents the relationship between population size and total output, rises less and less steeply as population size increases. The average output per capita (vertical axis, part b) for each population size is calculated by dividing total output Q by population P. Again reflecting the law of diminishing returns, the average output per capita curve AQ declines as population increases.

Notice that because of the law of diminishing returns, average output per capita decreases as the population size increases, as indicated by the declining AQ curve. For instance, when population is 7 million and total output equals 35 million, point e on TQ (part a), average output per capita is 5 units, point e' on AQ (part b).

THE SUBSISTENCE LIVING LEVEL

Another crucial ingredient of the classical theory of economic growth was the notion of a subsistence living level. *The* **subsistence living level** *may be viewed as the minimum standard of living necessary to keep the population from declining.* At the subsistence level the number of births would just equal the number of deaths. If the standard of living fell below the subsistence level, economic hardship would cause the death rate to rise above the birthrate and the population would decline. If the standard of living rose above the subsistence level, the death rate would fall below the birthrate and the population would increase.

The subsistence living level for our hypothetical economy is illustrated in Figure 16-5. The axes in parts a and b are exactly the same as those in parts a and b of Figure 16-4. Given any population size (horizontal axis), the subsistence total output curve SQ in part a indicates the minimum total output (vertical axis) necessary to maintain that population—that is, to keep it from declining. For example, the subsistence total output level necessary to sustain a population of 1 million is 5 million units of output, corresponding to point d on SQ. Similarly, the SQ curve indicates that it would take 10 million units of output to sustain a population of 2 million, 15 million units to sustain a population of 3 million, and so forth.

The subsistence living level also may be expressed in per capita terms. The average per capita subsistence level for any size population may be obtained by dividing the corresponding subsistence total output level by the population size. For example, for a population of 1 million requiring a subsistence total output of 5 million units (corresponding to point d on SQ), the average per capita subsistence level is 5 units of output per person. Alternatively, observe from the SQ curve that every additional 1 million

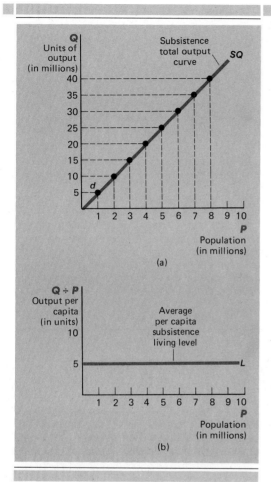

FIGURE 16-5 THE SUBSISTENCE LIVING LEVEL

The subsistence total output curve in part a shows the subsistence level of total output (vertical axis) associated with any given size population (horizontal axis) in a hypothetical economy. The subsistence level of total output for any given size population is that which provides a standard of living just sufficient to keep the total population from declining (the number of births just equals the number of deaths). The average per capita subsistence living level is equal to the subsistence level of total output for any given size population divided by the population. For the hypothetical economy shown here, the average per capita subsistence living level is 5 units of output per person, represented by the horizontal line L in part b.

people requires another 5 million units of total output to maintain a subsistence level of living. Hence, whatever the population size, the average per capita subsistence living level in our hypothetical economy is 5 units of output per person, represented by the horizontal line L in part b.

POPULATION GROWTH AND DIMINISHING RETURNS

The classical view of economic growth combined the law of diminishing returns with the notion of the subsistence living level. Figure 16-6 illustrates the classical view by combining the TQ and AQ curves of Figure 16-4 with the SQ and L curves of Figure 16-5.

Suppose the population is initially 1 million. Given the fixed quantity of resources and the state of technological know-how, the economy will be able to produce a total output of 10 million units, corresponding to point c on total output curve TQ (part a). However, the subsistence total output level needed for a population of 1 million is only 5 million units, point d on the subsistence total output curve SQ (part a). In terms of total output, the economy's standard of living exceeds the subsistence level by 5 million units, represented by the vertical distance between points c and d in part a. In per capita terms, the average output per capita of 10 units (point c' in part b) exceeds the per capita subsistence living level of 5 units (point d' in part b) by 5 units. Consequently, the death rate will be lower than the birthrate and the population will increase. Suppose the population increases to 2 million. The economy will produce a larger total output of 19 million units (point f in part a), which again exceeds the subsistence total output level of 10 million units (point g in part a), this time by 9 million units. In per capita terms, the average output per capita of 9.5 units (point f' in part b) again exceeds the per capita subsistence living level of 5 units (point g' in part b). Hence, the population will continue to increase.

According to the classical view, population and output will continue to grow as long as the economy's standard of living exceeds the subsistence living level. That is, population and total output grow as long as the total output curve TQ lies above the subsistence total output curve

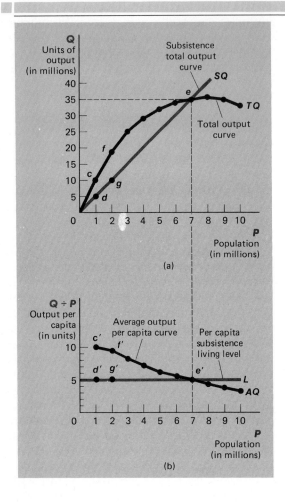

(a)

(b)

FIGURE 16-6 THE CLASSICAL VIEW OF ECONOMIC GROWTH

At any population size less than 7 million the total output curve *TQ* lies above the subsistence total output curve *SQ* in part a. Because the quantity of total output produced (vertical axis) exceeds the subsistence total output level, the classical view argued that the birthrate would be higher than the death rate. Hence, both the population (horizontal axis) and total output would grow. At any population size greater than 7 million the total output curve *TQ* lies below the subsistence total output curve *SQ*. Since the total output produced is less than the subsistence total output level, the death rate would exceed the birthrate. Hence, both the population and total output would decline. Long-run equilibrium occurs at the intersection of *TQ* and *SQ*, point *e*, where the total output level produced is just sufficient to support a population of 7 million at a subsistence living level.

The argument also may be represented in per capita terms, part b. Consider any population size less than 7 million. Average output per capita, given by the *AQ* curve, is greater than the per capita subsistence living level of 5 units of output per person, given by the horizontal line *L*. Hence population rises, causing average output per capita to fall toward the per capita subsistence living level. Now consider any population level greater than 7 million. Average output per capita is less than the per capita subsistence level—the *AQ* curve lies below *L*. Hence, population declines and average output per capita rises toward the per capita subsistence level. The long-run equilibrium occurs at a population size of 7 million, where average output per capita just equals the per capita subsistence level, corresponding to the intersection of *AQ* and *L* at *e*′.

SQ (part a). Putting it in per capita terms, they will continue to grow as long as the average output per capita curve *AQ* lies above the per capita subsistence living level curve *L* (part b). Once the population reaches 7 million, total output produced will be 35 million units (part a), which is just equal to the subsistence level of total output needed to sustain a population of 7 million. This level corresponds to the intersection of the *SQ* and *TQ* curves at point *e* in part a. In per capita terms, at a population of 7 mil-

lion, average output produced per capita is 5 units, which is just equal the per capita subsistence living level, corresponding to the intersection of *AQ* and *L* at point *e*′ (part b). At this point population and output will cease to grow. Economic growth stops. The economy has reached a static, or unchanging, equilibrium position.

What a dismal equilibrium it is, characterized by stagnation and a subsistence standard of living. If the population were to rise above 7 million, total output produced would be less than the subsistence total output level required to sustain the larger population (to the right of point e in part a, the TQ curve lies below the SQ curve). Average output per capita would be less than the per capita subsistence living level (to the right of point e' in part b, the AQ curve lies below L). Consequently, famine and disease would cause the death rate to rise above the birthrate and the population would tend to fall back to the 7 million level. On the other hand, if the population were to fall below the 7 million level, total output would exceed the subsistence total output required to sustain the smaller population (the TQ curve lies above the SQ curve to the left of point e in part a). Living standards would rise since the average output per capita would be above the per capita subsistence living level (the AQ curve lies above L to the left of point e' in part b). Unfortunately, according to the classical view, this would cause the birthrate to exceed the death rate. The population would tend to increase to 7 million again, and the standard of living would once again decline to the subsistence level.

THE "DISMAL SCIENCE"

If economic growth tended to lead society to such a dismal long-run equilibrium position, the prospects for ever improving economic well-being would seem dim indeed. It is this implication of the classical view of economic growth that earned economics its designation as the "dismal science." The classical view is still relevant today in the so-called underdeveloped countries of the world. The near subsistence living standards and the high rates of population growth that plague those countries do suggest a rush toward the dismal long-run classical equilibrium. But the classical view bears little resemblance to the spectacular rise in living standards and the sustained economic growth experienced by the present-day industrialized, or developed, countries.

Sources of Growth and Rising Living Standards

How can the long-run classical equilibrium and a subsistence living level be avoided? One way is for the total output curve, hence the average output per capita curve, to shift upward

fast enough to stay ahead of population growth. Obviously, it would also help if population growth didn't increase every time output per capita rose above the subsistence living level.

Economic growth with rising living standards is depicted in Figure 16-7. Suppose the population is initially P_1. Total output corresponding to point b on total output curve TQ exceeds the subsistence total output level corresponding to point a on the subsistence output curve SQ (part a). Hence, average output per capita corresponding to point b' on the average output per capita curve AQ exceeds the per capita subsistence level L by an amount represented by the vertical distance between b' and a' (part b). Assume this above-subsistence standard of living causes the population to rise to P_2 in the manner suggested by the classical view. However, in the meantime suppose the total output curve shifts up to TQ' and, hence, that the AQ curve shifts up to the position AQ'. Now, even though the population grows to P_2, the standard of living is not driven down to the subsistence level corresponding to points c and c'. Instead, total output rises to point d on TQ' and average output per capita rises to point d' on AQ'. The standard of living has actually increased, as represented by the fact that the vertical distance between c' and d' is greater than that between a' and b'.

What would cause economic growth to take place in this fashion, rather than along the lines suggested by the classical view? In particular, what causes the increase in productivity that allows any given size population to produce more, as represented by the upward shift in TQ and AQ? And what factors might inhibit the tendency for population growth to be so responsive to increases in the standard of living? While there is no hard and fast blueprint, most economists now agree that any list of the key elements in economic growth should include capital deepening, technological change and innovation, education or investment in human capital, rising aspirations for a better standard of living, and saving and investment.

CAPITAL DEEPENING

Capital deepening *is an increase in the stock of capital (machines, tools, buildings, highways,*

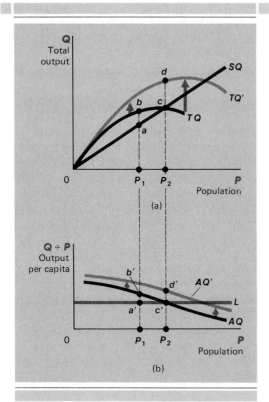

FIGURE 16-7 ECONOMIC GROWTH WITH RISING LIVING STANDARDS

When the total output curve TQ and, hence, the average output per capita curve AQ shift upward rapidly enough, economic growth will be accompanied by rising average output per capita.

Suppose the total output and average output per capita curves are in the positions TQ and AQ, respectively, and population is P_1. The standard of living exceeds the subsistence living level. Therefore, economic growth will tend toward the classical long-run equilibrium with population P_2 existing at a subsistence living level, corresponding to points c and c'. However, if in the meantime TQ and AQ shift up to TQ' and AQ', average output per capita will rise, as represented by the fact that the vertical distance between c' and d' is greater than that between a' and b'.

Upward shifts in AQ and TQ are caused by capital deepening, technological change and innovation, and an increase in the quality of the labor force caused by investment in human capital.

dams, and so forth) relative to the quantities of all other resources including labor. Capital deepening makes it possible for any given size population to produce a larger total output, so that average output per capita is increased. This, of course, is reflected in upward shifts of the TQ and AQ curves, such as shown in Figure 16-7. Given the size of the population, the state of technology, and the quantities of all other resources, there are diminishing returns to capital deepening just as there are to increases in the population. Increases in the quantities of the *same kinds* of machines, tools, buildings, highways, and dams beyond a certain point (that is, more of the same capital goods labor is already using) will obviously not yield further increases in total and per capita output. Why? Because there will not be enough population and quantities of other resources with which to combine them in productive activities. The emphasis on "same kinds" of capital brings us to the role of technological change and innovation.

TECHNOLOGICAL CHANGE AND INNOVATION

Invention and scientific discovery lead to technological change and innovation in production techniques. Even the most casual observer of economic life is struck by the changes that take place over time in the kinds of capital and procedures used to produce goods and services. When existing capital wears out, it is often replaced with *new kinds* of capital incorporating the new technology. Perfectly usable capital is often simply made obsolete by the development of new kinds of capital. As a result, even if the economy did not increase the quantity of resources devoted yearly to the replacement of worn-out or obsolescent capital, the productive capacity of the economy would grow. Hence, for any given size, population and quantity of all other resources total output would be larger. Again, this would be reflected in the upward shift of the TQ and AQ curves, such as that shown in Figure 16-7.

Some kinds of technological change are the result of changes in the form of a capital good, so-called **embodied technical change**. This is the kind of technological change that most often comes to mind. The diesel locomotive replaced the steam locomotive. Jet airliners have largely replaced the propeller variety. The electronic pocket calculator has made the slide rule almost obsolete. The list goes on and on.

Other kinds of technological change take the form of new procedures or techniques for producing goods and services, so-called **disembodied technical change**. Examples are the use of contour plowing to prevent soil erosion on farms, the development of new management techniques in business, and the pasteurization of milk. Such technological changes are not embodied in the form of a capital good. Of course, many types of embodied technical change make disembodied technical changes possible and vice versa. The electronic computer has made many new kinds of managerial procedures possible. And these procedures in turn make it possible to use new kinds of capital goods or embodied technical changes. For example, computers allow airlines to use sophisticated procedures for scheduling and controlling the flow of passengers between airports more efficiently. This efficiency makes it practical to use certain kinds of jet aircraft.

EDUCATION AND INVESTMENT IN HUMAN CAPITAL

Just as investment in capital goods increases productive capacity, so too does investment in human beings in the form of education, job training, and general experience. It is no accident that literacy rates and average years of schooling per capita tend to be higher in developed countries than in underdeveloped countries. Improvements in the quality of the labor force shift the TQ and AQ curves upward, as in Figure 16-7, in the same way that embodied and disembodied technical change do.

Improvements in sanitation, disease prevention, nutrition, and the general health of the population are also forms of investment in human capital. A healthier population is more capable of learning and generally gives rise to a more productive labor force less prone to absenteeism and accidents. In addition, increases in the average lifespan make it possible to develop a more experienced labor force and to provide the larger pool of able managers and leaders needed to fill administrative positions.

RISING ASPIRATIONS AND POPULATION GROWTH

If a society is to realize both economic growth and a rising standard of living, population growth must somehow be kept from literally "eating up" every increase in output per capita above the subsistence living level, as in the classical view. Countries that have experienced the industrial revolution and the progression from underdeveloped to developed status have somehow managed to escape from the drag of excessive population growth. One explanation is that once an economy realizes a rise in the standard of living above the subsistence level, the actual experience instills a taste for the "good life," or at least a better life. More and better food, clothing, and housing breeds a keen awareness that living *can be* more comfortable. People aspire to a better standard of living and become more aware of the relationship between curbing family size, and hence population growth, and the ability to realize these aspirations.

The effect of a rise in the aspiration level, measured in terms of average output per capita, on population size is shown in Figure 16-8. Suppose the aspiration level rises to AL. That is, people desire a standard of living, measured in terms of average output per capita, that exceeds the subsistence level by an amount equal to the vertical distance between AL and L. The population will not get larger than P_a, corresponding to the intersection of AL with the average output per capita curve AQ at point a. The long-run equilibrium average output per capita at point a is higher than that corresponding to the classical view at point b, where the larger population P_b exists at a subsistence living level. Now when capital deepening, technological change, and investment in human capital cause the AQ curve to shift upward, economic growth will cause population and output per capita to tend toward equilibrium positions corresponding to the intersection of the rising AQ curve with AL.

Another explanation of the decline in the population growth rate that tends to accompany economic development is that this decline is in part due to a change in the role of children. Such a change is brought about by the nature of economic development. The populations of un-

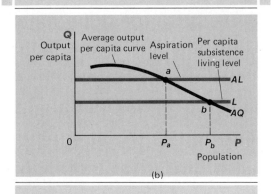

(b)

FIGURE 16-8 THE EFFECT OF A RISING ASPIRATION LEVEL ON POPULATION

Suppose the aspiration level, measured in terms of average output per capita, is AL. The population will not get larger than P_a, corresponding to the intersection of AL with the average output per capita curve AQ at point a. The long-run equilibrium average output per capita at point a is higher than that corresponding to the classical view at point b where a larger population P_b exists at a subsistence living level.

derdeveloped countries are largely involved in agricultural activities, eking out a meager living with primitive tools. It is argued that under such circumstances children are viewed as "another pair of hands," useful for the work they can perform starting at a relatively early age. In addition, they are insurance that there will be somebody to look after aging parents. As economic development progresses, an ever larger portion of the population becomes employed in the economy's expanding industrial sector. Families earning livelihoods in factories, stores, and trades servicing a more urbanized population no longer view children as contributors to the family's economic well-being. Rather a child is primarily a dependent to be fed, clothed, and housed until he or she enters the labor force as a self-sufficient young adult. In short, in an industrial and urban setting, children are more of an economic burden on the family. The incentive to have large families that exists in a rural, agricultural setting is greatly reduced. It is therefore

argued that as an increasing portion of the population moves into the industrial sector the birthrate, and hence population growth, tends to decline.

THE ROLE OF SAVING AND INVESTMENT

In the previous chapter we saw how saving, the refraining from consumption, makes it possible for investment to take place. Investment expenditures create new capital goods which both replace capital stock that is worn out or obsolescent, as well as increase the size of the economy's capital stock. Saving and investment are thus crucial to the capital formation and technological change that make possible economic growth and increasing output per capita.

Consider Figure 16-7 once again. The upward shift of TQ to TQ', and hence of AQ to AQ', requires saving and investment. When the population is P_1 and the total output curve is TQ, there is an excess of output above that required for subsistence. This excess is represented by the vertical distance between points a and b (part a). In order for capital formation to shift TQ up to TQ', the population must refrain from consuming all of the excess output that the economy is able to produce. That is, some of it must be saved. What is not consumed is available for investment or the formation of the capital goods that increase the economy's productive capacity, as represented by the upward shift of the total output curve from TQ to TQ'.

OTHER FACTORS IN ECONOMIC GROWTH

A distinguishing characteristic of developing economies is a growing *specialization of labor* accompanied by *increases in the scale of production*. In the early stages of economic development, a worker is typically engaged in many different tasks. For example, at the beginning of the Industrial Revolution in England (in the latter half of the eighteenth century), production was typically organized along the lines of the so-called cottage industry. A family occupying a cottage on a modest parcel of land would raise a small number of farm animals, tend a few crops, and engage in crafts such as spinning, weaving, and tanning. The family raised much of its own food and made a good deal of its own clothing.

ECONOMIC THINKERS

THOMAS R. MALTHUS
1766–1835

Malthus, a clergyman by training, was in many ways the epitome of the gentleman English scholar. Taking his A.B. degree from Jesus College, Cambridge, in 1788, he was appointed vicar at Albury near the family home and lived a quiet scholarly life. The economic views of Malthus fall into two broad categories, one, devoted to population problems, for which he is best known, and, two, his work on the inadequacy of aggregate demand, in which he was a forerunner of the great economist J. M. Keynes. His views on population were embodied in his famous work, *An Essay on the Principle of Population As It Affects the Future Improvement of Society* (1798), and his broader views were put forth in his book, *Principles of Political Economy,* published in 1820.

Malthus did not quarrel with the mildly cheerful view of Adam Smith relative to the future of humankind, but as he saw the future, it was a far cry from the optimistic picture drawn by his contemporaries Godwin, Condorcet, and their followers. Malthus forecast that the future was likely to be grim. He began with two postulates:

1. Food is necessary to people's existence.
2. The passion between the sexes is necessary and is likely to continue.

Following these basic postulates, he argued that "the power of the population is infinitely greater than the power of the earth to produce subsistence for man." That is, population would outstrip the ability of people to produce adequate food.

Since the science of keeping vital statistics was in its infancy and data relating to agricultural output were for all practical purposes nonexistent, the quantification of the theory was at best a theoretical approximation. This fact in no way inhibited Malthus, although later he did some empirical research to answer critical comment. His research may be summed up as follows:

Year	1	25	50	75	100	125	150	175	200	225
Population	1	2	4	8	16	32	64	128	256	512
Subsistence	1	2	3	4	5	6	7	8	9	10

That is, population, if unchecked, would increase 512 times after 225 years, the food supply only ten times.

If the means are available, population will naturally increase. There are, however, two kinds of checks on population. These checks are either "pre-

ventive", when they reduce birthrates, or "positive," when they affect the mortality rate. Among the lower classes the positive check is more common, since they suffer high rates of infant mortality and more often die from poor nutrition and general ill health resulting from lack of resources. On the other hand, those in the upper classes are more influenced by the preventive check since they tend to marry later and have fewer children, wishing to preserve their living standards. The poor have little to lose, so there is no reason to defer marriage.

As a further consequence, such policies as public relief (the "poor laws"), defeat their own purpose, resulting only in an upsurge of population. Generally, Malthus favored the preventive check over the positive. All this was, to be sure, unfortunate, for "to prevent the recurrence of misery is alas, beyond the power of man." For a man of the cloth to take such a dim view of the arrangements of Providence may seem to pose a bit of a problem, and Malthus tried to answer this seeming contradiction in the last two chapters of his *Essay* which attempt to mesh the principle of population with a view of a providentially ordered universe.

FOR FURTHER READING
Bonar, James. *Malthus and His Work.* New York: The Macmillan Company, 1924.

An individual worker typically performed many different tasks. With the advent of the Industrial Revolution and the advancement of production technology, greater specialization and increases in the scale of production took place, thereby reducing per unit (of output) costs of production. Lower-priced, mass-produced goods led to the expansion of markets, an integral part of the economic growth process.

Another important ingredient of economic growth is the *development of extensive capital markets,* that is, markets where savers lend funds to borrowers who make the investment expenditures that give rise to capital formation. The growth of banking and other financial institutions that pool the savings of a large number of small savers and lend them out to investors plays a crucial role in the development of capital markets. Some economists even suggest that the state of development of a country's financial institutions provides the single most revealing indication of a country's state of economic development.

Economic growth requires a *favorable cultural, social, and political environment.* Legal institutions are needed to provide law and order, and to enforce contracts between parties to economic transactions. Cultural attitudes toward work and material advancement are an important determinant of the incentives for economic growth. A social structure that allows reasonably fluid upward and downward mobility based on performance and merit is more conducive to economic growth than a rigid social structure that puts a premium on the station of one's birth. Finally, economic growth rarely takes place in societies racked by political instability.

■ CHECKPOINT 16-2

Do you think the law of diminishing returns is applicable to technological change and investment in human capital? Why or why not? What are the implications of your answer for economic growth?

ISSUES IN ECONOMIC GROWTH

What are the aspects of economic growth that are currently of most concern to industrialized

countries like the United States? As noted in the news item at the beginning of this chapter, policy makers are troubled by the implications of an apparent slowing down in U.S. economic growth. Quite aside from this issue, there has been considerable debate over whether the costs of continued economic growth in industrialized countries like the United States are worth the benefits. Finally, there is the question of the limits to economic growth. Will we literally run out of resources? Will there be a doomsday?

Recent Problems with Economic Growth in the United States

What are the causes of the recent slackening of growth in productivity in the United States noted in the news item? (See also Figure 16-2, part b.) Economists have offered several explanations for this trend. Among the most important are changes in the composition of the labor force, inadequate investment spending, reductions in research and development expenditures, and the increased government regulation of business.

CHANGES IN THE LABOR FORCE

Since the mid-1960s youths born during the postwar "baby boom" have represented a growing portion of the labor force. Their entry into the job market is at least part of the reason for the rise in the fraction of the population composing the labor force, as shown in Figure 16-2, part d (the other major cause is the increased labor force participation of women). Many of these young entrants to the labor force initially lack training and experience. It takes several years for them to become highly productive. The Council of Economic Advisors has estimated that industry's reliance on these inexperienced workers to fill jobs has the effect of shaving off a third of a point a year from the productivity index (Figure 16-2, part b). It is anticipated that as the "baby boom" population matures during the 1980s, it will cease to be a drag on productivity growth.

INADEQUATE INVESTMENT SPENDING

From 1948 to 1973 investment spending on new plant and equipment added 3 percent per year to the capital stock supporting each labor hour of work. Since 1973 this capital to labor hour ratio has increased only 1.75 percent annually. Some economists argue that the chief reason for this slow rate of increase has been tax policies that tend to discourage investment spending. Others claim it is business fear that recession or inflation, or both, will drastically reduce profit on new investment. In either case, the Council of Economic Advisors has concluded that the effect has been to slow the formation of cost-cutting, labor-saving capital. The end result, according to the Council, has been a reduction in the growth of productivity by a half a percentage point each year.

REDUCED RESEARCH AND DEVELOPMENT EXPENDITURES

Research and development (R and D) expenditures sow the seeds of technological change. It has been suggested that a decline in the intensity of research and development in the United States has been a factor contributing to the productivity slowdown. Measured as a percent of GNP, R and D spending reached a peak of 3 percent in 1964. By 1978 the R and D expenditure share of GNP had dropped to an estimated 2.2 percent. Federal spending on R and D programs dropped with the end of the Vietnam War and the cutting back of the space program. The financial squeeze on private universities has also hindered research activities. And it appears that in an inflationary era industry may judge the payoff on R and D spending to be too far in the future and uncertain. It is difficult to calculate the adverse effect of reduced R and D spending on productivity growth, since it would have to be measured in terms of inventions not made and technological advances not realized.

REGULATION AND POLLUTION CONTROL

Some economists believe that excessive government regulation hinders productivity growth. Companies have had to comply with an increasing number of antipollution regulations and health and safety rules, which has led to increased spending and time devoted to these areas. Funds have been diverted from buying productive machinery and developing more effi-

cient operating methods. Industrial accidents have undoubtedly been prevented and environmental damage reduced. But the Council of Economic Advisors estimates that compliance with such regulations may be cutting annual nonfarm productivity growth by four-tenths of a percentage point.

OTHER FACTORS CUTTING PRODUCTIVITY GROWTH

The sharp rise in energy costs during the 1970s has increased the cost of using labor-saving machinery. Some economists argue that companies are compelled to use more labor-intensive, less productive production techniques as a result. Another factor contributing to the productivity slowdown has been the growing relative importance of service industries in the economy. It is easier to raise (and measure) the productivity of auto or steelworkers than that of teachers, police officers, barbers, credit counselors, or lawyers.

Policies for Dealing with the Productivity Lag

What can be done about the productivity lag? One suggestion has been to change the methods of regulation used to enforce pollution controls. Specifically, government should set pollution standards and impose stiff fines for violations, but allow industry to devise the least costly methods of meeting the standards. It is argued that private enterprise, spurred by the prospect of stiff fines, would find more efficient ways to meet the standards than an army of government regulators specifying in great detail what equipment should be installed and how plants should be modified, as has been the practice.

Many economists argue that tax policy should be changed to provide greater incentives for investment spending. Among the proposals are further cuts in taxes on capital gains and corporate profits, and more generous investment tax credits—the reductions in a firm's taxes that are tied to the amount of the firm's investment spending. It has also been suggested that firms be allowed to use faster depreciation write-offs. That is, a larger portion of plant and equipment cost should be deducted from a firm's sales revenue. This effectively reduces the size of the firm's tax bill. Each of these proposals is aimed at increasing the after-tax return on investment, thereby encouraging more capital formation.

Tax credits to businesses for R and D spending are another possibility. Such credits work on the same principle as investment tax credits. That is, they allow reductions in a firm's taxes that are linked to the amount of the firm's R and D expenditures. Some economists also suggest that government provide universities with research funds to work on ways of increasing productivity in service industries where firms are too small to undertake such research themselves. A precedent is provided by the role land-grant colleges have played in pursuing research that has increased farm productivity.

Even if all these proposals were adopted immediately, the resulting increases in productivity growth would come slowly. The slowdown in R and D spending and technological change that occurred during the 1970s will be a drag on productivity growth for some time. But most economists agree that something must be done to reverse this trend. Otherwise, they foresee a prolonged era of slow growth with little rise in living standards, stubbornly high unemployment, and persistently high inflation—an era like the 1970s, but possibly even worse.

Costs and Benefits of Growth

The benefits of economic growth have always seemed quite obvious. The basic economic problem is to satisfy humanity's unlimited wants in the face of ever-present scarcity. Economic growth eases this problem by reducing scarcity. Without growth the only way one person can be made better off is by taking something away from another. With economic growth there can be more for everyone—the lot of all can be improved. However, it has become increasingly apparent in the more industrialized countries, where economic growth has been most spectacular, that there are also costs to economic growth. Among these are pollution and a possible decline in the quality of life.

POLLUTION AND THE ENVIRONMENT

When the economy produces "goods," it also produces by-products that are "bads"—smoke, garbage, junkyards, stench, noise, traffic jams, urban and suburban congestion, polluted water, ugly landscapes, and other things that detract from the general quality of life. In fact *all* output, both goods and bads, *eventually* returns to the environment in the form of waste. The more we experience economic growth, the more obvious this fact becomes. Many people are justifiably concerned about the undesirable effects of growth on the environment and the balance of the world's ecological system. There is concern about disappearing species of wildlife, and about the rising incidence of cancer related to synthetic products (both goods and bads). There is concern about the destruction of the earth's ozone layer by the use of aerosol spray cans. Scientists also allege that the large-scale burning of fossil fuels has increased the carbon dioxide content of our atmosphere to such an extent that the earth's average temperature has increased a few degrees. The list of such worrisome by-products of economic growth goes on and on.

Critics of economic growth argue that some curbs on growth are necessary if these increasingly undesirable aspects of industrialization are to be controlled. Others caution that we must be careful not to confuse the control of growth with the control of pollution. They argue that the additional productive capacity made possible by growth could at least in part be devoted to pollution control efforts and the correction of past environmental damage. They point out that pollution control and a clean environment cost something, just like any other good, and that economic growth and increased productive capacity make it easier for society to incur that cost. (Recall our discussion of the production possibilities frontier and the production of anti-pollution devices in Chapter 2.)

THE QUALITY OF LIFE—
PROGRESS VERSUS CONTENTMENT

Economic growth implies change. Change is often what is most desired and needed by an impoverished population in an underdeveloped country. But many question whether continual change is as obviously beneficial in advanced industrialized economies like the United States. Technological change, if anything, seems to have accelerated in the last half century. As a result, skills and training acquired in youth become obsolete more rapidly. There is more pressure to "keep current," to "retool," and to "update" one's skills. Fail to do so and you may be demoted or even out of a job. Such pressure creates anxiety and a sense of insecurity.

We have noted that an above-subsistence aspiration level may be necessary to avoid the tendency toward the long-run equilibrium of stagnation envisioned by the classical view. But some growth critics worry that aspiration levels in growth-oriented, industrialized countries are geared toward a "keep up with the Joneses" mentality. Goods may be valued more for the status they confer on the owner than the creature comforts they provide. ("I'd better get a new car this year or I may not look like I belong in this neighborhood.") Consequently, people work harder, produce more, enjoy it less, and complain about smog, traffic congestion, and the rat race. What there is of contentment, or peace of mind, may come largely from the sense that you're "making it," or better yet, that you've "arrived."

Since the beginning of the Industrial Revolution, many critics have argued that industrialization forces labor into dehumanizing jobs, requiring the performance of monotonous, mind-numbing tasks. Mass production, assembly-line jobs may provide bread for the table but little food for the soul. However, it has been said that those who make this criticism are not familiar with living conditions in countries where there is no industrialization.

How Serious Are the Limits to Growth?

Predictions of an end to economic growth are certainly not new. Indeed, the dismal classical view, nearly 200 years old, seems very relevant in many of today's underdeveloped countries, a fact sometimes easily forgotten by those living in the industrialized or developed countries of the world. But in recent years the hard facts of pollution, energy shortages, urban sprawl, and traffic congestion have served as increasingly insistent reminders that there may well be limits to economic growth.

RESOURCE LIMITATIONS AND DOOMSDAY PREDICTIONS

As we have already seen, the classical view of economic growth envisioned an inevitable tendency for countries to reach a point where both population and total output would cease to grow—a dismal long-run equilibrium of stagnation and misery. Due to the law of diminishing returns, output per capita would decline continuously until a subsistence standard of living was reached. However, capital deepening, technological change, investment in human capital, a rising aspiration level, and a favorable cultural, social, and political environment have all conspired to put off such a doomsday in the world's developed countries. But there are those who emphasize "put off." Put off for how long? It is undeniable that the earth's resources are limited. Therefore, these analysts argue that it is certainly not possible to beat the law of diminishing returns indefinitely. As the earth's resources are used up and population increases, the law of diminishing returns inevitably points to a declining per capita output.

Among the doomsday predictions, a group known as the Club of Rome (an international business association composed of business people, academicians, and scientists) has constructed an elaborate computerized model of world economic growth.[1] The Club of Rome model assumes that population and production grow at certain historically realistic percentage rates and that there are definite limits to world resources and technological capabilities. Given these assumptions, a computer is used to generate predictions of the future trends of industrial output per capita, the quantity of the world's resources, food per capita, population, and pollution. The predictions reach the alarming conclusion that the limits to growth will be reached somewhere in the years 2050 to 2100. The Club of Rome says that this conclusion follows largely from the depletion of the earth's nonrenewable resources—coal, petroleum, iron ore, aluminum, and so forth. Once the limit is reached, it is predicted that there will be an un-

---

[1] Dennis L. Meadows, and others, *The Limits to Growth* (Washington, D.C.: Potomac Associates, 1972).

controllable decline in population and productive capacity. If resource depletion does not trigger the collapse, then the precipitating factors will be famine, pollution, and disease.

What can be done to avert this doomsday prediction? Many of those who take the Club of Rome's predictions seriously argue that efforts should be made to establish zero population growth and zero economic growth. That is, establish a no-growth equilibrium. The Club of Rome suggests that by using appropriate technology, it may be possible to cut pollution, hold population growth in check, and reduce the amount of resources used per unit of output. In addition, investment in capital should be limited to the replacement of worn-out or obsolescent capital. Moreover, resources should be shifted away from the production of industrial products and toward the provision of more food and services.

PERSPECTIVE ON GROWTH AND DOOMSDAY

Many find such doomsday predictions quite unconvincing. They observe that modern-day doomsday predictions sound very similar to the classical view of economic growth. The economic growth of the countries of Western Europe, the United States, Canada, Japan, the U.S.S.R., New Zealand, and Australia is completely at odds with the classical view. This is so largely because the classical view did not foresee the tremendous advance of technology that has taken place over the last century or more. Critics of the "doomsdayers" argue that current doomsday predictions again vastly underestimate the potentials of science, innovation, and technological change.

This criticism may be well taken. One wonders what the classical economists of the early 1800s would have thought if one of their number had predicted that in the twentieth century: people would fly to the moon; jet aircraft carrying 450 passengers would cross continents in the time it takes a stagecoach to go 25 uncomfortable miles; in a split second an electronic computer would do calculations that would take a thousand clerks years; electronic communication would allow people to watch and hear a

live event on the other side of the world; or that most of the populous areas of the world could be obliterated in a few seconds by nuclear explosions. The list goes on and on. Imagine how farfetched such a list would seem to someone living in 1900, let alone the classical economists of the early 1800s. This puts a perspective on the pitfalls of making predictions about economic growth in the twenty-first century.

SUMMARY

1. Economic growth is the expansion of an economy's capacity to produce goods and services that takes place over prolonged periods of time. It may be viewed as a continual shifting outward of the economy's production possibilities frontier caused by growth in the quantity and quality of the economy's available resources (land, labor, and capital), and by ongoing improvement in the state of technological know-how.

2. The full benefits of growth will be realized only if there is an adequate expansion of total demand and an allocation of resources to those productive activities where the value of their contribution to total output is greatest.

3. The rate of growth of full-employment real GNP provides a measure of the growth in the economy's overall capacity to produce goods and services. The rate of growth of output per capita provides a rough measure of growth in the economy's standard of living. The rate of growth of output per labor hour provides a measure of the growth in the economy's productivity—the efficiency with which each labor hour combines with the capital stock and the existing state of technology to produce output.

4. Growth in the economy's full-employment total output may be viewed as the product of change in each of the following four components: (1) population; (2) the fraction of the population that participates in the labor force; (3) the average hours worked per laborer; (4) output per labor hour. The cumulative effects of seemingly small differences in growth rates become ever larger as time passes.

5. The classical economists' view of economic growth held that a nation's economic growth naturally tended toward stagnation and a subsistence standard of living. Citing the law of diminishing returns, they argued that as a larger and larger population works with a fixed amount of land and other resources the increase in total output becomes less and less, given the state of technological know-how. Consequently, average output per capita declines as population grows. Both output and population growth cease once output per capita has fallen to the subsistence level.

6. The drag on economic growth imposed by the law of diminishing returns and population growth can be overcome by capital deepening, technological change and innovation, and education and other forms of investment in human capital. The drag on rising living standards imposed by excessive population growth can be overcome by rising aspiration levels that tend to curb family size and, hence, population growth.

7. Saving and investment play an important role in economic growth because they are crucial to the process of capital formation and technological change that gives rise to sustained economic growth and increasing output per capita. Other important sources of economic growth are the increased specialization of labor, increases in the scale of production, the development of extensive capital markets, and the existence of a favorable cultural, social, and political environment.

8. During the 1970s there was an apparent slowdown in the growth of productivity in the United States. This slowdown may have been due to the influx of young, inexperienced workers into the labor force, inadequate investment spending, a slowdown in the growth of research and development expenditures, increased government regulation of business in the form of pollution control and health and safety standards, and the increased relative importance of service industries. It has also been argued that the rise in energy costs during the 1970s, and the resulting increase in the cost of using labor-saving machinery, has led companies to use more labor-intensive, less productive production techniques.

9. To deal with the productivity slowdown, it has been suggested that pollution controls and health and safety standards ought to be administered more efficiently, and that tax policy be changed to encourage investment and research and development spending.

10. Economic growth is beneficial in that it reduces the burden of scarcity by increasing output. However, in recent years industrialized countries have become increasingly aware of some of the undesirable by-products of growth—pollution, congestion, uncertain effects on the ecological system, and the sense of anxiety, insecurity, and lack of contentment that may afflict citizens in a growth-oriented society.

11. Doomsday predictors argue that the limits of economic growth are likely to be reached sometime in the latter half of the next century, largely as a result of depletion of the earth's nonrenewable resources. Critics of these predictions contend that such a forecast is most likely wrong because it grossly underestimates the advance of science, technology, and innovation, which has always been a major source of economic growth.

KEY TERMS AND CONCEPTS
capital deepening
disembodied technical change
economic growth
embodied technical change
productivity
subsistence living level

QUESTIONS AND PROBLEMS
1. The rate of growth of real GNP is frequently used as a measure of economic growth. If we view economic growth as an outward expansion of the production possibilities frontier, what shortcomings does this suggest are associated with the use of real GNP to measure economic growth?

2. It is technologically possible to produce

the *same* quantity of total output with different combinations of quantities of capital and labor. More capital may be used and less labor, or more labor and less capital. For example, a rise in the price of capital relative to the price (wage) of labor will typically cause firms to use more of the now relatively cheaper labor and less capital. Conversely, an increase in the price of labor relative to the price of capital would typically cause firms to use more of the now relatively cheaper capital and less labor. What are the implications of these possibilities for the use of output per labor hour as a measure of productivity? What bearing do these possibilities have on the apparent slowdown of U.S. productivity growth, given that energy prices increased dramatically during the 1970s?

3. Population growth can be both a blessing and a curse for economic growth. Explain.

4. In the last paragraph of the news item at the beginning of this chapter, it is argued that "in the short run, low productivity growth can create jobs because more workers will be required to satisfy rising demand." But it is then reported that in the long run, low productivity growth means a slower growth of total output,

which "hurts employment." Explain why you agree or disagree with this argument. What does a comparison of parts a, b, c, and d of Figure 16–2 suggest about the validity of this argument?

5. Can you explain why it might be possible for rising aspirations to cause the growth in total output to be *negative* and the growth in average per capita output to be *positive,* while at the same time there is technological progress? What are the implications of such a situation for population growth?

6. The classical view of economic growth envisioned a long-run equilibrium in which output per capita was just equal to the subsistence living level. However, if we consider the role played by saving and investment, is it really possible for long-run equilibrium to occur at such a position? Why or why not?

7. Despite the apparent slowdown in U.S. productivity growth, it appears that the growth of output per capita has not experienced a similar slowdown. How would you explain this? (Hint: Examine Figure 16–2). What does this suggest about the relative merits of each of these measures of economic growth?

■ NEWS ITEM FOR YOUR ANALYSIS ■

HOW ONE COMPANY COPES WITH PRODUCTIVITY SLOWDOWN

DETROIT, Mich., March 13—Three years ago Parker Hannifin Corp., a manufacturer of automotive parts and parts for industrial hydraulic and other fluid-power systems, was rebounding from the recession. Productivity boomed as experienced workers who had been laid off were recalled, and new, sophisticated machinery was put to fuller use.

The boom is over. "One of the toughest times to get productivity improvement is now, at the peak of a mature business cycle," says Patrick S. Parker, chairman and chief executive officer. "And the longer the recovery lasts the harder it gets."

In an attempt to improve productivity, most of the company's $47 million of investment expenditures this fiscal year is going into more-efficient machinery. For example, the company recently installed a new $50,000 "bending machine" at its Wickliffe plant. The machine can make 12,000 snakelike bends in steel tubing in about three days. Previously, when the job was done manually, it took the current operator of the new machine two weeks to make that many bends. Also, the company recently installed a $60,000 fittings packaging machine that completes 15 boxes per minute, compared with a manual output of just 4 per minute.

Not all capital spending is going into more efficient machinery, however. The Occupational Safety and Health Administration has requested that noise-abatement enclosures be installed on some machines at Parker Hannifin's Lewisburg plant. The devices would interfere with the work flow and reduce productivity by about 4 percent, according to H. L. Sullivan, general manager of the tube-fittings division. "If we ever lose the noise war," he adds, "it would be very costly. We'd probably go to court first."

While Parker Hannifin can step up capital spending and try to ward off burdensome regulations, it is having a more difficult time dealing with the problem created by the fact that an unusually high percentage of today's labor force are relatively unproductive. The coming of age of the "baby boom" generation has given rise to an unusually young and unskilled labor pool. Increasing numbers of untrained women are also flooding into the labor force. Some observers say the problem is aggravated because many workers are preoccupied with leisure time rather than job performance. "I'd feel pretty fortunate to get one exceptional worker out of 10 trainees," says Ned Rautsaw, a foreman at Parker Hannifin's Eaton, Ohio, plant.

Because of a shortage of experienced labor, younger workers are often put in jobs where they are more prone to damage the equipment, thus jeopardizing production even further. "We're forced to put guys on the machines before they're ready, and they end up busting tools," says Ken Gifford, a plant foreman. Moreover, inexperienced employees tend to increase the product scrap rate—another drag on productivity.

To cope with the skilled-labor shortage, Parker Hannifin is using formal classroom instruction to supplement routine on-the-job training. "We hope to make new employees more productive much faster with this extra education." But in the short run, time spent in class instead of on the factory floor also cuts productivity.

Production is frequently interrupted by bottlenecks when plants are running close to capacity. For example, heat-treating capacity has been inadequate at Parker Hannifin's tube-fittings plant in Eaton, and trays of steel parts tend to stack up awaiting processing. "You get to the point where just hiring more people won't do the trick," a plant official says.

Little, inexpensive innovations have been important to the company's productivity drive. Linda Moore suggested that she run both the bolt-sorter and the fault-detection equipment—two previously separate operations. This resulted in a productivity increase estimated to have saved $10,000 per year.

QUESTIONS

1. Which efforts undertaken by Parker Hannifin to improve productivity are examples of embodied technical change, and which are examples of disembodied technical change?

2. Cite any instances that suggest that Parker Hannifin is subject to the law of diminishing returns.

3. What are some examples at Parker Hannifin of the kinds of things that contribute to the upward shifting of the economy's average output per capita curve?

4. Parker Hannifin is balking at noise-control standards and their alleged impact on productivity. If you were called in as a consultant on this problem, would you agree or disagree with Mr. Sullivan's assessment? Why or why not?

FIVE

INTERNATIONAL ECONOMICS AND WORLD TRADE

17

INTERNATIONAL TRADE AND THE NATIONAL ECONOMY

STEELMAKERS BUY MORE LOW-COST FOREIGN COKE

WASHINGTON, Nov. 14—For months now, American steelmakers have been complaining loudly of unfair competition from abroad. They warn that cut-rate imports of foreign steel "dumped" on U.S. shores mean fewer jobs and, in the long run, a weaker American steel industry.

But when it comes to imported commodities the steelmakers use, such as coke, the steel companies aren't so upset. Several American steelmakers have been quietly buying ever-increasing amounts of coke from foreign sources. Moreover, to hear some U.S. coal producers tell it, the prices paid for the imported coke are not only lower than those paid for domestic coke, they are also lower than the foreign suppliers' cost of production. "We say it is being dumped," asserts William Mason, president of the Coal Exporters Assn., which today will consider filing an antidumping complaint.

The irony of the situation strikes some observers as humorous. For some steelmakers to rail at steel imports at the same time that they are buying more imported coke "is the funniest damn thing going," says Charles Bradford, a steel industry analyst at a large brokerage firm.

However, the situation is no laughing matter for many people. According to another coal trade group, the National Coal Association, thousands of U.S. workers who mine the metallurgical coal used to make coke have been laid off, partly because of rising coke imports. Echoing the plight of many middlemen, railroads that haul domestic metallurgical coal say their business is falling sharply. Some coke-oven makers contend that eventually the biggest loser could be the steel industry itself. They argue that because of the cheap foreign coke at their disposal, steelmakers are postponing much-needed construction of new coke capacity to replace old and inefficient ovens.

Even some steel officials worry about the risks of increased reliance on foreign coke supplies. "We're in a precarious situation," says one steel industry executive. "We're in a weak self-sufficient position in a basic commodity we can't function without."

Virtually every nation finds it advantageous to trade with other nations. To varying degrees, all are linked to one another by trade flows and financial networks that circle the globe. This and the next chapter will describe and analyze the nature of world trade.

In this chapter we will examine some of the following questions: How significant is international trade in the world economy? How does international trade affect a country's total income, output, and employment? What are the underlying reasons why nations trade with one another? Finally, as the news item at the beginning of this chapter indicates, international trade is not viewed favorably by everybody. The desire for protection from the rigors of foreign competition has frequently led nations to erect barriers to international trade. We will critically examine some of the more common arguments for such barriers.

THE IMPORTANCE OF INTERNATIONAL TRADE

International trade plays a significant role in the determination of living standards throughout the world. Though the United States is a relatively self-sufficient nation compared to most, its purchases of foreign cars, cameras, television sets, and oil are ever-present reminders of American dependence on foreign trade. Let's first look briefly at some of the quantitative dimensions of international trade. Then we will consider how foreign trade affects an economy's total income, output, and employment.

The Size of World Trade Flows

Table 17-1 provides an overall view of the magnitude of world trade, measured in dollars.

The table shows the total dollar value of exports of goods by the nations of the world—that is, the dollar value of goods produced by each nation and then sold abroad. Some perspective on the total value of world exports is provided by comparing this figure with the GNP of the United States. This comparison indicates that the $1,282.2 billion of total world exports was the equivalent of 61 percent of the U.S. GNP of $2,106.6 billion in 1978. It is also interesting to note that while the U.S. economy is not as dependent on international trade as many other countries, it does make a very large contribution to total world exports. The U.S. economy provided 10.9 percent of total world exports in 1978, only .1 percent less than the world leader, West Germany. Indeed, in 1977 the United States was actually the largest contributor to total world exports, just slightly ahead of West Germany.

The nations of the world differ greatly in regard to their dependence on foreign trade. This is illustrated in Table 17-2, which shows the value of exports of selected countries as a percentage of their respective GNP in 1977. For example, exports from the United States amounted to only 8 percent of its GNP in 1977, while exports for the Netherlands amounted to 54 percent of that country's GNP. The differences among countries in this respect largely reflect differences in size, the extent of development of their internal markets, and the quantity and diversity of their supply of resources. The United States is so fortunate in each of these respects that its economy is relatively self-sufficient. By contrast, the tiny but industrious Netherlands must engage in a significant amount of trade to get goods it cannot produce with reasonable efficiency. Clearly the United States is less dependent on trade (as measured by the size of total exports relative to GNP)

TABLE 17-1 WORLD TRADE EXPORTS, 1978

	Value (in Billions of Dollars)		Percentage of Total Exports
Developed Countries	$ 853.4		66.5
United States		$140.2	10.9
Canada		47.5	3.7
Japan		99.9	7.8
France		79.5	6.2
West Germany		142.1	11.0
Italy		52.5	4.1
United Kingdom		71.2	5.5
Other developed countries[a]		220.5	17.2
Developing Countries	296.1		23.1
OPEC[b]		145.0	11.3
Other		151.1	11.8
Communist Countries	133.3		10.4
USSR		52.9	4.1
Eastern Europe		63.8	4.9
China		9.9	.8
Other		6.7	.5
Total	$1,282.8		100.0

SOURCE: International Monetary Fund, Organization for Economic Cooperation and Development, and Council of Economic Advisers.

[a] Includes other OECD countries, South Africa, and non-OECD Europe (OECD: Organization for Economic Cooperation and Development).
[b] Organization of Petroleum Exporting Countries.

than the other countries in Table 17-2. Again, however, the sheer size of the U.S. economy is reflected by the fact that the total value of its exports exceeds that of any other country.

The Pattern of U.S. Trade

The pattern of U.S. trade with the rest of the world is illustrated by the export and import data in Table 17-3. There it can be seen that the

After reading this chapter, you will be able to:

1. Describe present-day world trade flows and the pattern of U.S. trade.
2. Explain how trade affects total income, output, and employment.
3. Explain why nations can have a larger total output if they each specialize according to comparative advantage and trade.
4. Describe the nature of the barriers to trade nations often erect to protect domestic industry from foreign competition.
5. Describe briefly the trends in trade policy since the 1930s.

TABLE 17-2 DOLLAR VALUE OF EXPORTS, AND EXPORTS AS PERCENTAGE OF GNP, SELECTED COUNTRIES, 1977

Country	Value (in Billions of Dollars)	Percentage of GNP
United States	$113,323	8
West Germany	102,032	26
Japan	67,225	14
France	55,817	20
United Kingdom	46,271	29
Netherlands	40,167	54
Canada	38,128	23
Italy	36,969	27
Norway	7,917	41

SOURCE: United Nations, *Yearbook of National Accounts Statistics, 1977,* New York 1978.

total dollar value of U.S. imports ($172.9 billion), the goods purchased abroad, was considerably larger than the total dollar value of U.S. exports ($136.9 billion) in 1978. The dollar value of U.S. exports to Western Europe was very nearly equal to the dollar value of imports from Western Europe. The same was true of U.S. trade with Canada, Australia, New Zealand, and South Africa. However, the value of U.S. imports from Japan was twice the value of U.S. exports to that country. And the U.S. economy's dependence on foreign oil is reflected in the fact that its imports from OPEC (the Organization of Petroleum Exporting Countries) were nearly two and a half times as large as the value of exports to those countries. Overall, the dollar value of U.S. imports from both the developed and the developing countries of the world was greater than its exports to those countries.

The composition of U.S. exports and imports by type of good is illustrated in Table 17-4. Imports of mineral fuels and related materials represented the largest share (30.2 percent) of purchases from abroad in 1977, again reflecting U.S. dependence on foreign oil. (The foreign coal imports discussed in the news item at the beginning of the chapter also fall in this category.) Next in importance among U.S. imports were machinery and transport equipment (motor vehicles, airplanes, and so forth), and other manufactured goods—combined, these categories represented roughly 50 percent of total imports of goods. On the export side, these categories accounted for nearly 60 percent of total exports of goods. It is notable that capital and manufactured goods represent a sizeable portion of U.S. imports. This testifies to the ability of other industrialized countries to compete head-on in U.S. markets with domestic manufacturers. The United States is also dependent on imports for such things as bananas, coffee, tin, nickel, tea, and diamonds. The prosperity of American agriculture benefits from exports of cotton, tobacco, wheat, and other foodstuffs.

Nations also buy and sell services from one another, such as shipping services, banking services, and so forth. For example, in 1978 the United States purchased (imported) $24.1 billion of services from other nations and sold (exported) $26.9 billion of services to other nations.

Trade Affects Total Income, Output, and Employment

Until now, our analysis of the determination of total income, output, and employment has assumed that the economy is isolated from international trade—that it is a **closed economy.** In reality, as we have just seen, ours is an **open economy**—one that trades with other nations. World trade affects the economy's total demand for goods and services and, hence, the levels of total income, output, and employment. Let's see how exports and imports can be incorporated into the analysis of income determination that we initially developed in Chapters 7, 8, and 9.

EXPORTS, IMPORTS, AND NET EXPORTS

Total expenditures on final goods and services in our economy include those arising from **exports**, the purchases of domestic output by foreigners. Hence, exports increase domestic production, incomes, and employment. They may be viewed as an injection into the econo-

TABLE 17-3 U.S. MERCHANDISE EXPORTS AND IMPORTS BY AREA, 1978

Exports to	Value (in Billions of Dollars)	Percent- age of Total	Imports From	Value (in Billions of Dollars)	Percent- age of Total
Developed Countries	$ 84.4	61.4	Developed Countries	$ 97.6	56.5
Canada	30.1	21.9	Canada	32.9	19.0
Japan	12.2	8.9	Japan	24.4	14.1
Western Europe	38.3	27.9	Western Europe	36.1	20.9
Australia, New Zealand, and South Africa	3.9	2.8	Australia, New Zealand, and South Africa	4.2	2.4
Developing Countries	48.5	35.3	Developing Countries	73.7	42.6
OPEC[a]	14.8	10.8	OPEC	33.2	19.2
Other	33.8	24.6	Other	40.6	23.5
Eastern Europe	4.5	3.3	Eastern Europe	1.4	0.8
Total	$136.9	100.0	Total	$172.9	100.0

SOURCE: Department of Commerce, Bureau of Economic Analysis.

NOTE: Data are on an international transactions basis and exclude military shipments. Data will not add to totals because of rounding.

[a] Organization of Petroleum Exporting Countries.

my's income stream, just like investment and government spending. **Imports**, on the other hand, represent expenditures by a country's citizens on output produced abroad. Such expenditures are a leakage from our economy's total income, just like saving. That is, imports also may be viewed as income *not* spent on domestically produced goods and services. As such, unlike exports, imports decrease domestic production, incomes, and employment. Therefore, the net effect of trade on a country's total income, output, and employment depends on whether the injections from exports are greater or less than the leakages due to imports. Recalling from Chapter 5 that net exports X equals exports minus imports, we may say that the net effect depends on whether net exports X is positive or negative. Exactly how does this difference affect total income level?

DETERMINANTS OF EXPORTS AND IMPORTS

To answer this question, we must first consider what determines the volume of a country's exports and imports. Certainly, differences between countries in terms of resource endowments, levels of industrial development, consumption patterns, and size are significant determinants. The extent and nature of barriers to trade are also important. We will examine the role of these considerations later in this chapter. In the next chapter we will see that exchange rates and differences in rates of inflation between nations also plays an important role.

However, given all these factors, the volume of a country's exports will depend mainly on income levels in other countries. For example, if Western European countries are in the expan-

TABLE 17-4 PERCENT DISTRIBUTION OF DOMESTIC EXPORTS AND GENERAL IMPORTS FOR THE UNITED STATES, BY BROAD COMMODITY GROUPS, 1977

Exports	Percentage of Total	Imports	Percentage of Total
Machinery and transport equipment	43.3	Mineral fuels and related materials	30.2
Other manufactured goods	15.8	Other manufactured goods	24.7
Food and live animals	12.0	Machinery and transport equipment	24.2
Crude materials except fuel	10.9	Food and live animals	8.5
Chemicals	9.2	Crude materials except fuel	5.4
Mineral fuels and related materials	3.5	Chemicals	3.7
Beverages and tobacco	1.6	Beverages and tobacco	1.1
Total	100.0	Total	100.0

SOURCE: U.S. Department of Commerce.

sion phase of a business cycle, the volume of U.S. exports to them will generally rise. Conversely, a recession in these countries will tend to lower their demand for U.S. exports. On the other hand, the volume of a country's exports typically will depend very little, if at all, on its own total income level. What about the volume of a country's imports? Like consumption spending, a country's imports generally vary directly with its total income level. As a country's total income rises, its purchases of foreign products tend to increase right along with purchases of domestically produced goods.

TRADE AND THE
EQUILIBRIUM LEVEL OF GNP

We can now examine exactly how trade affects the economy's total income level, or its level of GNP. We will use the leakages-injection approach that we developed in Chapters 8 and 9. Initially, suppose there are no exports or imports, that the economy is a closed economy. Suppose that sum of saving S and taxes T, the total leakages, varies with the level of GNP as shown by the upward-sloping $S + T$ function in Figure 17-1, part a. The sum of investment

spending I and government spending G, the total injections, is represented by the $I + G$ schedule. The equilibrium level of GNP is $1,500 billion, corresponding to point f, at which the $I + G$ schedule and $S + T$ function intersect. At this level of GNP, the injections from government and investment spending are just equal to the leakages due to saving and taxes. In this case, $I + G = S + T = $400 billion.

Now consider what happens when there are exports and imports—that is, when the economy is an open economy. At every possible level of GNP, the leakages due to imports must be added to those due to saving and taxes. Total leakages at each GNP level are therefore represented by the $S + T + Imports$ function shown in Figure 17-1, part a. The vertical distance between the $S + T$ function and the $S + T + Imports$ function represents the volume of imports at each level of GNP. Note that this vertical distance is greater at higher levels of GNP. This reflects the fact that the volume of imports varies directly with GNP so that the leakage from imports is greater at higher levels of GNP.

Now consider exports. At every possible level

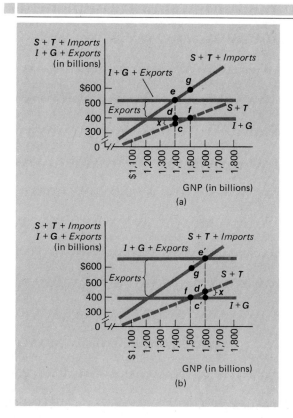

(a)

(b)

GNP (in billions)

FIGURE 17-1 TRADE AFFECTS THE EQUILIBRIUM LEVEL OF GNP

Exports, the purchase of domestic output by foreigners, are an injection into the economy's income stream just like investment and government spending. Imports, purchases by a country's citizens of output produced abroad, are a leakage from the economy's income stream just like saving and taxes. In an open economy equilibrium occurs at that level of GNP where the sum of the injections due to investment I, government G, and export spending are just equal to the sum of the leakages from savings S, taxes T, and imports.

If the economy is a closed economy (it neither exports nor imports), the equilibrium level of GNP would be $1,500 billion, corresponding to the intersection of the $I + G$ schedule and the $S + T$ function at point f, as shown in parts a and b. In equilibrium, $I + G = S + T = $400 billion.

If the economy is an open economy (it exports and imports) with exports of $120 billion (part a), the equilibrium level of GNP is $1,400 billion, corresponding to the intersection of the $I + G + Exports$ schedule with the $S + T + Imports$ function at point e. In equilibrium $I + G + Exports = S + T + Imports = $520 billion. The equilibrium level of imports, which is equal to $160 billion (the vertical distance between c and e), is larger than the $120 billion of exports (the vertical distance between d and e). Net exports X, therefore, are negative, or minus $40 billion (the vertical distance between c and d).

If exports were $260 billion, the equilibrium level of GNP would be $1,600 billion, corresponding to the intersection of the $I + G + Exports$ schedule and the $S + T + Imports$ function at point e' in part b. In equilibrium, $I + G + Exports = S + T + Imports = $660 billion. The equilibrium level of imports, which is equal to $220 billion (the vertical distance between d' and e') is less than the $260 billion of exports (the vertical distance between c' and e'). Net exports X are positive, or $40 billion (the vertical distance between c' and d').

In sum, positive net exports have an expansionary effect on GNP, and negative net exports have a contractionary effect on GNP.

of GNP the injections due to exports must be added to those due to investment and government spending. Total injections at each GNP level are represented by the $I + G + Exports$ schedule in Figure 17-1, part a. The vertical distance between the $I + G$ schedule and the $I + G + Exports$ schedule represents the volume of exports at each level of GNP. This vertical distance is the same at every level of GNP, a reflection of the fact that spending by foreigners on domestic output, or exports, is independent of the level of GNP. In part a, exports equal $120 billion.

Net Exports Negative. The equilibrium level of GNP is now $1,400 billion, corresponding to the intersection of the $S + T + Imports$ function and the $I + G + Exports$ schedule at point *e*. At this level of GNP, the sum of the injections due to investment, government, and export spending are just equal to the sum of the leakages from saving, taxes, and imports. In this case, $I + G + Exports = S + T + Imports = $520 billion. Note that the volume of exports, represented by the vertical distance between points *d* and *e*, is less than the volume of imports, represented by the vertical distance between points *c* and *e*. The difference, which is equal to the vertical distance between points *c* and *d*, equals net exports X (exports minus imports). In this case net exports are negative, minus $40 billion. The leakages due to imports are greater than the injections due to exports. Hence, when net exports are negative in an open economy, the equilibrium level of GNP ($1,400 billion) is lower than the closed economy equilibrium level of GNP ($1,500 billion).

Net Exports Positive. Alternatively, suppose the volume of exports were larger, or $260 billion, as shown in Figure 17-1, part b. Now the $I + G + Exports$ schedule intersects the $S + T + Imports$ function at point *e'*. The equilibrium level of GNP corresponding to this point is $1,600 billion. In this case, $I + G + Exports = S + T + Imports = $660 billion. The volume of exports ($260 billion), represented by the vertical distance between points *c'* and *e'*, now exceeds the volume of imports ($220 billion), represented by the vertical distance be-

tween points *d'* and *e'*. Net exports X are therefore positive, represented by the vertical distance between *c'* and *d'* ($40 billion). The injections due to exports exceed the leakages due to imports. When net exports are positive in an open economy, the equilibrium level of GNP ($1,600 billion) is greater than the closed economy equilibrium level of GNP ($1,500 billion).

Net Exports Zero. Finally, suppose that the level of exports were such that the $I + G + Exports$ schedule intersected the $S + T + Imports$ function at point *g*, in parts a and b of Figure 29-1. Then exports would equal imports, as represented by the vertical distance between points *f* and *g*. Net exports would be zero. The equilibrium level of GNP would be $1,500 billion, the same as the equilibrium level for the closed economy.

SUMMARY OF THE EFFECTS OF TRADE

In sum, when the net exports of an open economy are negative, the equilibrium level of GNP is lower than the equilibrium level that would prevail if the economy were closed. Conversely, when net exports are positive, the equilibrium level of GNP is greater than the closed economy level. When net exports are zero, the open economy and the closed economy level of GNP are the same. Hence, *the effects of trade on an economy's total income, output, and employment are expansionary when net exports are positive and contractionary when net exports are negative.*

■ CHECKPOINT 17-1

Suppose that the economy's citizens decide to reduce the volume of goods and services they buy from abroad, no matter what the level of GNP. Show how this would affect the equilibrium level of GNP in Figure 17-1, part a. At the $1,400 billion equilibrium level of GNP in Figure 17-1, part a, the leakages from imports exceed the injections from exports. How then can this be the equilibrium level of GNP? How is the effect of net exports (positive or negative) on the economy similar to the effect of a government budget deficit or surplus?

THE BASIS FOR TRADE: SPECIALIZATION AND COMPARATIVE ADVANTAGE

We have now looked at some of the overall quantitative dimensions of world trade, as well as the basic pattern of U.S. trade. And we have also examined the way in which trade affects the determination of total income, output, and employment. We now come to the question of why nations trade with one another. What is the basis of trade? In general, trade occurs because nations have different resource endowments and technological capabilities. Because of these differences, each nation can gain by specializing in those products which it produces relatively efficiently and by trading for those it produces inefficiently, or cannot produce at all. In short, international trade allows nations to increase the productivity of their resources through specialization and, thereby, to realize a higher standard of living than is possible in the absence of trade.

This general description of why nations trade sounds reasonable enough. However, to understand why it is correct requires an examination of the role of specialization and the important principle of comparative advantage. In essence, it is the principle of comparative advantage that makes it worthwhile for nations to specialize and trade.

In order to illustrate this principle and see why it leads to specialization and trade, let's consider the following *hypothetical* example. Suppose there are only two countries in the world economy, the United States and Venezuela. And suppose that each can produce both corn and oil, but with differing degrees of efficiency. The production possibilities frontier for each country is shown in Figure 17-2, parts a and b. (Recall from Chapter 2 that each point on a production possibilities frontier represents a maximum output combination for an economy whose available resources are fully employed.) Barrels of oil are measured on the vertical axis and bushels of corn on the horizontal.

Notice that each frontier is a straight line instead of a curve, as was the production possibili-

ties frontier discussed in Chapter 2. The frontiers here are straight lines because we are assuming that costs are constant. Along a straight-line frontier, a nation must give up the same amount of production of one good in order to produce an additional unit of the other, no matter which point on the frontier is considered. In other words, we are assuming that the law of increasing costs (see Chapter 2), which causes the frontier to be curved, does not apply here. The assumption of constant costs makes our discussion simpler but still allows us to illustrate the principle of comparative advantage.

Comparative Advantage: Differences in Opportunity Costs

As we can see, the production possibilities frontiers of the two nations differ. Observe that at any point on Venezuela's production possibilities frontier (part a), it is necessary to sacrifice 2 barrels of oil in order to have 1 more bushel of corn. For Venezuela, 1 bushel of corn, therefore, has an opportunity cost of 2 barrels of oil. Put the other way around, 1 barrel of oil has an opportunity cost of ½ bushel of corn. For the United States (part b), 1 barrel of oil must be given up to have 1 more bushel of corn. Hence, for the United States, the opportunity cost of 1 bushel of corn is 1 barrel of oil, or the opportunity cost of 1 barrel of oil is 1 bushel of corn. We can see from this that the opportunity cost of corn is higher for Venezuela than for the United States. While it costs Venezuela 2 barrels of oil for each bushel of corn, it costs the United States only 1. Conversely, the opportunity cost of oil is higher for the United States than for Venezuela. It costs the United States 1 bushel of corn for each barrel of oil, while it costs Venezuela only ½ bushel of corn for each barrel of oil.

In short, we can say that Venezuela has a *comparative advantage* (compared to the United States) in producing oil, and that the United States has a *comparative advantage* (compared to Venezuela) in growing corn. The difference in opportunity costs between the two nations reflects differences in their resource endowments, climates, and technological know-how.

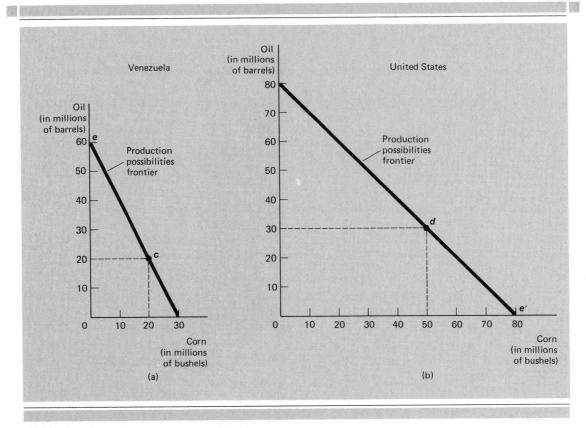

FIGURE 17-2 PRODUCTION POSSIBILITIES FRONTIERS FOR VENEZUELA AND THE UNITED STATES
(Hypothetical Data)

Each nation can produce both corn and oil. The production possibilities frontiers are straight lines because costs are constant—that is, the same amount of production of one good must be given up in order to produce an additional unit of the other, no matter which point on the frontier is considered.

The slope of Venezuela's production possibilities frontier (part a) indicates that 1 bushel of corn has an opportunity cost of 2 barrels of oil, or put the other way around, 1 barrel of oil has an opportunity cost of ½ bushel of corn. The slope of the U.S. production possibilities frontier (part b) indicates that the opportunity cost of 1 bushel of corn is 1 barrel of oil, or the opportunity cost of 1 barrel of oil is 1 bushel of corn. Since the opportunity cost of corn is lower for the United States than for Venezuela, the United States has a comparative advantage in producing corn. On the other hand, since the opportunity cost of oil is lower for Venezuela than for the United States, Venezuela has a comparative advantage in producing oil.

Inefficiency of Self-sufficiency—Efficiency of Specialization

As long as there is no trade between Venezuela and the United States, each is isolated and

must be self-sufficient. Each country is limited to choices along its own production possibilities frontier. Suppose Venezuela chooses to produce the output combination represented by point c

ECONOMIC THINKERS

DAVID RICARDO
1772–1823

Ricardo was born in London, the son of a merchant-stockbroker. At 14 (after a very brief commercial education in Holland), he entered his father's business, but for family reasons left the firm at 19 and went out on his own with borrowed funds. He was an immediate success, and in a decade he had amassed a fortune of some £2 million (an immense amount by the standards of the day). He retired from trade and in 1814 purchased a country estate and a seat in Parliament. Sensitive to his lack of education, Ricardo hesitated to put his views on paper, but began to do so in 1815. Despite stylistic shortcomings, Ricardo made major advances in the science of economics, and his contribution might well have been greater had he not died only eight years later.

While Adam Smith had argued that value was determined for the most part by labor and that labor was probably the best single measure of value, Ricardo went further. By a logical (but unrealistic) procedure, Ricardo tried to prove that *all* value is created by labor. Smith had said that in a primitive economy, where goods were exchanged by barter, land was free, and capital did not exist, labor was the sole measure, but in a modern economy where money was used there were complicating factors. Ricardo chose to ignore these complications.

One of Ricardo's most significant contributions was his theory of rent, which he approached by putting forth the theory of diminishing returns. He observed that successive applications of inputs to a productive process resulted in lower additional returns to output. That is, in agriculture, for example, more intensive use of manpower, fertilizer, and other inputs yielded larger output, but the increases were successively smaller than those at earlier stages of production. Thus, a point might be reached where output would reach an absolute level and, in fact, decline as more inputs were applied. For a

fixed resource such as land, it would be necessary over time to cultivate lands that were increasingly less productive in order to satisfy the pressing needs of increased population. As the demand for increased output rose, rent would rise (or increase) on that land of higher quality.

Ricardo was also the first to set forth the theory of comparative advantage in international trade in formal terms. According to this law, he argued, England would be better off if it imported food and exported manufactured goods. As a result, he was a supporter of the repeal of the tariff on grain as a method of lowering prices and thereby stimulating trade.

FOR FURTHER READING

St. Clair, Oswald. *A Key to Ricardo.* New York: Kelley & Millman, 1957.

Sraffa, Piero. *The Works and Correspondence of David Ricardo,* Vols. 1–9. London: Cambridge University Press, 1951–1955.

on its production possibilities frontier (Figure 17-2, part a), a combination consisting of 20 million barrels of oil and 20 million bushels of corn. Suppose also that the output combination the United States chooses to produce is represented by point *d* on its production possibilities frontier (Figure 17-2, part b), 30 million barrels of oil and 50 million bushels of corn.[1] Total "world" output is therefore 50 million barrels of

[1] Presumably each country's choice of output combination is made through its pricing system, as described in Chapter 2.

oil (the sum of 20 million barrels in Venezuela and 30 million barrels in the United States) and 70 million bushels of corn (the sum of 20 million bushels in Venezuela and 50 million bushels in the United States).

Figure 17-2 shows us that the world economy is not producing efficiently when each nation is isolated and self-sufficient, even though each nation is on its production possibilities frontier. Why do we say this? Suppose each nation specialized in the production of that product in which it has a comparative advantage. Venezuela would produce only oil, corresponding to point e (part a), and the United States would produce only corn, point e' (part b). Total world output would then consist of 60 million barrels of oil (Venezuela) and 80 million bushels of corn (United States). By specializing according to comparative advantage, total world output is greater by 10 million barrels of oil and 10 million bushels of corn as compared to what it is when each nation produces some of both products at points c and d. This example illustrates the principle of comparative advantage. *The principle of* **comparative advantage** *states that total world output is greatest when each good is produced by that nation which has the lower opportunity cost of producing the good—that is, by that nation which has the comparative advantage in the production of the good.*

When Venezuela produces 1 bushel of corn, the opportunity cost is 2 barrels of oil. It is clearly an inefficient use of the world's resources for Venezuela to produce corn when the United States can produce it at an opportunity cost of only 1 barrel of oil per bushel of corn. Similarly, it is an inefficient use of world resources for the United States to produce oil at an opportunity cost of 1 bushel of corn per barrel of oil when Venezuela can produce a barrel of oil at an opportunity cost of only ½ of a bushel of corn. If Venezuela produces corn, the world must give up more oil than is necessary to have corn. And if the United States produces oil, the world gives up more corn than is necessary to have oil. *The allocation of world resources is most efficient when each nation specializes according to comparative advantage.*

Since total world output of both goods is

greatest when each nation specializes according to comparative advantage, clearly there can be more of both goods for both nations if each specializes and engages in trade instead of remaining isolated and self-sufficient. Let's see what conditions will motivate them to specialize and trade.

Terms of Trade

Consider again the output combinations chosen by Venezuela and the United States when each is self-sufficient, represented by points c and d respectively in Figure 17-2. Note that Venezuela must forgo the production of 40 million barrels of oil in order to produce the 20 million bushels of corn associated with point c, since each bushel costs 2 barrels. The United States must forgo producing 30 million bushels of corn in order to produce 30 million barrels of oil—each barrel costs 1 bushel. If Venezuela could get corn by giving up *less* than 2 barrels of oil for each bushel, and if the United States could get oil by giving up *less* than 1 bushel of corn for each barrel, each would be eager to do so.

Is this possible? Yes, because of the difference in opportunity costs between the two nations. Let us now suppose that Venezuela offers to pay the United States 1½ barrels of oil for each bushel of corn it is willing to sell. For Venezuela this is cheaper than the 2 barrels per bushel that corn costs if Venezuela remains self-sufficient. For the United States, such a trade would mean that oil could be obtained at a cost of ⅔ of a bushel of corn for each barrel of oil. This is certainly cheaper than the 1 bushel of corn per barrel of oil it costs the United States if it tries to be self-sufficient. Therefore, the United States agrees to the terms of Venezuela's offer. The **terms of trade**, the ratio of exchange between oil and corn at which both nations agree to trade, would therefore be 1½ barrels of oil per bushel of corn or, equivalently, ⅔ bushel of corn per barrel of oil.

Specialization and Trade

Having established the terms of trade, Venezuela now specializes according to its comparative advantage in producing oil. It produces 60 million barrels of oil, which is the maximum it can produce on its production possibilities frontier. The United States now specializes according to its comparative advantage in growing corn, producing 80 million bushels, the maximum it can produce on its frontier. Though each nation specializes in production of one good, each nation's citizens want to consume both goods. This is possible, of course, because the nations can exchange goods at the agreed-upon terms of trade. This is shown in Figure 17-3, in which each nation's production possibilities frontier (exactly the same as in Figure 17-2) is shown along with its **trading possibilities frontier**. The trading possibilities frontier shows the choices that are open to a nation if it specializes in the product in which it has a comparative advantage and trades (exports) its specialty for the other product in which it has a comparative disadvantage.

When Venezuela produces 60 million barrels of oil, point *e* in part a, it can trade (export) this oil to the United States. Given the agreed-upon terms of trade of 1½ barrels per bushel, Venezuela can trade with the United States to get (import) 1 bushel of corn for every 1½ barrels of oil it exports to the United States. Starting from point *e*, such trade is represented by movement down the trading possibilities frontier as Venezuela gives up 1½ barrels for every bushel it gets. This is obviously better than the ratio of exchange along the production possibilities frontier which requires Venezuela to give up 2 barrels for each bushel it gets. Similarly, the United States produces 80 million bushels of corn, corresponding to point *e'* in part a. It can then move up the trading possibilities frontier by exporting 1 bushel of corn in trade for every 1½ barrels of oil it imports from Venezuela. Again, this beats the ratio of exchange along the production possibilities frontier which requires the United States to give up 1 bushel for every barrel it gets.

In sum, the terms-of-trade ratio of exchange along the trading possibilities frontier is better than the self-sufficiency ratio of exchange along each nation's production possibilities frontier. Hence, Venezuela can get *more* than 1 bushel of corn for 2 barrels of oil if it specializes in oil and trades for corn from the United States. On this two-way street, the United States can get *more* than 1 barrel of oil for every bushel of corn if it specializes in corn and trades for oil from Venezuela.

The Gains from Trade

Earlier we noted that if each nation specialized according to comparative advantage, total world output would be larger than if each produced some of both goods. Now we can see how trade makes this possible by allowing the citizens of each nation to consume more of both goods despite the fact that each nation produces only one of them.

Starting from point *e* (Figure 17-3, part a), Venezuela specializes in the production of oil (60 million barrels) which it trades to the United States for corn. Starting at point *e'* (part b), the United States specializes in the production of corn (80 million bushels) which it trades to Venezuela for oil. Given the mutually agreed-upon terms of trade of 1½ barrels per bushel, suppose Venezuela exports 36 million barrels of its oil to the United States in exchange for imports of 24 million bushels of corn. This gives Venezuela a combination of 24 million barrels of oil and 24 million bushels of corn, represented by point *d* on its trading possibilities frontier. Compared with the self-sufficient combination of 20 million barrels and 20 million bushels, represented by point *c* on its production possibilities frontier, Venezuela is now able to have more of *both* goods. The 4 million more barrels of oil and 4 million more bushels of corn represent the gains from trade to Venezuela. Similarly, the United States exports 24 million bushels of its corn to Venezuela in exchange for imports of 36 million barrels of oil from Venezuela. The United States thus has a combination of 36 million barrels of oil and 56 million bushels of corn, point *d'* on its trading possibilities frontier. This is clearly superior to the self-sufficient combination of 30 million barrels of oil and 50 million bushels, point *c'* on its production possibilities frontier. The gains from trade for the United States amount to 6 million more barrels of oil and 6 million more bushels of corn.

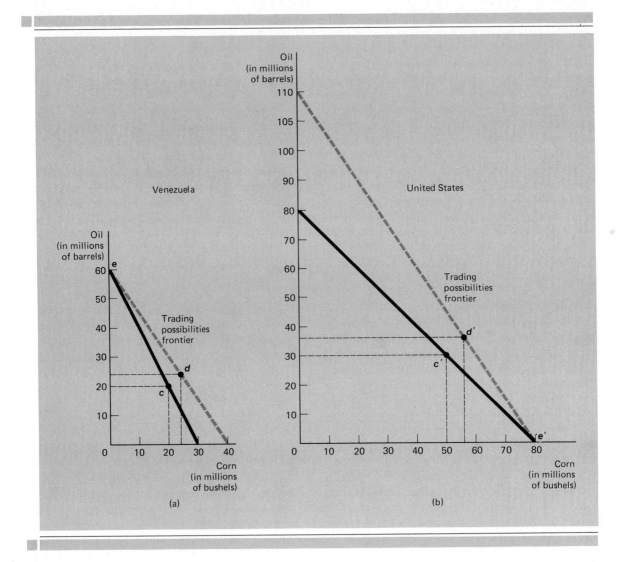

(a)   (b)

We noted earlier that if each nation specialized according to comparative advantage, total world output would be larger than if each produced the output combinations represented by points c and c′ in Figure 17-3. Specifically, we noted that specialization would increase total world output by 10 million barrels of oil and 10 million bushels of corn. Given the terms of trade (1½ barrels to 1 bushel), we now see how trade distributes this additional output—4 million barrels and 4 million bushels to Venezuela, and 6 million barrels and 6 million bushels to the United States. *Because of specialization and trade, there is an efficient allocation of world resources in production. Each good is produced by the nation that can produce the good at the lower cost. Consequently, each nation is able to have more of both goods.*

Finally, it should be noted that the United States is more productive than Venezuela in an absolute sense. The production possibilities frontiers in Figure 17-3 (or 17-2) show that the United States can produce any combination of corn and oil that Venezuela can *plus* more of

FIGURE 17-3 TRADING POSSIBILITIES FRONTIERS AND THE GAINS FROM TRADE
(Hypothetical Data)

Each nation can have more of both goods if each specializes according to its comparative advantage and trades with the other.

When each nation is isolated and self-sufficient, each is forced to choose an output combination on its production possibilities frontier. For example, Venezuela may choose to produce 20 million bushels of corn and 20 million barrels of oil (point *c*), and the United States may choose to produce 50 million bushels of corn and 30 million barrels of oil (point *c'*).

Alternatively, if each nation specializes according to its comparative advantage, Venezuela would produce 60 million barrels of oil (point *e*), and the United States 80 million bushels of corn (point *e'*). Then each nation could export some of its specialty in exchange for some of the other nation's specialty at terms of trade represented by the slope of the trading possibilities frontier. Such trade would move Venezuela down its trading possibilities frontier from point *e* to a point such as *d*, 24 million bushels and 24 million barrels. The United States moves up its trading possibilities frontier from point *e'* to a point such as *d'*, 56 million bushels and 36 million barrels. Each nation is able to have more of both goods. The gains from trade for Venezuela amount to 4 million bushels and 4 million barrels (point *d* compared to point *c*), and for the United States they amount to 6 million bushels and 6 million barrels (point *d'* compared to point *c'*).

both goods. This highlights the fundamental point that the incentive to specialize and trade stems from the fact that Venezuela and the United States have different opportunity costs in the production of corn and oil. For Venezuela the opportunity cost of producing corn is greater than for the United States, while for the United States the opportunity cost of producing oil is greater than for Venezuela. If the opportunity costs for Venezuela and the United States were the same, there would be no incentive to trade. However, because nations all differ in resource endowments, climate, size, and technological capabilities, it is little wonder that there is so much specialization and trade in the world.

Some Qualifications

So far in our discussion, we have simply assumed a particular ratio of exchange as the terms of trade. But what in fact determines the terms of trade? We have also assumed constant costs throughout our discussion so that the production possibilities frontier is a straight line. It is more realistic to assume increasing costs— that the production possibilities frontier is curved, bowed outward from the origin. How

does this affect the analysis? Let's consider each issue in turn.

DETERMINING THE TERMS OF TRADE

We have been assuming that the terms-of-trade ratio of exchange between Venezuela and the United States is 1½ barrels of oil per bushel of corn. However, in our hypothetical example both Venezuela and the United States would find trade beneficial at terms of trade lying anywhere between 2 barrels per bushel, the ratio of exchange along Venezuela's production possibilities frontier, and 1 barrel per bushel, the ratio of exchange along the U.S. production possibilities frontier. Any terms-of-trade ratio of exchange lying in this range allows each nation to obtain a good at a lower cost through trade than it costs to produce the good domestically.

The terms-of-trade exchange ratio within this range at which trade will actually take place depends on world supply-and-demand conditions for the two goods. If world demand for oil is strong relative to oil supply and the demand for corn is weak relative to corn supply, the price of oil will be high and the price of corn low. The terms of trade will be closer to the 1 barrel per bushel limit which is more favorable to Venezuela than to the United States. If world demand and supply conditions are the opposite, the price of oil will be low and that of corn high. Then the terms of trade will be closer to 2 barrels per bushel, which is more favorable to the United States. In any event, the terms of trade are determined competitively by consumers and producers in the two countries (not by their governments).

INCREASING COSTS

Suppose each nation's production possibilities frontier is curved so that it bows out from the origin. That is, each nation is faced with increasing costs as it expands production of the good in which it has a comparative advantage. Suppose Venezuela is initially at the point on its production possibilities frontier at which the cost ratio is 2 barrels of oil for 1 bushel of corn, and the United States is initially at a point on its frontier where the cost ratio is 1 barrel for 1 bushel.

Now suppose they begin to specialize and trade. As Venezuela expands its production of oil, the cost of producing it increases. That is, it will have to give up more than 1 bushel of corn to produce 2 barrels of oil. Similarly, as the United States expands production of corn, increasing cost will require it to give up more than 1 barrel of oil to produce 1 bushel of corn. Hence, the cost ratio for Venezuela goes from 2 barrels for 1 bushel, to $1\frac{7}{8}$ barrels for 1 bushel, to $1\frac{3}{4}$ barrels for 1 bushel, and so forth as it expands the production of oil. The cost ratio for the United States goes from 1 barrel for 1 bushel, to $1\frac{1}{8}$ barrel for 1 bushel, to $1\frac{1}{4}$ barrel for 1 bushel, and so forth as it expands the production of corn. The cost ratios of the two nations are now getting closer to one another.

At some point, after each nation has expanded the production of its specialty far enough, the cost ratios may become equal. At that point the basis for trade—a difference in opportunity costs between the two nations—will have been eliminated. Furthermore, at that point it is likely that each nation still produces both goods. Venezuela may still produce some corn along with its oil, and the United States

some oil along with its corn. *Hence, when there are increasing costs, specialization will not be as complete, nor the volume of trade as large, as is the case when costs are constant.*

The Argument for Free Trade

We now have seen how specialization and trade lead to an efficient allocation of world resources. They make it possible for each nation to have more of all goods than is possible in the absence of specialization and trade. While we have illustrated these points using only two nations and two goods, advanced treatments of the subject show that these conclusions hold for a multination, multiproduct world as well. Hence, it may seem odd that there are so many instances in which there is outright opposition to trade with foreign nations. The news item at the beginning of the chapter provides a fairly typical example. The rest of this chapter will focus on the barriers to trade that nations often erect as a matter of policy. We will examine critically the most often heard arguments in favor of restricting trade. But before considering these matters, we should state the argument for free trade from a somewhat different, yet compelling perspective.

When each nation specializes in production according to its comparative advantage and trades with other nations, each nation is able to move out beyond its individual production possibilities frontier. The effect of specialization and trade is therefore the same as if each nation had gained more technological knowledge or more resources, or both. That is, the effect is the same as if each nation experienced an outward shift in its production possibilities frontier (such as we discussed in Chapter 2). It is possible for each nation to have more of all goods, thereby lessening the problem of scarcity.

■CHECKPOINT 17-2

Suppose there are two pioneers in the wilderness. Each sets up a homestead and each chops wood and grows wheat. Construct an illustration showing why it would benefit both to trade with one another. Can you think of examples that illustrate the role of the principle of comparative

advantage in explaining trade between various regions of the United States?

BARRIERS TO TRADE AND ARGUMENTS FOR PROTECTION

The argument for free trade based on the principle of comparative advantage is one of the most solid cornerstones of economic analysis. No other issue seems to command such unanimous agreement among economists as the case for free trade. However, for a variety of reasons different groups in any economy are always prevailing on government to erect barriers to trade—that is, they want protection from the competition of foreign trade. We will first examine some of the most common barriers and then consider the merits of some of the most common arguments for protection.

Barriers to Trade

Tariffs and quotas are the main weapons in the arsenal of protectionism. More recently, so-called antidumping legislation has also been used as a barrier to foreign imports.

TARIFFS

A **tariff (or duty)** *is a tax on imports, most often calculated as a percent of the price charged for the good by the foreign supplier.* For example, if the price of a ton of imported steel were $100, a 10 percent tariff would require the domestic purchaser to pay an additional $10 per ton. This effectively raises the price of imported steel to $110 per ton. A tariff may obviously be used as a source of revenue for the government. However, a more common purpose of tariffs is protection against foreign competition. By raising the prices of imported goods relative to the prices of domestically produced goods, tariffs encourage domestic consumers to buy domestic rather than foreign products.

For example, suppose Japanese steel companies can produce steel at a lower cost than American producers, with the result that the price of imported Japanese steel is $100 per ton while the price of domestically produced steel is $102 per ton. Domestic buyers will import the lower priced Japanese steel. Sales of domestic

steel producers will suffer. Consequently, suppose domestic producers, both company officials and steelworkers unions, prevail on Congress to place a 10 percent tariff on imported steel. This raises the price of imported steel to $110 per ton, a price $8 higher than a ton of domestic steel. Domestic steel users now switch from importing Japanese steel to buying the cheaper domestic steel. Steel imports decline while sales and employment in the domestic steel industry rise. Recognize, however, that while domestic steel producers are better off, the rest of the nation's citizens will have to pay higher prices for all products containing steel.

Of course, tariffs need not completely eliminate imports. *As long as tariffs are not larger than the difference in production costs between domestic and foreign producers, tariffs will not completely eliminate imports.* In our example, suppose Japanese steel producers would just be able to cover costs as long as they receive a minimum of $92.73 per ton. Suppose American producers cannot afford to sell steel at a price less than $102 per ton. With a 10 percent tariff, Japanese producers would just be able to remain competitive with U.S. producers. Japanese steel unloaded on U.S. docks at a price of $92.73 would be taxed 10 percent by the tariff, or $9.27 (.1 × $92.73), thus costing American importers $102 per ton ($92.73 paid to Japanese producers plus $9.27 in tariff revenue paid to the government). However, if the tariff were greater than 10 percent, imports of Japanese steel would cease because Japanese producers would suffer losses if they sold their steel at less than $92.73. And this price plus a tariff *greater* than 10 percent would increase the price of imported Japanese steel to domestic buyers above the price of domestic steel of $102, making Japanese steel noncompetitive.

Finally, it should be noted that the use of a tariff as a source of tax revenue runs counter to the use of a tariff for protection. A tariff generates tax revenues only to the extent that there are purchases of imported goods on which tariffs can be collected. In general, to the extent tariffs successfully serve protectionist objectives by cutting back imports, the tax revenues from tariffs are also reduced. A tariff so high as to effectively block out all imports, giving complete protection from foreign competition, would generate no tax revenue at all.

IMPORT QUOTAS

Import quotas *limit imports by specifying the maximum amount of a foreign produced good that will be permitted into the country over a specified period of time (per year, for example).* Import quotas are a very effective tool of protection, unlike a tariff, the effect of which on the volume of imports can be hard to predict. After legislating a certain level of tariffs on a particular good, a class of goods, or even an across-the-board tariff on all goods, protectionists may find that imports are not limited to anywhere near the extent they had hoped for. Import quotas remove such uncertainty. Those favoring protection simply specify in the import quota legislation the exact quantity of a particular good that may be imported over a specified period of time. An import quota on Japanese steel, for example, might limit imports of such steel to 1 million tons per year.

ANTIDUMPING LAWS

Domestic producers of particular products often argue that they are unfairly victimized by competing foreign imports that are "dumped" in domestic markets. This type of complaint by both the domestic steel industry and domestic coal producers is reported in the news item at the beginning of this chapter. There the meaning of the term **dumping** is precisely captured by the complaint of U.S. coal producers. They claim that "the prices paid for the imported coke are not only lower than those paid for domestic coke, they are also lower than the foreign suppliers' cost of production."

Antidumping laws usually set a minimum price on an imported good. If the import enters the country at a price below that minimum, the law triggers a government investigation of possible dumping. Should it conclude that dumping is taking place, the imported good is not allowed to be sold at a price below the minimum, or "trigger," price. Actually, the United States has only one statute that deals with dumping. Prices are not set out in the statute. But in 1979,

the Carter administration introduced a trigger-price system covering steel imports to determine more quickly if a dumping investigation is warranted.

Difficulty of Detection. When domestic producers of any product cry "dumping," there is always reason to suspect they are simply campaigning for protectionist measures to shelter them from foreign competition. It may well be that foreign producers are not charging prices below their costs of production, but are simply more efficient than domestic producers. That is, foreign producers can charge prices that cover their costs but yet are still below the costs of domestic producers. In that case domestic consumers reap the benefit of lower prices for imported products that cost more when produced at home. Domestic producers' claims of dumping simply amount to "crying wolf" in that case. Furthermore, it is hard to establish whether or not foreign producers are selling their goods at prices below their costs. It is difficult if not impossible for an outsider to determine just what foreign producers' costs are. And just such information is necessary to determine whether dumping exists.

Export Subsidies and Dumping. Nonetheless, there are circumstances under which dumping can occur, and indeed does amount to "unfair" competition with domestic producers. In many nations it is not uncommon for the government to provide an **export subsidy**, or payment, to export industries to cover part of their costs of production. For example, suppose a government pays steel producers $10 for every ton of steel they export. If it costs the steel producers $90 to produce a ton of steel, the $10 subsidy from the government effectively reduces their cost to $80 per ton. Without the subsidy the steel producers could not sell steel abroad for less than $90 a ton. With the subsidy they can sell exported steel for as little as $80 a ton. Domestic steel producers in the nations importing this subsidized steel may be more efficient than the foreign producers. Let's say they can produce steel at a cost of $85 per ton. However, they will not be able to compete with the subsidized imported steel priced at $80 per ton. Domestic producers in a nation importing the subsidized steel have a legitimate complaint that imported steel is being dumped in their market.

Note that though foreign trade may increase as a result of export subsidies, it is not the kind of trade that gives rise to the world gains from trade due to specialization according to comparative advantage. In our example, the subsidized steel imports are in fact more costly to produce than the unsubsidized domestic steel. That is, the nation in which the subsidized steel is produced in fact has a comparative disadvantage in steel production relative to the nation importing the subsidized steel.

Protecting Employment and Jobs

One of the most common protectionist arguments is that importing foreign goods amounts to "exporting jobs." It is claimed that buying foreign goods instead of domestic goods creates jobs for foreign labor that would otherwise go to domestic labor. It is charged that domestic unemployment will increase as a result. The merits of this argument depend on whether it is made with reference to the short run or the long run.

THE SHORT RUN:
ADJUSTMENT PROBLEMS

There is indeed truth to this argument in the short run. Recall again our hypothetical example of trade between Venezuela and the United States. When each was isolated and self-sufficient, each had an oil industry and a farming industry growing corn. However, when the two nations began to trade, Venezuela's farmers could no longer compete with the corn imported from the United States. All resources previously devoted to farming, including labor, had to be shifted into Venezuela's specialty industry, oil production. Similarly, in the United States oil producers could no longer compete with imported Venezuelan oil. Labor and other resources in the oil industry had to shift into the United States's specialty, corn production.

The gains from trade *after* these shifts have occurred are clear. However, the transition period of readjustment and reallocation of resources within each country could be painful

and costly to many citizens. Workers experienced and trained in farming in Venezuela and in oil production in the United States would no longer have a market for their skills. With their old jobs eliminated, many would need retraining to gain employment in their country's expanding specialty industry. Many would have to uproot their families and move to new locations, leaving old friends and severing familiar community ties. While both nations would realize the material gains from trade in the long run, it is understandable that those threatened with loss of job and an uncomfortable and personally costly transition might well support protectionist measures.

Public policy in a number of nations recognizes that changing trade patterns typically impose transition costs on affected industries and workers. In the United States adjustment assistance is provided to workers and firms who suffer from increased imports resulting from government actions, such as tariffs and quotas, that lower trade barriers. Workers are eligible for lengthened periods of unemployment compensation, retraining programs, and allowances to cover costs of moving to other jobs.

The reasoning behind a policy of transitional adjustment assistance is this: The removal of trade barriers leads to increased trade. Since the whole nation realizes gains from increased trade, some of these gains can be used to compensate those citizens who suffer losses during the period of adjustment. *Quite aside from any issue of "fairness," it may not be politically feasible to lower trade barriers unless those injured by such a move are compensated. As long as not all of the gains from trade are needed to compensate (or possibly bribe) the injured parties, the gains left over after compensation payments still make it worthwhile to lower barriers to trade.*

THE LONG RUN

The news item at the beginning of this chapter reports that rising coal imports are at least partly to blame for the layoffs of "thousands of U.S. workers who mine metallurgical coal." If the United States has a comparative disadvantage in the production of metallurgical coal relative to foreign coal producers, the laid-off workers will have to make a transition to employment in other areas of the economy (unless domestic coal producers are protected from the imports). These workers will doubtless bear transition costs and may even require substantial assistance.

But is there any reason why these workers whose jobs have been eliminated by import competition should remain permanently unemployed? No, not as long as fiscal and monetary policy keep the economy operating near capacity. Workers displaced by import competition will have a more difficult time making a transition to other jobs if the economy is in a recession and unemployment is high. Adjustment assistance cannot overcome a lack of alternative jobs. However, in the long run, if fiscal and monetary policy keep the economy near full employment, workers displaced by foreign competition will become employed in other areas of the economy. Hence, if the argument prevails that protection from foreign competition is needed to protect domestic jobs and avoid unemployment, in the long run the nation will end up forgoing the gains from trade. *Unemployment that results from increased foreign competition should only be transitional. Any long-run unemployment problem should be blamed on fiscal and monetary policy and other domestic policies for dealing with unemployment, not on a policy of free trade.*

Protection from Cheap Foreign Labor

Another popular argument for protection is that we must protect domestic industries from competition from cheap foreign labor. This argument appeals to the labor vote in particular because they view cheap foreign labor as a threat to their standard of living as well as their jobs. The argument does not stand up, however. Let's see why.

Suppose two countries have exactly the *same size* labor force, but one's production possibilities frontier looks like that in part a of Figure 17-2, and the other's looks like that in part b. The labor force of part b is absolutely more productive because it can produce more of both goods. Hence, compared to the country of part a, the country of part b can pay its laborers more in both industries. Or, put the other way around, labor in the country of part a is cheaper than that of the country in part b.

But absolute differences in productivity are not the basis of trade—differences in opportunity costs are. Hence, despite the fact that labor in part b is more expensive than labor in part a, it pays for both countries to trade, as shown in Figure 17-3. Moreover, note that despite the fact that labor is cheaper in part a, it would cost the country in part b more to import corn from part a than to produce it itself. And despite the fact that labor is more expensive in part b, it still costs less for the country in part a to import corn from the country in part b than to produce it itself. Yes, it is true that the country in part b imports oil from part a *and* that labor is cheaper in part a than part b. But cheaper labor in part a is not the reason why part b imports oil from part a. It does so because the opportunity cost of producing oil in part a (2 barrels for each bushel sacrificed) is lower than it is in part b (only 1 barrel for each bushel sacrificed).

To clinch the point, suppose the cheap labor argument prevails and insurmountable tariff barriers are erected between the two countries so that trade ceases. In each country some labor that previously worked in the industry in which the country specialized according to comparative advantage would now have to work in the less efficient industry. Real wages (the quantity of goods that can be purchased with a given money wage) would *fall* in both countries because each now has *less* output. In terms of Figure 17-3, each country is now on its production possibilities frontier at points such as c and c', rather than on their trading possibilities frontiers at points such as d and d'. Living standards in both countries are reduced.

Protection for Particular Industries

Industries faced with competition from foreign imports naturally have a special interest in erecting barriers to such competition. The news item at the beginning of the chapter reports of warnings by American steelmakers "that cut-rate imports of foreign steel 'dumped' on U.S. shores mean fewer jobs and, in the long run, a weaker American steel industry." We should be suspicious of such statements, of course. Any industry seeking protection either can't operate efficiently enough to meet the market test of foreign competition or simply wants a larger share of the domestic market and a chance to milk it by charging higher prices. In either case consumers will have to pay higher prices for the industry's products if protectionist measures are enacted into law.

The protected industry and associated special interest groups stand to gain a lot from such legislation. Hence, they organize lobbies and campaigns to pressure Congress for tariffs, quotas, and other protective barriers. The rest of the nation's citizens are often not aware of the losses that trade restrictions imply for them. The forces that might oppose such legislation are often nonexistent, disinterested, or too disorganized to offset the industry and special interest groups who favor it. The problem is that protection provides relatively large gains to a few, while freer trade helps everybody a little.

But are there circumstances that might warrant protection for a special industry because it is in the best interest of everybody? Yes, some convincing arguments have been made for protecting industries important to national defense. There is also the so-called infant industry argument.

THE NATIONAL DEFENSE ARGUMENT

Certain industries are indispensable to any war effort—steel, transportation equipment, aircraft, mining of strategic materials, textiles, and so forth. Even though a nation may not have a comparative advantage in the production of any of these products, it may be difficult or impossible to import them when war disrupts world trade. In that case, protective tariffs and quotas may be justified to enable these industries to survive on domestic soil during peacetime. Defense considerations override the usual economic arguments. The difficulty is that many industries seek special protection in peacetime by arguing that they would be indispensable during wartime. Whether in fact they would be or not, the argument provides another vehicle for gaining protection from foreign competition.

Indeed, American steelmakers could make a compelling case for protection on these grounds.

THE INFANT-INDUSTRY ARGUMENT

It is sometimes argued that certain industries would develop into strong competitors in world markets if only they had a chance to get started. Unfortunately, so goes the argument, without protection from the competition of their already established counterparts in other countries, these infant industries never survive to the point where they can go head-to-head with foreign competition.

There may be some merit to this argument. However, the problem lies in correctly identifying those so-called infant industries that are destined, with the aid of temporary protective measures, to mature into productive enterprises in which the nation will definitely have a comparative advantage in a world of free trade. For example, how is it to be decided when maturity has arrived and protection can be removed? Will it eventually become the case that protective measures have simply spawned a mature special interest that is more efficient at maintaining continued protection for itself than it is at producing goods? In the meantime the nation loses in two ways. First, it forgoes the gains from trade available with the purchase of more efficiently produced foreign goods. Second, domestic resources tied up in the protected industry are not available for employment in more efficient industries elsewhere in the economy.

The Diversification-for-Stability Argument

An economy can be highly specialized in a few products, and depend to a large extent on its exports of these products for its ability to import the diversity of other goods it needs. Many developing nations fit this description. Brazil depends heavily on its coffee bean exports, New Zealand on exports of dairy products, and Saudi Arabia on its exported oil. Such nations often suffer from the risks inherent in having too many of their eggs in one basket. If world demand for their particular specialty fluctuates widely, real GNP and employment can be very unstable in these countries.

It is often argued that such nations could reduce this instability by diversifying their economies—that is, by encouraging the development of a variety of industries producing largely unrelated products. To do this it is argued that many of these industries would have to be protected from foreign competition by tariffs, import quotas, and other barriers. Otherwise, they would not be able to compete because of their relative inefficiency compared to their foreign counterparts. The main issue here is that there presumably is a trade-off between the gains from trade due to specialization according to comparative advantage on the one hand, and economic stability on the other. Some nations, like some people, prefer a higher *average* income level even though it means greater year-to-year income variability, rather than a lower average income with less year-to-year variability. The diversification-for-stability-through-protection argument obviously leans toward the lower average income, lower variability point of view.

Protection and Trade Policy

International trade is a two-way street. It requires that nations import as well as export. However, the history of trade policy among nations clearly indicates that their eagerness to export is not matched by a similar zeal for imports. While domestic producers welcome exports as a way of expanding their markets, they often view imports as a competitive threat to be stopped if at all possible. While policy makers frequently welcome exports as a way of increasing total income and employment, they may often be concerned about the fact that imports have the opposite effect (recall our analysis of Figure 17-1). Add to these considerations the often emotional, scare-type arguments for protection we have previously examined, and the basis for a nation's bias in favor of exports and against imports is readily apparent.

Unfortunately, if every nation indulges this bias in the long run, international trade must cease. Why? Because every nation's exports must be another nation's imports. For example,

if the United States doesn't buy goods from other nations (imports), then other nations can't earn dollars to buy goods from the United States (exports). Thus, if a nation raises tariffs, quotas, and other barriers to imports, that nation's export industries will eventually decline. Labor and other resources will have to be reallocated from the nation's shrinking export industries to its expanding industries that produce domestic goods protected by increased trade barriers. Hence, barriers to imports shift resources away from those industries in which the nation is so efficient as to have a comparative advantage. The gains from trade are lost and the nation's standard of living is diminished. If every nation cuts imports, then every nation's exports must eventually decline as well. Everyone loses the gains from trade.

TARIFFS OF RETALIATION

The process of shrinking world trade just described could begin with one nation's attempts to cut back its imports. Others might then retaliate by erecting their own barriers to imports. This has been an all too common occurrence in the history of world trade. Just as the Great Depression was beginning, Congress passed the Smoot-Hawley Tariff Act of 1930 which imposed some of the highest tariffs in U.S. history, as can be seen from Figure 17-4. If U.S. exports had remained the same, the reduction in imports caused by these tariffs would have increased net exports. This would have had an expansionary impact on total income and employment in the United States (recall our discussion of Figure 17-1). Of course, the levels of income and employment in other nations were adversely affected since a reduction in American imports meant a reduction in their exports. Hence, other nations raised trade barriers in retaliation, and U.S. exports also declined. Overall, the resulting contraction of world trade aggravated the decline in income and employment in many nations, making the Great Depression even worse.

REDUCING TRADE BARRIERS

Since the disastrous Smoot-Hawley Tariff Act of 1930, the United States has reduced tar-

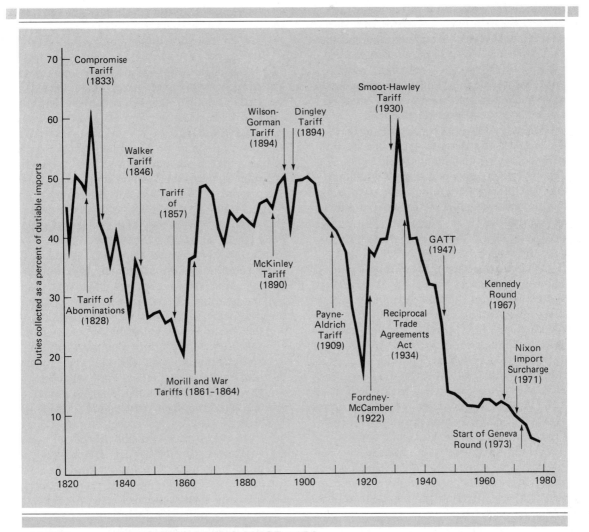

FIGURE 17-4 U.S. TARIFF RATES SINCE 1820

U.S. tariffs have fallen steadily since the Reciprocal Trade Agreement Act of 1934. In the postwar years they have been set at only a small fraction of the levels that prevailed throughout much of our history.

iffs dramatically, as can be seen from Figure 17-4. Compared with other nations, the United States today is one of the world leaders in the movement toward freer world trade. Congressional enactment of the Reciprocal Trade Agreement Act in 1934 was a major step in initiating tariff reductions in the United States. In 1947 the General Agreement on Tariffs and Trade (GATT) greatly enhanced the atmosphere for tariff reduction among nations. In the years since World War II, GATT has provided an ongoing forum for the multilateral negotiation of tariff reductions. Initially 23 nations were parties to GATT, but that number has expanded to the point where more than 90 nations are now members of GATT.

■CHECKPOINT 17-3

In the news item at the beginning of this chapter, coke-oven makers contend that the availability of "cheap foreign coke" is causing steelmakers to postpone "much-needed construction of new coke capacity to replace old and inefficient ovens." What do you think of the coke-oven maker's argument, and where do you think they would stand on the issue of whether or not an antidumping complaint should be filed against foreign coke producers? What is it that Charles Bradford finds so humorous in the protectionist positions of the coal and steel industries?

SUMMARY

1. The volume of world trade is roughly equivalent to 60 percent of the GNP of the United States. For many countries exports represent a sizeable portion of their GNPs—for some, as much as a half or more. Though U.S. exports and imports rarely exceed 10 percent of its GNP, the absolute dollar volume of its annual exports and imports typically exceeds that of any other nation. Roughly half of all U.S. exports and imports consist of capital goods and other manufactured goods. In recent years imports of oil have accounted for roughly a third of its total imports.

2. Exports may be viewed as an injection into the economy's income stream, just like investment and government spending. Imports are a leakage from the economy's income stream. The effects of trade on a nation's GNP are expansionary when net exports (exports minus imports) are positive, and contractionary when net exports are negative.

3. The basis for international trade lies in the fact that nations differ in their resource endowments and technological capabilities.

4. Differing resource endowments and technological capabilities typically make the opportunity cost of producing any given good different between nations. Because of this, nations that specialize according to comparative advantage and engage in trade can have a larger total output than is possible if they remain self-sufficient and isolated.

5. The terms of trade determine how the larger world output made possible by specialization and trade is distributed among nations. And the terms of trade between any two traded goods depends on world supply-and-demand conditions for the two goods. Increasing costs diminish the extent of specialization and trade relative to what it would be if costs were constant.

6. The argument for free trade is based on the fact that when nations specialize according to comparative advantage and trade, there is a more efficient allocation of resources. The resulting increase in world output lessens the problem of scarcity and makes possible a higher standard of living.

7. Nations often erect barriers to trade in the form of tariffs, import quotas, and antidumping laws. These measures effectively reduce the quantity of imports and allow domestic producers to sell more at higher prices. To the extent such barriers block trade, there is a less efficient allocation of world resources and a reduced level of total world output.

8. Most of the arguments for protection are flawed. However, short-run adjustment problems resulting from a reduction of trade barriers can cause real hardship for those in affected industries, possibly justifying short-run adjustment assistance. In the long run fiscal and monetary policy must keep the economy operating near capacity so that the full gains from trade may be realized. Protection may be justified where national defense considerations are concerned.

9. U.S. tariff rates have been declining ever since the Reciprocal Trade Agreement Act of 1934. In the postwar period world trade has been spurred by the General Agreement on Tariffs and Trade (1947).

KEY TERMS AND CONCEPTS

antidumping law
closed economy
comparative advantage
dumping
exports
export subsidy
import quotas

imports
open economy
tariff (or duty)
terms of trade
trading possibilities frontier

QUESTIONS AND PROBLEMS

1. Suppose that the level of a nation's exports fluctuates from year to year. Using a diagram like Figure 17-1, can you explain why the resulting fluctuations in the nation's GNP might be smaller if it imports goods than if it doesn't import? How might the composition of imports—whether the nation imports mostly consumption goods or mostly capital goods—affect your answer?

2. Why is it that a doctor hires a secretary even though the doctor may be a better typist than the secretary?

3. Suppose there are two nations, and that one is able to produce two goods, X and Y, and the other is able to produce only good X. Is there likely to be trade between these two nations? Why or why not? If you think they would trade, what do you think would be the terms of trade?

4. Is it conceivable that trade between Venezuela and the United States in Figure 17-3 could lead each nation to have more of one good and less of the other—that is say, as compared to the combinations c and c' which they have when there is no trade? If so, why is each still better off with trade than without it?

5. Suppose one nation (such as Australia) has a lot of land relative to the size of its population, and another nation (such as Japan) has a large population relative to the amount of its land. Suppose also that these two nations have similar levels of technological know-how. What do you think might be the pattern of trade between these two nations? If, on the other hand, the nation with the higher land to labor ratio also had a much higher level of technological know-how, how might this change your answer? Why?

6. It is sometimes argued that tariffs can force foreign exporters to provide their goods to us at a lower price. Can you explain why this is true?

7. One argument for protection runs as follows: "If I buy a car from Japan, Japan has the money and I have the car. But if I buy a car in the United States, the United States has the money and I have the car." Explain why you do, or do not, think this is a valid argument for putting a stiff tariff on imported cars.

■ NEWS ITEM FOR YOUR ANALYSIS ■

NEW ZEALAND STAGGERS FROM FARM PROTECTIONISM ABROAD AND INCREASED OIL PRICES

FEATHERSTON, New Zealand, Jan. 22—These two islands in the remote Pacific produce butter, cheese, meat, and wool worth nearly $2.5 billion per year. They ship it halfway around the world and sell it for less than competitors can charge in their own backyards. In short, New Zealand is the world's most efficient farm. Earning three-quarters of its export income from the land, of all the developed countries New Zealand alone hasn't industrialized heavily.

New Zealand depends on imports for nearly all its oil and a larger percentage of the manufactured products it needs. Ever since the oil crisis of late 1973, the prices of both have soared. However, unlike most countries, New Zealand was not able to defend itself by increasing the prices of its own exports. That's because stricken nations around the world erected especially high trade barriers against agricultural imports.

Today New Zealand's exports can buy only two-thirds of what they bought in 1973. Consequently, the economy's standard of living (measured by per capita GNP) has dropped from fourth in the world in the 1960s to twentieth.

Exports aren't going to recover as long as the industrial nations continue to shelter their less efficient farmers from New Zealand's produce. A New Zealand dairy farmer and a part-time helper milk an average of 116 cows per day. The average per farm in the United States is 30, and in West Germany 9. "Industrial countries," says a top Foreign Affairs Ministry official in Wellington, "expect rewards for industrial efficiency. Plant and equipment flow where the profits are. In agriculture they say this is different: 'High costs aren't the farmers' fault; you can't be too dependent on foreigners for your food.' "

New Zealand began scrambling for markets in the Third World after the developed countries started squeezing New Zealand out of their domestic markets with tariffs and import quotas (Japan and the United States have been just as unreceptive). Today, New Zealand sells 44 percent of its produce to 130 developing countries, including such nations as Senegal, Malta, Bangladesh, and Sikkim.

Yet even in the Third World, New Zealand is plagued by the policies of European Common Market countries. While using import quotas to shelter their farmers from the more efficient New Zealand farmer on the one hand, these countries have provided export subsidies to their farmers on the other. As a result, Common Market countries are dumping skim milk, butter, and cheese into the tiny alternative markets that New Zealand is laboring to cultivate, and prices are scraping bottom. "Export subsidization on this scale, and with these price effects," says a planning council report, "has materially undercut New Zealand's commercial interests."

The wage-earning New Zealand factory worker, sheltered by the country's own hard-line protectionism against manufactured imports, doesn't show much sympathy for the farmer's plight. "The rest of the community," says agricultural economist Ian McLean, "is not working as hard, is better rewarded and couldn't care less what happens to the farmer."

QUESTIONS

1. Do you think it is wise policy for New Zealand to protect its small industrial sector from foreign competition? Are there any arguments that might make this a sensible policy?

2. How are U.S. protectionist policies toward New Zealand affecting the American consumer?

3. What do you suppose are the possible reasons for the trade barriers erected by other countries against imports from New Zealand? Are any of these reasons justifiable as being in a country's best interests?

18

BALANCE OF PAYMENTS, EXCHANGE RATES, AND THE INTERNATIONAL FINANCIAL SYSTEM

DOLLAR'S WEAKNESS SEEN TO BE BEYOND EASY REMEDY

WASHINGTON, Sept. 18—The U.S. dollar's weakness on foreign exchange markets has emerged as a major concern of American economic policy makers. The problem won't be remedied easily or quickly say two important documents issued over the weekend: the annual report of the 134-nation International Monetary Fund and a policy paper on "The Floating Rate System" by the Atlantic Council, a private study group.

According to the IMF report, "Restoration of greater exchange rate stability probably awaits both the restoration of economic stability at the national level and a significant reduction of the existing large [imbalances]" in the international payments accounts of the leading industrial countries.

During the past year the dollar depreciated 17 percent against the West German mark, 32 percent against the Japanese yen, and 34 percent against the Swiss franc. Noting this fact, the Atlantic Council's international monetary affairs working group declared there is a need for "evidence that the adverse fundamental or basic factors are being corrected and that a better payments position (especially of the United States) is emerging." Indeed senior Carter administration officials echo this view, claiming that the dollar's decline has become a major consideration in economic policy making. According to one highly placed administration official, "The only real assurance of stability in the exchange markets in the future is to have a believable antiinflation policy that changes the psychology of those who look at the U.S. economy."

Both the Atlantic Council paper and the IMF report stressed that official intervention operations to prop up the dollar or any other currency can have only a limited effect, given differences in growth and inflation rates between countries. "While intervention may well have prevented exchange rates from fluctuating even more," the IMF said, "intervention alone hasn't been able to offset the other factors making for high volatility, and it isn't clear that it will be able to do so in the future, even if implemented on a larger scale."

In the previous chapter we focused on the real aspects of international trade. That is, we looked at the way in which nations can have a larger quantity of goods, or more real output, by specializing according to comparative advantage and trading with one another. But international trade also has a monetary aspect because goods are exchanged for money and each nation has its own unique money. For example, when Americans buy goods from Great Britain, they must pay for them with British money, or pounds. Similarly, when British citizens buy goods from the United States, they must pay for them with dollars. In short, every movement of goods and services between nations requires a financial transaction. The flow of goods and services in one direction requires a flow of money in the other.

In this chapter we will examine the different ways in which the international financial system may be organized to handle the financial transactions that accompany international trade. One of our main objectives is to be able to make sense out of the issues presented in a news item like the one at the beginning of this chapter. This will require that we become familiar with such concepts as the balance of payments, exchange rates and their determinants, and "official intervention operations." We also will examine why gold has often played an important role in international trade in the past, and how and why the present system of international financial arrangements evolved.

EXCHANGE AND THE BALANCE OF PAYMENTS

When Americans import goods and services from other nations, they must pay for these imports with foreign currencies, often called foreign exchange. For example, German marks must be paid for goods produced in Germany, French francs for goods produced in France, Japanese yen for goods from Japan, and British pounds for goods from Great Britain. Similarly, when Americans export goods to other nations, American suppliers want to be paid with dollars. Whatever the country, domestic producers selling goods abroad want to receive payment in domestic currency because that is what they must use to pay wages and all other factors employed in production. American workers don't want to be paid in French francs, nor do French workers want to be paid in dollars.

The fundamental point is this. If a nation wants to buy goods and services (imports) from other nations, it must somehow obtain the foreign currencies needed to make payment for these imports. Broadly speaking, the only way it can do this is to export some of its own goods and services to other nations and thereby earn the foreign currencies that it needs to pay for its imports. That is, to make payments for imports, a nation must use the payments received from exports—exports must finance imports. Hence, a nation's payments to other nations must be equal to, or balanced by, the payments received from other nations. It is in this sense that there is a balance of payments.

While basically correct, this is a very simplified description of how nations obtain foreign currrency. The nature of the balance of payments and the way it is calculated are also considerably more involved in reality. We need to look at currency exchange and the balance of payments in more detail.

Currency Exchange

Suppose an American firm wishes to buy a German machine. The German manufacturer ultimately will want to receive German marks from the sale of the machine. The American firm can go to its bank, buy the amount of marks needed to pay for the machine and send them to the German manufacturer. (The bank typically will charge the American firm a small fee for obtaining and providing the marks in exchange for dollars.) Alternatively, the American firm may pay the German manufacturer in dollars. The German manufacturer will then take the dollars to its own bank where it will exchange them for marks. Either way, dollars are exchanged for marks.

The **exchange rate** is the price of foreign currency. It is the amount of one currency that must be paid to obtain one unit of another currency. Suppose, in our example, that the exchange rate between U.S. dollars and German marks is $.50 for 1 mark. Equivalently, it may be said that 2 marks can be exchanged for $1. Suppose the price of the German machine is 100,000 marks. This means that the American firm will have to give its bank $50,000 in order to obtain the 100,000 marks needed to pay the German manufacturer. Alternatively, the American firm may give the German manufacturer $50,000. In that case, the German manufacturer will take the $50,000 to its own bank and exchange it for 100,000 marks. Either way the American firm pays $50,000 for the machine and the German manufacturer ultimately receives 100,000 marks.

Our example illustrates that *trade between nations requires the exchange of one nation's currency for that of another.* The American purchase of a German machine gives rise to a supply of dollars and a demand for marks. Similarly, a German purchase of an American product would give rise to a supply of marks and a demand for dollars. Hence, *international trade gives rise to the international supply and demand for national currencies, or a* **foreign exchange market**. *The exchange rates between different currencies are determined in the foreign exchange market.* We will investigate how foreign exchange rates are determined and what these rates mean for the balance of payments later in this chapter. First, however, we must become more familiar with the balance of payments concept.

Balance of Payments

The term **balance of payments** *means just what it says: a nation's total payments to other nations must be equal to, or balanced by, the total payments received from other nations.* When Americans supply dollars in foreign exchange markets, they are demanding foreign currencies in order to make payments to other nations. The currencies Americans receive in exchange for their dollars are supplied by foreigners who demand dollars in order to make payments to the United States. Every dollar sold must be bought, and every dollar bought must be sold.

After reading this chapter, you will be able to:

1. Explain the balance of payments concept and describe the major components of the balance of payments accounts.
2. Describe a balance of payments deficit and a balance of payments surplus.
3. Explain how flexible exchange rates eliminate balance of payments deficits and surpluses.
4. Describe how balance of payments adjustments are made under a system of fixed exchange rates.
5. Give the major arguments in the flexible-versus-fixed-exchange-rate debate.
6. Explain how a gold standard works.
7. Describe the Bretton Woods system and why it has been replaced by a mixed system of flexible exchange rates and managed floats.

Hence, U.S. payments to other nations must be matched exactly by payments from other nations to the United States.

We have already seen how nations keep national income accounts in order to measure domestic economic activity (Chapter 5). Similarly, nations also keep balance of payments accounts in order to keep track of their economic transactions with other nations. *A nation's* **balance of payments account** *records all the payments that it makes to other nations, as well as all the payments that it receives from other nations during the course of a year.* The total volume of payments made to other nations is exactly equal to the total volume of payments received from other nations.

The balance of payments account breaks down the nation's payments to other nations into the following categories: the amount spent on foreign goods; the amount spent on foreign services; the amount loaned to foreign businesses, households, and governments; and the amount invested abroad. Similarly, the account breaks down the payments received from other nations to show: the amount of foreign purchases of the nation's goods; the amount of foreign purchases of the nation's services; the amount of foreign lending to the nation's businesses, households, and government; and the amount of foreign investment in the nation. While the total volume of a nation's payments to other nations must always equal the total volume of payments received from other nations, individual categories in the balance of payments accounts need not and typically do not balance. For example, in any given year Americans may export a larger dollar volume of goods than they import, or buy more services from foreigners than are sold to foreigners.

The balance of payments account for the United States is shown in Table 18-1. International transactions that give rise to payments to other nations are recorded as debit items (designated by a minus sign) in the balance of payments account. Such transactions supply dollars to the foreign exchange market and create a demand for foreign currency because Americans must sell dollars to obtain foreign currency. The

import of a good is an example of a debit item. (Recall our example of an American business importing a German machine, which gave rise to a supply of dollars and demand for marks.) Transactions that give rise to payments to the United States from other nations are recorded as credit items in the balance of payments account. Such transactions supply foreign currency to the foreign exchange market and create a demand for dollars because foreigners must sell their currency to obtain dollars. The export of a good is an example of a credit item.

The credit and debit items in the balance of payments account are broadly divided into a current account and a capital account.

THE CURRENT ACCOUNT

The balance of payments on current account includes all payments received during the current period for the export of goods and services and all payments made during the current period for the import of goods and services.

Imports and Exports of Goods—Visibles. The largest portion of the current account is represented by merchandise imports and exports in row 1 of Table 18-1. These are the imports and exports of goods—the so-called visible items such as steel, wheat, tv sets, cars, and all the other objects that can be seen and felt. In 1978 the United States imported $176 billion of such merchandise and exported $141.8 billion. The difference between merchandise exports and merchandise imports is called the **balance of trade**. *When merchandise exports exceed imports, the nation has a balance of trade surplus. When imports exceed exports, the nation has a balance of trade deficit.*

In 1978 the United States had a balance of trade deficit of $34.2 billion ($141.8 billion of exports minus $176 billion of imports). As noted before, there is no particular reason why individual categories of a nation's balance of payments should in fact balance. However, when a nation has an overall balance of trade deficit, it is often said to have an unfavorable balance of trade. The balance is unfavorable in the sense that the nation is earning less from its merchan-

TABLE 18-1 UNITED STATES BALANCE OF PAYMENTS, 1978

Debits (−)		Credits			
U.S. Payments to Other Nations (in Billions of Dollars)		U.S. Receipts from Other Nations (in Billions of Dollars)		Balance (in Billions of Dollars)	
Current Account		**Current Account**			
(1) Merchandise imports	−$176.0	Merchandise exports	$141.8	Balance of trade	−$34.2
(2) Military spending	−7.2	Military sales	7.7		
(3) Income on foreign investment in United States	−21.6	Receipts of income on U.S. assets abroad	41.5		
(4) Services	−24.1	Services	26.9		
Unilateral transfers					
(5) Private	−2.0				
(6) U.S. government	−3.0				
(7) Imports of goods and services	−$233.9	Exports of goods and services	$217.9	Balance on current account	−$16.0
Capital Account		**Capital Account**			
(8) Change in U.S. assets abroad	−55.0	Change in foreign assets in U.S.	29.3	Balance on private capital account	−$25.7
(9) Change in U.S. govt. assets	−3.7	Change in foreign official assets	34.0	Balance on govt. capital account	$30.3
(10) Imports of capital	−$58.7	Exports of capital	$ 63.3	Balance on capital account	$ 4.6
(11)				Errors and omissions	$11.4
(12)		Row 7 plus row 10 plus row 11 =		Balance	$ 0.0

SOURCE: *Survey of Current Business*, April 1979.

dise exports than it is spending on its merchandise imports—exports of goods do not entirely finance imports of goods. However, it is not clear that it is unfavorable for a nation to get more goods from other nations than it gives in return. Besides, other categories in a nation's balance of payments will necessarily offset a balance of trade deficit because overall the balance of payments must balance. Similar observations may be made about a so-called favorable balance of trade, a balance of trade surplus.

Imports and Exports of Services—Invisibles. The import and export of services, or so-called invisibles, is another sizeable component of the current account. For example, Americans pay for tickets to fly on foreign airlines and pay foreign shippers to carry cargo. They also buy meals and pay for hotel rooms when traveling abroad and pay premiums for insurance provided by foreign insurance companies. All of these transactions are examples of imports of services. Like the payments for imported goods, payments for imported services give rise to a supply of dollars in the foreign exchange market and a demand for foreign currencies because foreigners want to be paid in their own currencies. Similarly, Americans also export services to foreigners. Like the export of goods, the export of services gives rise to a supply of foreign currencies in the foreign exchange market and a demand for dollars.

Like services, income from foreign investment in the United States is another invisible item on the current account. Such income consists of the payment of interest and dividends on American bonds (both government and private) and stocks held by foreigners, as well as the income earned by foreign-owned businesses on American soil. It can be thought of as payment for the import of the services of the financial capital provided by foreigners to American government and industry. Such payments give rise to a supply of dollars and a demand for foreign currencies in the foreign exchange market. Similarly, receipts of income on U.S. assets abroad represent payments received by Americans (government, firms, and households) for the services of capital exported to other nations. These payments to Americans give rise to a supply of foreign currencies and a demand for dollars in the foreign exchange market.

Table 18-1, row 4, indicates that the United States purchased slightly fewer services from other nations than it sold to them in 1978. Row 3 shows that payments to other nations for the services of foreign capital were about half as large as the payments received by Americans for providing capital to other nations.

Other Current Account Items. Military spending abroad by the United States, row 2, includes payments to other nations for both goods and services. Military sales to other nations represent payments received from other nations for military goods and services provided by the United States. These two items were almost balanced in 1978.

Unilateral transfers represent payments made to another nation for which nothing is received in exchange. Private unilateral transfers are gifts given by Americans to foreigners. Government unilateral transfers consist of foreign aid. It is a convention of balance of payments accounting that such gifts are recorded as credit items under merchandise exports, just as if goods had been sold abroad. A balancing entry is made under unilateral transfers.

Balance on Current Account. Row 7 shows that the total of the debit items on current account (− \$233.9 billion) was greater than the total of the credit items (\$217.9 billion) in 1978. In other words, the total payments made by the United States to other nations on current account exceeded the total payments made by other nations to the United States. On current account the United States supplied more dollars to the foreign exchange market than other nations demanded. Or equivalently, the United States demanded more foreign currency (to pay other nations) than other nations supplied (to get dollars to pay the United States). In short, on current account, payments received from other nations are not sufficient to finance U.S. payments to other nations. The deficit on current account amounted to − \$16 billion dollars in 1978.

THE CAPITAL ACCOUNT

There is no reason why there has to be a balance of payments on current account any more than there is a reason why merchandise imports should exactly equal merchandise exports. The current account is itself just a part of the balance of payments. Overall, however, the balance of payments must balance. Since the balance of payments is divided into the current account and the capital account, it follows that *if there is a deficit on current account, there must be a compensating surplus on capital account. Likewise, if there is a surplus on current account, there must be a compensating deficit on capital account.*

For example, if there is an excess of payments over receipts on current account (a deficit), then there must be a matching excess of receipts over payments on capital account (a surplus). That is, if more foreign currency is spent (in payments to other nations) than is earned (in payments from other nations) on current account, the difference must come from an excess of foreign currency earned over foreign currency spent on capital account. Alternatively, an excess of receipts over payments on current account (a surplus) must be matched by an excess of payments over receipts on capital account (a deficit). In that case, less foreign currency is spent than is earned on current account, and the surplus matches the deficit on capital account where more foreign currency is spent than is. earned.

Since the balance of payments is divided into the current account and the capital account, the capital account includes all international transactions not included in the current account. Specifically, the capital account includes all purchases and sales of assets, or what is termed capital.

Private Imports and Exports of Capital. When American businesses and households invest and lend abroad (to foreign businesses, households, and governments), they receive IOUs from foreigners in the form of stocks, bonds, and other debt claims and titles of ownership. Such investments and loans are entered as debit items in the capital account. They represent an increase in American ownership of foreign assets. For example, in 1978 American households and businesses invested and loaned $55 billion dollars abroad (Table 18-1, row 8). Why are such transactions recorded as a debit item, just like a merchandise import? There are two basic reasons. First, these transactions represent a payment to other nations. Second, they give rise to a supply of dollars in the foreign exchange market and a demand for the foreign currencies Americans need in order to pay for foreign stocks and bonds. Moreover, you can think of Americans importing stock certificates and bonds, just like they import merchandise. Both types of payment represent the acquisition of a claim of ownership or property right from a foreign nation.

Similarly, foreign businesses and households

also invest and make loans in the United States (to American businesses, households, and governments) for which they receive American stocks and bonds. These represent an increase in foreign ownership of American assets and are entered as credit items in the capital account. Such transactions give rise to a supply of foreign currencies in the foreign exchange market and a demand for dollars needed by foreigners to make payment for their investments and loans in the United States. In exchange the United States may be thought of as exporting stock certificates and bonds—that is, exporting property rights and ownership claims. Such transactions amounted to $29.3 billion in 1978 (Table 18-1, row 8).

In 1978 the United States had a deficit on its private capital account equal to $29.3 billion minus $55 billion, or −$25.7 billion (Table 18-1, row 8). This deficit on private capital account added to the deficit on current account (row 7) amounted to $41.7 billion. How were these deficits financed (or paid for) so that the balance of payments balanced? For the answer, we need to consider the government capital account.

Government Imports and Exports of Capital. Governments also make capital account transactions. These consist mostly of loans to or from other governments; changes in government holdings of official international reserve assets such as foreign currencies, gold, and reserves with the International Monetary Fund called Special Drawing Rights or SDRs (which we will discuss later); and changes in liquid claims on official reserve assets.

Loans to other governments are debit items on the government's capital account because they represent payments to other nations for the import of their IOUs, just like lending on the private capital account. Such lending gives rise to a supply of dollars and a demand for foreign currency in the foreign exchange market. Similarly, foreign governments make loans to the U.S. government. These are recorded as credit items on the government's capital account because they represent payments received from other nations in exchange for the export of U.S.

government's IOUs (such as U.S. government bonds and Treasury bills). Such transactions create a supply of foreign currency and a demand for dollars in the foreign exchange market.

The government capital account transactions in official reserve assets and liquid claims on official reserve assets play an accommodating role in the balance of payments. They adjust to satisfy the requirement that overall the balance of payments must balance. Therefore, they adjust because the total amount of foreign currency needed to make all payments to other nations *must* necessarily equal the total amount of foreign currency earned from all payments received from other nations.

For example, suppose there is a deficit on current account, a deficit on private capital account, and loans to foreign governments exceed loans received from them. The volume of foreign currency earned from other nations will be less than the volume of foreign currency paid to them. The difference will have to be made up either by using government holdings of official reserve assets or by giving other nations liquid claims on the government's holdings of official reserve assets. Payments out of holdings of reserve assets will, of course, reduce government holdings. Such payments are entered as a credit item on the government's capital account because they represent the export of official reserves (foreign currency, gold, or SDRs). Similarly, making payments by giving other nations liquid claims on holdings of official reserves is also a credit item. This item represents the export of an IOU, the liquid claim. The nation receiving the liquid claim may "cash it in" at any time (hence the term *liquid*) by demanding payment in official reserve assets.

Overall Balance. As already noted, in 1978 the U.S. deficit on current account (Table 18-1, row 7) plus the deficit on private capital account (row 8) totaled $41.7 billion. This deficit had to be matched by a surplus on the government capital account to give an overall balance of payments. However, we see from row 9 of Table 18-1 that the surplus on government capital account amounted to only $30.3 billion. Hence, the overall surplus on capital account (the sum of the private and government accounts, row 8 plus row 9) is $4.6 billion (row 10), which is less than the amount needed to match the $16 billion deficit on current account (row 7). The difference is due to errors and omissions amounting to $11.4 billion (row 11). These are errors in data collection and the government's inability to keep track of virtually all U.S. transactions with other nations. Taking these into account, the balance of payments balances (row 12), as it must.

Balance of Payments Deficits and Surpluses

In the news we often hear or read about this or that nation's balance of payments deficit or surplus. But if the balance of payments must balance, why the talk about deficits and surpluses? Sometimes commentators are referring to the balance of trade, row 1 of Table 18-1. (To avoid confusion, they should say so explicitly.) In general, however, such references are made with respect to the balance of payments *excluding* government capital account transactions in official reserve assets (foreign currency, gold, and SDRs) and liquid claims against these reserves.

Given this interpretation, a **balance of payments deficit** means that the government is reducing its holdings of official reserves assets or that the liquid claims of foreign governments against these reserves are increasing, or both. The deficit equals the excess of the nation's payments to other nations over the payments received from other nations, exclusive of government capital account transactions in official reserves and liquid claims. A **balance of payments surplus** means the government is increasing its holding of official reserves or its holdings of liquid claims on the official reserve assets held by foreign governments, or both. The surplus equals the excess of the payments received from other nations over the payments made to them, again exclusive of government capital account transactions in official reserves and liquid claims.

The news item at the beginning of this chapter is not entirely clear on what is meant by "imbalance in the international payments accounts of the leading industrial countries." But as we shall see later in this chapter, it will make sense to suppose that "imbalance" refers to deficits and surpluses as we have just defined them.

■ CHECKPOINT 18-1

Explain how you would classify the following international transactions on the balance of payments account, and why each is a credit or a debit item: as an American citizen you get a haircut in France; you give a birthday present to a cousin in Canada; you buy a Volkswagen and finance payments on it with a loan made to you by an American bank (instead, suppose you finance it with a loan made to you by Volkswagen); the government buys French francs and finances the purchase with a liquid claim.

EXCHANGE RATES AND BALANCE OF PAYMENTS ADJUSTMENTS

The size of balance of payments deficits and surpluses, as well as the adjustment process for their elimination, depends on the role which exchange rates are allowed to play in international transactions. At one extreme, exchange rates between national currencies can be freely determined by the forces of supply and demand in the foreign exchange market. At the other extreme, exchange rates can be rigidly fixed by government intervention in the foreign exchange market. We will now examine each of these extremes.

Flexible Exchange Rates

When exchange rates between national currencies are freely determined by supply and demand in the foreign exchange market, they are said to be **flexible (or floating) exchange rates**. They are free to change in response to shifts in supply and demand.

CURRENCY DEPRECIATION AND APPRECIATION

When the exchange rate between dollars and a foreign currency increases, the foreign currency gets more expensive in terms of dollars—it takes more dollars, or cents, to buy a unit of

foreign currency. Since this is the same thing as saying that a dollar will buy less foreign currency, we say that the value of the dollar has *depreciated* relative to the foreign currency. **Currency depreciation** *means that now more units of a nation's currency will be required to buy a unit of foreign currency.*

Conversely, if the exchange rate between dollars and a foreign currency decreases, it takes fewer dollars, or cents, to buy a unit of foreign currency. Since a dollar will now buy more foreign currency, the value of the dollar is said to have *appreciated* relative to the foreign currency. **Currency appreciation** *means that now less units of a nation's currency are required to buy a unit of a foreign currency.*

Note that *an appreciation in the value of one nation's currency is necessarily a depreciation in another's.* For example, suppose the rate of exchange between dollars and French francs is initially $1 per franc. Suppose the value of the dollar appreciates relative to the franc. For instance, say the rate of exchange decreases to $.50 per franc. It now takes half as many dollars to buy a franc. For French citizens this means the rate of exchange has risen from 1 franc per dollar to 2 francs per dollar. In other words, the value of the franc has depreciated relative to the dollar. It now takes twice as many francs to buy a dollar.

EXCHANGE RATES AND THE PRICE OF FOREIGN GOODS

Exchange rates allow citizens in one country to translate the prices of foreign goods and services into units of their own currency. Suppose $1 exchanges for 4 French francs on the foreign exchange market. If the price of a French-made car is 20,000 francs, its price in dollars is $5,000, or 20,000 multiplied by .25. Similarly, if the price of a ton of American wheat is $30, its price in francs is 120 francs, or 30 multiplied by 4.

Changes in exchange rates alter the prices of foreign goods to domestic buyers and the prices of domestic goods to foreign buyers. Suppose in the above example that the dollar depreciates so that $1 will now only exchange for 3 francs on the foreign exchange market. Now the French-made car selling for 20,000 francs will be more expensive for an American. It will cost $6,666 (.33 × 20,000). On the other hand, a ton of American wheat selling for $30 will be less expensive to a French citizen because the depreciation of the dollar means an appreciation of the franc. The ton of wheat will now cost a French buyer 90 francs (3 × 30).

FREE-MARKET DETERMINATION OF THE EXCHANGE RATE

In Chapter 4 we saw how supply and demand work in a freely operating market (one in which the government does not intervene) to determine the price of a good. The exchange rate is just the price of one currency stated in terms of another. And the determination of the equilibrium level of a flexible, or floating, exchange rate is determined by supply and demand just like the price of wheat or shoeshines.

For example, suppose the United States and France were the only two trading countries in the world. And suppose that the exchange rate between dollars and French francs is determined by supply and demand in the foreign exchange market as shown in Figure 18-1. (Our example uses hypothetical data.) The vertical axis measures the exchange rate, the price of a franc in terms of dollars. The horizontal axis measures the quantity of francs. The equilibrium level of the exchange rate is $.25 per franc, which corresponds to the intersection of the supply curve S and the demand curve D at point e.

The demand curve D shows the quantity of francs demanded by Americans at each possible level of the exchange rate. It comes from the desire on the part of Americans to exchange dollars for francs. The francs are needed to buy French goods and services and to pay interest and dividends on French loans and investments in the United States. They are also needed to make American military expenditures in France, to make unilateral transfers such as gifts and foreign aid grants, and to pay for the American acquisition (by government, businesses, and private citizens) of French assets. In short, the demand curve D represents the

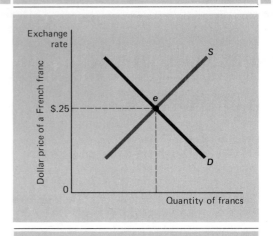

FIGURE 18-1 DETERMINATION OF THE EQUILIBRIUM LEVEL OF A FLEXIBLE EXCHANGE RATE

Underlying the demand curve D for French francs is the desire of Americans to exchange dollars for francs needed to buy French goods and services and to acquire French assets. Similarly, behind the supply curve S for francs is the desire of French citizens to exchange francs for dollars needed to buy American goods and services and to acquire American assets.

The equilibrium level of the exchange rate is $.25 per franc, determined by the intersection of the demand curve D and supply curve S at point e. If the exchange rate is less than $.25 per franc, the demand for francs in the foreign exchange market will exceed the supply and the rate will be bid up. If the exchange rate is greater than $.25 per franc, the supply of francs in the foreign exchange market will exceed the demand and the rate will be bid down.

American demand for francs needed to make payments to France—all the transactions with France that enter as debit items on the U.S. balance of payments account.

The supply curve S shows the quantity of francs supplied by French citizens at each possible level of the exchange rate. Underlying it are the desire of the French to exchange francs for dollars needed to pay for American goods and services and the French acquisition of American assets. These payments are represented by all the credit items on the U.S. balance of payments account.

The supply and demand curves have the usual slopes. If the exchange rate were below the equilibrium level, the quantity of francs demanded would exceed the quantity supplied, and the exchange rate (the price of a franc) would be bid up. If the exchange rate were above the equilibrium level, the quantity of francs supplied would exceed the quantity demanded, and the rate would be bid down. At the equilibrium exchange rate, there is no tendency for the rate to change because the quantity of francs demanded is just equal to the quantity supplied.

Flexible Exchange Rates and the Balance of Payments

The argument for flexible exchange rates is that they automatically adjust to eliminate balance of payments surpluses and deficits. Let's see how this happens.

The equilibrium in the foreign exchange market of Figure 18-1 (represented by the intersection of D and S at point e) is reproduced in Figre 18-2. In equilibrium there is no balance of payments deficit or surplus as we have defined these concepts. That is, there are no government capital account transactions in official reserves and liquid claims between the two nations. Moreover, the total of all other U.S. payments to France is exactly equal to the total of all payments received by the United States from France.

Now suppose Americans step up their imports of French goods (say because more Americans develop a taste for French wines and other French goods). Total payments to France will now exceed total payments received from France. American demand for francs needed to make these payments will increase, as represented by the rightward shift in the demand curve for francs from D to D' in Figure 18-2. At the initial exchange rate of $.25 per franc, there will now be a shortage of francs. Equivalently, we

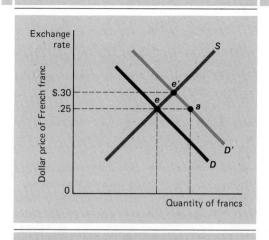

FIGURE 18-2 ADJUSTMENT OF A FLEXIBLE EXCHANGE RATE TO ELIMINATE A BALANCE OF PAYMENTS DEFICIT

An increase in American imports of French goods will cause the demand curve for francs to shift from D to D' because Americans now need more francs to make payments to France. At the initial exchange rate of $.25 per franc, the United States will have a balance of payments deficit. With a flexible exchange rate the excess demand for francs, equal to the distance between points e and a, will cause the rate to be bid up. The rise in the exchange rate will make French goods more expensive to Americans and American goods cheaper for French citizens. Therefore, American imports of French goods will decline, and French imports of American goods will rise. This adjustment will continue until the exchange rate has risen to the new equilibrium level of $.30 per franc (corresponding to the intersection of S and D' at point e'). At this point, the U.S. balance of payments deficit will be eliminated.

can say there will be an excess demand for francs equal to the distance between points e and a. The United States will now have a balance of payments deficit.

How will a flexible exchange rate eliminate this deficit? The excess demand for francs will cause the exchange rate, the dollar price of francs, to be bid up. But this will alter the prices of *all* French goods to Americans and the prices of all American goods to French citizens in the way we discussed earlier. Since Americans will now have to pay more for francs, the prices of French goods will now be higher when translated into dollars. Therefore, as the exchange rate is bid up, French goods will become more expensive for American buyers, and American imports will tend to decline. This decline is represented by a move from point *a* toward point *e'* along *D'* in Figure 18-2.

But a rise in the dollar price of francs is the same thing as a fall in the franc price of dollars. (The dollar depreciates relative to the franc, and the franc appreciates relative to the dollar.) French citizens will now find that they don't have to pay as much for dollars. The prices of American goods will therefore be lower when translated into francs. Since American goods are now less expensive for French citizens, French imports will tend to increase. This increase is represented by a move from point *e* toward point *e'* along *S* in Figure 18-2.

Hence, as the exchange rate rises to the new equilibrium position corresponding to *e'*, an exchange rate of \$.30 per franc, American imports from France decline while American exports to France increase. The result will be to eliminate the balance of payments deficit in the United States. In sum, *when exchange rates are flexible, or freely determined by supply and demand, balance of payments deficits and surpluses will be quickly eliminated. Indeed, it is often argued that foreign exchange markets adjust so quickly that there would be no deficits or surpluses if governments didn't interfere.* (Later in this chapter we will see how governments interfere with the mechanism.)

Factors Affecting Flexible Exchange Rates

We have just seen how a change in one nation's demand for the products of another can affect the exchange rate. Other factors can also cause shifts in supply and demand in foreign exchange markets and, hence, changes in flexible or floating exchange rates. Two of the more important factors in supply and demand are differences in rates of inflation between nations and changes in the level of interest rates in one nation relative to the interest rates in others.

DIFFERENCES IN RATES OF INFLATION

Assume again that the equilibrium exchange rate between dollars and francs is \$.25 per franc, determined by the intersection of *D* and *S* at point *e* in Figure 18-3. Now suppose the general price level in the United States (the prices of all American products) rises relative to the general price level in France (due to an expansionary American fiscal and monetary policy, say). As a result, French goods become less expensive relative to American goods, *given the exchange rate of \$.25 per franc.* Hence, Americans increase their demand for imports from France, thereby causing their demand for francs to increase, as indicated by the rightward shift in the demand curve for francs from *D* to *D'*. At the same time, the rise in the American price level causes French citizens to reduce their demand for American goods. This results in a reduction of their supply of francs (their demand for dollars), indicated by a leftward shift of the supply curve of francs from *S* to *S'*.

At the initial exchange rate of \$.25 per franc, there is now an excess demand for francs equal to the distance between points *a* and *b*. This excess demand will cause the exchange rate to be bid up from \$.25 per franc to \$.35 per franc, corresponding to the intersection of *S* and *D* at point *f*, Figure 18-3. The American demand for French imports will be cut back and the French demand for American goods will increase in exactly the manner already described in connection with Figure 18-2. In short, the rise in the general price level of American goods relative to French goods causes a depreciation of the dollar relative to the franc in the foreign exchange market.

Our hypothetical example illustrates a general observation about exchange rate movements in the real world. *Given a sufficient length of time, the exchange rate between the nations' currencies will tend to adjust to reflect changes in their price levels, all other things remaining the*

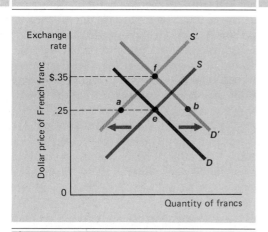

FIGURE 18-3 DIFFERENTIAL CHANGES IN THE PRICE LEVELS OF TWO NATIONS CAUSE THE EXCHANGE RATE TO CHANGE

The rise in the general price level of American goods relative to French goods causes a depreciation of the dollar relative to the franc in the foreign exchange market.

When the general price level in the United States rises relative to the general price level in France, French goods become less expensive relative to American goods. Hence, at the initial exchange rate of $.25 per franc American demand for French imports increases while French citizens reduce their demand for American goods. The demand curve for francs therefore shifts rightward from *D* to *D'* while the supply curve for francs shifts leftward from *S* to *S'*. The resulting excess demand for francs (equal to the distance between points *a* and *b*) causes the exchange rate to be bid up to $.35 per franc. This depreciation of the dollar relative to the franc cuts back the American demand for French imports and increases French demand for American goods in exactly the manner described in connection with Figure 18–2.

same. Of course, all other things typically do not remain the same. Hence, it is usually difficult to observe real-world adjustments that are as clear-cut as our hypothetical example.

The process of exchange rate adjustment due to differential changes in national price levels operates continuously when two nations experience different rates of inflation. *If two nations are each experiencing the same rate of inflation, the relation between their general price levels remains the same. The exchange rate between their currencies will therefore remain unchanged, all other things remaining the same. However, if a nation's rate of inflation is greater than that of a trading partner, the nation with the higher inflation rate will experience an increase in its exchange rate—a depreciation of its currency—all other things remaining the same.* For instance, in our example of the United States and France, suppose the American price level continued to rise relative to that of France. Then the rate of exchange between the dollar and the franc would continue to rise. The dollar would continue to depreciate relative to the franc.

CHANGES IN INTEREST RATES

In our discussion of the capital account of the balance of payments, we observed that money is loaned and borrowed across national borders. Some of these funds are moved around the globe almost continually in search of those highly liquid financial assets (such as short-term government bonds and commercial paper) that pay the highest interest rates. When the interest rates prevailing in one country change relative to those prevailing in another, funds tend to flow toward that country where interest rates are now highest, all other things remaining the same.

For example, suppose the interest rate on U.S. Treasury bills is 7 percent, the same as that on comparable short-term French government bonds. If the interest rate on Treasury bills suddenly drops to 6.5 percent (due to Federal Reserve open market purchases, say), short-term French government bonds paying 7 percent interest will look relatively more attractive to American investors. They will therefore increase their demand for francs in order to buy more French bonds. The demand curve for francs will shift rightward, just as in Figure 18–3. Similarly, French investors will reduce the supply of francs since Treasury bills will also be relatively less attractive to them. Hence, the supply curve for francs will shift leftward, again as in Figure 18-3. The result will be a rise in the exchange rate of dollars for francs, a depreciation of the dollar relative to the franc.

Since funds can be quickly transferred between countries, changes in the relative levels of interest rates between countries are a primary cause of day-to-day changes in flexible, or floating, exchange rates.

■CHECKPOINT 18-2

When one currency depreciates, why does another necessarily appreciate? In what sense is the supply curve in Figure 18-1 a demand curve for dollars, and the demand curve a supply curve of dollars? What would happen to the exchange rate of dollars for pounds if American authorities started to pursue a more expansionary monetary policy, all other things remaining the same? Why? What do you think would happen to the exchange rate of dollars for pounds if British authorities started to pursue a more restrictive fiscal policy, all other things remaining the same? Why?

Fixed Exchange Rates and the Balance of Payments

Governments have often chosen to fix or "peg" exchange rates, just the opposite of allowing the forces of supply and demand to freely determine rates in the foreign exchange market. *In order to fix the exchange rate at a level above, or below, the equilibrium level determined by supply and demand, governments must continually intervene in the foreign exchange market.* Let's see why this is so, and how governments must intervene.

FIXING THE RATE ABOVE EQUILIBRIUM

Consider the supply and demand for francs in Figure 18-4, part a. If the exchange rate were flexible, or floating, it would be equal to the equilibrium rate of $.25 per franc, as determined by the intersection of the demand curve D and supply curve S at point e. However, suppose the French government wants to fix, or peg, the exchange rate at $.30 per franc. At this

price the quantity of francs demanded by Americans in order to make payments to France equals Q_d, corresponding to point d on D. The quantity of francs supplied by French citizens in order to get dollars to make payments to the United States equals Q_s, corresponding to point s on S. The quantity of francs supplied exceeds the quantity demanded—payments by France to the United States are greater than payments by the United States to France. Therefore, France has a balance of payments deficit represented by the distance between points d and s (also equal to Q_s minus Q_d).

But what will keep market forces from bidding the exchange rate down to the equilibrium level at point e? The French government must buy up the excess supply of francs (equal to the distance between d and s) at a price of $.30 per franc using dollars out of its holdings of official reserve assets (foreign currencies, gold, and SDRs). The French government will be able to continue fixing the exchange rate above the equilibrium level only as long as it has reserves of dollars. Once it runs out, the exchange will fall to the equilibrium level of $.25 per franc. When the price of a currency (the exchange rate) is pegged above the equilibrium level that would prevail in a free market, the currency is often said to be overvalued. In this case the franc is overvalued relative to the dollar.

FIXING THE RATE BELOW EQUILIBRIUM

Now consider the opposite case, in which the exchange rate is fixed below the equilibrium level—the franc is undervalued relative to the dollar. For example, suppose the French government wants to peg the exchange rate at $.20 per franc, as illustrated in Figure 18-4, part b. In this case the quantity of francs demanded by Americans Q_d (corresponding to point d on D) exceeds the quantity supplied by French citizens Q_s (corresponding to point s on S). Payments by France to the United States are now less than payments by the United States to France. France now has a balance of payments surplus equal to the distance between points s and d.

How will the French government keep the excess demand for francs from bidding up the ex-

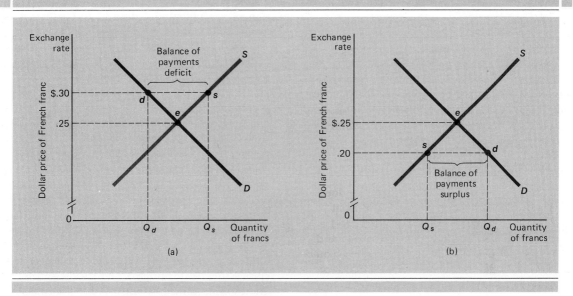

**FIGURE 18-4 FIXED EXCHANGE RATES:
BALANCE OF PAYMENTS DEFICITS AND SURPLUSES**

The equilibrium level of the exchange rate between dollars and francs would be $.25 per franc (the intersection at point e of the supply and demand curves for francs) if the forces of supply and demand were allowed to operate freely.

However, suppose the French government wants to fix, or peg, the exchange rate above the equilibrium level at $.30 per franc, as shown in part a. Then it will have a balance of payments deficit equal to the excess supply of francs, represented by the distance between points d and s. In order to maintain the exchange rate at $.30 per franc, the French government will have to buy up the excess supply of francs using dollars out of its holdings of official reserves.

Alternatively, suppose the French government wants to fix the exchange rate below the equilibrium level at $.20 per franc, as shown in part b. Then it will have a balance of payments surplus equal to the excess demand for francs, represented by the distance between points s and d. In order to maintain the exchange rate at $.20 per franc, the French government will have to supply the foreign exchange market with a quantity of francs equal to the excess demand.

change rate to the equilibrium level at point e? It will have to supply the foreign exchange market with a quantity of francs equal to the excess demand (the distance between points s and d). In exchange for these francs the French government will acquire dollars which will increase its holdings of official reserves.

**Policy Implications
of Fixed Exchange Rates**

It generally is easier for a government to keep its currency undervalued (the exchange rate is *pegged below the equilibrium level) than to keep it overvalued (the exchange rate is pegged above the equilibrium level).* As we have seen, a government must draw down its reserves of foreign currencies in order to keep its currency overvalued. Obviously, it can't do this indefinitely or it will run out of such reserves. It may be able to borrow more from other nations, but again not indefinitely. By contrast, in order to keep its currency undervalued, a government only has to supply its own currency to the foreign exchange market. And, as discussed in previous chapters, a government has unlimited capacity to do this.

OVERVALUED VERSUS UNDERVALUED CURRENCIES

Clearly, it is easier to keep currencies undervalued than to keep them overvalued. What are the policy implications of this fact? Suppose all nations are trading under a system of flexible exchange rates so that there are no balance of payments deficits or surpluses. Now suppose they all agree to fix exchange rates at currently prevailing levels. As time passes supply and demand curves in foreign exchange markets inevitably shift due to changing trade patterns and differing economic developments within each nation. Since exchange rates are fixed, some nations end up with overvalued currencies and balance of payments deficits while others have undervalued currencies and balance of payments surpluses.

Nations with overvalued currencies and payments deficits must do something to correct their situation or they will run out of official reserves. By contrast, those with undervalued currencies and payments surpluses are not under this pressure—they need only keep supplying their own currency to the foreign exchange market. Hence, to eliminate its payments deficits and preserve its reserve holdings, a nation with an overvalued currency is often forced to allow its currency to depreciate. In a world of fixed exchange rates, this is called a **currency devaluation**—the exchange rate is now fixed at a lower level. Of course, the problem could also be cured if nations with undervalued currencies allowed their currencies to appreciate, called a **currency revaluation** in a world of fixed exchange rates. Obviously, if one currency is overvalued, another must be undervalued. But the pressure on the nation with the overvalued currency to devalue is simply greater than that on the nation with the undervalued currency to revalue.

BIAS TOWARD CONTRACTIONARY FISCAL AND MONETARY POLICY

Unfortunately, devaluing a nation's overvalued currency is not a politically popular thing for the government in office. It is often seen as a sign of a weakening economy and a loss of international stature. Similarly, a nation with an undervalued currency faces political obstacles to revaluation because sales abroad by its export industries benefit when its currency is underpriced in the foreign exchange market.

But the nation with the overvalued currency and the balance of payments deficit must do something to avoid running out of official reserves. One possibility is to pursue a contractionary fiscal and monetary policy, thereby curbing total demand. As we saw in the previous chapter, this also will tend to reduce the nation's demand for imports. And a reduction in imports will help to reduce its balance of payments deficit. Unfortunately, however, curbing total demand will also increase the nation's unemployment rate and reduce its total output. Its domestic policy goals will have to be sacrificed to its international policy goal of reducing its payments deficit.

Of course, another possibility is for the nations with undervalued currencies and payments surpluses to pursue expansionary fiscal and monetary policies. Such a nation's total demand would rise causing an increase in its imports from the nations with overvalued currencies and payments deficits. Unfortunately, this might cause unacceptable inflationary pressures in the expanding nation. Such a nation is likely to be very reluctant to sacrifice its own domestic price stability for the sake of reducing another nation's balance of payments deficit, especially since this will reduce its own payments surplus as well. Consequently, the burden usually falls on the nation with the overvalued currency (the one running out of official reserves) to pursue contractionary fiscal and monetary policy in order to reduce its payments deficit. Hence, *many critics of a fixed exchange rate system contend that it is biased toward enforcing contractionary fiscal and monetary policies on nations with overvalued currencies and chronic balance of payments deficits. As a result, they claim worldwide unemployment rates are higher and worldwide output levels lower under such a system.*

Finally, what if a nation with an overvalued currency and a payments deficit is neither willing to devalue nor to curb total demand with restrictive fiscal and monetary policy? Such a nation may simply erect tariffs and other trade barriers to curb its imports. In that event everybody loses, as we saw in the previous chapter.

Flexible Versus Fixed Exchange Rates

Which is to be preferred, a system of flexible exchange rates or a system of fixed exchange rates?

FISCAL AND MONETARY POLICY CONSIDERATIONS

Under a system of fixed exchange rates nations will run balance of payments deficits and surpluses because exchange rates cannot automatically adjust to equalize supply and demand in the foreign exchange markets. As we have just seen, nations with chronic balance of payments deficits may have to sacrifice high employment in order to reduce their payments deficits. Hence, critics argue that fixed exchange rates interfere with a nation's freedom to use fiscal and monetary policy to pursue domestic policy goals. These same critics often advocate flexible exchange rates because they automatically eliminate balance of payments problems, thus freeing fiscal and monetary policy to focus strictly on domestic objectives. However, some advocates of fixed exchange rates argue just the opposite. They claim that the fear of running large balance of payments deficits serves as a check on governments that might otherwise pursue excessively expansionary fiscal and monetary policies that cause inflation.

STABILITY AND UNCERTAINTY

Critics contend that flexible exchange rates inhibit international trade because of the uncertainty about their future levels. For example, suppose an American woolens wholesaler puts in an order to purchase wool blankets from an English woolen mill. Suppose the current exchange rate is $2 per English pound, and that a wool blanket costs 20 pounds, or $40. At this price the American woolens wholesaler feels that the English blankets will be very competitive with American-made blankets that sell for $45. However, suppose that the blankets are delivered to the American wholesaler three

months after the order is placed, and that in the meantime the exchange rate has increased to $2.50 per pound. The English woolen mill contracted to sell the blankets for 10 pounds apiece. But in dollars it will now cost the American woolens wholesaler $50 per blanket ($2.50 × 20), a price that will no longer be competitive with comparable American-made wool blankets selling for $45. Clearly, fluctuations in flexible exchange rates can make international business transactions risky.

Advocates of flexible exchange rates argue that it is possible to hedge against the risks of changing exchange rates by entering into futures contracts. For instance, at the time the American woolens wholesaler placed the order for the wool blankets, a futures contract could have been obtained that guaranteed delivery of pounds to the wholesaler at a rate of $2 per pound three months hence. Whatever happens to the exchange rate between dollars and pounds in the meantime, the wholesaler will be assured of getting pounds at $2 per pound when it comes time to pay for the blankets. Who will enter into the futures contract agreeing to supply pounds to the wholesaler at this rate of exchange? Someone needing dollars three months hence who wants to be sure they can be obtained with pounds at a rate of $2 per pound. That someone might be an English firm that has ordered goods from an American firm to be delivered and paid for in three months.

While acknowledging the protection that hedging can offer, some critics still claim that flexible exchange rates can fluctuate wildly due to speculation—for example, the purchase of pounds at $2 per pound on the gamble that the rate will rise say to $2.25 per pound, yielding the speculator a profit of $.25 per pound. To the contrary, advocates of flexible exchange rates respond that speculative activity will tend to stabilize exchange rate fluctuations. They claim that speculators must buy currencies when they are low priced and sell them when they are high priced if they are to make money. Hence, it is argued that speculators will tend to push the price of an undervalued currency up and the price of an overvalued currency down, thus serving to limit exchange rate fluctuations.

It is often argued that fixed exchange rates

invite destabilizing speculation even more than flexible exchange rates. Suppose a currency is overvalued, such as the franc in Figure 18-4, part a. And suppose the word spreads that the French government is running out of the dollar reserves needed to fix the price of francs above the equilibrium level and finance its payments deficit. Anticipating a devaluation of the franc, holders of francs will rush to the foreign exchange market to get rid of their francs before the price of francs drops. This will shift the supply curve of francs rightward, making the excess supply even larger. With a larger payments deficit and reserves now declining faster, actual devaluation may be unavoidable.

■ CHECKPOINT 18-3

Describe what a government must do in order to fix an exchange rate. Why are balance of payments deficits and surpluses inevitable under fixed exchange rates? If a nation's currency was overvalued and it decided to tighten its monetary policy, what would happen to its official reserve holdings? Why?

THE INTERNATIONAL FINANCIAL SYSTEM: POLICIES AND PROBLEMS

The international financial system consists of the framework of arrangements under which nations finance international trade. These arrangements influence whether exchange rates will be fixed, flexible (or floating), or some combination of fixed and flexible, often called the *managed float*. The arrangements also influence the way balance of payments adjustments take place, and the way nations finance balance of payments deficits. We will now examine the principle ways in which the international financial system has been organized during the twentieth century. First we will briefly consider the gold standard which prevailed during the late nineteenth and early twentieth centuries. We will then examine the so-called Bretton Woods system which governed international transac-

tions from 1944 to 1971, and finally the mixed system which prevails today.

The Gold Standard

For about 50 years prior to World War II, the international financial system was predominantly on a gold standard. The United States was on a gold standard from 1879 to 1934 (except for two years, 1917–1918, during World War I).

GOLD AND A FIXED EXCHANGE RATE

Under a **gold standard** gold serves as each nation's money. Each nation defines its monetary unit in terms of so many ounces of gold. The use of this common unit of value automatically fixes the rate of exchange between different currencies. For example, suppose the United States defines a dollar to equal $\frac{1}{30}$ of an ounce of gold. This means the U.S. Treasury would pay $1 for every $\frac{1}{30}$ ounce of gold to anyone who wants to sell gold to it, or give $\frac{1}{30}$ of an ounce of gold for every dollar of its currency to anyone who wants to buy gold. U.S. currency (coins and paper money) would be redeemable in gold. Suppose Great Britain defines its monetary unit, the pound sovereign, to equal $\frac{5}{30}$ of an ounce of gold. The British Treasury would redeem its currency at the rate of $\frac{5}{30}$ of an ounce of gold for every pound sovereign (called a pound for short). What would be the international rate of exchange between dollars and pounds?

Obviously it would be fixed at $5 per pound. People who want pounds to buy British goods would never pay more than $5 per pound. Why? Simply because they could always go to the U.S. Treasury and get $\frac{5}{30}$ of an ounce of gold for $5, then ship the gold to Great Britain where they could exchange it at the British Treasury for a British pound. (For simplicity, we will ignore shipping costs.) Similarly, it would not be possible to buy a pound for less than $5. Why? Because no one would sell a pound for less than this when they could exchange it at the British Treasury for $\frac{5}{30}$ of an ounce of gold and then ship the gold to the United States where it could be exchanged at the U.S. Treasury for $5.

THE GOLD FLOW
ADJUSTMENT MECHANISM

Now that we see why the exchange rate was rigidly fixed under a gold standard, let's see how balance of payments adjustments took place under such a system.

Clearly, if the United States imported more from Great Britain than it exported, the United States would have to pay the difference by shipping gold to Great Britain. What would eliminate the U.S. balance of payment deficit and Great Britain's balance of payments surplus to assure that the United States wouldn't eventually lose all its gold to Great Britain?

When the United States ran a payments deficit, the nation's money supply, its gold stock, would decrease while that of its trading partner, Great Britain, would increase. Every time an American bought British goods, dollars (U.S. currency) would be turned in to the U.S. Treasury in exchange for gold. The gold would then be shipped to Great Britain and exchanged at the British Treasury for the pounds needed to pay British exporters. Similarly, every time a British citizen bought American goods, pounds (British currency) would be turned in to the British Treasury in exchange for gold. The gold would then be shipped to the United States and exchanged at the U.S. Treasury for the dollars needed to pay American exporters. If Americans bought more from the British than the British bought from Americans, more gold would be flowing out of the United States than was flowing into it. The reverse would be true of Great Britain—more gold would be flowing in than out. Hence, Great Britain's money supply would increase while that of the United States would decrease.

Now recall the effect of money supply changes on an economy, as discussed in previous chapters. If Great Britain's money supply was increasing, this change in the money supply would increase its total demand and income. Its price level would tend to rise and its interest rates to fall. As prices of its goods rose, they would become more expensive for Americans and lead to a reduction of American imports from Britain. Similarly, the fall in British interest rates would make British securities less attractive, so that American purchases (imports) of such securities would decline. At the same time, the rise in Britain's total demand and income would tend to stimulate its imports—its purchases of American goods and services. All of these factors would amount to a reduction in American payments to Britain and an increase in British payments to the United States. All these factors would work together to reduce the U.S. balance of payments deficit and decrease Great Britain's payments surplus.

Consider what would be happening in the United States at the same time. The U.S. money supply would be decreasing, reducing its total demand and income. This would put downward pressure on its price level. The reduction in its money supply would also tend to push U.S. interest rates up. To the extent U.S. prices fell, British citizens would find American goods cheaper and would therefore buy more of them. Similarly, higher interest rates would lead British citizens to step up their purchases of American securities. Finally, the reduction in total demand and income would tend to reduce American imports of British goods. Again, all these factors would contribute to an increase in Britain's payments to the United States and a reduction in American payments to Britain.

In short, the U.S. balance of payments deficit and the British payments surplus would automatically set in motion forces that would reduce America's payments deficit and Britain's payments surplus. And, as long as an American payments deficit and a British payments surplus exists, these forces would continue to operate until both the deficit and the surplus were eliminated. At that point, the flow of gold to the United States from Britain would exactly equal the flow of gold from the United States to Britain. Balance of payments equilibrium would be restored.

To summarize, *under a gold standard nations with balance of payments deficits would lose gold to nations with balance of payments surpluses. The increase in the money supplies of the surplus nations would tend to push up their price levels, reduce their interest rates, and increase their im-*

ports from deficit nations. The decrease in the money supplies of the deficit nations would tend to reduce their price levels, increase their interest rates, and reduce their imports from surplus nations. This process would continue until balance of payments equilibrium in all nations was restored.

SHORTCOMINGS OF THE GOLD STANDARD

The major difficulty with a gold standard is that balance of payments adjustments operate through interest rate, output, employment, and price level adjustments in each nation. Deficit nations may have to suffer recession and high rates of unemployment, while surplus nations experience unanticipated inflation with all the gains and losses which this bestows arbitrarily on different citizens. In short, domestic goals, such as the maintenance of high employment and output, as well as price stability, are completely at the mercy of the balance of payments adjustment process. Most economists feel that this amounts to letting the tail wag the dog.

Moreover, gold discoveries, which can happen at any time, can cause haphazard increases in money supplies and inflation. Cutting the other way, a lack of gold discoveries can result in money supply growth lagging behind worldwide economic growth. Consequently, tightening money supply conditions may trigger recessions and put a damper on economic growth.

DEMISE OF THE GOLD STANDARD

The Great Depression of the 1930s was the undoing of the gold standard. Many nations, faced with high unemployment, resorted to protectionist measures, imposing import tariffs and quotas and exchange controls (regulations that make it difficult to exchange domestic for foreign currency). Through such measures each hoped to stimulate sagging output and employment at home by maintaining exports and reducing imports. Clearly, this was no more possible than for each participant in a foot race to run faster than everyone else. In percentage terms, world trade fell even more than world output.

As the worldwide depression deepened, nation after nation had cause to fear that if its economy began to recover while those of its trading partners remained depressed, its imports would increase while its exports remained low. Under a gold standard such a nation would lose gold, and the resulting contraction of its money supply would drag its economy back into depression. This consideration, combined with the desire to stimulate exports, led nations to devalue their currencies in terms of gold throughout the 1930s. The resolve to keep the rates of exchange between national monetary units and ounces of gold permanently fixed (and, hence, permanently fix rates of exchange between currencies)—the essence of an orthodox gold standard—had been broken. This state of affairs persisted until the end of World War II.

The Bretton Woods System

In 1944 the industrial nations of the world sent representatives to Bretton Woods, New Hampshire, to establish a new international financial system for international trade. They set up a system of fixed exchange rates with the dollar serving as the key currency. That is, the United States agreed to buy and sell gold at $35 per ounce, while the other nations agreed to buy and sell dollars so as to fix their exchange rates at agreed-upon levels. Hence, all currencies were indirectly tied to gold. For example, someone holding marks could exchange them for dollars at a fixed exchange rate and then exchange the dollars for gold in the United States.

The agreements seemed a logical way to set up the new system for two reasons. First, the United States had the most gold reserves. Second, the war-ravaged economies of Europe viewed the dollar as soundly backed by the productive capacity of the American economy. The **Bretton Woods system** (sometimes called the *gold exchange system*) clearly reflected a widespread belief that international trade would function better under a fixed exchange rate system than under one of flexible rates. It also reflected an age-old belief that money should be backed by a precious metal such as gold.

ESTABLISHMENT OF THE INTERNATIONAL MONETARY FUND (IMF)

Recall from our earlier discussion of fixed exchange rates that if a nation's currency is fixed above the free-market equilibrium level, it will lose holdings of official reserves. When these are gone, it simply has to devalue its currency. The International Monetary Fund (IMF) was established to deal with this problem, as well as to supervise and manage the new system in general. Member nations were required to contribute funds to the IMF. Then to bolster its ability to keep exchange rates fixed, the IMF was given the authority to lend these funds to member nations running out of reserves. For example, if the British government used up its dollar reserves purchasing pounds to fix the dollar price of pounds above the free-market equilibrium level, the IMF would lend Britain dollars to continue its support operations. The situation should be temporary, and Britain eventually should earn enough dollars in world trade to repay the IMF. A nation would be allowed to devalue relative to the dollar only if its currency were chronically overvalued so that it continually ran a balance of payments deficit.

PROBLEMS WITH THE
BRETTON WOODS SYSTEM

We have already examined some of the major problems that plague a fixed exchange rate system. All of these troubled the Bretton Woods sytem until its demise in 1971. Nations often had to compromise domestic policy goals out of concern for balance of payments considerations. The burden of adjustment usually fell on the nations with overvalued currencies and balance of payments deficits. They often had to pursue more restrictive fiscal and monetary policies to curb total demand and income in order to reduce their imports. Deficit nations also had to devalue their currencies more often than surplus nations revalued. Deficit nations were the ones borrowing from the IMF and "allegedly" the source of difficulty. In addition, as it became more apparent that a currency would have to be devalued, the day of reckoning was hastened by those selling the currency to beat the fall in the exchange rate. Was a world of such sudden readjustments really more conducive to international trade than a world of flexible exchange rates? Was the uncertainty surrounding such abrupt adjustments really less than the uncertainty that would exist under flexible exchange rates? These questions were raised often.

THE END OF THE
BRETTON WOODS SYSTEM

As the postwar period unfolded into the 1960s, the fixed levels of exchange rates established after World War II became increasingly out of line with the levels that would give balance of payments equilibrium in most countries. Fixed exchanged rate levels established when Japan and European economies were still suffering from the ravages of war became increasingly unrealistic as these nations recovered and became more competitive with the United States. As a result, during the 1960s the dollar became increasingly overvalued and the United States ran chronic and growing balance of payments deficits. At the same time countries such as Germany and Japan ran chronic balance of payments deficits as their currencies were increasingly undervalued. They found themselves continually accepting dollar claims (IOUs) from the United States. In the meantime the United States lost more than half of its gold stock. More and more foreigners became nervous about holding overvalued dollars and forced the United States to honor its commitment to exchange gold for dollars at $35 per ounce.

What could be done? The dollar, the key currency of the system, was overvalued. The United States was not willing to sacrifice domestic policy goals, such as high employment, to reduce its payments deficit. Countries with undervalued currencies often found it difficult to revalue (increase the dollar price of their currencies) because their politically powerful export industries would lose sales as their goods became more expensive to foreign customers. Finally, in 1971 the United States government announced that it would no longer buy and sell gold. The link between gold and the dollar was broken and the era of the Bretton Woods system was over.

Flexible Exchange
Rates and Managed Floats

Despite initial attempts by the industrial nations to restore fixed exchange rates in late 1971, the international financial system has become a mixture of flexible exchange rates and managed floats. Some nations have allowed their exchange rates to float freely. Many others operate a **managed float,** a system whereby exchange rates are largely allowed to float but are subject to occasional government intervention. For example, a nation with an overvalued currency may from time to time use its holdings of foreign reserves to buy its own currency, thus easing its rate of depreciation. Such a managed exchange rate policy is sometimes termed a *dirty float.* In the spirit of Bretton Woods, some countries still attempt to peg their exchange rate more or less to the dollar.

THE DECLINING ROLE OF GOLD

What has happened to the role of gold in the international financial system? In 1968, before the link between gold and the dollar was broken, the IMF created a paper substitute called **Special Drawing Rights (SDRs).** SDRs serve as an official reserve in addition to gold and currency holdings. SDRs are really special accounts at the IMF that can be swapped among member nations in exchange for currencies. Since this is exactly what nations used to do with gold, the SDRs are popularly dubbed "paper gold." Unlike gold, however, the IMF can create SDRs whenever it feels more official reserves are needed to meet the financial needs of expanding world trade. In this sense the creation of SDRs to expand official reserves in the world economy is much like a central bank's creation of member bank reserves in a national economy. Since the elimination of the fixed rate of exchange between the dollar and gold in 1971, gold has become more like any other metal bought and sold in world markets. In recent years both the U.S. Treasury and the IMF have attempted to deemphasize the importance of gold as money by selling some of their gold holdings.

ADJUSTMENT IN
THE NEW ENVIRONMENT

The 1970s were turbulent years for the world economy. Oil prices quadrupled from 1973 to 1974 and abruptly rose again with the revolution in Iran in 1979. During 1974 and 1975 industrial nations experienced the severest recession since the Great Depression of the 1930s. Inflation emerged as a major problem for a number of nations such as the United States. And differences in domestic inflation rates between major industrial powers changed over the decade of the 1970s. All of these factors required continual readjustment of exchange rates. Many economists feel that the more rigid exchange rate structure of the Bretton Woods system would never have survived these stresses. Most feel that the mixture of managed floats and flexible exchange rates has probably served the world economy better.

An Illustration of Current Problems

The news item at the beginning of this chapter illustrates the kind of adjustment problems common to the world economy of the late 1970s. There it is reported that both an Atlantic Council policy paper and the annual report of the IMF "stressed that official intervention operations to prop up the dollar or any other currency can have only a limited effect, given differences in growth and inflation rates between countries."

In the previous chapter we saw that the United States, Germany, and Japan are the three largest participants in world trade, measured in terms of volume of exports. The "differences in growth and inflation rates" between these countries during the 1977–1978 period to which the article refers no doubt played some role in the reported facts that "the dollar depreciated 17 percent against the West German mark" and "32 percent against the Japanese yen." As we discussed earlier, whenever a nation's rate of inflation is greater than that of a trading partner, that nation will experience a depreciation of its currency, all other things remaining the same. Of course, other things did not remain the same during this period. Nonetheless, it is noteworthy that the U.S. rate of inflation was greater in both 1977 and 1978 than the rate in Germany and Japan in each of those years. The U.S. rate of inflation was 5.9 percent in 1977 and 7.8 percent in 1978, while in Germany it was 3.8 and 3.9 percent, and in Japan, 5.6 and 5.8 percent. No doubt it is facts such as these that prompted the "highly placed administration official" to comment: "The only real assurance of stability in the exchange markets in the future is to have a believable antiinflation policy that changes the psychology of those who look at the U.S. economy."

The news item points out that the Atlantic Council noted the plight of the depreciating dollar and declared the need for "evidence that the adverse fundamental or basic factors are being corrected and that a better payments position (especially of the United States) is emerging." What is meant by "a better payments position"? Recall that when we examined the U.S. balance of payments in Table 18-1, we observed that overall balance required a sizeable surplus on the government's capital account. In 1978 a large portion of this surplus represented transactions in official reserve assets to cover the U.S. balance of payments deficit. Specifically, these transactions consisted of the U.S. government using up some of its official reserves as well as an increase in the liquid claims of foreign governments against U.S. government holdings of such reserves. (The same thing had happened in 1977.) A better payments position for the United States would mean a reduction of its balance of payments deficit so that it doesn't use up its official reserves.

One possible solution is for the United States and other nations to allow the dollar to depreciate. That is, they must cease supporting the dollar by intervening in exchange markets to buy dollars with other currencies when it depreciates—stop the managed float of the dollar. Another possible solution is to curb the U.S. rate of inflation through the use of more restrictive fiscal and monetary policy, as discussed in Chapter 14. Of course, both approaches may be used simultaneously.

■ CHECKPOINT 18-4

Explain why and describe how the U.S. balance of payments deficit just discussed would be eliminated if it weren't for the managed float of the dollar. Some economists argue that the Bretton Woods system imposed a certain amount of fiscal and monetary discipline on governments that was missing in the world economy of the 1970s. What do they mean? Do you think the news item at the beginning of the chapter lends support to their view? Why or why not?

SUMMARY

1. International trade has a monetary aspect because trade between nations requires the exchange of one nation's currency for that of another. A nation's exports of goods, services, and financial obligations (IOUs) give rise to a demand for its currency and a supply of foreign currencies in the foreign exchange market. A nation's imports of goods, services, and financial obligations give rise to a supply of its currency and a demand for foreign currencies in the foreign exchange market.

2. A nation's balance of payments is an accounting statement that itemizes its total payments to other nations and the total payments it received from other nations. This statement reflects the fact that total payments to other nations must be equal to (or balanced by) total payments received from other nations.

3. A nation has a balance of payments deficit when its government must draw on its official reserves or issue liquid claims (to other nations) on these reserves, or both, to finance an excess of payments to cover payments from other nations. A balance of payments surplus occurs when payments from exceed payments to other nations, so that the government receives official reserves and liquid claims from other nations to finance the difference.

4. The forces of supply and demand automatically adjust flexible, or floating, exchange rates to eliminate balance of payments deficits and surpluses. They do this by changing the relative attractiveness of goods, services, and assets between nations. Flexible exchange rates tend to adjust to reflect differential rates of inflation and changes in relative interest rate levels between nations.

5. Exchange rates can be fixed or pegged only if

governments intervene in foreign exchange markets to buy and sell currencies. Fixed exchange rates give rise to balance of payments deficits and surpluses. Under fixed exchange rates deficits can be eliminated either by currency devaluation, or by pursuing a restrictive fiscal and monetary policy to curb total demand and income. Conversely, surpluses can be eliminated either by revaluation, or by an expansionary fiscal and monetary policy. Devaluation and revaluation are often resisted because of political considerations.

6. Critics contend that in practice a fixed exchange rate system tends to be biased toward forcing contractionary fiscal and monetary policies on nations with overvalued currencies. Advocates of fixed exchange rates argue that the uncertainty about future levels of flexible exchange rates tends to put a damper on international trade. Advocates of flexible exchange rates respond that it is possible to hedge against much of this uncertainty by entering into futures contracts. Moreover, they note, fixed exchange rates are not immune to uncertainty—namely, uncertainty about currencies that are likely to be devalued to eliminate chronic balance of payments deficits.

7. The gold standard has provided a system of fixed exchange rates in the past. However, balance of payments adjustments under this system often require severe changes in employment, income, and prices, thus sacrificing domestic policy objectives to balance of payments equilibrium.

8. The Bretton Woods system provided the financial framework for international trade from 1944 to 1971. Under this system nations fixed their exchange rates in terms of the dollar, the key currency, which was convertible into gold at a fixed rate of exchange maintained by the United States. The International Monetary System (IMF) was established to supervise the system, to lend official reserves to nations with temporary payments deficits, and to decide when exchange rate adjustments were needed to correct chronic payments deficits. The system eventually

foundered in 1971 due to chronic and rising U.S. payments deficits that led to growing concern about the dollar's continued convertibility into gold.

9. Since the demise of the Bretton Wood system, the international financial system has been a mixture of flexible exchange rates, managed floats, and continued attempts to fix some exchange rates in terms of the dollar.

KEY TERMS AND CONCEPTS

balance of payments
balance of payments account
balance of payments deficit
balance of payments surplus
balance of trade
Bretton Woods system
currency appreciation
currency depreciation
currency devaluation
currency revaluation
exchange rate
flexible (or floating) exchange rate
foreign exchange market
gold standard
managed float
Special Drawing Rights (SDRs)

QUESTIONS AND PROBLEMS

1. When a nation has a balance of payments deficit, would you say it is exporting or importing official reserves and liquid claims? Why?

2. Tell whether each of the following generates a demand for foreign currency (any currency other than dollars) or a supply of foreign currency on foreign exchange markets.

a. A German firm builds a plant in Hawaii.

b. A British firm transfers a million dollars from its bank account in a New York bank to its bank account in a London bank.

c. The U.S. government makes a foreign aid grant to the Phillippines.

d. An American firm transports goods from the East Coast to the West Coast through the Panama Canal on a Liberian freighter.

e. Belgium has a balance of payments deficit in its international transactions with the United States.

f. An American's French government bond matures.

3. Suppose you observe the following exchange rates: 5 French francs exchange for $1, 4 German marks exchange for $1, and 3 French francs exchange for 2 German marks.

a. Can you think of a way to make money out of this situation?

b. What would you expect to happen if exchange rates were flexible?

c. What would you expect to happen if exchange rates were fixed at these levels?

4. How would a nation's exchange rate likely be affected by each of the following, all other things remaining the same?

a. The nation's trading partners start to pursue relatively more expansionary monetary policies.

b. The nation increases its imports.

c. The nation experiences a decline in the growth of productivity relative to that of its trading partners, thus weakening its competitive position in the world economy.

d. The nation cuts its income taxes.

e. The nation has a recession.

f. The nation steps up its advertising about its tourist attractions.

5. Suppose Great Britain and the United States were the only two trading nations in the world. Suppose also that the exchange rate between pounds and dollars is fixed so that the pounds are overvalued in terms of dollars. Furthermore, suppose Britain decides to let its currency float but the United States wants to keep the dollar pegged. Will Britain lose dollar reserves? What will the United States get for its efforts? Which country do you think gets the "better deal" out of this situation and why?

6. Explain why exchange rates are fixed under a gold standard and describe how balance of payments adjustments takes place. Explain why you never hear about balance of payments adjustment problems between Texas and Wisconsin, New York and Pennsylvania, or between any of the other states of the Union? How does balance of payments adjustment take place between the states? How has balance of payments adjustment occurred between inner city slums and suburbia?

7. Compare and contrast a gold standard with the Bretton Woods system. Given that both operate under a system of fixed exchange rates, why could there be persistent balance of payments deficits and surpluses under the Bretton Woods system but not under a gold standard?

■ NEWS ITEM FOR YOUR ANALYSIS ■

BOLD CURRENCY SUPPORT ANNOUNCED BY THE UNITED STATES RAISES RECESSION RISKS

WASHINGTON, Nov. 12—The government has announced bold and sweeping moves to bolster the dollar. But the moves also increase the risks of recession.

Yesterday morning the White House announced a package of measures designed to increase U.S. interest rates, making dollar assets more attractive to hold, and also designed to give Washington some $30 billion in German marks, Swiss francs, and Japanese yen that can be used to purchase dollars in currency support operations. Administration officials also indicated that they are prepared to intervene in foreign exchange markets "massively," not only to stabilize the dollar but also to restore some of its lost value. (However, there is no intention to peg the exchange rate for the dollar at any specific level.)

President Carter described the dollar support effort as "a major step in the antiinflation program." Indeed, officials stressed that the dollar's sharp drop is itself inflationary because it increases the cost of U.S. imports and makes it easier for American manufacturers to raise prices of competing goods.

The Federal Reserve Board moves to increase interest rates won't trigger a downturn in the economy, according to administration officials. However, many private analysts as well as some government experts expressed concern that higher interest rates could bring on a recession. "Now, I think there will be a recession," declared Norman Robertson, chief economist of Pittsburgh's Mellon Bank. "Its the price we will have to pay for unwinding the inflationary spiral."

Measures jointly announced yesterday by the Treasury and the Federal Reserve were as follows:

—The discount rate at the Federal Reserve Bank of New York will be increased to 9.5 percent from 8.5 percent immediately.

—A "supplementary reserve requirement" equal to 2 percent of time deposits of $100,000 or more will apply to member banks of the Federal Reserve System. This will help moderate the recent relatively rapid expansion in bank credit. In addition, the Fed said, "It will also increase the incentive for member banks to borrow funds from abroad and thereby strengthen the dollar by improving the demand in Euromarkets for dollar-denominated assets."

—The Fed will increase its currency "swap" lines with the central banks of West Germany, Japan, and Switzerland to $15 billion from the current $7.4 billion. These short-term renewable credit lines would permit the United States to exchange dollars for foreign currencies, which the United States can then use to buy dollars in support operations.

—The United States will draw from its reserves at the IMF $3 billion in foreign currencies for use in dollar support operations. U.S. reserves in the IMF total $4.1 billion.

—The United States will sell $2 billion of its IMF Special Drawing Rights, an international reserve asset commonly referred to as "paper gold," for foreign currencies.

—The Treasury will expand its monthly gold sales to at least 1.5 million ounces per month. This increase will help reduce the U.S. trade deficit and sop up some excess dollars.

Senior officials here contend that these moves amount to "concerted and forceful action" to end speculation against the dollar now and reduce inflationary pressures in the longer run. However, there is widespread skepticism in the private sector that the Carter administration and the Fed will stick to a tighter-credit course if the economy starts to slump.

QUESTIONS

1. The news item reports that "officials stressed that the dollar's sharp drop is itself inflationary because it increases the cost of U.S. imports and makes it easier for American manufacturers to raise prices of competing goods." However, what effect will preventing the "dollar's sharp drop" have on the U.S. balance of payments deficit? And what effect will this have on further U.S. needs for foreign currency? How would you feel about preventing this sharp drop if you ran an American export business?

2. How does increasing the level of American interest rates help "to bolster the dollar"? If it bol-sters the dollar but increases the risk of a recession, how would a recession affect the value of the dollar in foreign exchange markets? Some would say that increasing the interest rate to bolster the dollar is just another way of saying you are going to fix the exchange rate and alleviate the associated payments deficit by pursuing a restrictive monetary policy. Would you agree or disagree with this point of view?

3. Explain how each of the measures listed in the news item would presumably work to bolster the dollar. Which of them run the risk of bringing on a recession?

4. What would an advocate of flexible exchange rates say about the likelihood of avoiding a recession if the managed float were simply abandoned and the dollar allowed to float? What would the advocate recommend about fiscal and monetary policy if, for some reason, it was desirable that the dollar not depreciate even under a system of freely floating exchange rates?

GLOSSARY

A

accelerator principle The relationship between changes in level of retail sales and the level of investment expenditures.

antidumping law Law that sets a minimum price on an imported good such that if the import enters the country at a price below the minimum, the law triggers a government investigation of possible dumping.

automatic stabilizers Built-in features of the economy that operate continuously without human intervention to smooth out the peaks and troughs of business cycles.

average propensity to consume *(APC)* The fraction or proportion of total income that is consumed.

average propensity to save *(APS)* The fraction or proportion of total income that is saved.

B

balanced budget A budget in which total expenditures equal total tax revenues.

balanced budget multiplier The ratio of the amount of change in GNP to the change in government spending financed entirely by an increase in taxes; indicates that a simultaneous increase, or decrease, in government expenditures and taxes of a matched or balanced amount will result in an increase, or decrease, in GNP of the same amount.

balance of payments A nation's total payments to other nations must be equal to, or balanced by, the total payments received from other nations.

balance of payments account Record of all the payments made by a nation to other nations, as well as all the payments that it receives from other nations during the course of a year.

balance of payments deficit The excess of a nation's payments to other nations over the payments received from other nations, exclusive of government capital account transactions in official reserve assets; means that the government is reducing its holdings of official reserve assets or that the liquid claims of foreign governments against these reserves are increasing, or both.

balance of payments surplus Excess of payments received from other nations over the payments made to them, exclusive of government capital account transactions in official reserves and liquid claims; means that the government is increasing its holdings of official reserves or its holdings of liquid claims on the official reserve assets held by foreign governments, or both.

balance of trade The difference between merchandise exports and merchandise imports.

bank note Paper money issued by a commercial bank.

barter economy Trading goods directly for goods.

Bretton Woods system System of fixed exchange rates in which only the dollar was directly convertible into gold at a fixed rate of exchange; all other currencies were indirectly convertible into gold by virtue of their convertibility into the dollar. Also called the *gold-exchange system.*

budget deficit Expenditures are greater than tax revenues.

budget surplus Expenditures are less than tax revenues.

business cycles The somewhat irregular but recurrent pattern of fluctuations in economic activity.

business fluctuations Recurring phenomena of increasing and decreasing unemployment associated with decreasing and increasing output. Also called *business cycles.*

C

capital consumption allowance See *capital depreciation.*

capital deepening An increase in the stock of capital (machines, tools, buildings, highways, dams, and so forth) relative to the quantities of all other resources including labor.

capital depreciation The wearing out of capital, often measured by its decline in value. Also called *capital consumption allowance.*

capital gains taxes Taxes levied on any gain one realizes from selling an asset at a price greater than the original purchase price.

capitalism Form of economic organization in which the means of production are privately owned and operated for profit, and where freely operating markets coordinate the activities of consumers, businesses, and all suppliers of resources.

certificate of deposit (CD) Special type of time deposit that depositor agrees not to withdraw for a specified period of time, usually three months or more.

ceteris paribus Latin expression for "all other things remaining the same."

closed economy An economy that does not trade with other nations.

coincidence of wants The possibility of barter between two individuals that occurs when each has a good that the other wants.

command economy An economy in which the government answers the questions of how to organize production, what and how much, and for whom to produce.

commercial bank Bank that can create money in the form of a demand deposit (checking account) by extending credit in the form of loans to businesses and households.

comparative advantage Theory holds that total world output is greatest when each good is produced by that nation which has the lower opportunity cost of producing the good—the nation is said to have a comparative advantage in that good.

complementary good A good which tends to be used jointly with another good.

consumption function The relationship between the level of disposable income and the level of planned consumption.

cost-push inflation Inflation that occurs when suppliers of factors of production increase the prices at which they are willing to sell them.

currency appreciation A rise in the free-market value of a currency in terms of other currencies, with the result that fewer units of a currency will

be required to buy a unit of a foreign currency.

currency depreciation A fall in the free-market value of a currency in terms of other currencies; means that more units of a currency will be required to buy a unit of a foreign currency.

currency devaluation A lowering of the level at which the price of a currency is fixed in terms of other currencies.

currency revaluation A rise in the level at which the price of a currency is fixed in terms of other currencies.

D

deduction Reasoning from generalizations to particular conclusions; going from theory to prediction.

deflation A general fall in prices which causes the value of a dollar measured in terms of its purchasing power to rise.

demand curve Graphic representation of the law of demand.

demand deposit A deposit from which funds may be withdrawn on demand, and from which funds may be transferred to another party by means of a check.

demand-pull inflation Inflation that occurs because the economy's total demand for goods and services exceeds its capacity to supply them.

demand schedule Numerical tabulation of the quantitative relationship between quantity demanded and price.

deposit multiplier Assuming banks are fully loaned up, the multiplier is the reciprocal of the required reserve ratio.

depreciation allowance Funds set aside for the replacement of worn-out capital equipment.

depression An unusually severe recession.

direct relationship Relationship between variables in which the value of each changes in the same way (both decrease or both increase).

discount rate The rate of interest that member banks must pay to borrow from Federal Reserve banks.

discount window A teller's window, figuratively speaking, at a Federal Reserve bank where a member bank may come to borrow money.

disembodied technical change Change that takes the form of new procedures or techniques for producing goods and services.

disposable income (DI) Personal income minus personal taxes.

dumping Selling a product in a foreign market at a price below the cost of producing the product.

E

economic efficiency Using available resources to obtain the maximum possible output.

economic growth An outward shift in the production possibilities frontier caused by an increase in available resources and technological know-how.

economic policy Proposed method of dealing with a problem or problems posed by economic reality which is arrived at through the use of economic theory and analysis.

economic problem How to use scarce resources to best fulfill society's unlimited wants.

economics A social science concerned with the study of economies and the relationships among economies.

economic theory A statement about the behavior of economic phenomena, often referred to as a law, principle, or model.

economy A particular system of organization for the production, distribution, and consumption of all things people use to obtain a standard of living.

embodied technical change Technological change that is embedded in the form of the capital good itself.

employment tax credit Program that allows firms to exclude from taxation an amount of income equal to some specified percent of the wages they pay labor, thereby effectively reducing the cost of labor and encouraging firms to hire more.

equation of exchange A relationship between the economy's money supply M, the money supply's velocity of circulation V, its price level p, and total real output Q; states that the total amount spent, $M \times V$, on final goods and services equals the total value of final goods and services produced, $p \times Q$—that is, $M \times V = p \times Q$.

equilibrium income level The level of total income that will be sustained once it is achieved. At equilibrium, the total income earned from production of the economy's total output corresponds to a level of total spending or demand just sufficient to purchase that total output.

equilibrium price Price at which market equilibrium is achieved.

equilibrium quantity Quantity of the good supplied and demanded at the point of market equilibrium.

equity The difference between a firm's total assets and its total liabilities.

escalator clause Clause in a labor contract that indexes wages to inflation by stipulating that wages must be periodically adjusted upward to keep pace with the rising cost of living.

excess reserves Total reserves minus required reserves.

exchange rate The price of foreign currency, or the amount of one currency that must be paid to obtain one unit of another currency.

exclusion principle Distinguishing characteristic of private goods, the benefits of which, unlike those of public goods, accrue only to those who purchase them.

expansion The upswing of a business cycle.

expected rate of return The amount of money a firm expects to earn per year on funds invested in a capital good, expressed as a percent of the funds invested.

exports The goods and services a nation produces and sells to other nations.

export subsidy Government payments to an export industry to cover part of the industry's costs of production.

F

factors of production The inputs (land, labor, and capital) necessary to carry on production. Also called *economic resources*.

fallacy of composition Error in reasoning which assumes that what is true for the part is true for the whole.

fallacy of division Error in reasoning which assumes that what is true for the whole is true for its individual parts.

federal funds The bank reserves that are loaned and borrowed in the federal funds market.

federal funds market Market in which borrowing and lending of reserves between commercial banks takes place.

federal funds rate Interest rate that banks borrowing reserves must pay to banks lending reserves in the federal funds market.

fiat money Money that is declared by the government to be legal tender—it is neither backed by nor convertible into gold or any other precious metal.

financial intermediary A business that acts as an intermediary by taking the funds of lenders and making them available to borrowers, receiving the difference between the interest it charges borrowers and the interest it pays lenders as payment for providing this service.

financial markets Markets that take the funds of savers and lend them to borrowers.

fiscal policy Government's efforts to use its spending and taxing authority to smooth out the business cycle and maintain full employment without inflation.

fixed-dollar assets Any kind of asset that guarantees a repayment of the initial dollar amount invested plus some stipulated rate of interest.

flexible (or floating) exchange rate Exchange rate freely determined by supply and demand in the foreign exchange market without government intervention.

flow A quantity per unit of time.

foreign exchange market Market in which exchange rates between different currencies are determined.

fractional reserve banking Managing a bank so that the amount of reserves on hand is only equal to a fraction of the amount of deposits.

free-market economy An economy in which what, how, and for whom to produce goods is determined entirely by the operation of free markets.

G

general equilibrium analysis Analysis of the adjustments a change in one market will cause in each and every other market.

GNP gap Potential GNP minus actual GNP, which is equal to the value of final goods and services not produced because there is unemployment.

gold standard A monetary system in which nations fix the rates of exchange between their currencies and gold and, hence, the exchange rates between their currencies.

government budget An itemized account of government expenditures and revenues over some period of time.

gross national product (GNP) The market value of all final goods and services produced by the economy during a year.

gross private domestic investment The total expenditures by business firms on new capital.

H

high-employment budget Difference between the actual level of government spending and the level of tax revenue that would be collected if the economy were at a high-employment level of GNP.

I

ideology Doctrine, opinion, or way of thinking.

import quotas Limitation on imports that specifies the maximum amount of a foreign produced good that will be permitted into the country over a specified period of time.

imports The goods and services a nation purchases from other nations.

indexing Program to keep the purchasing power of wages, taxes, and fixed-dollar, or nominal, assets constant by adjusting their dollar-denominated values to the change in the general price level.

indirect business taxes Sales and excise taxes and business property taxes.

induction Reasoning from particular facts and observations to generalizations.

inferior good A good that people typically want more of at lower income levels and less of at higher income levels.

inflation A rise in the general level of prices of all goods and services; this rise causes the purchasing power of a dollar to fall.

interest rate or **interest** The price of borrowing money, or the price received for lending money, expressed as a percentage.

inventory A stock of unsold goods.

inverse relationship Relationship between variables in which the value of one increases as the value of the other decreases.

investment Expenditures on new capital goods. Also called *capital investment.*

involuntary unemployment Occurs when workers willing to work at current wage rates are unable to find jobs.

L

labor force All persons over the age of 16 who are employed, plus all those actively looking for work.

laissez faire ("let [people] do [as they choose]") The belief that people should be allowed to conduct their economic affairs without interference from the government.

law of demand Theory that the lower the price of a good, the greater will be the demand for it and, conversely, the higher the price, the smaller will be the demand.

law of increasing costs The cost per additional good obtained, measured in terms of the good sacrificed, rises due to the different productivity of resources when used in different production processes.

law of supply Theory that suppliers will supply larger quantities of a good at higher prices than they will at lower prices.

liquidity The ease with which any asset may be converted into money without loss.

M

M_1 Money defined as currency plus demand deposits.

M_2 Money defined as M_1 plus time deposits.

M_3 Money defined as M_2 plus deposits at nonbank thrift institutions (mutual savings banks, savings and loan associations, and credit unions).

M_4 Money defined as M_2 plus large negotiable CDs.

M_5 Money defined as M_3 plus large negotiable CDs.

macroeconomics Branch of economic analysis that focuses on the workings of the whole economy or large sectors of it.

managed float Exchange rates subject to free-market forces modified by government intervention, but without any formal commitment to fix rates at specified levels. Also called *dirty float.*

manpower programs Job-training programs aimed at developing the job skills of the young and hard-core unemployed in order to increase their employability.

marginal propensity to consume *(MPC)* The fraction or proportion of any change in income that is consumed—equals the slope of the consumption function.

marginal propensity to save *(MPS)* Fraction or proportion of any change in income that is saved—equals the slope of the saving function.

margin requirement The minimum percentage of a stock purchase that must be paid for with the purchaser's own funds, as legally set by the Fed.

market An area within which buyers and sellers of a particular good are in such close communication that the price of the good tends to be the same everywhere in the area.

market demand curve The sum of all the individual demand curves for a good.

market equilibrium Equilibrium established at the price where the quantity of the good buyers demand and purchase is just equal to the quantity suppliers supply and sell.

microeconomics Branch of economic analysis which focuses on individual units or individual markets in the economy.

mixed economy An economy in which what, how, and for whom to produce goods are partly determined by the operation of free markets and partly by government intervention.

monetarism A school of thought that believes money is the main causal factor determining the level of economic activity.

money Anything that is generally acceptable in trade as a medium of exchange and that also serves as a unit of account and a store of value.

money GNP GNP measured in current prices or dollars.

money interest rate The interest rate calculated in terms of units of money, not purchasing power over goods.

multiplier The number of times by which the change in total income exceeds the size of the expenditure change that brought it about.

N

national bank Commercial banks that are chartered by the federal government and are required by law to be members of the Federal Reserve System.

national income (NI) Net national product minus indirect business taxes.

nationalized industry An industry owned by the government.

near money Assets that are like money except that they can't be used as a medium of exchange, though they are readily convertible into currency or demand deposits.

negotiable certificates of deposit CDs that are issued by commercial banks (usually in $100,000 denominations) and can be traded like bonds.

negotiable order of withdrawal (NOW) Deposits at savings banks from which the depositor may have funds transferred to a designated party by simply sending the savings bank a checklike form, the order of withdrawal.

net exports The difference between the dollar value of the goods produced and sold to foreigners and the dollar value of the goods foreigners produce and sell to us.

net national product (NNP) The dollar values of GNP minus capital depreciation or capital consumption allowance.

net private domestic investment The increase (decrease) in the economy's capital stock.

net worth See *equity*.

normal good A good which people typically want more of as their income rises.

normal profit Payments to financial capital and entrepreneurial skill that are just sufficient to keep them employed in a particular productive activity—that is, to keep them from leaving and going into some other productive activity.

normative statement A statement of what should or ought to be which cannot be supported or refuted by facts alone; a value judgment or opinion.

O

open economy An economy that trades with other nations.

open market operations The Fed's buying and selling of government securities in the open market in which such securities are traded.

opportunity cost The cost of a unit of a good measured in terms of the other goods which must be forgone in order to obtain it.

P

paradox of thrift If each household tries to save more, all households may end up saving and earning less.

partial equilibrium analysis Analysis of a change in one market and its consequences for that market, and possibly a few others. All other markets are assumed to remain unchanged.

peak The uppermost point in the upswing (expansion) of a business cycle.

per capita GNP An economy's GNP divided by the size of its population.

personal consumption Household expenditures on goods and services.

personal income (PI) National income plus transfer payments minus corporate income taxes, undistributed corporate profits, and social security contributions.

Phillips curve An alleged relationship between the rate of inflation and the rate of unemployment suggesting that they tend to move in opposite directions to one another.

positive statement A statement of what is, was, or will be that can be verified or refuted by looking at the facts.

post hoc, ergo propter hoc ("after this, therefore because of this") Error in reasoning which assumes that one event is the cause of another event simply because it precedes the second event in time.

potential GNP What GNP would be if the economy were "fully" employed.

precautionary demand The demand for money to cover unforeseen events or emergencies that require immediate expenditures.

price The exchange value of a good in terms of other goods, most often expressed as the amount of money people will pay for a unit of the good.

price index Ratio of current prices to prices in some base year.

production possibilities frontier A curve representing the maximum possible output combinations of goods for a fully employed economy.

productivity The efficiency with which each labor hour combines with the capital stock and the existing state of technology to produce output—often measured as output per labor hour.

progressive tax A tax that takes a *larger* percentage out of a high income than a low income.

proportional tax A tax that takes the same percentage of income no matter what the income level.

proprietors' income Income earned by the owners of unincorporated businesses.

public assistance programs Government programs aimed at providing help to dependent families, the sick, the handicapped, and the aged—those who for reasons largely beyond their control cannot work.

public goods Goods that will not be produced in private markets because there is no way for the producer to keep those who don't pay for the goods from using them—for example, the lighthouse beacon.

Q

quantity theory of money Asserts that veolcity, V, in the equation of exchange, $M \times V = p \times Q$, is stable and not just whatever number is necessary to make the equation true; therefore, changes in the money supply M are asserted to cause proportional changes in money GNP, $p \times Q$.

R

real GNP GNP measured in terms of prices at which final goods and services are sold in some base year. Changes in real GNP are due only to changes in the quantity of final goods and services, not changes in price.

real interest rate The annual percentage rate of increase in the lender's purchasing power on money loaned, or in other words, the interest rate calculated in terms of its purchasing power over goods and services.

realized investment Intended investment minus any unintended inventory reduction or plus any unintended inventory addition.

real wage The money wage divided by the price level.

recession A contraction or slowing down in the growth of economic activity.

regressive tax A tax that takes a smaller percentage out of a high income than a low income.

Regulation Q The regulation that gives the Fed the authority to put a ceiling on the interest rates that member banks can pay on time deposits.

required reserve ratio The ratio of required reserves to the total amount of demand deposits.

required reserves Reserves that a bank is legally required to hold against demand deposits—equal to the required reserve ratio multiplied by the amount of demand deposits.

reserves Defined by law as cash held in the bank's vault and the deposits of the bank at its district Federal Reserve bank.

resource misallocation See *underemployment*.

retained earnings Money saved by businesses out of sales revenue.

S

saving function The relationship between the level of disposable income and the level of planned saving.

Say's Law Supply creates its own demand.

scarce Existing in a limited amount.

scientific method Ongoing cycle of induction from observation to theory, followed by deduction from theory to prediction, and explanation and checking of predictions and explanations against new facts to see if theory is verified, refuted, or needs to be modified.

seasonal variation Regular patterns in economic data associated with custom and weather over the course of the year.

Special Drawing Rights (SDRs) Special accounts that the International Monetary Fund (IMF) creates for member nations, to be used as an official reserve to finance balance of payments deficits.

specialization of labor System of production in which each worker performs only one task for which he or she is specifically trained.

speculative demand The demand for money that arises from the anticipation that bond prices are more likely to fall than to rise.

stagflation The existence of high rates of inflation and unemployment at the same time.

state bank   Commercial banks that are chartered by a state; they may join the Federal Reserve System if they wish.

subsistence living level   The minimum standard of living necessary to keep the population from declining—the death rate just equals the birthrate.

substitute good   A good that can be used in place of another good because it fulfills similar needs or desires.

supply curve   Graphic representation of the law of supply.

supply schedule   Numerical tabulation of the quantitative relationship between quantity supplied and price.

T

tariff (or duty)   A tax on imports, most often calculated as a percent of the price charged for the good by the foreign supplier.

tax-based income policy (TIP)   Policies that use tax incentives to encourage compliance with wage guidelines; the carrot version of TIP rewards with tax credits (reductions in income taxes) those workers who keep their wage increases below the guideline rate for wage increases; the stick version of TIP punishes with tax penalties employers who grant wage increases in excess of the guideline rate for wage increases.

technology   The methods used to combine resources of all kinds, including labor, to produce goods and services.

terms of trade   The ratio of exchange between an exported and an imported good.

time deposit   A deposit at a commercial bank that earns interest, but is not legally subject to withdrawal on demand or transferable by check.

token coins   Coins that contain an amount of metal (or other material) that is worth much less than the face value of the coin.

trade credit   Credit extended by one business to another business, allowing the latter to buy goods from the former without making immediate full payment by check or with currency. Serves as short-term medium of exchange though it is not a store of value like money.

trading possibilities frontier   Graphical representation of the choices that a nation has by specializing in the product in which it has a comparative advantage and trading (exporting) its specialty for the product in which it has a comparative disadvantage.

transactions costs   The costs associated with converting one asset into another asset—brokerage fees, telephone expense, time and effort, advertising cost, et cetera.

transactions demand   Demand for money for its use as a medium of exchange to transact the purchase and sale of goods and services.

transfer payments   Payments characterized by the fact that the recipient is neither expected nor required to provide any contribution to GNP in return.

Treasury bill   A short-term government bond that matures either one, three, or six months after the day issued.

trough   The lower turning point of a business cycle.

U

unanticipated inflation   The amount of inflation that occurs that is unexpected.

underemployment   A condition in which available resources are employed in tasks for which other resources are better suited or in which the best available technology is not used in a production process. Also called *resource misallocation*.

unemployment   A condition in which available factors of production are idle; in reference to labor, unemployment is said to exist whenever workers are actively looking for a job but are unable to find one.

unemployment compensation   Payments to workers who are involuntarily unemployed (they want work but can't find a job).

V

value added   The difference, at each stage of production, between what the firm sells its product for and what it pays for all the materials it purchases to make the product.

variable-dollar asset   An asset that has no guaranteed fixed-dollar value.

velocity   The number of times a typical dollar of the money stock must go around the circular flow of money exchanged for final goods and services during a year.

W

wage insurance   A guarantee that the government will repay labor for the purchasing power lost if consumer prices rise faster than the guideline rate for wages.

wage-price controls   Government-specified rate of increase in wages and prices that it is illegal for business and labor to exceed—compliance is mandatory.

wage-price guidelines   Government-specified rate of increase in wages and prices that business and labor are requested not to exceed—compliance is voluntary.

INDEX